Feminist Research Practice

Second Edition

To my mother, Helene Skramko

Feminist Research Practice

A Primer

Second Edition

Sharlene Nagy Hesse-Biber

Boston College

Los Angeles | London | New Delhi
Singapore | Washington DC

Los Angeles | London | New Delhi
Singapore | Washington DC

FOR INFORMATION:

SAGE Publications, Inc.
2455 Teller Road
Thousand Oaks, California 91320
E-mail: order@sagepub.com

SAGE Publications Ltd.
1 Oliver's Yard
55 City Road
London EC1Y 1SP
United Kingdom

SAGE Publications India Pvt. Ltd.
B 1/I 1 Mohan Cooperative Industrial Area
Mathura Road, New Delhi 110 044
India

SAGE Publications Asia-Pacific Pte. Ltd.
3 Church Street
#10-04 Samsung Hub
Singapore 049483

Printed in the United States of America

Library of Congress Cataloging-in-Publication Data

Hesse-Biber, Sharlene Nagy.
Feminist research practice : a primer / Sharlene Nagy Hesse-Biber, Boston College. — Second Edition.

pages cm
Includes bibliographical references and index.

ISBN 978-1-4129-9497-2 (pbk.) —
ISBN 978-1-4833-1011-4 (web pdf) 1.

Women's studies. 2. Feminism—Research. I. Title.
HQ1180.H47 2013
305.4207—dc23   2013013954

This book is printed on acid-free paper.

SFI Certified Sourcing
www.sfiprogram.org
SFI-00453

Acquisitions Editor: Vicki Knight
Editorial Assistant: Jessica Miller
Production Editor: Libby Larson
Copy Editor: Ellen Howard
Typesetter: C&M Digitals (P) Ltd.
Proofreader: Bonnie Moore
Indexer: Michael Ferreira
Cover Designer: Karine Hovsepian
Marketing Manager: Nicole Elliott

13 14 15 16 17 10 9 8 7 6 5 4 3 2 1

Contents

Preface

What's New in the Second Edition?

The second edition of *Feminist Research Practice* brings a stellar group of new and returning scholars with newly revised chapters from the first edition as well as completely new chapters that cover some cutting-edge research methods. All chapters highlight the latest scholarship by a range of interdisciplinary scholars who bring together feminist issues and methods in the service of answering a range of complex issues that deeply impact the diversity of women's lives.

New Chapters to the Second Edition

I have added a number of new and timely chapters to the second edition that provide additional sets of analytical insights and research tools in the service of getting at complex and global issues. I have added two new theoretical chapters by leading scholars in feminist theory: Chapter 2, "Feminist Empiricism and Standpoint Theory" and Chapter 3, "Feminist Postmodernism, Poststructuralism, and Critical Theory." These chapters provide cutting-edge insights into the range of foundation issues feminist research grapples with, namely: How do we know what we know? Who gets to know? What theoretical lenses provide a window into subjected knowledges of women and other oppressed groups? What does it mean to take the standpoint of the most oppressed? This edition also includes a new chapter on "Ethics and Feminist Research" (Chapter 4) that covers a range of issues that are often not discussed in standard methods textbooks. This chapter explores the range of power and authority issues in social research and extends the discussion of ethics beyond "informed consent" issues to address the range of conundrums researchers face across any given research project. Another new chapter, "Feminist Practice of Action and Community Research" (Chapter 6), provides a set of analytical tools and methods that demonstrate how to specifically promote social change for women and other oppressed groups. This chapter provides strategies for including research participants more directly into the research process as well. Another new chapter, "Feminist Media Research" (Chapter 9), provides a set of analytical lenses and tools to engage with issues that deal with the growing influence of social media—Twitter, Facebook, and so forth. A new chapter on "The Feminist Practice of Program Evaluation" (Chapter 11) provides a feminist lens onto how to conduct an evaluation with the goals of social transformation and social change. The concluding new chapter, "Putting Together Your Research Project" (Chapter 13), provides the researcher with a "hands-on" step-by-step guide for conducting feminist research together with an in-depth example to follow that helps to solidify the concepts, ideas, and methods practices discussed throughout this book.

With the inclusion of more graphics, each chapter provides students with in-depth examples as guides to learning a specific method. We also provide a set of insightful discussion questions that are meant to be moments of reflection whereby students have an opportunity to put together what they have learned throughout the chapter and apply this learning to other research contexts. Each chapter also includes online resources for students to follow up on a specific method and its practice in other research contexts.

All new and returning chapters to this second edition have been revised to include the latest scholarship and feminist perspectives into a given research method. In addition, we have expanded a discussion of the impact of new technologies, such as online technologies that include online surveys, ethnographies, and interviews. We also review the advantages and disadvantages of employing these technologies with given methods practices. In addition, we have included a discussion of ethics throughout each of the methods chapters. Each methods chapter contains a discussion of the basic "how-to" of analysis, interpretation, and write-up of a given methods practice.

The second edition continues to provide students with more than a laundry list of methods alone. All the chapters bring a feminist theoretical perspective to methods practice. The first part of this second edition provides students with a range of feminist perspectives onto the social world that engage with a set of issues and problems that challenge the status quo and provide a new set of questions whose goals are to uncover "subjugated knowledge" of the situation of women and other oppressed groups.

A continued and expanded feature in each chapter is a set of in-depth examples that guide the reader toward a fuller understanding of how theory and method are brought together to answer specific research problems. Along the way, we provide sets of tips and even exercises that give students a way to personally engage with the methods discussed in each of the chapters. We provide a set of examples that includes the range of differences among women as well as examples that cross disciplinary divides.

GOING "BEHIND THE SCENES" OF A RESEARCH PROJECT

This book stresses a "hands-on" practice of feminist inquiry; and toward this end, we include a unique set of praxis tools. Inspired by Erving Goffman's concepts of "front stage" and "back stage," I wanted to provide the reader with a more holistic picture of just what it means on the "ground level" to conduct a research project. Very often we see only the "front stage" of a project—what we might read in, say, a journal article about a given research project. Yet, there is little discussion of the conundrums that may arise before, during, and after a given project's overall trajectory of tasks—what is often known as the "back stage" of a research project—where scholars need to confront issues and problems and opportunities that may arise as a project proceeds. This is information that is often hidden, yet critical for those who want to know the landscape they will traverse in the life of any given project. We cover a range of backstage research inquiries, asking questions such as: What guides researchers' topic selection? How do epistemological beliefs and theoretical commitments come to bear on the research process? What values, issues, and motivations do researchers bring to their projects? How do ethics play out in practice? What are the emotional aspects of a research project *really like?* Why do some researchers select particular methods, and how do those methods enable their research? These are critical questions and considerations in the practice of feminist research that explicitly require a synergy between the various components of the research process. In an attempt to get at some of these issues, I have invited well-known feminist researchers to contribute pieces about a range of epistemological and methodological concerns as well as "tales from the field," so to speak—experiences feminists have had employing some of the methodological options reviewed in this text. The rich texts they have generously shared with us are included throughout the book in what we call "Behind-the-Scenes" boxes. These boxes offer a glimpse behind the curtain of feminist research—a window into the feminist researcher's vantage point.

These "Behind-the-Scenes" vignettes relate the experiences of feminist scholars who are navigating and exploring new levels of feminist inquiry, and they share with their readers some of the "nuts and bolts" of doing a particular research project. Others share unique insights onto some feminist issues and concepts. Each chapter also contains a detailed set of thought-provoking discussion questions as well as a set of website information for further follow-up with regard to any given chapter specifics.

Sharlene Hesse-Biber, Editor
Brookline, MA

Acknowledgments

I appreciate the help of a number of people who supported the work toward this book. I am grateful to the many feminist scholars who let us go "behind-the-scenes" with them and shared their "insider" research stories and insights as they went about conducting their research. I also extend my heartfelt appreciation and thanks to all the feminist research experts who took the lead writing chapters for this book. Their expertise and wisdom contributed to enhancing our understanding of the feminist research process across a range of diverse methods.

I especially want to acknowledge the research assistance I received from so many. Several undergraduate research assistants from Boston College, Mary Downer, class of 2012, Lizzie Jekanowski, class of 2013, and Jessica Stevens, class of 2014, were invaluable in their energy and effort to make our manuscript sparkle. I especially want to commend Amelia Scott, class of 2013, for her excellent editorial expertise and assistance with the final phases of this manuscript. I extend my heartfelt appreciation to all of them for a job well done! Thanks as well to the Boston College graduate Hilary Flowers, class of 2009, for her stellar editorial assistance at the beginning stages of this project. I also want to thank the Boston College undergraduate research fellowship grants office, especially Dean William Petri.

I want to especially extend my gratitude to the academic reviewers of the second edition: M. Cristina Alcalde, University of Kentucky; Arlene Sgoutas, Metropolitan State University, of Denver; Jo Reger, Oakland University; M. Joan McDermott, Southern Illinois University Carbondale; Lena McQuade, Sonoma State University; Wendy Brandon, Rollins College; Rachel Sutz Pienta, Valdosta State University; Ann Marie Nicolosi, The College of New Jersey; Karrie Ann Snyder, Northwestern University; Jeanne Bickford, University of California, Irvine; John P. Bartkowski, University of Texas at San Antonio; Julia L. Offen, Cornell University; Linda E. Mitchell, University of Missouri, Kansas City; and Karen T. Keifer-Boyd, The Pennsylvania State University.

I want to enthusiastically thank the staff at Sage Publications. In particular, I want to express my utmost appreciation to my editor, Vicki Knight, for her editorial expertise and support of this manuscript. Thanks also to our copy editor, Ellen Howard, for her expertise in guiding this project toward completion. Much appreciation to Sage production editor Libby Larson for her professionalism and expert advice.

I want to expresses my love and deepest admiration to my family, in particular my daughters, Julia Ariel and Sarah Alexandra, for their patience, love, and forbearance. I especially value the friendship, love, and support of my husband, Michael Peter Biber, MD.

About the Editor

Sharlene Nagy Hesse-Biber is Professor of Sociology and the Director of Women's and Gender Studies Program at Boston College in Chestnut Hill, Massachusetts. She has published widely on the impact of sociocultural factors on women's body image, including her book *Am I Thin Enough Yet? The Cult of Thinness and the Commercialization of Identity* (Oxford, 1996), which was selected as one of *Choice Magazine's* best academic books for 1996. She recently published *The Cult of Thinness* (Oxford, 2007). She is the coauthor of *Working Women in America: Split Dreams* (Oxford, 2005). She is coeditor of *Feminist Approaches to Theory and Methodology: An Interdisciplinary Reader* (Oxford, 1999); *Approaches to Qualitative Research: A Reader on Theory and Practice* (Oxford, 2004); and *Emergent Methods in Social Research* (Sage, 2006). She is coauthor of *The Practice of Qualitative Research* (Sage, 2006; 2nd ed., 2010) and coeditor of *The Handbook of Emergent Methods* (Guilford, 2008; paperback ed., 2011). She is editor of the *Handbook of Emergent Technologies in Social Research* (Oxford University Press, 2011). Her most recent monograph, *Waiting for Cancer to Come: Genetic Testing and BRCA-Positive Women's Medical Decision Making,* is forthcoming in 2014 with The University of Michigan Press. Her forthcoming coedited *Handbook of Mixed and Multimethods Research in the Behavioral and Social Sciences* is scheduled for publication in 2014 with Oxford University Press.

Her most recent publications include editing the *Handbook of Feminist Research: Theory and Praxis* (Sage, 2007; 2nd ed., 2012), which was selected as one of the Critics' Choice Award winners by the American Education Studies Association, and was also chosen as one of *Choice Magazine's* Outstanding Academic titles for 2007. She is a contributor to the *Handbook of Grounded Theory* (Sage, 2008) as well the *Handbook of Mixed Methods Research* (2nd ed., Sage, 2010). She is author of *Mixed Methods Research: Merging Theory With Practice* (Guilford, 2010). She is a special issue editor for the July 2010 issue of *Qualitative Inquiry* on mixed methods research and coeditor of a special issue on Triangulation in Mixed Methods Research for the *Journal of Mixed Methods Research* in 2011.

She is a codeveloper of the software program HyperRESEARCH, a computer-assisted program for analyzing qualitative data, and the new transcription tool HyperTRANSCRIBE. A fully functional free demo of these programs is available at www.researchware.com. This website provides links to a free teaching edition for both programs (go to: www.researchware.com).

About the Chapter Contributors

Linda Bell is Principal Lecturer in the School of Health and Education, Middlesex University. She is an anthropologist whose publications relate to mothering, feminist research, ethics, and aspects of health and social care. Her University of London PhD dissertation, titled *My Child, Your Child; Mothering in a Hertfordshire Town in the 1980s*, was completed in 1994 and concerned women's support networks and the development of social capital in one locality in southern England. She teaches research methods to undergraduate and postgraduate students especially in the fields of social work, mental health, and complementary health disciplines. She works extensively with research students and currently chairs a university ethics committee for social work. Her recent research focuses on professional identity, including gender issues, and ethics. She has also researched interprofessionalism within social work education, care worker training, and women's experiences of a therapy centre concerned with male violence, when she was based at King's College, London. She is co–reviews editor for the *International Journal of Social Research Methodology* (Routledge); she is a long-standing member of the London-based *Women's Workshop on Qualitative Family and Household Research* and a contributor to the Workshop's publications, including *Ethics in Qualitative Research* (T. Miller et al., Eds.; 2nd ed., 2012, Sage). She is currently coediting (with Trish Hafford-Letchfield) a book titled *Ethics, Values and Social Work Practice* (McGraw-Hill, forthcoming).

Elana D. Buch is an assistant professor of Anthropology at the University of Iowa, with specializations in medical anthropology. She is interested in the intersections of aging, caregiving, and public policy in the United States. More specifically, her research examines the ways that caregiving intersects gender, race, and class while shaping peoples' abilities to be recognized as social persons and their relationships to the state. Her previous research examined these questions in the context of Chicago's paid home care industry, while her current project investigates the different experiences of caregiving among military veterans (and their families) from past and recent conflicts. An engaged and interdisciplinary feminist scholar, she holds an MSW and a Joint PhD in Social Work and Anthropology from the University of Michigan.

Alison Crosby is an associate professor in the School of Gender, Sexuality and Women's Studies (with a specialization in gender, violence, and transnationalism) at York University, Toronto, Canada. Her research interests include antiracist feminist contestations of ongoing histories of militarized, colonial, and imperial violence, and in particular, how we understand survivors' multifaceted struggles for agency and subjectivity; and the claiming, narration and performance of memory that challenges the hegemonic. As a feminist participatory action researcher, she is particularly interested in the politics of knowledge production and the complex and often contested role of multiple intermediaries in shaping such processes. She has published in journals such as the *International Journal of Transitional Justice* and *Feminism & Psychology,* and is currently working on a book manuscript with M. Brinton Lykes titled *Reparation Struggles: Mayan Women's Protagonism in Transitional Justice Processes in Guatemala,* which is based on four years of feminist participatory action research with Mayan women survivors of violence during the armed conflict in Guatemala. With her colleague Dr. Malathi de Alwis, she is developing a new comparative project on memorialization struggles by "communities of the sorrowing" in Guatemala and Sri Lanka. She also coordinates the Women in Conflict Zones Network (WICZNET) and is a member of the Advisory Board of the international organization Impunity Watch.

Lisa M. Cuklanz is Professor and Chair of the Communication Department at Boston College, where she has also served as Director of Women's Studies. Her research focuses on media representations of gender-based violence. She has published three books and numerous articles in journals within the field of Communication, including *Critical Studies in Media Communication, Communication Quarterly,* and *Women's Studies in Communication.*

Frauke Elichaoff is a graduate teaching assistant in the Psychology Department at Middlesex University. Her interests include research methods, feminism, and positive psychology, as well as autism in adolescents and adults. She has recently completed a BSc in Psychology with Counseling as a mature student and is currently considering topics for her PhD.

Nollaig Frost is a senior lecturer in the Psychology Department of Middlesex University, London, UK. She is interested in the (re)formulation of women's identity following transitional life events. More specifically, her work explores ways in which mothers experience having second and subsequent children, and women's experiences of mental illness. Such work has led to recent interest in how perception of maternal status, by mothers and by others, informs the constitution of choices available to women. The ways that women negotiate the choices and their outcomes is the focus of her research into shifts in the positionality of women researchers during the research process. She is currently developing research into the experiences of women migrants to the UK. Her background as a psychodynamic counsellor informs her interest in mental illness, and in teaching Counselling Theory and Skills. All of her research is underpinned by her broader focus on qualitative and pluralistic methodology; and she leads the Pluralism in Qualitative Research (PQR) Team, which explores the benefits and creative tensions arising from the combining of qualitative methods with each other. The work of the team has led to publications in *Qualitative Research, Qualitative Research in Psychology,* and other leading journals. Her edited book, *Qualitative Research Methods in Psychology: Combining Core Approaches* (Open University Press, 2011) details the work of the PQR team to date and is widely used in teaching and research.

Barbara Gurr is an Assistant Professor in Residence in the Women's, Gender and Sexuality Studies Program at the University of Connecticut. Her research on the intersections of race, class, gender, sexuality, and citizenship has been published in several journals, including *The International Journal of Sociology* and *Family* and *Societies Without Borders.* Her work on the applicability of human rights instruments for Native Americans, feminist methodology, and transgender children has been included in several edited collections. Her work on reproductive health care for Native American women has been recognized by the Health, Health Policy and Health Services Division of the Society for the Study of Social Problems; and her work on family identity tasks for parents of young transgender children has been recognized by the Feminism and Family Studies section of the National Council on Family Relations. She has also received numerous awards from the University of Connecticut, including recognitions from the Sociology Department and the Women's, Gender and Sexuality Studies Program.

Toby Jayaratne is an assistant research scientist in the Department of Health Behavior and Health Education in the School of Public Health at the University of Michigan. She has a long-standing interest in feminist methodology and has written and presented papers addressing issues central to that topic. Her work in this area specifically focuses on the importance and uses of both quantitative and qualitative methods for feminist researchers. She received her PhD from the University of Michigan and was trained in survey research at the Institute for Social Research (University of Michigan). She has directed or coordinated several large national surveys and is currently the Principal Investigator of a study examining the effects of the lay public's genetic explanations for obesity and type 2 diabetes on preventive attitudes and behaviors.

M. Brinton Lykes is Professor of Community-Cultural Psychology, Associate Director of the Center for Human Rights and International Justice, and Chair of the Department of Counseling and Applied Developmental and Educational Psychology at Boston College. She teaches participatory action research; critical psychological perspectives on race, gender, and class; and courses on human rights and international justice. She has worked with survivors of war and gross violations of human rights, using cultural resources, the creative arts, and participatory action research methodologies to analyze the causes and document the effects of violence and to develop programs that aspire to rethread social relations and transform social inequalities based on underlying structural injustices. Her current participatory and action research focuses on (1) migration, detention, and deportation and the effects of these U.S. policies and practices for women and children, with a particular focus on transnational and "mixed-status families" and (2) sexual violence against women in contexts of armed conflict and postconflict transition, and on women's struggles for truth, justice, healing, and reparations. She has published extensively in refereed journals and edited volumes, edited two books, and coauthored two others. She is cofounder and co-coordinator of several international NGOs and a member of the board of directors of *Women's Rights International* and of *Impunity Watch*. Her website is www2.bc.edu/~lykes

Heather McIntosh is a visiting assistant professor of mass communication in the Communication Department at Boston College. Her research explores documentary media in a converging media environment, focusing particularly on distribution and advocacy documentary. She earned her PhD in mass communications from The Pennsylvania State University.

Donna M. Mertens is a professor in the Department of Education at Gallaudet University, where she teaches advanced research methods and program evaluation to deaf and hearing students. She also serves as editor for the *Journal of Mixed Methods Research*. The primary focus of her work is transformative mixed methods inquiry in diverse communities that prioritizes ethical implications of research in pursuit of social justice. Her recent books include *Program Evaluation Theory and Practice: A Comprehensive Guide* (Guilford, 2012); *Transformative Research and Evaluation* (Guilford, 2009); *The Handbook of Social Research Ethics* (Sage, 2010); *Research and Evaluation in Education and Psychology: Integrating Diversity With Quantitative, Qualitative, and Mixed Methods* (3rd ed., Sage, 2010); *Research and Evaluation Methods in Special Education* (Corwin, 2004); and *Parents and Their Deaf Children: The Early Years* (Gallaudet University Press, 2003). She is widely published in the *Journal of Mixed Methods Research, American Journal of Evaluation, American Annals of the Deaf,* and *Educational Evaluation and Policy Analysis*.

Kathi Miner received her PhD in Psychology and Women's Studies from the University of Michigan and is currently an assistant professor of Psychology and Women's and Gender Studies at Texas A&M University. Her research focuses on the relationship between interpersonal mistreatment in organizations and occupational health. Most of her work has focused on incivility, harassment, and discrimination in work settings and how being a target or observer of such behavior affects employees' psychological, physical, and job-related well-being. She is especially interested in the degree to which individuals from low-status social groups (e.g., based on gender, race, sexual orientation) are disproportionately targets of mistreatment.

Jennie Munday is a postdoctoral teaching fellow in the Department of Sociology at Goldsmiths, University of London. She is interested in feminist theory and methodology, the focus group method, gender, identity, space (in particular, rural space), social movements, and political sociology. She is currently investigating how focus groups could be used to examine the ways in which different social groups construct the meaning of "human rights," and she teaches the undergraduate option course "Privacy, Surveillance and Security." She has previously written about gendered citizenship and how focus groups can be used to investigate the construction of collective identity. Her work has been published in *Sociology* and *Sociology Compass*.

Nancy A. Naples is professor of sociology and women's studies at the University of Connecticut where she also directs the Women's, Gender, and Sexuality Studies Program. Her research on citizenship, social policy, feminist methodology, immigration, and community activism has been published in numerous journals and edited books. Her scholarship includes more than fifty book chapters and journal articles. She is the author of *Grassroots Warriors: Activist Mothering, Community Work and the War on Poverty* and *Feminism and Method: Ethnography, Discourse Analysis and Activist Scholarship;* and editor of *Community Activism and Feminist Politics: Organizing Across Race, Class, and Gender;* and coeditor (with Karen Bojar) of *Teaching Feminist Praxis; Women's Activism and Globalization: Linking Local Struggles and Transnational Politics* (coedited with Manisha Desai); and *The Sexuality of Migration: Border Crossing and Mexican Immigrant Men* by Lionel Cantú (coedited with Salvador Vidal-Ortiz). She is series editor for *Praxis: Theory in Action* (SUNY Press) and *New Approaches in Sociology: Studies in Social Inequality, Social Change, and Social Justice* (Routledge). She received the 2008 Faculty Excellence Award in Research (Humanities/Social Sciences) given by UConn's Alumni Association and the 2011 Excellence in Research Award for Social Sciences from UConn's College of Liberal Arts and Sciences. She also received the 2010 Distinguished Feminist Lecturer Award and the 2011 Feminist Mentor Award from Sociologists for Women in Society. She has served as President of Sociologists for Women in Society, the Society for the Study of Social Problems, and the Eastern Sociological Society.

Karen M. Staller is an associate professor at the University of Michigan School of Social Work. She holds a PhD from Columbia University School of Social Work and a JD from the Cornell University Law School. She is curreny acoeditor of the international journal

Qualitative Social Work: Research and Practice. Her research interests include the history of social welfare problems, policies, and programs. She is particularly interested in those that have targeted runaway and homeless street youth. She has published two books: *Runaways: How the Sixties Counterculture Shaped Today's Practices and Policies* and, with a coauthor, *Seeking Justice in Child Sexual Abuse: Shifting Burdens and Sharing Responsibilities.* Currently, she is investigating the "newsies" and other child street vendors of the late nineteenth century. She has published numerous articles and book chapters on runaway and homeless youth, social welfare policy and services, as well as on qualitative research methods and methodologies. Her teaching interests include the history and philosophy of social welfare and social welfare policy, family policy, qualitative research methods, and the intersection of law and social work.

Nichole Stewart is a researcher, analyst, and evaluator experienced in data collection and analysis, performance management, and data visualization. She is currently the data manager for two initiatives housed at the Association of Baltimore Area Grantmakers (ABAG)—the Baltimore Integration Partnership, Baltimore's Living Cities revitalization initiative focused on linking workforce development and capital investment in targeted Baltimore City neighborhoods, and the Baltimore Workforce Funders Collaborative. She earned her master's in Community Planning at University of Maryland, College Park, in 2009, where she conducted cross-site evaluations of two Baltimore City HOPE VI developments to further contribute to the growing body of knowledge about poverty deconcentration and mixed-income development. She is currently a fourth year doctoral student in UMBC's Public Policy program with a focus on evaluation and analytical methods. Her current research interests involve studying the causal impact of mixed-income development, relocation, subsidized economic development, and developer locational incentives on employment outcomes.

About the Behind-the-Scenes Contributors

Y. Gavriel Ansara is a PhD candidate in the Department of Psychology at the University of Surrey in the United Kingdom. He completed his BA in the United States in Cross-Cultural and International Health. His current research focuses on cisgenderism, when people's biological sex and assigned gender differ from how they perceive their own gender. Adapted from: Surrey University (2009) *Psychology*. [Online] Available at https://www.surrey.ac.uk/psychology/people/phd_candidate_ansara_yousef_garviel_levi/index.htm (Accessed: 16th April)

Kimberlé Crenshaw is a Professor at both UCLA School of Law and Columbia Law School. She received a BA from Cornell, a J.D. from Harvard Law School, and an LLM from Wisconsin-Madison. She specializes in and has written about race, gender, civil rights, and legal issues. She has been a critical supporter and leader of the academic discipline known as Critical Race Theory. Adapted from: UCLA (2013) *School of law*. [Online] Available at: http://www.law.ucla.edu/faculty/all-faculty-profiles/professors/Pages/kimberle-w-crenshaw.aspx (Accessed: 16 April 2013)

Michelle Fine is Professor of Social Psychology, Women's Studies, and Urban Education at the Graduate Center of CUNY (City University of New York). Her more recent coauthored books include *Charter Schools and the Corporate Make-Over of Public Education* (Teachers College Press, 2012) and *Revolutionizing Education: Youth Participatory Action Research in Motion* (Routledge, 2008). She also received the Henry Murray Award in 2012 from the Society for Personality and Social Psychology of the APA. Adapted from: http://publicspace.commons.gc.cuny.edu/they-worked-with-us/michelle-fine/

Frida Kerner Furman is Professor in the Department of Religious Studies, the Women and Gender Studies Program, and the Peace, Justice, and Conflict Studies Program at DePaul University. She earned her PhD in Religion and Social Ethics at the University of Southern California. Her specializations include social and feminist ethics, religious and cultural identity, and peace-building, among others. One of her more recent books is called *Telling*

Our Lives: Conversations on Solidarity and Difference (Roman & Littlefield, 2005). Adapted from: http://offices.depaul.edu/svdpp/Members/Pages/Frida-Kerner-Furman.aspx

Peter Hegarty is Professor and Deputy Head of the Psychology Department at the University of Surrey in the United Kingdom. He received his BA in Psychology at Trinity College in Dublin, Ireland and earned his PhD at Stanford University in California. His research focuses on social psychology, LGBT (Lesbian, Gay, Bisexual, Transgender) psychology, and the history of psychology. His most recent book coming out in 2013 is called *Gentlemen's Disagreement: Alfred Kinsey, Lewis Terman and the Sexual Politics of Smart Men* (University of Chicago Press, 2013). Adapted from From: Surrey University (2009) Psychology. [Online] Available at: https://www.surrey.ac.uk/psychology/people/dr_peter_hegarty/index.htm (Accessed: 16 April 2013)

Lizzie Jekanowski is a senior at Boston College with a major in Political Science and minor in Women's and Gender Studies. As Chair of Boston College Students for Sexual Health, she emphasizes female empowerment through reproductive rights, comprehensive sexual health education, and sex-positive feminism. She has had the incredible privilege to work as Professor Hesse-Biber's Undergraduate Research Fellow for the past two years, and has published two papers on women's sexuality and public health concerns in BC's academic journals. This "Behind-the-Scenes" section originates from her original lecture titled "The F-Word: Why Men and Women Need Feminism Now More Than Ever," delivered at Boston College in November 2012.

David Karp is professor emeritus at Boston College. Karp's most recent book on mental illness, *Is It Me or My Meds? Living With Antidepressants* (2006, Harvard University Press), is based on in-depth interviews. This book explores the particularly powerful relationship between psychiatric medications and personal identity; the link between pills and personhood. He is author of *The Burden of Sympathy* (2002); *Speaking of Sadness: Depression, Disconnection, and the Meanings of Illness* (1997); *Being Urban: A Sociology of City Life* (1994); *Sociology in Everyday Life* (1993); *Experiencing the Life Cycle: A Social Psychology of Aging* (1993); and *The Research Craft: An Introduction to Social Research Methods* (1992). He received his PhD from New York University.

Veronica Magar is the Executive Director of **r e a c h** (research and action for change)— http://researchaction4change.wordpress.com/. Her technical areas of expertise include a range of applied-research methodologies in social development. These include both participatory/transformative and conventional research methods. Her areas of expertise, related to content, include gender/sexuality, equity, rights and social justice of marginalized groups within the health and HIV/AIDS sectors, community mobilization, structural interventions, violence against women, advocacy, and masculinity. She has conducted a range of evaluations, applying user-focused methodologies, at regional, national, and local levels, across Asia.

Haideh Moghissi is Professor of Sociology and Women's Studies at York University in Toronto. She currently serves as an executive committee member at the Centre for Refugee Studies. She has written numerous articles that have been published in books and journals that focus on Iran, women in the Middle East, and feminism and Islam. One of her recent books is *Muslim Diaspora, Gender, Culture and Identity,* (ed.) 2010. Adapted from From: Bechler,R (2013) Open Democracy. [Online] Available at: http://www.opendemocracy.net/author/haideh-moghissi (Accessed: 16 April 2013)And her website: http://www.atkinson.yorku.ca/~diaspora/team/haideh.htm

Mignon R. Moore is Associate Professor of Sociology and Director of Graduate Studies in African American Studies at UCLA. She received her PhD from the University of Chicago. She specializes in researching and writing about family, race, gender, sexuality, aging, and disadvantaged groups. She is the author of *Invisible Families: Gay Identities, Relationships and Motherhood among Black Women* (University of California Press, 2011). Adapted from: Moore, M.R. (2012) `Intersectionality and the study of black, sexual minority women,' Gender & Society, 26(1), pp.33–39.

Alexandra G. Murphy is an associate professor of Communication and the Director of Communication Studies in the College of Communication at DePaul University. She teaches undergraduate and graduate courses that focus on cultural and political issues within organizations such as organizational communication and culture, multiculturalism in the workplace, power and politics in organizations, and assessment and intervention in organizations. She received her PhD from the University of South Florida. Her research centers on organizational communication and culture, focusing on the risks that can occur in organizational and social contests when taken-for-granted communication practices are unquestioningly reproduced and institutionalized. In particular, she has a strong interest in organizational and social contexts where lives are on the line. She has worked on organizational development issues and improving communication among airline crews and medical staff in hospital emergency rooms. She has also worked extensively on public health communication programs for HIV/AIDS education in Kenya, Africa. Her work has been published in *Communication Monographs, Text and Performance Quarterly, Management Communication Quarterly, Journal of Applied Communication Research,* and *Journal of Contemporary Ethnography,* as well as edited books.

Andrea Nightingale is Associate Professor in the School of Global Studies at the University of Gothenburg in Sweden. She received her PhD in Geography from the University of Minnesota. While there, she researched environmental issues, resource management, development and progress, and social inequalities in Nepal starting in 1987. She is interested in mixing methods from both social and natural science disciplines. Adapted from her website: http://www.globalstudies.gu.se/english/staff/nightingale_a/

Brenda O'Neill is Associate Professor and Political Science Department Head at the University of Calgary. She earned her PhD in Political Science at the University of British Columbia. Her research interests include politics, research methods, and women and politics. She is coauthor of numerous publications including the books, *An Introduction to Government and Politics 9th edition* (Nelson Education, 2013), *Gender and Social Capital* (Oxford: Routledge, 2006), and *Citizen Politics: Research and Theory in Canadian Political Behavior* (Oxford University Press, 2002). In 2010, she was awarded the Calgary Institute for Humanities Annual Fellowship. Adapted from her website https://poli.ucalgary.ca/profiles/brenda-o-neill

Belen Sanz is the head of the Evaluation Office for the United Nations Entity for Gender Equality and the Empowerment of Women, also known as UN Women. She is also Chair of The United Nations Evaluation Group (UNEG).

Michelle Sheriff studied Psychology at Victoria University of Wellington in New Zealand where she wrote her master's thesis, "Making Age Relevant: A Discursive Approach to Age in Everyday Interaction." She now works as a policy analyst at the Ministry of Social Development in New Zealand. Adapted from From: Sheriff, M and Weatherall, A (2009) 'A Feminist Discourse Analysis of Popular-Press Accounts of Postmaternity,' *Feminism and Psychology,* 19 (1), pp.89–108

Inga Sniukaite is Evaluation Specialist in the United Nations Women Evaluation Office. She received her PhD in Sociology and has ample experience in social research and evaluation projects. She evaluates and provides advice for different local, national, and global programs. She currently provides support and advice for the initiative called Impact Evaluation Component of Safe Cities for Women and Girls Global Program.

Linda P. Thurston is a professor in the Department of Special Education, Counseling and Student Affairs and Associate Dean of the College of Education at Kansas State University. She was recently a program officer with the National Science Foundation (NSF) with the disability, gender, and evaluation programs for more than two years. Thurston is the founding director of the Office of Educational Innovation and Evaluation (OEIE), a mulitdisciplinary team of evaluators and researchers who provide evaluation services to programs across the United States and in other countries. OEIE grew from a staff of three to nearly 30, and more than $1 million in external funding since it was established in 2000. Thurston is a former teacher and entrepreneur with advanced degrees in experimental and behavioral psychology. She is the coauthor of *School Consultation, Collaboration and Teamwork,* in its 7th edition, and has authored or presented more than 150 publications and research papers at national and international conferences. Thurston has received grants for more than $10 million and has been honored and recognized for her innovative educational programs and leadership, including the development of Survival Skills for Women which was a significant part of welfare reform efforts in the 1980s and 1990s. Besides more than a decade of program evaluation, her research experiences include research on gender equitable strategies for science and math, disabilities education and teacher preparation, parent involvement in special education, and program development. Thurston has done research and writing on disability and gender issues for more than 35 years. She has received awards for women in leadership, educational research, and community leadership.

María Elena Torre is on the faculty of the Critical Social and Environmental Psychology Program and is Founding Director of the Public Science Project at The Graduate Center of the City University of New York. For the past 15 years, she has been engaged in critical participatory action research projects nationally and internationally with schools, prisons, and community-based organizations seeking to further social justice. Her work introduced the concept of "participatory contact zones" to collaborative research, and she continues to be interested in how democratic methodologies, radical inclusion, and notions of solidarity impact scientific inquiry (see www.publicscienceproject.org). She is a coauthor of *Echoes of Brown: Youth Documenting and Performing the Legacy of* Brown v. Board of Education and *Changing Minds: The Impact of College on a Maximum Security Prison.* Her writing can be found in volumes such as the APA *Handbook of Qualitative Research in Psychology; Participatory Action Research Approaches and Methods: Connecting People, Participation, and Place;* the *Handbook of Action Research;* and in journals such as *Feminism and Psychology,* the *Journal of Social Issues, Qualitative Inquiry,* and the *Journal of Critical Psychology.* She was a recipient of the American Psychological Association Division 35 Adolescent Girls Task Force Emerging Scientist award and the Spencer Fellowship in Social Justice & Social Development in Educational Studies, and is on the national board of the National Latino/a Education Research and Policy Project and What Kids Can Do.

Ann Weatherall is Associate Professor in the School of Psychology at the Victoria University of Wellington. She earned her BA from Otago University and her PhD from Lancaster University. Her research interests include social psychology, gender, sexuality, and language. She has received numerous awards, including the 2004 Research Excellence Award from Victoria University of Wellington and the 2009 Fulbright Travel Award. Adapted from: http://www.victoria.ac.nz/psyc/about/staff/ann-weatherall

Amy Wilson is Associate Professor at Gallaudet University and Program Director of the International Development Program in Washington, DC. She earned her BA from Illinois State University in Deaf Education, her MA from the University of Illinois Chicago in Learning Disabilities, and her PhD from Gallaudet University in Deaf Education. She specializes in teaching and writing about international development, disability, and evaluation and program management. Adapted from: http://www.gallaudet.edu/x1736.xml

CHAPTER 1
A Re-Invitation to Feminist Research

Sharlene Hesse-Biber

Are You a Feminist? A Classroom Reflection

I can vividly remember the first day of teaching my undergraduate course titled Women and Work: I start by introducing myself to the students, and I talk a little about my research on gender. I then provide them an overview of the course and end my introduction by asking the students in my (all female) class the following set of questions:

"Do you believe in equality?" Response: Everyone's hand goes up.

"Do you believe in social justice?" Response: All eagerly raise hands.

"Are you a feminist?" Response: Stark silence ensues, as some students slowly begin to raise their hands.

Looking back on that first day of class, I remember asking myself why so few students self-identify as feminists. As I contemplated this quandary that day, I tell my class that in fact if they answered in the affirmative to the first two questions—which all of them did—they are well on their way to being feminists! This idea caught many in the room by surprise.

After student introductions, I ask the students to break into small circles to discuss the questions that I raised at the beginning of the class. After private dynamic debate, the groups come together into one large circle to share their thoughts and ideas with the entire group if they wish to do so. Some students repeat what they had said earlier, namely they feel feminism is no longer relevant because women have gained equality. Feminism for them is a fight that has been "won," and now it is time that society in general needs to move on from feminism. One woman explains her beliefs by noting that her own mother had no trouble achieving a high-powered law position while at the same time having children. She goes on to say that her mother had employed a full-time nanny. Another student quickly adds that in fact her mother decided to stop working once her kids were born, and she went back to work after they were of school age. Both students ask the class, "What is the problem with women now?"

The room is silent before another hand rises. This time, the story told is different. One woman states that her experience growing up was different: for her, feminism is just as relevant today as it was decades ago. This woman grew up in poor circumstances, and her dad left her mother before she was five years old. Her mother wound up working two different jobs in order to support her family while her grandmother took care of her. She came to Boston College on a scholarship, and must work 15 hours a week to support herself. She continues, saying she feels the state of women in American society is dismal; she especially notes the increasing incidents of violence against women and children, as well as the large number of women and children living below the poverty line. As for her own mother, this woman states, she is still working two jobs and is more or less in the same place as when she started out ten years ago.

Another student's hand goes up. She asks the class: "How can this class of students have such different views on the state of women's lives in contemporary America?"

This brief remembrance of the first day of my class came to mind as I began to think of a way to provide you, the reader, with a re-invitation to feminist research. While each student's experience is real, it also arises out of very different life circumstances. While most women in my class start out with the common goals of equality and of social justice for all women, they do not share the same lived reality; these differences cause these women to provide different answers to the question of whether or not feminism is still needed and relevant today. Critical contrasts in life dimensions especially create varied experiences: in particular, differences by race, ethnicity, social class, sexual preference, religion, and so forth.

Social realities of women's lives, then, are different; yet there is a tendency for women to treat all women as if they are the same. Even if many of the students feel feminist issues have been won, this does not make that belief real for those women who continue to struggle with gender-related discrimination and bias in their own daily lives. Yes, the gains and contributions that feminist researchers and activists have made toward overcoming widespread gender stereotypes and improving women's rights and equality across the globe are significant, and some of the women in my very class are the beneficiaries of these hard-won gains. But it is essential to note that much more needs to be accomplished. Toward this end, feminist research plays a crucial role.

What Is Feminist Research?

Feminist research positions gender as the categorical center of inquiry and the research process. By using a variety of research methods—quantitative, qualitative, mixed—feminist researchers use gender as a lens through which to focus on social issues. Research is considered "feminist" when it is grounded in the set of theoretical traditions that privilege women's issues, voices, and lived experiences.

From data collection to data analysis and interpretation, the process by which feminist researchers conduct their research projects—feminist research praxis—centralizes the relationship between the researcher and researched to balance differing levels of power and authority. Researchers practice reflexivity, a process by which they recognize, examine, and understand how their social background, location, and assumptions can influence the research. From the selection of the research problem and method(s) to the analysis and interpretation of findings, researchers' agendas can impact the research process. Reflexivity is a way for researchers to account for their personal biases and examine the effects that these biases may have on the data produced.

One of the main goals of feminist research projects is to support social justice and social transformation; these projects seek to study and to redress the many inequities and social injustices that continue to undermine and even destroy the lives of women and their families. Researchers look at patterns and trends within the population of all women, and they draw conclusions based on the varied range of women's unique circumstances. They are frequently concerned with the intersections of gender with other identity standpoints, such as sexual orientation, race, ethnicity, class, or nationality. Feminist researchers have unique angles of theoretical perspectives that they use to assess women's status within society and to formulate particular questions that might not otherwise be tackled by the hegemonic ideas that reinforce the existing system of gender inequality.

Many different research methods are employed to gather both qualitative and quantitative data in the service of uncovering "subjugated" knowledge. For example, feminist research work has uncovered a discrepancy between how the law is enacted and how it is practiced. While the past decades of women's advocacy have been influential in enacting protection against sexual harassment in the workplace, feminist research finds that laws such as these do not necessarily translate into practice: women (overwhelmingly more so than men) still experience sexual harassment at work, and they oftentimes face backlash when it is reported. While women are entering male-dominated professions such as law, business, and medicine in increasing numbers, they still face gender-based discrimination in hiring and promotions. Women as a group continue to earn only 70% of the salary men earn in equivalent positions, and they are underrepresented in fields of science and engineering, as well as upper-level positions such as business CEOs and law firm partners. There remains a lack of affordable child care, and inflexible corporate environments make it difficult for women to balance their work and family lives. Furthermore, the feminization of poverty—meaning women and girls make up the large and growing percentage of the world's poor—and violence against females continue to expand globally in new and particularly virulent forms (Hesse-Biber & Carter, 2005).

In order to address these and related issues, this book is an invitation for you to learn more about feminist research and the range of methods feminists employ in the services of social change and social justice for women and other oppressed groups.

Feminist Empiricism: Uncovering Male Bias in the Sciences and Social Sciences

Over the course of the 1960s, 1970s, and 1980s, feminist researchers reacted against the pervasive "androcentric, or male bias" that was characteristic of published research findings. Feminist empiricists sought to "correct" such biases. They diversified research samples by including women and began to ask new questions that would enable women's voices to be heard. Feminist empiricists wanted to eradicate sexist research by introducing women's perspectives into research projects across many academic disciplines: psychology, philosophy, history, sociology, education, anthropology, language and communication, and the fields of law and medicine.

During the 1970s and 1980s, many groundbreaking anthologies of feminist research were published. Authors such as Gloria Bowles and Renate Duelli-Klein, Marcia Millman and Rosabeth Kanter, Helen Roberts, and Nancy Tuana compiled these anthologies that were simultaneously critical of androcentric bias and of traditional knowledge frameworks. In the 1980s and 1990s, feminist researchers took a different approach in challenging traditional research, creating a new foundational question for their work: *What is the nature of social reality?* From this, they developed new sets of feminist epistemologies (ways of knowing) and methodologies (ways of asking questions) that interrogated, disrupted, and modified dominant models of knowledge building.

These, at times, radical challenges to traditional research began from a critique of positivism, the mainstream research paradigm based in the scientific method. The basic tenets of positivism are (1) scientific objectivity—the concept of "value-free" science that stresses the detachment of the researcher from the researched, and (2) universality—the concept that the researcher can discover the "Truth" of the "social reality" that exists outside of the researcher (Comte, 1896/2000; Durkheim, 1895/1938). The new epistemologies and methodologies challenged both of these premises.

In the past, feminist empiricists had worked to improve the accuracy, objectivity, and universality of mainstream positivist research by including women in their samples. In the 1980s and 1990s, however, feminist researchers began to question this very same strategy. These feminists argued that knowledge is achieved not through "correcting" or supplementing mainstream research studies by including women, but by paying close attention to the specificity of women's individual lived experiences.

Centering Women's Issues and Lived Experiences as a Basis for Knowledge Building

Objectivity, a central principle of positivism, was transformed into "feminist objectivity" by researchers such as Donna Haraway, Sandra Harding, and Kum-Kum Bhavnani. Haraway describes feminist objectivity through the concept of "situated knowledges," in which concepts such as knowledge and truth are always partial and inseparable from the lived experience of the researched; that is: subjective, power-imbued, and relational. In this schema, the denial of values, biases, and politics is unrealistic and undesirable (Haraway, 1988).

In particular, the historian Joan Scott disputed the positivist belief that there is a one-to-one correspondence between experience and social reality. Scott introduced a "linguistic turn" to our understanding of social reality by making two arguments: (1) the specific circumstances, conditions, values, and relations of power influence one's particular context, and (2) experience is discursively constructed by dominant ideological structures. Scott traced the discourse surrounding experience in order to examine the underlying mechanisms of oppression, thereby opening up new avenues of resistance and transformation (Scott, 1999). Categories like "experience" are redefined in feminist research projects and, subsequently, new methods emerge that can enable the researcher to develop new forms of knowing.

Some feminist researchers go beyond valuing women's unique and situated experiences as knowledge. Feminists like Alison Jaggar recognized emotion as a critical aspect of knowledge seeking, and made the case that the importance of emotions and values should be validated within the research process. According to Jaggar, it is unrealistic to assume that emotions and values will not affect the data, especially because emotions often motivate the researcher's selection of topics and questions as well as the methods by which those topics and questions are studied (Jaggar, 1997). For these feminist researchers, the dualism between the rational and the emotional, as proposed by positivism, is a false dichotomy (Sprague & Zimmerman, 1993).

To be clear, positivism per se is not necessarily antithetical to feminist inquiry. Apart from challenging androcentrism, some feminist researchers utilize positivistic methodology in order to add validity to their projects because positivism remains well-respected within androcentric research frameworks. In fact, some feminist research questions may rely on such a framework. This is especially the case when the goal of the research project in question requires testing a hypothesis on a broad spectrum of data in order to generalize to a wider population.

Feminist research underwent yet another turn toward alternative models of knowledge building with the emergence of feminist standpoint epistemology (Harding, 1993; Smith, 1990). Feminist standpoint epistemology is rooted in the shared Marxist and Hegelian idea that an individual's material and lived experience structures his or her understanding of his or her social environment. For example, the worker/slave's perspective is more complete than the master's alone, because the worker/slave must comprehend both his or her own world and that of the master's in order to survive. By placing value on victims of oppression, feminist standpoint epistemology follows the feminist tradition of bringing in voices of the silenced and/ or oppressed to mainstream dialogue. Thus, for feminist standpoint theorists, women's oppressed position within society is precisely what allows women to harbor rich insights into society as a whole. Because they are structurally oppressed in relation to the dominant group (men), women have access to a more enhanced and more nuanced understanding of social reality than men.

Sociologist Dorothy Smith, an early advocate of standpoint epistemology, emphasizes that feminist research projects must begin with women's lives. Smith is interested in the dissonances that occur in women's everyday lives when they attempt to reconcile their experiences with the dominant culture's conceptualization of their experiences. By locating and examining the gaps that emerge in this process, the researcher is able to gain an accurate and theoretically rich set of explanations regarding the relationships between the oppressors and the oppressed (Harding, 1993; Naples, 2003).

Standpoint epistemology faced early critiques that focused on difference. One critique was that standpoint epistemology unfairly collapses all women's experience into a single experience; this collapse neglects the diversity of women's lives in terms of, for example, race, class, and sexual orientation. Further questions were raised, such as, "If knowledge begins with the oppressed, how does one ascertain who is the most oppressed?"

Difference Matters: Feminist Research and the Turn Toward Difference

Both feminist empiricists and feminist standpoint theorists sought to give voice to the women who had been left out of mainstream research models by recognizing women's life stories as valuable forms of knowledge. But, both feminist empiricists and standpoint theorists had not yet answered some important questions, such as: *Which women's stories were being told? Whose life experiences were included? Whose are excluded?* The increasing attention paid to these questions indicated that feminist researchers were becoming conscious of the diversity of women's experiences. This consciousness was elevated further through feminism's interactions with a multitude of social justice movements—postcolonialism, poststructuralism, postmodernism—and, in this way, feminist research took a turn toward "difference research."

Feminist researchers' concern with difference provoked them to disagree with the idea that there is one essential "woman's experience." In place of one experience, they recognized a plurality. With multiple standpoints that accounted for the interlocking relationships between racism, sexism, heterosexism, and class oppression, additional starting points from which to understand social reality emerged.

The critical insights of feminists of color—Deborah King, Patricia Hill Collins, Chandra Mohanty, bell hooks, Gloria Anzaldua, to name a few—emerged from their research to address the interconnections among categories of difference such as gender, ethnicity, nationality, and class. The sociologist Patricia Hill Collins, for example, highlights the significance of black feminist thought. According to Collins, black women, or "outsiders within," must navigate the rules of the privileged white world, while always being aware of their marginalization in terms of race and gender (Collins, 1990). Black feminists' contributions are so important because sociological insiders, due to their privileged social positions, cannot understand the African American experience. Those in power tend to generalize without regard to diversity, and so black feminists must voice their experiences of the intersections between race and gender.

Additionally, Collins suggests that it is only by exploring the intricate matrix of difference that we can truly understand a given individual's lived experience. Collins' outsider/insider distinction was taken a step further by feminists like Michelle Fine, who emphasizes the distinction's fluidity: one can be an outsider in one social context, while being an insider in another (Fine, 1992).

Feminist theorists and researchers continue to work with these categories of difference, and the first two decades of the 21st century see feminists expanding their definition of difference by applying it to a global context.

Global Feminist Research

There is also a growing awareness among feminist researchers of the importance of women's experiences in a global context with respect to issues of imperialism, colonialism, and national identity. Postcolonial feminist Gayatri Chakravorty Spivak (1990) notes:

> On the other side of the international division of labor, the subject of exploitation cannot know and speak the text of female exploitation even if the absurdity of the nonrepresenting intellectual making space for them to speak is achieved. The woman is doubly in shadow. (p. 894)

Historian Deniz Kandiyoti (1999) discusses the tendency of some Western feminist researchers to "universalize" disciplinary concepts, ignoring the ethnocentrism that lies deep within constructs such as patriarchy. Kandiyoti also calls for the employment of a historical–comparative lens to strengthen our understanding of the cross-cultural context of conceptual meaning across Western and non-Western societies (see also Mohanty, 1988).

Frequently, analyses that incorporate race, class, and gender differences tend to ignore the diversity of women in terms of their particular geographical and cultural placement across the globe. Feminist researchers attempt to work against this tendency by asking questions such as:

How do we conceptualize and study difference in a global context?

What research frameworks serve to empower women and promote social change?

The expansion of feminist praxis across international and multicultural borders has helped to raise awareness about issues of power and authority regarding the relationship between the researcher and the "other(s)" for whom the research speaks. For example, this expansion has raised the question, "How does the researcher give voice to the 'other(s)'?"

Feminist researchers who work in a global context call for a heightened attention to power and difference across nation-state boundaries, and they use the intersections of difference as starting points. The creation of links between different strands of knowledge, however, remains a challenge for feminist research. For example, many studies concerning women in global contexts are somewhat fragmented; and black feminists, Third World feminists, and feminists studying global/postcolonial/transnational issues, in many cases, remain unaware of each other's theories and methodologies. In order to cultivate a complex, nuanced understanding of the interlocking mechanisms of racism, imperialism, and neocolonialism across historical and cultural borders, feminist researchers must continue to find new ways to put multiple analyses of difference in dialogue with each other.

The Development of *Feminist Research Practice*

So far, I have very briefly outlined the historical patterns that define the evolution of feminist research theory and praxis. Feminists continue to develop new ways of critically contemplating and understanding the nature of the social world. The creation of new questions and new angles through which to understand social reality is always, for feminist researchers, in service of promoting social justice for women.

By putting together this edited volume, *Feminist Research Practice*, I intended to provide theoretical and methods tools to feminist research scholars across disciplinary divisions. After many semesters teaching both undergraduate and graduate methods courses, I discovered that the topic of feminist research was too often neglected in standard research methods books. This edited volume is the direct result of that discovery. Teaching at the Graduate Consortium of Women's Studies, which began in 1992 and was then housed at Radcliffe College, I cultivated an appreciation for an interdisciplinary approach to studying and teaching feminist perspectives on theory and methods. Now housed at the Massachusetts Institute of Technology, the mission of the Graduate Consortium is to bring together faculty from a variety of disciplines in order to "discuss ways of consolidating and increasing the availability of feminist research and teaching across the disciplines and across institutions" (Hesse-Biber, Gilmartin, & Lydenberg, 1999, p. 5).

In particular, I co-taught a course titled Feminist Perspectives in Research: Interdisciplinary Practice in the Study of Gender with the historian Christina Gilmartin at Northeastern University and with the literary critic Robin Lydenberg at Boston College. Our coedited book, *Feminist Approaches to Theory and Methodology* (Hesse-Biber, Gilmartin, & Lydenberg, 1999), was based on our collaborative teaching experience and gathered together a wide range of interdisciplinary scholarship that found its intersection in feminist research and activism. As we note in our introduction, teaching within an interdisciplinary framework presented its own unexpected challenges:

> Over the three years during which the editors of this volume revised and taught this course, we were surprised to discover that as contested as the terrain of feminism has become, the interdisciplinary aspects of the course proved equally, if not more, problematic. While we eventually reached some shared understandings about feminism—that although its methodologies were rooted in social activism, it could not be reduced to an easily defined set of propositions, theoretical claims, or research methods—the nature and practice of interdisciplinarity remained elusive. (pp. 5–6)

I applied my experiences of teaching and learning in an interdisciplinary environment to a broader scope of research processes in a second anthology that I coedited: *Feminist Research Perspectives on Social Research* (Hesse-Biber & Yaiser, 2004). All aspects of the research process were taken into account in this second anthology, which was especially interested in the linkages between epistemology, methodology, and methods. Additionally, this anthology stressed the critical difference in research projects between acknowledging and practicing difference:

> Feminist research has taught us that it is not enough to merely acknowledge the importance of difference. Difference is critical to all aspects of the research process. It is important to

incorporate difference into our views of reality, truth, and knowledge. We must examine the difference that difference makes. (p. 117)

One organizing principle of this volume is that while any given feminist perspective may guide how a given method is put into practice, no feminist perspective precludes the use of specific methods. Pairing a perspective with an unexpected method may provide rich data. Theory and practice (and their interplay) are ever changing in feminist research, and this continuous shifting of knowledge is, according to Teresa de Lauretis (1988), "not merely an expansion or reconfiguration of boundaries, but a qualitative shift in political and historical consciousness" (pp. 138–139).

Organization of This Book

The organization of the book reflects the elements of the research process from a feminist standpoint. The first part of the book focuses on the major epistemological and theoretical groundings that guide many feminists in their research. In Chapter 2, Nancy Naples and Barbara Gurr expand upon the theories of feminist empiricism and feminist standpoint theory by questioning the "objective" truth, and they note that this dominant form of knowledge building has a history of propagating hegemonic power dynamics. They note that the development of standpoint theories and methodologies centers women's lived experiences in order to uncover "subjugated knowledge" that often remains hidden when utilizing traditional positivistic approaches. Chapter 3 by Nollaig Frost and Frauke Elichaoff introduces feminist poststructuralist and postmodernist theoretical approaches as well as the development of critical theory. Originating from French philosophical thinkers, postmodernism and poststructuralism challenged traditional biological essentialism and binaries that dictated gender characteristics and roles and questioned the notion that all women were the same. In contrast to feminist empiricism and standpoint theory, the developments of critical theory and feminist approaches to postmodernism and poststructuralism stress methods for deconstructing the gender binary and its inherent oppression. All these theoretical approaches emphasize the diversity of women's experiences over a single collective narrative. Both theoretical chapters provide a range of perspectives regarding the social world that privilege the diversity of women's lived experiences over a single collective narrative and stress the pursuit of social justice by challenging the oppression of women.

The next set of chapters analyzes a diverse array of research methods employed by feminist researchers, and it addresses the linkages between particular methods and feminist epistemological frameworks and perspectives. Chapter 4, by Linda Bell, addresses the ethics of feminist research and offers examples of feminist researchers embedding ethics in the research process; they are able to do this by carefully tending to power dynamics, the intricacies of obtaining "informed consent," and potential obstacles to maintaining confidentiality. Chapter 5, by Elana Buch and Karen Staller, expertly traces the development and practice of feminist ethnography and walks the reader through the process of preparing and utilizing this research method. Chapter 6, by M. Brinton Lykes and Alison Crosby, tackles participatory action research: "Insiders" of a problem collaborate with "outsiders" with different skills or techniques in order to expose the various forces promoting inequality. In Chapter 7, I introduce the method of in-depth interviewing by exploring a holistic step-by-step approach to conducting an interview, with a series of exercises for you to practice along the way. Chapter 8, by Jennie Munday, addresses focus groups and their importance to feminist research before describing how one would find and prepare a sample, be an effective moderator, and analyze the received data. Chapter 9, by Heather McIntosh and Lisa Cuklanz, focuses on feminist media research, which is overridden by gender stereotypes of women and female appearances and behavior. After an introductory explanation of feminist media theory, the chapter contextualizes feminist media theory methods within different media—such as the Internet and material culture—and then outlines the process by which one could follow such methods. Chapter 10, by Kathi Miner and Toby Jayaratne, deals with feminist approaches to surveys, both quantitative and qualitative, and the processes of these methods. In Chapter 11, "The Feminist Practice of Program Evaluation," Donna Mertens and Nichole Stewart expertly introduce the nuts and bolts of conducting a feminist evaluation, as well as the feminist principles and the axiological, ontological, epistemological, and methodological questions that are crucial to evaluation. In Chapter 12, I bring an introductory perspective onto feminist approaches to mixed methods research, in which the qualitative and quantitative methods are combined in a single study. I highlight the various types of mixed methods research designs and their advancement of feminism's social justice goals using multiple case studies. Finally, in Chapter 13, I tie the strands of feminist practice together by providing an extended case study example to illustrate how to put your feminist research project together—step-by-step.

I hope that in reading this book, you will come to realize the many different ways that feminist research can serve as a vehicle for women's empowerment. All the authors of this volume extend to you their personal invitation to make this exciting research journey!

We end this introduction as we began, with a story. This was a story written by a Women's and Gender Studies minor undergraduate senior at Boston College who was inspired to write this "Behind-the-Scenes" piece that discusses the necessity of feminism in today's society.

Behind the Scenes With Lizzie Jekanowski

The Necessity of Feminism Today

Today, I observe how common it is for my peers to erroneously believe that feminism is passé. Many women voice that their singular experiences of being a certain race, class, and nationality will speak for the lived realities of all women. Thus, because one woman does not experience or recognize sexist oppression, then it simply could not exist. From my perspective as a white, middle-class Boston College student, I see that this type of thinking serves to silence the diversity of women's voices. It is for this reason that we need feminism NOW more than ever.

While the American feminist movement has fought for and obtained significant advancements, some critical things remain resistant to change. Many individuals from my own generation have grown up without the feminist history of what life was like before the circumstances we have now. We may often see the gains, but we may not see the past struggles and inequities. We do not see that I would not have been allowed to occupy a place at my own university fifty years ago, simply because I am a woman. I would argue that many of my generation take the opportunities we now have for granted. Thus, gratitude and constant vigilance against the resurgence of sexist forces is imperative to bring about an equal world.

For me, to be a feminist is to continue to reflect upon the historical legacy of those feminists who came before us and to be cognizant of the work and research they have done. As a feminist now, I am obligated to understand the knowledge of women's lived realities. This is the significance and legacy of feminist research: It delves into the complexities, differences, and intersections of oppression within women's lives. It is fundamentally crucial to the understanding of inequality around us, so that together we all may move forward in the pursuit of social justice.

Author's note: A portion of this chapter was adapted from: Hesse-Biber, S.N. 2012. "Feminist research: Exploring, interrogating, and transforming the interconnections of epistemology, methodology and method." In S. Hesse-Biber (Ed.), *The handbook of feminist research: Theory and praxis* (pp. 2–26). Thousand Oaks, CA: Sage

REFERENCES

Collins, P. H. 1990. *Black feminist thought: Knowledge, consciousness, and the politics of empowerment.* Boston, MA: Unwin Hyman.

Comte, A. 2000. *The positive philosophy of August Comte* (Vol. 1, H. Martineau, Trans.). Kitchener, Ontario, Canada: Batoche Books. (Original work published 1896)

de Lauretis, T. 1988. Displacing hegemonic discourses: Reflections on feminist theory in the 1980s. *Inscriptions, 3/4,* 127–145.

Durkheim, É. 1938. *The rules of sociological method.* Glencoe, IL: Free Press. (Original work published 1895)

Fine, M. 1992. *Disruptive voices: The possibilities of feminist research (Critical Perspectives on Women and Gender Series).* Ann Arbor: University of Michigan Press.

Haraway, D. 1988. Situated knowledges: The science question in feminism and the privilege of partial perspective. *Feminist Studies 14,* 575–599.

Harding, S. 1993. Rethinking standpoint epistemology: What is "strong objectivity"? In L. Alcoff & E. Potter (Eds.), *Feminist epistemologies* (pp. 49–82). New York, NY: Routledge.

Hesse-Biber, S., & Carter, G. L. 2005. *Working women in America: Split dreams.* New York, NY: Oxford University Press.

Hesse-Biber, S., Gilmartin, C., & Lydenberg, R. (1999). Introduction. In S. Hesse-Biber, C. Gilmartin, & R. Lydenberg (Eds.), *Feminist approaches to theory and methodology* (pp. 1–11). New York, NY: Oxford University Press.

Hesse-Biber, S., & Yaiser, M. L. 2004. *Feminist research perspectives on social research.* Oxford, England: Oxford University Press.

Jaggar, A. M. 1997. Love and knowledge: Emotion in feminist epistemology. In S. Kemp & J. Squires (Eds.), *Feminisms* (pp. 188–193). Oxford, England: Oxford University Press.

Kandiyoti, D. (1999). Islam and patriarchy: A comparative perspective. In S. Hesse-Biber, C. Gilmartin, & R. Lydenberg (Eds.), *Feminist approaches to theory and methodology* (pp. 219–235). New York, NY: Oxford University Press.

Mohanty, C. 1988. Under Western eyes: Feminist scholarship and colonial discourses. *Feminist Review, 30,* 61–88.

Naples, N. A. 2003. *Feminism and method: Ethnography, discourse analysis, and activist research.* New York, NY: Routledge.

Scott, J. 1999. The evidence of experience. In S. Hesse-Biber, C. Gilmartin, & R. Lydenberg (Eds.), *Feminist approaches to theory and methodology* (pp. 79–99). New York, NY: Oxford University Press.

Smith, D. E. 1990. *The conceptual practices of power: A feminist sociology of knowledge.* Boston, MA: Northeastern University Press.

Spivak, G. C. 1990. *The postcolonial critic: Interviews, strategies, dialogue.* New York, NY: Routledge.

Sprague, J., & Zimmerman, M. K. 1993. Overcoming dualisms: A feminist agenda for sociological methodology. In P. England (Ed.), *Theory on gender/Feminism on theory* (pp. 255–280). New York, NY: Aldine de Gruyter.

CHAPTER 2

Feminist Empiricism and Standpoint Theory

Approaches to Understanding the Social World

Nancy A. Naples and Barbara Gurr

Introduction

Over twenty-five years ago, feminist philosopher Sandra Harding (1987) asked: "Is there a distinctive feminist method of inquiry?" In answering the question, she distinguished between epistemology ("a theory of knowledge"), methodology ("a theory and analysis of how research does or should proceed"), and method ("a technique for . . . gathering evidence"; pp. 2–3). She pointed out the important connections between epistemologies, methodologies, and research methods (p. 3l). The specific methods researchers choose and how they employ those methods are informed by their epistemological stance. Epistemological assumptions also influence how researchers define their roles, what they consider ethical research practices, and how they interpret and implement informed consent or ensure the confidentiality of their research subjects. In this chapter, we describe two major epistemological approaches within feminist research, namely, empiricism and standpoint theories; and we illustrate these approaches with recent developments in feminist research.

The burgeoning women's movements of the 1960s and 1970s brought with them challenges to traditional forms of social science. One of the primary challenges put forth by feminist scholars has been to prevailing understandings of the nature of knowledge and knowledge production. As sociologist Patricia Hill Collins (2000) points out, "what to believe and why something is true are not benign academic issues. Instead, these concerns tap the fundamental question of which versions of truth will prevail and shape thought and action" (p. 203). The fundamental feminist assertions that "truth" can be multiply defined or understood and that knowledge is political (as opposed to existing in a pure state outside of social contexts) have motivated scholars to explore a variety of questions such as: Who benefits from traditional forms of knowledge production, and who may be disadvantaged by these? If knowledge is differentially produced and claimed, how are feminists, with a concern for social justice grounded in gendered experiences, to understand "truth" in knowledge? In other words, how do scholars evaluate knowledge validity, particularly if there are competing claims? And, methodologically, how can scholars seek out knowledge from a variety of perspectives?

How do feminist scholars account for their methodological practices in ways that do not reproduce the power imbalances potentially embedded in more traditional theoretical and methodological approaches? These questions/problems and their focus on power dynamics in research have led to at least three important developments in feminist theory and methodology: a broad and deep critique of traditional approaches to objectivity; intense scrutiny of epistemic privilege in the production of knowledge; and an increased attention to standpoint and positionality, particularly as they relate to the first two.

What Is Knowledge and How Do We Know? Empiricism as One Answer

The questions of what knowledge is and how it is produced to organize all endeavors to understand the social world, whether we recognize the epistemological underpinnings of our efforts or not. For much of the Western world, "science" has been historically examined through an empirical lens, which claims that all knowledge is based on experience, and particularly the experience of the five commonly recognized physical senses. This epistemology or "way of knowing" is called empiricism. Empiricism is the doctrine that all knowledge derives from sensory experience, exists relatively uniformly outside of social contexts, and is validated as true by its replicability through objective measurements.

Empiricism emerged from the universities of Renaissance Europe, privileged centers of learning for men of economic means. The emphasis in empiricism on replicability of experience promoted the development of the scientific method, with its reliance on hypotheses and experimental situations. The scientific method continues to dominate the physical sciences today, although it is also utilized in social sciences such as sociology, economics, and education. Empirical scientists understand that experience is measurable, finite, and replicable—anyone with the prerequisite skills can reproduce this same knowledge given the right circumstances, and, in fact, its very validity as knowledge rests on its replicability. In this framework, although individuals exist within social contexts, knowledge or "truth" is separable from individual knowers. The empirical approach follows Rene Descartes' 17th century belief that the mind and body are separate one from another, and that rationality (mind) is more valued as a means of knowing than corporeality (body). The Cartesian dualism embedded in the idea that knowledge is separate and separable from society is reflected in classical notions of objectivity in research as unbiased, value-free, and asocial; the researcher is a learned investigator, but not a participant in knowledge production, because truth already exists outside of social contexts. It is the job of the researcher to discover this truth without imposing her own ideas, values, or social frames on it.

In the early 20th century, the scientific method and its empirical underpinnings became linked to positivism, an epistemological theory that holds that *only* knowledge that can be proven experientially—through the physical senses—is scientifically valid. French philosopher Auguste Comte proposed in the mid-19th century that positivism would eventually become the guiding framework of sociology and other social science endeavors, an assertion that Karl Marx rejected, although Emile Durkheim further developed a positivist approach to social science research. Anthropology and geography, as well as sociology, grew increasingly positivist in their accounts of social and human phenomena throughout the 20th century, relying, for example, on observation and forms of measurement such as quantitative analysis and computer-derived geographic information systems. During the early to mid-20th century, in particular, the growing emphasis on positivism elevated the status of particular methods such as experimental and survey research.

Following the empirical paradigm, early ethnographic research, a multimethod approach that includes observation of everyday activities, saw as its goal the development of truth about certain communities or institutions. Although ethnographic work has become increasingly complicated by feminist calls for reflexivity and postmodern understandings of positionality, classic forms of ethnographic observation leading to generalizable conclusions continue to dominate (see, e.g., Dean, 2009; see also Merry, 2000). Nonetheless, despite its reliance on observation, ethnography is often considered to be lacking scientific rigor due to its lack of replicability or control over variables and its potentially subjective conclusions (Atkinson & Hammersley, 2007; Brewer, 1994). This may be due in part to reliance on the body in ethnographic research, which privileges participant observation as a means of knowing (Conquergood, 2003; see also Goffman, 1989).

Many feminist scholars have embraced the basic tenets of empiricism and attempt to use the methodological norms of scientific inquiry to uncover and correct sexist and androcentric assumptions in method, theory, and findings. In some ways, this is a very pragmatic response to the institutionalization of these biases, in that feminist scholars can potentially open dialogues with other scientists as well as justify particular findings with methods deemed generally acceptable. As Nelson (1990) argues, "The point of feminist science criticism must, in the end, be to change science, and changing science requires changing the practices of scientists. Hence, scientists must be brought into the dialogue" (p. 6).

However, feminist uses of empirical methods do more than promote dialogue and potential change; they can also reveal the androcentric biases inherent in much of the physical sciences. For example, evolutionary biologist Elisabeth Lloyd (2005) asserts that theories about female orgasm from evolutionary biology reflect an androcentric bias toward heterosexuality which privileges male sexual experiences. She argues that these theories simply fail to adequately explain the existence of female orgasms, or the range of orgasm experiences women have. This assertion, which rejects the evolutionist stance that biological adaptation must have a survival function, opens up new ways of understanding female sexuality, including destigmatizing women who do not regularly have orgasms as well as destigmatizing women's same-sex erotic attractions by de-linking orgasms from evolutionary necessity (and thus de-linking women's sexuality from male orgasm).

Feminist scholars in the physical and biological sciences have been working to produce an agenda of feminist empiricism, which challenges traditional models while still relying on empirical methods. Physicist Vandana Shiva (2005, 2010) foregrounds an ecofeminist perspective in her examinations of consumption, sustainability, and the oppression of women. She uses a gendered, postcolonial approach to argue that the physical world and the social world must be understood as deeply and inextricably linked. Biologist Anne Fausto-Sterling (2000) provides an in-depth examination of the ways in which biologists have historically politicized the body in particularly gendered ways. Using historical data, media reports, structured interviews, and informal conversations with scientists, health professionals, and social researchers, Fausto-Sterling reveals the complex "politics of sexuality and the making and using of knowledge about the biology of human behavior" (p. 5).

Geneticist and sociologist Tom Shakespeare (2006) works from a feminist perspective to interrogate the intersections of the body with the social world, revealing how ideas about ability and disability are complexly informed by biology, medicine, and social expectations. Drawing on a long-term ethnographic investigation of organizations and nongovernmental organizations serving individuals with disabilities, as well as interviews with people with disabilities, disability studies researchers, philosophers, and policy makers, Shakespeare explores the diverse views held by different constituencies who have influenced contemporary medical, social, and policy approaches to disabilities. The work of these and other scholars challenges the wisdom received from traditional positivist science as well as the means of deriving this wisdom.

However, feminist empiricism has been heavily criticized by some feminist scholars for failing to perceive the links between science and politics (see, e.g., Hartsock, 1983;

Hekman, 1992). In the late 1980s and early 1990s, feminist scholars such as Ruth Behar (1993, 2007), Joan Scott (1988), and Dorothy Smith (1987, 1992) increasingly began to challenge finite categorizations of knowledge systems in ways that called into question the validity of empirical measurements. In the context of these challenges, Harding (1991) and others questioned whether or not there could be a feminist empiricism. This was contemporaneous with the development of emerging postmodern theories that challenged previous conceptions of knowledge as static, measurable, and linked to prevailing notions of objectivity.

Feminist Analyses of Objectivity

As sociologist Joey Sprague (2005) argues, "[A]t the heart of positivist epistemology is an emphasis on objectivity. Positivism assumes that truth comes from eliminating the role of subjective judgments and interpretations; . . . subjectivity is an obstacle to knowledge" (p. 32). Yet as feminist researchers have long argued, it is the very assumption that an objectivity which is free of social context can be achieved that both privileges a certain way of conducting research—primarily through a positivist, empirical frame reliant on replicability and a Cartesian split between knower and known—and discredits other ways of learning and knowing, which may rely upon or conjure networks of relationship, community knowledges, and subjective experiences. Educational theorist Patti Lather (2003) explains that "feminist research, neo-Marxist critical ethnography, and Freirean 'empowering' research all stand in opposition to prevailing scientific norms. . . . [E]ach argues that scientific 'neutrality' and 'objectivity' serve to mystify the inherently ideological nature of research in the human sciences and to legitimate privilege based on class, race, and gender" (p. 186). Harding (1995) refers to this as the rule of "might makes right in the realm of knowledge production" and points out that, after all, "observations are theory-laden; our beliefs form a network such that none are in principle immune from revision; theories are underdetermined by any possible set of evidence for them" (p. 331). Given the potential tensions of such a positivist approach to objectivity, many feminist theorists have sought to develop other conceptualizations of what objectivity is, what it can be, and perhaps what it should be. According to historian Joan Scott (1991), the feminist reimagination of knowledge includes efforts to "unmask all claims to objectivity as an ideological cover for masculine bias by pointing out the shortcomings, incompleteness, and exclusiveness of 'mainstream' history" (p. 786; see also Proctor, 1991).

Harding (1995) is perhaps one of the most well-known feminist theorists of objectivity. She argues that many of the weaknesses feminists have previously identified in classical notions of objectivity can in fact be reconfigured to open up new spaces for theorizing, if and when they can be recognized and examined. She is particularly interested in the politics of androcentrism and eurocentrism as these are "exercised less visibly, less consciously, and *not on but through* the dominant institutional structures, priorities, research strategies, technologies and languages of the sciences—through the practice and culture that constitute a particular scientific episode" (p. 335, emphasis original) and whereby the social actually constitutes scientific projects. Harding explains that due to the inherent limitations of such science, the equation of objectivity with a sense of neutrality can never succeed, but rather works to hide the politics of power at play. As one potential way to address this, Harding urges the development of "strong objectivity," which is neither classical objectivity nor what is often taken for its opposite, relativity. Strong objectivity acknowledges the politics of knowledge production and claims that greater attention to the social locations of knowledge producers and to the social contexts of knowledge production will contribute to a more transparent and thus potentially ethical result. Strong objectivity involves acknowledging the political, social, and historical aspects of all knowledge (Longino, 1993).

STANDPOINT EPISTEMOLOGY AND STRONG OBJECTIVITY

One aspect of traditional approaches to science and knowledge production that contributes to a weak form of objectivity is found in the movement toward greater and greater generalization, as scholars seek to produce insights which can be applied in a wide variety of contexts. This focus on theoretical applicability results in the privileging of certain kinds of knowledge—namely, that which is more and more widely applicable—and thereby knowledge that emerges from or applies only to very specific contexts remains invalid in the eyes of academia or, at the very least, is undervalued. As a result, material reality is replaced with abstractions that bear little resemblance to the phenomenon originally under examination. Feminist standpoint theorist Dorothy Smith (1987) explains that the traditional androcentric approach to sociology that privileges a white, middle-class, and heterosexual point of view produces results that are both alienating and colonizing (see also Stanley, 1990). Harding (1998) has also been concerned with the role of colonization in marginalizing the situated knowledges of the targets of colonization. Western science has developed through the exploitation and silencing of colonial subjects. In this way, much useful knowledge has been lost or rendered suspect (see Sachs, 1996).

Like Harding, feminist scholars who approach the research process from the point of view of strong objectivity are interested in producing knowledge for use as well as for revealing the relations of power that are hidden in traditional knowledge production processes. Strong objectivity acknowledges that the production of power is a political process and that greater attention paid to the context and social location of knowledge producers will contribute to a more ethical and transparent result. In fact, Harding (1991) argues, an approach to research and knowledge production that does not acknowledge the role that power and social location play in the knowledge production process must be understood as offering only a weak form of objectivity.

Feminist empiricists take up the positive approach but introduce the importance of social context for shaping knowledge. They are attentive to the ways that assumptions about gender and other categories of difference influence the construction of scientific practices and data collection. They are also concerned about the lack of epistemic authority granted to women and others historically marginalized within the fields of philosophy, social science, science, and technology. In providing a corrective to the classical approach to empirical inquiry, feminist empiricists emphasize the role of the situated knower and situated knowledge to reflect the importance of diverse ways of knowing for improving the production of knowledge. However, feminist empiricism continues the earlier emphasis on the ability to generate objective knowledge, or knowledge as separate from or independent of the knower (Nelson, 1990). Their neo-positive approach, while recognizing the need to locate research in the specific cultural and regional context, remains linked to the classical positivist notion of objectivity that holds to the belief that truth can be discerned by adherence to a system of inquiry that controls for different variables. It does expand the variables to be considered but ultimately remains in dialogue with the traditional scientific approach. This is not to say that feminist empiricism is not an important feminist framework. In fact, it remains a significant way of generating knowledge about a wide range of topics including demographic, economic, and epidemiological diversity and change.

While feminist empiricism does address questions related to diversity and change, feminist standpoint theorists include attention to diversity of individual experiences as well as the specific social context as identified by economic, demographic, and other measures. For feminist standpoint theorists, the strongest approach to knowledge production is one that takes into account the most diverse set of experiences. Harding follows this line of inquiry into practices of strong objectivity in her book *Is Science Multicultural? Postcolonialisms, Feminisms, and Epistemologies* (1998), this time with a focus on colonialism and ethnocentrism in research as well as sexism and other institutional biases. She explains that ethnocentrism is more than a set of "false beliefs and bad attitudes" held by individual scholars; it is structured into the institutional and academic practices so as to produce relationships oppressive to indigenous cultures in the so-called first world as well as third world countries. In her book, *Sciences From Below: Feminisms, Postcolonialities, and Modernities*, Harding (2008) demonstrates the link between imperialism, contemporary globalization, and inequalities in evaluations of different systems of knowledge. She concludes by offering a vision of a democratic future in which different knowledges are valued and put into action for a sustainability and social justice.

Additionally, Harding argues that more objective and more relevant knowledge is produced by starting inquiry from the lived experiences of women and others who have been traditionally outside of the institutions in which knowledge about social life is generated and classified. Harding (1986) and political theorist Nancy Hartsock (1983) emphasize that knowledge produced from the point of view of subordinated groups may offer stronger objectivity due to the increased motivation for them to understand the views or perspectives of those in positions of power. This argument, discussed further below, also leads to interrogations of epistemic authority and epistemic privilege.

What Are Epistemic Authority and Epistemic Privilege?

The question of epistemic authority, or whose knowledge is recognized and validated and whose is silenced, as well as related questions of methodology, complicate reliance on empirical knowledge gained from the scientific method of inquiry. As Mariane Janack (1997) points out, epistemic privilege and epistemic authority, although linked, are not the same, and the differences between them must be teased out in order to develop a nuanced understanding of the nature of standpoint and objectivity. According to Janack (1997), "epistemic authority is conferred . . . as a result of other peoples' judgment of our sincerity, reliability, trustworthiness, and 'objectivity'; . . . certain people are [understood to be] in a better position to 'see' the world than are other people" (p. 133). This privileged social location imparts a level of authority to knowledge claims. Epistemic privilege, on the other hand, is perhaps more socially complex, in that it refers to those who have and use (or are used by others who have) the opportunity to be *known* as authorities, and in being known as authorities, become privileged to speak further. Epistemic privilege can be provided, enforced, occluded, or restricted in a myriad of shifting social contexts, including race, class, gender, and sexuality; cognitive and physical ability; citizenship; communities of knowledge production and knowledge sharing such as university departments and activist organizations; and so on. For example, anthropologist Victoria Sanford (2008), whose work focuses primarily on violence and narratives of memory, argues that "individual, communal, and national memories . . . offer trajectories of meaning. . . . [O]ne's location on a given trajectory of meaning determines one's structure of understanding—which ultimately shapes the contours of 'understandable' truth" (p. 21; see also Thomasson, 2003).

Many postcolonial and indigenous feminist theorists further locate the consequences of epistemic privilege in geopolitical structures of dominance and control (see also Collins, 2000; Sanford, 2008). Linda Tuhiwai Te Rina Smith (2002) asserts that "the critique of positivism by feminist theorists, ethnic minorities and indigenous peoples has emerged from the experience of people who have been studied, researched, written about, and defined by social scientists" and that "as Europeans began to explore and colonize other parts of the world, notions of rationality and conceptualizations of knowledge became the convenient tool for dismissing from serious comparison with Western forms of thought those of 'primitive' thought which were being encountered" (pp. 169–170). Furthermore, in a global system of knowledge production dominated by Western methods, "a process which tends to give greater legitimacy to written sources. . . . [T]he potential to reproduce colonizing ideologies and colonizing perspectives is always present" (p. 172). In this way, knowledge production becomes an act of silencing as much as an act of discovery, and the politics of knowledge production serve the politics of imperialism.

Feminists are not immune to this process. For example, feminist scholar Chandra Mohanty (2006) critiques the construction by Western feminists of a "composite, singular, third world woman" through "assumptions of privilege and ethnocentric universality [which] lead to the construction of a . . . reductive and homogeneous notion of . . . 'Third World difference' " (p. 19). Historian Devon Mihesuah (2003) argues that a similar construction of a "monolithic Indian woman" (p. 15) by largely non-Native academics limits knowledge of Native America to that produced and controlled by dominant frames.

As feminist scholars have pointed out, epistemic privilege—the right and ability to be heard—has frequently resulted in "knowledge" that is, in fact, demonstrably limited. For example, in her foundational interrogation of previously unchallenged theories of moral development, psychologist Carol Gilligan (1982) argued that the typically accepted trajectory of moral development was, in fact, based on androcentric projects that eschewed traits and characteristics more commonly associated with girls and women, such as relationality and conflict avoidance. She found that young girls developed a moral sensibility that was essentially different from young boys', but was neither deficient nor inadequate to social tasks. Rather, she argued, socialization into hegemonically feminine behaviors provided girls with a strong relational logic, while socialization into hegemonically masculine behaviors provided boys with a strong rational logic based on individualism; in a patriarchal society, it is the masculine-associated rationality that is validated, while other moral logics are infantilized. Gilligan's work is often cited as an exemplar of feminist research due to her challenges to the assumed universality of male experience. Similarly, Belenky, Clinchy, Goldberger, and Tarule (1986) examined women's ways of gaining and experiencing knowledge. Belenky and colleagues did not explicitly argue that these "ways of knowing" belonged only or even primarily to women. Their findings offered alternative understandings of knowledge that expanded more positivist epistemologies, which, they argued, had relied on empirically positivist ideals.

Epistemic privilege does not belong only to individuals who produce knowledge; it can be located also in academic disciplines. For example, philosophers Sarah-Marie Belcastro and Jean Marie Moran (2003) argue that reconceptualizing knowledge in the physical sciences comes with distinct challenges for feminists. One of these challenges is the very nature of training in the physical sciences, which they argue is dominated by men and wherein "physical scientists are not necessarily trained in recognizing or acknowledging biases in their work or in admitting blind spots in how they conducted experiments and interpreted their results" (p. 28). They argue that this may be one reason why so few active physical scientists are simultaneously engaged with their primary discipline and with feminist philosophies of science. Similarly, Martha Whitaker (2001) discusses her graduate training in Women's Studies and Hydrology and notes the disciplinary training required from singular disciplines (rather than interdisciplinary endeavors such as Women's Studies) may limit feminists who wish to produce scholarship that expands traditional means of knowledge production. In fact, Belcastro and Moran (2003) assert, such expansion may not even be possible in the physical sciences, particularly for those who may not "have the freedom to explore new paradigms in [their] respective academic environments" (p. 28). The disciplinary training of many physical scientists eschews alternative paradigms of knowledge production and produces structural challenges to thinking and researching outside of these frames, thereby potentially limiting opportunity and ability to develop feminist ways of knowing in these disciplines.

Despite ongoing efforts by feminists in the physical and natural sciences, the social sciences have perhaps seen a greater impact on the potential to reimagine knowledge and knowledge production. For example, geographer Mei-Po Kwan (2002) demonstrates that geographic information systems and other visual technologies can be used by feminist researchers for a variety of purposes, including deconstructing binaries in geographical discourse such as divisions between quantitative and qualitative data collection and analysis. She asserts that a feminist geographic vision reveals previously unconsidered aspects of social lives and social justice. Anthropology in particular has progressed an agenda of seeking out and validating alternative ways of knowing that critique and elaborate on traditional empirical forms. For example, anthropologist Renato Rosaldo (1989) expands traditional anthropological perspectives by foregrounding both multiply situated social identities and the larger political and social processes that constitute cultural structures. He argues, "[A]lthough the classical vision of unique cultural patterns has merit, it also has serious limitations. It emphasizes shared patterns at the expense of processes of change and internal inconsistencies, conflicts and contradictions. . . . [C]lassic forms of analysis make it difficult to study zones of difference within and between cultures" (pp. 27–28). Ruth Behar (1993, 2007) experiments with hybrid methods of data collection and analysis in which she incorporates sustained attention to her own role in the production of knowledge. Behar's work exemplifies another aspect of contemporary feminist standpoint approaches that attend to the role of emotions and of the body in constructing different experiences and different ways of knowing.

Feminist researchers who are interested in shifting the standpoint on knowledge also use a critical analysis of discourse to reveal the way in which power is lodged in categories of analysis and in science. For example, Emily Martin (2001) and David Valentine (2007) interrogate the role of discourse in shaping knowledge and experiences in different fields. Martin examines the gendered nature of knowledge in biology and medicine and the consequences of the gendered discourses, which organize prevailing knowledge production and medical treatment. Valentine's (2007) work on transgender identity and experience, specifically locating the trans-gendered body in multiple social contexts, reveals the links between the social production of knowledge, embodiment, and medicalization of the body.

In sociology, feminist scholars have advanced intersectionality as one means of addressing the nuances of knowledge production. Intersectionality, first theorized by legal scholar Kimberle Crenshaw (1991), foregrounds the complications of multiply situated identities and the social contexts in which these identities are experienced. Collins (2000) refers to this as a matrix of domination. Intersectional theorists use a variety of methods from interviews and observations (Cantú, 2009; Gurr, 2011; Kang, 2010; Naples, 1998; Purkayastha, 2005); content analysis and historical sociology (Collins, 2004; Nagel, 2003); discourse and policy analysis (Baker, 2007; Gurr & McGary, 2009; Holmes, 2005; Naples, 1998; Shakespeare, 2006); and quantitative analysis (McCall, 2001) to bring to light different ways of knowing and experiencing the social world.

Feminist Standpoint Epistemology and Methodological Innovations

Feminist standpoint theory is a broad categorization that includes somewhat diverse theories ranging from Hartsock's (1983) *feminist historical materialism* perspective, Donna Haraway's (2003) analysis of *situated knowledges*, Patricia Hill Collins's (1990) *black feminist thought*, Chela Sandoval's (2000) explication of third world feminists' *differential oppositional consciousness,* and Smith's (1987, 1990a, 1990b) *everyday world sociology* for women. Many theorists whose work has been identified with standpoint theory contest this designation; for example, Smith (1992) has been particularly vocal about the limits of this classification. She explains that it was Harding (1986) who first named feminist standpoint theory as a general approach within feminism to refer to the many different theorists who argued for the importance of situating knowledge in women's experiences.

Feminist standpoint theory was initially developed in response to debates surrounding Marxist feminism and socialist feminism in the 1970s and early 1980s. In reworking Marx's historical materialism from a feminist perspective, standpoint theorists' stated goal is to explicate how relations of domination are gendered in particular ways. Standpoint theory also developed in the context of third world and postcolonial feminist challenges to the so-called dual systems of patriarchy and capitalism. The dual systems approach was an attempt to merge feminist analyses of patriarchy and Marxist analyses of class to create a more complex socialist feminist theory of women's oppression. Critics of the dual systems approach pointed out the lack of attention paid by socialist feminist analyses to racism, white supremacy, and colonialism. In contrast, feminist standpoint theory offers an intersectional analysis of gender, race, ethnicity, class, and other structural aspects of social life without privileging one dimension or adopting an additive formulation (e.g., gender plus race). Standpoint theory retains elements of Marxist historical materialism for its central premise: knowledge develops in a complicated and contradictory way from lived experiences and social historical context.

Feminist standpoint scholars often use diverse qualitative methods to shift the standpoint to knowers whose vantage point has been ignored or discredited for producing knowledge. In *Bodies in Crisis: Culture, Violence, and Women's Resistance in Neoliberal Argentina,* Barbara Sutton (2010) foregrounds women's experiences in Argentina during a time of major social change and economic crisis. Her analysis centers women's accounts through an examination of embodiment that she defines in multiple ways. Sutton examines how women's lives were affected by the political context, including the toll it took on them, and the embodied strategies they developed to resist the repressive environment. She marshals her evidence to reveal the specific mechanisms that contribute to the different bodily effects and resistance strategies. Her analysis offers new insights for a number of important areas of academic knowledge including social movements, sexuality, health, and cultural studies to produce a rich understanding of women's lives and political activism.

In her study of Latinas who are experiencing violence against them, Roberta Villalón (2010) used participant observation, interviews with attorneys and other relevant actors, and archival research to explore their experiences as well as the personal, social, economic, and political contexts that shape them. Through this multimethodological approach, Villalón was able to uncover the myriad of ways that staff attempt to support these women's rights and to negotiate the relevant laws and social policies as well as the obstacles the women face as undocumented immigrants. However, the staff inadvertently makes judgments regarding which immigrant women are deserving of assistance and which legal cases should be pursued. Villalón examines the effect on the women's lives as well as the advocacy work of nonprofit organizations at the local level to understand how social policy reproduces inequalities and leaves immigrant women vulnerable to further abuse. Her discussion of the historical, cultural, and geographical context is especially powerful in that it provides a rich and multilayered understanding of the processes by which Latinas attempt to challenge the violence in their lives. Her attention to the methodological dilemmas she faced as an activist–scholar highlights the importance of reflexive practice for qualitative research.

In his book *Imagining Transgender: An Ethnography of a Category*, Valentine (2007) maintains a visible presence as a researcher and as a participant in the lives of his informants. Using reflexive practice, he reveals his own struggles as a gay man conducting research among transgender communities in New York; and he incorporates not only empirical data from interviews, observations, and discourse analysis, but also his own perspective on this data and the processes of obtaining it. Importantly, he also makes visible the ways in which his perspective and his research methods are influenced by his informants, their experiences, and their opinions of his work, thereby maintaining an emphasis on their subjectivity. Sociologist Julie Bettie (2003) uses similar methods to analyze the intersections of race, class, gender, and sexuality for young women in her book *Women Without Class: Girls, Race, and Identity*, reflexively considering her data, her own ongoing responses to the data as a researcher, and the subjectivity of her informants. Sociologist Barbara Gurr (forthcoming) relies on autoethnographic methods to develop an accountable, strong objectivity in her research on the family identity tasks of parents of transgender children, thereby resisting positivist notions of objectivity as neutral and unbiased by openly asserting her own location in the research process and as the parent of a transgender daughter. These scholars attempt to make clear their own situated locations as well as the ways in which these locations may impact their data collection and analysis, thereby eschewing what Haraway (2003) has referred to as the "God trick" of omniscience implied by classical standards of objectivity.

Feminist scholars argue for a self-reflexive approach to theorizing in order to foreground how relations of power may be shaping the production of knowledge in different contexts (Naples, 2003). The point of view of all those involved in the knowledge production process must be acknowledged and taken into account in order to produce strong objectivity. In this way, knowledge production should involve a collective process, rather than the individualistic, top-down, and distanced approach that typifies the traditional scientific method. For Harding (1991), strong objectivity involves analysis of the relationship between both the subject and object of inquiry. This approach contrasts with traditional scientific method that either denies this relationship or seeks to achieve control over it. However, as Harding and other standpoint theorists point out, an approach to research that produces a more objective approach acknowledges the partial and situated nature of all knowledge production (see also Collins, 1990; Haraway, 2003; Hartsock, 1983).

Science studies scholar Donna Haraway (2003) describes the feminist work to understand and develop a feminist sense of objectivity as a kind of split personality, in which feminists have "alternatively, or even simultaneously, held on to both ends of the . . . greased pole leading to a usable doctrine of objectivity" (p. 26). She asserts that "feminist objectivity means quite simply *situated knowledges*" (p. 27), a recognition of objectivity as "about particular and specific embodiment and definitely not about the false vision promising transcendence of all limits and responsibility." Rather than a claim to a social dislocation, which is value-free and replicable, "feminist objectivity is about limited location and situated knowledge, not about transcendence and splitting of subject and object. It allows us to become answerable for what we learn and see" (p. 28). However, sociologist Jayati Lal (1996) cautions us that because "all of us live in contradictory locations," (p. 199) thus "one's identity in the research project is . . . neither fixed nor predetermined" (p. 197). Consequently, feminist researchers must take special care to adequately understand and transparently analyze their own (multiple) locations; otherwise, we avoid the accountability urged by Haraway.

Postmodern critics of this approach point out that the goal of producing a strong objectivity replicates the limitations of traditional scientific methods, namely, privileging one or another account as most "accurate" or true (Hekman, 1992). Postmodern theorists argue that all social positions are fluid. Such fluidity makes it impossible to identify individual knowers who can represent any particular social group. Furthermore, they insist, the search for truth, even one that is partial, is fraught with the danger of marginalizing other accounts.

Similarities Across Different Standpoint Approaches

Despite the shared themes outlined above, the notion of standpoint is conceptualized differently by different standpoint theorists. Nancy Naples (2003) has identified several different approaches to the construction of standpoint: as embodied in women's social location and social experience, as constructed in community, and as a site through which to begin inquiry. Many feminist theorists understand standpoint as embodied in specific actors who are located in less privileged positions within the social order and who, because of their social locations, are engaged in activities that differ from others who are not so located. The appeal to women's embodied social experience, as a privileged site of knowledge about power and domination, forms one central thread within standpoint epistemologies.

Critics of this approach to standpoint theory point out that the reliance upon a notion of women or any other marginalized group as having an identifiable and consistent standpoint leads to the trap of essentialism. For example, feminist scholars who center the role of mothering practices in generating different gendered ways of knowing (e.g., Belenky et al., 1986; Ruddick, 1989) or who argue that there are gendered differences in moral perspective (Gilligan, 1982) have been criticized for equating such gendered differences with an essentialized female identity (Spelman, 1988). However, many feminist theorists who contribute to the embodied strand of standpoint theorizing argue that due to relations of domination and subordination, women, especially low-income women of color or others located in marginalized social positions, develop a perspective on social life in the United States that differs markedly from that of men as well as middle- and upper-income people (Collins, 1990; Moya, 1996; Sandoval, 2000). Black feminist and Chicana standpoint theorists argue that the political consciousness of women of color develops from the material reality of their lives rather than a shared essential nature and reflects both the diversities of their experiences as well as the commonalities.

However, Collins as well as Hartsock emphasize that there is a difference between a so-called women's standpoint and a feminist standpoint. Jaggar (1989) points out that a feminist standpoint is different from women's viewpoint or women's specific experiences. In contrast, they argue, a standpoint is achieved as a consequence of self-reflective analysis from a specific social actor, social group, or social location rather than available simply because one happens to be a member of an oppressed group or share a social location (see also Weeks, 1998). Rather than view standpoints as individual possessions of disconnected actors, most standpoint theorists attempt to locate standpoint in specific community contexts with particular attention to the dynamics of race, class, and gender.

This second strand of feminist standpoint epistemology understands standpoint as relational accomplishment. Using this approach, the identity of "woman" or class or other embodied identities are viewed as constructed in community and therefore cannot be interpreted outside the shifting community context. Collins (1990), for her analysis of black feminist thought, draws on the construction of community as a collective process through which individuals come to represent themselves in relation to others with whom they perceive they share similar experiences and viewpoints. Collins (1997) argues that a standpoint is constructed through "historically shared, *group*-based experiences" (p. 375, emphasis original). Like the embodied approach to standpoint theorizing, group-based approaches have also been criticized for unproblematically using women's class and racial identities to define who is or is not part of a particular group. However, those who draw on a relational or community-based notion of standpoint, emphasize the collective analytic process that must precede the articulation of a standpoint. Both Sandoval (2000) and Collins (1990) utilize this approach to standpoint. (Although Sandoval does not describe her approach as a "standpoint epistemology," it does share many of the features outlined above.)

Sandoval's (2000) analysis of oppositional consciousness has much in common with Hartsock's and Collins's approaches, in that her analysis of oppositional consciousness focuses on the development of third world feminism as a methodology by which oppressed groups can develop strategies for political resistance. Sandoval's model offers a methodological strategy that contests previously taken-for-granted categorizations of women's political practice such as liberal, radical, or socialist. The oppositional methodology she presents draws on multiple political approaches such as equal rights or liberal, revolutionary, and separatist political strategies. Rather than privilege one approach, Sandoval argues that oppressed peoples typically draw on multiple strategies to form an oppositional methodology. Sandoval treats experience as simultaneously embodied and strategically created in community and concludes that this dynamic interaction affects the political practice of third world women. Although Sandoval locates her analysis in a postmodern frame and Hartsock resists such a move, the legacy of historical materialism links their work within a broadly defined feminist standpoint epistemology. In fact, Hartsock (1996) acknowledges the power of Sandoval's analysis for challenging essentialized views of identity and identity politics.

The third strand of feminist standpoint epistemology provides a framework for capturing the interactive and fluid conceptualization of community and resists attaching standpoint to particular bodies, individual knowers, or specific communities or groups. Standpoint is understood as a site from which to begin a mode of inquiry as in Smith's everyday world institutional ethnographic approach to epistemology. Smith (1992) explains that her approach does not privilege a subject of research whose expressions are disconnected from her social location and daily activities. Rather, Smith starts inquiry with an active knower who is connected with other people in particular and identifiable ways. This mode of inquiry calls for explicit attention to the social relations embedded in women's everyday activities. Smith's (1992) analysis of standpoint as a mode of inquiry offers a valuable methodological strategy for exploring how power dynamics are organized and experienced in a community context.

Despite the diverse perspectives that are identified with standpoint epistemology, all standpoint theorists emphasize the importance of experience for feminist theorizing. In this regard, many point out the significance of standpoint analysis's connection to consciousness raising, the women's movement's knowledge production method. Consciousness raising (CR) was a strategy of knowledge development designed to help support and generate women's political activism. By sharing what appeared as individual-level experiences of oppression, women recognized that the problems were shaped by social structural factors. The CR process assumed that problems associated with women's oppression needed political solutions and that women acting collectively are able to identify and analyze these processes (Fisher, 2001). The consciousness-raising group process enabled women to share their experiences, identify and analyze the social and political mechanisms by which women are oppressed, and develop strategies for social change.

Standpoint theorists assert a link between the development of standpoint theory and feminist political goals of transformative social, political, and economic change. From the perspective of feminist praxis, standpoint epistemology provides a methodological resource for explicating how relations of domination contour women's everyday lives. With this knowledge, women and others whose lives are shaped by systems of inequality can act to challenge these processes and systems (Weeks, 1998, p. 92). One example of this point is found in Pence's (1996) work to create an assessment of how safe battered women remain after they report abuse to the police. Pence draws specifically on Smith's (1987) approach to shift the standpoint on the process of law enforcement to the women whom the law attempts to protect and to those who are charged with protecting them. Pence developed a safety audit to identify ways criminal justice and law enforcement policies and practices can be enhanced to ensure the safety of women and to ensure the accountability of the offender. Police departments, criminal justice and probation departments, and family law clinics have used Pence's safety audit in diverse settings across the country. Pence asserts that her approach is not an evaluation of individual worker's performances but an examination of how the institution or system is set up to manage domestic violence cases.

Intersectional Theorizing: Toward a Queer Standpoint Epistemology

In exploring the epistemological grounds for different intersectional perspectives, Naples (2009) conceptualized a fourth framework that, she argues, offers more analytic power than the other approaches in that it brings into view the multiple dimensions of intersectionality. She calls this type of intersectional analysis an epistemological approach. An epistemological approach draws on the theoretical perspectives developed to analyze gender, race, and class inequalities as well as sexuality and culture. For example, she draws on insights from materialist feminism, racialization theory, political economic theory, and queer theory for her intersectional research on social policy, citizenship, and community activism (Naples, 2009).

An epistemological view is evident in both Patricia Hill Collins's and Smith's approaches. Collins's (2000) intersectional approach centers the construct "matrix of domination." She identifies four dimensions of power that are woven together to shape black women's social, political, and economic lives: a structural dimension (i.e., "how social institutions are organized to reproduce Black women's subordination over time" (p. 277); a disciplinary dimension, which highlights the role of the state on other institutions that rely on bureaucracy and surveillance to regulate inequalities; a hegemonic dimension, which deals with ideology, culture, and consciousness; and an interpersonal dimension, the "level of everyday social interaction" (p. 277). Collins argues that "[b]y manipulating ideology and culture, the hegemonic domain acts as a link between social institutions (structural domain), their organizational practices (disciplinary domain), and the level of everyday social interaction (interpersonal domain)" (p. 284).

Smith's approach to intersectionality includes attention to historical, cultural, textual, discursive, institutional, and other structural dimensions that contour the intersection of race, class, gender, sexuality, national and religious identity, among other social phenomena. She uses the term, "relations of ruling," to capture the ways in which these different dimensions shape everyday life. Her institutional ethnographic approach is especially powerful for revealing how interactions within and across these different dimensions of social life produce contradictions and tensions that can create the grounds for resistance and politicization.

In her social structural approach to the intersection of gender, race, and class in contemporary economic arrangements, Leslie McCall (2001) draws on quantitative data in her empirical examination of what she terms "configurations of inequality." She analyzes the ways "in which race, gender, and class intersect in a variety of ways depending on underlying economic conditions in local economies" (p. 6) and emphasizes the importance of regional variation in labor markets. McCall differentiates between anticategorical and intracategorical approaches to intersectionality. She finds both approaches inadequate for her purposes. She offers a third strategy she calls intercategorical, which she applies to what she calls the new inequality within the American labor market. By incorporating a gendered lens that is attentive to the intersection of class and race, McCall's comparative method reveals the importance of examining the intersection of race, class, and gender in a regional context.

Since the 1980s, there has been increasing attention in feminist scholarship to queer theory and queer methodologies. Geographers Kath Browne and Catherine Nash (2010) argue that "queer theorizing initially gained greater visibility more quickly in the humanities than the social sciences" (p. 4); and it contributed to debates about "the supposedly unassailable 'objective researcher' inexorably uncovering a knowable reality" (p. 4). In the social sciences, queer theory has been particularly visible in intersectional studies, which consider the matrix of gender and sexuality.

For example, in *The Sexuality of Migration: Border Crossing and Mexican Immigrant Men* by Lionel Cantú (2009), Naples and coeditor Salvador Vidal-Ortiz explain how Cantú's intersectional standpoint approach takes up insights from theories of political economy and migration, and places them in dialogue with feminist and queer theories to produce a new framework for understanding the immigration of Mexican men who have sex with men. Cantú also drew on the scholarship of Gloria Anzaldúa (1987), Cherríe Moraga (1981), and Collins (1990), among other Latina and black feminist scholars, to capture "the multiplicity of sexualities as they intersected with class, race, national origin, and other dimensions of social and political life" (Naples & Vidal-Ortiz, 2009, p. 9). While Cantú approached his analysis of standpoint from three different angles—as embodied the immigrant men's social location and social experience, as constructed in community, and as a site through which to begin inquiry—his use of an intersectional epistemological approach also enabled him to reveal the complex ways that sexuality influences the experience of migration through attention to the powerful intersection of political, economic, social, cultural, and sexual practices. As Naples and Vidal-Ortiz explain:

> Cantú resisted the reductive reading of standpoint that is often criticized by postmodern critics of standpoint epistemology. . . . Taking inspiration from Anzaldua's (1987) analysis of *mestiza consciousness* and Moraga's "theory of the flesh," Cantú's queer materialist framework maintains sensitivity to the fluidity of identity, the community context for the development of standpoints, as well as the structural relations of power that contours everyday life. (p. 11)

Geographer Lorena Munoz's (2010) research on queer gendered "street-scapes" in Los Angeles is similarly intersectional in its attention to the fluidity of identity in shifting community contexts. Her research was profoundly influenced by her decision as a researcher to come out as a lesbian to some, although not all, of her informants, which forced her to "renegotiate [her] own subjectivity, reflexivity and identity construction . . . to understand the everyday economic spatial practices of Latina vendors" (p. 56). She argues that although feminist methods have "re-centered the marginalized 'other' by making space for multiple voices," they nonetheless "often reinforce gender and sexual categories even as they seek to redefine categorical structures" (p. 56). Her efforts to negotiate her own shifting positionality produced a deeply intersectional research project informed by queer theories of subjectivities. She concludes that "queer of color methodology can expand the possibilities of further accepting and understanding that researchers co-create data with their subjects, thus adjusting the lens so that multiple ways of 'knowing' and 'being' become visible" (p. 66).

CONCLUSION

In sum, both feminist empiricist and feminist standpoint epistemologies remain important approaches for uncovering different aspects of the "relations of ruling" (Smith, 1987) that contour everyday life. Feminist standpoint theorists typically resist focusing their analyses on individual actors removed from their social context. Knowledge generated from embodied standpoints of subordinates is powerful in that it can help transform traditional categories of analyses that originate from dominant groups. However, as many feminist standpoint theorists argue, it remains only a partial perspective (Haraway, 2003). Naples (2003) argues that by placing the analysis within a community context, it is possible to uncover the multiplicity of perspectives along with the dynamic structural dimensions of the social, political, and economic environment that shape the *relations of ruling* in a particular social space. Haraway (2003) explains that situated knowledges are developed collectively rather than by individuals in isolation. Hartsock (1983) and Collins (1990) both emphasize that standpoints are achieved in community, through collective conversations and dialog among women in marginal social positions. According to Collins, standpoints are achieved by groups who struggle collectively and self-reflectively against *the matrix of domination* that circumscribes their lives. Hartsock (1987) also emphasizes that a feminist standpoint is achieved through analysis and political struggle. Given standpoint theory's emphasis on a process of dialogue, analysis, and reflexivity, the approach has proven extremely vibrant and, over time, open to reassessment and revision. As a consequence, standpoint theory remains an extremely important approach within feminist theory.

Strong objectivity, like Haraway's situated knowledge, emerges from and is linked with standpoint epistemology. The development of standpoint theory is another feminist effort to reconceptualize ways of knowing, producing, and validating knowledge. Standpoint theory argues that the knowledge and theories of marginalized populations (women, people of color, gender and sexual minorities, etc.) hold more epistemic authority than the knowledge and theories developed by dominant groups. It is assumed within standpoint theory that dominant groups will be limited in their epistemic perspectives to their own values and perspectives, unable to gain a wider view of interests and experiences, but that marginalized groups are able to attain a more global perspective that not only begins in their own experiences but also includes consideration of the dominant ideologies to which they are subjugated. Thus members of marginalized groups have a kind of double vision that allows them to understand social contexts broadly because they not only experience their own realities, but also witness other realities through their engagement with dominant groups. Members of dominant groups have a more restricted perspective, limited by their avoidance of "downward mobility" and the invisibility of the work performed by those in other social classes.

To help illustrate this, imagine Paris Hilton's life: her meals are prepared by others; her clothes are cleaned, pressed, and returned to their closets by others; her bed is made by others; her travel arrangements are made by others; and so forth. Paris Hilton does not see these people accomplish these tasks; she may not know their names, or what their lives are like, or even how many of them are involved in the management of these details. But these people know Paris Hilton's name; they have an understanding of what her life is like (even if they are not privy to her innermost thoughts and feelings); they move about the physical environment of Paris Hilton's life invisibly and perhaps largely unnoticed, but they notice; and they see the contrasts between their own and Paris Hilton's life. Standpoint theory argues that this grants a particular epistemic perspective to marginalized populations such as those who invisibly manage the smooth running of Paris Hilton's life.

However, many feminist theorists including Harding (1993), Hennessy (1993), Janack (1997), Lal (1996), Munoz (2010), and Collins (1997) are uncomfortable with the absolutism of such claims. They point out that power and knowledge are not necessarily static within or between groups, and therefore standpoint theory must be contextual, responding flexibly to shifts in power and agency. Haraway (2003) further argues that although "there is good reason to believe vision is better from below the brilliant space platforms of the powerful, . . . [t]he standpoints of the subjugated are not 'innocent' positions" (p. 229). As Harding (1998) reminds us, "what the standpoint of any particular group consists in must be determined by empirical observation and theoretical reflection" (p. 150).

This leads us to conclude that diverse ways of knowing must also include different epistemological foundations for the production of knowledge. Feminist empirical approaches remain essential for uncovering some larger patterns of inequality, discrimination, and change. For example, as anthropologist Susan Greenhalgh (2008) demonstrates in her work on the one-child policy in China, we would not know about the missing girls without the methodological tools of demography.

This effort to recognize and incorporate diverse ways of knowing has been particularly relevant to marginalized communities; as anthropologist Victoria Sanford (2008) learned by collecting narratives from local villagers in her study of human rights violations and genocide in Guatemala, these previously silenced narratives brought to light new ways of understanding violence, memory, and the possibilities of reparations. Importantly, feminist scholars increasingly recognize the epistemic value of community knowledges in both research and practice. For example, Native American health activists on Akwesasne Reservation identified the links between the toxic pollution of the St. Lawrence River and increasing rates of miscarriage, infant mortality, childhood cancer, and cancer among women. These findings were established in part through the Mother's Milk Project, in partnership with the U.S. Environmental Protection Agency and Cornell University (Grinde & Johansen, 1995; LaDuke, 1999; Silliman, Fried, Ross, & Gutierrez, 2004); but the findings began with midwives on the reservation who noted the increasing number of reproductive problems in their community. Using environmental testing together with local records, interviews, and focus groups, the Mother's Milk Project revealed the impacts on the bodies of Mohawk and other women of the legal and illegal dumping of toxic wastes by multinational corporations such as General Motors, Alcoa, and Reynolds Metals in and near local water sources (Grinde & Johansen, 1995; Silliman et al., 2004). Similarly, sociologist Barbara Gurr's work on Native

American women's reproductive healthcare (2009, with Nikki McGary, 2011), which began by listening to the stories of Native women, eventually led to her institutional ethnography of the Indian Health Service that revealed the role of race, gender, and citizenship discourses in restricting Native women's access to contraception and other forms of reproductive healthcare. By beginning with recognition of the epistemic authority of Native women's stories, the Mother's Milk Project and Gurr were able to ascertain both some of the causes of health disparities in Native communities as well as potential strategies to address these disparities.

The work of feminist scholars to develop new ways of understanding knowledge production has had a profound impact on the social sciences, as demonstrated by the continuing debates around theory and methods over the last four decades. The linking of epistemology with feminist praxis in particular has encouraged the development of new methodological approaches as well as theoretical perspectives. Taken together, these present a rich and complex array of epistemological possibilities, which feminist scholars continue to explore, debate, and expand upon.

Authors' Note. Portions of this chapter were excerpted from writings by Nancy A. Naples: "Teaching Intersectionality Intersectionally," (2009), *International Feminist Journal of Politics, 11,* 566–577; "Feminist Standpoint Theory" and "Strong Objectivity," (2007), in G. Ritzer (Ed.), *Encyclopedia of Sociology,* Hoboken, NJ: Wiley-Blackwell; and *Feminism and Method: Ethnography, Discourse Analysis, and Activist Research,* (2003), New York, NY: Routledge.

DISCUSSION QUESTIONS

1. How are epistemology and research methods related?

2. How is scientific objectivity distinguished from truth and certainty by feminist scholars?

3. How have the meanings associated with objectivity evolved at the hands of feminist scholars?

4. Much of the scholarship by feminists on empiricism is concerned with recognizing and disrupting power imbalances. How can feminist theory and research potentially contribute to this project, and where might it potentially fail?

5. What is to be gained from standpoint epistemology? What are the risks of such an approach?

6. Is it possible to recognize the epistemic authority of whole communities? How? What are the potential strengths and weaknesses of such an approach?

WEB RESOURCES

- http://faculty.maxwell.syr.edu/mdevault/default.htm

This website is hosted by sociologist Marjorie Devault and offers resources and discussions about Institutional Ethnography, originally developed by Dorothy Smith as a "sociology for people."

- http://plato.stanford.edu/entries/feminism-epistemology/

The *Stanford Encyclopedia of Philosophy* provides an extensive discussion of standpoint epistemologies.

- http://tcs.sagepub.com/content/23/7-8/135.full.pdf

This links to an open access interview with Donna Haraway originally published in *Theory, Culture & Society, 23*(7–8), 135-158 (2006).

- http://mantlethought.org/content/conflict-and-resolution-moment-victoria-sanford

This links to a podcast featuring an interview with Victoria Sanford in which she discusses, among other things, alternative approaches to ethnography and fieldwork.

FOR FURTHER READING

Collins, P. H. 2000. *Black feminist thought: Knowledge, consciousness, and the politics of empowerment* (2nd ed.). New York, NY: Routledge.

Denzin, N., & Lincoln, Y. (Eds.). 2003. *Turning points in qualitative research: Tying knots in a handkerchief.* Walnut Creek, CA: AltaMira Press.

Naples, N. A. 2003. *Feminism and method: Ethnography, discourse analysis, and activist research.* New York, NY: Routledge.

Sprague, J. 2005. *Feminist methodologies for critical researchers: Bridging differences.* Walnut Creek, CA: AltaMira Press.

REFERENCES

Anzaldúa, G. (1987). *Borderlands/la frontera: The new mestiza.* San Francisco, CA: Spinsters/ Aunt Lute.

Atkinson, P., & Hammersley, M. (2007). *Ethnography: Principles in practice* (3rd ed.). New York, NY: Routledge.

Baker, C. N. (2007). *The women's movement against sexual harassment.* New York, NY: Cambridge University Press.

Behar, R. (1993). *Translated woman: Crossing the borders with Esperanza's story.* Boston, MA: Beacon Press.

Behar, R. (2007). *An island called home: Returning to Jewish Cuba.* Piscataway, NJ: Rutgers University Press.

Belcastro, S.-M., & Moran, J. M. (2003). Interpretations of feminist philosophy of science by feminist physical scientists. *NWSA Journal, 15*(1): 20–33.

Belenky, M., Clinchy, B., Goldberger, N., & Tarule, J. (1986). *Women's ways of knowing: The development of self, voice, and mind.* New York, NY: Basic Books.

Bettie, J. (2003). *Women without class: Girls, race, and identity.* London, England: University of California Press.

Brewer, J. D. (1994). The ethnographic critique of ethnography: Sectarianism in the RUC. *Sociology, 28*, 231–244.

Browne, K., & Nash, C. (Eds.). (2010). *Queer methods and methodologies: Intersecting queer theories and social science research.* Surrey, England: Ashgate.

Cantú, L. (2009). *The sexuality of migration: Border crossings and Mexican immigrant men.* N. A. Naples & S. Vidal-Ortiz (Eds.). New York: New York University Press.

Collins, P. H. (1990). *Black feminist thought: Knowledge, consciousness, and the politics of empowerment.* Boston, MA: Unwin Hyman.

Collins, P. H. (1997). Comment on Hekman's "Truth and Method": Feminist standpoint revisited: Where's the power? *Signs: Journal of Women in Culture and Society, 22*, 375–381.

Collins, P. H. (2000). *Black feminist thought: Knowledge, consciousness, and the politics of empowerment* (2nd ed.). New York, NY: Routledge.

Collins, P. H. (2004). *Black sexual politics: African Americans, gender, and sexuality.* New York, NY: Routledge.

Conquergood, D. (2003). Rethinking ethnography: Towards a critical cultural politics. In Y. S. Lincoln & N. Denzin (Eds.), *Turning points in qualitative research: Tying knots in a handkerchief* (pp. 351–374). Walnut Creek, CA: AltaMira Press.

Crenshaw, K. (1991). Mapping the margins: Intersectionality, identity politics, and violence against women. *Stanford Law Review, 43*, 1241–1299.

Dean, B. (2009). *Urarina society, cosmology, and history in Peruvian Amazonia.* Gainesville: University Press of Florida.

Fausto-Sterling, A. (2000). *Sexing the body: Gender politics and the construction of sexuality.* New York, NY: Basic Books.

Fine, C. (2010). *Delusions of gender: How our minds, society, and neurosexism create difference.* New York, NY: Norton.

Fisher, B. M. (2001). *No angels in the classroom: Teaching through feminist discourse.* Lanham, MD: Rowman & Littlefield.

Gilligan, C. (1982). *In a different voice: Psychological theory and women's development.* Cambridge, MA: Harvard University Press.

Goffman, E. (1989). On fieldwork. *Journal of Contemporary Ethnography, 18*, 123–132.

Greenhalgh, S. (2008). *Just one child: Science and policy in Deng's China.* Berkeley: University of California Press.

Grinde, D., & Johansen, B. (1995). *Ecocide of Native America: Environmental destruction of Indian lands and peoples.* Santa Fe, NM: Clear Light.

Gurr, B. (2011). Mothering in the borderlands: The policing of Native American women's reproductive healthcare. *The International Journal of Sociology of the Family, 31*(1), 69–84.

Gurr, B. (forthcoming). Queer mothering or mothering queerly? Motherwork in transgender families. In M. Gibson (Ed.), *Queering maternity and motherhood: Narrative and theoretical perspectives on queer conception, birth, and parenting.* Toronto, Ontario, Canada: Demeter Press.

Gurr, B., & McGary, N. (2009). Restricted access: The intersections of reproductive health, rights, and policy for minors and Native American women. *The Journal of the Association for Research on Mothering, 11*(1), 110–121.

Haraway, D. (2003). Situated knowledges: The science question in feminism and the privilege of partial perspective. In Y. S. Lincoln & N. Denzin (Eds.), *Turning points in qualitative research: Tying knots in a handkerchief* (pp. 21–46). Walnut Creek, CA: AltaMira Press.

Harding, S. (1986). *The science question in feminism.* Ithaca, NY: Cornell University Press.

Harding, S. (1987). *Feminism and methodology.* Bloomington: Indiana University Press.

Harding, S. (1991). *Whose science? Whose knowledge?* Ithaca, NY: Cornell University Press.

Harding, S. (1993). Rethinking standpoint epistemology: What is strong objectivity? In L. Alcoff & E. Potter (Eds.), *Feminist epistemologies* (pp. 49–82). New York, NY: Routledge.

Harding, S. (1995). Strong objectivity: A response to the new objectivity question. *Synthese, 104,* 331–349.

Harding, S. (1998). *Is science multicultural? Postcolonialisms, feminisms, and epistemologies.* Bloomington: University of Indiana Press.

Harding, S. (2008). *Sciences from below: Feminisms, postcolonialities, and modernities.* Durham, NC: Duke University Press.

Hartsock, N. (1983). *Money, sex and power: Toward a feminist historical materialism.* New York, NY: Longman.

Hartsock, N. (1987). The feminist standpoint: Developing the ground for a specifically feminist historical materialism. In S. Harding (Ed.), *Feminism and methodology* (pp. 157–180). Bloomington: Indiana University Press.

Hartsock, N. (1996). Theoretical bases for coalition building: An assessment of postmodernism. In H. Gottfried (Ed.), *Feminism and social change: Bridging theory and practice* (pp. 256–274). Urbana: University of Illinois Press.

Hekman, S. J. (1992). *Gender and knowledge: Elements of a postmodern feminism.* Boston, MA: Northeastern University Press.

Hennessy, R. (1993). *Materialist feminism and the politics of discourse.* New York, NY: Routledge.

Holmes, J. (2005). Power and discourse at work: Is gender relevant? In M. Lazar (Ed.), *Feminist critical discourse analysis: Gender, power and ideology* (pp. 31–60). New York, NY: Palgrave MacMillan.

Jaggar, A. (1989). Love and knowledge: Emotion in feminist epistemology. In A. M. Jaggar & S. R. Bordo (Eds.), *Gender/body/knowledge: Feminist reconstructions of being and knowing* (pp. 145–171). New Brunswick, NJ: Rutgers University Press.

Janack, M. (1997). Standpoint epistemology without the "standpoint"? An examination of epistemic privilege and epistemic authority. *Hypatia, 12,* 125–139.

Kang, M. (2010). *The managed hand: Race, gender, and the body in beauty service work.* Berkeley: University of California Press.

Kwan, M.-P. (2002). Feminist visualization: Re-envisioning GIS as a method in feminist geographic research. *Annals of the Association of American Geographers, 92,* 645–661.

LaDuke, W. (1999). *All our relations: Native struggles for land and life.* Cambridge, MA: South End Press.

Lal, J. (1996). Situating locations: The politics of self, identity, and "other" in living and writing the text. In D. Wolf (Ed.), *Feminist dilemmas in fieldwork* (pp. 185–215). Boulder, CO: West-view Press.

Lather, P. (2003). Issues of validity in openly ideological research: Between a rock and a soft place. In N. Denzin & Y. Lincoln (Eds.), *Turning points in qualitative research: Tying knots in a handkerchief* (pp. 185–216). Walnut Creek, CA: AltaMira Press.

Lloyd, E. A. (2005). *The case of the female orgasm: Bias in the science of evolution.* Cambridge, MA: Harvard University Press.

Longino, H. E. (1993). Feminist standpoint theory and the problems of knowledge. *Signs: Journal of Women in Culture and Society, 19,* 201–212.

Martin, E. (2001). *The woman in the body: A cultural analysis of reproduction.* Boston, MA: Beacon Books.

McCall, L. (2001). *Complex inequality: Gender, class, and race in the new economy.* New York, NY: Routledge.

McCall, L. (2005). The complexity of intersectionality. *Signs: Journal of Women in Culture and Society, 30,* 1771–1800.

Merry, S. E. (2000). Crossing boundaries: Ethnography in the twenty-first century. *PoLar: Political and Legal Anthropology Review, 23*(2), 127–133.

Mihesuah, D. (2003). *Indigenous American women: Decolonization, empowerment, activism.* Lincoln: University of Nebraska Press.

Mohanty, C. T. (2006). *Feminisms without border: Decolonizing theory, practicing solidarity.* Durham, NC: Duke University Press.

Moraga, C. (1981). Introduction. In C. Moraga & G. Anzaldúa (Eds.), *This bridge called my back: Writings by radical women of color* (pp. xiii–xix). Watertown, MA: Persephone Press.

Moya, P. M. L. (1996). Postmodernism, "realism," and the politics of identity: Cherrie Morago and Chicana feminism. In M. J. Alexander & C. T. Mohanty (Eds.), *Feminist genealogies, colonial legacies, democratic future* (pp. 125–150). New York, NY: Routledge.

Munoz, L. (2010). Brown, queer and gendered: Queering the Latino/a "street-scapes" of Los Angeles. In K. Browne & C. Nash (Eds.), *Queer methods and methodologies: Intersecting queer theories and social science research* (pp. 55–68). Surrey, England: Ashgate.

Nagel, J. (2003). *Race, ethnicity, and sexuality: Intimate intersections, forbidden frontiers.* New York, NY: Oxford University Press.

Naples, N. A. (1998). *Grassroots warriors: Activist mothering, community work, and the War on Poverty.* New York, NY: Routledge.

Naples, N. A. (2003). *Feminism and method: Ethnography, discourse analysis, and activist research.* New York, NY: Routledge.

Naples, N. A. (2006). Feminist standpoint theory. In G Ritzer (Ed.), *Encyclopedia of Sociology*. Hoboken, NJ: Wiley-Blackwell.

Naples, N. A. (2007). Strong objectivity. In G. Ritzer (Ed.), *Encyclopedia of Sociology*. Hoboken, NJ: Wiley-Blackwell.

Naples, N. A. (2009). Teaching intersectionality intersectionally. *International Feminist Journal of Politics, 11,* 566–577.

Naples, N. A., & Vidal-Ortiz, S. (Eds.). (2009). Editors' introduction. In Lionel Cantú (Author), *The sexuality of migration: Border crossings and Mexican immigration men* (pp. 1–20). New York: New York University Press.

Nelson, L. H. (1990). *Who knows: From Quine to feminist empiricism*. Philadelphia, PA: Temple University Press.

Pence, E. (1996). *Safety for battered women in a textually mediated legal system* (Unpublished doctoral dissertation). University of Toronto, Ontario, Canada.

Proctor, R. (1991). *Value free science? Purity and power in modern knowledge*. Cambridge, MA: Harvard University Press.

Purkayastha, B. (2005). *Negotiating ethnicity: Second-generation South Asians traverse a transnational world*. Piscataway, NJ: Rutgers University Press.

Rosaldo, R. (1989). *Culture and truth: The remaking of social analysis*. Boston, MA: Beacon Press.

Ruddick, S. (1989). *Maternal thinking: Toward a politics of peace*. New York, NY: Ballantine Books.

Sachs, C. (1996). *Gendered fields: Rural women, agriculture and environment*. Boulder, CO: Westview Press.

Sandoval, C. (2000). *Methodology of the oppressed*. St. Paul, Minneapolis: University of Minnesota Press.

Sanford, V. (2008). Excavations of the heart: Reflections on truth, memory, and structures of understanding. In V. Sanford & A. Angel-Ajani (Eds.), *Engaged observer: Anthropology, advocacy, and activism* (pp. 19–41). New Brunswick, NJ: Rutgers University Press.

Scott, J. W. (1988). *Gender and the politics of history*. New York, NY: Columbia University Press.

Scott, J. W. (1991). The evidence of experience. *Critical Inquiry, 17,* 773–797.

Shakespeare, T. (2006). *Disability rights and wrongs*. New York, NY: Routledge.

Shiva, V. (2005). *Globalization's new wars: Seed, water and life forms*. New Delhi, India: Kali/Women United.

Shiva, V. (2010). *Staying alive*. Cambridge, MA: South End Press.

Silliman, J., Fried, M. G., Ross, L., & Gutierrez, E. R. (2004). *Undivided rights: Women of color organize for reproductive justice*. Cambridge, MA: South End Press.

Smith, D. E. (1987). *The everyday world as problematic: A feminist sociology*. Toronto, Ontario, Canada: University of Toronto Press.

Smith, D. E. (1990a). *Conceptual practices of power*. Boston, MA: Northeastern University Press.

Smith, D. E. (1990b). *Texts, facts, and femininity: Exploring the relations of ruling*. New York, NY: Routledge.

Smith, D. E. (1992). Sociology from women's experience: A reaffirmation. *Sociological Theory, 10*(1), 88–98.

Smith, L. T. T. R. (2002). *Decolonizing methodologies: Research and indigenous peoples.* London, England: Zed Books.

Spelman, E. V. (1988). *Inessential woman: Problems of exclusion in feminist thought.* Boston, MA: Beacon Press.

Sprague, J. (2005). *Feminist methodologies for critical researchers: Bridging differences.* Walnut Creek, CA: AltaMira Press.

Stanley, L. (Ed.). (1990). *Feminist praxis: Research, theory, and epistemology in feminist sociology.* New York, NY: Routledge.

Sutton, B. (2010). *Bodies in crisis: Culture, violence, and women's resistance in neoliberal Argentina.* New Brunswick, NJ: Rutgers University Press.

Thomasson, A. L. (2003). Realism and human kinds. *Philosophy and Phenomenological Research, 67,* 580–609.

Valentine, D. (2007). *Imagining transgender: An ethnography of a category.* Durham, NC: Duke University Press.

Villalón, R. (2010). *Violence against Latina immigrants: Citizenship, inequality, and community.* New York: New York University Press.

Weeks, K. (1998). *Constituting feminist subjects.* Ithaca, NY: Cornell University Press.

Whitaker, M. (2001). Oases in a desert: Why a hydrologist meanders between science and women's studies. In M. Whitaker (Ed.), *Feminist science studies: A new generation* (pp. 48–54). New York, NY: Routledge.

CHAPTER 3

Feminist Postmodernism, Poststructuralism, and Critical Theory

Nollaig Frost and Frauke Elichaoff

The question is always whose interests are being served and whose side is one taking.

—Haideh Moghissi, 1999

Introduction

Feminist postmodernism and poststructuralism challenge the basis on which essentialist claims arising from feminist standpoint and feminist empiricism are made. They are approaches that emphasize specificity of context and time and recognize these influences in shaping a multiplicity of realities. Instead of accepting notions of universality of difference, feminist postmodernism and poststructuralist approaches seek to highlight the variations of women's lives and identities and to ask how they are perceived and shaped, both by themselves and by others. In this recognition of differences among women, critical theory emerged as a tool that allowed identification and detailed examination of the multiple axes of difference that constitute women's identities. Exploring interactions between axes such as gender, sexuality, class, race, and ableism provides more informed insight to the ways in which culture, history, and society shape identity.

In this chapter, we explore some of the ways in which these three approaches enable not only women's differences from men but women's differences from each other to be acknowledged and better understood. We show how critique of the postmodern approach originated from black feminism and led to the development of intersectionality. We show how intersectionality offers ways of challenging power relations within different dimensions of identity, and in their intertwinement. We provide insight to ways in which knowledge and understanding of different aspects of women's being can be furthered and enhanced in a way that is sensitive to the contexts that are of most relevance.

What Are Postmodernism and Poststructuralism?

Postmodernist thinking proposes that instead of the existence of one essential truth, there are multiple subjective, relative truths of personal construction. These realities are shaped not just by subjective experience, but also by what is available from society, culture, the spoken and written word. Thus, postmodernist thinking moves away from the empiricist quest for objective truth and opens up possibilities for women's experiences and behavior to be explored in relation to the context in which they are taking place rather than within a framework of assumed hegemonic norms that sees women as members of a group that is deviant from the norm.

Postmodernism refocuses the relative experience of each individual and moves away from an often arbitrary and artificial (binary) categorizations, such as "man" and "woman." It questions the validity of distinctions and assumptions based on cultural, societal, and class distinctions; and it deconstructs these socially constructed categories to explore variations in individual experience within these groupings. In doing so, it questions and makes obsolete the groupings themselves.

Poststructuralism has been described as "a loose collection of theoretical positions" (Gavey, 1989, p. 460). It rejects objectivity and the notions of an absolute truth and a single reality, upon which modernist claims are based. It challenges the notion of "essentialism" that describes "woman" as an identity category that is fixed and unchanging. Instead, it recognizes the social construction of realities and the risk of maintenance and perpetuation of constructions arising from power interests. As such, poststructuralism provides a useful conceptual foundation for feminist research practice. It provides ways of examining dominant male constructions of realities that emerge from and serve male power interests. The poststructuralist paradigm regards knowledge as unstable and informed by the social and material world. For feminist researchers, this means the exploration of the power of patriarchy and its role in constructing social structures.

At the heart of feminist poststructuralism is the belief that there are more satisfactory ways to theorize gender than those reliant on patriarchal or essentialist claims. The exploration of women's experiences highlights their complexity and variation as women draw on cultural, historical, political, and personal constructs to make sense of themselves and their relations to the world they inhabit. The plurality of meanings of realities that emerge allow for the inclusion of traditional scientific approaches to find out what is known, but feminist poststructuralists regard this as only one discourse among many that are available. By perceiving knowledge as socially produced, unstable, and contextualized, an emphasis is placed on language and discourse. Language is regarded as constitutive of experience and not simply representative of it. Language is not separate from experience because the way it is understood and expressed is reliant upon it.

Thus many feminist writers and researchers have focused on the language used to describe the world and the people in it, to show how understanding and perceptions are developed and then become accepted and reinforced. Foucault (1971) was among the first to show how individual realities are shaped by constant shifts in power and that the access to and creation of power lies in its relationship to language. Combined with Derrida's (1976) work on deconstruction, which seeks to dismantle the male/ female binary (and all other binaries) within language, Foucauldian discourse analysis has become a key method of research in feminist postmodern work.

There is not space in this chapter to do more than highlight the work of the many prominent and influential feminist researchers who contribute to and apply the theories that underpin feminist postmodernism and poststructuralism. In the hope that mention here will provoke reading of their work, we highlight Hélène Cixous, Luce Irigaray, and Julia Kristeva. These writers all use and describe language and its relation with power to confront and deconstruct meanings, practices, and taken-for-granted understandings of women.

Hélène Cixous (2003) explores the binary male/female taxonomy that writing develops and reinforces. She argues that in order to represent the feminine voice, writing needs to be informal, illogical, and organically flowing. This contrasts with the formal, traditional style of writing that has emerged from and is representative of the male voice. The binary taxonomy set up by the dominance of one writing style over the other reinforces differences between genders and creates categories of "man" and "woman."

Luce Irigaray (1996, with M. Whitford) is a feminist writer who also centers her work around binary language and its influences on gender identity, experience of the self, and the shaping of identity. Irigaray extends Derrida's findings of hierarchical power imbalances to criticize Freud's binary-based categorizations of the masculine and the feminine. She suggests that only a gender-neutral language can eventually "undo" the pervasive gender identities that are formed by binary thinking to enable, eventually, a pluralistic, postmodern understanding of individual voices. Irigaray goes further to suggest that feminine stereotypes created in language need to be exaggerated and reflected back in order to challenge them. Although this suggestion is criticized by some feminists, who argue that women should not be put under the same pressure to

conform by feminists that they experience from wider society, Irigaray's work is important in highlighting the repressive structures of language and in effecting changes to
gender-neutral language.

Julia Kristeva (1981), like Cixous and Irigaray, considers language as responsible for
creating repressive structures by equating biological gender with femininity and masculinity. Kristeva sees language as the tool that enables power structures to operate; but
unlike her contemporaries, she does not advocate the creation of a gender-neutral language. Instead she suggests that gender be allowed to emerge through unrepressed writing. Kristeva argues that language that conforms to traditional norms of grammar and
style is repressed, and that writing that is nonconformist and, if necessary, illogical is
unrepressed.

The focus on language that these and other writers have developed is based on the
premise that there is an inextricable link between language (or knowledge, expressed
through language) and power. Feminist postmodernism and poststructuralism
approaches position themselves against feminist empiricism and standpoint epistemology by exploring ways in which language serves to create and reinforce the essentialist views of women simply as "different from men." Instead these approaches
invite the exploration of diversity in womanhood and seek out the multiple truths,
viewpoints, and voices that describe the range of women's experiences.

A large body of work that illustrates applications of this thinking can be seen in
feminist studies of women's use of cosmetic surgery. Kathy Davis (2003, 2008) conducts her work on embodiment by exploring meanings of cosmetic surgery. She is
critical of the cosmetic surgery industry; but she features poignant accounts from
women who have undergone breast augmentation, often to strive for a more "normal"
appearance. Her work is considered vital by many researchers for its innovative use of
feminist research methods and its efforts to wrestle with women's embodiment from a
feminist perspective. Various feminist approaches to embodiment are featured in her
edited volume *Embodied Practices* (1997).

Susan Bordo (1993) offers a feminist perspective on embodiment that differs from
that of Davis (see *Dubious Equalities and Embodied Differences,* 2003, by Davis for more
on this debate). Further work has been carried out by Joan Cassell (*The Woman in the
Surgeon's Body,* 2000), who provides a full analysis of the intersection between gendered
organizations, gender identity, and embodiment.

Finally, in this all-too-brief overview of feminist work, bell hook's prolific output
(e.g., 1982, 1994, 2000a, 2000b) as a feminist writer must be mentioned. Hooks is one
of the most recognized and cited African American authors, much of whose work
considers the failings of feminism toward black women. Her work also focuses on
education and pedagogy, which hooks holds key to improving gender and race
inequalities. hooks took on her great-grandmother's name as her *nom de plume*
because of her admiration for her. She chooses not to capitalize it, partly to distinguish

herself from her namesake, but also to draw attention to the greater importance of the content of her work over who she is as a person. Her 1982 book *Ain't I a Woman* (1982) is considered by many to be the defining work on the relationship between feminism and black women. In the book, hooks disseminates the interconnection between slavery, black women's roles, and capitalism; and she compellingly highlights how these issues still affect black women today.

How Are Postmodernist and Poststructuralist Ideas Brought to Research?

One of the most commonly utilized methods in feminist postmodern research is discourse analysis. This approach allows for the analysis of language, spoken or written, and of images, symbols, and other media representations. Discourse analysis aims to understand how realities are constructed through these media, and to observe cultural and societal influences on subjective experiences.

The analysis of discourse offers a collection of approaches (e.g., Gavey, 1989; Holt, 2011) with which to gain insight to how experiences are constructed through language. Like the concept of poststructuralism, discourse analysis is a conglomerate of approaches and methodologies, each with clearly defined frameworks and theories. Although some are given labels, such as feminist discourse analysis, discursive psychology, Foucauldian discourse analysis, and feminist poststructuralist discourse analysis, all share a focus on questioning the questions that are asked about women's experiences rather than on looking for answers. With this approach, prevailing theories can be deconstructed into their constituent parts, and insight to the power dynamics and other factors that have informed their makeup highlighted. The possibility of different constructs is enabled, and power to change a restrictive and discriminative construct into one that supports and nurtures is created. Although clearly not exclusive to feminism, discourse analysis enables the change of discriminatory constructs. Discourse analysis adheres to the poststructuralist assumptions of the existence of a plurality of possible truths and serves as an approach that yields findings to be acted upon. This provides it with a political agenda alongside its expectations of finding alternative constructions of experiences. Feminist discourse analysis aims to effect change in perception and action of and against women.

Thus feminist researchers do not regard discourse analysis as a method per se (e.g., Gavey, 1989, 2011; Holt, 2011); instead, they see it as an underpinning influence on all the questions that they ask. In so doing, it changes the nature and the focus of the questions. As one feminist discourse analyst said in a personal communication to us:

As I know you know, there are many feminisms and many forms of discourse analysis! I also think that feminism is inherent within doing discourse analysis, [DA], since DA seeks to uncover hidden oppressions etc., so it would be impossible to perform DA without taking a feminist stance. (Personal communication, 2012)

Discourses arise from the coherence of description and evaluation of actions and events. They can be understood to be patterned ways of understanding (Sheriff & Weatherall, 2009). Discourse analysts look for sense-making practices formed by the cohesion of clusters of terms and phrases, referred to as *interpretative repertoires*. The analytical approach is framed by key notions of construction, function, and variability (Potter & Wetherell, 1987). Attention is paid to the selection of the words and phrases used by the narrator as well as to the way meaning is given to the concepts it constructs. It is assumed that descriptions of experiences and events are designed by the narrator to accomplish actions, such as to persuade or to argue. Language is regarded as performing a function, and the function is achieved by the words used to construct the description.

Proposed discourses are thought of as *practical ideologies*; practical because they provide commonsensical ways of making experiences meaningful, and ideological because of their support of systems of belief that perpetuate oppression or inequality. Gavey (1989) highlights the idea that the power of some dominant discourses lies in their apparent common sense. Billig and colleagues (1988, cited in Sheriff & Weatherall, 2009) suggest that the term *ideological dilemmas* be adopted to describe competing ways of making sense of the same action.

Foucauldian discourse analysis (Parker, 1992; Burman & Parker, 1993) assumes that individuals are subject to the constructs of discourse and take up subject positions accordingly. The available positions determine their further actions, and the actions serve as perpetuating discourses. Discursive psychology (Potter & Wetherell, 1987; Wetherell & Potter, 1992) focuses more on how language is utilized to navigate the subject positions created by discourses and how individuals use language to explain and justify their positions.

Commonalities between the two approaches can be seen in the role of reflexivity, which takes account of the researcher's own subject position in relation to the discourse the person is researching. The subject position of the researcher inevitably influences which discourses receive greater attention and which ones may be disregarded. An awareness of this by the researcher is paramount (Holt, 2011).

Discourse analysis offers the opportunity to ask new and relevant questions by reexamining and listening to the diverse women's voices to create a rich tapestry of women's experiences. Feminist postmodern analysis opens the doors to a dialogue that values and counts all women's experiences within their cultural and societal contexts.

Behind the Scenes With Michelle Sheriff and Ann Weatherall

A Feminist Discourse Analysis of Popular-Press Accounts of Postmaternity

Introduction: The researchers regard "motherhood" as a patriarchal institution, which not only shapes women's experience but also directly fuels feelings of ambiguity and guilt when they make choices that do not fall into the category of what is "natural" for women. Within this context, the study explores variable meanings ascribed to "postmaternity"—the time when children leave home and begin to lead independent lives. The study focuses on how variation in language in the media is used to make sense of descriptions of postmaternity.

Method: A feminist discourse analysis approach is used to explore the perception that postmaternity is most commonly associated with negative emotions, and that this is an experience exclusive to women. With the goal of constructing a corpus of data that captures a diversity of personal views on postmaternity, accounts were gathered from popular press articles about postmaternity in the USA, the UK, Australia, New Zealand, and Canada. The press included weekly newspapers, women's magazines, and general magazines. Covering a time span between 1997 and 2006, key words such as "empty nest, postmaternity, adult children, and postparenting" were used to source articles. Some were written by men or from the male perspective, but 90% appeared to have been written by women or to be giving the female perspective. Articles written in the USA dominated, with 50% of the final data corpus ($N = 49$) coming from there.

Analysis: The analysis highlighted the various meanings ascribed to postmaternity and showed the different ways in which it was construed to be important. Different emotions evoked in response to experiencing postmaternity were reported. Conflicting discourses of a "modern" versus a "traditional" woman were identified as producing an ideological dilemma, and one requiring delicate identity management. "Empty nest" was considered as a metaphor.

Findings: Key themes included:

Adjustment to Significant Change

Meanings and Emotional Responses

Individual Differences

Conflicting Positions

Gender Differences

The Imagined Life of Birds

Discussion: The pervasiveness of the expression "empty nest" was seen to encapsulate an assumption that a home without children is notable, and is a topic worthy of journalistic exploration. "Empty nest" was the dominant way of referencing adult offspring leaving home. The notion of Individual Differences was used to explain different reactions to children's departures. This is a practical ideology used to undermine the principle of equality in discussions of positive attitudes toward women (Billig et al., 1988). In this study, it served to hide a gendered division of labor where women shouldered more of the burden of responsibility for child care than the men. Where men were construed as more likely to suffer than women, it was because of their regret at having been absent fathers and their inability to discuss their emotions. "Empty nest syndrome" was raised only in relation to women.

In contrast to the dominant discourses of sadness and upset at children leaving home, positive feelings were also reported. Such feelings included pride in a parenting job well done and relief at being free to pursue interests outside the domestic sphere. These positive reactions were construed by women as counter to expectations and were frequently disclaimed against an inference of being a "bad" mother, or as a more shallow response than the deeper ones of loss.

Conclusion: The researchers conclude that the inextricability of womanhood with motherhood that is exerted by cultural assumptions continues to bring powerful pervasive discursive influences to perceptions of women, and of mothers. However discourses of "social fitness" and modern women, in which successful women are seen to have friends and a full and busy life outside the domestic sphere, contends with mandated motherhood discourses of full and exclusive emotional binding to one's children. The dilemma of being both emotionally bound to, and emotionally independent of, adult offspring is managed with the concept of adjustment, which provides an opportunity for, and an exit from, the socially mandated grief at children leaving home.

(For full details, see M. Sheriff and A. Weatherall, 2009, A Feminist Discourse Analysis of Popular-Press Accounts of Postmaternity. *Feminism & Psychology, 19*, 89–108.)

Feminist Poststructuralist Discourse Analysis: A Critique of Critical Discourse Analysis

Feminist poststructuralist discourse analysis (FPDA), developed by Baxter (2005, quoted in 2008), is defined by her as

an approach to analysing intertextualised discourse in spoken interaction and other types of text. It draws upon the poststructuralist principles of complexity, plurality, ambiguity, connection, recognition, diversity, textual playfulness, functionality and transformation. The feminist perspective on poststructuralist discourse analysis considers gender differentiation to be a dominant discourse among competing discourses when analysing all types of text. FPDA regards gender differentiation as one of the most pervasive discourses across many cultures in terms of its systematic power to discriminate between human beings according to their gender and sexuality. (p. 245)

In contrast to some other forms of discourse analysis, it has a "transformative quest." Rather than following an agenda of emancipation and risk, creating a new "will to truth" (Foucault, 1980, p. 109), FPDA uses poststructuralist principles to support small-scale, bottom-up, localized social transformation, believing that these hold the promise of developing a richer, multiperspective, and multidimensional understanding of the particularities of context in which social interventions are delivered. Approaches to their investigation have been shown to benefit most from paying attention to issues of salience and appropriateness (e.g., Frost & Nolas, in press; Hansen & Rieper, 2009). New interventions often develop from small ideas, requiring a lot of work in terms of proof of concept and program theory development in order to attract more funding and to be rolled out on a wider basis. Feminist poststructuralist discourse analysis seeks to develop this work by giving space to marginalized and overlooked women in contexts in which they have a degree of agency to change their conditions.

Furthermore, FPDA challenges the oppositional pairing that polarizes discourses by selecting which to deconstruct on behalf of oppressed social groups. It does this by valuing the complexity of female subject positions and recognizing that the existence of competing discourses means constant fluctuation between subject positions within matrices of powerfulness and powerlessness (Baxter, 2008). By examining text and speech from this perspective, the multiply located, variable, and complex positions that women inhabit across speech events can be better illuminated.

Rather than assuming that discourses work dialectically, valuing difference and thriving on tension (Johnson, 2012), FPDA adopts an antimaterialist stance that regards discourses as always being shaped and adjusted through the lens of other discourses. This offers a useful way to understand feminist research practice. Baxter (2008) argues that with an antimaterialist approach FPDA regards research practices themselves as highly discoursal and textualized. It extends the principle of self-reflexivity to place the research analyst as an author of the text and therefore constrained by the number of subject positions available to her, much as the narrator of the text is. Conventions of academic research dissemination and publication limit the researchers to presenting their research as coherent and complete. The value of the self-reflexive practice ensures that the process of reaching this is made more transparent—a key evaluation criterion of the quality of qualitative research.

Thus FPDA highlights the provisional constructed nature of all research and its status as a textualizing and fictionalizing process. Feminist postconstructuralist discourse analysis provides ways of broadening the range of possible meanings within accounts by creating and allowing space for competing voices and diverse accounts. It refuses to constitute gender in binary terms and so explores and highlights differences within and between girls and women. It aims to support transformative feminist processes that are specific and localized. FPDA supplements the grand narratives of other discourse analysis approaches by offering an alternative set of strategies that can be used alongside them.

Without feminist postmodern research methods, repressive structures could be understood only within the context that created them in the first place, and without the option for radical change. Discourse analysis offers ways of challenged accepted norms through the exploration of language and its role in creating, maintaining, and reinforcing discourses. In so doing, discourse analysis highlights constituent parts that form identity and perceptions of identity and allows for the range of voices, views, and beliefs that better represent the formation of self to be illuminated.

What Are the Limits of Postmodernism and Poststructuralism?

Despite the advances in understanding that the postmodern and poststructuralist approaches enabled, their politicized standpoint has drawn criticisms of feminist postmodern research. However the main critiques of feminist postmodernism can also be regarded as its greatest strengths: the acceptance that there is no universal truth, the aim to deconstruct power structures within discourse, the understanding that there is no one "woman's voice." Criticism of feminist postmodernism is more concerned with the effects of this approach and with asking, "Is it detrimental to the goals of feminism?" and to a lesser extent with the actual methodology.

Feminist postmodernism suffers from its very tenet that there is no such thing as a "woman's experience," that we can only explore what it means to be a woman by listening to the many different voices that come from women from different cultures, classes, and societies. The postmodern view that there is no such thing as a universal truth, that we can only examine collections of individual truths has been considered harmful to feminism, because it robs the movement of a sense of community, of a common goal.

In a vast body of work that space prevents us from exploring here, Judith Butler offers a detailed and informative critique of feminist postmodernism. Although some see it as offering an alternative to the empirical positivist objectivity that dominated traditional research into human behavior and saw women's identity only in terms of men's identity, others reject the label as being too inclusive. Butler suggests that the labeling as "postmodern" those theories and understandings that oppose existing theories acts as a violent reduction of alternative interpretations and reinterpretations of identity and behavior

(Butler, 1990). She argues that for feminists the label of postmodernist risks creating a separate whole theory which, while oppositional in content, is similar in representation to the cultural dominant grand narratives of hegemony that it set out to challenge.

Feminist postmodernism explicitly acknowledges and invites a variety of women's experiences, voices, and narratives, and encompasses a diverse group of viewpoints within its framework. This also represents the main criticism levied at feminist postmodernism—the lack of a unifying philosophy and defined goals that threatens to minimize the effect on the impact of feminist postmodernism on societal and cultural change.

The criticism of relativism is a valid one, but at the same time, it needs to be acknowledged that the attention given to the variety of different voices accentuates the complexity of human experience and allows for inclusion of those who would be otherwise marginalized. Feminist postmodernism and poststructuralism within research practice focuses on this complexity as a strength in order to gain an understanding of a multifaceted representation of the experience that cannot be shoehorned into one truth.

Feminist postmodern research is in essence not about finding an absolute truth, but about effecting a change within the political, social, and cultural structures it examines. In reverse, feminist postmodernist research cannot exist without having this aim at its very core. However, caution in recognizing the limits of this approach is urged to avoid imposing minority world ideas on others in an uninformed and potentially damaging way. Using the work of Haideh Moghissi as a case study, we can see some of the limitations of feminist postmodern analysis with regard to Islamic fundamentalism (Moghissi, 1999).

Behind the Scenes With Haideh Moghissi

Feminism and Islamist Fundamentalism: The Limits of Postmodern Analysis

Moghissi suggests that the "vagaries of academic fashion" (Moghissi, 1999, p. 8), including postmodern relativism, anti-Orientalism, and identity politics, share with debates on the "Muslim woman" a hostility toward the social, political, and cultural processes of modernity. She lists some of the similarities between postmodernists and fundamentalists and goes on to say:

I propose that anti-Orientalism and postmodernism may have opened new possibilities for cultural inquiry but in their rush to give voice to those constructed as Other, they have entrapped themselves in the headlong pursuit of the "exotic" and the "native." If the Orientalists created an illusory, shimmering image of Oriental Muslim women, postmodernists confront them by turning the genre on its head. In the process of validating "Muslim women's" experience, the harsh edges of fundamentalism are softened; and the image that fundamentalists transmit of

Muslim women as emblematic of cultural revival, integrity and authenticity is validated. In the end, the postmodern relativists collude with the fundamentalists' culturalist solutions to crises of modernity and modernisation. (p. 8)

These salutary words are extended into an exploration of the "possibilities and limits" of Islamic feminism. Here Moghissi asks whether Islam can develop an alternative paradigm to Western feminism without Islam being pushed on feminists in Islamic societies, thus reducing their identities to Islam once again and erasing difference across region, ethnicity, religion, class, and culture.

She concludes by reminding us that despite many challenges to misogyny in Islamic societies, none were carried out in the name of Islamic feminism. By imposing this label onto the struggles against oppression,

we see the political and discursive influence of Islamic fundamentalism as supporters of this line invade the agenda of secular intellectuals, including feminists. In truth the "exuberant" accounts of Islamic feminism reflect a profound defeatism which presumes the end of secular nationalist liberal and socialist projects in Islamic societies. (p. 10)

Although these words were written in 1999 and much has happened since, within Islamic societies, and between them and the Western world, it seems that there is great value in adopting the substance of these words in the pursuit of postmodern feminist research.

(For full details, see H. Moghissi, 1999, *Feminism and Islamic Fundamentalism: The Limits of Postmodern Analysis*, London, England: Zed Books.)

The Emergence of Critical Theory

As feminists were grappling with the recognition that postmodernism was threatening to fragment and further disempower communities of women, critical theory began to emerge as a way of identifying processes underlying oppression and subjugation.

WHAT IS CRITICAL THEORY?

Like postmodernism, critical theory has no single definition or epistemological underpinning and was developed to challenge assumptions and practices that oppress and discriminate. Critical theory highlights ways in which differences and diversity are at best obscured and at worst marginalized or pathologized because of assumptions of universal behaviors and experiences contained within traditional research approaches. The critical tradition embraces plurality of experience and therefore is made up explicitly of many theories (Kincheloe & McLaren, 2011). In response to the complexity of culture and life as lived, it is always changing and evolving. Critical theory research practice is particularly concerned with exploring issues of power and justice and ways in which matters of class, gender, race, sexuality, ableism, and nation intersect with ideologies and discourses. Critical theory seeks to understand how cultural dynamics interact to construct social systems. Above all, critical theory aims to change practices by challenging assumptions and biases that obscure difference and diversity through the development of power relations. Critical theory was originally explained by Marx as "the self-clarification of the struggles and wishes of the age" (Marx, 1943; cited in Fraser, 1985, p. 97); and many researchers still regard the overtly political character that this understanding espouses as being at the very core of their work.

With many women experiencing oppression, either overtly or as an outcome of living in predominantly patriarchal societies, feminist researchers quickly came to see the value of using critical tools to understand more about the experiences of women. By carefully constructing research questions that enable firsthand accounts to be gathered and perspectives that do not position women as other by comparing them and their experience to men, ways in which cultural assumptions, powers, discourses, and social structures work for women to be oppressed and to perpetuate their own oppression could be explored.

Such an approach led to the development of global feminism research, feminist critical race theory, feminist transformative justice research, and cisgenderism research—to name but a few. These uses of critical theory as a tool to explore lived worlds of women enable a diverse range of research questions to be asked. Examples include:

- What is the gendered nature of natural disasters on women? (Neumayer & Plümper, 2007)

- How are lesbian, gay, transsexual, and queer sexualities constructed and portrayed in museums? (Mertens, Fraser, & Heimlich, 2008)

- What role does cisgenderism play in the ways that mental health professionals communicate with each other? (Ansara & Hegarty, 2012)

- What are the challenges and strategies for conducting feminist research in African contexts? (Mama, 2012)

HOW DO FEMINIST RESEARCHERS WORK WITH CRITICAL THEORY?

As we have identified above, the very essence of critical theory is to respond and adapt to perceived power relations and resulting subjugations and oppressions of individuals and groups. It does this by examining the role of social and historical contexts in shaping power relations that inform the ways in which people's lives and identities are interpreted. Since its inception, critical theory quickly developed a feminist trajectory that enabled feminist research to construct new theories and paradigms with which to examine and explore the lives of women. In the following section, we shall explore a few of these to consider how they enable critical feminist research practice.

Critical theory allows feminist researchers to highlight the ways in which women were regarded as different from an assumed norm that placed men at the center of research and research findings. With the publication of Carol Gilligan's groundbreaking book *In a Different Voice* (1982), the problems with the tradition of psychological research that treated women as if they were men began to be highlighted. The book focused on moral development and found that gender differences played an important role. Crucially, however, Gilligan pointed out that rather than there being something wrong with women for not developing in the same way as men, there must instead be something wrong with a theory that suggests that they do.

The publication of that work enabled a detailed focus on the experiences of women and arguably launched the advent of "difference" research.

What Is Difference Research?

Difference research acknowledges and works with structural axes of difference. Originally differentiating women from men on the basis of gender alone, difference research focused on gathering firsthand accounts from women about their experience and on finding ways to interrogate and interpret these accounts without recourse to the existing patriarchal norm. This meant explaining women's experiences in terms of their gender and of acknowledging that gender was formed as a social construct in response to cultures within which women lived. On one hand, this approach to researching women's lives and the power relations that constructed their sense of self-enabled insight to the complexity of women's experiences as women and not as other than men; but, on the other hand, this approach risked obscuring or, worse, further perpetuating the subjugation of other aspects of women's identity. With the recognition of the diversity of women's identities as women but also as mothers, partners, members of different races, classes, and nations came recognition of the risks of developing an "essentialist" approach to feminist research that saw women simply as women and fixed this category alone as key to their identity and to informing all that they do and how they construct themselves.

Feminist difference researchers propose that gender forms a site of power that can be oppressed or subjugated. They seek to enable difference and to draw it out from obscurity or marginalization. They attend to difference by constructing research questions that ask about genderized experiences. The "discourse of difference" (Burman, 2006, p. 294) sets out to challenge uniformity and generalization that sees women positioned as other and all the same. Difference research aims to illuminate the complexity of experiences of women without reference to an assumed patriarchal norm.

To do this, difference research demands thoughtful research design and methodology that allows the taken-for-granted assumptions of hegemony to be identified and challenged. Careful and reflective attention is paid to power relations within and between the groups under study and within the research process. Power relations may be those created by the social structures of the culture in which the research is taking place, or those within the research process itself that can position the participant and researcher in a power hierarchy that sets the researcher as expert on the experiences of others.

There are important ethical considerations within this approach. Feminist researchers seek to flatten hierarchies within the research, perhaps by adopting an openness to questioning by research participants (Marshall, Woollett, & Dosanjh, 1998) or using data provided from their own experiences as in memory-work research (Haug, 1987). A reflexive stance is taken to make explicit researchers' motivations for the research and their role throughout it to consider the impact of the researchers on the research process. Such ethical care reduces the imposition of others' experiences or of researcher bias onto the research process and enhances the credibility of the research outcomes. However, approaches that seek to "give voice" to those considered to be otherwise marginalized can have other consequences of which feminist researchers have recently been made aware. Burman (2006) points out that with seeking to give voice to those who are different comes an accompanying decision about whom not to include and with this, the threat of perpetuating marginalization of some groups and erasing the agency and powers of the selected ones. Instead of flattening hierarchies and facilitating a challenge to subjugation, the decision to give voice to one form of difference over another positions the "voice-giver" in a privileged role that itself reinforces the paternalistic relationship it set out to challenge. Ryan-Flood and Gill (2010) highlight that for some women, the best way they can give voice is through secrecy and silence. In some cultures, this can be a more challenging and more powerful stance for women to take. Feminist researchers have a responsibility not to represent as commonplace that which is not, to respect that there may be essential reasons for secrecy and silence, and that the silences and secrets can be the researcher's as much as the participant's. Silence can be an important part of identity or survival for participants, such as those who choose to remain silent about their sexuality in restrictive societies (e.g., Parpart, 2010). Similarly, choices about whether to remain silent about issues such as female circumcision challenge researchers with questions about their role in apparently condoning practices with which they disagree (e.g., Moore, 2010).

As difference research has proliferated, the axes of difference have, too, so that now they are likely to include sexuality and ableism in addition to gender, class, and race. Burman (2006) points to the risk of overproliferation of lists of difference that become so long that they serve to reinforce the notion of otherness that the research set out to challenge. With increasing lengths of lists of differences comes the risk of increased pathologization of all difference and of the diversity of differences being unified into one. The ever-increasing number of axes of difference risks fragmenting difference so that the experience of others becomes difficult to engage with. Burman highlights that since the 1980s, modernist political movements such as Marxism and feminism have been fragmented because of accusations of overlooking or even downplaying oppressions accorded to black and working-class women and lesbians (Burman, 2006, p. 296).

Black Feminism and Intersectionality

This potential for conflict of research agendas and the very real threat of reinforcing subjugation led to critiques of feminist difference research by black feminist researchers, notably Patricia Hill Collins and Kimberlé Crenshaw. They argued that grouping all women together as different set up a further oppression of black women because it overlooked race as an identity category. Consider this extract from a publication by Moore (2012):

> Asked how she thought of race, gender and sexuality as identities that described her, Zoe said, "If I had to number them one, two, three? Probably Black and lesbian—real close, to be honest with you. I don't know which would come up as one. Probably Black Woman last." When I asked, "What makes you say that?" she replied:

> Because that is just what it is. People see your Blackness, and the world has affected me by my Blackness since the very inception of my life. . . . My sexuality is something that developed later on, or I became aware of later on, [because] I think *it's always been what it's been*, but I think that it was just something that developed in my psyche. But being Black is something that I've always had to deal with: racism since day one and recognizing how to navigate through this world as a Black person, and even as a Black woman. (p. 33)

This highlights the importance of considering race when exploring the shaping of identity. Black feminist researchers argue that race is intertwined with gender for black women and so by examining the intersection of these dimensions, their relations with discourse of power and their relation with each other enable the question to be asked: "How would gender and race aid exploration into the lives of Black women?" (Higginbotham, 2012). As Burman (2006) states, "[T]he question becomes not whether but 'how' we are raced" (p. 299).

As recently as the late 1980s, black women were perceived as a group that deviated from the (white women) norm. The extent of this perception was such that the legitimacy of research into the lives of black women was questioned. At the same time realities for many black women researchers were that professional positions and status were compromised with differing workloads and foci from those of their white counterparts in academe (Higginbotham, 2012). The knowledge that black women researchers within academe gained about being outsiders enabled them to use the identification of power relations with race and gender as sources of empowerment rather than of subjugation. They took a standpoint to develop their own voices as black women rather than to work within white feminist theory. They took up the quest for social justice within universities by highlighting that existing frameworks of difference offered no context for understanding the lives and identities of women of color.

An important publication by Collins in 1992, *Black Feminist Thought,* focused on the interplay between black feminism, postcolonial theory, and feminist theory. Collins's work identified a standpoint that allowed for an identification and examination of how social location makes for a perspective connected to lived experience. This approach allowed critical questions about knowledge and the role of power in constructing knowledge to be asked. The public definition of the knowledge, how it was acquired, and how it was constructed was expanded. Empirical work to identity and dispel myths about black women and their families was enabled, as well as the employment experiences and contributions of black women to community and to politics. Importantly the invisible history of black women started to be uncovered through the adoption of the intersectionality approach. This groundbreaking work of Collins's led to identity politics being established as a key source of understanding identity construction through the intersection of axes of race, class, and gender. It has since led to the interrogation of color blindness, analysis of black sexual politics, and examination of the shifting terrain of oppression in a postracial American nation.

Crenshaw (1991) proposes that gender and class act as intrinsically negative frameworks within which social power works to exclude those who are different and that such gender politics can ignore intragroup differences, usually to the further cost of the black woman. Crenshaw suggests that adopting intersectionality as both a theoretical framework and an empirical research approach enables a focus on the intersections between categories. At these sites, identity politics take place and allow for a reconceptualization of identity by acknowledging differences among group members and enabling a renegotiation of the means by which differences find expression to construct identity.

Crenshaw (1991) identified three forms of intersectionality.

Structural intersectionality, in which the location of women of color intersects the axes of race and gender. This separates the experiences of black women from those of white women and enables them to be regarded as qualitatively different.

Political intersectionality, which challenges the disempowerment of groups with different political agendas arising from a focus on one discourse over another. Crenshaw argues that by intersecting competing discourses, differences within the group are made apparent and the diversity of the different aspects of identity made salient. This avoids the strategic silences that arise when the political agenda of one group is pursued over that of another, such as for example antiracists working to challenge perceptions of black men.

Representational intersectionality, an approach that challenges the cultural representation of women of color and contestations of these to suggest that responses to the portrayal of either race or gender must be a response to each of these but also a response to both in order to avoid marginalization. Crenshaw illustrates this point with a discussion of the obscenity charge brought against a black rap group for lyrics about violence toward women used in their songs. Her position is summarized below.

Behind the Scenes With Kimberlé Crenshaw

The 2 Live Crew Controversy

Crenshaw argues that criticism of the prosecution against the band focused on concern for the women to whom the actions of the songs were directed. However, attacking the singers for this overlooks the race of the women, positions them alongside white women, and therefore flattens difference between white women and black women, reinforcing the assumed norm that black women's lives should be like white women's lives. In this case, black and white women are brought together as being under threat from the violence of black men.

However Crenshaw's research had shown that in reality, the prosecution and sentencing of black men for violence against women was in proportion to the race of the women they were accused of attacking. Therefore by grouping women together with a criticism solely of the misogyny of the songs reinforces the black man/white woman dyad that sees black women as excluded from both the race and gender categories. The racialized sexual politics are reinforced and work to perpetuate the exclusion of the black woman.

(Continued)

(Continued)

Instead, Crenshaw proposes that an inclusive response to the actions of the band and to the charge against them is to acknowledge that sexism has fueled the antiracism discourse that allows the stereotype of the violent black men to be challenged and to avoid women serving as the vehicle for this to happen by also addressing the explicit misogyny of the rap band's lyrics and their connotations.

(For full details, see K. Crenshaw, K., 1991, Mapping the Margins: Intersectionality, Identity Politics, and Violence Against Women of Color, *Stanford Law Review, 43*(6), 1241–1299.)

The theory of intersection stresses complexity by examining the relations between intersecting sites of structural axes. It does not necessarily incorporate all the dimensions of identity; so, for example, African American feminist researchers emphasize racism and sexism by focusing on race and gender categories and identities (e.g., Crenshaw, 1995; McCall, 2005). Thomson (1997) has used the intersection of gender, disability, and sexuality to focus on marginalized female bodies (Thomson, 1997). By providing insight to the discourses of power of each axis and how they intersect, insight to how they serve to shape identity and to perpetuate marginalization and oppression is gained.

Despite the obvious extension in scope and focus that the intersectionality approach facilitated, it attracted criticism for being particularistic from some quarters. Criticisms were leveled at intersectionality for viewing the particular experiences of black women in a vacuum that worked ultimately to compare their experiences to those of white women. However, the intersectionality approach enabled black women to reposition themselves in a matrix of domination based on reality and to move away from explanations based on their failure to construct conventional families or as victims of the legacy of slavery. Instead, intersectionality enabled them to examine the realities of their lives in contemporary contexts relevant to their lives (Higginbotham, 2012).

Intersectionality research addresses some of these critiques of difference research by seeking not to privilege one axis of difference over another (race over class, e.g.) but instead by recognizing that different identities that one individual may have are likely to overlap with each other and intersect in a dynamic way. The intersectionality approach places the site of power at the junction where the axes overlap and intertwine and enables the relations between the axes to be examined. Using this approach enabled researchers such as Collins (1992) to highlight the multiple identities and discriminations against women of color. The move away from focusing on one identity category over another worked to include recognition of the saliency of multiple dimensions of identity and how they intertwine to shape experience and practice.

Categories are not positioned as competing with or in opposition to each other, and neither is one or another reduced to an essentialist fixed form (Brah, 1996; Somers, 1994). Instead, intersectionality research becomes about more than a study of gender differences between men and women. Intersectionality research aims to examine "the relationships between sociocultural categories and identities" (Knudsen, 2006, p. 61). It seeks to combine axes of difference in order to reflect the complexity and transient nature of identity and of experience.

Over the past few decades, researchers such as Crenshaw (1991), Meyer (2002), and Lykke (2005) have variously added dimensions of class, ability, and sexuality to the initial focus on the intersection of race with gender.

Transversal intersectionality (Knudsen, 2006) seeks to gain insight to how the categories of identities within the same group overlap and intertwine and how they pervade and transform each other (Lykke, 2005). The experiences of black women who are lesbians is an example (Moore, 2011). This approach allows questions such as "How is ethnicity gendered and how are masculinity and femininity ethnicized and racialized?" (Mørch & Staunæs, 2003) to be asked. Transversal intersectionality allows for a detailed focus on the relationships between categories and enables a troubling of one taken-for-granted category to inform the troubling of other categories connected to it by power discourse. Judith Butler's "Gender Trouble: Feminism and the Subversion of Identity" (1990) troubled gender and problematized heterosexuality. Knudsen (2006) argues further that troubling ethnicity problematizes gender and heterosexuality.

Behind the Scenes With Mignon R. Moore

Intersectionality and the Study of Black, Sexual Minority Women

Moore's work focused on black women with same-sex desire and their families. She highlights that sexuality is a site where heterosexism, class, race, gender, and nation as systems of power converge. Here the relations work to shape the experience, identities, and behavior of black women who are lesbians within a context dependent on geographical location, racial socialization, and racial hierarchy. Drawing on Patricia Hill Collins's work that promotes the exploration of women's experiences through a racialized lens, Moore argues that

(Continued)

(Continued)

black feminist thought allows the study of lesbian women of color with black feminist ideologies, race consciousness, and structural experiences with racial discrimination—and not with
lesbian feminism at the foundations and its connotations of comparison with white women's
experiences. The framework for understanding other statuses of black women as women, gay,
and mothers, for example (Moore, 2011), guides their interpretations of how gender, sexuality, social class, and other axes shape their lives. Black women's experiences of being gay are
separated from comparison with experiences of white women who are gay, and they highlight instead that black heterosexism is the assumed norm within this group.

(For full details, see M. R. Moore, M. R., 2012, Intersectionality and the Study of Black, Sexual
Minority Women, *Gender & Society, 26*, 33–39.)

What Are the Next Steps in Feminist Critical Theory?

Intersectionality research has undoubtedly enabled new ways of exploring and gaining understanding of the lives and identities of women and how they have been marginalized. From its origins within black feminism in the United States, its outcomes can be seen internationally and in a diverse range of areas relating to gender and sex. Two such areas currently emerging are those of transfeminism and transformative justice research, which we shall briefly consider below.

TRANSFEMINISM

Transfeminism is the adoption of the female gender by those who have not had this gender biologically assigned to them. For feminist researchers who recognize the social construction of gender and the role of language, critical theory allows for inclusion and detailed exploration of the experiences of this community. Research has found that transgender people suffer extreme levels of violence because of "transphobia." Transphobia has been described as "an emotional disgust toward individuals who do not conform to society's gender expectations" (Hill & Willoughby, 2005, p. 534). Furthermore, children usually self-assign their gender at an average age of five years (Kennedy, 2012), although they may not be able to tell anyone about this for lack of the language to describe what they are understanding about themselves.

In recognition of the power held by the academic and clinical disciplines of psychology, the American Psychological Association (APA) recently addressed the need for professionals to attend to the way in which they were disseminating and constructing knowledge about children who self-assign their gender. Furthermore, in efforts to reduce discrimination against this community, the APA called for psychologists to take a "leadership role in working against discrimination toward transgender and gender variant individuals" (APA, 2008, para. 17). In light of the issuance of these guidelines Ansara and Hegarty (2012) conducted extensive research to examine the role of language in literature written by psychology professionals working with children who self-identify their gender. Details are displayed below.

Behind the Scenes With Y. Gavriel Ansara and Peter Hegarty

Cisgenderism in Psychology: Pathologizing and Misgendering Children From 1999 to 2008

The Study

In agreement with the assumptions of feminist research that scientific language about groups both represents and perpetuates ideology, these researchers investigated whether cisgenderism was increasing or decreasing over time, whether cisgenderism was unevenly distributed across subdisciplines of psychology and was particularly prevalent in mental health literature, and whether an invisible college of authors existed that served to increase the impact of the literature.

The Findings

The researchers conducted a content analysis on literature ($N = 49$) drawn from a wide range of academic and professional journals and a broad scope of terms related to boys, girls, gender, and gender expression. Their results showed that cisgenderist language is commonplace in professional communications between psychologists about children who self-defined their gender, that the most pathologizing language is found in literature by mental health professionals, and that those most closely tied to the most prolific author in the field through publication are most likely to use language that pathologizes and misgenders children.

The Impact

The impact of these findings on the professional services offered to children is profound, and the authors usefully delineate practical and conceptual ways in which cisgenderism discourses are perpetuated and reinforced through psychological literature and research. Among these

(Continued)

(Continued)

are the measures of assessment value placed on academic and clinical publications that, in turn, inform the allocation of research funding and leadership position appointments.

Wider implications

The invisible college is defined as a collection of authors grouped around a leading published writer. Through self-citations and coauthorships, the Impact Factor of journals in which their work is published is increased. With this comes the repetition of ideas on which the college members agree. Funding bodies and employers look to the apparent leaders in the field when making financial decisions, seeking reviews of proposals, appointing people to committees, and seeking advice on policy and practice development. The work of this group of people comes to dominate the field and obscure that of others who may have minority views. Hegarty and Ansara highlight that psychological knowledge constructed and disseminated this way works to obscure the views of individuals who are likely to be experiencing discrimination and pathologizing as a result of the perpetuation of these discourses—people of transgender and variant gender.

(For full details, see Y. G. Ansara and P. Hegarty, 2012, Cisgenderism in Psychology: Pathologising and Misgendering Children From 1999 to 2008, *Psychology & Sexuality, 3,* 137–160.)

This study and its findings can, of course, be easily equated with the origin of feminist research, in which the experiences and discrimination of women were obscured by dominant discourse originating within a college of members coalescing around others with similar approaches and language. As intersectionality theory has helped advance insight to the diversity of women's experience and developed out of a critique of the lack of recognition of intragroup differences, the approach can also shine a light on the experiences of other people who are marginalized, such as those with self-assigned gender. Ansara and Hegarty highlight the danger of "coercive queering," an apparently positive and affirming response to those who self-assign gender that places them with the lesbian, gay, bisexual and transgender (LGBT) group. In a suggestion that mirrors that of Crenshaw's (1991) notion that black women's experiences are compared to those of white women if the focus is on a single discourse (that of feminism in Crenshaw's argument, and of homonormative gender in the argument of Ansara and Hegarty), children placed in this group are placed at risk of further oppression as they become the pathologized members by being seen as deviating from the homonormative norm. In another useful implication derived from the adoption of an intersectional approach to understanding the lives and experiences of self-assigned gender children, Ansara and Hegarty point out the intersection between cisgenderism and ethnocentrism. They highlight the value of recognizing the dominance of the minority worldview (by which they mean the Western world and developing countries) that gender is a psychomedical assignation and that deviation from this assignment is a disorder. The majority world (made up of the remaining 83% of the world) does not universally subscribe to this view. These researchers suggest that further research attend to the fact that use of biological attributes to assign gender is not a universal cultural practice and that the researchers use this fact to guide the conduct of their research.

The value of findings from intersectional research has been illustrated using research with women, with black women, and with children who self-assign their gender. Such findings are crucial, and sometimes lifesaving, for those who have participated. Ansara and Hegarty (2012) remind us of the United Nations Convention on the Rights of the Child (UNCRC, 1989) that guarantees all children the right to unrestricted freedom of play and expression. Crenshaw (1991) highlights the risk to life and well-being posed to women under threat of violence by the lack of understanding that enables constructive and accessible interventions to be developed for these women. Collins (1992) shows how finding ways to understand the experiences of black women by viewing them through a racialized lens allows insight to issues such as family development and formation by black women with same-sex desire.

Much of the research cited above has focused on American culture and groups residing within that culture. However, feminist critical theory has enabled development of new understandings and research approaches across the world. One such example is transformative justice research (e.g., Mertens, 2009).

FEMINIST TRANSFORMATIVE RESEARCH

Transformative justice research is an emerging approach that seeks to blend the academic genre of research with community conventions and beliefs in pursuit of bringing about change for social justice (Mertens, 2009). Using critical theory as a framework, transformative justice research aims to enable difference, examine power relations with axes of difference, and explore the ways that they intersect to shape behavior and identity. The research is explicitly guided by individuals who are included as partners and whose beliefs are utilized to inform the research direction in pursuit of social justice. The priority of transformative research is the furtherance of social justice and human rights. The greatest involvement possible of community members along with employment of multiple methodologies in ways that are culturally appropriate ensure that an advance toward the realization of social change emerges from the research. Transformative justice approach sees the potential for power to effect positive change in communities and seeks to utilize positive psychology principles to move research away from a deficit focus that sees only the problems of a community and not its strengths (Mertens, 2009).

The transformative justice paradigm extends the thinking of democratic inquiry by exploring the similarities in beliefs underlying critical, feminist, critical race theory, and many other approaches that focus on dimensions of diversity. It ensures that a range of people who are excluded from society are included in the research by making explicit that the axes of difference that are historically associated with discrimination are included.

Transformative justice research challenges academe and researchers within it to accept research approaches that fall outside the conventional academic genre. It prioritizes the involvement of community members as partners and seeks to develop community solidarity. In common with much qualitative research, transformative justice research processes do not proceed in a linear fashion. However in this paradigm, it is the researched rather than the researcher who guides the direction of the process. As with all research, effort is made to pay attention to the ethical stance and rigor of the research process to ensure its credibility. In transformative justice research, three key themes underlie this ethical stance and rigor (Mertens, 2009).

- Assumptions brought to the research are explicitly ethically inclusive so that community members are given a voice and share in the research from its development to its dissemination. This may include, for example, sharing royalties with the community.

- The researchers have responsibility for ensuring they know enough about a community to develop an entry point into the community that will build trust and make goals and strategies apparent.

- The researchers have responsibility for dissemination of the findings of the research in ways that ensure social justice and human rights are advanced within that community.

Transformative justice research spans a wide range of discrimination and oppression. Examples of questions that it asks include:

- What do women engineers experience at work? (Watts, 2009)

- What is mental health service provision for Native American women like? (Duran & Duran, 2000)

- What cultural conflicts exist in reactions to the death of a child between the dominant and Maori populations? (Clarke & McCreanor, 2006)

CONCLUSION

Feminist postmodernism offered an innovative and exciting approach to addressing the positioning of women as Other and as members of a group that deviated from the norm. Three decades ago, it enabled women to confront pathologizing labels, to challenge accusations of abnormality and disorder, and to highlight their identities as unique. Postmodernism's contribution to enabling reinterpretation of women's lives is immense and the thinking fostered by postmodernism pervades much of feminist practice and research today. Acknowledgment of the risk of recreating an Othering of all women and of erasing difference among communities of women enabled postmodernism to evolve into intersectionality and, in turn, to foster a culture of recognition and respect for the other dimensions of identity that intertwine with gender. In contemporary practice, intersectionality has gone beyond the racialized focus of the black feminists and can now be brought to consider the experiences of a wider range of groups. Although a relatively recent development, intersectionality has demonstrated a new way of thinking that challenges much of what has preceded it in the search for more understanding of women.

Underlying all of the approaches brought from feminist postmodern, poststructuralist, and critical thinking is the desire to identify and challenge oppressive practice against women. It is this that inspires and motivates feminist researchers—but also challenges them—to move out of academe in their work and to be truly inclusive in their research practice. Transformative justice research explicitly challenges the conventions of academic research to work as partners with members of the communities in which they have research interest and, crucially, to bring about change for social justice. This important and contemporary step forward in the development of feminist postmodernist thinking may well prove to be the vanguard for innovative and life-changing research for women all around the world.

DISCUSSION QUESTIONS

When discussing the applications of feminist postmodernism in terms of research, a number of possible questions arise.

1. Can a feminist postmodernist approach ask and answer questions that remain unsatisfactory in other approaches, such as feminist empiricism and feminist standpoint epistemology?

2. When taking into account the criticism against feminist postmodernism of being too vague and of being without a unifying goal or tenet, consider in what ways these effects can offer a positive advantage when exploring feminist issues in research.

3. What new perspectives can feminist postmodernism add to existing research and its associated methods?

4. How can feminist critical thinking bring about social change in communities where for women to have their voices heard can endanger their lives?

WEB RESOURCES

- Feminist Research Group: http://www.uwindsor.ca/feministresearchgroup/frg-history

A group of feminist researchers based at the University of Windsor, Canada, who have organized 10 annual conferences where feminist researchers can present their work, and who now focus on encouraging feminist knowledge by holding a variety of community--based and academe-based events. The detailed website includes links to the conference programs and to a Feminism 101 Blog.

- The Feminist Majority Foundation: http://feminist.org/default.asp

An American-based consciousness-raising network of more than 120 leading research, policy, and advocacy centers that aim to bridge differences across sectors and silos and to foster collaboration among researchers and change agents. The network is dedicated to women's equality, reproductive health, and nonviolence by utilizing research and action to empower women economically, socially, and politically. The website links to resources including feminist books, magazines, and research centers across the United States.

- Global Feminisms Collaborative: http://www.vanderbilt.edu/gfc/

Based at Vanderbilt College of Arts and Sciences, this group of feminist researchers aims to raise the visibility of scholarship in this field within their own institutions and globally. It seeks to work transinstitutionally with global, national, and institutional partners through scholarly and ethical reflections on feminisms and their worlds. The website includes links to global partners and to previously held Workshops on Gender and the Environment.

- Psychology of Women Section (POWS) of the British Psychological Society: http://pows.bps.org.uk/

This Section aims to bring together everyone with an interest in the psychology of women to provide a forum for the psychology of women in research, teaching, and professional practice. It aims to increase awareness and action around gender and inequality issues within the British Psychological Society, the psychology profession, and the teaching of psychology. The website is regularly updated with news of competition and funding opportunities that support feminist research practice.

REFERENCES

American Psychological Association (APA). (2008). *APA policy statement: Transgender, gender identity, & gender expression non-discrimination.* Retrieved from http://www.apa.org/about/policy/transgender.aspx

Ansara, Y. G., & Hegarty, P. (2012). Cisgenderism in psychology: Pathologising and misgendering children from 1999 to 2008. *Psychology & Sexuality, 3,* 137–160.

Baxter, J. (2008). Feminist post-structuralist discourse analysis: A new theoretical and methodological approach? In K. Harrington, L. Litosseliti, H. Sauntson, & J. Sunderland (Eds.), *Gender and language research methodologies* (pp. 243–255). Basingstoke, England: Palgrave Macmillan.

Billig, M., Condon, S., Edwards, D., Gane, M., Middleton, D., & Radley, A. (1988). *Ideological dilemmas: A social psychology of everyday thinking.* Beverly Hills, CA: Sage.

Bordo, S. (1993). *Unbearable weight: Feminism, Western culture and the body.* Berkeley: University of California Press.

Brah, A. (1996). *Cartographies of diaspora, contesting identities.* London, England: Routledge.

Burman, E. (2006). From difference to intersectionality: Challenges and resources. *European Journal of Psychotherapy and Counselling, 6,* 293–308.

Burman, E., & Parker, I. (1993). *Discourse analytic research : Repertoires and readings of texts in action.* London, England: Routledge.

Butler, J. (1990). *Gender trouble: Feminism and the subversion of identity.* New York, NY: Routledge.

Cassell, J. (2000). *The woman in the surgeon's body.* Cambridge, MA: Harvard University Press.

Cixous, H. (2003). *Rootprints: Memory and life writing.* London, England: Routledge.

Clarke, E., & McCreanor, T. (2006). He wahine tangi tikapa . . . : Statutory investigative processes and the grieving of Maori families who have lost a baby to SIDS. *Kotuitui: New Zealand Journal of Social Sciences Online, 1,* 25–43.

Collins, P. H. (1992). *Black feminist thought.* London, England: Routledge.

Crenshaw, K. (1991). Mapping the margins: Intersectionality, identity politics, and violence against women of color. *Stanford Law Review, 43*(6), 1241–1299.

Crenshaw, K. W. (1995). Intersections of race and gender. In K. W. Crenshaw, N. Gotanda, G. Peller, & K. Thomas (Eds.), *Critical race theory: The key writings that formed the movement* (pp. 357–383). New York, NY: New Press.

Davis, K. (1997). *European Journal of Women's Studies Readers series: Vol. 1. Embodied practices: Feminist perspectives on the body.* London, England: Sage.

Davis, K. (2003). *Dubious equalities and embodied differences: Cultural studies on cosmetic surgery.* Lanham, MD: Rowman & Littlefield.

Davis, K. (2008). Intersectionality as buzzword: A sociology of science perspective on what makes a feminist theory successful. *Feminist Theory, 9,* 67–85.

Derrida, J. (1976). *Of grammatology.* Baltimore, MD: Johns Hopkins University Press.

Duran, B., & Duran, E. (2000). Applied postcolonial research and clinical strategies. In M. Battiste (Ed.), *Reclaiming indigenous voice and vision* (pp. 86–100). Vancouver, Canada: University of British Columbia.

Foucault, M. (1971). *The order of things: An archaeology of the human sciences.* New York, NY: Pantheon Books.

Foucault, M. (1980). *Power/knowledge.* Brighton, England: Harvester Press.

Fraser, N. (1985). What's critical about critical theory? The case of Habermas and gender. *New German Critique, 35,* 97–131.

Frost, N. A., & Nolas, S.-M. (in press). The contribution of pluralistic qualitative approaches to mixed methods evaluations [Special issue]. *New Directions for Evaluation.*

Gavey, N. (1989). Feminist poststructuralist and discourse analysis: Contributions to feminist psychology. *Psychology of Women Quarterly, 13,* 459–475.

Gavey, N. (2011). Feminist poststructuralism and discourse analysis revisited. *Psychology of Women Quarterly, 35,* 183–188.

Gilligan, C. (1982). *In a different voice: Psychological theory and women's development.* Cambridge, MA: Harvard University Press.

Hansen, H. F., & Rieper, O. (2009). The evidence movement: The development and consequences of methodologies in review practices. *Evaluation, 15,* 141–163.

Haug, F. (1987). *Female sexualization.* London, England: Verso.

Higginbotham, E. (2012). Reflections on the early contributions of Patricia Hill Collins. *Gender & Society, 26,* 23–27.

Hill, D. B., & Willoughby, B. L. B. (2005). The development and validation of the genderism and transphobia scale. *Sex Roles, 53,* 531–544.

Holt, A. (2011). Discourse analysis approaches. In N. A. Frost (Ed.), *Qualitative research methods in psychology: Combining core approaches* (pp. 66–90). Berkshire, England: Open University Press.

hooks, b. (1982). *Ain't I a woman. Black women and feminism.* Boston, MA: South End Press.

hooks, b. (1994). *Teaching to transgress: Education as the practice of freedom.* New York, NY: Routledge.

hooks, b. (2000a). *Feminism is for everybody: Passionate politics.* London, England: Pluto Press.

hooks, b. (2000b). *Feminist theory. From margin to center.* London, England: Pluto Press.

Irigaray, L., & Whitford, M. (1996). *The Irigaray reader.* Oxford, England: Blackwell.

Johnson, R. B. (2012). Dialectical pluralism and mixed research. *American Behavioral Scientist, 56,* 751–754.

Kennedy, N. (2012). Transgender children: More than a theoretical challenge, presented at POWS Annual Conference, Windsor, July 11–13.

Kincheloe, J. L., & McLaren, P. (2011). Rethinking critical theory and qualitative research. *Key Works in Critical Pedagogy, 32,* 285–326.

Knudsen, S. V. (2006). Intersectionality–A theoretical inspiration in the analysis of minority cultures and identities in textbooks. In E. Bruillard, B. Aamotsbakken, S. V. Knudsen, & M. Horsley (Eds.), *Caught in the Web or lost in the textbook?* (pp. 61–76). Contributions presented at the 8th IARTEM (International Association for Research on Textbooks and Educational Media) Conference, October 2005, Caen, France. Online: IARTEM, Stef, & Iufm. Retrieved from http://www.iartem.no/documents/caught_in_the_web.pdf#page=61

Kristeva, J. (1981). Women's time. *Signs: Journal of Women in Culture and Society, 7,* 13–35.

Lykke, N. (2005). Nya perspektiv på intersektionalitet. Problem og möjligheter" [New perspectives of intersectionality. Problems and possibilities]. *Kvinnovetenskaplig tidsskrift, 2–3,* 7–17.

Mama, A. (2012). Where we must stand: African women in an age of war. *AWID International Forum Transforming Economic Power to Advance Women's Rights and Justice.* Retrieved from http://www.opendemocracy.net/5050/amina-mama/where-we-must-stand-african-women-in-age-of-war

Marshall, H., Woollett, A., & Dosanjh, N. (1998). Researching marginalized standpoints: Some tensions around plural standpoints and diverse experiences. In K. Henwood, C. Griffin, & A. Phoenix (Eds.), *Standpoints and differences: Essays in the practice of feminist psychology* (pp. 115–134). London, England: Sage.

McCall, L. (2005). The complexity of intersectionality. *Signs: Journal of Women in Culture and Society, 3,* 1771–1800.

Mertens, D. M. (2009). *Transformative research and evaluation.* New York, NY: Guilford Press.

Mertens, D. M., Fraser, J., & Heimlich, J. E. (2008). M or F? Gender, identity and the transformative research paradigm. *Museums and Social Issues, 3*(1), 81–92.

Meyer, B. (2002). Extraordinary stories: Disability, queerness and feminism. *Nordic Journal of Feminist and Gender Research, 10,* 168–173.

Moghissi, H. (1999). *Feminism and Islamic fundamentalism: The limits of postmodern analysis.* London, England: Zed Books.

Moore, M. R. (2010). Articulating a politics of multiple identities: Sexuality and inclusion in black community life. *Du Bois Review: Social Science Research on Race, 7*(2), 1–20.

Moore, M. R. (2011). Two sides of the same coin: Revising analyses of lesbian sexuality and family formation through the study of black women. *Journal of Lesbian Studies, 15,* 58–68.

Moore, M. R. (2012). Intersectionality and the study of black, sexual minority women. *Gender & Society, 26,* 33–39.

Mørch, Y., & Staunæs, D. (2003). Introduction: Gender and ethnicity. *Nordic Journal of Feminist and Gender Research, 11,* 67–68.

Neumayer, E., & Plümper, T. (2007). The gendered nature of natural disasters: The impact of catastrophic events on the gender gap in life expectancy. *Annals of the Association of American Geographers, 97,* 551–566.

Parker, I. (1992). *Discourse dynamics: Critical analysis for social and individual psychology.* London, England: Routledge.

Parpart, J. L. (2010). Choosing silence: Rethinking voice, agency and women's empowerment (pp. 1–15); Kabeer, N., Voice, agency and the sounds of silence: A comment on Jane L. Parpart's paper (pp. 16–20); Parpart, J. L., Response to Kabeer (pp. 21–24). *Gendered perspectives on international development* (Working Paper 297). East Lansing: Michigan State University, Center for Gender in Global Context.

Potter, J., & Wetherell, M. (1987). *Discourse and social psychology: Beyond attitudes and behaviour.* London, England: Sage.

Ryan-Flood, R., & Gill, R. (2010). *Secrecy and silence in the research process: Feminist reflections.* London, England: Routledge.

Sheriff, M., & Weatherall, A. (2009). A feminist discourse analysis of popular-press accounts of postmaternity. *Feminism & Psychology, 19,* 89–108.

Somers, M. R. (1994). The narrative constitution of identity: A relational and network approach. *Theory & Society, 23,* 605–649.

Thomson, R. G. (1997). *Extraordinary bodies: Figuring physical disability in American culture and literature.* New York, NY: Columbia University Press.

United Nations. (1989). *Convention on the rights of the child.* Retrieved from http://treaties.un .org/doc/publication/UNTS/Volume%201577/v1577.pdf

Watts, J. H. (2009). "Allowed into a man's world." Meanings of work–life balance: Perspectives of women civil engineers as "minority" workers in construction. *Gender, Work & Organization, 16,* 37–57.

Wetherell, M., & Potter, J. (1992). *Mapping the language of racism: Discourse and the legitimation of exploitation.* Hemel Hempstead, England: Harvester Wheatsheaf.

CHAPTER 4

Ethics and Feminist Research

Linda Bell

Imagine this scenario. Knowing that you are a feminist researcher, male colleagues invite you to join them in a project investigating intimate partner violence. Male research participants in this study are all attending a therapy center in an attempt to reduce their violent behavior. One therapist offers a list of the men's phone numbers and asks you to use this list to make direct contact with their assumed female partners. (No consideration is given to same-sex partnerships.) [*Partner violence project, England*]

This is a true story; it happened to me. This situation raises many ethical issues. Here are three, which I immediately considered at the time:

- What would a female partner think about her privacy being invaded by some unknown, female researcher who has obtained her phone number from a male therapy center?

- Does her male partner know she is being contacted? What are his views, and is the situation likely to trigger further violence?

- How is the female researcher going to introduce herself and explain to the female partner what is going on? (For example: "Hello, I'm a researcher, I understand your partner is attending therapy because he is acting violently towards you. . . .")

When these issues were pointed out to male colleagues involved, it was clear they had not considered them at all. As a feminist researcher, I worked hard to grapple with all of these issues, to avoid breaking confidentiality with either the women or their partners and to ensure that potential research participants were able to consent freely to taking part in the research. This example also shows that ethical issues are embedded within feminist ways of doing research; they cannot be easily separated from issues of research methodology or epistemology. This is an important first point that will be demonstrated throughout the case examples presented in this chapter.

Why Has Ethics Become Important to Social Research?

Over the past few decades, ethics has become increasingly important to social research, including feminist research. The above example illustrates some reasons why this might be, especially when researchers are working together, yet they seem to be taking very different ethical perspectives (like my male colleagues and me). Ethics generally means moral principles or rules of conduct. But one must distinguish between *ethics* and *morality*. Beauchamp and Childress (2001) define ethics as "a generic term for various ways of understanding and examining the moral life" (p. 4), while morality is the identification and practice of what one *ought* to do. "Morality refers to social conventions about right and wrong human conduct that are so widely shared that they form a stable (though usually incomplete) communal consensus" (p. 5).

Clearly morality can therefore differ between societies, because what a person believes she ought to do can vary between whole societies, religions, or cultural groups. In terms of doing research, including doing feminist research, there are conventions or ethical principles that have been developed over many years to help do research in what is believed to be the right way. What is considered to be ethical research practice in particular circumstances will depend on what is considered to be good, moral conduct, whether this is founded on social, religious, or cultural grounds (see for example Paradis, 2000).

Attention to research ethics first began when the Nuremberg Code was established in 1948, following Nazi trials in Nuremberg after World War II. The Code states that voluntary consent by human subjects is essential and is a key principle in research. This Code was the first international document advocating voluntary participation and informed consent in research (see also Boulton & Parker, 2007). Since that time, many organizations concerned with research in different countries have now produced publications and guidelines about ethical conduct of research by individuals or research teams, with which feminist researchers must engage. See, for example, American Sociological Association (1999), *Code of Ethics*; and Economic and Social Research Council (ESRC, UK), *Framework for Research Ethics* (2010). Alongside this, research governance has become increasingly important over the past decade. The term *governance* refers to the government or management of research via committees or frameworks, whether nationally or locally. Such frameworks aim to uphold high standards of research conduct and can require all researchers within an institution (including students) to apply for ethics approval before they can carry out research projects.

Researchers, including feminists, have discussed or criticized implementation of these changing aspects of research ethics (e.g., Boulton & Parker, 2007; Dench, Iphofen, & Huws, 2004; Hammersley, 2009; Hedgecoe, 2008; Iphofen, 2009; Truman, 2003). Many authors have tried to develop ideas about how ethics should work in practice, especially to help researchers improve their social research practices in various ways (e.g., Mauthner, Birch, Jessop, & Miller, 2002; Miller, Birch, Mauthner, & Jessop, 2012). Hammersley (2009), in particular, states that much current focus on ethics, involving procedures, rules, and governance (instead of focusing on *research practice*) is unhelpful to all researchers. There has been controversy about these developments (see, e.g., Hammersley, 2009; Hedgecoe, 2008) because they have a considerable and increasing impact on social researchers, including student researchers doing projects, by regulating their need to obtain approval to carry out research projects or to obtain funding to do so (see also Halse & Honey, 2005; Munro, 2008).

Social research in some circumstances, and especially for feminist researchers, has almost become a battleground where researchers and those who control funding or policy agendas fight over how and why research should be done and how risk can best be avoided (for research participants, researchers, or other stakeholders in research). Miller and Boulton (2007) have identified this as a *fundamental shift* from a moral discourse for research ethics, which focuses on how individuals or teams can carry out research ethically, to a discourse of regulation for research ethics, where those who control research can exercise power over researchers by regulating their practice through committees and formal requirements to obtain ethics approval.

Well-developed ethics approval systems are now based around Institutional Review Boards (IRBs, in the United States). Federal laws (e.g., the National Research Act, Pub. L. No. 99-158) aim to protect the rights and privacy of people involved in research. There are rules about how these IRBs operate, and most institutions such as universities will have local instructions for students and staff who need to apply for ethics approval to do a project. For example, while all federally funded research must be approved by an IRB, increasingly many universities or other institutions also require students to engage with these IRB processes when doing research projects.

In the United Kingdom (UK), the Research Governance Framework for Health and Social Care links to a network of Research Ethics Committees operating in various institutions, including Health Trusts and universities. This Framework aims to set standards, improve research quality, and safeguard the public (UK Department of Health, 2005).

Both the United States and the United Kingdom systems resulted partly from health research scandals, which had detrimental effects on patients and research participants. Governmental or federal agencies therefore tried to devise ways to prevent such risks and to clarify the terms of individual research participation. Within these governance systems, researchers (including students) are expected to make a formal, detailed application to carry out a specified research project. This includes providing documentation such as information sheets for research participants, consent forms, and often a full research proposal or protocol.

While some of the specific protocols for applying for ethical approval of your project may differ depending on your unique university and country context, there are some basic steps you might consider when thinking of gaining ethical approval from your university for your research project.

Steps to Obtain Ethics Approval for Research Projects at the University Level

Step 1. The first and most important step is to prepare a full proposal (protocol) demonstrating what you intend to do in your research project. Show awareness of issues such as

- Considering the privacy and dignity of potential respondents, for example, by approaching them respectfully with your request for their participation;
- Ensuring that participants give consent (usually written), for example, to be interviewed;
- Maintaining confidentiality, for example, about what is said in interviews; and
- Storing or disseminating research findings or information about participants in ways that are legally required, for example, according to the Data Protection Act (1998) in the United Kingdom.

Step 2. You should always contact your supervisor or adviser before making an IRB or ethics committee application.

Step 3. You should check what your institution requires for IRB or Ethics Committee submission. Requirements will usually include

- Completing an application form and attaching your research proposal;
- Deciding (with supervisor's help) whether your application needs to go for a full or partial review, and whether you will also need to apply for external review (outside your institution), for example, to the national IRAS (Integrated Research Application System) in the United Kingdom. More detailed review may be needed if you are intending to carry out research that carries more risks, for example, if you intend to interview children or vulnerable adults (see, e.g., Walliman, 2005, pp. 334–369);

- Submitting the form on time (depending upon when the Board/Committee meets) and to an appropriate IRB or Ethics Committee representative; and

- Responding to any requirements that the IRB or Ethics Committee has made after reviewing your application.

Background on Feminist Ethics and Ethics for Research

This chapter will center on a discussion of how feminist researchers and theorists have grappled with challenges of linking issues of ethics, morality, politics, and research; and it will set these challenges within the wider context of increasing concerns that all forms of research may now be seen as a risky activity, which needs to be controlled. Some feminist authors (e.g., Miller & Boulton, 2007) suggest that there has recently been a fundamental shift from seeing ethics mainly as moral discourse (based largely on ideas about what researchers *ought to* do, and on their own values and integrity) to a discourse of regulation (where those with power over researchers' activities also seek to control and judge what they do in advance).

There are many aspects of research ethics of interest to feminists. For instance, what does informed consent to participation in research actually mean? In the example with which we started this chapter, the feminist researcher was in fact being asked to compromise ethical principles, particularly about confidentiality and informed consent, in order to make quicker progress with research interviews.

Edwards and Mauthner (2012) suggest the focus on ethics in research is "rooted in a genuine and legitimate concern with issues of power" that researchers themselves share (p.17). (See also Mauthner & Bell, 2007.) More widely, however, there are increasing concerns about risk and litigation internationally (see, e.g., Adam, Beck, & Loon, 2000), including instrumental and procedural issues involved in controlling research. This is what Miller and Boulton (2007) mean when they talk about a shift to a "discourse of [research] regulation" (p. 2202). In other words, researchers and those who control their activities are becoming much more focused on regulating research and are perhaps in danger of being less concerned about dealing with issues like power, which underpin feminist research agendas.

Feminist researchers are involved in these crucial debates about what ethics can or should currently mean in practice to social research (see, e.g., Halse & Honey, 2005; Mauthner et al., 2002; Miller & Boulton, 2007; Miller et al., 2012). These debates include a focus on gender in areas of participation in health research (Ballantyne, Bennett, Karpin, & Rogers, 2008). Health researchers have attempted to provide guidelines that sometimes deal with power relationships between researchers and those with whom they research; these take account of feminist research practice, though sometimes in a limited way (see, e.g., Karnieli-Miller, Strier, & Pessach, 2009).

What Is Feminist Ethics Practice?

We will take up some critical dimensions of ethics practice that are of particular concern to feminist researchers.

FEMINIST CRITIQUES OF VALUE-FREE WAYS OF DOING RESEARCH: PRINCIPLES AND DILEMMAS

Feminists have for many years challenged notions of value-free ways of doing research. They have already been concerned with issues of power relations, confidentiality, and antioppressive practices, which all involve consideration of ethics and personal values in research; all of these issues were raised by our initial example relating to partner violence research. Positivist approaches to research, on the other hand, tend to be concerned with universal notions about truth and science. A long-standing, broadly feminist critique of positivism might be summed up as the rejection of

- the idea that hard science is the best model for social research;
- the idea that social research's primary goal should entail seeking universal laws involving relationships between fixed variables; and
- a belief in objectivity separate from politics, power, social relationships, ethics, and values.

One of the goals of feminist research is to reveal the subjugated voices of women with an emphasis on tending to the range of differences among those they study with regard to race, class, and sexual orientation (see Gillies & Alldred, 2012). The practice of feminist research is designed to include greater emphasis on inclusivity (and thereby increase ethical forms of research practice), often by innovating or adapting existing methods such as ethnography (Lather, 2001; Stacey, 1988) or research based on interviewing (Mauthner & Doucet, 1998) or diaries (Bell, 1998, reprinted in 2012). However, a quantitative theoretical lens does not need to be antithetical to feminist research practice. In fact, Oakley (1999) suggests how a positivist approach can also serve feminist research ends:

Women and other minority groups, above all, need quantitative research, because without this it is difficult to distinguish between personal experience and collective oppression. Only large-scale comparative data can determine to what extent the situations of men and women are structurally differentiated. (p. 251)

In addition, a feminist perspective on research has much to offer those who engage in quantitatively driven research (see also Crocker, 2010). Demographer Williams (2010), proposes that feminist approaches to research have much to offer scientific disciplines precisely because they allow scientific researchers to address questions of ethics, especially when considering issues relating to power, politics, and globalization: "[F]eminist-demographers must realize that the demographic conceptualization of women's empow-erment in developing countries generally measures women's power against an unstated Western model of the empowered women" (p. 206). Williams therefore suggests that if we are to avoid holding Western women as an implicit norm for all women, research design must emphasize the significance of contextual and culturally specific knowledge.

The feminist research lens can address many ethical conundrums within issues of power and authority presented by the process of obtaining informed consent for research participation. Boulton and Parker (2007) identify several key themes that demonstrate how social research differs from research in biomedicine, which suggests the ethics issues are also likely to be different. Given the range of different forms of gath-ering data (especially in open-ended forms of qualitative research), obtaining informed consent only at the start of a project may not be possible or desirable (for an example in ethnography, see also Murphy & Dingwall, 2007, p. 2224). Boulton and Parker also sug-gest that relationships in social research should be potentially negotiable and equal, allowing and encouraging participants to challenge researchers to continually reflect on their activities. They also note that social scientists as well as many working in bioethics now challenge "the dominance of the rights-and-justice-based model of ethics under-pinning the concept of informed consent in biomedical research" (Boulton & Parker, 2007, p. 2191; see also Ballantyne et al., 2008).

Mixed methods are advocated by a number of feminist researchers (e.g., Brannen, 1992; Hesse-Biber, 2010; Mason, 2006) as a way of addressing the need for flexibility, which can more easily incorporate attention to ethical practices. This also reflects recent growth in interdisciplinary research in areas of women's studies (Evans, 2011; see also Boulton, Haynes, Smyth, & Fielder, 2006). In relation to ethics in this context, Dench and colleagues (2004) have brought together (as part of the RESPECT project) ethics guidelines that amalgamate various national and professional codes, to develop common European standards and benchmarks for socioeconomic research.

Whatever research methods are chosen, feminists are already promoting research practices that *cannot* be considered value-free, but that take account of, reflect on, and uphold human values (Letherby, 2002, 2003). For example, many researchers might agree with Iphofen (2009) when he says that in general terms: "Ethical practice in social research is about being a 'good' researcher at the same time as being a 'good' human being" (p. 3). But, of course, it depends what one means by "good." Edwards and Mauthner (2012) have identified four approaches to thinking about research ethics. They relate these ethics models to feminist research as follows:

1. A deontological ethics model, which can potentially apply to all circumstances (is universalist) and is based on *intended* principles such as honesty, justice, rights, and respect. In other words, this model suggests that the best way to act ethically is always to follow an intended principle, like justice. However, a danger for feminist researchers if they follow this kind of approach is the potential of following absolute principles of right action, *regardless of any possible consequences*. It might be difficult to reach a consensus to determine exactly "What does justice mean?" Using a research example could lead to ignoring the need to obtain consent from participants whose behavior one might want to analyze: A researcher might observe the participants covertly on the grounds that the principle of justice requires obtaining a wide and varied sample of respondents.

2. A utilitarian or consequentialist ethics model, which is also universalist, on the other hand, "prioritizes the 'goodness' of *outcomes* [emphasis added] of research such as increased knowledge . . . . [T]he rightness or wrongness of actions are judged by their *consequences* [emphasis added] rather than their intent" (Edwards & Mauthner, 2012, p. 19). In following this kind of approach focused on *consequences*, feminist researchers could risk taking action that might not be considered ethical, so long as the ends justify the means and the consequences seem to be right. An example is, using individual medical records for research without consent because the *consequences* of a study would benefit the whole community and data would be limited if restricted to participants who agreed to take part.

3. Virtue ethics, unlike the two previous models, is not supposed to apply in all circumstances; it focuses instead on the attributes of the researcher. This model "stresses a contextual or situational ethical position, with an emphasis on researchers' moral values and ethical skills in reflexively negotiating ethical dilemmas" (Edwards & Mauthner, 2012, p. 19). This kind of approach may appeal to feminist researchers because it would allow them to focus on their own moral or value base; but this may also raise issues where they are working with others who do not share their same values.

4. A feminist ethics of care is a model that emphasizes responsibility and caring relationships rather than more abstract ideas about rights, justice, virtues, or outcomes. According to Edwards and Mauthner (2012), taking this approach would allow feminist

researchers to consider various issues more specifically during research practice, such as: "who are the people involved in and affected by the ethical dilemma raised in the research? what is the context for the ethical dilemma in terms of the specific topic of the research and the issues it raises . . . ? and what is the balance of personal and social power between those involved [in the research]?" (Edwards & Mauthner, 2012, p. 26).

Some feminist researchers have explicitly adopted this kind of approach to connect their own forms of practice with the subject focus of their study (see, e.g., May, 2008; Ribbens McCarthy, Edwards, & Gillies, 2000; Rogers & Weller, 2013).

Developments in Feminist Ethics

Feminist ethics has become a distinct area within philosophy in recent years (Tong & Williams, 2009), as noted by Brennan (1999; see also Hoagland, 1988; Jaggar, 1991, 1992, 1994; Koehn, 1998; Porter, 1999). Brennan also suggests there has been a "blurring of boundaries between feminist ethics and the rest of ethics" (p. 858). Other related literature has highlighted the development of feminist ways of thinking about knowledge production (epistemologies), including links to research practice and ethics (e.g., Doucet & Mauthner, 2012; Harding, 1998; Lennon & Whitford, 1994; Morley, 1999; Tanesini, 1999).

In terms of feminist research practice, while one should take account of issues raised specifically by feminist ethicists, feminist researchers need to address and reflect upon ethical concerns commonly found during direct research practice or the formal management of research (governance). These can include dealing in practice with confidentiality, ownership of research, and responsibilities toward and between research participants and coresearchers (i.e., consent to participate in research projects). As we have seen, feminist researchers also have to meet institutional requirements to obtain approval for their projects—often by demonstrating, through a formal application to an ethics committee, that they have addressed any potential ethical issues relevant to their project. However, this may involve grappling with situations where feminist researchers and ethics committees see a particular situation very differently. For example, being able to access research participants who are considered vulnerable may be very difficult if the researchers are trying to follow one set of (feminist) ethical principles while the ethics committee does not acknowledge the relevance of those principles to the research situation (see Halse & Honey, 2005).

Such issues become more complex where researchers are also professional practitioners working in a specific occupation such as nursing or social work; these researchers can often have divided loyalties toward their profession, their research, and their research participants, as noted elsewhere (Bell & Nutt, 2012). In this example, Bell and Nutt write about how they both had to address ethics issues in relation to social work. Bell had to assist professional colleagues to produce an appropriate set of research ethics guidelines for social work students, while Nutt was faced with a professional dilemma relating to potential risk to children while undertaking doctoral research. Complicated negotiations were required to reconcile divided loyalties between being a professional social worker and a researcher. This reflects a broader concern with potential ethical dilemmas and power issues, as noted earlier (Edwards & Mauthner, 2012, p. 26), and links to ideas about virtue ethics (the morally good researcher) to the ethics of care.

Feminists who were writing in the early 1980s first developed a concept of a feminist ethics of care (e.g., Gilligan and Noddings). This was followed by another loose wave of writers from the 1990s onwards, such as Tronto and Sevenhuijsen. (For a recent discussion of these developments, see Philip, Rogers, & Weller, 2013.) It was developmental psychologist Carol Gilligan (1983, 1995) who suggested there could be gender differences in moral reasoning. Her work has influenced other feminists writing more recently about the ethics of care, such as Held (2006), as well as those concerned with more practical aspects of research methodology like data analysis (see Mauthner & Doucet, 1998, on using Gilligan's Voice-centered relational method). Noddings (2003), whose work has also been influential in the field of education, provided a more "phenomenological account of what is involved in the activities of care" (according to Held, 2006, p. 28). Noddings discusses responding to others in encounters that seem to reflect a notion of caring that is particularly rooted in women's experiences. Although sometimes criticized for highlighting women's natural caring abilities, Noddings usefully identifies a distinction between "caring for and caring about" others, which is another essential component of current thinking in feminist ethics.

Tronto's earlier work (1993; Fisher & Tronto, 1990) further contributed to this broad field of feminist ethics of care by identifying how the distribution of caring work in society reflects power relations. For example, those with more power are often able to prevail upon others to do their caring work for them. For Sevenhuijsen (1998, 2000, 2002), power relations and politics dovetail with issues about caring and feminist ethics. Women's emancipation has been linked to the idea of freeing them from caring responsibilities, but Sevenhuijsen (1998) argues that care is and should be important to everyone. While embodying insights from feminist ethics and implying a redistribution of paid work and caring between women and men, Sevenhuijsen looks for ways to characterize the concept of care politically, within democratic citizenship. She suggests that we should see justice as a process that involves an ethics of care, and not merely a set of rules. So we return to the idea that care is based on collective and relationship-based activities (see also Robinson, 2011; Scheyvens & Leslie, 2000; Zembylas, 2010).

Writing recently about feminist ethics, Walker (2007) for example proposes that we should "locate morality in *practices of responsibility* that implement commonly shared understandings about who gets to do what to whom and who is supposed to do what for whom" (p.16). Walker suggests that feminist ethical principles should be grounded in actual situations (empirically grounded) and that this has implications for the ways individuals construct their identities, relationships, and values. Responsible ethical theory ought to allow us to both question and reveal the moral significance of these kinds of social differences.

Feminists such as Walker have engaged with, but also criticized, more universalist forms of ethics principles that we noted earlier, such as consequentialist theory (the second ethics model by Edwards & Mauthner, 2012). Such ethics theories are based mainly on abstract ideas about logic or argument that do not connect directly with specific social situations and are focused on the abstract idea of goodness, whether in relation to the self or other people. These forms of ethics theorizing have also not, it can be argued, sufficiently considered gendered power imbalances and oppressions. The feminist ethicist Hoagland (1988), while promoting and developing a separate lesbian ethics, suggests that the key moral question for lesbians is whether something contributes to their self-creation, freedom, and liberation, rather than asking in a more abstract way, "Is this good?" or "Am I good?"

A research illustration based on Hoagland's approach is Chalmer's interview-based work (2002) with Japanese lesbians. Here we read that if these women have children, they need to socialize with each other, in order to challenge the more rigid aspects of Japanese society based around the family. They must "self create spaces for 'belonging'" (p.104). However, at the same time, they are "more than aware of how the moral precepts that define the idealized 'Japanese family' and 'motherhood' might affect their children" (p. 116). So this would represent a dilemma between the need to be good in social terms and principles based more closely on Hoagland's (separatist) lesbian ethics.

Despite these developments in more distinctively feminist forms of ethics theorizing, a recent view by Driver (2005) suggests that an ethics model focusing on consequences (consequentialism), as we discussed earlier, does still offer some positive benefits to feminists. Although this approach has been criticized for focusing on impartial norms instead of actual, caring relationships, Driver suggests that feminists can still be consequentialists while at the same time they can "be responsive to concerns laid out in feminist scholarship relating to partiality and the demands of morality. Universal benevolence does not lead inevitably to disavowal of the ties of friends and family or to rejection of special obligations" (p. 197). Driver therefore suggests most people can acknowledge the benefits to others as well as to themselves of taking a special interest or focus on their own children or their friends; this does not have to mean they would not also care about others in a wider sense. Feminist researchers may even turn situations in which the consequences of caring for friends can involve including them as potential research participants (Browne, 2005).

Extending the notion of ethics of care, Porter (1999) suggests that while care may seem irrelevant to politics (which seems to be about power and wider human relationships across society), a politics of compassion is possible; she uses attitudes toward asylum seeking as an example. She argues that a compassionate approach involves active listening to those who are suffering. Some researchers have challenged the whole idea of a feminist ethics of care. In one research example, Hughes, McKie, Hopkins, and Watson (2005) propose there could be a more mutually beneficial relationship, for example, between carer and cared for in situations where people with disabilities would reject the "dis-abling" connotations of the concept of care.

What characterizes an overall feminist approach to ethics seems to involve paying more attention to context, relationships, and power issues. This is often more important than seeking absolute, universal norms presented in some ethical theories, such as a deontological or rights-based approach. This has important implications for feminist researchers seeking to apply such principles in their practice. Some researchers have sought to develop a separatist or feminist standpoint model based, for example, on the notion of lesbian ethics (Hoagland, 1988). Some other feminist researchers have specifically followed an ethics of care model, while others have adapted this or tried to reinstate other more universalist ethics models such as consequentialism so as to make them acceptable to feminist researchers.

These central ethical dilemmas and how feminist researchers engage with them in their own research practice is presented as a series of ethical dilemmas. Contained within each dilemma are in-depth case studies that illustrate how feminist researchers reflect on ethics principles and the research strategies they employ in the service of ethical praxis.

HOW HAVE FEMINIST RESEARCHERS ENGAGED WITH ETHICS PRINCIPLES AND ETHICAL DILEMMAS IN THEIR RESEARCH PRACTICE?

During the past decade, feminists have continued to engage in many fields of social sciences, health, and humanities research. Women's Studies, with its key focus on gender, continues to thrive in the United States and globally (Evans, 2011). Some areas of continuing feminist research interest, particularly where researchers connect their work to questions of ethics, include the relevance of gender to studies of globalization, development, and international relations (Ackerly & Attanasi, 2009; Ackerly & True, 2008; Desai, 2007; Jouili, 2011); studies of embodiment, sexualities, or disability (Halse & Honey, 2005; Pedwell, 2007; Rice, 2009; Scully, 2010); as well as continuing focus on an ethics of care in various settings (Datta et al., 2010). Interdisciplinary feminist research has become more important. It has linked social to health or biomedical research, raising epistemological and methodological as well as ethical issues (e.g., Bailey, 2011; Ballantyne et al., 2008; Boulton et al., 2006; Boulton & Parker, 2007; Shildrick, 2004). Evans (2011) notes that "feminist scholarship is increasingly organized in terms of cross-disciplinary 'themes' rather than in the discussion of more precise 'disciplinary concepts'" (p. 609).

In engaging with such dilemmas, feminist researchers have not always found it easy or straightforward to carry out research or to disseminate research findings in ways that meet feminist ideals. It is clear that the rise of risk and governance agendas places new constraints on feminists, as on other researchers, both inside and outside academia (see Gillies & Lucey, 2007). Halse and Honey (2005) had to engage not only with the challenge of obtaining a suitable sample that did not restrict their feminist ideals, but also with the challenge of an ethics committee whose officers could not see the relevance of their arguments. Yet this ethics committee had the power to permit or deny approval for the research to take place. However, it can also be argued that these governance agendas requiring formal ethics approval also provide researchers with opportunities and encouragement to act in caring ways toward research participants, fellow researchers, or colleagues—enabling researchers to adopt critical *reflexivity* in their research practice (see also Hedgecoe, 2008).

Ethics codes, standards, and other agendas have changed the ethics landscape for feminist researchers: Miller and Boulton (2007) identified this as a fundamental shift for research ethics from a moral discourse to discourse of regulation. In the future, alongside methodological integrity being an integral part of doing ethical research, feminist researchers will be expected to reflect on and apply appropriate, formalized aspects of research ethics, such as obtaining informed consent from participants (see Boulton & Parker, 2007; Miller & Boulton, 2007).

Key aspects of ethical practice feminist researchers focus on are: (1) Do no harm (beneficence); (2) confidentiality, privacy, and anonymity; (3) informed consent; (4) disclosure and potential for deception (e.g., relating to overt or covert research practices); (5) power between researcher and subject; (6) representation or ownership of research findings; (7) ensuring respect for human dignity, self-determination, and justice, including safeguards to protect the rights of vulnerable subjects; (8) demonstrating that the researcher has engaged with the above six issues, in order to obtain required formal ethics approval and/or show adherence to professional codes/guidelines.

These eight key ethics points are intended to be "signpost issues" during discussion of research examples given in the rest of this chapter. This list is intended particularly for first-time researchers or students wanting to identify some areas of research process where ethical issues may arise during their own research projects. (For a more detailed checklist intended for those formally preparing research project proposals and protocols, see also Iphofen, 2009).

The following section takes us to the praxis of ethics as they unfold in empirical research projects. We take the range of specific ethical dilemmas that can arise in a research project and demonstrate how feminist researchers engage with ethics across the research process. We take you "behind the scenes" by revealing researchers' own discussions of the ethical dilemmas they have personally faced and provide examples of ethical dilemmas at different stages in the research process.

The Application of Feminist Ethics Across the Research Process

PLANNING RESEARCH AND ACCESSING PARTICIPANTS IN AN ETHICAL MANNER

When feminist researchers describe how they have planned their research, especially when they access potential research participants, they may be particularly concerned with trying to minimize power differences between themselves and the potential participants. For most feminist researchers, this is important because they are specifically concerned with challenging power issues that would privilege the place of the researcher over any participants. This may be even more difficult when recruiting vulnerable participants.

For various reasons, researchers sometimes want to begin by using their own social network contacts in studies relying on volunteers. Student researchers, for example, may want to start with a project that seeks to recruit volunteers where their fellow students could participate. This approach may also be used to avoid any problems about obtaining ethics approval to access other kinds of participants, although ethics committees may not always be sympathetic to this view. While this approach may allow researchers to get started quickly, it can also lead to further ethical issues.

Would students feel coerced if approached by a fellow student? Are they free to refuse to participate in a fellow student's project? Do tutors or teachers have any influence (or perhaps even undue influence) over this situation? Nevertheless, students should surely draw from their teachers' research experiences, and most teachers will understand the issues likely to arise and be willing to support all their students with their project work in resolving these kinds of problems.

More generally, as a feminist researcher, is the use of existing contacts for research purposes acceptable? Are these people too close to you, even if you intend to snowball to other contacts later on? Could this approach backfire by allowing research participants to block access to others?

CONFRONTING ETHICAL DILEMMAS INVOLVED IN USING PERSONAL CONTACTS IN RESEARCH

In a reflexive account of her study of nonheterosexual women, Browne (2005) discusses how she accessed many of her research participants because they were her friends. She used a form of snowball sampling to recruit her participants, a technique that depended very clearly on these interpersonal relations. This also meant she recruited women who already knew each other, but not necessarily her. She explains the methodological as well as ethical advantages to this approach. For example, it allowed participants to trust her, and she found some were more willing to make disclosures.

> As I was considered a friend, "Andie" did not distinguish the focus group from other interactions we may have had such as sitting in the pub having a conversation. As a result, she said things she might not otherwise have said had the group been conducted by and consisted of strangers. (p. 55)

There were other advantages to the researcher being "embedded in the social networks" from which Browne (2005) was recruiting research participants. "Being rooted in social networks was significant because participants were able to 'check out' the research and me both as a researcher and a person" (p. 50). Browne also feels that by using personal contacts, she was able to reach women whose voices might not have been heard in this context, such as those who did not openly identify as lesbian. However, Browne also acknowledges that her sample was "inevitably limited" (particularly in terms of age, but also by ethnicity) due to her focus on her own social contacts (who were mainly young, white women). Some potential local participants who were not part of this group would therefore have been excluded. Some friends or contacts actively excluded themselves from the study:

> [O]ne woman excluded herself because, although she was a friend of another participant, she said she did not know me. She told her friend, who participated in the study, that she did not wish to discuss her private life in front of me. Another couple did not want to be involved because, as friends, they did not want to reveal "too much" to me. In this way they created a boundary between our friendship and the research relationship. (p. 53)

ETHICAL ISSUES AND RESEARCH STRATEGIES TO OVERCOME THEM WHEN WORKING WITH VULNERABLE POPULATIONS

It is likely that where potential research participants are designated as somehow vulnerable, ethics committees may have concerns about researchers accessing these people. However, there may also be some unexpected ethical issues to confront in these circumstances, linking for example to other feminist concerns about knowledge production. This can reveal important divides between feminist ways of researching in a caring way and other more traditional ethical or methodological concerns, as illustrated in the next dilemma.

ACCESSING VULNERABLE PARTICIPANTS AND ABIDING BY ETHICS COMMITTEE REQUIREMENTS

Halse and Honey (2005) described their experiences when applying for ethics approval to do research in Australia with women involved in self-starvation. This involved a clash of perspectives between these feminist researchers and research officers representing the ethics committee to which they applied for ethics approval. Halse and Honey start by explaining that "[d]efining the research population is an act of category construction with profound intellectual and moral implications" (p. 2145). How should they describe anorexia nervosa in their ethics application and in the information letter to participants? As a physical or psychological condition, or an illness, or "should it be presented as a label or rhetorical device that positions young women as abnormal, deviant, and in need of treatment when they defy socially constructed notions of normal, healthy eating behaviors?" (p. 2145). The researchers were keen to maintain a principle of respect for their study participants, so they were concerned about how to name those who participated.

> To brand a girl anorexic without consent was to deny her selfhood—one of the very issues the study aimed to address. To include only those girls who acknowledged their diagnosis would affect the research by failing to capture the complex spectrum of "anorexic" experiences. (p. 2146)

The researchers therefore consulted ethics officers in their institution, whose task was to help researchers sort out any problems before they made a formal application for review by the ethics committee. Although the officers were sympathetic, their view was that the researchers needed to find an overarching definition, saying "If you can't label the population, then the research isn't possible" (Halse & Honey, 2005, p. 2146). To proceed with the research, Halse and Honey felt there were two options: either to privilege the girls' own definitions, or to limit the study only to those girls who had been diagnosed as anorexic (p. 2146). While the first option would have excluded some participants the researchers wanted to include (or potentially cause harm where girls might have had a different, undiagnosed medical condition), the second option could not guarantee the definitive, homogenous population that ethics policy and our ethics officers invoked us to find. Both options censored the particularity of some girls' experiences, and both required us to abandon our sensibility and moral responsibility to some potential participants. (p. 2147)

A potential compromise using multiple descriptions to address the particularity/diversity of potential participants was unacceptable to the ethics officers, who said: "That would mean they're different populations. So you'll need separate ethics applications and approvals for each group" (Halse & Honey, 2005, p. 2147). The researchers therefore decided to use as a compromise the broadest, most inclusive category available: "girls who have received a medical diagnosis of anorexia nervosa" (p. 2147). This definition satisfied the ethics committee and allowed the project to take place, but it left the researchers feeling uncomfortable about the potentially dishonest way (intellectually and morally) in which they had felt obliged to define their sample. "Our positioning as actively complicit in perpetuating this story undermined our ethical and moral responsibility to our participants and had troubling moral implications for our desired identities as ethical, feminist researchers" (pp. 2147–2148).

This research example raises important wider issues for feminist researchers: Whose interests do ethics standards and systems of governance, like committees, represent? How should feminist researchers tackle these concerns, and does this have to be simply on a case-by-case basis (as in the example above)?

Ethical Issues and Research Strategies in Dealing With Gatekeepers

For many feminist researchers, finding a way in to access research participants may involve the use of gatekeepers, who control access to potential participants, for example, as an employer or manager granting access to employees; or a health or social care professional in relation to their clients/service users. This frequently raises ethical issues affecting all sides. It is important when gatekeepers are involved that consent is obtained *directly* from research participants themselves, and that they are reassured they are not being coerced into entering or staying in the study. Careful preparation and direct negotiation with participants (following initial permission from a manager or other authority figure) may take longer, but it is a more satisfactory (and more ethical) way of gaining access.

ACCESSING WOMEN PARTICIPANTS VIA MALE GATEKEEPERS

There may be particular ethical issues for feminist researchers who are dealing with men acting as gatekeepers to women who are potential participants. In Bell's

(Miller & Bell, 2012) research involving a center that offered therapy to men who acted violently toward their female partners, there were potentially two layers of male gatekeepers: "The therapists and male researchers had designed a project into which the women were then 'fitted' and for whom they acted as gate-keepers. A second layer of 'gate-keeping' involved the violent men themselves" (Miller & Bell, 2012, p. 65).

Bell refused the offer of a list of men's phone numbers, even though the consequence of this action was to restrict potential access to female participants, partly because she felt that this would compromise the women's right to refuse to take part in the research. As already noted at the beginning of this chapter, there were other, equally serious ethical dilemmas involved in simply accepting the list of phone numbers.

The solution to this situation involved the researcher distancing herself as far as possible from the men's center, in order to recruit women independently through her university. This approach was also intended to assist in maintaining confidentiality for any women who participated in the research. Because of these attempts to maintain confidentiality, only a few women were recruited to the project. The male therapists again criticized Bell for the reduced sample of participants. However, the project eventually produced valuable lessons for the research team, especially about ethical and practical considerations they and the therapists needed to show toward female partners; these were acted upon successfully in conjunction with a women's support center (see also Miller & Bell, 2012).

USING FORMAL AND INFORMAL GATEKEEPERS TO AVOID ETHICAL PROBLEMS IN ACCESSING MARGINALIZED PARTICIPANTS

Bhopal (2010) describes accessing research participants from a Gypsy (traveller) community site, using gatekeepers. She reports that her own (female) gender and ethnicity were crucial to developing rapport with her respondents. As we might expect, working with marginalized communities involves developing a high degree of trust, so Bhopal initially needed to use both formal (Traveller Education Service [TES]) and informal gatekeepers to access her research participants. Bhopal describes how she began with the formal approach via TES because they were trusted by the traveller families and also because TES had an emancipatory agenda.

The TES agreed to negotiate access to the Gypsy families. One reason for this may have been the recognition that the research was funded and supported by the local education authority (Ethnic Minority Achievement Service) and would be instrumental in improving the educational experiences of Gypsy children and their families. I was accompanied by the TES to the site to meet with the families and was introduced to the families by the TES. (Bhopal, 2010, p. 189)

A second, equally important informal gatekeeping stage involved developing trust within the community through using the right channels and contacts. Bhopal was also made aware that it was not considered respectable for Gypsy women to be alone with a male interviewer. Ethically, she as the female researcher would need to carry out interviews herself. She reports community members also carefully checked her out during her visits to the site.

> I was introduced first to Mrs. Smith who was the matriarch of the community. It was evident that I had to be accepted first by her, and seen as "legitimate" in my role as researcher before I was given access to other families on the site. . . . Mrs. Smith was quite happy that I wanted to speak to members of the community and indicated that if there was anyone I needed to speak to, she would happily put in a "good word" for me. (p. 190)

Bhopal indicates that in complex research situations such as this, in addition to gaining the trust of community participants, it is very important for the researcher(s) to keep formal organizations/representatives (such as the TES in this case) in agreement, because they often have powerful sanctions they could use either to permit or stop the research altogether.

ETHICAL ISSUES INVOLVED IN GAINING INFORMED CONSENT FROM PARTICIPANTS AND DEVELOPING STRATEGIES TO ADDRESS THEM

Despite its long history in biomedical research, feminist researchers have become increasingly skeptical about the possibility of working with notions of prior, informed consent in practice (Boulton et al., 2006; Halse & Honey, 2005). Boulton and colleagues (2006) caution that in some ways, consent may even have become distracting and over-emphasized as an ethical issue. Informed consent first implies that potential participants need to be given sufficient information about the project and what will be required of them *in advance*; but this participant information may not necessarily tell the full story, either by accident or design.

Getting written, informed consent from participants may be difficult. When researchers are working with marginalized populations, or if people are concerned with activities that are illegal or dangerous, they may not wish to sign a consent document formally. Many feminist researchers (e.g., Bhopal) build on initial, formal ethics requirements by developing rapport with their participants *during the research project* in order to develop and ensure their participants' continuing consent. This approach is not without difficulties (see Duncombe & Jessop, 2012) yet is probably a useful way to proceed (see Mayes, Lle-wellyn, & McConnell, 2011; Miller & Bell, 2012).

Some researchers might argue that the "ends (of the research) justify the means"; in doing so, they could be focusing on *consequentialist* ethics principles. They could argue that some topics would become impossible to research without forgetting about consent altogether and using completely covert research methods. There are clearly ethical dilemmas here, due to the possibility in this approach for deceiving partici-pants. Despite these kinds of arguments, obtaining consent of some kind from partic-ipants seems to remain a key tenet of ethical research practice for most feminist researchers.

Ethical Issues That Arise During the Process of Data Collection and Strategies for Maintaining Ethical Awareness

Once feminist researchers are in a position to collect data from participants, many other ethical issues arise. In qualitative research, these issues may arise principally from tensions within interpersonal relationships between researchers and research partici-pants. There are many examples where researchers reflect on these issues, for example in trying to develop rapport (see, e.g., Duncombe & Jessop, 2012; Lather, 2001; Luff, 1999; Ribbens & Edwards, 1998; Ward, 2008). Sometimes these issues dovetail with wider moral concerns that are part of the research itself (Ribbens McCarthy, Edwards, & Gillies, 2000).

Emotions loom large in discussions about direct contacts with research participants, as Holland (2007) has pointed out, although the ethical implications may not always be directly addressed. Through what Holland terms "the ethics of empathy," we see not only that feminist researchers have the opportunity to develop rapport with their participants (especially where these are other women) but also that this is a potentially exploitative relationship fraught with ethical dilemmas. If interviewing encourages friendship, it can also allow researchers to exploit that connection in order to gain data.

ETHICAL DILEMMAS INVOLVED IN FEMINIST RESEARCH WITH ANTIFEMINIST WOMEN

In her study of women employed by politically right-wing moral lobby organizations, Luff (1999) describes ethical difficulties involved in researching with women whose ideas were opposed to her own in many respects. Although she acknowledges moments of rapport she experienced with these research participants and says they sometimes led to her rethinking some aspects of her research, she also struggled with the idea that "in practice, in my research the whole idea of *deceit* became quite intense and complex" (p. 698). Luff suggests, for example, that while the researcher's power with respect to participants can come from their overall responsibility for reflection and analysis of research findings, "feminist strategies to disrupt this power imbalance may be more complicated when working with relatively powerful women who are also actively hostile to many aspects of one's own standpoint" (p. 699).

Nevertheless Luff was aware that some views women expressed, especially about feminism, could leave them in vulnerable positions within their own organizations; and this left her with a personal dilemma.

> I had no desire, as a feminist, to encourage women to remain, unchallenged, in such organizations but, on the other hand, as a researcher, I had ethical commitments to them as participants in the research. In the end this latter concern won out, though I was left with a sense of unease, not least about the potential identity conflicts and contradictions of being a "feminist researcher." (Luff, 1999, pp. 699–700)

For Luff, we can see that taking a position during her research related to virtue ethics, which involved her own integrity. Taking a position, therefore, placed her in a difficult situation, while simultaneously allowing her to argue for the significance of her own values and ethical commitments to the research.

Ethical Issues of Representing the Views or Voices of Participants and How to Be Reflective on Issues of Power and Control Over Whose Voices Are Heard in the Research Project

Many feminist researchers have discussed the ethical issues of representing participants' views through data analysis and presentation of research findings (Alldred & Gillies, 2012; hooks, 1989; Rice, 2009; Robinson, 2011; Standing, 1998). In previous examples, feminist researchers attempt to grapple with nonexploitative ways of representing the voices of participants, especially where these voices appear to be silenced or are otherwise unheard.

PROTECTING THE IDENTITIES OF PARTICIPANTS WHEN RESEARCHING WOMEN'S EXPERIENCES OF VIOLENCE AND DISPLACEMENT

Oo and Kusakabe's (2010) description identifies a number of ethical issues the researchers had to address during their project on strategies of Karen mothers who have experienced displacement in Burma (Myanmar) due to violence and conflict. The first key ethical issue encountered was the protection of participants' identities, because they were caught up in violent conflict. The researchers had to ensure no individuals were identifiable, and even the names of their villages were not identified for security reasons (one of the authors is herself from the Karen people). Initially, gatekeepers (from the local Anglican church diocese) were used to access potential participants. After the researchers developed good rapport, through learning the participants' language, they were able to speak freely with little interruption.

> Because of security concerns and heavy [military] surveillance, it was not possible to live with the women or tape-record their narratives. The first author commuted to the relocation sites every day and stayed there from morning till evening for four months, spending time with the women and taking notes on every informal conversation to record their experiences. (Oo & Kusakabe, 2010, p. 486)

Researchers' notes were cross-checked with informants from the Anglican diocese who knew the participants well. The researchers declared that despite these restrictions, oral testimony can "give voice to those marginalized individuals and communities who are not able to express themselves in writing" (p. 486).

We have identified morality as a term that usually indicates what we *ought* to do, often in relation to conduct in a particular society or setting. Oo and Kusakabe felt they behaved morally. Below I have chosen examples of feminist scholarship where the authors have focused in different ways on an aspect of morality, closely linked to their research practices.

Exploring Human Rights Activism and the Experiences of Palestinian Women

Shalhoub-Kevorkian and Khsheiboun (2009) use an explicitly critical feminist analysis when discussing Palestinian women's experiences during the past decade, based on the notion that gendered subjects are constructed in relation to various positionings (e.g., ethnicity), within contested social situations and representations. They draw on and interrelate two main bodies of theoretical literature:

- feminist writing dealing with silence, speech, and the importance of "talking back" (see, e.g., hooks, 1989); and

- work relating to human rights (ethics) discourse, especially in relation to localized justice (see, e.g., Merry, 2006).

Shalhoub-Kevorkian and Khsheiboun (2009) ask whether localized justice and human rights can lead to new political opportunities, as suggested by Merry (2006), or whether for Palestinian women, "it further maintains the existence of unequal local and global distribution of power and resources, generating more despair for the already silenced Other" (p. 358).

Shalhoub-Kevorkian and Khsheiboun use an innovative methodology, juxtaposing data from three projects they conducted from 2003 to 2006 that includes individual narratives and focus groups data from more than 250 young Palestinian girls and women affected by the building of the Israeli Separation Wall (ISW) or the Israeli house demolition policy.

The article uses direct quotes from individual women; but these are attributed only by first name and age, so as not to be directly identifiable. This procedure enables confidentiality to be maintained as far as possible. In working with all these data, the authors intended to produce an overall account that is "presenting law from above (the global human rights discourse) and law from below (the perspectives of Palestinian women whose voices, analyses and interpretations give meaning to localized human rights laws and activism)" (Shalhoub-Kevorkian & Khsheiboun, 2009, p. 357).

Some events witnessed during their research shed further light both on the researchers' explicitly stated intentions to empower their research participants, and on other ethical issues. For example, one evening while they were listening to women's stories in preparation for a public hearing that was to be broadcast on a radio station,

> a group of young girls (8–12 years old) came into the room against their parents' consent in order to give us a written letter addressed to "human rights organizations." The letter not only drew our attention to the needs of young girls fearing and suffering from the loss of their homes, but the letter showed us that they also have the agency and power to raise their voices and share their ordeals. The letter was signed: "the girls from the neighborhood." (Shalhoub-Kevorkian & Khsheiboun, 2009, p. 358)

Despite describing this as "an act of agency and resilience," the authors also acknowledge that actions such as this

> situated the many activists in helpless situations as they know that their ability to prevent further housing demolitions is minimal. In many other instances, the arrival of human rights activists and organizations was perceived as an invasion of privacy, and was treated with much anger and hostility. Many women and young girls stated that human rights activities and interventions enhanced their feeling of loss and made them angrier. (Shalhoub-Kevorkian & Khsheiboun, 2009, p. 358)

The researchers became involved in several ethically sensitive situations involving dilemmas (such as perceived invasion of privacy), for which they were not responsible. However, these events reinforced the researchers' determination to take a moral stand in defense of these women. "Palestinian women's voices of dissent are in reality still unheard voices" (p. 356).

They argue that revealing these Palestinian women's voices shows limitations to the "transformative" potential of the human rights approach to ethics to change the social hierarchy within which these women have become marginalized. It also shows how spontaneous actions of research participants (e.g., the young girls) can produce important insights for researchers, in this case allowing them to connect their research findings with a more globalized aspect of morality (human rights ethics discourse). This suggests again the limitations—yet also the possibilities of feminist researchers linking to universalist ethics (see also Shalhoub-Kevorkian, 2006).

Engaging With New Technologies and Forms of Communication Without Violating Participants' Confidentiality

With the rapid current development of communication technologies, more research-ers will be attempting to use digital, virtual, or cyber means to carry out research. In many previous examples in this chapter, researchers were engaging in research prac-tices such as interviewing focused around interpersonal relationships; and this may imply face-to-face contact, which some still see as essential for developing rapport (see also Olivero & Lunt, 2004).[1] We should also note two sides to the use of newer technologies: sometimes the subject/topic being researched lies in cyberspace, and/ or the means to carry out the research can also lie within this domain. For example, feminist researchers have recently been exploring newer forms of communication such as blogging (Doucet & Mauthner, 2013; Friedman & Calixte, 2009; Lopez, 2009) or using adaptations of established research methodologies, such as cyber-ethnography (Ward, 1999), as well as exploring research ethics implications (Buchanan, 2004; Mauthner, 2012).

Ward (1999), for example, argues that cyber-ethnography is not entirely separate from other forms of ethnography, and she questions the idea that "cyberspace is cast as having accentuated egalitarian properties" (Ward, 1999, para. 1.5). Technological devel-opments potentially bring with them even more complex ethical dilemmas. For exam-ple, issues like covert approaches to research have greater complexity in cyberspace, where global links are possible yet people can potentially remain anonymous. As Ward

(1999) comments: "[M]any observers of cyber-culture celebrate the possibilities for identity play.... In this light, what responsibility does the cyber-ethnographer have; should s/he reveal his/her true intentions?" (Ward, para. 1.10).

These developments also suggest opportunities for researchers, as well as for those involved in formal Ethics Committees or IRBs, as Miller and Boulton (2007), among others, have suggested.

[C]hanges in communication technologies, for example email, can offer researchers new opportunities to document the *process* of consent—the invitation, the response from the participant, the questions asked and the answers given, the negotiation of dates and times of interviews and so on. This is potentially a much more appropriate and useful way of working towards (and documenting) participation in research which is both informed and voluntary than asking participants to sign a consent form at the start of a study. (Miller & Boulton, 2007, p. 2209)

The following illustrates how new technologies are leading to new perspectives on what constitutes ethical feminist research practice.

RESEARCHING ETHICALLY WITH ADULTS AND CHILDREN IN CYBERSPACE/VIRTUAL REALITIES

In Ward's (1999) study of two (adult) feminist online communities, she was aware that in exploring the possibilities of research in cyberspace, she was moving into uncharted territory.

I felt uncomfortable pioneering research that moved against the grain of ethical research practice. I suggest that the researcher informs the participants of his/her intentions, but this is problematic in cyberspace, when the researcher has no way of proving his/her purity of intention. I decided to inform participants, via the BBS [bulletin boards] and email lists, that I was a PhD student carrying out research CMC [computer-mediated communication]. I posted messages to the BBS and email lists to which I was subscribed, and then *it became the participants' responsibility to read the message* [emphasis added]. (para. 1.10)

To an extent, Ward feels that research participants and others using these ephemeral spaces had power and responsibilities, which arose from being part of a dynamic set of relationships. The researcher then had to acknowledge this and adapt her research practice in order to act appropriately. Cyberspace allowed greater reflexivity, sharing of ideas and questions, as well as letting participants have instrumental choices to stay or leave these networks, using their resources as needed. "If the participants perceive their online aggregation to be a community, then they have the power, through the reflexivity of the method, to define it as such" (Ward, 1999, para. 6.2).

However, participants' experiences were not always positive and were certainly gendered. "[H]arassment in text-based virtual space is experienced as a reality. In short, members of this online community perceived themselves to be open to harm. Consequently, the gendered self remains a significant player in social interaction on the electronic frontier" (Ward, 1999, para. 5.12).

Bober's (2004) discussion focuses on a key area of interest to researchers in virtual environments, researching with children and youth. Her own online study of young people's use of the Internet raised additional ethical issues compared to working with adults, or working directly with young people face-to-face. Good ethical practice with children in offline contexts has suggested giving them more rights when participating in research, as well as treating them with respect, and taking issues like privacy seriously (see, e.g., Alderson & Morrow, 2011). Parental consent may also be required before young people can participate directly in research, and researchers with youth are usually subject to various legal checks. Bober states that

> my experience of online research demonstrates that the protection of children and adolescents is less effective in a virtual environment, and the researcher is left alone with his/her moral values.... It is fairly easy to access this age group online.... With no stringent checks present, which researchers normally have to face before being granted offline access to children and young people, online researchers are in danger of forgetting to take precautions to protect their subjects of study. (Bober, 2004, p. 302)

Bober suggests moral considerations alone should not be allowed to stop research projects merely because youth are perceived to be more vulnerable than adults. However, she raises (and responds to) a number of useful ethical questions, focusing around issues of access, parental consent, confidentiality, and power relationships between the young person and the researcher in virtual environments. There may be issues for the researcher if a young person disclosed something indicating they were "at risk."

Should researchers attempt to contact young participants online directly or only via online gatekeepers? Bober suggests this depends on the topic and sensitivity of the research and perceived maturity and/or potential vulnerability of the young people.

Do young people fully comprehend the idea of informed consent to participation in research? Are they fully aware of issues of privacy, for example, in relation to home pages, Facebook, and so forth? Bober says it is the *researcher's responsibility*, if it seems the young people are not fully aware, to take steps to protect these participants by ensuring confidentiality and/or anonymity.

Should parental consent be sought? In virtual environments, it is difficult to obtain this, as a practical basis. Bober provided full information about her research, but she did not seek parental consent from participants.

CONCLUSION

In this chapter, we considered some key aspects of research ethics currently linked to feminist research practices. We saw how ethical issues are embedded within feminist research; they cannot be easily separated from issues of research methodology or epistemology. We also explored what has been called the shift from seeing ethics *mainly* as moral discourse (based largely on what researchers ought to do, and on their own values and integrity) to a discourse of regulation (where those with power over researchers' activities also seek to control and judge what they do in advance). This means that feminist researchers must not only continue to behave ethically, they must now respond to the requirements of research regulation and governance as part of this ethical behavior.

The key ethical dilemmas and the range of in-depth examples we have provided demonstrate that feminist researchers take account of power issues as part of the research process. The significance of various social contexts is clear when considering what ethical issues may be embedded within feminist research examples. Feminist researchers, whose work was considered, demonstrate different ways of dealing with these issues, depending upon what kinds of ethical principles they adhere to, or develop during research. Stages in research are also key to what kinds of ethical issues arise: accessing participants, working with them to gather or interpret data, or attempting to represent or give voice to women, especially those from marginalized groups.

These dilemmas and in-depth examples illustrate the key ethical issues, in addition to power, that feminist researchers need to engage with. In addition to doing no harm and ensuring respect for participants (and researcher colleagues), these key ethical issues also include ensuring confidentiality, privacy, and informed consent. In addition, they include developing reflexivity and ethical awareness with regard to issues about disclosure or deception, protecting vulnerable subjects, and issues of representation. These key dilemmas are embedded within the research examples presented in this chapter, to varying degrees. They serve to underscore the feminist ethical principle of praxis, namely that it is impossible to separate ethical issues from other epistemological or methodological issues when carrying out research from feminist perspectives.

DISCUSSION QUESTIONS

1. Using ONE example of feminist research, why do you think ethical issues are, or are not, embedded within other methodological processes, such as analyzing and reporting participants' accounts, and accessing research participants?

2. Are research governance and control processes (e.g., IRBs) helpful or a hindrance in setting out detailed practices of responsibility for feminist researchers in relation to feminist research?

3. Is covert research always unethical?

4. How does the feminist researcher demonstrate her/his own integrity in virtual environments?

WEB RESOURCES

- http://www.afeast.org/

The Association for Feminist Ethics and Social Theory (FEAST) is a professional organization that aims to promote feminist ethical perspectives in various areas including philosophy, public policy, and political life.

- http://appeonline.com/

The Association for Practical and Professional Ethics (APPE) is an international organization based at Indiana University advancing scholarship, education, and practice in practical and professional ethics, including research ethics.

JOURNAL RESOURCES

- *Hypatia: A Journal of Feminist Philosophy*
- http://depts.washington.edu/hypatia/
- *International Journal of Feminist Approaches to Bioethics*
- http://www.ijfab.org/
- *Research Ethics*
- http://www.uk.sagepub.com/journals/Journal202119

NOTE

1. "E-mail interviews require . . . a degree of active participation that must rely on motivational components, rather than initial agreements on a research contract and that can only exist within the gratifying, trusted reciprocal exchange indicated by the feminist perspective" (Olivero & Lunt, 2004, p.107).

REFERENCES

Ackerly, B., & Attanasi, K. (2009). Global feminisms: Theory and ethics for studying gendered injustice. *New Political Science*, 31, 543–556.

Ackerly, B., & True, J. (2008). Reflexivity in practice: Power and ethics in feminist research on international relations. *International Studies Review, 10,* 693–707.

Adam, B., Beck, U., & Loon, J. (Eds.). (2000). *The risk society and beyond: Critical issues for social theory.* London, England: Sage.

Alderson, P., & Morrow, V. (2011). *The ethics of research with children and young people.* Thousand Oaks, CA: Sage.

Alldred, P., & Gillies, V. (2012). Eliciting research accounts: Re/producing modern subjects? In T. Miller, M. Birch, M. Mauthner, & J. Jessop (Eds.), *Ethics in qualitative research* (2nd ed., pp. 140–156). London, England: Sage.

American Sociological Association. (1999). *Code of Ethics.* Washington, DC: Author.

Bailey, A. (2011). Reconceiving surrogacy: Toward a reproductive justice account of Indian surrogacy. *Hypatia, 26,* 715–741.

Ballantyne, A., Bennett, B., Karpin, I., & Rogers, W. (2008). Introduction to special issue: Women, sex and gender in biomedical research. *International Journal of Feminist Approaches to Bioethics, 1*(2), 1–4.

Beauchamp, T., & Childress, J. (2001). *Principles of biomedical ethics* (5th rev. ed.). New York, NY: Oxford University Press.

Bell, L. (1998). Public and private meanings in diaries: Researching family and childcare. In J. Ribbens & R. Edwards (Eds.), *Feminist dilemmas in qualitative research* (pp. 72-86). London, England: Sage. Also reprinted in J. Goodwin (Ed., 2012). *Sage biographical research* (Vol. 3). London, England: Sage.

Bell, L., & Nutt, L. (2012). Divided loyalties, divided expectations: Research ethics, professional and occupational responsibilities. In T. Miller, M. Birch, M. Mauthner, & J. Jessop (Eds.), *Ethics in qualitative research* (2nd ed., pp. 76–93). London, England: Sage.

Bhopal, K. (2010). Gender, identity and experience: Researching marginalised groups. *Women's Studies International Forum, 33,* 188–195.

Bober, M. (2004). Virtual youth research: An exploration of methodologies and ethical dilemmas from a British perspective. In E. A. Buchanan (Ed.), *Readings in virtual research ethics: Issues and controversies* (pp. 288–316). Hershey, PA: Information Science.

Boulton, M., Haynes, L., Smyth, D., & Fielder, A. (2006). Health-related quality of life of children with vision impairment or blindness. *Developmental Medicine & Child Neurology, 48,* 656–661.

Boulton, M., & Parker, M. (2007). Introduction: Informed consent in a changing environment [Special issue]. *Social Science & Medicine, 65,* 2187–2198.

Brannen, J. (Ed.). (1992). *Mixing methods: Qualitative and quantitative research.* Aldershot, England: Avebury Press.

Brennan, S. (1999). Recent work in feminist ethics. *Ethics, 109,* 858–893.

Browne, K. (2005). Snowball sampling: Using social networks to research non-heterosexual women. *International Journal of Social Research Methodology, 8,* 47–60.

Buchanan, E. A. (Ed.). (2004). *Readings in virtual research ethics: Issues and controversies.* Hershey, PA: Information Science.

Chalmers, S. (2002). *Emerging lesbian voices from Japan.* New York, NY: Routledge Curzon.

Crocker, D. (2010). Counting woman abuse: A cautionary tale of two surveys. *International Journal of Social Research Methodology, 13,* 265–275.

Datta, K., McIlwaine, M., Evans, Y., Herbert, J., May, J., & Wills, J. (2010). A migrant ethic of care? Negotiating care and caring among migrant workers in London's low-pay economy. *Feminist Review, 94,* 93–116.

Dench, S., Iphofen, R., & Huws, U. (2004). *An EU [European Union] code of ethics for socio-economic research* (Institute for Employment Studies Report No. 412). Retrieved from http://www.respectproject.org/main/index.php

Desai, M. (2007). The messy relationship between feminisms and globalizations. *Gender & Society, 21,* 797–803.

Doucet, A., & Mauthner, N. S. (2012). Knowing responsibly: Ethics, feminist epistemologies and methodologies. In T. Miller, M. Birch, M. Mauthner, & J. Jessop (Eds.), *Ethics in qualitative research* (2nd ed., pp. 122–139). London, England: Sage.

Doucet, A., & Mauthner, N. (2013). Tea and Tupperware: Mommy blogging as care, work, and consumption. In C. Rogers & S. Weller (Eds.), *Critical approaches to care: Understanding caring relations, identities and cultures* (pp. 92–104). Oxford, England: Routledge.

Driver, J. (2005). Consequentialism and feminist ethics. *Hypatia, 20,* 183–199.

Duncombe, J., & Jessop, J. (2012). "Doing rapport" and ethics of "faking friendship." In T. Miller, M. Birch, M. Mauthner, & J. Jessop (Eds.), *Ethics in qualitative research* (2nd ed., pp. 107–128). London, England: Sage.

Economic & Social Research Council (ESRC). (2010, 2012 rev.). *ESRC framework for research ethics.* Swindon, England: Author. Retrieved from http://www.esrc.ac.uk/_images/Framework-for-Research-Ethics_tcm8-4586.pdf

Edwards, R., & Mauthner, M. (2012). Ethics and feminist research: Theory and practice. In T. Miller, M. Birch, M. Mauthner, & J. Jessop (Eds.), *Ethics in qualitative research* (2nd ed., pp. 14–28). London, England: Sage.

Evans, M. (2011). Doing gender: Gender and women's studies in the twenty-first century. *Women's Studies International Forum, 34,* 603–610.

Fisher, B., & Tronto, J. (1990). Toward a feminist theory of caring. In K. E. Abel & M. K. Nelson (Eds.), *Circles of care* (pp. 35–62). Albany: State University of New York Press.

Friedman, M., & Calixte, S. L. (Eds.). (2009). *Mothering and blogging: The radical act of the MommyBlog.* Bradford, Ontario, Canada: Demeter Press.

Gillies, V., & Alldred, P. (2012). The ethics of intention: Research as a political tool. In T. Miller, M. Birch, M. Mauthner, & J. Jessop (Eds.), *Ethics in qualitative research* (2nd ed., pp. 43–60). London, England: Sage.

Gillies, V., & Lucey, H. (Eds.). (2007). *Power, knowledge and the academy: The institution is political.* Basingstoke, England: Palgrave Macmillan.

Gilligan, C. (1983). *In a different voice: Psychological theory and women's development.* Cambridge, MA: Harvard University Press.

Gilligan, C. (1995). Moral orientation and moral development. In V. Held (Ed.), *Justice and care: Essential readings in feminist ethics* (pp. 31–46). Boulder, CO: Westview Press.

Halse, C., & Honey, A. (2005). Unravelling ethics: Illuminating the moral dilemmas of research ethics. *Signs: Journal of Women in Culture and Society, 30,* 2141–2162.

Hammersley, M. (2009). Against the ethicists: On the evils of ethical regulation. *International Journal of Social Research Methodology, 12,* 211–225.

Harding, S. (1998). *Is science multicultural? Postcolonialism, feminisms and epistemologies.* Milton Keynes, England: Open University Press.

Hedgecoe, A. (2008). Research ethics review and the sociological research relationship. *Sociology, 42,* 873–886.

Held, V. (2006). *The ethics of care: Personal, political, and global.* Oxford, England: Oxford University Press.

Hesse-Biber, S. N. (2010). *Mixed methods research.* New York, NY: Guilford Press.

Hoagland, S. L. (1988). *Lesbian ethics: Toward new value.* Palo Alto, CA: Institute of Lesbian Studies.

Holland, J. (2007). Emotions and research. *International Journal of Social Research Methodology, 10,* 195–209.

hooks, b. (1989). *Talking back: Thinking feminist, thinking black.* Boston, MA: South End Press.

Hughes, B., McKie, L., Hopkins, D., & Watson, N. (2005). Love's labours lost? Feminism, the Disabled People's Movement and an ethic of care. *Sociology, 39,* 259–276.

Iphofen, R. (2009). *Ethical decision-making in social research: A practical guide.* Basingstoke, England: Palgrave MacMillan.

Jaggar, A. M. (1991). Feminist ethics: Projects, problems, prospects. In C. Card (Ed.), *Feminist ethics* (pp. 78–106). Lawrence, KS: University Press of Kansas.

Jaggar, A. M. (1992). Feminist ethics. In L. Becker & C. Becker (Eds.), *Encyclopedia of ethics* (pp. 363–364). New York, NY: Garland Press.

Jaggar, A. M. (1994). *Living with contradictions: Controversies in feminist social ethics.* Boulder, CO: Westview Press.

Jouili, J. S. (2011). Beyond emancipation: Subjectivities and ethics among women in Europe's Islamic revival communities. *Feminist Review, 98,* 47–64.

Karnieli-Miller, O., Strier, R., & Pessach, L. (2009). Power relations in qualitative research. *Qualitative Health Research, 19,* 279-289.

Koehn, D. (1998). *Rethinking feminist ethics.* London, England: Routledge.

Lather, P. (2001). Working the ruins of feminist ethnography. *Signs: Journal of Women in Culture and Society, 27,* 199–227.

Lennon, K., & Whitford, M. (Eds.). (1994). *Knowing the difference: Feminist perspectives in epistemology.* London, England: Routledge.

Letherby, G. (2002). Claims and disclaimers: Knowledge, reflexivity and representation in feminist research. *Sociological Research Online, 6*(4). Retrieved from http://www.socresonline.org.uk/6/4/letherby.html

Letherby, G. (2003). Whose life is it anyway? Issues of power, empowerment, ethics and responsibility. In *Feminist research in theory and practice* (pp. 99–121). Buckingham, England: Open University Press.

Lopez, L. K. (2009). The radical act of "mommy blogging": Redefining motherhood through the blogosphere. *New Media & Society, 11,* 729–747.

Luff, D. (1999). Dialogue across the divides: "Moments of rapport" and power in feminist research with anti-feminist women. *Sociology, 33,* 687–703.

Mason, J. (2006). Mixing methods in a qualitatively driven way. *Qualitative Research, 6,* 9–25.

Mauthner, M., & Bell, L. (2007). Power relationships in research teams. In V. Gillies & H. Lucey (Eds.), *Power, knowledge and the academy: The institution is political* (pp. 88-104). Basingstoke, England: Palgrave Macmillan.

Mauthner, M., Birch, M., Jessop, J., & Miller, T. (Eds.). (2002). *Ethics in qualitative research.* London, England: Sage.

Mauthner, N. S. (2012). "Accounting for our part of the entangled webs we weave": Ethical and moral issues in digital data sharing. In T. Miller, M. Birch, M. Mauthner, & J. Jessop (Eds.), *Ethics in qualitative research* (2nd ed., pp. 157–175). London, England: Sage.

Mauthner, N. S., & Doucet, A. (1998). Reflections on a voice-centered relational method: Analysing maternal and domestic voices. In J. Ribbens & R. Edwards (Eds.), *Feminist dilemmas in qualitative research* (pp. 119–146). London, England: Sage.

May, V. (2008). On being a "good" mother: The moral presentation of self in written life stories. *Sociology, 42,* 470-486.

Mayes, R., Llewellyn, G., & McConnell, D. (2011). "That's who I choose to be": The mother identity for women with intellectual disabilities. *Women's Studies International Forum, 34,* 112–120.

Merry, S. (2006). *Human rights and gender violence: Translating international law into local justice.* Chicago, IL: University of Chicago Press.

Miller, T., & Bell, L. (2012). Consenting to what? Issues of access, gate keeping and "informed" consent. In T. Miller, M. Birch, M. Mauthner, & J. Jessop (Eds.), *Ethics in qualitative research* (2nd ed., pp. 61–75). London, England: Sage.

Miller, T., Birch, M., Mauthner, M., & Jessop, J. (Eds.). (2012). *Ethics in qualitative research* (2nd ed.). London, England: Sage.

Miller, T., & Boulton, M. (2007). Changing constructions of informed consent: Qualitative research and complex social worlds. *Social Science & Medicine, 65,* 2199–2211.

Morley, L. (1999). *Organizing feminisms: The micro-politics of the academy.* New York, NY: St. Martin's Press.

Munro, E. R. (2008). Research governance, ethics and access: A case study illustrating the new challenges facing social researchers. *International Journal of Social Research Methodology, 11,* 429–439.

Murphy, E., & Dingwall, R. (2007). Informed consent, anticipatory regulation and ethnographic practice. *Social Science & Medicine, 65,* 2223–2234.

Noddings, N. (2003). *Caring: A feminine approach to ethics and moral education* (2nd ed.). Berkeley: University of California Press.

Oakley, A. (1999). Paradigm wars: Some thoughts on a personal and public trajectory. *International Journal of Social Research Methodology, 2,* 247–254.

Olivero, N., & Lunt, P. (2004). When the ethic is functional to the method: The case of e-mail qualitative interviews. In E. A. Buchanan (Ed.), *Readings in virtual research ethics: Issues and controversies* (pp. 101–113). Hershey, PA: Information Science.

Oo, Z. M., & Kusakabe, K. (2010). Motherhood and social network: Response strategies of internally displaced Karen women in Taungoo district. *Women's Studies International Forum, 33,* 482–491.

Paradis, E. K. (2000). Feminist and community psychology ethics in research with homeless women. *American Journal of Community Psychology, 28,* 839–858.

Pedwell, C. (2007). Ethics of the body: Postconventional challenges. *Feminist Review, 85,* 134–136.

Philip, G., Rogers, C., & Weller, S. (2013). Understanding care and thinking with care. In C. Rogers & S. Weller (Eds.), *Critical approaches to care: Understanding caring relations, identities and cultures* (pp. 1–12). Oxford, England: Routledge.

Porter, E. (1999). *Feminist perspectives on ethics.* Harlow, England: Pearson Education.

Ribbens, J., & Edwards, R. (Eds.). (1998). *Feminist dilemmas in qualitative research.* London, England: Sage.

Ribbens McCarthy, J., Edwards, R., & Gillies, V. (2000). Moral tales of the child and the adult: Narratives of contemporary family lives under changing circumstances. *Sociology, 34,* 785–803.

Rice, C. (2009). Imagining the other? Ethical challenges of researching and writing women's embodied lives. *Feminism and Psychology, 19,* 245–266.

Robinson, F. (2011). Stop talking and listen: Discourse ethics and feminist care ethics in international political theory. *Millenium, 39,* 845–860.

Rogers, C., & Weller, S. (Eds.). (2013). *Critical approaches to care: Understanding caring relations, identities and cultures.* Oxford, England: Routledge.

Scheyvens, R., & Leslie, H. (2000). Gender, ethics and empowerment: Dilemmas of development fieldwork. *Women's Studies International Forum, 23,* 119–130.

Scully, J. L. (2010). Hidden labor: Disabled/Nondisabled encounters, agency, and autonomy. *International Journal of Feminist Approaches to Bioethics, 3*(2), 25–42.

Sevenhuijsen, S. (1998). *Citizenship and the ethics of care: Feminist considerations on justice, morality and politics.* London, England: Routledge.

Sevenhuijsen, S. (2000). Caring in the third way: The relation between obligation, responsibility and care in Third Way discourse. *Critical Social Policy, 20,* 5–37.

Sevenhuijsen, S. (2002). A third way? Moralities, ethics and families: An approach through the ethics of care. In A. Carling, S. Duncan, & R. Edwards (Eds.), *Analysing families* (pp. 129–144). London, England: Routledge.

Shalhoub-Kevorkian, N. (2006). Counter-spaces as resistance in conflict zones: Palestinian women recreating a home. *Journal of Feminist Family Therapy, 17*(3–4), 109–141.

Shalhoub-Kevorkian, N., & Khsheiboun, S. (2009). Palestinian women's voices challenging human rights activism. *Women's Studies International Forum, 32,* 354–362.

Shildrick, M. (2004). Genetics, normativity, and ethics: Some bioethical concerns. *Feminist Theory, 5,* 149–166.

Stacey, J. (1988). Can there be a feminist ethnography? *Women's Studies International Forum, 11,* 21–27.

Standing, K. (1998). Writing the voices of the less powerful: Research on lone mothers. In J. Ribbens & R. Edwards (Eds.), *Feminist dilemmas in qualitative research* (pp. 186–202). London, England: Sage.

Tanesini, A. (1999). *An introduction to feminist epistemologies.* Oxford, England: Blackwell.

Tong, R., & Williams, N. (2009). Feminist ethics. In E. N. Zalta (Ed.), *The Stanford encyclopedia of philosophy.* Retrieved from http://plato.stanford.edu/entries/feminism-ethics/

Tronto, J. (1993). *Moral boundaries: A political argument for an ethic of care.* New York, NY: Routledge.

Truman, C. (2003). Ethics and the ruling relations of research production. *Sociological Research Online, 8*(1). Retrieved from http://www.socresonline.org.uk/8/1/truman.html

UK Department of Health. (2005). *Research governance framework for health and social care* (2nd ed.). Retrieved from http://www.dh.gov.uk/en/Publicationsandstatistics/Publications/PublicationsPolicyAndGuidance/DH_4108962 and http://www.dh.gov.uk/prod_consum_dh/groups/dh_digitalassets/@dh/@en/documents/digitalasset/dh_4122427.pdf

Walker, M. U. (2007). *Moral understandings: A feminist study in ethics* (2nd ed.). Oxford, England: Oxford University Press.

Walliman, N. (2005). *Your research project: A step-by-step guide for the first-time researcher* (2nd ed.). Thousand Oaks, CA: Sage.

Ward, J. (2008). Researching drug sellers: An "experiential" account from "the field." *Sociological Research Online, 13*(1), 14. Retrieved from http://www.socresonline.org.uk/13/1/14.html

Ward, K. J. (1999). The cyber-ethnographic (re)construction of two feminist online communities. *Sociological Research Online, 4*(1). Retrieved from http://socresonline.org.uk/4/1/ward.html

Williams, J. (2010). Doing feminist demography. *International Journal of Social Research Methodology, 13*(3), 197–210.

Zembylas, M. (2010). The ethic of care in globalized societies. *Ethics and Education, 5,* 233–245.

CHAPTER 5

What Is Feminist Ethnography?

Elana D. Buch and Karen M. Staller

D efining feminist ethnography is difficult in practice because the forms of feminist ethnography are nearly as diverse as feminist ethnographers themselves. The diversity among feminist ethnographies reflects the wide variety of feminist theories presented in this book. Ethnography is a flexible, responsive, and *iterative* form of research and is well suited to feminist researchers' interests. In this chapter, we explore this exciting, dynamic, and evolving methodology. In particular we examine the questions: What is feminist ethnography? How do ethnographers prepare for ethnographic fieldwork? How do ethnographers collect evidence? How do ethnographers turn evidence into feminist ethnography? Finally, we close with some concluding observations.

What Is Feminist Ethnography?

Ethnography is a form of research that attends to the social relations and cultural practices of groups of people, and works to understand these aspects of social life within broader political, economic, and historical contexts. Ethnographies describe and analyze the dynamic and meaningful connections among and between different aspects of social life including religion, work, kinship, politics, and language. Feminist ethnography attends to the ways in which gender is understood and made meaningful in social life, as well as the ways that gender is related to the distribution of power and resources. In short, "Ethnographic research aims to get an in–depth understanding of how individuals in different subcultures make sense of their lived reality" (Hesse–Biber & Leavy, 2006, p. 230).

Sherry Ortner (1995) notes that "minimally [ethnography] has always meant the attempt to understand another life world using the self . . . as the instrument of knowing" (p. 173). There are two significant parts to this "minimal" definition of ethnography. First, it is the "attempt to understand another life world." Thus, ethnographers study the lived experiences, daily activities, and social/political context of everyday life from the perspectives of those being studied. To do so, ethnographers typically conduct their research by going to the environments or *natural settings* where social life occurs, immersing themselves in those environments for long periods of time in order to gain a deep understanding of people's lives.

Second, ethnographers gain their knowledge by "using the self" as much as possible. Ethnography rests upon the assumption that researchers can come to have a productive understanding of lived realities very different from their own through careful participation and observation of daily life. Much of what sets ethnographic research apart from other research methods is that ethnographic knowledge is created in and through the ethnographer's relationships with those he or she studies. By this we mean that ethnographers study human social relations and culture by both observing and participating in social relationships with those whose lives we are interested in. By engaging in these relationships as well as observing them, ethnographers are able to both experience and record the social norms, rules, and practices that shape diverse forms of human sociality. Ethnography depends on cultivating a range of interpersonal as well as research skills. In addition to asking incisive, careful questions and maintaining an observant eye, ethnographers need to cultivate empathy, imagination, and open–mindedness. Moreover, ethnographers cultivate a sense of skepticism about their own culturally conditioned common sense, recognizing that people from different backgrounds might understand and organize the world in radically different ways. Because of the critical role the self plays in generating ethnographic knowledge, each feminist ethnographer must also carefully attend to the ways in which his or her position in the world might impact what and from whom he or she is able to learn. Since individual history and identity patterns what can be learned, any individual ethnography can offer only one possible window of understanding into the lives of the people it portrays.

Ethnographic research can be distinguished from most other forms of research by the presence of long–term engagements and relationships between the researcher and those being studied. Of course, ethnographers do not have equally durable or close relationships with every individual in their studies; however, ethnographers typically engage with a subset of people in the field over a period of months or years. Through these relationships, ethnographers are able to understand the findings from shorter term methods of collecting evidence—for example, evidence gathered through surveys, focus groups, or interviews—within their broader social context. For example, an ethnographer conducting research in a medical clinic might conduct relatively brief interviews with hundreds of patients, but he or she would typically seek to contextualize these interviews through ongoing participant observation (described below) with clinic staff and with a subset of patients observed in their homes and communities.

Like all forms of research, ethnography has limitations. It is difficult to make generalizations based on ethnographic research, because ethnography does not use representative sampling. Rather, ethnographic studies can be used comparatively to see what is shared and what is unique among diverse peoples. Although ethnographies often provide historical and narrative explanations for events and processes, it is difficult to prove causation because the method does not test the impact of different factors on a given outcome. Ethnographies are virtually impossible to replicate or verify because they depend so greatly on personal interactions.

TOWARD FEMINIST ETHNOGRAPHY: TRACING THE FEMINIST ETHNOGRAPHIC TRADITION

While the ethnographic method was initially developed by anthropologists, it has been used and refined by researchers working in disciplines ranging from sociology, social work, public health, and women's studies to political science, psychology, nursing, education, and business. Researchers with both humanistic and social science backgrounds find ethnography useful for gathering information about and analyzing social life around the world because this method offers scholars the chance to engage directly and for a sustained period of time with the people they are studying. In doing so, researchers often come away from projects feeling like they have a much deeper and richer understanding of how life is lived in a particular time and place. Ethnographic methods can also be used flexibly to accommodate a number of epistemologies and research paradigms. Mixed method researchers often use ethnographic methods before and after conducting survey research as a way to generate socially grounded research questions or contextualize survey findings.

Common accounts typically trace the origins of the method to the early 20th century when European and American sociologists and anthropologists sought ways to understand the lives of people who seemed very different from themselves. A number of scholars played a critical role in developing the method. Franz Boas, an American anthropologist writing between 1888 and 1942 emphasized the importance of history, flux, migration, and social contact between groups and of social change in understanding contemporary social life. Early female scholars also played an important role in developing the theoretical foundations for this method (Reinharz, 1992). For example, in 1838, Harriet Martineau, a British theorist often considered a founder of contemporary sociology, wrote *How to Observe Morals and Manners*, emphasizing the importance of observing local manners and mores on their own terms. Martineau outlined key domains for observation ranging from inquiries into religion, discourse, family life, and the treatment of criminals to the organization of work and the notion of liberty (Martineau, 1838). Martineau was particularly interested in examining the relationship between morality, social progress, and racial, class, and gender inequality. Alice Fletcher, an American anthropologist who conducted ethnological research on newly formed Omaha, Nez Percé, and Sioux reservations from the 1870s through the mid–1920s, brought an archaeological interest in categorizing and comparing cultural practices to the observation of living humans. Like others of her era who assisted with projects of colonial governance, Fletcher worked for the U.S. government to develop and implement highly controversial land reform policies on the newly formed Indian reservations. Fletcher was one of the first ethnographers to practice a deeply relationship–based form of ethnography, and she viewed (at least some of) her research subjects as intellectual peers. As evidence of this, Fletcher collaborated and coauthored a number of publications with her adopted son, Francis La Flesche, who was a member of the Omaha tribe (making La Flesche one of the first *native ethnographers;* Mark, 1988). These women and others such as Helen Merrell Lynd and Faith Williams emphasized the importance of the ethnographer actually going to the *field* and relied on interviews and observations with local people to find out about their lives, customs, and beliefs (Reinharz, 1992).

Although many female pioneers of the ethnographic method did not specifically focus their research on issues of gender and sexuality, one notable exception was Elsie Clews Parsons, an American who worked as an anthropologist from 1910 to 1941. Parsons emphasized the ways in which women were limited by, "taboos, constraints, and exclusionary practices, often centering on women's bodies, their sexuality, and their reproductive roles as mothers" (Lamphere, 1995, p. 98). Lesser known early female ethnographers focused on the lives of women around the world, including the Australian scholar Phyllis Kaberry, who studied the ritual lives of Aboriginal women and the economic position of women in British Cameroon in the 1930s through the late 1950s (Lewin, 2006, p. 7).

While Boas, Fletcher, Clews, Parsons and other early ethnographers conducted fieldwork while living among the people they wrote about, they tended to rely on surveys and interviews to collect evidence. The cornerstone of the ethnographic method, *participant observation,* was developed by Bronislaw Malinowski during a famous and extended stay on the Trobriand Islands during World War I. Malinowski emphasized the importance of the researcher using him– or herself as a primary tool for data collection by engaging directly in social life, and then using these experiences to provoke discussion and debate among those studied. Malinowski argued that

> [d]irect questioning of the native about a custom or belief never discloses their attitude of mind as thoroughly as the discussion of the facts connected with the direct observation of a custom or with a concrete occurrence, in which both parties are materially connected. (cited in Stocking, 1983, p. 97)

The notion of gathering information about social life in a particular place by directly participating in it has become a central feature of contemporary ethnographic methods. While ethnographers continue to collect information using a number of techniques, most ethnographers place a great deal of emphasis on their own direct experiences of social relations to formulate their analyses.

Although women have been working as ethnographers since the earliest advent of the method, *feminist* ethnographers did not begin to formally distinguish their approach to research from other forms of ethnography until the early 1970s. It was at this point that feminists began systematically rethinking the male–centered perspective that had dominated the development of the method. With notable exceptions, such as Margaret Mead, who had begun to explore the social, cultural, and political importance of domestic life and women's daily activities, most ethnographic research reflected Euro–American male researchers' assumptions that economic, political, and religious life would be observable through men's public activities. By the 1970s, feminist ethnographers simultaneously began challenging the male–centric thinking that shaped early ethnography and began asking how being a woman might impact the experience of fieldwork (Lewin, 2006). In doing so, feminist concerns moved from implicit to explicit in the design and execution of research studies.

Feminist researchers during the 1970s and 1980s often extolled the virtues of ethnography for its potential to create interpretive and intersubjective understandings of social lives. Thus, feminist researchers began to influence the actual methods associated with ethnography itself. They expressed concern that traditional research methods treated the people being studied as silent and inactive objects to be observed and analyzed rather than as social actors, actively engaged in shaping the conditions of their own lives. Moreover, they argued that traditional methods tended to benefit powerful and privileged academics rather than those they studied. As feminists became increasingly concerned about the politics of research and committed to producing research that improved the lives of women, feminist researchers began to look for suitable methods. As Judith Stacey has argued, "discussions of feminist methodology generally assaulted the hierarchical, exploitative relations of conventional research, urging feminist researchers to seek instead an egalitarian research process characterized by authenticity, reciprocity and intersubjectivity between the researcher and her subjects" (Stacey, 1991, p. 112). The feminist tradition of ethnography has developed in the context of multiple and sometimes competing goals: to ensure the inclusion of women in the ethnographic method, to better understand the workings of gender and sexuality in social life, and to develop more egalitarian approaches to research, among others.

Traditionally, ethnography involved people from North America and Europe travelling to conduct research in small villages in exotic and remote locations. Since then, various forms of ethnography have been developed, especially by feminist researchers looking to minimize the deeply ethnocentric assumptions that shaped early ethnographic practice and reform ethnography to better reflect the complex world in which we live. *Native ethnographers* conduct their research in familiar settings. Thus, while traditional ethnography strove to describe foreign ways of life, *native ethnographers* work to denaturalize taken–for–granted aspects of their own social worlds, often revealing unseen workings of power or shared social norms. *Urban ethnographers* study aspects of social life in cities, generally attending to the ways that underprivileged people or neighborhoods are (or are not) integrated into city life. *Urban ethnographers* also examine the ways that global flows of people, money, and goods are implicated in the complexities of city life. *Global ethnography* seeks to describe how people in multiple places are tied together through global processes and practices, including the circulation of foods, global banking systems, migration, and notions of humanitarianism. In *critical ethnography* and *applied ethnography*, the researcher often collaborates with community members, and together they focus on solving a social problem or evaluating social policy. According to Robert Trotter and Jean Schensul, the goal of applied ethnographers is to, "conduct research so that the implications of their research can be used for direct interventions or to lead to recommendations for policy change" (2000, p. 691). In *visual ethnography*, researchers use images (photographs, films, social media) to study cultures. For example, they might use building and subway graffiti to study urban youth culture or body tattoos to study prison gangs. In *auto–ethnography*, the researcher uses personal lived experiences as the source of ethnographic data.

More recently, ethnographers are engaged in *digital ethnography*, which explores the cultures and worlds that exist in cyberspace, including sites such as Facebook or Second Life (Boellstorff, 2010). Among the pioneers in digital ethnography is Michael Wesch, a cultural anthropologist and major innovator in the field, with his creative work on, in, and about YouTube (2008). In his brilliant early work, "The Machine is Us/ing Us," he explores the implications of decoupling the form of text from its content in the digital age. His YouTube posting of his final product is better visited online and witnessed in its web space than described in the linear textual space offered by this book (see http://www.youtube.com/watch?v=NLlGopyXT_g). Tom Boellstorff has studied Second Life. Second Life is a complete virtual world with geographic features, social and business institutions much like you would find in the real world. People create one or more avatars to live and interact in this virtual world. In doing so, they create residents of Second Life who interact with other people's avatars in this "third place." Boellstorff (2010) conducted an ethnography of the virtual world of Second Life. He created an avatar and participated in (and studied) Second Life for three years. Like any ethnographer, he argued that studying the culture of Second Life required active participation, being emerged in the culture for an extended period of time, and he attempted to understand social interactions that were occurring within their own cultural (in this case virtual) environment. Among other things, he reported on such important topics as personhood, intimacy, and community as they were created and shaped in Second Life. Digital ethnography may open up whole new opportunities to combine feminist approaches with ethnographic research.

Feminist Practices of Ethnography

What makes an ethnography *feminist* is a contested issue. Rather than speaking of a single feminist practice of ethnography, it is more accurate to think about multiple feminist practices, each shaped by the different perspectives and approaches encompassed within feminist research and theory. Hesse–Biber and Leavy (2006) note:

> What unites these approaches is a deep commitment to understanding the issues and concerns of women from their perspective, and being especially attentive to the activities and the "goings on" of women in the research setting. The work of early feminist ethnography did much to unearth the "invisible" aspects of women's roles in the ethnographic setting. (p. 237)

There are three principle ways in which *feminist* ethnography might be distinguished from other ethnography. They include

- focusing on women's lives, activities, and experiences or on highly gendered settings;
- methods or writing styles informed by feminist theories and ethics; and
- analysis that uses a feminist theoretical lens and/or attends to the interplays between gender and other forms of power and difference.

We briefly consider examples of each.

FOCUSING ON WOMEN'S LIVES AND EXPERIENCES

One of the earliest academic ethnographies to include detailed analysis of women's activities was Audrey I. Richard's (1939/1995) *Land, Labour and Diet in Northern Rhodesia*. Richards was one of Malinowski's students, and her study of agriculture and nutrition among Bemba people was one of the first to provide a detailed account of women's domestic labor and responsibilities. Richards (1956/1982) complemented the many accounts of male initiation rituals when she published one of the first ethnographic accounts of female initiation ceremonies in her description of the Bemba "Chisungu" ceremony. This work showed that women's maturation was marked as a spiritually important event central to understandings of sexuality, marriage, and matrilineal kinship. Through her work, Richards showed that attending to women's lives and experiences was crucial to understanding aspects of social life—such as politics and economics—that early ethnographers assumed were dominated by men. Richards showed that without including women's experiences in ethnographic analyses, the theories scholars develop about social life are inherently incomplete.

Recently, feminist ethnographers have explored women's experiences of their bodies, work, family, and reproduction. In *Birthing a Mother* (2010), Elly Teman intervenes in broader debates about the merits and morality of surrogate pregnancy by focusing on the lived experiences and moral understandings of surrogates and intended mothers in Israel, where the pronatalist state is heavily involved in legislating surrogacy and approving surrogacy contracts. Teman's research is based on eight years of ethnographic fieldwork, including long–term relationships with individual surrogates and intended parents; participant observation with both online and face–to–face surrogacy support groups; and extended formal interviews with surrogates, intended parents, doctors, lawyers, agency directors, social workers, and others. Teman's ethnography describes the ways in which Jewish surrogates and intended mothers in Israel negotiate the emotional and relational challenges involved in the cooperative process of having a baby through surrogacy.

Teman describes a series of processes and practices through which surrogates relinquished maternal claims to the babies they were carrying and developed emotional bonds with intended mothers, who were themselves developing connections to the pregnancy and baby. These processes involved surrogate mothers reimagining their bodies by conceptually dividing body parts into those connected to their body and those more connected to the intended mothers. At the same time, intended mothers engaged in bodily and relational processes that established their roles and status as mothers. After a baby was born, relationships between surrogates and intended mothers seemed to depend on whether intended mothers accepted surrogates' understanding of surrogacy as a gift relationship that extends beyond the limited parameters of the financial contract. Teman argues that surrogates often view the process as one of self–discovery, even though many elements of the process are potentially disempowering. By focusing on women's experiences of surrogate pregnancies, Teman provides detailed evidence and careful analysis regarding a complex and controversial public issue that has significant consequences for women's health and well–being. Moreover, Teman helps us better understand how new medical technologies like surrogacy are reshaping the human relationships that make reproduction possible.

METHODS AND WRITING STYLES INFORMED BY FEMINIST THEORIES AND ETHICS

In the classic and controversial feminist ethnography *Translated Woman* (2003), Ruth Behar weaves together the life story of Esperanza, a Mexican peddler woman and her own experiences as a woman, immigrant, and academic. Behar's approach to her fieldwork with Esperanza, her literary writing style, and biographical research reveal Behar's deeply personal approach to ethnography; they also help reveal both the similarities and differences in Esperanza's and Behar's experiences of rage, power, and redemption. Even more, Behar explicitly examines how she came to be a scholar with the power to "transport Esperanza's story across the border" (2003, p. xvii), and how her own life history influenced her telling of Esperanza's story. In contrast to the approach of ethnographers who say little about their own lives in order to maintain focus on the "other" being studied, Behar probingly, sometimes uncomfortably describes how her relationship with Esperanza impacted both their lives. Behar's inclusion of her personal narrative promotes a feminist agenda of breaking down analytical boundaries between women's experiences through writing that explicitly acknowledges the *intersubjectivity of knowledge production.*

In most research (including ethnographic research), the research agenda, questions, methods, analysis, and final presentation are all determined by the researcher. Thus, the people and communities being studied traditionally have little ability to decide what kinds of knowledge are produced about them. Many feminists are interested in using collaborative *participatory* ethnographic methods that involve academic researchers working in collaboration with researchers from the communities being studied. Typically, in participatory ethnographic methods, researchers collaborate with individuals who live or work in the field site at every step of the research process, ideally enabling research that addresses the needs and interests of community members as well as academic debates. Participatory methods aim to change the relationships between the researcher and subjects, and to build participants' capacity to conduct their own research and change their own communities.

For example, Caitlin Cahill (2007) collaborated with six young women of color who had grown up in New York's Lower East Side to investigate the gentrification of their neighborhood. Members of the research team were paid a stipend for their participation, and Cahill collaborated with them to develop and implement the project at each stage. The research team collected evidence in and about their neighborhood in the form of mapping, photographs, focus groups, observations, and reflective writing. This project explored the relationship between processes of gentrification, disinvestment, public (mis)representations, and young women's self–understanding (Cahill, 2007, p. 206). To share their project with members of their community as well as the scholarly community, the team members collectively created a stereotype sticker campaign, two websites, and a report distributed to local youth organizations and community centers;

presented at a number of academic conferences; and coauthored book chapters. Cahill argues that in the process of "investigating the contradictions of their everyday lives, the young women came to understand their individual experiences as shared, social, and also political" (2007, p. 206). As a result of their research and their own personal concerns, the research team developed a project titled "Makes Me Mad: Stereotypes of Young Urban Womyn of Color." Although not all participatory research is explicitly feminist, Cahill's work suggests the possibilities for participatory ethnography to connect personal and local experiences of gender with broader efforts at social change.

ANALYSIS THAT USES A FEMINIST THEORETICAL LENS AND/OR ATTENDS TO INTERPLAYS BETWEEN GENDER AND OTHER FORMS OF DIFFERENCE

A number of feminist ethnographies focused on people's experiences of gender, sexuality, race, ability, difference, and power to build upon feminist theories. These ethnographies may or may not focus on women's lives, and yet by exploring understandings of gender, they contribute to feminist thinking. For example, in *Dude, You're a Fag* (2011), C. J. Pascoe draws on eighteen months of fieldwork in a racially diverse, working–class high school to show how adolescent boys become masculine through the continual repudiation of a "fag" identity. Arguing that masculinity is not a social category attributed to individuals just because they have male bodies, Pascoe shows how masculinity was constructed in this school through "practices and discourses" that boys and girls embodied in different ways and to different degrees (2011, p. 5). Pascoe argues that boys achieve a masculine identity by continually repudiating the "specter of failed masculinity," which can be accomplished by "lobbing homophobic epithets" at one another and by engaging in heterosexist discussions of girls' bodies (2011, p. 5). These masculinizing practices were experienced differently by white and black boys, as the latter were more likely to be disciplined by the school for participating in them. Pascoe's work contributes to feminist discussions about the ways that gender, sexuality, and heteronormativity are constructed and performed.

A pioneer in feminist methods, Shulamit Reinharz (1992) wrote of feminist ethnography: "My view on this matter is that there is no agreed on definition of feminism, but that there are many people who call themselves feminists and whose ethnographic research follows their own definition of feminism" (p. 74). Rather than trying to isolate a single definition or a single tradition, it is best to embrace a diversity of approaches—we can evaluate the scholar and the scholarship by understanding how the ethnographer him- or herself situates and integrates his or her feminist views with his or her methodological approach. Reinharz concludes that it is not the ethnography per se that is feminist, but rather, it is "ethnography in the hands of feminists that renders it feminist" (p. 48).

As can be seen from the examples above, feminist ethnography is an open and flexible method. Each ethnographer tailors her methodological choices to reflect both her theoretical interests and the particular constraints of the question and field she chooses. Nonetheless, most ethnographers follow similar steps. Next, we outline these steps: preparing for the field, collecting ethnographic evidence, and turning evidence into feminist ethnography.

How Do Ethnographers Prepare for Ethnographic Fieldwork?

Feminist ethnography is a *practice*. We mean this in two ways. First, feminist ethnography is a practice in the colloquial sense that ethnography is something learned in the doing. Yet each ethnographic moment, each encounter with a new research participant, each field site, and each project require the ethnographer to begin anew—as each situation requires the ethnographer to navigate ever–changing social relationships and contexts. Because ethnographers build knowledge through relationships, ethnographers are necessarily part of the situations they study; and they have deep responsibilities to the people with whom they work. So ethnography is also a practice in the sense advocated by Pierre Bourdieu (1990) and Sherry Ortner (1996) in that it is a form of human action that can both reproduce and transform the social and cultural orders that constrain our lives.

No book chapter can tell you how to make the myriad decisions that face the ethnographer. Feminist theory can inform the research questions you choose to study, the way you conduct yourself in the field, the relationships you develop with the people you study, the analytical tools you use to make sense of ethnographic data, and your final analysis and description. Researchers will use feminist theory at different stages of the ethnographic process. Thus, this chapter strives to help you to prepare for feminist ethnographic research by giving you a sense of the common problems encountered, as well as the strategies commonly used to gather and analyze ethnographic evidence.

Successful and responsible ethnography requires both careful preparation and exploratory steps. One strength of ethnography is that community engagement can enable the researcher to continually refine questions meaningful to the community, but a first step necessarily involves learning enough to begin to ask questions.

FORMULATING A RESEARCH PROBLEM

Every research project starts with something that the researcher is curious about. Often ethnographers don't start with a specific, inflexible question but with large and intersecting domains of interest. These domains can include types of people, places, customs, ideas, practices, or attitudes, among other things. For example, Beth Montemurro (2005) was interested in studying changes in gender roles and social practices. So she examined what happened when men were included in wedding showers, a ritual that in the United States is traditionally reserved for women. Elana Buch was interested in how caregiving shaped people's experiences of aging, gender, and race, as well as how care shaped people's understandings about the role of government and family in daily life. Thus, she conducted ethnographic research with paid home care workers and older adults in Chicago (2010) and is developing a project focused on care provided to injured military veterans by family members and government employees. Through the process of ethnographic research, these general domains of interest give way to more specific research questions. In fact, researchers frequently use ethnographic methods because they don't yet know how to frame good research questions; ethnography can be used to explore broadly and develop better, more nuanced questions.

When defining an ethnographic problem, most researchers rely either implicitly or explicitly on theory to help them decide which domains of social life they are interested in studying. Personal or informal theories about how the world works are often drawn from the ethnographer's understanding of his or her own everyday experiences. These informal theories can be useful, yet an ethnographer should expect that his or her experiences in the field will challenge cultural assumptions that often lie underneath informal theories. Formal theories are explicit explanations of the relations between domains of social life, often drawn from the work of other scholars. Sometimes researchers design their studies in ways intended to challenge or refine formal theories and to contribute to theory development. Others draw from formal theory in order to find out if it is applicable to a specific situation. When doing applied ethnography, scholars use theory both to help them understand the social phenomenon they are studying as well as to guide their thinking about programs or interventions that might benefit the people with whom they work. Because ethnography often involves an *iterative* process in which emerging evidence helps refine or reformulate theoretical ideas, ethnographers find it useful to be aware of a variety of formal and informal theories that can help them understand encounters in the field.

Feminist theories often direct ethnographers to ask questions about the contexts of women's lives, the ways that women experience and resist gender norms, and the ways in which difference is organized across lines of gender, race, class, and sexuality. For example, Emily Martin's *The Woman in the Body* (1987) is informed by feminist theories about how popular and medical discourse constructs gender and ideas about women's bodies. This ethnography shows how women both subscribe to and resist dominant medical discourses (created by male doctors) that alienate women's bodies by describing them as productive machines. In her ethnographic study of a women's self–defense course, Kristine De Welde (2003) framed the study using "feminist theories that focus on women's power and agency" and used a feminist lens to aid in final interpretation (p. 248). De Welde's feminist perspective influenced the way she designed the study at the outset and the way she interpreted her evidence at the end. For example, her feminist perspective allowed her to focus on interactions of gender and power and thus "examine how gender ideologies and resistance to them manifested in women's everyday lives" (p. 254). In doing so, De Welde recognized that women were socialized into gender narratives about femininity that had implications for their understandings of sexual coercion. These taken–for–granted understandings were necessarily challenged during the self–defense course, which resulted in subverting gender in the process.

While feminist research is no longer unusual within the academy, feminist areas of interest can be met with skepticism and resistance, particularly when studying seemingly mundane aspects of everyday life. For example, Frida Furman (1997), who was interested in learning about "meaning and experience of the female body for older—mostly Jewish—women in the context of a youth–loving, male–dominated society" (p. 5), studied a beauty salon where the customers were primarily older Jewish women.

Behind the Scenes With Frida Furman

Feminist Topics in a Patriarchal and Ageist Society

Furman wrote of her own initial concern about the study:

> I remember asking a friend, an academic also involved in feminist work, "Do you think it is serious enough?" I had evidently internalized mainstream values and was nervous about how such work would be perceived in the academy....I soon discovered that on the face of it, a study of a beauty salon populated by older Jewish women was not taken seriously by everyone; for some, it was a source of amusement. For example, when I answered my home phone one day, a male university colleague's first words were "Is this Frida Furman's beauty parlor?"...When I told a colleague in sociology about the study, he assured me, with a laugh, that he knew all about that generation of Jewish women; he was alluding to his mother. (Furman, 1997, p. 4)

Although feminist ethnographers may experience resistance regarding the legitimacy of their research, rather than be discouraged, they are likely to agree that such resistance indicates the importance and necessity of their research.

DEFINING THE FIELD

Once a general area of study is defined, an ethnographer must decide the community, institution, or setting in which she will investigate it. This is referred to as the *field*. The *field* is the natural setting of the people and processes the ethnographer is interested in learning about. *Fieldwork* can be done in an urban neighborhood, a rural village, a beauty parlor, a clothing store, a displaced persons camp, and so on. In *multi–sited ethnography*, the field is constructed by tracing how widespread processes or the circulation of objects connect people in a variety of places. For example, Jane Collins (2003) used a *multi–sited* approach to trace the links between women's participation in southern Virginia and Aguascalientes, Mexico, apparel factories. By examining the diverse ties that link working–class women, managers, and consumers across national borders, Collins was able to explore how the transnational economics of the apparel industry made it possible for firms to move their manufacturing anywhere in the world and thus weaken workers' abilities to demand improved working conditions or better pay.

Several criteria may influence an ethnographer's selection of the field, but the first criterion is to pick a field site in which you can successfully investigate your research interest or question. Given Furman's (1997) interest in women's experiences of aging in a culture that tends to worship youth, Furman chose a beauty parlor frequented by older women as her field site. Furman's choice of field site allowed her access to a large number of women experiencing aging, as well as to the stylists who serve these women. Moreover, because the beauty industry plays a substantial role in perpetuating the idealization of youth, conducting fieldwork in a beauty parlor enabled Furman to directly examine the ways older women and their stylists resist, perpetuate, or otherwise engage these ideals. When feminist ethnographer De Welde (2003) identified an interest in the "tradition of feminists who reconceptualize power and place women's agency and resistance at the forefront" (p. 249), she selected a dojo that specialized in women's self–defense courses at which to study. Conducting fieldwork in this dojo gave De Welde regular access to both students and instructors committed to women's physical empowerment, and thus she was able to learn more about the kinds of feminist (or other) ideological commitments and personal histories that motivated dojo participants.

Reinharz (1992) argues that feminist ethnography is "research carried out by feminists who focus on gender issues in female–homogeneous traditions or nontraditional settings, and in heterogeneous traditional and nontraditional settings" (p. 55). Selection of the field is often, but not always, part of a feminist approach to the ethnographic project. It is the focus on gender issues, rather than the gender–composition of a particular field site that distinguishes feminist research projects. Consider the differences between Marisa Corrado (2002) who studied a bridal shop and Montemurro (2005) who studied bridal showers. They both meet Reinharz's characterization of "female–homogeneous traditions" and settings. However, Corrado was interested in the way salespeople control their customers' behavior. She selected a bridal dress shop because it offered an "unfamiliar sales setting" and therefore a unique site in which to witness the interactions between customer and salesperson. Corrado specifically denied interest in the "gendered processes of buying and selling wedding dress[es]." Instead she examined the generic social processes at play. In contrast, Montemurro (2005) studied bridal showers specifically for the gendered nature of the ritual. Interested in the growing practice of men attending showers, she wanted to see whether it "is indicative of gender convergence or if couples showers replicate traditional gender roles" (p. 7).

Practical considerations also go into selecting a field site. Ethnographies require a great deal of time—frequently, years—to conduct. Thus, time and money are very practical issues that must be factored into field selection. Language skills must also be taken into consideration because ethnography relies on communication between the ethnographer and those he or she is studying. Distance and access to transportation are also important factors in choosing the field. So too are positionality and status, since feminist ethnographers pay keen attention to issues of power and exploitation (Nader, 1988; Spivak, 1988). It is critical that feminist ethnographers consider how their own identities—class, race, gender—will impact their evidence collection and influence how people interact with them.

Safety concerns, including that of both researcher and participant, are also critical concerns when choosing a field site. Sometimes, participation in a research project with an unknown outsider is dangerous. For example, researchers studying domestic abuse might inadvertently put an abused woman in greater danger if her abuser learned she was speaking frankly with a stranger. Because of their outsider status and habit of asking strange or intimate questions, ethnographers are frequently suspected of being undercover agents for law enforcement agencies. Research participants can then come under suspicion of collaborating, placing them at risk of violence and censure. Ethnographers must give the safety of those they work with the highest consideration when designing a research project, even if this limits fieldwork opportunities. For example, when conducting research on international nongovernmental organizations' (NGOs') environmental projects in Iraq from 2005 to 2007, Bridget Guarasci learned that her presence at the project sites might place project staff at risk of being violently targeted as collaborators with the United States. Instead, Guarasci conducted the majority of her fieldwork in Amman, Jordan, and in various sites in Europe, focusing on the experiences of NGO officials, project administrators, and affiliated scientists (Guarasci, 2011).

Feminist ethnographers must mind their own safety as well. Reinharz (1992) writes,

[M]uch feminist ethnographic writing includes a frank, reflexive discussion of these problems, particularly sexual harassment, physical danger, and sex stereotyping. In a society that is ageist, sexist, and heterosexist, the researcher who is female and young may be defined as a sex object to be seduced by heterosexual males. (p. 58)

Thus, the relative safety of the field site is a reasonable and important consideration. Considerations should include both the ethnographer's physical and mental well–being. Given the importance of ongoing and close relationships between ethnographers and those they study, and the fact that many ethnographers participate in the everyday lives and activities of those they study, ethnographic research may be mentally and emotionally challenging for researchers. Even seemingly safe settings can be unsafe at times. Ethnographers may choose to study refugee camps rather than war because it is safer to do so. Some study topics that put them in harm's way—such as drug cultures, gangs, prostitution, or disease epidemics. In evaluating field choices, it is important for ethnographers to consider if there are safer ways to study their questions or if danger is an inherent aspect of it (e.g., studying disease or war). In addition, ethnographers should think about what kinds of training or knowledge would help them remain safe in their field of choice, including back–up plans and ways to extricate themselves from the field if necessary.

In short, ethnographic researchers should select the field with care. Consider all the possible field sites where you could see intersections between your domains of interest, and then ask:

- Where can I successfully answer my research questions?
- Who am I? How might I be positioned by others while in the field?
- Where can I conduct my study safely?
- What personal risks am I willing to take?
- What privileges am I assuming when I think I can gain access to the field?

PRELIMINARY FIELDWORK AND GAINING ACCESS

Ethnographic research is *iterative* and does not proceed in a linear order. This iterative process begins with formulating a question and choosing the field, but it also continues throughout the collection of evidence and writing up. At the preliminary stages, the ethnographer focuses on finding out whether a field site is suitable and refines her research questions or changes the focus of study to better address the broader problems she is interested in. Thus, many ethnographers undertake an initial, comparatively brief period of preliminary fieldwork before making a final decision about a field site. Of course, the duration of preliminary fieldwork may depend on the ease of access.

Preliminary research conducted in local communities may be briefer than that needed to scout potential regions, towns, cities, or neighborhoods when doing research far from home.

Just because a certain field location looks perfect does not mean an ethnographer will automatically have access to it. The process of gaining access and building rapport with gatekeepers and potential research participants begins during the preliminary stage, but it often continues throughout fieldwork. Brooke Harrington (2003) draws distinctions among the concepts of access, entry, and rapport. She argued that "access" related to the "social scientific goals of ethnography," and specifically meant gaining *access to information*, while *entry* commonly referred to "the initial act of entering the field or gaining permission from participants to start a study" (p. 599). Finally, *rapport* referred to "the quality of the researcher–participant relationship itself and is often likened to friendship" (p. 599).

For example, Jennifer Lois (2001), who studied a mountain search–and–rescue team made up of volunteers, describes each of these ideas in her methodology section—although she does not use Harrington's terminology. Lois began the process of gaining access by volunteering with the search and rescue group herself. She attended "bi-weekly business meetings, weekly training sessions, social hours at the local bar and some missions" for several months before she even approached the board of directors about the possibility of conducting research (p. 136). She received permission to proceed, thus gaining initial *entry* into the field. Finally, she spent 5 1/2 years going on search and rescue missions with volunteers, building *rapport* with them over time. This rapport building continued to help deepen her *access to information*.

Yet, like every method of building rapport and gaining access, Lois's method of entry has substantial consequences for her research. By aligning herself early on with the board of directors of the search and rescue group, Lois's method holds the potential of limiting her access to the points of view from other members of the organization. However, in this case, Lois's extensive and long–term ethnographic participation as a member of the search and rescue team might well have mitigated against any initial entry bias. However, it's critical to remember that every avenue of gaining entry opens some possibilities for gaining access to information and closes others. Given the social and political realities of the chosen field site, ethnographers strive to make choices about gaining entry and access that will best enable them to address their research questions.

Ethnographers frequently refer to individuals who hold key positions either formally or informally within the environment and help facilitate their access to people and information as *gatekeepers*. They often serve a *gatekeeping* function that can help or hinder access to the setting. Furthermore, they can challenge a researcher to a public test as part of their way into the community.

Behind the Scenes With Alexandra Murphy

Gatekeeping and Access

Alexandra Murphy (2003) was tested by the manager of the strip club she was studying. She reports:

> During those initial visits, I felt uncomfortable, conspicuous, I felt like I had entered a male fantasy cliché: football played on a gigantic television screen adjacent to a main stage where a topless woman danced around a pole filled with bubbling water. My fourth visit marked a turning point in my research. At one point in the evening, Bob, the manager of the club, came over and told me to take a seat in a chair he had retrieved from a nearby table. In front of me was a blonde woman wearing a black Lycra bra and G-string bottoms and holding a tray full of shots in test tubes. "What do you want, sex on the beach?" Bob asked as I tried to figure out what was going on. "Sex on the beach is fine," I replied, still not knowing the full implications of that response. The woman took one of the liquid-filled test tubes off her tray and with her head tilted back lowered the test tube down her throat and back up again; then, with the end of the tube still in her mouth, she leaned over me putting the other end in my mouth, forcing the alcohol down my throat. Cheers rang out as I finished the shot. I was no longer watching the spectacle; I had become part of the show. Later, I realized the importance of that shot. If I had turned it down, I would have rejected the lifestyle of the organizational members I was trying to understand. After that evening, I had open access to the club. (p. 332)

Not only can gaining access be very time–consuming and cumbersome, it may not yield entry. Ethnographers may have to work very hard to establish trust among those they wish to study. For example, Buch (2010) struggled to figure out a way to gain access to the home care workers she studied, primarily because of the decentralized nature of this employment context and the hesitancy of home care agencies to allow a researcher to study their employees. One reason agencies were unwilling to allow Buch to study their workers was their concern that she would evaluate the workers, the care they provide, or the agencies' administrative practices negatively. Workers, who were mostly black and immigrant women earning near–poverty level wages, were often suspicious that Buch—who is white and middle class—would not respect them or their expertise. Buch was partly able to overcome these challenges by working with agencies whose managers believed both that their organization had nothing to hide and who believed that the research might help them identify areas for improvement. Of course, this meant that the agencies she worked with were notably different from others both in their interest in transparency and in making improvements. Buch asked the home attendants to treat her as a trainee, and she participated in any of the care tasks that the older adults were comfortable with her doing. By asserting that her position was subordinate to the workers, Buch was able to build greater rapport with them over time.

In order to ease access to the field, sometimes ethnographers rely on gatekeepers who seem to make access easier, such as friends, family, or other personal acquaintances. There are risks associated with this method of gaining access that are worth considering at the outset. While using a familiar insider may seem to save time and hassle, it can create other problems. It may be harder to access people with opposing points of view if the researcher is perceived by the community to be too closely allied with the gatekeeper. For example, Karen Staller (2002) attempted to conduct an ethnographic study of a police unit by relying on "permission" from a friend who was a sergeant in the unit. Police organizations, like military units or some businesses, are very hierarchal. In Staller's study, the beat officers were reluctant to cooperate with the research project because they feared consequences from the unit's lieutenant who ranked higher in the departmental pecking order than the sergeant who had first permitted access. Thus, working through a known gatekeeper who had apparent authority to grant access did not guarantee the ability to conduct the study as it was planned.

In keeping with feminist interest in how gender, race, and class shape power dynamics, the feminist ethnographer must always be aware of the power dynamics including formal and informal relationships between and among the people that she studies. Gaining entrance through one set of institutional players may preclude or impede gaining access to another set that may have different kinds of information, as was demonstrated in Staller's failure to win over the beat officers. Therefore, ethnographers typically give a great deal of thought to how to gain access because it will be directly related to the kind of evidence that they will be able to collect. Choosing access through one entry point may end up precluding or limiting access to other viewpoints. Furthermore, ethnographers typically stay on the lookout for both the formal and informal social relationships of the community or institution that they are studying. In short, be aware that the pathway utilized to get into the community can have a direct relationship on what information can be gathered during the course of fieldwork.

PRACTICAL CONSIDERATIONS

Before entering the field, there are a number of practical aspects to research that are important to consider. They may include attending to ethical concerns, obtaining research equipment, anticipating health needs, and, when conducting research abroad, obtaining necessary research visas and immunizations.

Regardless of field site location, ethnographers typically need to procure research ethics approval from an institutional review board (IRB). In addition, they might need to obtain ethics oversight/permission from a local sponsoring institution's IRB. These processes can be lengthy and complex; ethnographers are advised to allot ample time to complete the tasks. It is fairly uncommon that ethnographic projects proceed through the IRB process without revisions or clarifications. Some of this process can be stream-lined by consulting ahead of time with IRB staff. New ethnographers may find that it helps to discuss their project with others that have successfully navigated an ethno-graphic research project through their institution's IRB.

Although ethnography can be a fairly low-tech research method—and indeed a note-book and pen are perhaps the most important research equipment you'll need—most ethnographers supplement written field notes (see below) with photographs as well as voice or video recording. Procuring research equipment may be easy. Alternatively, it may take a considerable amount of time to weed through the myriad choices of digital cameras, voice recorders, video recorders, and other possible equipment. Ethnographers conducting interviews or observing formal interactions, will most certainly want either an audio recorder or video camera—which an individual ethnographer chooses typically depends on how important capturing body language, setting, and so forth is to her or his research question. In either case, ethnographers should choose peripheral micro-phones that will enable them to capture the best sound quality possible given the partic-ular conditions of the field site. Ethnographers conducting relatively short-term projects might consider asking to borrow needed equipment from the university. For lengthier projects, ethnographers typically need to invest in their own equipment (or look for grant money to cover some of these costs).

Many ethnographers depend a great deal on recording equipment to help them col-lect evidence, which must thus be both easy to use and reliable. Because this equipment creates one of the permanent records of fieldwork, the quality of recordings is critical. For example, ethnographers must be able to enter a variety of settings with diverse field conditions and be able to collect data spontaneously as they present themselves. This is a necessary step in data collection; but, in addition, how well data are captured also has implications for their analysis, their interpretation, and their reporting. The rigor of the entire study will be assessed relative to the strength of its methods and to how well the methods relate to the methodological approach. So while other methodological approaches might utilize tape recorders to capture data, the recorder and recordings may not be so integrally related to the overall methodology as in ethnography.

Many ethnographers need to carry multiple devices with them at the same time, as well as various chargers, spare batteries, microphones, notepads, and other materials. If fieldwork occurs mostly in a fixed location, having bulky equipment may not be a prob-lem; however, if fieldwork requires an ethnographer to move around a great deal, size and weight become greater concerns. Moreover, ethnographers need to consider how using/carrying particular equipment might impact their positions or relationships in the field. For example, Buch (2010) initially purchased an entry–level digital single lens reflex (SLR) camera to take photographs of home care workers, elders, and their neighborhoods. She quickly learned that although this camera took beautiful photographs, its strong resemblance to a professional camera intimidated her participants. Thus, it was impossible for her to capture candid images with this camera. Participants were substantially more relaxed when she used a less sophisticated point–and–shoot camera. Moreover, several participants warned Buch that if she walked their neighborhoods with the SLR camera visible, she would potentially make herself a target of crime.

Ethnographic research fosters deep engagements between researchers and participants. While these engagements are ethically and intellectually important, it is also critical to prepare for the possible impacts such engagements might have on a researcher's mental and emotional well–being. Ethnographic research often involves stepping out of your comfort zone to observe and participate in ways of life that are very different from your own. This can create (sometimes productive) psychological stress. For some ethnographers, this experience is disorienting and lonely. Even when surrounded by research participants, ethnographers often feel like outsiders and emotionally isolated. Ethnographers who conduct research in settings characterized by violence or suffering may struggle with not having the resources or ability to improve the situations they observe. Moreover, ethnographers cultivate empathy and often develop deep relationships with research participants, leaving them emotionally connected and vulnerable to their struggles. For these and other reasons, it seems that ethnographic research may render researchers somewhat more susceptible to mental health concerns than other forms of research. While each person reacts differently and each ethnographic setting makes different demands on ethnographers, it is important for ethnographers to attend to their mental well–being and seek help if needed.

It is also important to make preparations for any predictable physical health issues you may experience in the field. For example, when working in underdeveloped areas, ethnographers may need to prepare to provide themselves with clean drinking water. Ethnographers working with young children may find themselves susceptible to more minor infections and illnesses than they are accustomed to, and they need to anticipate this when preparing fieldwork schedules. Ethnographers working with vulnerable older adults or others with compromised immune systems may be unable to conduct fieldwork whenever they could spread an infection, no matter how mild. In other settings, ethnographers may want to prepare for possible contact with environmental irritants. For example, when conducting ethnographic research with hotel housekeepers, Buch quickly learned that some of the cleaning products gave her severe headaches. While she eventually limited her contact with particular solvents, this embodied experience also provided her with important ethnographic information about the bodily risks of this kind of work. This experience also provided an explanatory context for her observation that housekeepers seemed to experience a large number of unexplained health conditions ranging from severe rashes and headaches to immune conditions.

Working abroad necessitates a number of additional preparations. Procuring research visas, for some countries, can take many months. Ethnographers will also want to inquire about any vaccinations necessary for living in the intended field site, and obtain health and travel insurance. Researchers working abroad may also be required to affiliate with a local educational or research institution that will provide ethical oversight and, ideally, help make sure that research plans are viable and appropriate in the local cultural context.

Ethnography is a responsive form of research and the researcher needs to be able to adjust flexibly as his or her circumstances and knowledge of the field change. That said, advanced planning might make this flexibility easier to achieve.

Questions that must be asked before entering the field include:

- What pathway will I use to gain access?

- What are the benefits and risks of my choice of access?

- How will the methods I use to gain access affect the evidence I am able to collect?

- What resources and equipment do I need to successfully collect, record, and protect evidence?

- What is my back–up plan if things don't work the way I've planned or I find myself in an unsafe situation? What resources will be available to me?

How Do Ethnographers Collect Evidence?

Ethnographers typically use multiple strategies to collect evidence while in the field; and ethnography should be considered a research practice or approach, rather than a specific method. While ethnographers rely heavily on participant observation, they frequently also make use of informal and formal interviews as well as collect evidence in the form of social artifacts such as photographs, media, or other documents. In this section, we focus primarily on doing participant observation and additionally touch on some of the ways ethnographers incorporate document collection and interviews into their research. Any individual ethnographer's methods of collecting evidence will depend on his or her research questions and field site.

Most ethnographers use a rich combination of empirical evidence. For example, Corrado (2002) spent many hours observing bridal store salespersons interact with brides, fiancés, bridesmaids, mothers, and other members of the bridal party in one particular bridal shop. She conducted formal, semistructured interviews with the sales help; she traveled to five other bridal shops in the region as a client; and she used secondary resources such as bridal magazines, videotapes, and Internet bulletin board postings, which helped contribute to her understanding of people's experiences in bridal shops. Lois (2001) spent 5 1/2 years as a volunteer in the mountain rescue group she was studying, keeping detailed field notes of her experiences, as well as collecting thank–you notes from victims, and conducting in–depth interviews with rescue team members. In addition to extensive participant observations in a beauty shop serving older Jewish women, Furman (1997) used photo elicitation because she discovered "that asking women to reflect on their facial wrinkles and other marks of aging was too intrusive and intimidating" (p. 10). She asked them to select photographs of themselves from youth, middle age, and current periods and asked them to reflect on their appearance. She noted that "by treating the photograph as a kind of artifact, participants were able to gain some distance from it and to feel less self–conscious" (p. 10).

As these examples illustrate, researchers often modify their original plans as they come to learn more about people in their field site. Often ethnographers find themselves in unexpected places or gathering unexpected kinds of information as they recognize new connections and possibilities in their field site. It is important for ethnographers to think broadly and creatively about the ways they can obtain evidence, and what types of documents, observations, or interviews might be useful. Moreover, it is important for ethnographers to continuously reevaluate whether their planned approach is acceptable to those they are working with and is helping them better understand their ways of life.

In the following sections, we focus on aspects of evidence collection unique to ethnography (such as participant observation) but refer the reader for detailed descriptions of other aspects of the research process to other sources.

PARTICIPANT OBSERVATION AND FIELD NOTES

Ethnographers rely heavily on participant observation to collect evidence about social life. When doing so, the ethnographer actively engages in the everyday lives of those he or she studies while simultaneously observing the details about the social dynamics and patterns he or she encounters. Ethnographers are keen observers of social settings. They watch mundane, everyday activities as well as special events and rituals that have particular significance.

Ethnography, and participant observation in particular, is a deeply relational form of research, meaning that participant observation creates knowledge about social relations through social relationships. The relationships ethnographers develop with people in the field thus determine what kinds of things they are able to say and write about social life afterwards. For these reasons, it is essential that ethnographers consider their roles and relationships in the field both before and throughout the research process, adjusting research plans as participants help the ethnographer understand what they consider appropriate roles and possible relationships to be.

One measure of the variety of roles that an ethnographer can play involves the degree to which the researcher becomes involved in the day-to-day activities of those people and institutions under investigation. Sometimes these different *researcher roles* are described as complete observer, observer-as-participant, participant-as-observer, and complete participant (Hesse-Biber & Leavy, 2006, pp. 245-251). Note that this ranges from a complete, detached observer to a complete and fully integrated participant. Choices about how to balance participation versus observation are likely to be based partly on your research questions, partly on your theoretical position, and partly on what is possible in the field. No one balance of these roles will work equally well in all sites or to answer all questions.

Oftentimes the researcher's role will evolve as she becomes increasingly familiar with her field site and her informants become increasingly accepting of her. For example, Corrado's (2002) role changed with time. In her study of the bridal shop, she started out as a complete observer; however, as time passed and she came to know the social actors and the business, she began to help out as an "assistant" to the two women who ran the shop; performing tasks such as "fetching and restocking dresses the workers needed" (p. 38). In doing so, her role became more participatory in nature. Yet, Corrado never became a full-time employee of the shop and thus never reached a "complete participant" status.

Another role dimension to consider is whether the researcher is an *insider* or *outsider* of the community under investigation. Murphy (2003) chose not to become a stripper herself in her study of the strip club, thus remaining an outsider. Alternatively, Lois (2001) was an insider and played an active role in the respective community. Often, these choices regarding how much of an insider to become can have complicated ethical, legal, or moral aspects. For example, if you want to study homeless women, must you become homeless yourself? If you are studying low-income workers who travel to work on public transportation, must you forsake the use of your car? If you are studying drug use, must you experiment with the drugs yourself? Of course, making these decisions has a direct impact on the evidence an ethnographer can collect and thus requires careful and thoughtful balancing of alternatives.

Another dimension to consider has to do with attributes that the community may ascribe to the researcher. So while the ethnographer may enter the field with a general idea of the role he or she would like to play in the community he or she studies, members of the community may end up defining it themselves. It is likely that community members will expect that female researchers act similarly to other women in the community (and that male researchers' behavior will conform to local expectations of men). As discussed above, it is fairly common that single women doing ethnographic fieldwork are approached as possible partners for marriage, dating, or sexual activity. The decision to accept or reject the roles can have a significant effect on the kind of access the ethnographer will have in the community. Moreover, conscious attention should be paid to the processes involved when a community places the ethnographer in particular social roles, for they can illuminate a great deal about gender and other roles associated with life in the community.

A number of very important and often difficult ethical questions can be encountered while in (and after leaving) the field. One involves the level of intervention or assistance an ethnographer is willing to provide. For example, if the people the ethnographer is studying use public transportation daily to get to work, should the ethnographer offer to give them a ride in her car on a cold, snowy day? What if they ask for a ride? This seemingly innocent intervention changes the environment and experiences of those the ethnographer is studying. What if the ethnographer witnesses an act of violence, such as domestic violence, elder abuse, or child abuse? Or what if the ethnographer is studying a teenage gang that plans to engage in criminal activity? As a researcher and feminist, should the ethnographer intervene by calling the police, reporting the case to child welfare authorities, taking the victim to a shelter, or warning potential victims? It is important to be aware of the legal, ethical, and research implications of the answers to these questions. For example, if an ethnographer chooses to give a person he or she is working with a ride, the ethnographer changes the experience she or he is studying. But is it changed in significant or important ways? If an ethnographer witnesses some form of abuse, he or she may have to balance confidentiality agreements, legal reporting requirements (which may apply to health, education, and social work researchers, among others), and his or her own ethical stance.

Another significant ethical dilemma can arise from the personal relationships that develop during the period of fieldwork. Oftentimes, the people an ethnographer is "studying" forget that the ethnographer is "researching" them. Since the ethnographer is in the field for long periods of time and will continually meet new people in new situations, he or she will have an ongoing responsibility of introducing him- or herself and the project to those being studied. How often should he or she remind them?

Ethnographers rarely rely exclusively on information from single individuals; nonetheless, key informants can be critical. They may act as guides and interpreters and help you make contact with individuals you might not otherwise have access to. Key informants may be individuals who have special knowledge or long–term experience. As such, they may be particularly eager to participate in a research project; however, these individuals may also have a political or personal stake in the research that motivates their participation. Indeed, it is common that nearly everyone who participates in ethnographic research projects has some opinion about the research. When using key informants who have obvious biases, it's worth taking note of the ways in which this informant's perspective and relationships may be directing your research and attempt to encourage participation from those with different points of view.

Many feminist ethnographers consider it critical to account for the ways relationships with key informants may impact their analysis later on. Feminist ethnographers typically also play close attention to their own positionality, which means keeping a written record of how their own backgrounds, identities, and opinions may be influencing how people relate to them and what they are willing to share, as well as how the ethnographer's own emotional reactions and opinions change over the course of fieldwork. Many feminists argue that all knowledge reflects particular social positions, and this kind of evidence can be used during analysis and write–up to contextualize your research as a product of the changing positionality of both yourself and those you are studying.

While the primary empirical evidence used by ethnographers is obtained by talking with and observing people, it is important that this evidence is systematically and thoroughly collected and preserved. Thus ethnographers rely on *field notes* in order to preserve their day–to–day observations. Field notes must be recorded as soon after the experience as possible; events must be fresh in the ethnographer's mind. This is particularly true because ethnographic analysis and writing depend on vivid and detailed descriptions of everyday life that are likely to be forgotten if not immediately recorded.

Field notes are often written as a two–part process. While in the field, many ethnographers write *jottings* in a pocket–sized notebook or on scrap paper to help them remember unique turns of phrase or interactions that they will further elaborate on in field notes written up later. Jottings help the ethnographer capture the immediacy of field experiences in an accurate manner. Often the significance of a particular conversation or event may not be evident at the time it occurs. It is only during the process of reviewing the entire field experience that its relevance becomes apparent. Thus, field notes serve as a comprehensive, chronological log of the ethnographer's perceptions of everything that has happened in the field. They can be extremely tedious to write, and sometimes what to focus on is not apparent. Ethnographers frequently spend a long day in the field, only to have to spend equally long hours at night writing down what happened.

Field notes may be descriptive as well as analytical. The field notes might record what the ethnographer observed (who was there, what they were wearing, what happened) but they may also include interpretations, hypotheses, or speculations about what was happening. The ethnographer may begin to record tentative interpretations (perhaps beginning hypotheses) after a day in the field, but these may change over time. In this way, the process of ethnographic analysis begins immediately and is ongoing. Furthermore, good ethnographers will continue to challenge their own interpretations as they spend more time in the field.

Behind the Scenes With Alexandra Murphy

Field Notes

Murphy (2003) reports the following observations in her field notes of a strip club:

A football game on a big-screen TV silhouettes a half-nude woman dancing for a row of cheering men. Waitresses wander through the club in white lace G-string lingerie. One asks what I want to drink. Her name is Ilona, and she speaks with a soft Spanish accent. $4.50 for a Miller Lite! "PUT THE GREENERY ON THE SCENERY," I hear an amplified voice ring out over the sound of Madonna singing, "Like a Virgin." "COME ON GENTLEMEN, THESE WOMEN DON'T GET A SALARY FROM THIS ESTABLISHMENT. THEY RELY ON GENEROUS TIPS FROM YOU!" Though stimulated by vision, the customers are controlled by sound. A dancer performs a table dance for the man next to me. He is alone. She is called the "Polynesian Queen." In this dark room full of smoke, he can pretend to be her king. Her breasts appear too round. Are they real? He doesn't seem to care. He watches her body move to the beat as Janet Jackson sings "Nasty Girl." She leans forward and presses perfectly round breasts together—in his face. She bends down—her head in his lap. Her hair hides what she is not doing—mock fellatio. She turns around. With her back to the patron, she bends over again. This time I see her face. She looks disinterested. He looks impressed. I'm impressed with her ability to walk in four-inch heels. Music pounds so loudly it vibrates my chair. "Welcome to Paper Dolls," a sign out front declares. "The Hottest Show on Earth." (p. 306)

In writing these notes Murphy creates a rich description of what she observed. We get a sense of the sights and sounds of the place. Note that she records factual observations, such as the price of a can of Miller Lite; but by using the exclamation point, she also records her interpretation, opinion, and responses to this pricing. Note how she adds to her interpretation that patrons are "stimulated by vision" but "controlled by sound" and reproduces the sound control in capital letters in her field notes. Also notice how she offers an interpretation of how three different individuals are responding in the moment, writing that the dancer "looks disinterested" and the patron "impressed," and her own passing thought about the skill it takes to walk in "four–inch heels."

Ethnographers also use field notes to reflect on their own position in the field. This might include describing and creating preliminary analyses about how they gained access or built rapport. Field notes might also record the roles the ethnographer has been given or chosen in the field, and the ways that this seems to be influencing what kinds of interactions she is able to observe and participate in. This kind of reflection about the ethnographer's own power, position, and influence in the field is known as *reflexivity*. So, for example, in Furman's (1997) study of older women and beauty shop culture, she records the following in her field notes:

> What is so safe there? Is it something about the shop culture that reminds me of my childhood in its more positive moments—time with grandmothers, aunts? What is so comforting and satisfying about talking about coat sales? Or exchanging, in a somewhat competitive mood, our latest physical maladies? There is something very affirming there. It is as if one feels nurtured without having to do anything in exchange, save nurture others, which comes naturally and is self–confirming, too. Why does the concern expressed feel so warming? (p. 1)

Note that Furman uses reflexivity to relate the way she feels in the field to her own childhood experiences. In this way, she is attempting to make sense of her field experiences. However, she is also posing important questions for herself—such as "Why does the concern expressed feel so warming?"—which will drive her study forward. She will continue to seek answers to this question and therefore a better understanding of the culture in which she is immersed.

Perhaps the most important thing to remember about participant observation is that it is an active, not passive, process. The ethnographer must always be watchful and mindful of what is going on. She or he must continually observe with a critical and analytical eye, even while participating in everyday social life. He or she needs to actively remember or make jottings of conversations while in the field. There is a continual back–and–forth process of participating and observing that must be maintained. Ethnography requires a very special kind of "being there."

INTERVIEWS (FORMAL AND INFORMAL)

Ethnographers often use formal or informal interviews with research participants in conjunction with participant observation to gather information about social life. Interviews allow ethnographers to explore participants' explicit understandings and compare these with their observations of behavior.

Formal interviews are interviews that have been planned ahead and occur outside the normal course of social interaction. Other chapters in this book offer techniques for conducting formal interviews. Informal interviews may take place during the course of participant observation when the researcher asks participants to discuss their perspectives on ongoing activities. Informal interviews can occur in the course of normal conversation, but they differ from it because the researcher is largely directing the discussion and asking explicit questions of participants. It is important that ethnographers note when they are conducting this kind of questioning and note that the answers to these questions occurred as a direct response to their questions, rather than arising naturally. Because informal interviews can occur spontaneously, you may not be able to use recording devices to create an audio or video record of the interview, and thus it is essential that you take careful notes documenting both the questions you asked and the answers you received for later use.

Feminist ethnographers may find that they are interested in using participatory interview methods to collect ethnographic evidence. These might include asking participants to conduct their own interviews, interview one another, or asking participants to work collaboratively to design interview schedules with you. For example, in her study of the communicative practices of girls in inner city Naples, Heather Loyd conducted *radio workshops,* in which the young girls she was studying used an audio recorder to interview each other. This method gave the girls agency to set the frame of the interviews and the power to interview whomever they wanted, yielding insights into culturally significant issues that they found relevant (Loyd, 2012). Note that when using participatory methods of collecting evidence, ethnographers typically observe and write field notes both about the evidence that participants collect and the social processes involved in that collection. This method is laid out in greater detail by Tobias Hecht (1998).

COLLECTING SOCIAL ARTIFACTS AND TAKING PHOTOGRAPHS

Feminist ethnographers may collect a variety of social artifacts from their field sites to supplement observations. Social artifacts could range from collecting newspaper articles, marketing materials, pamphlets, or policy documents to collecting recipes, items of clothing, or empty food containers. What each ethnographer collects will depend to some degree on her research interests. For example, a researcher interested in studying baby showers to examine the role of babies' sex during pregnancy and infancy might collect shower invitations, copies of gift registries, store advertisements, and local magazine or newspaper articles about baby showers in addition to attending baby showers and interviewing shower participants. Artifacts may be the physical material created through the social processes being studied (e.g., shower invitations, gift registries), which the researcher could analyze for patterns in the kinds of images, colors, products and words that are used depending on the racial, ethnic, or class background of the family. Artifacts might also include items that structure the processes being studied (e.g., store advertisements, magazine articles with advice for throwing showers) that can be analyzed to understand how powerful institutions like governments, corporations, and media outlets that produce these artifacts shape social life.

Ethnographers also use photography (both still and video) to collect evidence about social artifacts that cannot be easily removed. For example, extending the baby shower study, the ethnographer might also take photographs of store windows or displays, or record television advertisements. The ethnographer might also take photographs of the shower gifts both wrapped and unwrapped. Ethnographers also frequently take photographs of the people they study and important places (such as homes, parks, communal spaces). While these photographs serve as evidence in their own right (e.g., documenting what people were wearing, their expressions), they can also be important illustrations to supplement written ethnographies. However, any analysis of photographs should account for how people changed their demeanor when they know a photograph was being taken. Of course, researchers taking photographs of people are required to secure their permission (and publishing such photographs may require written permission).

Feminist ethnographers may also be interested in incorporating participatory methods of collecting social artifacts and photographs. Ethnographers might ask research participants to help determine what kinds of artifacts are important for understanding a particular social event or process, or ask participants to collect artifacts from their homes and daily lives. This can be beneficial because it offers ethnographers the opportunity to analyze how participants are conceptualizing the event or process being studied and to elicit an explicit discussion from participants about the meaning and value of the selected items. One example of participatory methods is Photovoice, in which researchers offer participants training in photography, ask them to take photographs of their lives and communities, and then use these photographs to facilitate ongoing discussion and analysis (Hergenrather, Rhodes, Coward, Bardhoshi, & Pula, 2009; Wang & Burris, 1997).

How Do Ethnographers Turn Evidence Into Feminist Ethnography?

ANALYSIS

Analysis of ethnographic evidence starts immediately on collection and is iterative. Good ethnographers start to ask questions to themselves about what they are seeing and experiencing, thus beginning the *interpretive process*. However, at some point all ethnographers are faced with the nearly overwhelming prospect of returning to all their data (which can include years of chronological jottings and field notes, thousands of pages of interview transcripts, and collections of artifacts including documents, photographs, etc.) and somehow make sense of it all. This part of the ethnographic process is both interpretive and analytical. Ethnographic analysis techniques are sometimes borrowed from, or at least shared with, other methodological discussions. For example, some use grounded theory (Charmaz, 2003; Glaser & Strauss, 1967), others narrative analysis (Bruner, 2003; Garro & Mattingly, 2000; Labov & Waletzky, 1967), and many a more generic thematic approach. So, for example, De Welde (2003), who studied narratives and self–defense using a feminist lens, first needed to decipher the dominant stereotypical social scripts around femininity and victimizations. Next, she could analyze how women who participated in a self–defense course ended up subverting and resisting these dominant narrative scripts through a three–step process that resulted in the women "reframing victimization," "liberating the self" (by incorporating a defender narrative), and finally "enabling the body." Thus, during her analysis, De Welde was able to analyze her data in ways that revealed patterns in narrative construction that resisted and replaced the dominant social scripts by comparing and contrasting them.

Ethnographers will frequently compare and contrast ideas during their analyses in order to establish how different behaviors, ideas, and social structures are related to one another. Feminist analysis in ethnography often involves sustained attention to the ways that difference, power, and privilege are organized through sex and/or gender. In analyzing their evidence, ethnographers also work to *contextualize* incidents and experiences, meaning that ethnographic analysis attends to the ways in which observations from the field might be connected to broader social and political trends. Feminist ethnographers often pay attention to the ways that social and political contexts contribute to or are influenced by gendered differences and other kinds of discrimination.

There is some folklore among anthropologists about sorting ethnographic evidence by using index cards with holes punched to represent topical or theoretical codes, which were then grouped by pulling a knitting needle through the holes. More recently, these low–tech physical approaches have been supplemented (and in some cases supplanted) by electronic versions of coding and sorting offered by computer software programs. Computers can be a great help in maintaining, organizing, and sorting large amounts of evidence. However, it is critical to remember that unlike quantitative software analysis (in which the researcher essentially feeds in numerical data, asks the software to perform a mathematical function, and then interprets the results), no such mechanical step exists in the process of qualitative analysis. Thus, ethnographic researchers who use qualitative software must be constantly interacting with their evidence and interpretations. So, for example, the qualitative researcher who is coding his or her text using qualitative software must make a decision about where to place an electronic marker that begins and ends a segment of text encompassed by that code. Yet, because computer software analysis often rests on the proximal relationships of coded text (i.e., Do codes overlap? Do codes always or never appear together? Are they near to each other?), the researcher's judgment about where to place the initial code boundaries is directly related to the results that the computer program will generate about their relative relationships. The qualitative researcher must necessarily engage in further interpretive analysis of the meaning to be made of these proximal findings. Of course, in the end, the results of quantitative analysis must also be interpreted. However, when using quantitative software, interpreting the statistical result is often aided by reference to an external objective cutoff point or probability standard.

As ethnographers work, and rework, their way through the evidence, they often find their research questions becoming more focused, more concrete, more complicated, and often more interesting. It is hoped that the ideas that emerge from ethnographic field-work more closely reflect the experiences and understandings of the people studied, rather than the *a priori* beliefs of the ethnographer. Some argue that one purpose of ethnographic studies is not only to answer some questions the researcher had in mind at the outset but also to learn enough to ask better, more sophisticated, and more nuanced questions at the end.

Reinharz (1992) argued that

> a feminist perspective on data analysis includes many components such as understanding women in their social contexts and using women's language and behavior to understand the relation between self and context. It includes the problem of finding a way not to omit any person's voice while still having a manuscript of manageable length. It includes the use of feminist theory to analyze data. (p. 71)

In short, one of the big projects during analysis is to move from having piles and piles of chronological data, individual people, and events to reorganize it in a way that is topical, thematic, and interpretive. This also involves the often painful process of data reduction, which necessitates taking complicated, rich, and contextual information and reducing it to smaller sets of ideas that can be reported to an audience. Buch (2010) refers to this deci-sion–making process as choosing "which thread she will pull" in order to report her study after she has first been confronted with an entire interwoven tapestry of ideas. There are always many threads from which to choose. So ethnographers, like all other researchers, face decisions about which stories get told. Feminist ethnographers often choose which stories to tell in ways that reflect their feminist theoretical and ethical positions.

WRITING UP

As with any research project, the goal of a feminist ethnographer is to write up an interesting and accurate (although what constitutes accuracy is contested) narrative report about what the researcher discovered. Feminist ethnographers may be particu-larly concerned that their written report leads to social change that decreases gender inequality and/or improves the lives of research participants. Ethnographers pride them-selves on providing *thick descriptions* of social life, which include rich contextual detail along with clear analysis (Geertz, 1972). This is easier said than done. Ethnographers may consider such questions as the following:

- How do I tell a readable and accurate story?
- How should I represent the voices and the perspectives of the people I study?
- What are the ethical and political implications of telling the story the way that I do?

- How much control should the community have over the final interpretation?

- How much control should I have over the final interpretation?

These questions are fundamentally about how the ethnographer goes about *representing* her participants and their communities.

Feminist ethnographers have particularly struggled over methods of representing the people they study in ways that seek to balance the visions of the author with the visions of those they study. In this vein, feminist ethnographers have pioneered several alternative methods of writing ethnographies, some of which more closely approach humanistic writing (e.g., poetry, novel, biography) than traditional scientific reporting. These kinds of ethnographies emphasize the subjective and intersubjective aspects of human experience and attempt to capture it by using emotive and personal language rather than detached or analytical prose. Nevertheless, such forms of ethnography share with others the goal of portraying the rich and varied experiences of people in their social contexts.

Even when the communities studied are familiar, ethnographies often present and analyze aspects of community life that challenge common sense ideas about these people and places. Of course, the best way of learning about "writing up" ethnographic research is to read some of the wonderful studies that women have produced both historically and currently.

Feminist Ethics and Ethnographic Representation

Feminist ethnography requires attention to ethical approaches both in collecting evidence and in reporting results. There is a plethora of ethical questions that arise at every stage of the ethnographic research project. Frequently, these dilemmas are not well addressed by the university IRBs, which usually frame ethical issues within other kinds of research paradigms. Resolving ethical dilemmas in research can be particularly challenging, especially when feminist researchers consider the relative positions of power and authority between themselves and those they study. Daphne Patai (1991) writes that if the idea of feminism is to have any meaning,

it must involve a critique of traditional concepts and structures that have marginalized women materially and psychologically, in the world and even in their own souls. . . . Because feminism has challenged the pose of neutrality and objectivity that for so long governed positivist social science, it has forced us to scrutinize our own practice as scholars. . . . Is it possible—not in theory but in the actual conditions of the real world today—to write about the oppressed without becoming one of the oppressors? (p. 138)

Patai further argues that feminists often make the mistake of imagining that simple participation in the discourse of feminism protects them from the possibility of exploiting other women even when their research practices are predicated on privilege. Regardless of your feminist positions, it is essential that you consider how dynamics of power, including hierarchies of class, race, education, and access will affect the lives of those you study.

Given the fact that ethnographers spend so much time with the people they work with in the field, most want and feel obligated to continue important relationships from the field for many years. It is critical to be aware of how the research you write and publish might affect both the people you worked with and the possibility of working with them in the future. Given the complexity of ethnographic work and the variety of participants, it may be impossible to write up a single narrative that will satisfy everyone. Some ethnographers have been surprised by the response that they encountered when they returned to the communities in which they had spent a great deal of time (Ellis, 1995; Scheper–Hughes, 2000). Even the most well–intentioned ethnographers sometimes describe communities or people in ways that those they write about find unfair or hurtful, often for reasons the ethnographer did not anticipate. At other times, the ethnographer may find herself intentionally critiquing practices of dominance, discrimination, or coercion in the community. Each ethnographer must make her own decision about publishing potentially hurtful or embarrassing analyses of the community she studies. Many ethnographers emphasize the importance of obligation and responsibility in deciding what to publicize. Such ethnographers argue that their ability to do research depended (and in the future depends) on the voluntary contributions and participation of those being studied. Without them, these ethnographers acknowledge, we would have nothing to write about.

Most ethnographers agree that it is important not to publicize material that would put those they work with at risk of violence, economic hardship, or severe emotional trauma. Many ethnographers also share their findings with the community they study before they publish any writing to get feedback from the community, both about the accuracy of their portrayal and about the potential risks involved for community members if the work is published. Regardless of how you choose to negotiate the many ethical challenges of ethnographic fieldwork, it is important to be aware that what you do in the field and write about it afterwards can have serious consequences for your research and those with whom you work in the field.

CONCLUSION

Ethnography is a flexible, iterative method that enables researchers to gain a nuanced, contextualized understanding of the everyday social lives and relationships of those they study. Feminist researchers have found ethnographic methods particularly attractive due to the central role that relationships play in creating ethnographic knowledge. This emphasis enables feminist researchers to examine the dynamic interactions of gender and other forms of social difference, power and privilege as they occur in the ebb and flow of daily life. Ethnographic research can stand on its own but is also well suited to mixed method studies, as it enables researchers to refine research questions for future studies and to contextualize the findings of previous work. Ethnography is also particularly adaptable to studying cultural environments being created by the Internet as it opens up new frontiers of virtual place and space filled with social interactions.

Conducting feminist ethnographic research, however, is no simple task. Ethnography is extremely time–consuming and requires careful practical, intellectual, ethical, and emotional preparation. Ethnography is an iterative method, in which researchers are continually re–evaluating both research questions and strategies in light of their experiences in the field. At each stage of the research—choosing a field site, negotiating access, building rapport, conducting participant observation, analysis, and write–up—feminist researchers must continually reexamine their own positionality as well as emerging ethical issues in order to ensure that both the process and product reflect their feminist ethics and theories. Nonetheless, excellent feminist ethnographic research will undoubtedly continue to keep issues of relationship, gender, and power central to discussions of knowledge development and dissemination even as the social and political conditions of women continue to evolve.

DISCUSSION QUESTIONS

1. Assume you would like to study the spirit of sisterhood as it is expressed in hospital settings. Consider the advantages and disadvantages of gaining access to the hospital through a male administrator, a female doctor, a male nurse, and a female social worker. How would it influence the evidence you would be able to collect? How might you predict it would change access to information? If you switched the genders of the gatekeeper, would it matter?

2. Suppose you are conducting an ethnography of gendered play behavior on school playgrounds and you witness some children bullying a youngster. Do you intervene? If so, how? What would be the consequence of that intervention to your study?

3. Visit a local automobile repair shop or showroom. Take field notes of the experience, paying particular attention to the gender and other characteristics of the customers and salespeople. How might you begin to make sense of your observations?

4. Suppose you are interested in studying power, sexuality, morality, and femininity. What field site might you select in order to begin asking questions about these large domains of interest? How would the different possible sites influence the more specific research questions you would ask?

WEB RESOURCES

- *Mediated Cultures* is the website for Michael Wesch's digital ethnography project at Kansas State University: www.mediatedcultures.net

- *Photoethnography* is a website run by Karen Nakamura at Yale University that focuses on the art and science of analyzing and representing other cultures visually: www .photoethnography.com

- *Savage Minds* is a collective weblog dedicated to connecting the public to recent developments in anthropology. Savage Minds frequently covers fieldwork, research ethics, and related topics: www.savageminds.com

JOURNAL RESOURCES

- *Ethnography* is a journal focused on innovations in the theory and practice of ethnographic research: eth.sagepub.com

- *Field Methods* publishes articles focused on practical issues and methodological advances in ethnographic methods: fmx.sagepub.com

- *Journal of Contemporary Ethnography* is an interdisciplinary journal publishing research using ethnographic methods: jce.sagepub.com

- *Signs: Journal of Women in Culture and Society* is an interdisciplinary journal publishing innovative research concerning men's and women's lives across the globe: www .signs.rutgers.edu

REFERENCES

Behar, R. (2003). *Translated woman: Crossing the border with Esperanza's story* (10th anniv. ed.). Boston, MA: Beacon Press.

Boellstorff, T. (2010). *Coming of age in second life: An anthropologist explores the virtually human.* Princeton, NJ: Princeton University Press.

Bourdieu, P. (1990). *The logic of practice.* Cambridge, England: Polity Press.

Bruner, J. (2003). The narrative construction of reality. In M. Mateas & P. Sengers (Eds.), *Narrative intelligence* (pp. 41–62). Amsterdam, Netherlands: John Benjamins.

Buch, E. (2010). *Making care work: Sustaining personhood and reproducing inequality in home care of older adults in Chicago, IL* (Unpublished doctoral dissertation). University of Michigan, Ann Arbor.

Cahill, C. (2007). Negotiating grit and glamour: Young women of color and the gentrification of the Lower East Side. *City & Society, 19*(2), 202–231.

Charmaz, K. (2003). Qualitative interviewing and grounded theory analysis. In J. A. Holstein & J. Gubrium (Eds.), *Inside interviewing: New lenses, new concerns* (pp. 311–331). Thousand Oaks, CA: Sage.

Collins, J. L. (2003). *Threads: Gender, labor, and power in the global apparel industry.* Chicago, IL: University of Chicago Press.

Corrado, M. (2002). Teaching wedding rituals: How bridal workers negotiate control over their customers. *Journal of Contemporary Ethnography, 31,* 33–67.

De Welde, K. (2003). Getting physical: Subverting gender through self-defense. *Journal of Contemporary Ethnography, 32,* 247–278.

Ellis, C. (1995). Emotional and ethical quagmires in returning to the field. *Journal of Contemporary Ethnography, 24,* 68–98.

Furman, F. K. (1997). *Facing the mirror: Older women and beauty shop culture.* New York, NY: Routledge.

Garro, L. C., & Mattingly, C. (2000). Narrative as construct and construction. In C. Mattingly & L. Garro (Eds.), *Narrative and the cultural construction of illness and healing* (pp. 1–49). Berkeley: University of California Press.

Geertz, C. (1972). *The interpretation of cultures.* New York, NY: Basic Books.

Glaser, B. G., & Strauss, A. (1967). *The discovery of grounded theory: Strategies for qualitative research.* New York, NY: Aldine.

Guarasci, B. (2011). *Reconstructing life: Environment, expertise and political power in Iraq's marshes 2003–2007* (Unpublished doctoral dissertation). University of Michigan, Ann Arbor.

Harrington, B. (2003). The social psychology of access in ethnographic research. *Journal of Contemporary Ethnography, 32,* 592–625.

Hecht, T. (1998). *At home in the street.* Cambridge, England: Cambridge University Press.

Hergenrather, K. C., Rhodes, S. D., Coward, C. A., Bardhoshi, G., & Pula, S. (2009). Photovoice as community-based participatory research: A qualitative review. *American Journal of Health Behavior, 33,* 686–698.

Hesse-Biber, S., & Leavy, P. (2006). *The practice of qualitative research.* Thousand Oaks, CA: Sage.

Labov, W., & Waletzky, J. (1967). Narrative analysis: Oral versions of personal experience. In C. B. Paulston & G. R. Tucker (Eds.), *Sociolinguistics: The essential readings* (pp. 74–104). Oxford, England: Blackwell.

Lamphere, L. (1995). Feminist anthropology: The legacy of Elsie Clews Parsons. In R. Behar & D. A. Gordon (Eds.), *Women writing culture* (pp. 85–103). Berkeley: University of California Press.

Lewin, E. (Ed.). (2006). *Feminist anthropology: A reader.* Oxford, England: Blackwell.

Lois, J. (2001). Managing emotions, intimacy and relationships in a volunteer search and rescue group. *Journal of Contemporary Ethnography, 30,* 131–179.

Loyd, H. (2012). *Growing up fast: The rhetoric of resilience among inner city Neapolitan girls* (Unpublished doctoral dissertation). University of California, Los Angeles.

Mark, J. (1988). *A stranger in her native land: Alice Fletcher and the American Indians.* Lincoln: University of Nebraska Press.

Martin, E. (1987). *The woman in the body: A cultural analysis of reproduction.* Boston, MA: Beacon Press.

Martineau, H. (1838). *How to observe morals and manners.* London, England: Charles Knight.

Montemurro, B. (2005). Add men, don't stir: Reproducing traditional gender roles in modern wedding showers. *Journal of Contemporary Ethnography, 34,* 6–35.

Murphy, A. (2003). The dialectical gaze: Exploring the Subject–object tension in the performances of women who strip. *Journal of Contemporary Ethnography, 32,* 305–335.

Nader, L. (1988). Up the anthropologist—Perspectives gained from studying up. In J. B. Cale (Ed.), *Anthropology for the nineties* (pp. 470–485). New York, NY: Free Press.

Ortner, S. B. (1995). Resistance and the problem of ethnographic refusal. *Comparative Studies in Society and History, 37,* 173–193.

Ortner, S. B. (1996). *Making gender.* Boston, MA: Beacon Press.

Pascoe, C. J. (2011). *Dude, you're a fag: Masculinity and sexuality in high school.* Berkeley: University of California Press.

Patai, D. (1991). U.S. academics and third world women: Is ethical research possible? In S. B. Gluck & D. Patai (Eds.), *Women's words: The feminist practice of oral history* (pp. 137–153). New York, NY: Routledge.

Reinharz, S. (1992). *Feminist methods in social research.* Oxford, England: Oxford University Press.

Richards, A. I. (1982). *Chisungu: A girl's initiation ceremony among the Bemba of Zambia.* New York, NY: Tavistock. (Original work published 1956)

Richards, A. I. (1995). *Land, labour and diet in Northern Rhodesia: An economic study of the Bemba Tribe* (2nd ed.). Munster–Hamburg, Germany: LIT Verlag, with the International and African Institute. (Original work published 1939)

Scheper–Hughes, N. (2000). Ire in Ireland. *Ethnography, 1,* 117–140.

Spivak, G. C. (1988). Can the subaltern speak? In C. Nelson & L. Grossbert (Eds.), *Marxism and the interpretation of Marxism* (pp. 271–316). Basingstoke, England: Macmillan Education.

Stacey, J. (1991). Can there be a feminist ethnography? In S. B. Gluck & D. Patai (Eds.), *Women's words: The feminist practice of oral history* (pp. 111–120). New York, NY: Routledge.

Staller, K. (2002). Working the scam: Policing urban street youth. *Qualitative Inquiry, 8,* 550–574.

Stocking, G. W., Jr. (1983). Fieldwork in British anthropology. In G. W. Stocking, Jr. (Ed.), *Observers observed* (pp. 70–120). Madison: University of Wisconsin Press.

Teman, E. (2010). *Birthing a mother: The surrogate body and the pregnant self.* Berkeley: University of California Press.

Trotter, R., & Schensul, J. (2000). Methods in applied anthropology. In H. R. Bernard (Ed.), *Handbook of methods in cultural anthropology* (pp. 691–735). New York, NY: AltaMira Press.

Wang, C., & Burris, M. A. (1997). Photovoice: Concept, methodology and use for participatory needs assessment. *Health Behavior and Health Education, 24,* 369–387.

Wesch, M. (2008). An anthropological introduction to YouTube. You Tube.

CHAPTER 6

Feminist Practice of Action and Community Research

M. Brinton Lykes and Alison Crosby

We [Mayan] women... who have endured *la violencia* [36-year armed conflict] are remembering, through means of the PhotoVoice project, what we have seen or experienced and we are establishing a memory of it. This is very important because there are many young people who are growing up now who did not see this suffering and, because they didn't live through it they doubt that it happened. In contrast, people like us, who lived and suffered in our own flesh, remember it very well. And so, interviewing the people who suffered through it and who saw their family members die offers a sort of relief for them, because they recount what happened to another person. You think or feel that in sharing that person is asking, hoping, that this violence, this war, never again return.

This PhotoVoice project is our search for... support so that this violence and the massacres that took place never happen again. That is why this project is so very important for us. (Women of PhotoVoice/ADMI & Lykes, 2000, p. 103)

As feminist participatory action researchers currently employed by universities in two countries of the global north (the United States and Canada), we have worked much of our professional lives among communities of the global south or majority world, and in particular with Mayan communities in rural Guatemala (Blacklock & Crosby, 2004; Crosby, 2009; Crosby & Lykes, 2011; Lykes, 1994, 2001, 2010; Lykes & Cabrera Pérez-Armiñan, 2008; Lykes & Crosby, in press; Melville & Lykes, 1992; Women of PhotoVoice/ADMI & Lykes, 2000). This country of approximately 13 million people has endured the brutality of nearly four decades of armed conflict from the 1960s, to the signing of final peace accords in 1996, which resulted in the deaths of over

200,000 people, the displacement of nearly a million more, and the destruction of over 600 rural Mayan communities through genocidal violence (Commission for Historical Clarification [CEH], 1999). This violence was gendered as well as racialized, and Mayan women were marked in particular ways by these gross violations of human rights (Fulchiron, Paz, & Lopez, 2009). Much of our research has focused on collaborative endeavors with Mayan women—and with locally based organizations with whom they have organized.

Our decision to locate our praxis at the interface of feminist, community-based, and participatory action research stems from the fundamental epistemological and methodological challenges that arise in undertaking research in contexts that continue to be overshadowed by ever-present histories of colonization and imperial intervention, which include the hegemonic power of Northern academics—and in particular North American academics—to know the Guatemalan Other. As such, a feminist, anti-racist, anticolonial, and anti-imperial epistemological framework informs our work (Mohanty, 2003). Through our research, we seek to explicitly problematize the encounter between the Western self and the colonized Other, and to contest power and acknowledge systemic privilege, as well as oppression. Such an approach requires attention to the interlocking and intersecting relations of power, including gender, racialization, class, sexuality, and ability. These tenets frame and inform the research processes described in this chapter. A standpoint encompassing feminism and community-based participatory action research argues that all who are engaged in the research process are "knowers," and indeed, they coconstruct knowledge together. How to develop and engage these dialogical relationships in order to create new and transformative forms of knowledge is a central concern, and it is these processes, with their accompanying dilemmas and challenges, that are the central focus of this chapter. Thus, this chapter draws from feminist postcolonial and intersectional theory, and situates praxis at the interface of feminist and community research that is participatory and activist. It presents a set of resources for researchers seeking to coconstruct knowledge in critical solidarity with, and across, local and transnational communities with the aspiration of redressing injustice and engaging transformative praxis for change.

What Is Feminist Community-Based Participatory and Action Research?

DEFINITIONS

Community- and organization-based research activities, through which community residents and university-based researchers seek to analyze injustices and redress social inequalities, have been described variously as action research (AR), participatory research (PR), or participatory action research (PAR). Eikeland (2001) traces these approaches to knowledge generation and social change to early Greek philosophers or to indigenous communities; in comparison, most historians of science trace the beginnings of these approaches to 20th-century social scientific research, more specifically to the work of Kurt Lewin in the 1940s and the experiential learning and inquiry communities of the 1960s (see Adelman, 1993; Greenwood & Levin, 1998; Gustavsen, 2008). Those who live and work in Latin America, Africa, and Asia and engage in AR, PR, or PAR are more likely to trace the origin of their work to Paulo Freire (1970), Orlando Fals-Borda (1985), and Mohammad Anisur Rahman (with Fals-Borda, 1991). In the late 1960s and 1970s in India and Latin America, Paulo Freire's understanding of critical consciousness—that is, *conscientização* [conscientization]—influenced educators and social change advocates. They sought to create participatory processes that include and engage local knowledge systems in order to effect transformations in inequitable social relations and structures of power. Participatory rural appraisal (PRA) within the context of community development and humanitarian aid initiatives in rural communities of Africa and Asia embraces similar values. Although each has a distinct origin story and disciplinary context, they share basic assumptions about power inequalities and social oppression, as well as frequently overlapping values and goals; this has contributed to our decision to use these terms interchangeably.

PAR, AR, and PR are resources through which coresearchers[1] with indigenous or local knowledge and/or those directly affected by an issue or problem that becomes the focus of the project (often called insiders, participants, community members) *and* others with differing, sometimes technical, skills and formal knowledge and expertise (often called outsiders, researchers, facilitators, catalysts) collaborate in learning and teaching activities to systematize and construct knowledge, enhance consciousness, and engage in transformative action for change. PAR, AR, and PR emphasize the processes as well as the outcomes of research and the sharing of results within and beyond the participating communities.

PAR, AR, and PR seek to promote collective processes of inquiry that expose the ideological, political, and social processes underlying and permeating systems of inequality. They seek solutions to everyday problems and—to a greater or lesser extent—to transform the social inequalities exposed through research, by facilitating and engaging in specific actions that contribute toward human well-being and a more just and equitable world. These projects seek to generate knowledge and practice that is of genuine interest to all involved, and thus require "mutually dependent and cooperative relationships" (Martin, 1996, p. 88). Participants who engage in PAR, AR, and PR are transformed at a very personal level, and the process typically politicizes them in regard to their desired outcomes (Khanna, 1996). The shared space wherein the various knowledge systems and skill levels of all coresearchers can be valued, shared, and exchanged is critical to this work, as it is where coresearchers develop procedures for generating, evaluating, and reflecting upon the data gathered, and generate processes for interpretation and diffusion of the knowledge generated.

Adelman (1993) defined action research as "the means of systematic enquiry for all participants in the quest for greater effectiveness through democratic participation" (p. 7), thereby clarifying the link between systematic inquiry and democracy. Action research significantly contributed to work in organizational behavior and human development by introducing strategies for enhancing communication and cooperation. Zeichner (2001) identified five major educational AR traditions in the English-speaking world, and argued that some draw on emancipating practices developed in Asia, Africa, and Latin America, which extend their focus beyond the school to the local community (see also Brydon-Miller, Greenwood, & Maguire, 2003, for a brief historical overview). This emancipating perspective explicitly explored "power bases that define social roles and strongly influence the process of any change" (Adelman, 1993, p. 10). As a methodology and epistemology, action research challenges the myth of neutrality and objectivity that exists in much of the empirical social scientific and educational research. It emphasizes coresearchers' performances of their multiple subjectivities; institutional, professional, or personal interests and choices are negotiated within the primary commitment to gather knowledge and to address immediate social issues.

Thus, the AR, PR, and PAR methods are relational; and they reflect collaborations and partnerships within and across linguistic, cultural, gendered, classed, and racialized communities. The following values characterize most AR, PR, and PAR:

1. The democratization of knowledge production and use: The data collected, the analyses and interpretations generated, and the conclusions drawn are focused on the needs and priorities of all participants and coresearchers, with priority given to their use-value for addressing the community's problem focus, that is, the issue or problem that generated the research collaboration.

2. Ethical fairness in the benefits of the knowledge generation process: The processes and outcomes of the collaboration should benefit those most in need, and should "do no harm" to participants and coresearchers.

3. An ecological stance toward society and nature: The work is sensitive and responsive to micro-, meso-, and macro-level contexts in which it is carried out, including both the natural and human environments.

4. The processes and outcomes reflect an appreciation of, and engagement with, the diversities of capacities of all involved: It affirms our individual and collective abilities to reflect, learn, teach, and change, irrespective of formal education, skills, and/or training.

5. The participatory and transformative processes and outcomes are characterized by critical and constructive engagement, reflexivity, and humility throughout.

Most AR, PR, and PAR reflect an understanding of knowledge as constructed in particular social, cultural, and linguistic communities. This has contributed to Peter Reason and Hilary Bradbury's (2008) argument that PAR, AR, and PR have embraced the mid-20th century postmodern linguistic and cognitive turn within social science. Despite this, the problem-posing methods inherent in these methodologies presume that there is a "reality," that is, a set of social structures and institutions that support and sustain an unequal distribution of resources, and through which power circulates in ways that facilitate and constrain all social relations. These "circuits of dispossession" then contribute to action researchers' embrace of at least one of the basic assumptions of positivism, that there is a "real" and material social world (Fine & Ruglis, 2009). The turn toward action, characteristic of all PAR, AR, and PR, enriches the interface of the modern and postmodern, and it creates a synergy that informs diverse action and community researcher praxis.

Yet, despite these strengths, as PAR and AR methods have become increasingly established in the work of schools, universities, community–university partnerships and governments, international organizations (e.g., the World Bank), and nongovernmental organizations (see, e.g., Dick, 2004, for a review), there is a growing concern that PAR, AR, and PR risk becoming depoliticized tools. Thus, rather than facilitating the active participation of those marginalized from decision making and the exercise of power, including women, indigenous communities, and racialized minorities, PAR, AR, and PR have been increasingly used to gather data for, in the words of Orlando Fals-Borda (2001), "education, information, research and scientific work . . . geared to the upkeep of unjust power structures" (p. 33). The research presented in this chapter seeks to repoliticize PAR, AR, and PR through their alliance with critical community praxis and postcolonial feminisms. Importantly, this critical gaze also needs to be turned onto university-based research itself (Levin & Greenwood, 2008; Yee, 2011).

WHO, WHAT, AND WHERE IS "COMMUNITY"?

Much PAR and AR emerges through partnerships and collaborations between institutionally based researchers and local communities, nongovernmental organizations, and/or communities of professional practice (e.g., school, health clinics) or those served by and organized through these systems. Despite the diversities of these partners, AR, PR, and PAR are frequently referred to as community-based or community research. Various understandings of community—and how these have changed over time—are discussed below.

The term "community" initially referred to a group of people historically formed and rooted around geographic places (Duffy & Wong, 1996). Because of these geographic and historical continuities, residents, organizers, community psychologists, and researchers tended to focus on social similarities within and across these groupings. McMillan and Chavis (1986) identified four characteristics or "senses" of community: membership, influence, integration and fulfillment of needs, and shared emotional connection; suggesting that members of any given community holistically share these experiences and feelings of belonging. Mid-20th century communes, or alternative communities, harkened back to 19th-century utopian initiatives within the United States, and were sites where political and environmental activists sought an alternative lifestyle.

Widespread and large-scale, identity-based social movements were organized by African Americans, Asian Americans, Latinos, women, gays and lesbians, and/or people with disabilities within the second half of the 20th century. These movements built upon, yet shifted, the earlier ideas of community by focusing less on physical space and more on social similarities—and contrasts with other groups—emphasizing issues of social inequalities, marginalization, or oppression organized around identities.[2] These initiatives dislodged the term community from geographies of place, and instead emphasized belongingness along a single, identity dimension. More recently, activists and scholars have opposed these essentialist understandings of community, arguing that they reduce diversities and interlocking systems of oppression to a single, underlying dimension; this pushes activists toward a misguided search for a primary, underlying source of oppression and inequality. Moreover, there can be a tendency to essentialize and polarize within particularly focused communities; one salient challenge to this more singular understanding of identity can be seen in the lesbian, gay, bisexual, transgender and queer movements, in which many people experience, identify, and perform multiple sexualities or genders within continuums (Billies, Johnson, Murungi, & Pugh, 2009; Cruz, 2011). This critique has thus contributed to understandings of community as a "discursive invocation" (Stommel, 2008) or as a "performance of belongingness" (Fortier, 1999).

Community-based, participatory, and action researchers engage with members of these diverse communities in partnerships and collaborative projects focused on social issues and/or problems that emerge within such communities, particularly those marginalized from access to power, resources, and decision making. The sites of these partnerships include educational and health-related organizations or institutions, nongovernmental community-based organizations, local urban and rural communities or neighborhoods, and informal groups including, for example, asylum seekers and refugees, among others. Irrespective of the specific site or focus of the collaboration, however, these partnerships strive to promote the development of leadership within the individualized unit, to advance their agenda, and to develop solidarity through which coresearchers can (1) identify and document a social problem, issue, or concern; (2) encounter and document circuits of power within the community; (3) generate new understandings and interpretations of the sources of inequalities, oppression, or violation; and (4) identify and take steps toward self- and social transformation.

HOW CAN COMMUNITY AND PARTICIPATORY AND ACTION RESEARCH BE FEMINIST?

As discussed in earlier chapters within this volume, there is considerable epistemological diversity within and across feminist research. Academics and scholars who infuse their work with feminist values and ideals seek—at the minimum—to find what has been excluded from previous research, and to use gender as an analytic tool (see Stewart, 1998) in order to generate critical consciousness—their own and that of others with whom they work—about gendered oppression and how it constrains women's and men's lives. Others argue that feminist research is not solely about gender differences, and that it is also about critically exploring aspects of social status and the participants' positionalities (see Collins, 1990; Naples, 2003; Smith, 1989, 1991).

Feminist community-based, participatory, and action researchers have developed multiple ways to analyze the various epistemological and methodological resources identified above. Hill, Bond, Mulvey, and Terenzio (2000) identified seven themes, which they argue cross over the terrains in which community and feminist researchers work:

1. Integrating a contextualized understanding;

2. Paying attention to issues of diversity;

3. Speaking from the standpoint of oppressed groups;

4. Adopting a collaborative approach;

5. Utilizing multilevel, multimethod approaches;

6. Adopting reflexive practices; and

7. Taking an activist orientation and using knowledge for social change. (p. 760)

Through empirical studies, these seven themes emphasize and exemplify the earlier feminist theory that resisted defining feminist research exclusively—or even primarily—in terms of methods, and that also sought to avoid essentializing gender. Thus the work, presented in a special issue of the *American Journal of Community Psychology,* reflects a diversity of methods, but it also emphasizes the reflexive practices of the researchers, all of whom are described as striving to generate a "body of work that presents a rich, multitextured tapestry of the lives of the participants and that is used to improve those lives" (Hill et al., 2000, p. 770).

As PAR and AR have increasingly informed work by feminists and community-
-based researchers, the utilization of the language of participants and researchers
has been contested. Brydon-Miller, Maguire, and McIntyre (2004) write about "travelling companions," reflecting not only the various models for building research
relationships, but also the ways in which those positioned differently at the outset of
a negotiated research project shift in roles and responsibilities through teaching–
learning processes. In this way, they "hope to influence feminist scholarship to be
more participatory and action-oriented, and participatory action research to be
more grounded in feminist theories and values" (p. ix).

Reid and Frisby (2008) push this further, suggesting that feminist researchers and
participatory action researchers should become "allies," arguing that despite many
epistemological and methodological similarities, both have particular contributions
that can strengthen the other. Specifically, they emphasize feminism's particular contributions to the field: feminism's theoretical and epistemological debates, the promises and challenges of intersectional analyses, the emphasis on researcher positionality
and reflexivity, and the foregrounding of agency and lived experiences of women as
resources to strengthen AR and PAR. Similarly, they suggest that the emphasis within
AR and PAR on understanding stakeholders' multiple locations and the implications
therein, as well as the longstanding prioritization of praxis and of action–reflection
dialectics, are potential contributions to facilitating alliances between feminists and
local communities and activists. According to Reid and Frisby, FPAR (feminist participatory action research) is performed at the intersections of six interrelated dimensions that include:

- Centering gender and women's diverse experiences while challenging forms of
  patriarchy (p. 97),
- Accounting for intersectionality (p. 97),
- Honoring voice and difference through participatory research processes (p. 98),
- Exploring new forms of representation (p. 99),
- Reflexivity (p. 100), and
- Honoring many forms of action (p. 101).

Despite the importance of each dimension—which is explored through a set of proposed
questions as guidelines for feminist participatory action researchers—the authors caution against a rigid or singular model, suggesting instead the multiple ways of embodying these principles, and thus sharing the aforementioned tendencies to eschew methodological or epistemological rigidity.

Lykes and Hershberg (2012) have built on these diverse recommendations, but they
seek to capitalize on the tensions between feminist research and participatory and action

research in order to press both toward more transformative praxis. Specifically, they suggest that feminist-infused PAR and AR constitute an iterative set of processes and outcomes performed to critically reposition gender, race, and class; excavate indigenous cultural knowledge and generate voices; and/or deploy intersectionality as an analytic tool for transformation.

Similarly, recent work by Creese and Frisby (2011) centers postcolonial feminist scholarship, and suggests that its focus on community, and on race and racialization in the intersection of other oppressions, emphasizes the historical sites in which relations of power are embedded and operationalized. Postcolonial feminist research deconstructs these structures of power, and "creates space in a constructive maneuver for agency of subaltern and subjugated knowledges" (p. 21). Some features of this work have been identified above (e.g., recognizing intersectional oppressions, listening to silenced voices); but Creese and Frisby stress not only the research methods, but also the multiple ways in which power is structured within these processes and the relationships formed therein. Thus, reflexivity in the feminist research process is critical to this study, particularly the acknowledgment of outsider research privilege. Postcolonial feminist research emphasizes "accounting for vestiges of colonialism, including racialization and classism; recognizing shifting, hybrid identities for women; [and] tracking the influence of history and place" (p. 26). It incorporates many of the critiques of community research's aforementioned tendencies to "essentialize community," and it turns its critical lens, as do Mohanty (2003), Alexander (2005), and Yee (2011), onto the academy itself; and, in the case of Creese and Frisby, onto the academic researcher's discourse of "community partnership." See the "Behind the Scenes" box in this chapter for further discussion of feminist practice in addressing questions of privilege and positionality when outsider researchers engage with insider communities for the advancement of social change.

Behind the Scenes

Feminism in Practice

The following is based on a conversation between M. Brinton Lykes (MBL), Michelle Fine (MF), and María Elena Torre (MET) that took place on January 12, 2012, in New York City. Dr. Michelle Fine is a Distinguished Professor of Psychology at The Graduate Center of the City University of New York, where she teaches social personality psychology, urban education, and women's studies. Dr. María Elena Torre is Director of the Public Science Project at The Graduate Center of the City University of New York.

(Continued)

(Continued)

MBL: Alison Crosby and I are interested in how you think about yourselves as feminists and whether you think identifying as such facilitates or hinders your activist scholarship. When Erzulie Coquillon and I did that first handbook chapter on feminism and PAR (Lykes & Coquillon, 2007), we tried to present a typology for "feminist PAR." Alison and I have just completed a chapter exploring creative resources (theater, drawing, photography, etc.) and Mayan practices and beliefs in Guatemala in PAR with Mayan women, including those in Chajul with whom I worked over a decade ago.

I was impressed by how the Maya Ixil and K'iche' women had incorporated creative resources into their current work and adapted them in their local communities where women continue to live in extreme poverty with very few NGO [nongovernmental organization] or government resources. The women of PhotoPAR have organized women's groups in these rural villages, deploying indigenous Mayan beliefs and embodied practices (theater, dramatic play) and creative storytelling and drawings as resources for organizing and education. Their drawings and dramatic presentations affirmed their sense of themselves as indigenous women, of being able to go out of their houses, participate in meetings, and say what's on their minds. The self-confidence and protagonism—absent 20 years ago—now permeated the workshops. They also expressed empathy for the women whose husbands continue to restrict their movements, with one woman representing these gender dynamics in a drawing of her head on top of a man's head (Figure 6.1). The man is looking one way, and she is looking the other. In the group discussion, she and others described husbands who control their wives' every movement, including through violence.

We also documented women revindicating the struggles and the resistance through which they and the men in their communities demanded their rights and economic justice, demands to which the Guatemalan government responded with repressive violence. All had been victimized by state-sponsored violence, rape as a tool of war, and genocide. But they were—and are—protagonists whose lives and stories we seek to re-present through these PAR processes. . . . I never used the word feminist, or womanist in Chajul—nor did they—but we met where they were, as they articulated who they were. Yet the framework that I brought with me was feminist and informed by postcolonial theory, participatory action research methodologies, and psychologies of liberation.

In contrast, Alison and I are currently collaborating with a feminist organization in Guatemala that has strong Marxist roots. Young Mayan women activists who have integrated embodied therapeutic practices and traditional Mayan beliefs in interesting, dynamic ways have been part of this work (see, e.g., Grupo de Mujeres Mayas Kaqla, 2004, 2009). This project engages us in complex relations among women differently racialized and classed, some of whom are Guatemalan ladinos whose parallel challenges as "outsiders" working with indigenous Mayan women resonate with some we have as Unitedstatesian and Canadian. Despite shared feminist assumptions, as Northern academics our gendered, racialized and classed privileges and constraints are also points of tension. Thus we are challenged by these mobile but deeply structured relations of power as we seek to engage feminist antiracist community and action research.

MET: In terms of being a feminist or claiming yourself as a feminist, I was raised by a woman who was deeply involved in the feminist movement, so I don't know that I spent a lot of time questioning that. I just *am* a feminist; it informs everything that I do.

Some of us recently went to San Juan del Sur, Nicaragua, to do a PAR project with workers in a community center who were documenting the intersections of a burgeoning tourism industry and a spike in violence against women and children. We were women, all Spanish-speaking with roots in Spanish-speaking countries, with deep commitments to feminism—even though we never had an explicit conversation about feminism or our relationship to it. But feminist theory overwhelmingly informed our work, as did critical race theory, critiques of power, and anticolonial frameworks. The same is true for indigenous theory, which without question, informed everything we did there. As did our North American perspectives, as we all have lived in the United States or Canada for the majority of our lives. These theories and perspectives pulsated through our bodies, our actions, how we spoke with people, and our practice of PAR. . . .

Figure 6.1 Drawing From Creative Workshop

The project in San Juan del Sur took on a solidarity framework, which has been a useful framing to help us open up new kinds of relationships through research. The project brought together very differently situated people—into a participatory contact zone—and theorizing it as a space of solidarity encouraged us to think about what we had to offer each other, what resources we could leverage, and how we could pool our collective knowledge and skills to engage and challenge the current conditions through research.

Since then, we've held onto the idea of "solidarity research"—not so much research *on* than *in* solidarity—and migrated it into a study we are conducting on aggressive policing with a

(Continued)

(Continued)

collective of community members in a neighborhood near Yankee Stadium in the Bronx. Like in Nicaragua, our research team is made up of very differently situated members. Two thirds of us live in the neighborhood where we are conducting the research—a neighborhood under attack by the NYPD—and one third live in different sections of the city.

When our group was first getting to know each other, we shared our experiences and outrage at the police, and the differences were stark. Young men and their mothers spoke of violent stops and regular, almost weekly, harassment. I told my only story of being stopped by police. It was a long time ago, when I was probably about 19. I was walking from East Harlem over to the West Side to visit a friend, and it was around 10 pm on a weeknight. In the middle of my walk, a police car pulled up alongside me, and the two officers yelled, "Get into the car! Get into the car!" in really loud, booming voices. Bewildered, and probably because of the power of their authority, I listened and I got into the car. They then proceeded to tell me how lucky I was that they had saved me, that they had *rescued* me; and they explained that they do this periodically. They called them "rescue missions" where they pick up people that look like me, light-skinned women who are "walking in places they shouldn't be walking." And then they let me out. So that was my experience of being stopped: I was stopped and "rescued." This is not what the young people or my other colleagues in the Bronx are living.

Through our research, we are creating a space of solidarity, where some members of the group are simply fed up with being terrorized by the policing of their community, and others are fed up with living in a society where these practices are tolerated, or worse where they are supported, and celebrated for increasing our "safety." Through our collective research, we bring these differences together and *use* them—these and all of the other differences we carry—as tools of research, they shape and inform our methods, our analyses. We use these differences, and the histories and knowledges connected to them to theorize every aspect of our work. But like I said, we are not simply coming together in a partnership—we're engaged around an issue that we want to change, regardless of where we are positioned to it. And we keep all of our differences alive—recognizing where and how they come about and all the structures, policies, and practices that sustain them. We use these differences to understand each other's lives, to understand our data, to think differently, to question, and at times to bridge.

At a recent meeting, we were interviewing a mother whose son is repeatedly getting picked up by the police. She shared an experience of being called at home one afternoon by an officer at the local police precinct to see if her child had been picked up—the officer was not calling to report it, but to ask if he had been, as if out of concern. I listened and asked naïvely, "How did she [the officer at the precinct] know your number? What do you mean she just called you?" The mother described the officer's tone to be like that of a friend saying "Hey, where's your son?" After we talked a while, the mother paused and said, "You know, I never thought of that. Why *do* they have my number? Is there a list that I'm on?" Because she and I have really different experiences, we prompted each other to ask questions about the kinds of information and records the police precinct keeps. And though this is an example of an "outsider," to use old language, seeing into a dynamic that has been normalized by constant repetition, these insights happen in all directions in our work because we are explicit and value *all* of our ways of knowing—different histories, ideas, understandings, and even desires.

MF: So let me hitchhike a little on María, and speak to the older version of "Why feminism"? You know, it must happen to you all the time, when people say: "Is this a feminist project?" or "Whose theory is this based on?" and I resist a simple classification; but when I have to default, I default to feminism. Even though I feel like our work, my work, is deeply informed by feminism *and* critical race theory *and* indigenous and postcolonial theory; but if it has a pulse and a heart, it's a feminist pulse and heart, but not the white, elite feminism, but a fleshy, activist feminism, the one where bodies, politics, lives and silences are connected to structures, histories, and to social movements. The kind of feminism that knows there is desire, yearning, and capacity, if you dare to imagine, to create the space for someone to sing through her story of pain, survival, and laughter. Our feminist analyses are also a little suspicious of taken-for-granted categories, even the categories we use in our work. We understand that lives are not lived in categories and are not situated in structures and histories, but are dynamic and fluid—not fixed, not wholly known or knowable....

But, I now know that I have written too much on voice, and I now know there is much wisdom in silence, under the skin, in touch, and images, and dreams and in breaths. My 96-year-old mother is very sick right now. As we lay in bed, eating ice cream for the past month, for breakfast, in the rehab center, I feel like I have been blanketed and warmed and frightened. I bear witness to her breaths that carry along her-story of immigration, yearnings, passions; you know her silences, her dream states—these feel like feminist fluids running through my/her body....

In our research, critical race, neo-Marxist, queer, critical disability, and postcolonial theory complicate our feminist understandings, populating our analyses with critical intersecting questions. A lot of the work in Nicaragua that María describes was informed by a class-based analysis of how tourism and economic "progress" transforms women's lives on the ground—and not always for the good....

Yesterday we were invited into a conversation with activist women's organizations: thinking

(Continued)

(Continued)

about how to document the circuits of domestic violence that are electrifying and threatening the city as jobs evaporate and austerity consumes the soul of our communities; listening to these stories of Ecuadorian women, undocumented women from Africa, those living in orthodox Jewish communities or on Native Indian reservations, or formerly incarcerated women being beaten, Arab women. None of them can call the police, or easily secure an order of protection without massive collateral damage to themselves, their children, and/or their families. All of their bodies are being sacrificed to a failing economy. These women are the first responders to neoliberalism. It's their bodies, their human (in)security that haunts the city; they worry that if they call the police, they will be deported, their children may be taken, they may be incarcerated for "engaging in domestic violence." If they don't call the police, they worry about how vulnerable they are to their men. . . .

[T]o do this work requires a feminist analysis that takes seriously how neoliberalism, a racialized prison industrial complex, virulent xenophobia, and the heavily invested rise of the Security State all contribute to the shape of women's lives; how austerity cuts the threads of the fragile safety net women once enjoyed; how class, gender, sexuality, (dis)ability, immigration status, and women's yearnings carve the opportunities and constraints in which they find themselves searching simply for safety. . . .

Feminism is about a commitment to narratives, structural analysis, and action; to understanding how precariously and passionately women's lives are situated in what Martín-Baró called "limit situations." For us, feminist research is also designed for radical accountability, as an intellectual, theoretical, and political debt to the women who scrub the surfaces of the inequality gaps that organize our nation. Feminist research stands for our collective commitment to take up the questions that haunt and threaten the most vulnerable women. Feminist research presumes that we all have a right, indeed a responsibility to analyze and resist social oppression.

I remember leaving the prison, when we were involved with *Changing Minds* (Fine et al., 2001) and confused about our role as outsiders. I turned to María and said, "Maybe we're just ventriloquists." And María said, "No. Actually, as nonprisoners, we ask naïve questions; we can carry the critical analysis of gender and mass incarceration to places where the women can't speak" (Fine & Torre, 2006). Through the *Public Science Project* (www.public scienceproject.org), we believe that the CUNY Graduate Center has a debt to the city and to the poorest people of the city and that our status as academics obligates us to document, theorize, and interrupt the relationship of privilege and dispossession; to examine and contest how unevenly power, public resources, and human security are distributed.

Once we understand that we are all in these circuits, then we recognize that it's our responsibility to gather stories or other forms of evidence, place them in time and space, archive the forgotten stories, and then migrate these analyses into communities, dining rooms, state legislatures, and protest movements where they couldn't easily travel (or be believed) on their own. As feminist scholars we help to carry the water of women's lives during incredibly difficult times, in impossible circumstances. And when we publish these stories, we honor them, preserve her-story, stories that might otherwise get washed out by the next regime in Nicaragua or New Jersey. Or when Yankee Stadium buys up the whole neighborhood and all that policing stops because the new gentry will move in, we will re-member the bodies taken away. It feels to me like teaching, researching, organizing, and publishing are political acts, and reclaiming psychology as intellectual, historic, and political is a profoundly, old-fashioned feminist act of revenge, liberation, and collective laughter from generations of women who have been the undisciplined objects of our discipline.

The remainder of this chapter describes selected processes that contribute to developing the feminist practice of action and community research. It begins by discussing how researchers develop and engage the dialogical relationships needed in order to create new and transformative forms of knowledge, and continues with how they address some of the dilemmas and challenges that they face in this process.

EXPLORING FEMINIST PRACTICES IN ACTION AND COMMUNITY RESEARCH

a. Dialogical relationships.

i. Who are the researchers? Positivist social science research is most typically designed by university-based academic researchers who invite members of a wider community to participate as subjects of a "study." Whether through laboratory experiments, surveys, in-depth questionnaires, or focus groups, these "subjects" have relatively little to do with the researchers beyond agreeing to respond to a series of prompts or questions, completing the assigned task, and being "debriefed" about the scientific objectives of the project.

As argued above, feminist practice of action and community research challenges these assumptions of objectivity and seeks to develop participatory processes among all research collaborators, often shifting from a researcher–participant dialogue to one involving coresearchers. Thus, participating insiders from a local community are invited to collaborate with outsider researchers in addressing a social issue or problem of interest to both and, in most cases, with particular consequences for the community. Postcolonial feminism further contests the borders of these collaborative relationships, in light of the growing numbers within the community- and identity-based groups that are naming problems and are seeking human and social capital within and beyond their borders, in order to cooperatively generate knowledge and to forge actions to redress injustices.

ii. Forming relationships, identifying partners. Patricia Maguire (1987) designed what many have acknowledged to be the first feminist participatory and action research project in collaboration with Native American women. From the perspective of forming relationships, this project has some of the classic characteristics that action researchers might associate with "insider-outsider" research (Bartunek, 2008). Maguire was a PhD student who sought to work with Native women who were survivors of sexual violence. Unlike many other research projects that report only findings, Maguire described the multiple challenges she encountered as she sought to develop "just enough trust" with local Native women who later became participants in her dissertation research project. She reported multiple "decision points," during which she was pulled between wanting to provide resources to the survivors of sexual violence—either through child care, rides to activities, and so forth—and withholding services in order not to influence her research findings.

Pierrette Hondagneu-Sotelo (1996, 2001/2007) similarly worked with undocumented immigrant women in paid domestic work in California. She identified herself as a *servidora* or informal social worker, which facilitated her access to this community and also helped her to better understand their lives. Significantly, she positioned herself through action, as someone who could contribute to their work through developing novellas—"booklets with captioned photographs" (1996, p. 106)—that reported the domestic workers' stories and served as organizing resources for her project.

Lykes (Lykes, in collaboration with Caba Mateo, Chávez Anay, Laynez Caba, Ruiz, & Williams, 1999) entered a rural Guatemalan community as an activist volunteer. She accompanied local Mayan women in developing a women's group and, over time, in creating a local nonprofit that sponsored educational and economic development projects. As local women developed essential leadership skills and self-confidence, they formed partnerships. Over time, they designed PhotoPAR, a project that incorporated photography and oral history interviews to document Mayan women's experiences of, and responses to, armed conflict in the rural community of Chajul (Women of PhotoVoice/ ADMI & Lykes, 2000).

Each of these relationships forged in community-based and participatory action research was done so at the intersection of action and reflection; yet in each case, the researcher was an outsider to the community, although she shared similarities as well as differences along various axes of racialization, gender, language, nationality, and social class. Each researcher was challenged to develop "safe enough" spaces in which potential participants (for Maguire and Hondagneu-Sotelo) and coresearchers (for Lykes) could value their own diverse strengths and capacities, and with whom outsider and insider coresearchers could engage in reflective critical practices that problematized the matrices of power, privilege, and domination that circulated throughout the social worlds of the colonized Other into which differently positioned and more privileged women entered. Feminists have characterized these research relationships in a variety of ways, such as "friendship" or a "family" (McIntyre & Lykes, 2004), which stretch the boundaries of a hypothesized insider–outsider dichotomy. In the words of Michelle Fine (1994), coresearchers "work the hyphen" as relationships between the two groups shift (p. 70). By utilizing these methods of reflexivity, Maguire, Hondagneu-Sotelo, and Lykes were able to name their relative privileges vis-à-vis the women with whom they partnered; in Lykes's work particularly, these reflexive practices extended, in some limited ways, to the coresearchers (see Lykes, 2010, for a discussion of the limits and possibilities of shared reflexive praxis).

As suggested above, these relationships deeply implicate us (Lykes and Crosby) as white, privileged, university-based researchers working with Mayan women of Guatemala. Sherry Gorelick (1996) cautions those who seek to forge relationships beyond those sites of privilege, suggesting that the external researcher's "relationship to oppression, as either privileged or oppressed . . . is contradictory, complex, and, to some degree, up to us" (p. 40). Chavez, Duran, Baker, Avila, and Wallerstein (2003) suggest that for "professionally trained researchers who are white or otherwise advantaged, privilege is one of the most important and difficult arenas . . . to address, as it in part defines who [the researchers] understand [themselves] to be" (p. 91).

The work of independent researcher and activist Susan Stern exemplifies some of these challenges "at the hyphen." As a white woman, her activist research in a predominantly black suburban neighborhood school near Washington, D.C., in the early 1980s, required continual conversation with other predominantly black parents and teachers about the implications of race and racism for their partnership. As Stern (1998) explains: "[A]t the personal level, our different racial backgrounds threatened to maintain a barrier between us. At the social level, racial[ized] differences and race-based policies and procedures were at the core of the problem at hand [in the] children's school" (p. 115). Although Stern was an insider in the school community due to her status as the parent of a student, she was an outsider as a white, Euro-American in an almost exclusively black community. These identities positioned her differently and had implications for the research relationships she cultivated, the knowledge she generated, and the actions in which she engaged through the research process.

The relationships among the Sangtin Writers and Richa Nagar further exemplify feminist participatory researchers' dynamic relationships, as embodied through collective actions. Antecedents that informed their work include Latin American *testimonio* (see, e.g., Menchú, 1983); autobiographical work of many women of color; the lesbian and black women's 1978 Combahee River Collective's Statement (http://circuitous.org/ scraps/combahee.html); as well as the collective research endeavors of some white women, including the Personal Narratives Group (1989). The social movement *Sangtin*

Yatra, or Playing With Fire, thus emerged as an alliance of a university-based researcher (Nagar), a district level NGO activist, and seven village-level activists in Uttar Pradesh, Sittapur District, India. Through autobiographical writing about poverty, caste, violence, privilege, and group processes over a three-year period, together they generated structures of accountability and transparency for the world to see, demystifying for themselves and for their readers the intricacies of the power embedded within the interstices of their individual lives and their social structures and institutions. Thus, utilizing their participatory- and action-based methodology, they narrated their lives, theorized women's empowerment, and critiqued the hegemonic power of international aid donors and development agencies (Sangtin Writers & Nagar, 2006). Chandra Mohanty described their work as envisioning new forms of solidarity grounded "on place-based struggles for social and economic justice—struggles that are rooted in the particularities of place-based needs but that simultaneously map and engage political processes at all geographical scales" (Sangtin Writers & Nagar, 2006, p. xv).

Researchers and participants are situated in the matrices of intertwining social interactions that both constrain and facilitate the relationships they develop, as well as the action and research processes they generate. Feminist community-based and action research challenges delineated and static notions of insider and outsider, or researcher and participant, and emphasizes instead the mediated and progressive nature of our relationships and our shared action–reflection processes. Indian action researcher Anisur Rahman (2004) well understood these processes, and he suggested that the "desired relation between external activists and people is best expressed by the term *uglolana,* meaning 'sharpening each other'" and by a "companion concept . . . *uakana,* meaning 'to build each other'" (p. 17). He embraced these two South African Bantu terms as "the profoundest articulation of the participatory development paradigm" (p. 17). These lived experiences not only redefine the insider–outsider dialectic of coresearchers, but also refashion the discourse of power at the intersection of feminisms, community-based, and participatory and action research.

iii. Identifying a shared question/focus. Within these complex and dynamic relationships that are established over time, coresearchers are challenged to identify a shared research question or focus. The classic outsider researcher typically enters a community with a question already in mind, often one that is based upon a careful reading of previous work about a personal issue of concern, and one that is deemed to be important to the community (Maguire, 1987). Alternatively, some community-based organizations have begun to develop their own research agenda and to seek collaborators from nearby universities or NGOs who could contribute to their work (see, e.g., Institute for Community Research, http://www.incommunityresearch.org/about/about.htm). In some cases, for example, Lykes in Chajul, Guatemala (see fuller discussion of this project below), a researcher is invited into a community because of a set of nonresearch skills he or she possesses and, over a period of collaborative activities, they develop a shared research question/focus (Lykes, 1999).

In all cases, it is critical that the focus or question, around which research processes and actions are organized, must be something that is negotiated among all involved parties. Levin and Greenwood (2008) emphasize the importance of pragmatism within the problem identification processes; these collaborations are typically characterized by working *with* people, not *for* them. The research or issue focus emerges when coresearchers listen to themes that come from group discussions—particularly concerning issues about which community members feel strongly—and when they privilege voices who are frequently marginalized or unheard. Importantly, those facilitating these processes may be from the community or beyond, and they must attend to the silences, noting who is speaking and who feels less empowered or entitled to state concerns. Participation may be observable on anticipated axes of power—for example, older women speak less than younger women, nonnative speakers less than native speakers, literate more than nonliterate, and so forth. These conversations thus require cultural literacies as well as a commitment to shared participation.

The processes utilized to search for community problems or issues must be creative, thoughtful, and, most importantly, familiar to the diverse members of the community. They might include focus groups, brainstorming exercises, or dramatic play (see "Generating and analyzing data," below, for examples). Equally important, the processes must be dialogical and organized in ways that demonstrate mutuality and shared roles as colearners through which we iteratively and dynamically generate a research question or focus.

iv. Designing the project. In the research design process, community-based and participatory and action researchers must decide how they will proceed to gather information, systematically organize it, analyze it, and interpret what has been found. In so doing, the coresearchers may decide to gather information from a larger group of participants, in addition to those individuals already identified as participants or coresearchers. For example, 50 high school students were invited to collaborate with CUNY researchers to form a "Youth Research Community" in which they explored their perceptions of social class, race, gender, ethnicity, and opportunity (Torre, 2008; Torre & Fine, 2003). They then extended their work to include 9,174 youth from fifteen New York and New Jersey urban and suburban districts as respondents to a survey regarding a shared research focus on educational opportunities—or lack thereof—for urban youth. A team of youth and university-based coresearchers analyzed this data in addition to that gathered in focus groups, observations, archival research, and from the youth coresearchers' creative writing (Fine et al., 2001; Torre, 2008; see also the discussion with Torre and Fine in the "Behind-the-Scenes" box in this chapter).

The PhotoPAR process in the rural Mayan community of Chajul, Guatemala (Lykes, 2001), reflects such an iterative research design process. There, Lykes collaborated with a local organization with which she had had prior involvement, in order to identify 20 Mayan women coresearchers to participate in the PhotoPAR process (Lykes, 1999). Training for the project involved a series of participatory workshops through which they designed the research. Some of the workshops were open to all women in the wider organization, and some were developed exclusively with the 20 coresearchers. Within that context, Lykes and the coresearchers designed a methodology that they utilized in order to collaboratively identify themes that they felt would address their research focus, which included documenting both the effects of armed conflict on the community of Chajul and local women's responses to these changes. Additional participants in the study included men, women, and children who were photographed and interviewed about their experiences, yet the number of coresearchers remained stable throughout the three-year project. As will be discussed below, the various processes that helped shape these relationships, and the training workshops in which women participated, all constituted data, which was documented and analyzed in this PhotoPAR project.

b. Generating and analyzing data.

As suggested above, data is constituted through a wide range of activities that can be documented, systematized, analyzed, and interpreted. Because the feminist practice of action and community research necessitates the involvement of multiple parties, data are thus generated through highly participatory processes. These include the methods identified and described in other chapters of this volume; for example, interviews (in-depth, oral history, structured, or semistructured; see chapters 7 and 10), focus groups (see chapter 8), ethnography (see chapter 5), and/or evaluation processes (see chapter 11). The remainder of this section also describes a selection of the additional activities engaged to gather and analyze data, which significantly respond to the pragmatism of the feminist practice of action and community research.

i. Mapping as a resource in data collection. One of the many resources available to better understand an identified issue or problem is mapping. Although maps today are typically designed with sophisticated technological resources and are used to represent complex economic and political relationships of power, they have served for centuries as resources for communicating stories, songs, and dreams related to space (Blanchet-Cohen, Ragan, & Amsden, 2003). Increasingly, researchers who have embraced visual techniques use them for mapping concepts in analyzing qualitative interviews (Butler-Kisber & Poldma, 2010). Maps have also been found to be particularly useful in participatory research working with children and/or within and across diverse linguistic groups. Maps have been generated in the sand using sticks, with paper and pencils, or using sophisticated computer programs. Maps take many forms, represent a wide range of individual and social experiences, and mapmaking can be deeply relational.

A *genogram* is a map of a family, and it can be developed to include one or multiple generations within the family.

The map in Figure 6.2 was completed as part of an interview with a 10-year-old girl, Maria (not her real name), whose genogram exemplifies a family structure common to many Latin American migrant families. At the time of the interview, Maria was living outside Zacualpa, in the Southern Quiché region of Guatemala, while her parents resided in a northeastern region of the United States. Maria's visualization of the two generations of her nuclear family also includes a cousin Kate (name has been changed), and Kate's mother, who is raising Kate and Maria together in Guatemala, while Kate's father also lives in the United States. Maria also has two siblings in the United States whom she has never met. Her family is thus both *transnational,* meaning the parents and children live on different sides of a national border; and *mixed status,* signifying that some members are U.S. citizens (her siblings), but others are not (her parents). The PAR project in which this map was generated was designed collaboratively with migrants in the United States and in Guatemala, in order (1) to better understand the effects of U.S. detention and deportation processes upon families (see, e.g., Brabeck, Lykes, & Hershberg, 2011) and (2) to listen to the marginalized voices within migration studies—that is, those of the children and youth left behind (Lykes & McDonald, in press), paying particular attention to the voices of young girls (Hershberg & Lykes, 2012).

Figure 6.2 Family Mapping: Guatemala and United States

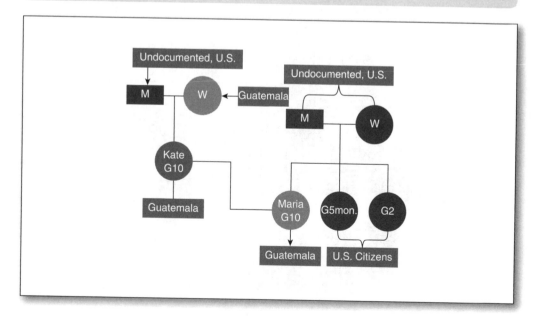

Community maps are often tools coresearchers utilize in order to identify features of their ecological and social environments, which provide key information that serves as bedrock for the successful implementation of projects in the studied area. Participants can identify current realities or envision future dreams. Kretzman and McKnight (1993) embraced mapping as a resource through which communities could map assets as a starting point for community development projects. For example, some coresearchers use community maps to identify places where residents and/or participants feel safe—or threatened—in a local community, or to ensure the inclusion of all members of the community (Figure 6.3).

The coresearchers who designed this map were living and working in urban Johannesburg, South Africa, where they sought to identify the places in their community where they felt at risk for contracting HIV/AIDS, and the sites where they felt safe. The former included street corners where buying and selling of drugs, and needle exchanges among addicts occurred, whereas the latter encompassed a local church that ran a drop-in center and a local health clinic. The coresearchers then sought to interview key informants at each location, with the goal to systematically understand the specific risks at those sites that were perceived to be "dangerous" and the reasons why some sites were considered "safe." Armed with the necessary information, local interventions were then designed to reduce the risks at the former category and to strengthen the safe areas as a whole.

Some coresearchers employ *body mapping and drawing* to facilitate projects involving survivors of sexual violence and those with other health-related concerns. Andrea Cornwall (1992) and her colleagues used body mapping collaboratively with rural farming

Figure 6.3   Community Mapping: South Africa

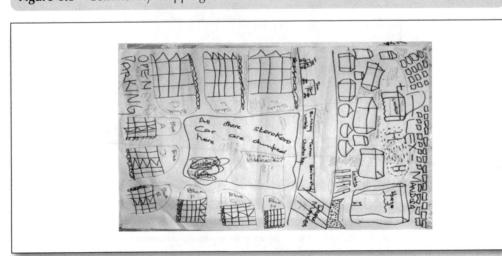

women. Using paper or the dirt, the local women were asked to draw their reproductive organs in order for those facilitating the project to better understand indigenous notions of reproduction and birth control. These exercises are important teaching–learning opportunities for both insiders and outsiders—and they significantly contribute to later projects. Within our own work in Guatemala, survivors of sexual violence in armed conflict participated in a range of mapping and body mapping exercises; one invited the women to partner and to draw the outline of each other's body on large life-sized sheets of newsprint. Each participant was then asked to represent her experiences on her drawing (Figure 6.4).

These drawings were displayed to all workshop participants, and those who had drawn them were invited to share their stories. These images and stories were important indicators of the change experienced within and across the survivors of sexual violence, who for several years had been participating in multiple collaborative research and action processes to move toward healing (for examples, see Equipo de Estudios Communitarios y Accion Psicosocial [ECAP], 2009; Fulchiron, et al., 2009; Lykes & Crosby, in press).

ii. Creative techniques as resources for data generation and analysis. As the previous example suggests, the various strategies described throughout this chapter can be used individually, or in combination, to both generate and analyze data. In addition to mapping and drawings, creative techniques within community and action research can be organized along three axes: *corporal expression*, including role playing or dramatic play, theater, and dramatic multiplication (Pavlovsky, Martinez Bouquet, & Moscio, 1985); *drawing*, and all forms of physical creativity "outside of ourselves," including drawings, models made with

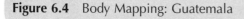

Figure 6.4   Body Mapping: Guatemala

newspapers or other materials, and collages (Butler-Kisber & Poldma, 2010); and *verbal techniques*, the playing with words in ways that reveal their liberating character (Rodari, 1996; Zipes, 1995; see also Goudvis, 1991, for a discussion of the intersection and application of these techniques), as well as narratives, storytelling, and careful description or analysis of previously presented work and photographs.

Photography in particular can be used as a highly effective research method, and examples abound with its utilization in feminist research projects. One that is especially well known was developed by public health researcher Caroline Wang and her colleagues in rural China (*Visual Voices*, 1995; Wang, 1999). Rural women took pictures and described them in short captions, and then they re-presented them to policy makers in China with the goal of improving rural child care. Ximena Bunster and Elsa Chaney (Bunster & Chaney, 1989) in urban Peru used photographs in their project as "talking pictures." They had photographs taken by professionals, further selected them through focus group activities with urban peasants, and then utilized the photographs as prompts to elicit stories from local market women about the challenges they confronted as urban indigenous women. In a feminist PAR project with Latina and African American health promoters in post-Katrina New Orleans, coresearchers took pictures and interviewed survivors of Hurricane Katrina in a participatory data collection and analysis process through which they sought to document health disparities and community health promotion in response to a humanitarian disaster (Scheib & Lykes, 2013). The resultant photonarratives—which incorporated individual stories of survival, analyses of the underlying structural causes of racism in New Orleans, as well as the racialization of survivors and the stories of resistance—were blown up on banners in English and Spanish and presented to the photographed neighborhoods and to the wider New Orleans community.

Individual and collective drawings are also used regularly in participatory and action research, specifically with women and children in rural communities in order to address the traumatic effects of conflict. Figure 6.5 is typical of many images that are drawn to represent life during war. In one of a series of workshops conducted to assess local understandings of the contributions of these creative techniques to women's postconflict recovery and rethreading of community, the women of a village near Chajul in the Ixil region of northern Quiché, Guatemala, represented life before they participated in feminist community workshops. When discussing their collective drawing as represented in Figure 6.5, the women spoke of how the "military entered the daily lives of what women do every day, such as the soldier killing a woman who is washing her clothes," or "soldiers coming into the house while women are making tortillas." They depicted helicopters dropping bombs, houses burning, and people fleeing to the mountains or into the town. There is deep sadness and "many people are burned inside their houses and in their *temazcales* [traditional steam baths]." They explained how "women had to cook for the soldiers" while fathers and brothers, some of whom were only

Figure 6.5 Remembering Violence Against Mayan Communities During Guatemala's Armed Conflict

12 years old, were forcibly conscripted into the civil patrols.[3] In the group conversation about this drawing, the village women noted that the "soldiers raped the women. The violence always existed. Sometimes they raped a woman and then killed her right away" (Lykes & Crosby, in press).

c. Interpreting findings within and across differences.

Feminists engaged in community and action research projects strive to engage local participants and coresearchers in all phases of the process, and sometimes the most challenging stage in this process is in the analysis and interpretation of data. Throughout the PhotoPAR project in Chajul, the coresearchers collaborated by analyzing the phototexts generated by individual photographers in small group discussions. Together, they coded the context; the actors or people involved; their feelings, actions, and thoughts; and the reasons, causes or explanations for the event(s) portrayed in the photographs, which were complemented by the original texts from the photographer and the personal interviews with those depicted (see Lykes, Coquillon, & Rabenstein, 2010, for a detailed explanation of this process). Within these projects, data analysis is a teaching–learning method, through which coresearchers engage in action–reflection iterative processes in order to generate knowledge. Thus, data gathering and interpretation are procedures of conscientization or developing critical consciousness and also opportunities for learning skills. Here, women have the opportunity to perform their multiple self-understandings, increasing self-confidence and participation.

These interpretative processes result in products that are frequently performed in public spaces by the coresearchers. As described above, the women in New Orleans presented their collective story in many community contexts. In workshops we conducted in Guatemala in 2011 to reflect back on the experience of the PhotoPAR project in Chajul (see Lykes & Crosby, in press), Mayan women highlighted the significance of the product, that is, the book that resulted from the action–reflection process in which they had participated. They described how the book helped them to "remember others and what happened to them, to remember the dead," and noted that "it's like a museum so that youth can see what happened in our community." Another coresearcher referenced the public presentation of the book in Guatemala City, an important moment of breaking through the generalized silence about the violence suffered by Mayan women in Chajul and its villages during the war. The book was compared to the military archive that had recently been opened, in that it provided a means through which "we can demand justice for the victims." In the book's concluding sections, individual participants describe its significance as their "*nunca más*"—in English, "Never Again"—which was the title of the Catholic Church's Recovery of Historical Memory (REMHI) truth-telling report. As suggested in the quote at the beginning of this chapter, in this way, the book is the coresearchers' own truth-telling report, conveying to people in Guatemala City and beyond—including the transnational—what happened to them, and demanding that it will never happen again (Women of Photovoice/ADMI & Lykes, 2000).

In discussions about the significance of the PhotoPAR project, the women also explained how the sale of the book has allowed them to continue their economic development work. By participating in PhotoPAR—including taking photographs, and interviewing women, men, and children in the villages surrounding Chajul—coresearchers learned to multiply their experiences and subsequently ran workshops with women in the villages. As one woman put it, "lots of people in the villages had these same experiences and invited me to come back to do workshops with them so they could tell their stories and to feel better by being involved in mental health workshops." These workshops allowed the women of Chajul to see themselves reflected in others, and thus, they were an important reflexive and community-building experience for all.

Developing processes of shared learning and *conscientization* are not without conflict. As suggested in this chapter, coresearchers are challenged to cross and contest borders of racialization, gender, social class, sexualities, and abilities (among others); and solidarity takes shape in dialogical relationships formed within the terrain of ever-present histories of colonization. Yet, when coresearchers succeed in creating collaborative collective processes and actions that they utilize to challenge systems of power and structures of domination, they can begin to redress social inequality and cocreate personal and social change.

Concluding Reflections: Challenges Toward the Future

This chapter provides examples of how the interstices of feminist and community-based participatory action research provide a rich border space in which to engage the community in knowledge creation and challenge systems of power and structures of domination. This final section discusses two sets of ongoing challenges in this work that can move the work described forward in new directions. First, a challenge remains in linking the community to broader processes of organizing toward societal transformation; and second, despite discourses of reflexivity and the cocreation of knowledge, power tends to remain firmly in the hands of academic coresearchers. The question of how to "work the hyphen" (Fine, 1994), discussed earlier in this chapter, remains a central dilemma to those who are situated within academic institutions of the North. It is a dilemma that still requires the shifting of margins to center that bell hooks (1984/2000) pressed for nearly three decades ago, and the related decentering of privilege.

Despite an overt commitment to social change, all too often, coresearchers working within the contexts described throughout this chapter engage in ameliorative rather than transformative practices. Some are involved in processes of change that are limited solely to personal transformation, which, while extremely important, fail to incorporate the material conditions that sustain systems of oppression and marginalization; this ultimately maintains an institutional *status quo*. As important, many local actions, such as some described earlier, are not necessarily yoked to social movements that might further influence the wider societal levels or broader based constituencies. An exception is the *Sangtin Yatra* or Playing with Fire initiative discussed in this chapter, where there was a linking of "place-based" strategies (Mohanty, 2003) to broader alliances, and in the process, a social movement was formed. Building on such an approach, contemporary action researchers, while continuing to collaborate with community- or identity-based groups, aim to connect similar efforts to these broader movements and networks, a strategy that enhances possibilities for systemic change and social transformations (see Hale, 2008, for examples). This activist framework to the work described has thus alternatively been labeled social change research (Seedat, Cloete, & Shochet, 1988; Snowden, 1987), social justice research (Prilleltensky, 2001; Prilleltensky & Nelson, 1997), social activism (Bhana & Kanjee, 2001), or activist scholarship (Hale, 2008). Despite differences in emphasis or approach, the framework stresses core values of justice, equity, and transformation. Change then occurs at multiple levels, including that of the individual, the small organization, the neighborhood, social institutions, and the wider society.

Drawing on this change-justice-activism model, Seedat (1997); Comas-Díaz, Lykes, and Alarcón (1998); and Watts and Serrano-Garcia (2003), among others, situate contemporary community research within a liberatory framework. Seedat (1997) broadly defines this new model as one that respects indigenous knowledge systems, critically engages Euro-American theory, and resists the hegemony of dominant institutional power structures. Theorists and researchers from the majority world, including South Africans Berger and Lazarus (1987), Bulhan (1985), and Seedat (1997), have been informed by liberation struggles in North Africa and Latin America which advocate for a redistribution of resources, and for the liberation of oppressed groups from the psychological and material effects of colonization (see Ngonyama ka Sigogo et al., 2004, for a fuller description).

Such postcolonial theories, movements, and strategies have deep implications for the so-called Northern Hemisphere. Morten Levin and Davydd Greenwood (2008) urge those located within universities to create teaching–learning communities and to alert us to the growing intrusion of the corporate model of accountability and quality assurance within higher education. They embrace action research as a potential resource for institutional transformation and knowledge generation that are responsive to the public good and to practical problem solving. The "Behind-the-Scenes" descriptions by Fine and Torre regarding AR facilitated by and out of the Graduate Center of the City University of New York are concrete examples of such university responsiveness.

In the edited volume *Feminism FOR REAL: Deconstructing the Academic Industrial Complex of Feminism* (2011), indigenous feminist activist Jessica Yee and her colleagues have turned a similarly critical lens onto feminism itself, particularly as it is taught within the academy. This questioning of the institutionalization of feminism calls for the problematizing of the position of power and privilege of those of us situated within academia—and for a recentering of knowledge production into the community itself, which remains a central tenet of action research.

These actions of critique and recentering are at once radical, political, and critical; and they have as their aim the construction of knowledge and the development of praxis that are geared toward the creation of social justice by communities themselves, as well as a radical decentering of notions of academic privilege. Through such processes, community research can engage feminism in order to progress toward a next iteration: the further development of postcolonial feminist action and community research. As we continue our work with rural Mayan women in Guatemala, we are challenged (1) to center the knowledge they have generated in documenting and naming the effects of war, including the material conditions of impoverishment that constrain their community's life circumstances, and (2) to support Mayan women's activism through social movements in Guatemala and transnationally.

DISCUSSION QUESTIONS

1. What do feminist community and participatory and/or action research bring to the table in terms of methodologies for linking theory and practice?

2. How do you see an intersectional analysis shaping and informing feminist community and/or participatory and action research? Does the "community" with whom the research is being conducted have to be feminist? What is "feminism" to you, "for real" (Yee, 2011)?

3. What constitutes "action" within feminist community and/or participatory and action research?

WEB RESOURCES

- *COMMUNITY TOOL BOX*

http://ctb.ku.edu/en/default.aspx

This is a global resource for free information on essential skills for building healthy communities. It offers more than 7,000 pages of practical guidance in creating change and improvement. It includes exercises, background readings, and practical tips for changing real-world communities. Topic sections include step-by-step instruction, examples, and checklists. The Community Tool Box is a service of the Work Group for Community Health and Development at the University of Kansas.

- *HIGHLANDER RESEARCH AND EDUCATION CENTER*

http://highlandercenter.org

Highlander serves as a catalyst for grassroots organizing and movement building in Appalachia, the South, and beyond. Through popular education, participatory research, and cultural work, it develops leadership and helps create and support strong, democratic organizations that work for justice, equality, and sustainability.

- *INCITE! WOMEN OF COLOR AGAINST VIOLENCE*

http://www.incite-national.org

This is a U.S.-based organization of radical feminists of color who are working to advance "a movement to end violence against women of color and our communities through direct action, critical dialogue, and grassroots organizing." The site includes a useful resource directory.

- *PARTICIPATORY FEMINISM (PARFEM)*

http://atlas.geo.cornell.edu/parfem

This site is an online participatory feminist resource where colearners can contribute materials and ideas and carry on dialogue. The site includes an online bibliography, case studies, and live events such as presentations and discussions that can be downloaded.

- *RACIALICIOUS*

http://www.racialicious.com/

This blog provides antiracist commentary (mainly from the United States and Canada) on popular culture. Includes a regular blog by Jessica Yee, editor of *Feminism for REAL* (2011).

- *RADICALLY QUEER*

http://radicallyqueer.wordpress.com/

This U.S.-based blog discusses queerness, sexuality, gender, violence, and desire.

- *SEEDS FOR CHANGE*

http://www.seedsforchange.org.uk/free/resources

This site provides resources for grassroots activists (based in the United Kingdom).

JOURNALS RESOURCES

Action Research

Feminism & Psychology

Feminist Studies

International Journal of Qualitative Studies in Education

Women's Studies International Forum

NOTES

1. Within this chapter, the term "coresearcher" is used to refer to all engaged in the research endeavor, both those traditionally labeled "researchers" and those traditionally labeled "participants."

2. See Stanford Encyclopedia of Philosophy for more details: http://plato.stanford .edu/entries/identity-politics/

3. The military government established the civil patrols (PAC) in most of rural Guatemala in the early 1980s as compulsory militias for all adolescent and adult men. In many places, the PAC was associated as the direct perpetrator (under military orders) of war crimes, although participants were often forced to commit such crimes under threat of death. The army formally disbanded the PAC in 1996.

AUTHORS' NOTE

Portions of this chapter are revisions based on a chapter by M. Brinton Lykes and Rachel Hershberg (2012) in Sharlene Hesse-Biber (Ed.), *Handbook of Feminist Research: Theory and Praxis* (2nd ed.). Reprinted with permission from Sage.

REFERENCES

Adelman, C. (1993). Kurt Lewin and the origins of action research. *Educational Action Research, 1,* 7–24. doi:10.1080/0965079930010102

Alexander, M. J. (2005). *Pedagogies of crossing: Meditations on feminism, sexual politics, memory, and the sacred.* Durham, NC: Duke University Press.

Bartunek, J. M. (2008). Insider/Outsider team research: The development of the approach and its meanings. In A. B. Shani, N. Adler, S. A. Mohrman, W. A. Pasmore, & B. Stymne (Eds.), *Handbook of collaborative management research* (pp. 73–91). Thousand Oaks, CA: Sage.

Berger, S., & Lazarus, S. (1987). The views of community organizers on the relevance of psychological practice in South Africa. *Psychology in Society, 7,* 6–23.

Bhana, A., & Kanjee, A. (2001). Epistemological and methodological issues in community psychology. In M. Seedat, N. Duncan, & S. Lazarus (Eds.), *Community psychology: Theory, method and practice. South African and other perspectives* (pp. 135–158). Cape Town, South Africa: Oxford University Press.

Billies, M., Johnson, J., Murungi, K., & Pugh, R. (2009). Naming our reality: Low-income LGBT people documenting violence, discrimination and assertions of justice. *Feminism & Psychology, 19,* 375–380. doi:10.1177/0959353509105628

Blacklock, C., & Crosby, A. (2004). The sounds of silence: Feminist research across time in Guatemala. In W. Giles & J. Hyndman (Eds.), *Sites of violence: Gender and conflict zones* (pp. 45–72). Los Angeles: University of California Press.

Blanchet-Cohen, N., Ragan, D., & Amsden, J. (2003). Children becoming social actors: Using visual maps to understand children's views of environmental change. *Children, Youth and Environments, 13*(2), 278–299. Retrieved from http://colorado.edu/journals/cye

Brabeck, K. M., Lykes, M. B., & Hershberg, R. (2011). Framing immigration to and deportation from the United States: Guatemalan and Salvadoran families make meaning of their experiences. *Community, Work and Family, 14,* 275–296. doi:10.1080/13668803.2010.520840

Brydon-Miller, M., Greenwood, D., & Maguire, P. (2003). Why action research? *Action Research 1,* 9–28. doi:10.1177/14767503030011002

Brydon-Miller, M., Maguire, P., & McIntyre, A. (2004). *Traveling companions: Feminism, teaching, and action research.* Westport, CT: Praeger.

Bulhan, H. A. (1985). *Frantz Fanon and the psychology of oppression.* New York, NY: Plenum Press.

Bunster, X., & Chaney, E. M. (1989). Epilogue. Taking pictures: A new methodology. In X. Bunster & E. M. Chaney (Eds.), *Sellers & servants: Working women in Lima, Peru* (pp. 217–233). Granby, MA: Bergin & Garvey.

Butler-Kisber, L., & Poldma, T. (2010). The power of visual approaches in qualitative inquiry: The use of collage making and concept mapping in experiential research. *Journal of Research Practice, 6*(2), Article M18. Retrieved from http://jrp.icaap.org/index.php/jrp/article/view/197/196

Chavez, V., Duran, B., Baker, Q. E., Avila, M. M., & Wallerstein, M. (2003). The dance of race and privilege in community based participatory research. In M. Minkler & N. Wallerstein (Eds.), *Community-based participatory research for health: From process to outcomes* (pp. 81–97). San Francisco, CA: Jossey Bass.

Collins, P. H. (1990). *Black feminist thought: Knowledge, consciousness, and the politics of empowerment.* Boston, MA: Unwin Hyman.

Comas-Díaz, L., Lykes, M. B., & Alarcón, R. (1998). Ethnic conflict and the psychology of liberation in Guatemala, Perú, and Puerto Rico. *American Psychologist, 53,* 778–792.

Commission for Historical Clarification (CEH). (1999). *Guatemala: Memoria del silencio (Tz'inil Na'Tab'Al)* [Guatemala: Memory of Silence]. Retrieved from http://www.usip.org/publications/truth-commission-guatemala

Cornwall, A. (1992). Body mapping in health RRA/PRA. *RRA Notes, 16,* 69–76. London, England: IIED.

Creese, G., & Frisby, W. (Eds.). (2011). *Feminist community research: Case studies and methodologies.* Vancouver, Canada: University of British Columbia Press.

Crosby, A. (2009). Anatomy of a workshop: Women's struggles for transformative participation in Latin America. *Feminism & Psychology, 19,* 343–353. doi:10.1177/0959353509105625

Crosby, A., & Lykes, M. B. (2011). Mayan women survivors speak: The gendered relations of truth telling in postwar Guatemala. *International Journal of Transitional Justice, 5,* 456–476. doi:10.1093/ijtj/ijr017

Cruz, L. E. (2011). Medicine bundle of contradictions: Female-man, Mi'kmaq/Acadian/Irish diasporas, invisible disAbilities, masculine-feminist. In Jessica Yee (Ed.), *Feminism FOR REAL: Deconstructing the academic industrial complex of feminism* (pp. 49–60). Ottawa, Ontario, Canada: Canadian Centre for Policy Alternatives/DLR International Printing.

Dick, B. (2004). Action research literature: Themes and trends. *Action Research, 2,* 425–444.

Duffy, K. G., & Wong, F. Y. (1996). *Community psychology.* Boston, MA: Allyn & Bacon.

Eikeland, O. (2001). Action research as the hidden curriculum of the Western tradition. In P. Reason & H. Bradbury (Eds.), *Handbook of action research: Participative inquiry and practice* (pp. 145–156). Thousand Oaks, CA: Sage.

Equipo de Estudios Comunitarios y Accion Psicosocial (ECAP). (2009). *Mujeres Rompiendo el Silencio—Intervencion psicosocial con sobrevivientes de violencia sexuales durante el conflicto armado en Guatemala* [Women Breaking the Silence—Psychosocial intervention with survivors of sexual violence during the armed conflict in Guatemala]. Guatemala: Serviprensa.

Fals-Borda, O. (1985). *The challenge of social change.* London, England: Sage.

Fals-Borda, O. (2001). Participatory (action) research in social theory: Origins and challenges. In P. Reason & H. Bradbury (Eds.), *Handbook of action research: Participative inquiry and practice* (pp. 27–37). Thousand Oaks, CA: Sage.

Fals-Borda, O., & Rahman, M. A. (Eds.). (1991). *Action and knowledge: Breaking the monopoly with participatory action research.* New York, NY: Apex Press.

Fine, M. (1994). Working the hyphens: Reinventing the self and other in qualitative research. In N. Denzin & Y. Lincoln (Eds.), *Handbook of qualitative research* (pp. 70–82). Newbury Park, CA: Sage.

Fine, M., & Ruglis, J. (2009). Circuits and consequences of dispossession: The racial realignment of the public sphere for U.S. youth. *Transforming Anthropology, 17,* 20–33.

Fine, M., & Torre, M. E. (2006). Intimate details: Participatory action research in prison. *Action Research, 4,* 253–269. doi:10.1177/1476750306066801

Fine, M., Torre, M. E., Boudin, K., Bowen, I., Clark, J., Hylton, D. . . . Upegui, D. (2001, September). *Changing minds: The impact of college in a maximum security prison.* Retrieved from http://web.gc.cuny.edu/che/changingminds.html

Fortier, A-M. (1999). Re-membering places and the performance of belonging(s). *Theory, Culture & Society, 16*(2), 41–64. doi:10.1177/02632769922050548

Freire, P. (1970). *Pedagogy of the oppressed.* New York, NY: Seabury Press.

Fulchiron, A., Paz, O. A., & Lopez, A. (2009). *Tejidos que lleva el alma: Memoria de las mujeres mayas sobrevivientes de violación sexual durante el conflicto armado* [Weavings of the soul: Memories of Mayan women survivors of sexual violence during the armed conflict]. Guatemala City: Community Studies and Psychosocial Action Team, National Union of Guatemalan Women and F&G Editores.

Gorelick, S. (1996). Contradictions of feminist methodology. In H. Gottfried (Ed.), *Feminism and social change: Bridging theory and practice* (pp. 23–45). Chicago: University of Illinois Press.

Goudvis, P. (1991). *Trabajando para un futuro mejor: Talleres creativos con niños [Working for a better future: Creative workshops with children;* Motion picture]. Available from author.

Greenwood, D. J., & Levin, M. (1998). *Introduction to action research: Social research for social change.* Thousand Oaks, CA: Sage.

Grupo de Mujeres Mayas Kaqla. (2004). *La palabra y el sentir de las mujeres mayas de Kaqla* [The words and feelings of the Mayan women of Kaqla]. Guatemala: Netherlands: Oxfam.

Grupo de Mujeres Mayas Kaqla. (2009). *Mujeres Mayas: Universo y vida. Kinojib'al Qati't* [Mayan women: Universe and life. Kinojib'al Qati't]. Guatemala: Iximulew.

Gustavsen, B. (2008). Action research, practical challenges and the formation of theory. *Action Research, 6,* 421–437.

Hale, C. R. (2008). (Ed.). *Engaging contradictions: Theory, politics, and methods of activist scholarship.* Berkeley, CA: University of California Press.

Hershberg, R. M., & Lykes, M. B. (2012). Redefining family: Transnational girls narrate experiences of parental migration, detention, and deportation. *FQS—Forum: Qualitative Social Research Sozialforschung, 14*(1), Art. 5. Available from http://www.qualitative-research.net/index.php/fqs/article/view/1770/3476

Hill, J., Bond, M. A., Mulvey, A., & Terenzio, M. (2000). Methodological issues and challenges for a feminist community psychology: An introduction to a Special Issue. *American Journal of Community Psychology, 28,* 759–772.

Hondagneu-Sotelo, P. (1996). Immigrant women and paid domestic work: Research, theory and activism. In H. Gottfried (Ed.), *Feminism and social change: Bridging theory and practice* (pp. 105–122). Urbana: University of Illinois Press.

Hondagneu-Sotelo, P. (2007). *Domestica: Immigrant workers cleaning and caring in the shadows of affluence.* Berkeley: University of California Press. (Original work published 2001)

hooks, b. (2000). *Feminist theory: From margin to center.* Cambridge, MA: South End Press. (Original work published 1984)

Khanna, R. (1996). Participatory action research (PAR) in women's health: SARTHI, India. In K. de Koning & M. Martin (Eds.). *Participatory research in health: Issues and experiences* (pp. 62–71). London, England: Zed Books.

Kretzman, J., & McKnight, J. (1993). *Building communities from the inside out: A path toward finding and mobilizing communities' assets.* Chicago, IL: ACTA.

Levin, M., & Greenwood, D. (2008). The future of universities: Action research and the transformation of higher education. In P. Reason & H. Bradbury (Eds.), *The SAGE handbook of action research: Participative inquiry and practice* (2d ed., pp. 211–226). London, England: Sage.

Lykes, M. B. (1994). Terror, silencing, and children: International multidisciplinary collaboration with Guatemalan Maya communities. *Social Science and Medicine, 38,* 543–552.

Lykes, M. B. (2001). Creative arts and photography in participatory action research in Guatemala. In P. Reason & H. Bradbury (Eds.), *Handbook of action research: Participative inquiry and practice* (pp. 363–371). Thousand Oaks, CA: Sage.

Lykes, M. B. (2010). Silence(ing), voice(s) and gross violations of human rights: Constituting and performing subjectivities through PhotoPAR. *Visual Studies, 25,* 238–254.

Lykes, M. B. (1999), in collaboration with A. Caba Mateo, J. Chávez Anay, I. A. Laynez Caba, U. Ruiz, & Joan W. Williams. Telling stories—rethreading lives: Community education, women's development and social change among the Maya Ixil. *International Journal of Leadership in Education: Theory and Practice, 2*(3), 207–227.

Lykes, M. B., & Cabrera Pérez-Armiñan, M. (2008). *Compartir la memoria colectiva: Acompañamiento psicosocial y justicia integral para mujeres víctimas de violencia sexual en conflictos armados* [Sharing our collective memory: Psychosocial accompaniment and integral justice for women, victims of sexual violence in armed conflict]. Guatemala: PCS-Consejeria en Proyectos.

Lykes, M. B., & Coquillon, E. D. (2007). Participatory and action research and feminisms: Towards transformative praxis. In S. Hesse-Biber (Ed.), *Handbook of feminist research: Theory and praxis* (pp. 297–326). Thousand Oaks, CA: Sage.

Lykes, M. B., Coquillon, E. D., & Rabenstein, K. L. (2010). Theoretical and methodological challenges in participatory community-based research. In H. Landrine & N. F. Russo (Eds.), *Handbook of diversity in feminist psychology* (pp. 55–82). New York, NY: Springer.

Lykes, M. B., & Crosby, A. (in press). Creative methodologies as a resource for Mayan women's protagonism. In B. Hamber (Ed.), *Trauma, development, and peacebuilding: Towards an integrated psychosocial approach.*

Lykes, M. B., & Hershberg, R. (2012). Participatory action research and feminisms: Social inequalities and transformative praxis. In S. Hesse-Biber (Ed.), *Handbook of feminist research: Theory and praxis* (2nd ed., pp. 331–367). Thousand Oaks, CA: Sage.

Lykes, M. B., & McDonald, E. (in press). Exploring meaning making with adolescents "left behind" by migration. *Education Action Research.*

Maguire, P. (1987). *Doing participatory research: A feminist approach.* Amherst: Massachusetts Center for International Education, University of Massachusetts.

Martin, M. (1996). Issues of power in the participatory research process. In K. de Koning & M. Martin (Eds.), *Participatory research in health: Issues and experiences* (pp. 82–93). London, England: Zed Books.

McIntyre, A., & Lykes, M. B. (2004). Weaving words and pictures in/through feminist participatory action research. In M. Brydon-Miller, P. Maguire, & A. McIntyre (Eds.), *Traveling companions: Feminism, teaching, and action research* (pp. 73–110). Westport, CT: Praeger.

McMillan, D. W., & Chavis, D. M. (1986). Sense of community: A definition and theory. *Journal of Community Psychology, 14*, 6–23.

Melville, M., & Lykes, M. B. (1992). Guatemalan Indian children and the sociocultural effects of government-sponsored terrorism. *Social Science and Medicine, 34,* 533–548. doi:10.1016/0277-9536(92)90209-9

Menchú, R. (1983). *I, Rigoberta Menchu: An Indian woman in Guatemala.* (E. Burgos-Debray, Ed.; A. Wright, Trans.). London, England: Verso.

Mohanty, C. T. (2003). *Feminism without borders: Decolonizing theory, practicing solidarity.* Durham, NC: Duke University Press.

Naples, N. A. (2003). *Feminism and method: Ethnography, discourse analysis, and activist research.* New York, NY: Routledge.

Ngonyama ka Sigogo, T., Hooper, M., Long, C., Lykes, M. B., Wilson, K., & Zietkiewicz, E. (2004). Chasing rainbow notions: Enacting community psychology in the classroom and beyond in post-1994 South Africa. *American Journal of Community Psychology, 33,* 77–89.

Pavlovsky, E., Martinez Bouquet, C., & Moscio, F. (1985). *Psicodrama. Cuando y par que dramatizar* [Psychodrama: When and why to dramatize]. Buenos Aires, Argentina: Ediciones Busqueda.

Personal Narratives Group. (1989). *Interpreting women's lives: Feminist theory and personal narratives.* Bloomington: Indiana University Press.

Prilleltensky, I. (2001). Emancipation, epistemology, and engagement: Challenges for critical psychology. *International Journal of Critical Psychology, 1,* 106–110.

Prilleltensky, I., & Nelson, G. (1997). Community psychology: Reclaiming social justice. In D. Fox & I. Prilleltensky (Eds.), *Critical psychology: An introduction* (pp. 166–184). London, England: Sage.

Rahman, A. (2004). Globalization: The emerging ideology in the popular protests and grassroots action research. *Action Research, 2*(1), 9–23.

Reason, P., & Bradbury, H. (Eds.). (2008). *The SAGE handbook of action research: Participative inquiry and practice* (2nd ed.). London, England: Sage.

Reid, C., & Frisby, W. (2008). Continuing the journey: Articulating dimensions of feminist participatory action research (FPAR). In P. Reason & H. Bradbury (Eds.), *The SAGE handbook of action research: Participative inquiry and practice* (2d ed., pp. 93–106). London, England: Sage.

Rodari, G. (1996). *The grammar of fantasy: An introduction to the art of inventing stories* (J. Zipes, Trans. & intro.). New York, NY: Teachers & Writers Collaborative.

Sangtin Writers & Nagar, R. (2006). *Playing with fire: Feminist thought and activism through seven lives in India.* Minneapolis: University of Minnesota Press.

Scheib, H. A., & Lykes, M. B. (2013). African American and Latina community health workers engage PhotoPAR as a resource in a post-disaster context: Katrina at 5 years. *Journal of Health Psychology, 18.* doi:10.1177/1359105312470127

Seedat, M. (1997). The quest for a liberatory psychology. *South African Journal of Psychology, 27,* 261–270.

Seedat, M., Cloete, N., & Shochet, I. (1988). Community psychology: Panic or panacea. *Psychology in Society, 11,* 39–54.

Smith, D. E. (1989). Sociological theory: Methods of writing patriarchy. In R. A. Wallace (Ed.), *Feminism and sociological theory* (pp. 34–64). London, England: Sage.

Smith, D. E. (1991). Writing women's experience into social science. *Feminism & Psychology, 1,* 155–169. doi:10.1177/0959353591011019

Snowden, L. R. (1987). The peculiar successes of community psychology: Service delivery to ethnic minorities and the poor. *American Journal of Community Psychology, 15,* 575–586.

Stern, S. P. (1998). Conversation, research, and struggle over schooling in an African American community. In N. A. Naples (Ed.), *Community activism and feminist politics: Organizing across race, class, and gender* (pp. 107–128). New York, NY: Routledge.

Stewart, A. J. (1998). Doing personality research: How can feminist theories help? In B. McVicker Clinchy & J. K. Norem (Eds.), *The gender and psychology reader* (pp. 54–68). New York: New York University Press.

Stommel, W. (2008). Conversational analysis and community of practice as approaches to studying online community. *Language@Internet, 5,* article 5. Retrieved from http://www.languageatinternet.org/articles/2008

Torre, M. E. (2008). Participatory action research and critical race theory: Fueling spaces for *nosotras* to research. *Urban Review, 41,* 106–120.

Torre, M. E., & Fine, M. (2003). Youth reframe questions of educational justice through participatory action research. *The Evaluation Exchange, 9*(2), 6, 22. Harvard Family Research Project.

Visual voices: 100 photographs of village China by the women of Yunnan Province. (1995). Yunnan, China: Yunnan People's Publishing House.

Wang, C. C. (1999). Photovoice: A participatory action research strategy applied to women's health. *Journal of Women's Health, 8,* 185–192.

Watts, R., & Serrano-Garcia, I. (2003). The quest for a liberating community psychology: An overview. *American Journal of Community Psychology, 31,* 73–78.

Women of PhotoVoice/ADMI & Lykes, M. B. (2000). *Voces e imágenes: Mujeres Mayas Ixiles de Chajul/Voices and images: Mayan Ixil women of Chajul.* Guatemala: Magna Terra.

Yee, J. (2011). (Ed.). *Feminism FOR REAL: Deconstructing the academic industrial complex of feminism.* Ottawa, Ontario, Canada: Canadian Centre for Policy Alternatives/DLR International Printing.

Zeichner, K. (2001). Educational action research. In P. Reason & H. Bradbury (Eds.), *Handbook of action research: Participative inquiry and practice* (pp. 273–285). Thousand Oaks, CA: Sage.

Zipes, J. (1995). *Creative storytelling: Building community/changing lives.* New York, NY: Routledge.

CHAPTER 7

Feminist Approaches to In-Depth Interviewing

Sharlene Hesse-Biber

The Cult of Thinness: Delia's Story

The "Cult of Thinness" offers a perspective on young women's problems with eating and their desire to attain a "slender" body image to the point of risking their health and in some cases their lives. The term, "cult of thinness," is a theme that arose from the interviews I conducted with a range of college-aged women; this theme describes the day-to-day rituals that many college-aged women like Delia engage in to attain a slender body ideal. Joining the "cult of thinness," as I came to find out from analyzing these interviews, is a process, and there is a *continuum* along which different women, depending upon their age, race, and sexual orientation, fall in the cultural quest for the ideal body. The extent to which women are drawn into or avoid this form of body obsession often depends on their perception and willingness to rely on alternative socioemotional resources by which they measure their sense of self-esteem beyond the number that comes up on their bathroom scale.

The following interview with Delia, a Caucasian undergraduate senior attending an Ivy League school, offers a glimpse into her lived experiences with "being a body" in Western culture.

An excerpt from Delia's interview (from Hesse-Biber, 2007, pp. 11–14):

Delia: I mean, how many bumper stickers have you seen that say "No Fat Chicks," you know? Guys don't like fat girls. Guys like little girls. I guess because it makes them feel bigger and, you know, they want somebody who looks pretty. Pretty to me is you have to be thin and you have to have like good facial features. It's both. My final affirmation of myself is how many guys look at me when I go into a bar. How many guys pick up on me. What my boyfriend thinks about me.

Interviewer: I see, can you tell me a bit more about that?

Delia: I've never been deprived of anything in my entire life, you know. I was spoiled, I guess, because I've never felt any pressure from my parents to do anything. My dad would say, "Whatever you want to do, if you want to go to Europe, if you want to go to law school, if you don't want to do anything, . . . whatever you want to do, just be happy." No pressure.

I am so affected by *Glamour* magazine and *Vogue* and all that, because that's a line of work I want to get into. I'm looking at all these beautiful women. They're thin. I want to be just as beautiful. I want to be just as thin. Because that is what guys like.

Interviewer: Umm.

Delia: My mom wants me to be nice and pretty and sweet and thin and popular and smart and successful and have everything that I could ever want and just to be happy.

She says to only eat small amounts. "Eat a thousand calories a day; don't overeat." My mom was never critical like, "you're fat." But one time, I went on a camping trip and I gained four pounds and she said, "You've got to lose weight." I mean, she watched what I ate. Like if I was going to get a piece of cake she would be, "Don't eat that."

Interviewer: Can you tell me more about this?

Delia: When I first threw up I thought, "well, it's so easy." My mom told me. "I can eat and not get the calories and not gain weight." And I was modeling at the time, and I wanted to look like the girls in the magazines.

When I was sixteen I just got into this image thing, like tiny, thin. . . . I started working out more. I was Joe Healthy Thin Exercise Queen and I'd just fight eating because I was working out all the time, you know? And so I'm going to aerobics two or three times a day sometimes, eating only salad and a bagel, and like, no fat. I just got caught up in this circle.

Interviewer: Umm.

Delia: The most stressful thing about college for me is whether I'm going to eat that day, and what am I going to eat, more than getting good grades.

Freshman year, I know I weighed like 93 or 94 pounds, which to me was this enormous hang-up, because I'd never weighed more than 90 pounds in my entire life. And I was really freaked out. I knew people were going to be looking at me in the crowd and I'm like, I've got to lose this weight.

Interviewer: Can you tell me more about what that was like?

Delia: So I would just not eat, work out all the time. I loved being on the cheerleading squad, but my partner was a real jerk. He would never work out, and when we would do lifts he'd always be, "Delia, go run. Go run, you're too heavy." I hadn't been eating that day. I had already run seven or eight miles and he told me to run again. And I was surrounded by girls who were all so concerned about their weight, and it was just really this horrible situation.

When I was eight I wanted to be President of the United States. As I grew older and got to college I was like, wow, it's hard for women. I mean, I don't care what people say. If they say the society's liberated, they're wrong. It's still really hard for women. It's like they look through a glass window [sic]. They're vice presidents, but they aren't the president. And I just figured, God, how much easier would it be for me to get married to somebody I know is going to make a lot of money and just be taken care of. . . . I want somebody else to be the millionaire.

What Is a Feminist Approach to Interviewing?

As a feminist interviewer, I am interested in uncovering the *subjugated knowledge* of the diversity of women's realities that often lie hidden and unarticulated. I am asking questions and exploring issues that are of particular concern to women's lives. I am interested in issues of social change and social justice for women and other oppressed groups. As a feminist interviewer, I am aware of the nature of my relationship to those whom I interview, careful to understand my particular personal and researcher standpoints and to understand what role(s) I play in the interview process in terms of my power and authority over the interview situation. I am cognizant, for example, in my interview with Delia, a college student, that I am both an "insider" and an "outsider." I am an "insider" in that Delia and I are part of the academic world in that I am a faculty member and Delia is a student. Yet we inhabit distinct roles in that world and also differ from one another in terms of age, marital status, and a range of other differences that also make me an outsider to her world. Within the interview situation, we also occupy different roles—as I become the interviewer and she, the interviewee. As the interviewer, I have the authority and power to, if I wanted to, set the specific agenda for the interview—for example, the questions I want to ask, or not ask, and when I choose to ask these questions.

Let's look at the structure of the excerpt from the interview I conducted with Delia. While I do have any agenda that I want to pursue, you will notice that during the interview I don't ask many questions, but instead, I listen to Delia's story and support her in helping her tell her story. I do not ask her to answer a question with a fixed number of choices. Instead, I am conducting what in interviewing terminology is called an *unstructured interview*. Sometimes my questions are in response to what she tells me or I am asking for clarification of one of her answers. While I do have some specific ideas I want to find out, I do not have a specific set of questionnaire items with which I begin. I tend to "go with the flow" of the interview, seeing where it takes me.

Interviewing is a particularly valuable research method feminist researchers can use to gain insight into the world of their participants. It is a method used by feminists who are in a range of social and natural science disciplines, from anthropology where the researcher conducts field work within a given culture, to sociology where the feminist researcher wants to gain a new perspective on the lives of participants living in a particular community or society, to the field of nursing and medicine where nurses and doctors want to understand, for example, the impact of certain illnesses and treatments on the ability of patients to cope in their daily lives.

Feminist approaches to survey and market research also center women's issues and concerns, but the goal in utilizing these types of data collection techniques is to enable feminist researchers to generalize their findings to a wider population. Often the goal is to promote social policy changes on issues of particular importance to women where there is a need to gather an overview of the extent of a given problem, such as violence against women, to provide some quantitative assessment of the scope of the problem. In addition, a survey would be important in understanding the public's attitudes toward violence against women, and whether or not the public would support increased funding and programs to address the range of issues with regard to violence against women. These are only a few of the disciplines in which interviewing plays an important role in better understanding the human condition. We can see that the range of interviews feminists conduct span from the unstructured, in-depth variety to a much more specific set of questions that fit into a survey format.

What Are the Different Types of Interviewing Forms?

Interviews come in a series of formats. We can think of the interview method running along a "continuum" from "informal" to "formal." The *informal* interview has little structure. Very often this type of interview is used to build a relationship with your participant, to explore what might be the relevant topics of interest to them, and to uncover topics that might otherwise be overlooked by the researcher. So, for example, I didn't have any prior contact with Delia, and I knew very little about her body image issues. While not shown in this excerpt, given that I don't personally know Delia, I might start out my interview by asking a set of questions to establish some trust and reciprocity between Delia and myself. The questions I ask would, hopefully, open up a space to get to know a little about her situation, and I might begin with some questions about her current life as a student. I might begin the interview with the following types of open-ended questions:

- How are things going for you this semester?
- What courses are you currently enrolled in?
- How did you happen to select this school?

Unstructured interviews are like the one I conducted with Delia, in which I have a basic interview plan in mind, but I have a *minimum of control* over how the participant should answer the question. I am often taking the lead from my participants—going where they want to go, but keeping an overall topic in mind. Therefore, I might ask the following questions:

- Do you think women are concerned with their appearance at this school?
- Why do you think this is (or is not) the case?

Once I feel I have gained some rapport with Delia, I might begin with asking her a simple open-ended question such as: Can you tell me about what it's like to be a female at this particular college? From there, I would see my job as deeply listening to Delia and seeing where she takes this question. To deeply listen means that you, the interviewer, are focused on what it is your participant is saying. You are not thinking about what it is you want to ask next (your agenda), but you are instead providing support for your participant to tell his or her story. This means maintaining eye contact and nonverbal cues that you are listening, such as nodding to affirm that you understand. As the interview progresses, and I feel that Delia has told me in some detail what her life has been like at her school, I might then begin to ask a few more of my own agenda questions with regard to such issues as her feelings about her own body image.

A *semistructured* interview is conducted with a *specific interview guide*—a list of written questions that I need to cover within a particular interview. I am not too concerned about the order of these questions, but it is important that I cover them in the interview. I have *some control* then in how the interview is constructed in terms of, for example, the sequence of questions and the specific content of each question. However, I am still open to asking new questions, on-the-fly, throughout the interview. I have an agenda; but it is not tightly determined, and there is room left for spontaneity on the part of the researcher and interviewee.

- How much time and energy Delia spends on her appearance. Questions such as: Do you worry about your weight?

- To what extent (if any) do you feel pressure to be thin at this school? (If yes: In what sense?)

- To what extent, if any, has your perception of your body changed from high school to college? (If yes: In what way(s)? If no change: Why do you think that's the case?)

These are some of the questions I might try to interject during the interview with Delia (my agenda). Ideally, I would try not to disrupt the flow of the interview but would do my best to interject these questions at a time when I felt some new space opened up in our conversation.

Structured interviewing is where the researcher has total control over the agenda of the interview. A survey is a good example of this type of interview structure. All participants are asked the same set of questions in a specific order. Sometimes the questions are *open-ended*, such as the ones I asked Delia, but many of them are *closed-ended* questions with a set of fixed choices, such as

- On the average, how many times a week do you exercise? Would you say (1) I don't exercise; (2) one to two times a week; (3) three to five times a week; (4) more than five times a week.

- On the average, how long is your exercise routine? (1) Less than one hour; (2) one hour up to two hours; (3) over two hours, but less than three hours; (4) three hours or more.

- Which of the following describes how you are currently feeling about your body image? "Very happy," "happy," "somewhat happy," "unhappy," "very unhappy."

I would ask a participant to pick just one of these choices when answering the questions. We can use the first two questions to gauge the frequency with which certain behaviors occur. Consequently, we are creating a more standardized way to compare and contrast frequency of certain behaviors, such as exercising, across the different interviews. We can think of the third item as more of an attitudinal question that captures Delia's feelings about her own body image. In this question, I am not asking Delia to go into detail about her feelings but, instead, I want her to respond to a specific *fixed-choice response*. I am asking for a single response that best captures how she feels and that will allow me to compare her assessment with others I interview about this particular issue. I would ask these questions in the order that they are presented here and would not waver from this sequence as I begin to interview other undergraduate women.

We can see from Figure 7.1 that interviews themselves take on a specific structure that can be depicted by a triangle. At the top are those interviews that contain only close-ended questions that are standardized for all participants. There is no leeway in how the interviewer asks the question, and there is usually a set of forced-choice responses to the question from which the participant can select. At the bottom of the triangle is a set of open-ended questions. Very often there is no standard way of asking this type of question, and its placement can vary. Then there is the middle of the triangle where there is often a combination of both closed and open-ended questions asked during an interview situation. Where these questions are placed in the interview is less standardized. Given the variety of types of questions, one might ask: Which is best? The answer to this question depends on the *overall goals of your research project*. A move from the informal end (bottom of the triangle) of interviewing to the more formal, structured end (top of the triangle) is to move from an *exploratory data gathering and*

Figure 7.1   Types of Interview Structures

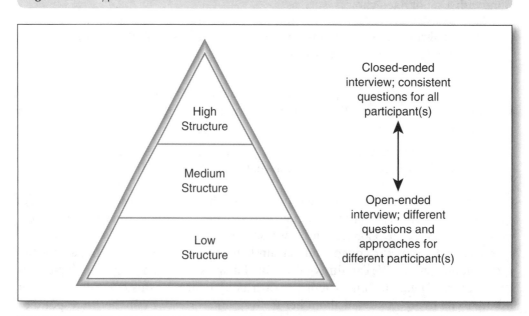

Adapted from: Hesse-Biber and Leavy (2011).

in-depth understanding goal of a project to a more *theory-testing set of goals.* Feminist researchers use both of these interview formats. As we shall observe in Chapter 10 on survey research in this volume, feminists ask questions that require structured interviews to test out the relationships within their data. These structured interviews require large-scale data sets with fixed-choice items. Feminists who carry out mixed methods research, as we will see in Chapter 12, may also have to integrate both types of interviewing styles, with one type of interview illuminating another. For example, feminists can gain insights from unstructured interviews. These interviews can reveal to them what specific questions they need to ask in a survey and what fixed-choice items they should include.

These interview styles, then, often complement one another or are even integrated in a given research project. What is feminist about each of these interview styles, however, are the *types of questions* feminists ask. Research that gets at *an understanding of women's lives and those of other oppressed groups*, research that promotes *social justice and social change*, and research that is mindful of the *researcher–researched relationship* and the *power and authority* imbued in the researcher's role are some of the issues that engage the feminist researcher. Feminist researchers practice *reflexivity* throughout the research process. This practice keeps the researcher mindful of his or her personal positionality and that of the participant. Feminist researchers focus on representation of the researched. Their research praxis strives to place the researcher and research on the "same plane," being mindful of the differences in authority and power that lies within the researcher–researched relationship. It is to these issues that we now turn.

In-Depth Interviewing: A Feminist Perspective

In this chapter, we will focus on the in-depth interview, which is one of the three types of interviews covered in this book. (In the next we will review oral history and focus group interviews.) The *in-depth interview* seeks to understand the "lived experiences" of the individual. We are interested in getting at the "subjective" understanding an individual brings to a given situation or set of circumstances. In-depth interviews are often *issue oriented.* In other words, a researcher might use this method to explore a particular topic and gain focused information on the issue from the participants. The *oral history* method of interviewing usually covers a participant's entire life story. A *focus group* interview provides the researcher with an opportunity to gain information from a group of people in a short period of time. The researcher can also observe the types of interactions among group members concerning a given topic or issue.

THE IN-DEPTH INTERVIEW PROCESS

The interview method remains one of the most popular tools that feminist researchers employ to get at subjugated knowledge and, in turn, feminist principles of praxis continue to be "enhanced rather than impeded by the many discussions and debates about the ethics and relevance of these methods" (O'Shaughnessy & Krogman, 2012, p. 516).

Feminists are particularly concerned with getting at experiences that are often hidden. In-depth interviewing allows the feminist researcher to access the voices of those who are marginalized in a society; women, people of color, homosexuals, and the poor are examples of marginalized groups. Shulamit Reinharz (1992) explains how interviewing is a way feminist researchers have attempted to access women's hidden knowledge:

> Interviewing offers researchers access to people's ideas, thoughts, and memories in their own words rather than in the words of the researcher. This asset is particularly important for the study of women because in this way learning from women is an antidote to centuries of ignoring women's ideas altogether or having men speak for women. (p. 19)

However, there is always a tension in having women speak and you, the researchers speaking for them. The feminist researcher needs to be mindful and reflexive on issues of authority and power within the interview situation. Who has the authority and power to make meaning? There is a "first-level" meaning to your interview that consists of the words your participant tells you, the way he or she puts together his or her story. There is, however, a second level of meaning by which you, the researcher, may read into this interview. This is the meaning you construct that is filtered through your own personal biography and expertise as a researcher. It is important that both the researcher and researched meanings be in conversation with one another. It is in this dialogue, in fact, that new ways of understanding the interview may arise. We take up these issues of analysis and interpretation in more detail in Chapter 13.

DESIGNING AN IN-DEPTH INTERVIEW STUDY

- What is your research question?

It is important to point out that your research question will most often determine your research method. Suppose you want to study eating disorders among college students from a feminist standpoint. Given this perspective, your research goal becomes understanding from the point of view of those you are studying. So, for example, you might ask the following research question:

- What is the "lived experience" of college women's relationship to food and to their body image?

Conducting a survey with closed-ended questions gleaned from the research literature on this topic would *not* capture the lived experiences of these college students. We are interested in their story. We might decide to begin with an unstructured interview that would maximize our understanding of the process by which eating and body issues become gendered and perhaps even begin to build some *theoretical ideas* concerning this topic as we go along. The overall format of the interview process would be along the lines of having a conversation, with some give-and-take between the researcher and the participant as depicted in the following diagram (Figure 7.2).

Figure 7.2 Model of Interview Process as a "Give-and-Take" Model of Gathering In-Depth Interview Data

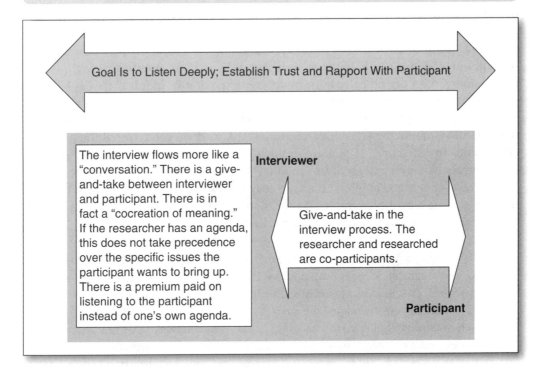

SAMPLING

The logic of qualitative research is concerned with in-depth understanding and usually involves working with *small samples*. The goal is to the look at a "process" or the "meanings" individuals attribute to their given social situation, not necessarily to make generalizations. For example, we investigate women's attitudes toward their bodies, not to make overall generalizations about *how many* women have problems with their body image, but to understand how women *experience* being overweight, for example, in a thin culture. Here, we would be interested in the process by which women do or do not cope with their body image and the ways in which they interact with cultural messages of thinness from the media and significant others in their lives.

Qualitative researchers are often interested in selecting *purposive* or *judgment samples*. The type of purposive sample chosen is based on the particular research question as well as consideration of the resources available to the researcher. Patton (2002, pp. 243–244), in fact, has identified 16 different types of purposive samples, and more than one purposive sampling procedure can be used within any given qualitative study.

While many qualitative interviews are conducted face-to-face, some may be conducted via telephone and even over the Internet. Interviews that are not conducted in person often make it more difficult for the interviewer to establish rapport with the participant, and the researcher also loses the impact of visual and verbal cues, such as gestures and eye contact. In this chapter, I am going to focus on in-person interviewing, although we want to bring these other options to your attention as well. Patton (2002) notes "there are no rules for sample size in qualitative inquiry" (p. 244). Patton goes on to note that part of determining the size of your sample depends on your research question, your specific economic resources, and the particular context within which you are practicing your research project. (Ask: Have you covered the phenomenon under investigation? If you are doing a grounded theory analysis, did you add new samples based on emergent information?) If you are funded by a private or governmental agency, for example, the agency may have strict criteria established for what it believes to be a credible sample size for a qualitative project. Patton leaves us with the following advice with regard to sample size:

> Sample size adequacy, like all aspects of research, is subject to peer review, consensual validation, and judgment. What is crucial is that the sampling procedures and decisions be fully described, explained, and justified so that information users and peer reviewers have the appropriate context for judging the sample. The researcher or evaluator is obligated to discuss how the sample affected the findings, the strengths and weaknesses of the sampling procedures, and any other design decisions that are relevant for interpreting and understanding the reported results. Exercising care not to overgeneralize from purposeful

samples, while maximizing to the full the advantages of in-depth, purposeful sampling, will do much to alleviate concerns about small sample size. (p. 246)

OBTAINING INFORMED CONSENT

It is important to obtain the *informed consent* of each participant after explaining the nature of your research project in advance. If your project is conducted under the auspices of a university or other organizations, each of these institutions will most likely have some type of review board that must approve your study to ensure that you are following the ethical guidelines set forth by that specific institution to protect human subjects. Even though the study and the participant's informed and voluntary participation have been discussed in advance, it is important to reiterate these points prior to beginning the interview. Interviewees should be given every opportunity to ask questions and should also feel free not to answer any question they may not feel comfortable with.

WHEN WOULD I USE AN INTERVIEW GUIDE?

If you have a specific set of issues and concerns to discuss with your participant, you might find a more structured interview to be the best research method for your purposes. In other words, if you have a specific agenda that you want to explore in the interview, you might find it helpful to prepare an *interview guide*. An interview guide is a set of topical areas and questions that the interviewer brings to the interview. Weiss (1994) suggests beginning with a "substantive frame" and then using that to create a guide for the interview process. It is often helpful to think topically before creating and choosing the specific questions you'd like to address in your interview. This can make the creative process of preparing an interview guide much simpler and better organized. In other words, guides can be constructed by first focusing on broader, more abstract areas of inquiry and by then creating a series of interview questions. To begin, write down a "topics-to-learn-about" list. The topics you select become a "line of inquiry" or "domain of inquiry" that you might pursue during the interviews with participants. You can then construct and organize your interview questions to "get at" the information that might relate to each of these "lines." The interview guide is ultimately a list of topics with or without specific questions under each topic that speak to the lines of inquiry that were suggested during the initial drafting of the guide (p. 48). The process of creating an interview guide, even if it remains unused, is an important tool that you might use in preparation for the interview, for it often helps the researcher isolate key issues and consider the kinds of things he or she might like to ask participants. Pilot interviews are an opportunity for researchers to test out the effectiveness of their research guide:

- Is the guide written well? Does the participant understand the question asked? Is the level of the language used devoid of unclear or unfamiliar terms?

- Is the guide complete? Have you covered all of the areas and issues you want to address?

- Does the guide work to answer your research problem? Are there any topical areas or general questions missing from the guide?

Based on early experiences with an interview guide, you can then modify the guide to better suit your needs.

David Karp talks about creating interview guides as an *analytical process* in the following Behind-the-Scenes piece.

Behind the Scenes With David Karp

[I'm] looking for major themes, what I think of as "domains of inquiry." Of course, they do not just come out of nowhere, because I have done so much preliminary work before this. And this is really critical, because too often when people do in-depth interviews, they see putting together the interview guide as, "Well, I've got to get this out of the way." And I see this task of discovering the areas of inquiry as an incredibly important analytical step in the process of doing this work. And if we talk about the full process, when you get to the point of writing, in my case books or articles, it comes full circle because the amount of time and energy that I put into getting this interview guide together really previews what will be the central pieces that I ultimately will write about. Now, in the end, it's just a guide, and in any interview, maybe 60% of the questions I ask are not on that guide. You are sitting, having a conversation with a person, and the artfulness of doing that in-depth interview is to know when to follow up on what a person is saying in the moment. By the end of the interview, I want to make sure that all the areas that I want to have covered are covered. But you would be missing the whole deal if the only questions you asked were the questions on your guide.

It is important that interview guides do not become too long or detailed. Consider the interview guide as a shorthand reference that you may rely on from time to time but are clear not to have this guide take over your connection and "in the moment" connection to your participant. The interview guide can also be a quick "checklist" you consult to make sure you have touched on the most important topics you felt were important to cover during any given interview (see also Weiss, 1994).

Conducting an In-Depth Interview

The in-depth interview can be particularly helpful when the feminist researcher wants to focus on a particular area of an individual's life. The interview tends to occur in one session, although multiple follow-up sessions may occur to expand or develop the ideas from the initial session. The goal of intensive interviews is to gain rich data from the perspectives of selected individuals on a particular subject. For example, in my own research on body image among different populations, I became interested in how college-aged women experienced living with eating disorders while going to college. Let us take a look at a transcript excerpt from an interview with Alison, a white, middle-class, 20-year-old college student. I am interested in knowing more about Alison's experiences with eating disorders in college and specifically how her transition from high school to college affected how she negotiated her eating issues. She is Asian American and the second oldest of five sisters, one of whom is a half-sister from her father's second marriage. Alison has been bingeing and purging since she was in high school. Her father remarried when she was in the fifth grade; in Alison's words, "That's about the time of the onset of my eating problem." In this excerpt, Alison talks about her eating problems and their current manifestation in her life as a college coed. Alison's mother is a compulsive binge eater whose eating issues apparently began after her divorce from Alison's father. We enter the conversation as Alison begins to talk about her binge-eating disorder and her mother's problems with food.

Alison: My mother was binge eating at night. She's a compulsive eater. And I'd watch her, and I thought it was normal. And just in spurts. At night, she'd get up by herself and get a big bowl of something, and just like, eat it all. I can remember the sounds very well. That, in addition to me thinking I was fat because I was eating so much, and my stomach was hurting and I would feel bad. You know . . . I was obsessed with food all throughout high school. I had not vomited except, you know, a good amount, but I wouldn't say it was bulimia. Once every month, 2 weeks, something like that.

So what happened when you made the transition from high school to college?

Alison: First year of college was OK. I was a little obsessed with food as I always am, but I never vomited. My sophomore year, after, you know, I told you about my boyfriend, and he wasn't there, but I was, you know, that was my crutch, you know, I used it exactly the way an alcoholic would alcohol. So that's what I was doing.

Can you tell me how you were feeling during this time?

Alison: A lonely Friday night, I was in a single room by myself at a school I didn't like, you know. I didn't have a big social life. I had a close friend but that wasn't enough. I had lots of good acquaintances, one close, best, trustworthy friend, but I don't know; it just didn't seem like enough somehow.

So when you said, "It didn't seem like enough somehow," what did you mean?

Alison: Mealtime was always hard because I'd always overeat, and the problem was I would always go to classes from like 9:00 until 12:00, or whatever, and then I would have like the whole rest of the day. And, like, I liked high school because you are supposed to do this from this time to that time, and then you're supposed to do homework, but then you have to organize your own time, set your own schedule, and I just don't know what to do, and I'm always thinking, am I studying too much? I feel like I've been studying forever, but if I don't then I'll feel guilty. And I just didn't know what to do with myself. Today it's easier, because I have a tight schedule now.

So you'd go home and eat?

Alison: So I guess around dinnertime I would eat and then, you know, being premed, you have to study all the time. And the only break you can take without feeling guilty is mealtime or exercise time. But I guess if you are bingeing, that's not really mealtime. I don't know. After dinner I would just, I think it was physical after a while. I honestly was compelled to go back down, you know, I have a food card. I can put anything on my food card. Of course, later I did spend lots of cash I didn't have, and then I would just go to the bathroom, which was the community bathroom for the floor.

Right after you ate?

Alison: Yes. And after, my friend and I would do study sessions. I would come back at like 10 p.m., and I had a refrigerator in my room, and I grocery shopped, and I would make like bread with peanut butter and jelly, or jelly and butter, just whatever I had. I knew there was a vending machine in our building, and I would go down there and I'd come back up, and I'd go down there, and I'd come back up. And also, my best friend who lived next door to me in her single, she went home a couple of weekends, once a month or so, and I would be there. I felt alone. There were people I could hang out with. But nobody who really knew me, and so I would go down to the vending machines, and I can remember thinking, "This just isn't going to do it for me. It's not going to make my Friday night that exciting, but then again, why not?" So . . . . I would binge four times a week. Sometimes I stopped.

Uh-huh. So for how long?

Alison: Most of my sophomore year, and a good part of that summer.

So you also binged when you went home as well?

Alison: I remember when I went home for Christmas my sister. . . . Oh, Christmas was the worst at my house. That's where all the memories came back. My family left for Florida. I was there by myself with my brother. It was the house, the emptiness, the food. You know, it was just the worst. It was an awful Christmas. My boyfriend was seeing these other girls and I was in town, and I had no friends left that I kept in touch with. It was just really awful. My sister, I remember, mentioned it to me. She said, "Are you bulimic?" She knew I was defending my food. I told her, I said, "Yes." And she started crying and she got real upset, and she said, "Would you please make an effort, or something like that?" And so, when I went back to college, I stopped being bulimic for a couple of months.

In looking at Alison's transcript, several points can be made. First, the in-depth interview is a way of gaining information and understanding from individuals on a *specific topic*. In this example, we were interested in understanding Alison's transition from high school to college and her experience with bulimia. Second, the in-depth interview is a very particular kind of interaction, a particular kind of conversation. The in-depth interview dialogue is one where the researcher asks a question or seeks some clarification or amplification on what the participant is saying. The role of the researcher is to listen to the participant's story. If we look at the sheer number of words coming from the interviewer and the participant, we cannot help but note that most of the conversation is coming from the participant. The researcher often seeks to gain more insight into the participant's life by asking questions that probe, in a neutral way, for more information or understanding. The researcher is engaged with the participant and shows this by listening and providing signs of engagement. These include gestures such as nodding or asking the participant to clarify a point or term. We can think of "probing" as an essential tool for an effective interview. *Probes* are also critical to a good interview, and you should be able to distinguish between when a marker has been dropped that you want to pick up on and when you should probe further into a participant's response. Probes are particularly helpful and important during an in-depth interview; if it is a low-structure interview requiring you to ask fewer questions, you will find it very important to delve deeper into what the participant is choosing to discuss. A probe is the researcher's way of getting a participant to continue with what he or she is talking about, to go further or to elaborate, perhaps by virtue of an illustrative example. Sometimes a probe is simply a sign of understanding and interest that the researcher puts forward to the interviewee. Let's look back to a snippet of our talk with Alison to examine the various types of probing you might employ in this type of interview.

The Art of Probing

Probes allow researchers to provide the participant with support and encouragement without pushing their own agenda into the conversation. The following are some common ways you might employ probing in your own in-depth interviews.

A silent probe. You remain silent, but gesture with a nod. You might also convey your interest and support by maintaining eye contact with the participant while she is speaking.

Echo probe. This is where you may repeat what the participant has just said and ask the participant to continue. Such an example might be where I ask Alison, *So when you said "it didn't seem like enough somehow," what did you mean?* You can see that I repeated what she had said before asking her to clarify what she meant by this statement. I asked a new question but followed the direction of her general concern by asking her to elaborate on this. A neutral probe does not create a new agenda, but it is a way of keeping the conversation going and encouraging participants to continue with their agendas.

Uh-huh probe. This is where you can encourage your participants to continue to tell their stories by providing an affirmation sound like "uh-huh," "yes," or "uhmm, I understand." We can find an example of this probe in my interview with Alison. After she spoke, I said: *Uh-huh, so, for how long?* This is a "neutral probe," in that you are not trying to steer the conversation in a specific direction, but rather you are encouraging the participants to continue with their stories. It is a sign that you are listening and supporting their telling of their story.

Probing by leading the participant. Here you are being a bit more explicit about your probing. You want to lead the participant toward a specific question or touch on a specific issue. In the interview with Alison, I might go on to ask a specific question about her relationship with her mother.

- "Was your mother ever critical about your body?"
- "If so, in what sense?"

I might probe further with this line of questioning by asking Alison a few more questions that would depend on her answer. If, for example, she tells me that her mother was critical and the ways in which she was critical about her body, I might be interested in knowing how often she was and when this tended to occur—as a young child, all throughout her childhood, and so on. I am taking a particular thread of the interview and following up with several other questions I consider pertinent to the specific issue. In this sense, I am following where Alison is taking me, but I am also mindful of my interests and research agenda regarding her mother's attitude toward her body.

Researcher–Researched Relationship in the In-Depth Interview

Feminist researchers are particularly concerned with reducing the hierarchy between the researcher and the researched. In fact, there is concern among feminists that the researcher and the researched are not on the same plane, and there is much attention paid to the interview as a "coconstruction" of meaning. Early on, feminist researcher Ann Oakley (1981; see also Reinharz, 1983) advocated a "participatory model" that stresses the importance of the researcher sharing his or her own biography with the researched. The idea of sharing identities and stories with one another is thought to increase reciprocity and rapport in the interview process, thus breaking down the notions of power and authority invested in the role of the researcher. In particular, there is concern regarding the *power and authority* issues that can ensue between the researcher and the researched. These issues might interfere with the ability of those researched to provide a subjective account of their understanding on a specific issue, their life story, or a specific topic. To further balance out the inequities of power between the researcher and the researched, some feminist researchers and others advocate the process of giving back their research findings and interpretations to the participant to get his or her input and to resolve possible disagreements between their interpretation and that of their participants.

However, there are some feminist researchers who caution against getting too close to your participant. They argue that closeness alone can determine whether or not you will obtain the participants' subjective understandings and perspectives. Feminist sociologist Judith Stacey (1991) suggests that while self-reflection is important to decreasing the power differentials between the researcher and the researched, being too personal with a participant can provide a false illusion that there is no power and authority. This case might make the participants more vulnerable, encouraging them to reveal the more intimate details of their lives. The researcher, however, still has the power to analyze and interpret the participants' stories in a way that renders them with little or no voice in this process. Daphne Patai (1991) argues that giving back one's research findings to participants as a way to address any power imbalances in the researcher–researched relationship may serve only as a "feel good measure." In doing so, the researcher may forgo his or her intellectual responsibility of interpretation to gain rapport and approval from the participant (p. 147). Feminist researchers have suggested a number of important factors to consider throughout the interview process to make sure the participant's stories are heard.

Knowing Your Own Position as a Researcher: Reflexivity in the Research Process

The feminist, reflexive researcher's perspective begins with an understanding of the importance of one's own values and attitudes in relation to the research process. This recognition begins prior to entering the field. Reflexivity means taking a critical look inward and reflecting on one's own lived reality and experiences; this self-reflection or journey can be extremely helpful in the research process. Consider the following questions: How does your own biography affect the research process? What shapes the questions you chose to study and your approach to studying them? How does the specific social, economic, and political context in which you reside affect the research process at all levels? Reflexivity is the process through which a researcher recognizes, examines, and understands how his or her own social background and assumptions can intervene in the research process. Like the researched or participant, the researcher is a product of his or her society's social structures and institutions. Our beliefs, backgrounds, and feelings are part of the process of knowledge construction. To practice reflexivity means to acknowledge that "all knowledge is affected by the social conditions under which it is produced and that it is grounded in both the social location and the social biography of the observer and the observed" (Mann & Kelley, 1997, p. 392). The following is an excerpt from a reflection memo I wrote concerning being a white middle-class researcher who is interviewing adolescent girls in the heart of an inner-city black community center.

Behind the Scenes With Sharlene Nagy Hesse-Biber

Can a White Middle-Class Researcher Interview African American Teens?

I walked into the community center in the heart of an African American community in a medium-sized inner city located in the Northeast. I was scheduled to meet with a group of African American teens between the ages of 13 and 17 to talk with them about their experiences in "coming of age" in their community and their attitudes about school as well as their hopes and concerns for the future. I was definitely the "outsider." I was the researcher and the only white person in the community center that day. My concerns centered around trying very hard not to have a strict agenda—a set of prepackaged questions I would ask all of them, reminiscent of a survey where there is little room for the voices of those I interview to be heard outside of my own agenda of questions. I also wanted to find a way to position myself in the setting so that I would be able to break down somewhat the power and authority that is often inherent in the researcher–researched relationship.

I remember the first day I came to the center. The director piled us all into a room she had reserved for us; after initial introductions, I provided more detailed information about myself, telling them I was a researcher and a teacher, that I was not the expert, but rather they were the experts on their own lives. I wanted to begin to shift the emphasis and flow of conversation around their concerns and hopes; I was to become the learner, bearing witness to their lives. What was important to them? How did they see their lives unfolding at home? At school? During the course of the interview, they asked me questions: What do you teach? Are you married? Do you have children? Sometimes they would ask me to join them in playing basketball or to look at something they had drawn, and we would engage each other in conversation. I volunteered one day a week at one of the community centers, where I tutored several of the younger children, helping them with their homework assignments. Yet I was concerned about whether or not I was listening in a way that the girls felt they were being heard. How do I listen to them across the many differences I bumped up against with them—my race, my class, my age, my position as a researcher? (Hesse-Biber & Leavy, 2007, p. 13)

Reflexivity goes to the heart of the in-depth interview; it is a process whereby the researcher is sensitive to the important "situational" dynamics that exist between the researcher and the researched that can affect the creation of knowledge. Reflexivity is particularly important when conducting team-based research as well. Pezalla, Pettigrew, and Miller-Day (2012) remind us that the researcher is an instrument in the data collection and analysis process, especially when working in research teams. These authors provide a glimpse at how they came together as researchers to reflect on the variation of differences among them that might facilitate the interview process by having a participant connect to different interviewer characteristics that resonated with them and also served to enhance the interview process and opened up new spaces for obtaining sensitive information.

To understand what biases you bring to a research project, and what specific power and privilege you might impose onto your own research, you might try the following exercise before you begin your research. This simulation could be particularly helpful as you prepare to begin the interviewing phase of your research.

RESEARCH EXERCISE: FINDING YOUR RESEARCH STANDPOINT

Take 10 minutes and write down the various ways your social position affects the way you observe and perceive others in your daily life.

- What particular biases do you bring to and/or impose onto your research?
- How does this affect the types of questions you ask in your own research?
- How does this influence the research style you take on?

As reviewed in the chapter on feminist standpoint epistemology, Sandra Harding (1993) introduces the concept of "strong objectivity" and argues that considering one's own standpoint during all phases of a research project "*maximizes* objectivity" for the researcher. This also ensures that the participant's voice is represented, listened to, and understood throughout the research process. Harding urges researchers to examine the questions they ask during interviews and notes that these questions are not "value free," for they often reflect the values, attitudes, and agendas of the researcher. Researchers who practice strong objectivity might ask the following questions:

- How do my values, attitudes, and beliefs enter into the research process? Do I only ask questions from my perspective?
- How does my own agenda shape what I ask and what I find?
- How does my positionality affect how I gather, analyze, and interpret my data, and from whose perspective?

These are "reflexivity points," that you may want to consider at the beginning stages of your research project. Practicing reflexivity should be kept in mind when carrying out your entire research process.

The Importance of Listening

Sociologist Marjorie DeVault (2004; with Glenda Gross, 2012) urges researchers to pay attention to the language with which a participant expresses his or her reality. She is particularly interested in not just what is said but what is not said or what might come across as "muted" language. For example, in my interview with Alison, she uses the phrase "You know?" many times. Let's take a snippet from her interview to illustrate what DeVault means:

Alison: A lonely Friday night, I was in a single room by myself at a school I didn't like, you know. I didn't have a big social life. I had a close friend but that wasn't enough. I had lots of good acquaintances, one close, best, trustworthy friend, but I don't know, it just didn't seem like enough somehow.

What DeVault would note is the hesitation that becomes evident in Alison's interview through her use of language; this is especially clear when she begins to talk about her loneliness. She uses the term *"you know"* when she begins to describe the lonely Friday night in her dorm room. In transcribing Alison's interview, the researcher may in fact decide to omit the term *"you know"* since it appears to be irrelevant. Yet DeVault (2004) notes, "I believe, this halting, hesitant, tentative talk signals the realm of not-quite-articulated experience, where standard vocabulary is inadequate, and where a participant tries to speak from experience and finds language wanting" (p. 235).

DeVault (2004) suggests we should honor hesitant language and terms like *you know* during the interview process. This can be done by acknowledging this language not only when it occurs in the interview but also when the time comes to represent our participant's voices in writing up our research findings. She discusses what she has done in a similar interview situation:

I nodded, "um hmm," making the interview comfortable, doing with my participant what we women have done for generations—understanding each other. But I fear that the request is too often forgotten when, as researchers, we move from woman talk to sociology, leaving the unspoken behind. In some sense, this is a betrayal of the participant—I say I understand, but if I later "forget," her reality is not fully there in what I write. (p. 236)

A feminist perspective regarding in-depth interviewing would see the interview process as a *cocreation of meaning*. The researcher must stay on his or her toes and listen intently to what the interviewee has to say, for the researcher should be prepared to drop his or her agenda and follow the pace of the interview. The interview and conversations with the researched will assume an agenda independent of that of the researcher, and researchers should be ready to work with these changes. This can be difficult to do, and Kathryn Anderson ran into this kind of problem in her research. Anderson, a speech communications expert, wanted to document the lives of farmwomen living in northwest Washington State for the Washington Women's Heritage Project (Anderson & Jack, 1991). During the course of her research, however, her focus on the rural farmwomen's attitudes and feelings was often displaced by her personal agenda. Anderson hoped to find specific descriptions of women's farm life activities that could be used as material for an exhibit. She notes:

> In retrospect, I can see how I listened with at least part of my attention focused on produc-
> ing potential material for the exhibit—the concrete description of experiences that would
> accompany pictures of women's activities. As I rummage through the interviews long after
> the exhibit has been placed in storage, I am painfully aware of lost opportunities for women
> to reflect on the activities and events they described and to explain their terms more fully
> in their own words. (Anderson & Jack, 1991, p. 13)

Let us listen in on one of Anderson's interviews. She interviews a farmwoman named Verna, who candidly discusses how difficult life has been for her as a mother. Verna opens up to Anderson in the following excerpt, but notice Anderson's response to Verna's emotional remarks.

> [Verna:] There was times that I just wished I could get away from it all. And there were times
> when I would have liked to have taken the kids and left them someplace for a week—the
> whole bunch at one time—so that I wouldn't have to worry about them. I don't know whether
> anybody else had that feeling or not but there were times when I just felt like I needed to get
> away from everybody, even my husband, for a little while. Those were times when I just felt
> like I needed to get away. I would maybe take a walk back in the woods and look at the flow-
> ers, and maybe go down there and find an old cow that was real and gentle and walk up to
> her and pat her a while—kind of get away from it. I just had to, it seems like sometimes. . . .
>
> [Anderson:] Were you active in clubs? (Anderson & Jack, 1991, p. 16)

We can use this excerpt as an example of how a researcher's agenda can interfere with the interviewing process. This interview demonstrates Anderson's pursuit of her own agenda, and we can see that, given her next question, she appears not to be really "listening" to Verna's heartfelt remarks. Instead, she follows her own agenda and fails to acknowledge the powerful emotions Verna has discussed. Anderson's follow-up question on clubs is an excellent example of how personal research agendas can conflict with the intimacy and spontaneity of the interviewing process. While it appears that this type of interview was more structured, we can see that when emotional topics do come up in a structured inter-view, it may serve to "shut down" the interviewee who may find it difficult not to have her story acknowledged.

Perhaps the format of this type of interview needs to take on an in-depth interview struc-ture instead. A feminist perspective on the in-depth interview process is more like a conver-sation between coparticipants than a structured question and answer session. Instead, information flows back and forth throughout the interview, but it is important to underscore the role of the researcher in this process. The researcher's primary job is to listen carefully, discerningly, and intently to the comments of the researched. Researchers may want to ask specific questions that relate to their field or area of study, but it is important that their questions evolve as cues from the researched. This keeps the researcher from asserting his or her own agenda while emphasizing the researcher's role as a listener. Anderson and Jack (1991, p. 24) offer us a guide to sharpening our listening skills during the interview process. This guide is especially helpful in listening across our differences.

- Have an open-ended interview style to enable your interviewees to express their attitudes and feelings.
- Probe for feelings, not just facts. For example: How does the participant understand what is happening? What meaning does she give to the course of events in her life?
- What is not said?

Anderson and Jack (1991) also suggest consulting the following checklist *before* you conduct your interviews:

- Be mindful of your own agenda.
- Go with your own "hunches, feelings, responses that arise through listening to others" (p. 24).
- If you are confused about something, don't be afraid to follow up on an issue or concern.
- What about your own discomfort and how this might affect the interview situation? Can your personal discomfort also provide you with a clue as to where you need to look at "what is being said" and what the participant is feeling?

I have also provided you with a "listening exercise" you might want to practice with a researcher partner (see the following boxed text).

Developing Good Listening Skills

Introduction

Good interviewing starts with good listening. This exercise is intended to help you practice your listening skills. You will need one person who will be the interviewer, another who will be the participant, and another who will serve as a timekeeper. The interviewer will start out

(Continued)

(Continued)

by asking only one question of the participant; after that it is important that the interviewer not think about what he or she wants to ask next (your agenda). The interviewer should concentrate on what is being said and try to remain silent during the interview process itself.

The Listening Exercise

1. Pair off with a research partner.

2. Position yourself in the interview situation so that you are facing one another at a distance that feels comfortable.

3. Flip a coin to decide who will first take on the role of interviewer, with the other taking on the role of participant.

4. The participant should talk for 30 seconds on a specific topic that the interviewer will determine. It should be a fairly neutral topic such as "my favorite restaurant" or "my favorite vacation spot."

5. A moderator will call time out after 30 seconds have elapsed.

6. At this point, the interviewer should repeat what it is that he or she heard the participant say.

7. Now reverse roles.

8. After this is complete, the time will increase to 60 seconds; you should inquire concerning a more personal issue, such as "something you are concerned with about yourself" or "the most difficult challenge faced in the past year."

9. Some questions you might want to ponder: What differences, if any, did you notice happening in the interview situation between the 30-second interviews and the 60-second interviews? Did your body language change? Did you make more or less eye contact? Did your verbal expressions change? How? How much were you able to recall in the 30-second encounters versus the 60-second interview? Was it hard to listen? In what sense?

There are other tools you can use to conduct a successful interview. Picking up on *markers* is one way to show a participant that you are listening and interested in what is being said. Markers are also a valuable source of information and often lead to the thick descriptions that characterize and enrich qualitative interview data.

Picking Up on "Markers": A Strategy for Listening

Markers are important pieces of information that participants may offer while they are discussing something else. Weiss (1994) explains the marker and its appearance as

> a passing reference made by a participant to an important or feeling state. . . . Because markers occur in the course of talking about something else, you may have to remember them and then return to them when you can, saying, "A few minutes ago you mentioned. . . ." But it is a good idea to pick up a marker as soon as you conveniently can if the material it hints at could in any way be relevant for your study. Letting the marker go will demonstrate to the participant that the area is not of importance to you. It can also demonstrate that you are only interested in answers to your questions, not in the participant's full experience. . . . Participants sometimes offer markers by indicating that much has happened that they aren't talking about. They might say, for example, "Well, there was a lot going on at that time." It is then reasonable to respond, "Could you tell me about that?" (p. 77)

Let's revisit the interview with Alison and examine the markers that appear in this discussion. There is a moment in the interview where Alison describes her loneliness. This issue comes up several times during the course of my interview with her. Here is one snippet from the excerpt you have already read:

Alison: Yes. And after, my friend and I would do study sessions. I would come back at like 10 p.m., and I had a refrigerator in my room, and I grocery shopped, and I would make like bread with peanut butter and jelly, or jelly and butter, just whatever I had. I knew there was a vending machine in our building, and I would go down there and I'd come back up, and I'd go down there, and I'd come back up. And also, my best friend who lived next door to me in her single, she went home a couple of weekends, once a month or so, and I would be there. I felt alone. There were people I could hang out with. But nobody who really knew me, and so I would go down to the vending machines, and I can remember thinking, "This just isn't going to do it for me. It is not going to make my Friday night that exciting, but then again, why not?" So. . . . I would binge four times a week. Sometimes I stopped.

Uh-huh. So for how long?

In this particular exchange, I heard Alison's concern about how empty and lonely she felt. She notes above, "I felt alone. There were people I could hang out with. But nobody who really knew me. . . . " It would be important for the interviewer to pick up on this "marker" shortly after she finished her response. I might follow her marker and ask, "Can you tell me more about your feeling lonely?" Alison mentions her loneliness at several points throughout the interview, but she never fully describes what she is feeling. It appears, however, that these feelings are strongly associated with her bulimic behaviors. By listening for these markers, you are showing the participant that you are in fact listening very carefully to the hints and issues that matter to them.

At this point, let us join David Karp behind the scenes (Karp, as cited in Hesse-Biber & Leavy, 2006) to get a glimpse at how he conducts an interview and addresses some of the following issues:

- How do you get someone to start talking?
- Is it hard to be an active listener while in the role of interviewer?
- Do participants want to share their stories?
- What do participants get out of this process?

Behind the Scenes With David Karp

Well, I think you should be making it easy on people. You should begin by asking the easy questions. You know, "What religion did you grow up with, etc.?" And not to ask threatening questions, and to give people a sense about what you are doing because what they are trying to figure out, just like in any interaction, is, who is this guy? What is he after? Is he genuine? Are his intentions good? Does he listen? Does he seem to care about what I'm saying? And when you do an interview, you must make that person feel that he or she is the only person in the world at the time that you are talking to. I could never do more than one interview a day, never! Because the amount of energy that is required to really listen, to really pay attention, is enormous. And to know just when to ask a lot of questions.

Part of this conducting thing is to reach a balance . . . You should be respectful of the story that the person you're interviewing wants to tell. See, people come into your office and they have a story that they want to tell. And when they walk in, at the beginning, maybe they want to talk about how medicine screwed them over, or something like that. That's what they really want to talk about. I have to go with that at the beginning. I'm not going to turn them off. I'm not going to say, "Well, I didn't want to talk about that until 2 hours into the interview." And I think it's reaching balance between allowing people to be heard, to tell the parameters of the story that they really want to tell—and every story is to some degree idiosyncratic in meaning—and at the same time, as I said, to know what you want to get covered before you're done with this person.

I find in doing interviews that if you ask the right question at the beginning of the interview, once you really get into the substance of it, you often don't have to ask much more. In the depression stuff, the first question I typically asked people was, "You may not have called it depression, but tell me about the first moment it entered your head that something was wrong. What was the first time there was any kind of a consciousness that something was wrong?" Sometimes I didn't have to say much of anything else for the next 3 hours. People had a way of telling their story, and they spontaneously covered all of those domains of inquiry that I wanted to have covered. And the other thing I would say about this is that people really do want to tell their stories. Almost invariably, people thanked me at the end of their interview for giving them a chance to tell their story. And to have a sociologist ask them questions . . . . They often got a different perspective on their life than they could have gotten through years of therapy, because I was asking questions that only a sociologist would ask.

Feminist Perspectives on "Difference" in the Interview Process

Feminist researchers view social reality as complex and multidimensional, and this perspective shapes their opinion of the interview process. The researcher and the researched come together for an interview with different backgrounds in terms of gender, ethnicity, and sexual preference. Class status and other differences might also affect the flow and connection of the interview.

Researchers often pay little attention to how these differences might affect or define the interview situation. Positivist researchers are especially apt to overlook these differences, for traditional positivistic research deals with the issue of difference by *minimizing* its effects. Positivistic researchers standardize their participation in the interview situation by being "objective" or "bracketing off" these differences in their positionality vis-à-vis their participant, so as not to influence the interview process itself. This minimizes the effects of difference, but it also means that the following questions are rarely considered:

- Can a single, white, middle-class, male researcher interview a black, working-class mother?

- Can a middle-class, white female interview a woman from the Third World who is living in poverty?

- Can a straight, white, middle-class male interview a gay working-class male?

Feminist researchers argue that "bracketing" off attitudes is not as easy as it may seem, for it is difficult to overlook the attitudes and values that emanate from any given individual's mix of positional ties. In fact, acknowledging the similarities and differences between the interviewer and the participant allows the researcher to assess the impact of difference on the interview situation. Issues of difference affect all phases of the research process, from the selection of a particular research question, the formation of a hypothesis, to the overall process of data collection. The ultimate analysis, interpretation, and the writing up of our research findings are all affected by our perception of difference; and they should include awareness of this difference.

INSIDER/OUTSIDER?

Some researchers have found ways to overcome the impact of difference in the interview process. One way this can be done is to "match" the interviewer's more important status characteristics (race, age, gender, or sexual preference) so that they use their *insider status* to gain access to an interview. This might also help the researcher obtain cooperation and rapport within the situation that would help him or her to better understand his or her participants. After all, the researcher is an insider and should be familiar with the participant's group situation. It is also important to achieve a balance in some of these status markers to decrease the possibility of power and authority imbalances negatively affecting the interview situation (Oakley, 1981). If the interviewer is perceived as an *outsider,* it is generally thought that his or her differences might make it more difficult to gain access to and understand the situation of "the other." But does an "insider" status guarantee a more valid and reliable interview? How might differences affect the research process?

Embedded in this example of difference is the realization that from the beginning of our research project, whom and what we choose to study is grounded in an appreciation of difference. Likewise *what* and *whom* we study affects our cognizance of difference and our general approaches to these issues. An appreciation of difference allows us to ask the questions: Which women? Are all women around the world the same? How are they different and what differences are important to my research question?

Difference is also critical in terms of the *interview situation.* Can a researcher from a First World country truly understand and relate to the plights of women working in the global marketplaces of the Third World? Suppose the researcher is a white middle-class male conducting a research project. How might his gender, race, ethnic background, and social class affect the interview process? Can the researchers "overcome" differences between themselves and those they research? Does the researcher want to "overcome" all of these differences?

If the interviewer and the interviewee are of the same gender, class, and ethnicity, it is easy to assume that an open dialogue would quickly be established. This situation might also provide a maximum opportunity for the voice of the participant to be heard and represented. These are not unreasonable suppositions. In her field research among Gullah women, Beoku-Betts (1994) found that her research was enhanced when she informed her participants that she, too, was raised in a rural community with similar cultural practices. This revelation of her social positionality and background helped her to make contacts and gain data that would not otherwise have been available. Kath Weston (2004) is very reflexive about her identity as a lesbian and how it has influenced her research. She notes that while she still would have chosen to study gay families, her project would have been very different if she were not a lesbian. Weston also recognizes that her position within the homosexual community was the reason she had little trouble finding lesbian participants. These women seemed virtually invisible to her male colleagues who were also conducting sexuality research. She notes: "In my case, being a woman also influenced how I spent my time in the field: I passed more hours in lesbian clubs and women's groups than gay men's bars or male gyms" (p. 202).

Sometimes sharing some insider characteristics with a participant is not enough to ensure that the researcher can fully capture the lived experiences of those he or she researches. Catherine Kohler Riessman (1987) researched divorce narratives, and she provides an example of this instance. Riessman found that just being a woman was not enough for her to understand the experiences of divorced women whose class and ethnic backgrounds differed from hers. Her status position as an Anglo, middle-class, highly educated individual prevented her from fully understanding the particular ways these women structured their divorce narratives (episodically instead of chronologically). The researcher realized the challenge of separating her own cultural expectations from the narratives that were shared with her from women of different ethnic and class backgrounds.

Beoku-Betts (1994) confronted a similar scenario in her field research among Gullah women. Beoku-Betts is a black female researcher, and her race helped her secure insider status in the black community she was studying. Beoku-Betts relates how one of her participants told her that "she preferred a black scholar like myself conducting research in her community because 'black scholars have a sense of soul for our people because they have lived through it'" (p. 416). However, Beoku-Betts found that her racial insider status was intertwined with other differences in class and cultural backgrounds. These differences created considerable resistance within the community toward her fieldwork activities.

> My shared racial background proved instrumental in providing access to research participants and in reducing the social distance at a critical stage of the researcher process. However, my identity as an outsider was also defined by other subgroups within that identity.

For example, my gender, marital status (unmarried), and profession status as a university researcher often operated separately and in combination with my race to facilitate and complicate the research process. (p. 420)

Beoku-Betts (1994) also provides vivid illustrations of how difference created conflict in her research. Her status as an unmarried female created some tensions in one of the communities she studied, and she relays how difference created the following incidents in the field.

In one community a local man visited the family with whom I was staying. When we were introduced, he recalled that he had heard about me and shared with me the rumor in the community that I was there to look for a husband. . . . Another incident occurred in church one Sunday with an African American minister who invoked the topic of the Anita Hill/Clarence Thomas hearing after I was asked to introduce myself to the congregation. At first, the minister was very supportive and welcomed me warmly into the community as an African coming to study aspects of a common historical heritage. However, he soon switched to the Hill/Thomas hearings and began to remark on the fact that Anita Hill was also an educated woman who had used that privilege to accuse and embarrass Clarence Thomas (whose hometown was not far from this community). (p. 428)

Beoku-Betts (1994) realized that she needed to negotiate her differing statuses if she was to obtain interviews with her participants that reflect how they actually felt about her. It was only after she completed this negotiation process that she was given full access to her research subjects and could begin to cocreate meaning and understanding.

While it is important to familiarize yourself with the challenges of difference, it should also be noted that being an outsider can actually be an advantage. This hinges on the research problem and population you have chosen to study, but not belonging to a specific group can make you appear more unbiased to your participant. Similarly, being an outsider might encourage you to ask questions you might otherwise have taken for granted as "shared knowledge," and you might discover the unique perspectives your participants have on a particular issue. Sociologist Robert Weiss (1994) comments on issues of difference between the interviewer and the participant as follows:

One way to phrase this issue is to ask to what extent it is necessary for the interviewer to be an insider in the respondent's world in order to be effective as an interviewer. It is difficult to anticipate what interviewer attributes will prove important to a respondent and how the respondent will react to them. . . . There are so many different interviewer attributes to which a respondent can react that the interviewer will surely be an insider in some ways and an outsider in others. . . . I have generally found it better to be an insider to the milieu in which the respondent lives, because it is easier then for me to establish a research partnership with the respondent. But some of my most instructive interviews have been good just because I was an outsider who needed instruction in the respondent's milieu. (p. 137)

INTERSECTIONALITY AND DIFFERENCE

It is interesting and important to note that an individual's status as an insider/outsider is fluid and can change even in the course of a single interview. The concept of intersectionality is a critical insight black feminist theorists stressed early on (Baca Zinn, Cannon, Dill, & Higginbotham, 1986; Dill, 1979; Dill & Kohlman, 2012), and it captures the complexity of status positions (e.g., race, ethnicity, gender) that shape women's experiences and attitudes. Difference matters. Bonnie Thornton Dill and Marla H. Kohlman (2012) stressed the importance of analyzing the "interlocking effects" that race, class, gender, and sexuality—as primary status differences—serve to inflect one another. In the case of in-depth interviewing, the researcher (interviewer) and researched (interviewee) can hold a variety of status characteristics that may come into play over the course of any given interview situation (see Figure 7.3), as we have noted, for example, in the discussion of Beoku-Betts's (1994) research study. Depending upon the path a given interview takes, similarities and differences

Figure 7.3 Intersectionality (Interaction of Two or More Differences) and Difference During the Interview

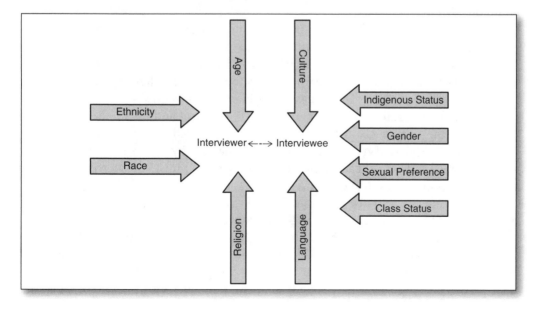

between interviewer and participant may come into play. So, we can think of the differences and similarities we share with our participant as fluid over the course of a given interview. It is critical to note that when conducting any interview, your role/ status might be shared with your participant on some issues, but you might also discover that glaring differences exist on other particularities of your research question or a topic of conversation. In other words, you may become an "insider" with your participant because you share the same race or ethnic background, but may differ from your participant in terms of your age or class standing.

A good example of such a situation comes from research conducted by Rosalind Edwards (1990). Edwards is an educated, middle-class, white woman who is interested in conducting unstructured interviews with mature, Afro-Caribbean mothers who are also students. She wanted to understand the lived experiences of these women around issues of education, work, and family life, but she had trouble accessing the population and gaining their trust in interview scenarios. She and her participants finally acknowledged these differences in an open discussion, and it was then that they were able to candidly discuss their experiences. Edwards experienced an ebb-and-flow feeling from insider to outsider status that shifted as she discussed different issues with her participants. She notes that she felt more like an insider when the discussion was focused on motherhood: "The black women did indicate some common understandings and position between us" (p. 488). A noticeable shift occurred when the discussion reverted to a more "public" realm like their educational experiences. Even though Edwards also shared the status of having been a mature mother and student, the conversation became one where "black women were least likely to talk to me about what we had the most in common" (p. 488).

Sometimes differences that occur between interviewer and interviewee may seem particularly challenging, especially with regard to interviewing across gender lines and/ or dealing with interview topics that may be extremely sensitive to deal with. Campbell, Adams, Wasco, Aherns, and Sefi (2010) discuss the challenges they encountered when interviewing rape survivors. The focus of their interviews was on survivors' lives postas-post-assault, with regard to their experiences with medical and mental health providers. One of the biggest challenges these researchers faced was how to prevent the women they interviewed from becoming re-traumatized by the interview experience itself. Campbell and her colleagues employed a range of feminist interviewing strategies to combat this negative interview outcome.

Their first interview strategy was to reduce the hierarchy between themselves and the women they interviewed by being consciously aware of the different statuses they occupied with regard to their participants. They sought to reduce the hierarchy of these status positions by, in their words, trying to "emphasize to participants their choice, power and control during the interview" (2010, p. 72). They engaged in a "mutual disclosure" with their participants, by which they sought to answer any questions interviewees had on both the personal and professional levels. They also pointed out resources in their community that might help on a particular issue their participants were dealing with. One of the most important things they did was simply listen deeply and emphatically to their participants' experiences. At the end of the interviews, the participants felt that their stories were heard and that the interviewer was empathetic to their situation. The researchers noted:

> For so many of the survivors . . . the experience of being able to talk about the assault, to have someone really listen to their story, to see that their words have touched someone else, and that someone really cares, helped ease the burden of surviving rape. (p. 76)

These important feminist principles of interview praxis were also echoed in yet other research studies across a range of other differences, such as interviewing across differences in sexual identities (Allen, 2010); as well as interviewing across gender, while also dealing with sexually sensitive interview content (Gailey & Prohaska, 2011).

As in-depth interviewing moves to a *team-based interviewing* approach, issues of difference are magnified as the number of interviewers increases on any given research project. Anne Pezalla and her colleagues (2012) analyzed how their three different interviewing styles and differences impacted the overall team-based research project. Each of them reflected on each others' interviews and on the variety of strategies for dealing with differences they each brought to the interview situation that might later impact their research findings. They noted that in doing this reflexive analysis, they could in fact build on the interviewing strengths each researcher brought to the project. They could take advantage of particular interviewer characteristics: for example, which researchers may be more effective than others in eliciting detailed narratives from participants depending on the perceived sensitivity of the topic. In these instances, variation in interviewer characteristics may benefit rather than detract from the goals of team-based qualitative inquiry. The authors call for the inclusion of enhanced self-reflexivity in interviewer training and development activities and argue against standardization of interviewer practices in qualitative research teams.

REFLEXIVITY AND DIFFERENCE

The concept of reflexivity, then, is crucial when we discuss studying across difference. Reflexivity can be an important tool, as we saw in the above studies, that allows researchers to be aware of their status differences along gender, race, ethnicity, class, and any other factors that might be important to the research process. We can use the previously discussed research projects to see how similarities and differences affect the interview process. Each of the above researchers had to face how they were similar and different from those they researched and then channel varied similarity and difference factors into their research. *Doing reflexivity* in fact empowered both the researcher and the researched within the interview situation. Reflecting on difference allowed Beoku-Betts (1994), Campbell and her colleagues (2010), Edwards (1990), Riessman (1987), Weiss (1994), and Weston (2004) to *negotiate their differences and similarities* with their participants to *gain access* and *obtain data* that would not have been available to them otherwise. They were also able to *gain new insight* into their data from the perspective of difference. Kath Weston's (2004) reflexivity concerning her lesbian identity and its impact on her research allowed her to easily obtain access to the lesbian community. Edwards's (1990) recognition of the similarities and differences she shared with her Afro-Caribbean population offered her a more in-depth understanding of how her population talks about public and private issues. Weiss (1994) and Edwards (1990) also realized the fluidity of being an insider or outsider, which can shift depending on the given research topic and the individual current of the actual interview. Campbell and colleagues (2010) were able to reduce the hierarchy between themselves and rape survivors in a way that prevented them from feeling re-victimized by the interview process.

Reflexivity also reminds us of the important role difference plays in our research project as a whole. Difference enters every facet of our research process. It guides the projects we select, informs the questions we ask, and directs how we collect, analyze, write, and interpret our data. Differences should be explored and embraced, for ignoring and disavowing them could have negative effects on your data and overall project, as we noted earlier with Beoku-Betts's research experience.

WHEN REFLEXIVITY IS NOT ENOUGH

There are, however, important *limits to the power of reflexivity* within the interviewing process, with some researchers, early on, noting that the praxis of reflexivity had its limitations (Reinharz, 1993; Rose, 1997; Wasserfall, 1993). These scholars express reservations that, especially in more asymmetrical power relations between the interviewer and interviewee, it might be illusionary to believe that reflexivity alone would be able to bridge some of the differences both the participant and researcher bring to the interview situation itself.

Bosworth, Hoyle, and Dempsey's (2011) research on trafficked women notes the limitations on reflexivity in working with vulnerable populations. They argue that feminist researchers must be mindful to also engage with other research actors such as those "institutional gatekeepers" who can and do limit access to those vulnerable populations feminist researchers seek to interview. All the reflexive practices we have discussed thus far may be upended by those in power who often work with vulnerable populations. The gatekeepers are in a position to determine access to these vulnerable populations whose experiences feminist researchers seek. There can be distrust over the necessity of interviewing vulnerable populations for fear that they become re-victimized during the research process and because of concerns about protecting them socially and legally from any fallout that may occur from having been interviewed. Part of the issue is also one of practicing reciprocity—What is it that researchers can give back to these vulnerable communities that may serve as a longer lasting resource than that of a research article? The researchers note:

> Part of the work that needs doing, in other words, is a political one: a more open discussion from all sides over the nature, causes, and effect of sexual violence and prostitution. So, too, our experiences on this project suggest that it may be necessary in some research to devise a series of publications, some of which are not purely academic. Perhaps, we could have been more persuasive if we had been able to offer the organizations more than a set of scholarly articles. (p. 776)

Peer-to-Peer Reciprocal Interviewing

Porter, Neysmith, Reitsma-Street, and Baker Collins (2009) suggest a novel way to bridge the authority and power-divide between the researcher and participants. It is what they term the "participatory model," whereby research participants interview each another as a way to create more symmetry in power relations. A peer-designed reciprocal interview model strives to break down the hierarchal relationship between interviewer and interviewee (see Figure 7.4).

Peer interviewing may also be a way to enable individuals to talk about highly sensitive topics especially to someone who might have experienced a similar sensitive issue. Such was the case with Highet's (2003) study of the social context of adolescents' (13 to 15 years of age) smoking and marijuana (cannabis) usage. The researcher paired up individuals based on their friendship choices, and these reciprocal dyads primarily consisted of the same sex. The researcher noted that being paired with someone they knew provided a degree of stability and comfort to the interview situation, such that this "facilitated a better balance in the relationship between interviewer and participant. This interview design also facilitated the process of developing trust and rapport, and helped to generate high quality data" (pp. 111–112). It also served to enhance access and recruitment of young adolescents into the study. Highet asserts that the strength of the mutually-paired interviews lies in their ability

Figure 7.4   "Peer-to-Peer" Reciprocal Interviewing

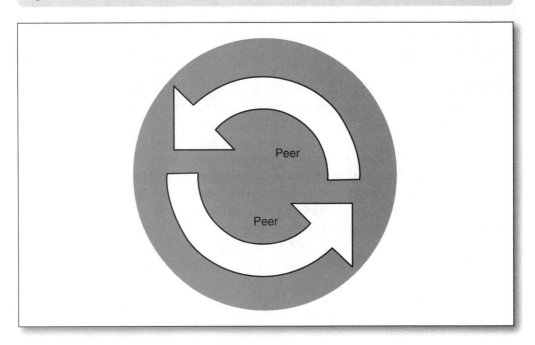

to connect to adolescents around difficult and sensitive issues and to provide them a more welcoming and safe environment in which to talk about their more private experiences with smoking and marijuana use. Highet (2003) suggests that it is the specific pairing of close friends that appears to provide an interview context that allows for the subjugated social and cultural worlds of young adolescents to be exposed and provides a more "insightful understanding of young people's social relationships with one another . . . and could perhaps lead to the development of more interactive forms of health education/promotion which draw on this sort of dynamic" (p. 117).

Each person in this reciprocal peer interviewing "dyad" is trained in interviewing skills by the researcher who is heading up the study. Each peer is "matched" on a series of crucial status factors the researcher feels pertains to the research problem focus. The interview process design is "reciprocal," meaning that each participant takes a turn asking and responding to interview questions that take on a "dialogic" co-creation of meaning during the interview process. This form of reciprocity interviewing has a highly "active" quality in that there is a strong "give-and-take" among the co-participants.

STUDENT EXERCISE: PEER-TO-PEER INTERVIEW

One important way students can gain valuable interviewing skills is to practice inter-viewing with their peers. The following set of loose guidelines is meant to facilitate this process. This is a short exercise that you can do with a classmate in your current meth-ods course. The overall goal of the interview is to get acquainted with what your and your peer's experiences have been like academically, by talking about your first-year college classroom experiences.

The purpose of this exercise is to get you acquainted with the interviewing process and to have you both take turns at being the "interviewer" and "interviewee." Spend ten minutes each asking some general "starter open-ended questions" such as "Can you tell me about one positive and one negative experience you encountered in the academic classroom this past year?" Make sure the person who is doing the interview keeps time and stops at the end of 10 minutes. Switch roles after that, and go for another 10 minutes.

Now spend 10 additional minutes de-briefing one another on what it was like to be the interviewer and the interviewee in terms of some of the issues of difference and reflexivity that we have discussed so far in this chapter.

What do you perceive as the positive aspects of peer interviewing?

What do you perceive as some negative aspects?

What did you learn by doing this exercise with regard to the interviewing process?

What questions do you come away with that you would like to bring up for class dis-cussion?

LIMITATIONS AND RISKS OF PEER INTERVIEWING

It is important to note, however, that while the peers are leveled on some status dimensions, there remain other ways in which peers will differ. These differences may also come into play in the interview process; thus, each interviewer also needs to be aware, practice reflexivity across the interview process, and not take for granted that a peer feels the same way you might feel.

Peer interviewing also requires an additional layer of resources and time for training and recruiting peer interviewers and following with a debriefing on how things went. It requires that the researcher to identify those who would be viable candidates for this type of interviewing position. Ethical issues need to be carefully addressed, especially those that concern confidentiality. In many cases, if there is familiarity among the peers in the dyad, this may heighten researcher concerns about not having confidential information becoming more public knowledge among peer interviewers' network. Decisions also need to be made in terms of whether or not peer interviewers will receive compensation for their work on the research project and if so, what type and amount of compensation. Failure to pay careful attention to these tasks and issues may give rise to some unintended negative consequences during and after the research project. For example, if interviewers are not adequately trained, they may find themselves feeling disempowered by the interview process.

Taking Your In-Depth Interview Online

While we have been discussing in-depth interviews as a face-to-face situation, where you are physically present talking with your participant, there is an increasing movement to take research projects and conduct them online (see James & Busher, 2009). Internet-mediated research is already transforming the way social science research is practiced. Traditional research methods such as survey research and increasingly qualitative approaches to research such as ethnographies and in-depth interviews are going online as researchers confront the new challenges (Denissen, Neumann, & van Zalk, 2010; Dicks & Mason, 2008; James & Busher, 2009; Robinson & Schultz, 2011). An online study can vary in its time-dimension from synchronous to asynchronous mode. A synchronous mode of data collection is ongoing and streaming, while an asynchronous data collection mode (such as conducting an e-mail survey) has a time lag in communication between the researcher and the participant. One major decision in going online is to decide the type of time-dimension that is most relevant to your research problem. Do you want to set up an interview in real time, or would you rather set it up in asynchronous time—such as providing your participant with a question, and then he or she can answer it offline and send it back to you via e-mail or by some other way?

In this aside, we will take up a range of specific issues that feminist researchers in particular may confront as they take their in-depth interviews online. While we will not go into this particular aspect of in-depth interviewing in detail, we want to briefly note some of the possible advantages and disadvantages to conducting an in-depth interview over the Internet. In doing so, we will look at how feminist principles of praxis with regard to issues of reflexivity and tending to power differentials in the research process may be impacted by the nature of the Internet as a medium of communication.

LACK OF VISUAL CUES

One important issue and challenge that feminist researchers who conduct online interviews face is the lack of visual cues that a face-to-face interview provides. Face-to-face interviewing allows the researcher to assess the overall tenor and tone of the interview through nonverbal cues. As we noted earlier, nonverbal as well as verbal cues are crucial in assessing the emotional climate of the interview situation in terms of the degree to which the researcher feels he or she has built up rapport and trust during the interview process as a way to reduce some of the power dynamics between researcher and researched. We noted earlier, that in Campbell and her colleagues' study (2010), it was important for the researchers to express empathy with their participants physically by their presence, demonstrating their verbal and nonverbal support for them, in order for their participants to feel safe to tell their stories.

However, in some instances it can, in fact, be the case that taking an interview online might better suit the needs of both the researcher and participant, especially regarding issues about sensitive topics. Such was the case with Catherine Cook's (2012) study of women who were diagnosed with a sexually transmitted disease (STD). Cook conducted in-depth e-mail interviews with 26 women from a range of countries spread across the world—New Zealand, the United States, Canada, and England—who had been diagnosed with an STD. She found that this type of online interviewing design allowed her to recruit women from a range of geographical regions, who also resided in different time zones. She found, in fact, that utilizing an asynchronous model of data collection, whereby the participants could answer their question offline and send it to the researcher at any given time via e-mail, generated a high participation rate. The women in her study expressed a sense of high satisfaction with this mode of interviewing, feeling that it provided them with a sense of anonymity. Many interviewees felt that the emotional distance of e-mail interaction gave them a sense of protection. Cook discovered that conducting asynchronous interviews allowed her time to consider more deeply her participants' answers by providing her with the time to think about what her participants were saying and to respond in a much more reflective way.

BENEFITS TO DOING ONLINE RESEARCH

Conducting online interviews may cut down the costs of recruiting and travelling to a physical site, making the logistics of setting up an interview less time-consuming and costly. If you want to build in a face-to-face element to your online interview, you might want to consider a program like Skype that allows you visually to connect to participants over the Internet. Interviewing online can also allow you to interview across time zones more easily by selecting an asynchronous mode of connecting with your participant as was done in the Cook (2012) study. It can also provide you with a quick way to recruit participants in a short period of time, as was the situation in Cook's research study. She could contact participants more directly and even bypass medical gatekeepers. This can often be done by placing webposts or blogs and websites that specifically draw members based on a common type of issue they face or a concern where they want to connect to others with a similar issue.

DRAWBACKS OF ONLINE INTERVIEWS

If you decide to move your interview to cyberspace, you will need to assess how the medium will affect the type of participants you will be able to recruit and what types of participants you are most likely to miss in your study.

Part of assessing the advantages and disadvantages to going online depends on your research problem and also the resources both you and your participants have at their disposal in terms of whether or not they have the computer skills and economic means to engage in online communication. Engaging in an online study may, in fact, limit the type of participant you are able to reach in your study, especially those who are poor and/or lack the skills to engage in this type of online project.

As research moves online, the ability of the researcher to garner the overall tenor, and the form of interaction between researcher and researched begins to shift, especially as new forms of social networking communication tools like blogs and Twitter arise. These Internet-mediated communication boundaries between researcher and researched may become more fluid, such that there is a blurring of the line between the real world and the cyber-world, whereby new forms of social networking (interaction) can cross over into the real world as researcher and researched communicate offline (Hine, 2008). There is also the possibility that a lack of face-to-face interaction may cause meaning to be lost in the collection of data because nonverbal cues are missing from the interaction, thus perhaps compromising the ability of the researcher to adequately analyze interactions.

Analysis and Interpretation of Interview Data

In this section, I will provide you with some general concepts to consider as you analyze your interview data. The sociologist David Karp (as cited in Hesse-Biber & Leavy, 2006, pp. 142–144) advocates a step-by-step approach to use as you begin the analysis of your interview data (see text box below). He stresses the importance of starting your analysis early, for qualitative data analysis is an *iterative process* of data collection along with data analysis. These two processes should proceed almost simultaneously. Karp suggests *memoing* throughout your research process to trace how your data do or do not fit together. Memoing will help you track your project's progress, and it is also a fine time to jot down any hunches and ideas you might have about connections within your data. You can reflect on breakthroughs in your memos, but the memoing process will also help you become more reflexive about your own positionality and how it might affect your research. Karp also underscores the importance of purposely seeking "negative cases" that do not fit cohesively or create problems in your research. You can find these cases by asking yourself: What doesn't support my interpretation?

David Karp's Tips for Successful Analysis of Your In-Depth Interview Materials

Remember that the analytical work you do along the way is every bit as important as the task of data collection. Never subordinate the task of data collection to thinking about and analyzing your data. The great strength of methods such as in-depth interviewing is that you can engage simultaneously in the processes of data collection and analysis. The two processes should inform each other.

Start writing memos with the very first interview. Let your early data tell you which of your ideas seem sensible and which ones ought to be reevaluated. Especially at the beginning, you will hear people say things that you just had not thought about. Look carefully for major directions that it had just not occurred to you to take. The pace of short memo writing ought to be especially great toward the beginning of your work. I advocate "idea" or "concept" memos that introduce an emerging idea. Such memos typically run two to three pages.

Reevaluate your interview guide after about 10 interviews. Ten interviews ought to give you enough information to do a major assessment of what you are learning or failing to learn. This is probably a good point at which to take a close look at your research questions and emerging themes.

If you think that you have been able to grab onto a theme, it is time to write a "data" memo. By this, we mean a memo that integrates the theme with data and any available literature that fits. By a data memo, I mean something that begins to look like a paper. In a data memo, always use more data on a point than you would actually use in a

(Continued)

(Continued)

research paper. If you make a broad point and feel that you have 10 good pieces of data that fit that point, lay them all out for inspection and use later. Also, make sure to lay out the words of people who do NOT fit the pattern.

Once themes begin to emerge, go out of your way to find cases that do not fit. You must try as hard as you can to disprove your ideas. Do not be afraid of complexity and ambiguity about themes. The world is complicated and your writing must reflect that complexity. There is a tendency of social scientists to describe patterns as if they were uniform and monolithic. To do that slights the complexity of things. Don't fall in love with early, plausible theories.

After 15 to 20 interviews, it is probably a good idea to create coding categories. Here the task is to begin by creating as many categories as you can that seem sensible. Coding is another way of "getting close to the data" and telling you what you know. You can eventually use these codes as you go through the data for paper and memo writing.

Write a fairly complete memo every time your work takes on a new direction (say, a major change in sampling procedure). Provide a full explanation for changes in analytical directions. Your memos can constitute an "audit trail" for people who want to retrace your steps. People who do qualitative research should be as fully accountable for their procedures as those who employ more standardized procedures.

If you think you have a theme significant enough to write a paper on for publication, do it. Getting papers published is very affirming and brings your ideas to a point of high refinement. You do not have to wait until all your data are in to write papers. You will find that some of your papers will be on "subsamples" within the larger sample.

Periodically, write outlines for what a book, thesis, or report from your data might look like. Draw up preliminary prospectuses. Pretend that you were about to sit down and write a book. This is a good exercise that requires you to paint the total picture.

Do not get crazy about getting exactly the same data from every participant. You will find that each participant's story is to some degree unique. In your writing, you will want to point out here and there the unique story. It is probably a good idea to write up a summary sheet of about one page that describes the main themes in each interview.

Test out your hypotheses on your participants. Incorporate your hypotheses into questions ("You know, several of the people with whom I have talked tell me that . . . . Does this make sense to you?"). There is no reason to hide or conceal hypotheses, ideas, and concepts from subjects.

Pay attention to extreme cases, because they are often the most informative. Be on the lookout to do "negative case analysis."

Analyzing In-Depth Interviews Using Computer-Assisted Software

New technologies can play a significant role in the process of data analysis. (See Chapter 13 for an in-depth description of the different types of software programs for your analysis of qualitative interviews.) The following list of research tasks by Miles and Huberman (1994) suggests how you might want to use a computer-assisted software program in the analysis and interpretation of your qualitative data from your interviews.

Uses of Computer Software in Qualitative Studies

— Making notes in the field

— Writing up or transcribing field notes

— Editing: correcting, extending, or revising field notes

— Coding: attaching keywords or tags to segments of text to permit later retrieval

— Storage: keeping text in an organized database

— Search and retrieval: locating relevant segments of text and making them available for inspection

— Data "linking": connecting relevant data segments to each other, forming categories, clusters, or networks of information

— Memoing: writing reflective commentaries on some aspect of the data as a basis for deeper analysis

— Content analysis: counting frequencies, sequence, or locations of words and phrases

— Data display: placing selected or reduced data in a condensed, organized format, such as a matrix or network, for inspection

— Conclusion-drawing and verification: aiding the analyst to interpret displayed data and to test or confirm findings

— Theory-building: developing systematic, conceptually coherent explanations of findings; testing hypotheses

— Graphic mapping: creating diagrams that depict findings or theories

— Preparing interim and final reports

Source: Miles and Huberman (1994, p. 44).

There is a growing and extensive international community of software users, as the field of qualitative software development has grown over time (Fielding & Lee, 1998). As the usage of computer software programs as tools in qualitative analyses increases, so too does the number of methodological and theoretical concerns regarding the analysis and interpretation of qualitative data. Sharlene Hesse-Biber (1995) discusses five fears that critics of computer software express. First, there is the fear that computer programs will preclude the creative process. Some analysts see their qualitative work as "artistic," and there is the belief that computer technology is incompatible with art. Second, there is the fear that computer programs will turn the researcher into an "unthinking and unfeeling human being." Third, critics are concerned that the line between quantitative and qualitative analysis will be blurred with the introduction of software, as the logic of survey research will be imposed onto qualitative data and as in-depth analysis may be sacrificed for a larger data sample. These specific concerns react to the fact that software programs now permit the coding and storage of a large volume of data, and large sets of data are more typically associated with quantitative research projects. Fourth, critics fear that the use of computers may define a particular field of study, as they often dictate the direction and structure of a research project's proceedings. Here, computer software programs are perceived as able to influence both questions and methods of analysis. Fifth, critics fear that computer programs require the researcher to be more explicit about the procedures and analytical processes they went through in order to collect and interpret their data. Controversies arise when interpretations are accountable to tests of validity and reliability: Should qualitative data be subjected to such strict tests?

WHAT COMPUTER SOFTWARE PROGRAMS ARE OUT THERE, AND WHICH ONE SHOULD I CHOOSE?

The following set of reflective questions to consider when choosing a qualitative software program is suggested by Hesse-Biber and Crofts (2008). These questions are derived from Renata Tesch (1990) and Eben Weitzman and Matthew Miles (1995). The work of Weitzman (2000) and Creswell and Ray Maietta (2003) on computer software usage and evaluation may be helpful to consider here as well. Hesse-Biber and Crofts ground their perspective in that of the user. The user should prioritize which questions are most relevant to his or her research projects:

"What type of computer system do you prefer to work on or feel most comfortable working on? Does the program support your operating system? Do you need to upgrade your system or perhaps purchase a new computer to meet the requirements of a specific program? Do you like the look and feel of a program's interface? What excites you about this program at a visceral level?"

"Does the look and feel of the program resonate with your own research style? What is your analysis style? How do you plan to conduct your analysis, and how might computers fit into that style? How might each program enhance (or detract from) your analysis? In what sense? For example, do you plan on coding most of your data—what type of coding do you want to do? How do you prefer your data be retrieved and how important is it to you to be able to look at the full context from which the data was taken? Are you a visual person? Do you like to see relationships and concepts selected in some type of diagram or network? Do you anticipate quantifying any of your data?"

"What research project or set of projects do you anticipate using a computer software program? For example what type of data does your project consist of—textual, multi-media?"

"How do you want a computer program to assist you? What tasks do you want to mechanize? What specific tasks do you want computerized? You may not want all the features espoused by these programs. What are your expectations of what the program will be able to assist you in doing? Are your expectations realistic?"

"What resources are available to you? Which programs can your computer support? Which programs can you afford? What resources (time, personnel, material) necessary for learning how to use this program are available to you?"

"What are your preconceptions about these programs? How have other users' opinions, product marketing, or other sources of information about qualitative data analysis software programs influenced your preferences? Are your assumptions about programs accurate? What more would you like to learn about particular programs?"

"What of the above questions/concerns are most important to you? How would you rank-order what are your most important factors in considering a software purchase? What questions have been left out?" (Hesse-Biber & Crofts, 2008, p. 665)

If users reflect on these concerns before selecting a qualitative data analysis program, they can critically evaluate for themselves how each program might impact their research. The user can get a sense of how different kinds of programs might operate in his or her research project by trying free demos, reading through user's manuals, and thinking about the ways in which one's colleagues use similar programs. The above set of questions enhances user empowerment and program accountability. Users should remember that ultimately there is no technological tool that can independently perform analysis (Hesse-Biber and Crofts, 2008).

Computers can revolutionize the ways in which researchers carry out their analysis, but there are also some accompanying caveats that the qualitative analyst should remember. Researchers should assess the strengths and weaknesses of these program, and analyze how these programs are working within their projects. Free demonstration copies of commercial and freeware products known as CAQDAS (Computer Assisted Qualitative Data Analysis Software) are available at http://caqdas.soc.surrey.ac.uk/. This website hosts a variety of resources, including guides on how to select software packages and workshop information on software demonstration.

CONCLUSION

In-depth interviews capture an individual's lived experiences. Feminist researchers bring a unique perspective to the practice of in-depth interviewing, for they are often cognizant of issues of power and authority that might affect the research process. These researchers are mindful that they must consider their own standpoints. Feminist researchers are able to discern how their own values and biases affect their research at all points along the research continuum. This includes the types of research questions that are asked and how data are to be gathered, analyzed, and interpreted. Feminist research is committed to getting at the subjugated knowledge that often lies hidden from mainstream knowledge building. Feminist researchers are particularly interested in issues of social justice and social change for women and other oppressed groups.

In the next chapter, we turn to other forms of feminist research that involve interviewing as a means of data collection. We will first consider feminist oral history research and then turn to feminist focus group interviewing. We will focus on how these methods can be employed in the service of feminist concerns.

Author's note: Portions of this chapter are adapted from and apart from the joint co-authorship a chapter on the Practice of Qualitative Interviewing in Hesse-Biber and Leavy, (2011) with permission from Sage Publications, Inc.

DISCUSSION QUESTIONS

1. Describe and provide examples of three different interview structures. Is one structure "better" than another? Why or why not?

2. What are the main characteristics of a feminist approach to interviewing?

3. What does this process of "deep listening" entail? Provide three strategies for specifically how this can be carried out in an interview situation.

4. Describe three examples of how feminist researchers deal with issues of difference in the interview process.

5. What is reflexivity and why is it important to be reflexive when conducting your research project? Provide two examples of reflexive practice.

6. Why is in-depth interviewing a particularly important method for feminist researchers?

7. What are some research dilemmas feminist researchers confront as they conduct an in-depth interview?

8. Describe the benefits and drawbacks of utilizing computer-assisted software to analyze your interview data.

WEB RESOURCES

- Doing Feminist Interviewing.

http://www.esds.ac.uk/qualidata/support/interviews/feminist.asp

This website provides the reader with the basic resources on the "how-to's" for conducting an interview using feminist principles of praxis discussed in this chapter. The website goes through a specific study that employs a feminist approach to interviewing.

- Education Online: "Collecting data by in-depth interviewing."

http://www.leeds.ac.uk/educol/documents/000001172.htm

Website provides basic information on conducting in-depth interviews. It provides the reader with a step-by-step process of how to do this.

REFERENCES

Allen, L. (2010). Queer(y)ing the straight researcher: The relationship(?) between researcher identity and anti-normative knowledge. *Feminism & Psychology, 20,* 147–165.

Anderson, K., & Jack, D. C. (1991). Learning to listen: Interview techniques and analyses. In S. B. Gluck & D. Patai (Eds.), *Women's words: The feminist practice of oral history* (pp. 11–26). New York, NY: Routledge.

Baca Zinn, M., Cannon, L.W., Dill, B. T., & Higginbotham, E. (1986). The costs of exclusionary practices in women's studies. *Signs: Journal of Women in Culture and Society, 11,* 290–303.

Beoku–Betts, J. (1994). When black is not enough: Doing field research among Gullah women. *NWSA Journal, 6,* 413–433.

Bosworth, M., Hoyle, C., & Dempsey, M. M. (2011). Researching trafficked women: On institutional resistance and the limits to feminist reflexivity. *Qualitative Inquiry, 17,* 769–779.

Campbell, R., Adams, A. E., Wasco, S. M., Aherns, C. E., & Sefi, T. (2010). "What has it been like for you to talk with me today?" The impact of participating in interview research on rape survivors. *Violence Against Women, 16,* 60–83.

Cook, C. (2012). Email interviewing: Generating data with a vulnerable population. *Journal of Advanced Nursing, 68,* 1330–1339.

Creswell, J. W., & Maietta, R. C. (2003). Qualitative research. In D. C. Miller & N. J. Salkind (Eds.), *Handbook of research design social measurement* (pp. 143–180). Thousand Oaks, CA: Sage.

Denissen, J. J. A., Neumann, L., & van Zalk, M. (2010). How the Internet is changing the implementation of traditional research methods, people's daily lives, and the way in which developmental scientists conduct research. *International Journal of Behavioral Development, 34,* 564–575.

DeVault, M. (2004). Talking and listening from women's standpoint: Feminist strategies for interviewing and analysis. In S. Hesse-Biber & M. Yaiser (Eds.), *Feminist perspectives on social research* (pp. 227–250). New York, NY: Oxford University Press.

DeVault, M., & Gross, G. (2012). Feminist qualitative interviewing: Experience, talk, and knowledge. In S. Hesse-Biber (Ed.), *Handbook of feminist research: Theory and praxis* (2nd ed., pp. 206–236). Thousand Oaks, CA: Sage.

Dicks, B., & Mason, B. (2008). Hypermedia methods for qualitative research. In S. N. Hesse-Biber & P. Leavy (Eds.), *Handbook of emergent methods* (pp. 571–600). New York, NY: Guilford Press.

Dill, B. T. (1979). The dialectics of black womanhood. *Signs: Journal of Women in Culture and Society, 4,* 543–555.

Dill, B. T., & Kohlman, M. H. (2012). Intersectionality: A transformative paradigm in feminist theory and social justice. In S. Hesse-Biber (Ed.), *Handbook of feminist research: Theory and praxis* (pp. 154–174). Thousand Oaks, CA: Sage.

Edwards, R. (1990). Connecting methods and epistemology: A white woman interviewing black women. *Women's Studies International Forum, 13,* 477–490.

Fielding, N., G., & Lee, R. M. (1998). *Computer analysis and qualitative research.* London, England: Sage.

Gailey, J. A., & Prohaska, A. (2011). Power and gender negotiations during interviews with men about sex and sexually degrading practices. *Qualitative Research, 11,* 365–380.

Harding, S. (Ed). (1987). *Feminism and methodology.* Bloomington: Indiana University Press.

Harding, S. (1993). Rethinking standpoint epistemology: What is "strong objectivity"? In L. Alcoff & E. Potter (Eds.), *Feminist epistemologies* (pp. 49–82). New York, NY: Routledge.

Hesse-Biber, S. (1995).Unleashing Frankenstein's monster: The use of computers in qualitative research. In R. G. Burgess (Ed.), *Studies in qualitative methodology: Computing and qualitative research* (Vol. 5, pp. 25–41). Westport, CT: JAI Press.

Hesse-Biber, S. (2007). *The cult of thinness*. New York, NY: Oxford University Press.

Hesse-Biber, S. N. (Ed.). (2011). *Handbook of emergent technologies in social research*. New York, NY: Oxford University Press.

Hesse-Biber, S., & Crofts, C. (2008).User-centered perspectives on qualitative data analysis software: Emergent technologies and future trends. In S. N. Hesse-Biber & P. Leavy (Eds.), *Handbook of emergent methods* (pp. 655–673). New York, NY: Guilford Press.

Hesse-Biber, S. N., & Leavy, P. (2006). *The practice of qualitative research*. Thousand Oaks, CA: Sage.

Hesse-Biber, S. N., & Leavy, P. (2007). *Feminist research practice: A primer*. Thousand Oaks, CA: Sage.

Hesse-Biber, S. N., & Leavy, P. (2011). *The practice of qualitative research* (2nd ed.). Thousand Oaks, CA: Sage.

Highet, G. (2003). Cannabis and smoking research: Interviewing young people in self-selected friendship pairs. *Health Education Research: Theory & Practice, 18,* 108–118.

Hine, C. (2008). Internet research as emergent practice. In S. N. Hesse-Biber & P. Leavy (Eds.), *Handbook of emergent methods* (pp. 525–542). Thousand Oaks, CA: Sage.

James, N., & Busher, H. (2009). *Online interviewing*. Thousand Oaks, CA: Sage.

Mann, S. A., & Kelley, L. R. (1997). Standing at the crossroads of modernist thought: Collins, Smith, and the new feminist epistemologies. *Gender & Society, 11,* 391–408.

Miles, M. B., & Huberman, A. M. (1994). *Qualitative data analysis: An expanded sourcebook*. Newbury Park, CA: Sage.

Oakley, A. (1981). Interviewing women: A contradiction in terms. In H. Roberts (Ed.), *Doing feminist research* (pp. 30–61). London, England: Routledge and Kegan Paul.

O'Shaughnessy, S., & Krogman, N. T. (2012). A revolution reconsidered? Examining the practice of qualitative research in feminist scholarship. *Signs: Journal of Women in Culture and Society, 37,* 493–520.

Patai, D. (1991). U.S. academics and Third World women: Is ethical research possible? In S. B. Gluck & D. Patai (Eds.), *Women's words: The feminist practice of oral history* (pp. 137–153). New York, NY: Routledge.

Patton, M. Q. (2002). *Qualitative research and evaluation methods* (3rd ed.). Thousand Oaks, CA: Sage.

Pezalla, A. E., Pettigrew, J., & Miller-Day, M. (2012). Researching the researcher-as-instrument: An exercise in interviewer self-reflexivity. *Qualitative Research, 12,* 165–185.

Porter, E., Neysmith, S. M., Reitsma-Street, M., & Baker Collins, S. (2009). Reciprocal peer interviewing. *International Review of Qualitative Research, 2*(2), 291–312.

Reinharz, S. (1983). Experiential analysis: A contribution to feminist research. In G. Bowles & R. Duelli-Klein (Eds.), *Theories of women's studies* (pp. 162–191). New York, NY: Routledge.

Reinharz, S. (1992). *Feminist methods in social research*. New York, NY: Oxford University Press.

Reinharz, S. (1993). Neglected voices and excessive demands in feminist research. *Qualitative Sociology, 16,* 69–76.

Riessman, C. K. (1987). When gender is not enough: Women interviewing women. *Gender & Society, 1,* 172–207.

Robinson, L., & Schulz, J. (2011). New fieldsites, new methods: New ethnographic opportunities. In S. N. Hesse-Biber (Ed.), *The handbook of emergent technologies in social research* (pp. 180–198). New York, NY: Oxford University Press.

Rose, G. (1997). Situating knowledges: Positionality, reflexivities and other tactics. *Progress in Human Geography, 21,* 305–320.

Stacey, J. (1991). Can there be a feminist ethnography? In S. B. Gluck & D. Patai (Eds.), *Women's words: The feminist practice of oral history* (pp. 111–119). New York, NY: Routledge.

Tesch, R. (1990). *Qualitative research: Analysis types and software tools.* Abingdon, Oxford, England: Routledge Falmer.

Wasserfall, R. (1993). Reflexivity, feminism and difference. *Qualitative Sociology, 16,* 23–41.

Weiss, R. S. (1994). *Learning from strangers: The art and method of qualitative interview studies.* New York, NY: Free Press.

Weitzman, E. A. (2000). Software and qualitative research. In N. K. Denzin & Y. S. Lincoln (Eds.), *Handbook of qualitative research* (2nd ed., pp. 803–820). Thousand Oaks, CA: Sage.

Weitzman, E. A. & Miles, M. (1995). *Computer programs for qualitative data analysis: A software sourcebook.* London, England: Sage.

Weston, K. (2004). Fieldwork in lesbian and gay communities. In S. Hesse-Biber & M. Yaiser (Eds.), *Feminist perspectives on social research* (pp. 198–205). New York, NY: Oxford University Press.

CHAPTER 8

The Practice of Feminist Focus Groups

Jennie Munday

What Is a Focus Group and Why and How Would Feminist Researchers Want to Use Them?

At its most basic, a focus group is a small group discussion focused on a particular topic and facilitated by a researcher (Tonkiss, 2004). As Kitzinger (1994) explains it, "The group is 'focused' in the sense that it involves some kind of collective activity—such as viewing a film, examining a single health education method or simply debating a particular set of questions" (p. 103).

Focus groups have not always been a popular method among feminist researchers. Writing in 1999, Wilkinson noted that focus groups were relatively neglected in feminist research, and that feminist methods textbooks rarely included a chapter on focus groups. Similarly Montell (1999) comments that focus groups began to gain popularity in academic research while remaining obsolete in feminist research. Because of this distinction, she viewed her advocacy of the focus group method as arguing for a "new feminist method." I will explain in this chapter how traditional conceptions of the focus group method could be considered opposite to the concerns of feminist research practice and praxis, therefore making the method unappealing to feminist researchers.

However, by 2001, Rose reported that focus groups were gaining in popularity among feminist researchers—even arguing that they could be seen as one of the most appropriate methods for use in feminist research. Writers such as Madriz (2000), Montell (1999), and Wilkinson (1999) argued that focus groups particularly helped feminist researchers address issues of feminist praxis. These issues include researching the experiences and empowerment of marginalized groups, rejection of essentialism and exploration of the social as constructed rather than pregiven, consideration of the collective as opposed to individual nature of social life, contextualization of data, and addressing the power inequalities that exist between the researcher and the researched.

When conducting my own research on British rural identity, I was drawn to the claims that the focus group had the potential to be used in a way that corresponds to feminist research practice. I decided to explore these claims and set out to develop my own distinctively feminist way of conducting focus groups. I conducted a pilot study that consisted of one focus group with members of The Women's Institute (WI), which aimed to investigate how these women negotiated and produced a collective identity that revolved around their gender, living in a rural location, and their belonging to the WI, an organization specifically for rural women. During the pilot study, a pressure group called the Countryside Alliance was protesting legislation that would ban fox hunting in the United Kingdom (UK). In light of the protests, the pilot study helped inform the use of focus groups in another project that looked at the production of rural identities among different social groups.

This chapter draws on my own experiences of conducting this research, as well as the work of other feminist academics who have been drawn to the focus group method, to explore and examine some of the issues that are raised by the above question: Why and how would feminist researchers want to use focus groups?

What Is the History of the Focus Group?

Robert K. Merton initially developed focus groups for use in social science research during his time at the Bureau of Applied Social Research, Columbia University, in the 1940s. However, as Jowett and O'Toole (2006) comment, initially focus groups were never seen as an appropriate primary research method in their own right. Rather they were considered a method used to supplement others to provide preparatory or exploratory support. By the 1970s, the use of focus groups had become synonymous with market research and marketing, where they are generally used to study public opinion and the potential reception of new products and services. In recent years, focus groups have become increasingly popular in a variety of fields and used in a number of diverse settings for different purposes.

Those working in the field of media and communications used focus groups to investigate audience reception. Focus groups are also used in organizational research to generate data on staff views and experiences, while in consultation and evaluation research they have been used to gain information on the experiences and views of service providers and users. Focus groups are often used in the context of health and medicine for a variety of purposes, including evaluating the impact of health education programs or gaining the views of patients who have received a particular type of treatment.

This increasing popularity of the focus group has included its rediscovery by social scientists, who have reexamined its characteristics and are now more prepared to use focus groups as a primary research method and accept findings produced using this method as valuable and useful (Kitzinger, 1994). Today, focus groups are used as the sole research method (Munday, 2006) or are successfully combined with other methods (Skeggs & Woods, n.d.). They are an important tool in the process of triangulation, whereby different research methods are used to produce data on the same research question and the data gained from each method are compared. Focus groups are utilized at different points during the research process—as a pilot to help inform the formulation of future research questions, as the main method to address the research question, or as a follow up to further explore points of interest raised at earlier times during the research. It is also possible to conduct longitudinal research using focus groups. In these cases, a series of focus groups are conducted with the same participants at given intervals. They are useful if the researcher wants to investigate how the opinions and beliefs of a given set of people may change over time or after exposure to specific events.

According to Gofton (n.d.) the rise in the interest of focus groups among social scientists can be dated to the 1980s, and this increased interest was often for practical reasons associated with appealing to funding bodies that wanted speedy, value-for-money research. Given that a focus group enables the researcher to work with a number of participants at the same time, it is a method that can effectively meet both these requirements. It was initially practical concerns rather than questions of epistemology and methodology that prompted a return to the focus group method.

However, focus groups have much more to offer than just being quick, efficient, and good value for the money. Social scientists have now become much more interested in recognizing and investigating the distinct epistemological and methodological characteristics of the focus group—most notably its collective, interactive nature—and the way that these impact the data and knowledge produced. The use of focus groups in the social sciences is now generally associated with the qualitative, interpretive study of social and cultural life—for example, investigating the construction of collective identities.

As will be seen in the next section of the chapter, feminist researchers have been at the forefront of how the focus group has been reconceived—seeing it as an important and useful method for achieving the goals of feminist research and praxis.

Why Are Focus Groups Attractive to Feminist Researchers?

It must be stressed that no method is inherently feminist, and no method is inherently superior or inferior to any other (Denmark & Pauldi, 2008; Kimmel & Crawford,

1999). Rather, feminists use a wide variety of methods and adapt them to suit their own aims, goals, and research questions. I now move on to discuss the characteristics of focus groups that make them such a potentially potent tool for use in feminist research and feminist praxis.

It is interesting that such strong claims about the suitability of focus groups for feminist research have been made, considering that as traditionally conceived, focus groups can initially appear to be an unappealing method, unsuited for use in feminist research. Indeed, as stated in the introduction, even as focus groups became more popular in academic research during the 1980s, it took longer for feminist researchers to begin using the method.

As stated above, focus groups have become synonymous with market research. Morgan (1993) and Kitzinger and Barbour (1999) comment that it is the market research model that tends to predominate and to be accepted as the norm. They argue this led to the creation of certain myths about how focus groups should be conducted, which has limited how academic researchers have used focus groups. Researchers can be left feeling that they have to stick to "the Rules," which, while appropriate for market research, are not necessarily suitable for academic research. Social researchers and market researchers possess different research skills, and they conduct and analyze focus groups in different ways and seek to generate different types of data (Krueger, 1998a). Nevertheless, as Kitzinger and Barbour (1999) explain, "[S]ocial scientists are in danger of uncritically adopting market researchers' models of such research rather than adapting and expanding them, taking into account our own purposes and theoretical traditions" (p. 1).

In terms of epistemology, focus groups used within market research are associated with a positivist research paradigm (Cunningham-Burley, Kerr, & Pavis, 1999) whereby the researcher can elicit objective facts about the attitudes and opinions of the members of the group. The researcher can access the true feelings and beliefs of the participants. As Liamputtong (2011) explains, the chief aim of market research is to provide clients with accurate opinions from prospective customers about how new products will be received. Because the client will be basing subsequent decisions about marketing and the potential viability of new products on this information, the moderator must control and direct the group so that the data produced provide an accurate, objective account of the participants' views. Similarly Johnson argues that the traditional use of focus groups is associated with "assumptions of positivism, behaviourism and empiricism" (Johnson, 1996, p. 517).

The traditional use of focus groups is associated with a skilled moderator who controls the research process, thus producing objective knowledge about the research participants. This has had particular consequences for feminist researchers because, while there is no overarching approach to, or definition of, feminist research practice, overriding concerns have challenged the notion of objective social research in favor of praxis.

The combination of theory and research with practice as an explicit aim to understand the world and then change it (Stanley, 1990) disrupts and challenges the hierarchies of power that exist between the researcher and those being researched.

Thus, in order to be successfully used in an appropriate manner, feminist researchers have to be willing to break with commonly held assumptions about the nature of focus groups and how they should be conducted. Pini (2002) calls for what she refers to as a "paradigmatic shift" in their use. She draws on Johnson's (1996) idea that focus groups can be used in such a way that they are informed by the politics and knowledge of movements of resistance, which, for Pini, meant that her use of focus groups could be informed by her own commitment to feminism. She rejected the idea that research should be about producing objective knowledge, but rather embraced the belief that research should be informed by the subjectivity, values, and politics of the researcher. She argues that if focus groups are to be used in a way that corresponds to feminist research practice, then the method has to be reconceptualized in terms of ontology, epistemology, and methodology.

In order to do this, many feminist researchers have paid attention to aspects already inherently part of the focus group method, but often ignored by the traditional model—in particular the collective, interactive nature of the focus group. In the traditional model, the context in which attitudes and opinions are expressed is not usually taken into consideration; and the focus group is treated as a resource rather than a topic, with the emphasis on content (the expressed reality) rather than process (how participants constructed that reality).

However, it is surprising that it should be this version of the focus group method, which emphasizes content over context, that predominates in social research since it is the ability to observe interaction between participants and to analyze the context in which speech is produced that are the distinctive characteristics of focus group research. This enables the researcher to generate data that could not be produced using any other type of interview technique (Blee & Taylor, 2002; Krueger, 1998a). Importantly, this aspect of interaction between participants means that a focus group should not be seen as the same as a group interview, which is conducted as a series of separate one-to-one interactions between the researcher and each participant (Bertini, 2011).

This aspect of interaction, through which participants come to negotiate and construct their own meanings, indicates that focus groups are actually more appropriate to a social constructionist paradigm. In reality, it is socially produced by individuals interacting with one another, and it is only when this important aspect of focus group research is ignored that focus groups appear to fit a positivist approach to research. While market research orthodoxy may stress that it is possible to elicit an objective truth from participants via careful moderating, it is more appropriate to see focus groups as social contexts in themselves through which partial and multiple versions of social reality are constructed, thus rejecting any idea of there being one, ultimate, objective truth of social reality. This may be important to feminist researchers because it provides a way to challenge essentialism. If they accept that categories such as "woman" are socially constructed, then there can be no natural or essential character- istics of women, and the ideas and values generally associated with that term can be challenged. In the context of a focus group, women are given the chance to coconstruct and negotiate meanings rather than having meanings imposed on them by the researcher. The task, then, for feminist researchers is not to use focus groups as a means of eliciting some objective truth about the nature of social reality but rather to investi- gate how the participants understand and actively construct social categories and phenomena. The focus group provides a means for the researcher to observe these processes as they actually happen. Researchers can thus generate data not just on con- tent but on the processes through which that content is produced.

However, while researchers pay lip service to the presence of interaction in focus groups, what often happens is that in analysis, this aspect is ignored (Kitzinger, 1994). This leads to a situation where "[m]ore commonly, the focus is on *content,* rather than the *process,* of interaction" (Wilkinson, 1999, p. 77). The idea that mean- ing and knowledge is coconstructed through social interaction is lost—who has power among the group to impose their own ideas? How is conflict managed and consensus achieved? Wilkinson goes on to explain that many researchers actually treated the data produced using focus groups as if they were analyzing one-to-one, in-depth interviews. She also notes that most feminist researchers were also initially guilty of doing this.

However, writers like Wilkinson have been particularly influential for a later genera- tion of feminist researchers, including myself; and it is now the case that feminist researchers have come to realize that interaction is an incredibly valuable and distinctive aspect of focus groups. Indeed, many feminist researchers now state that it is one of the main reasons that they choose to use the method. The idea that research should be con- textualized and involve processes of everyday interaction is an important aspect of fem- inist research practice (Kimmel & Crawford, 1999). Wilkinson (1998) argues that despite this concern to contextualize research data, feminist research has been domi- nated by individualistic methods; and she points to the need for the use of more socially situated methods, focus groups being seen as a particularly valuable tool. While the focus group cannot be seen as a truly naturalistic method, it can be seen and analyzed as a particular social context in its own right.

It is interesting to note that while social researchers are seeking to break the rules of market research orthodoxy, those involved in market and consumer research are now increasingly willing to acknowledge the problems and limitations associated with their conception of focus groups and to learn from social researchers. Most commonly it is the interactive and collaborative nature of focus groups that market researchers are being encouraged to recognize and exploit (Catterall, Maclaran, &

Stevens, 1999). Sunderland and Denny (2007) provide a thoughtful and interesting account of the influence that anthropology and its associated research methods (including focus groups) have had on consumer research. Importantly, their work clearly demonstrates that not all contemporary market and consumer research is conducted along the didactic lines that are associated with the more traditional use of focus groups in these fields, although it still has to be borne in mind that market researchers and academics are trying to achieve very different outcomes for different audiences through their research.

When Should You Use Focus Groups and When Should You Not?

As with all research methods, focus groups are not suitable for use in every situation. Focus groups are more appropriate for some research questions than others. Focus groups are not suitable if you want to produce statistical data or data that is generalizable to a wider population. While focus groups are seen as "naturalistic" and therefore somehow a reproduction of wider society in miniature, they are discrete and specific contexts, which do not necessarily act as a mirror for the population as a whole.

However, focus groups are particularly appropriate if you want to produce in-depth data about how the social world is constructed collectively. For example, in my own research (Munday, 2008), it was the collective nature of focus groups and the ability to see process in action that made them particularly appropriate for use in this particular project. Because my understanding of identity was informed by the New Social Movement Theory of Touraine (1981), Melucci (1989, 1996), and Castells (1997)—an identity that is constructed rather than pregiven and collective rather than individualistic—focus groups provided a means of accessing the negotiations and processes through which participants produced their collective identity, and I could investigate questions of both process and content.

It has also been argued that the collective nature of focus groups makes them particularly useful for the research of sensitive topics. In her work with victims of domestic violence, Fielding (1993) argued that the shared experiences of the women facilitated discussion and made the women feel more relaxed and willing to participate and talk about what could be seen as a sensitive and difficult topic. However, as Owen (2001) points out, conducting focus groups with vulnerable and marginalized groups of women is by no means straightforward. For example, a great deal of time and effort has to be invested in the recruitment process; despite shared experiences, the participants may still feel reluctant to discuss difficult issues in front of one another; and the line between research and therapy may become blurred.

The appropriateness of focus groups to research sensitive topics remains controversial and open to debate. While some participants clearly feel at ease in the focus group setting and are able to talk openly about their experiences in front of others—although this may raise issues about "overdisclosure"—some can feel intimidated and unwilling to speak because other participants are present. This highlights one of the distinctive ethical problems associated with conducting focus groups—participants not only share information with the researcher but they also share information with each other. While researchers may be bound to confidentiality and anonymity by formal ethical guidelines and procedures, other participants are not; and once information has been disclosed, no one can control how fellow participants treat this knowledge outside of the research setting.

Similar difficulties concerning overdisclosure, feelings of intimidation, and questions of how participants treat information outside of the research context are also experienced when running focus groups that consist of participants who already know one another. Market research orthodoxy advocates that all participants, although sharing similar characteristics, should be strangers to one another (Morgan, 1993, 1998). Some researchers argue that it is inappropriate to use focus groups when participants already know one another. Preexisting relationships and hierarchies of status and power, which will be present among such participants, will be detrimental to the research process and "contaminate" the data produced (Krueger & Casey, 2000). As mentioned above, Pini (2002) experienced just such problems when the existing difficult relationship between two of her participants adversely impacted the focus group. However, as Morgan (1993) states with regard to the market research orthodoxy of ensuring all participants are strangers to one another, "This is an example of a useful rule of thumb that has become an overly rigid restriction on when to use focus groups" (p. 6), and researchers should not be deterred from using this method when working with participants who know one another.

Social research often necessitates the use of preexisting groups, and focus groups can be successfully used in these circumstances. However, a focus group that consists of people who know one another must be approached in a slightly different manner from one that consists of strangers (Morgan, 1993). The researcher needs to be particularly alert to established hierarchies and patterns of interaction, which may impact the data produced. Indeed, this very impact may in itself provide a valuable source of knowledge—for example, revealing how power is used and maintained among the participants. From a more practical perspective, working with preexisting groups affords a number of advantages. These include ease of recruitment, the fact that participants already feel relaxed with one another and need little time to warm up, and the way that discussion can be prompted by reference to shared stories and experiences. These advantages can outweigh any difficulties that might occur (Bloor, Frankland, Thomas, & Robson, 2001).

Behind the Scenes With Jennie Munday

In my Women's Institute focus group, all the participants were members of the committee, and the focus group was piggybacked onto one of their committee meetings. This meant that all the participants knew one another and were already used to working as a group. They shared a wealth of stories and experiences, which helped to facilitate good interaction between the participants, and the focus group produced very rich, in-depth data. Although all the participants were members of the committee and therefore all had a degree of status and authority within their WI branch, one of the members was the chairman and thus in overall charge of this particular WI branch. (Despite being an organization solely for women, the WI continues to use the title chairman rather than chairwoman or chairperson.) She clearly held power and influence among these women, but I do not feel that her actions caused any sense of false or enforced consensus between the women. However, at times she did appear to adopt the role of spokesperson, as if she felt it was her responsibility to speak on behalf of the organization and present it in a good light. Therefore, although working with an organization presented many advantages—ease of access and recruitment of participants; ease of organizing and arranging the date, time, and place of the focus group; and the ease of interaction among participants who already knew one another—it did have an impact on the research process, and it was necessary to be particularly reflexive with regard to these issues when analyzing the data.

I was also aware of the need to be particularly reflexive about my own role in the research. Every researcher plays an active part in the research process and generation of data, but I had to be particularly aware of the impact of my own personal biography because, not only were all the participants known to each other, but in many cases I already knew them as well. In the WI group, the chairman was my grandmother, and all the others were family friends who knew me during my time growing up in the village. While there were some advantages to this—again ease of access and recruitment, ease of interaction, and shared experiences and stories facilitating understanding on my part—I was very aware that I did not want to use my relationships with these people in an exploitative manner, for example, by making people feel pressured to participate just because they knew me. However, some participants whom I knew did drop out at the last minute, leaving me with somewhat mixed feelings—relief that I had obviously not put too much pressure on the participants and they felt able to drop out of the research but also annoyance at the inconvenience caused and a wish that I had perhaps been a bit more forceful in my recruiting technique. So, while knowing your participants may facilitate access and recruitment, it does not guarantee success.

(Continued)

(Continued)

Additionally, while common knowledge may be seen as an advantage to facilitating inter-action and understanding, it is possible that familiarity can lead to both the participants and researcher erroneously thinking that the researcher understands something, where really further exploration and explanation is required in order to prevent important details being glossed over. I was also faced with the difficult task of having to bracket off what I thought I knew through prior knowledge from the data that was generated within the context of the focus group. There were frustrating moments when participants did not disclose within the focus group views and opinions that I heard them express outside of the research context and that would have been invaluable for the project, but that could not be used.

Focus Groups, Empowerment, and Feminist Praxis

For many researchers, the appeal of the focus group is its distinctive interactive and collective nature. For feminist researchers, this appeal may not just be linked to the fact that this aspect of the focus group method provides the best means of producing the type of data required to investigate a particular research question. Rather, their collective and interactive nature is important in and of itself. For many feminist researchers, the importance of the collective nature of focus groups is that they bring women together and through discussion can reach a point where they realize that their experiences are not just individual but collective. Discussions between participants can make explicit meanings and realities that were previously hidden, thus promoting a new and greater understanding of their social position as women constrained within patriarchal social structures. In other words, the collective and interactive nature of focus groups is par-ticularly appealing to feminist researchers because it links to ideas of empowerment and feminist praxis.

Montell (1999), in her exploration of the relationship between popular culture and the construction of normative sexuality, explicitly refers to focus groups as a tool for "con-sciousness raising," a term often associated with second-wave feminism, now much cri-tiqued and challenged. Who decides what is best for women? What happens to the women after the research has finished, when they realize their situation but may lack the cultural, social, and economic capital to do anything about it? Here lie the practical difficulties of translating academic knowledge produced through research into meaningful social and political change.

Despite these concerns, the collective and interactive nature of focus groups, and how this links to ideas of empowerment and praxis, remains appealing. Examples of such projects, which explicitly incorporate the goal of achieving social change through the use of focus groups, include Pini's (2002, 2005) research with women working in the male-dominated sugar industry. Pini's research was undertaken in partnership with an agri-political organization called Canegrowers. No women held any of the elected leadership positions in the organization, which was a concern to the organization itself. Thus, there was an explicit aim to promote women's active participation in the organization and get them promoted to positions of power. Sampling was purposive, and only women who expressed an interest in becoming actively involved in industry forums and politics were chosen. Pini herself recognizes that this may have skewed the sample and may have actually disempowered and marginalized even further those who did not want to be formally involved in the running of Canegrowers. For Pini, empowerment is not about what we, as researchers, can do *for* our participants; but rather it is about giving them the power to act for themselves. She argues that it is the collective nature of focus groups that makes them particularly potent tools for empowering marginalized groups. Her argument is that it is easier for women to become empowered in a collective and supportive setting as opposed to an individualistic and isolating environment.

Not all feminist researchers accept that social research can be empowering. Culley, Hudson, and Rapport (n.d.) conducted focus groups with Asian women who were suffering from fertility problems. While they acknowledged that participation in the research did have an impact on the lives of these women, infertility is a condition often stigmatized and little understood in the women's own ethnic communities. Consequently, many of the participants were misinformed or knew very little about the condition. The researchers decided they would take it upon themselves to provide the participants with accurate information, but they were careful to avoid any claims that they empowered the women or in any way significantly altered their social position. While the women became more informed about infertility, the research process did little to alter their standing in their ethnic communities or prevent them from becoming the victims of social stigma.

Similarly, I would not wish to claim that the women who participated in the WI focus group were in any way empowered or that their social situation changed as a result of taking part in the research. However, I do believe that my participants enjoyed taking part in the research process. All the participants wrote to me after the event, both to thank me for the voucher that they had been given for participating and to say how much they had enjoyed the experience. They valued the fact that they were given time just to talk to one another and, in particular, that they were listened to and their views considered important enough to be included in an academic research project. This is a concrete example of positive outcomes that can stem from bringing women together collectively to share their experiences and from listening to and taking seriously the experiences of members of marginalized groups.

Behind the Scenes With Jennie Munday

What happens when we work with people whom we do not want to actively help? Surely we don't just ignore groups or individuals whose position we don't agree with?

My own decision to research British rural identities was far from a neutral or value-free decision. My background of growing up in a small village where many of my family and friends continue to live informed my decision. Given that my academic discipline of sociology is most associated with studying the urban, I wanted to research a group that was important to me but that I felt was overlooked and neglected in traditional sociological research. Additionally, the research was conducted at a time when rural issues were becoming increasingly prominent in the British media and politics. The then Labour government was in the process of implementing legislation that would ban the practice of fox hunting. The Countryside Alliance was publicly protesting against the legislation, arguing that the ban was an attack on the traditional rural way of life by an urban, metropolitan government who did not understand or care about the countryside. The Countryside Alliance was trying to produce a representation of rural identity in the public sphere that supported fox hunting at its heart. Although I have spent much of my life living in rural areas, I oppose fox hunting on the grounds that it is a cruel and ineffective method of controlling the fox population and that fox hunting is an exclusionary social practice, particularly in terms of class and ethnicity. I thus wanted to challenge the idea that support for fox hunting is fundamental to rural identity and to explore the idea that rural identities are in practice more varied and diverse than that of the representation produced by the Countryside Alliance.

In some ways, I agreed with my participants and wanted to promote their point of view—particularly around ideas that rural problems were being dealt with poorly or were completely ignored by the Labour government—but at the same time, while I always treated them ethically and with respect, I in no way wished to actively help or empower the Countryside Alliance.

This was further complicated by the fact that explicit in the New Social Movement Theory (NSMT) was the assumption that researchers would actively want to help the movement they are researching. Indeed, it is an explicit aim of NSMT research to produce knowledge and, thus, actively help the movement to progress and ultimately achieve their aims of bringing about change in the wider social world. In other words, this was a prime example of praxis.

Often there is an assumption that we will be working only with people whom we actively support, agree with, and wish to help; but I suggest that in reality the situation is more complicated than this. How do we, as feminists, work with groups whom we actively dislike and don't wish to help? I was also aware that although I didn't want to help the Countryside Alliance, I had no control over what, if anything, they learned from the process of being involved in this research and how they used any resulting knowledge.

I think that feminists should not shy away from researching subjects and people with whom they disagree. Indeed, in many cases it strikes me as being particularly important that we do not do so. However, the issue does raise interesting and difficult questions around the role of empowerment and praxis and whether this should always be a central aim in feminist research.

Practicalities of Running a Feminist Focus Group

Questions of praxis and empowerment also impact how feminist researchers choose to practically run focus groups. The potential to run focus groups in a nonhierarchical manner that empowers and actively involves participants in the research process has made the focus group a particularly appealing method to feminist researchers.

The next section of this chapter will look at how these practical issues impact each stage of conducting focus group research, and examine how feminist researchers have actively put the focus group method into practice.

FOCUS GROUPS AND TECHNOLOGY

Technology plays an important role in the running of focus groups as, in almost all cases, a recording—audio and/or visual—of the focus group will be made and the data analysis will be based on this recording.

Audio recordings can be made using a digital voice recorder while the most appropriate type of microphone used is an omnidirectional boundary microphone. They tend to be small and unobtrusive and are better at picking up multiple voices coming from different directions than unidirectional microphones. It is now becoming increasingly common to video focus groups. This has the advantage of allowing the researcher to analyze body language, gestures, and interaction (process as well as content) and can make it easier for the researcher to identify who is speaking, compared to audio recordings. Before conducting a focus group, it is important to practice using the equipment and to test it in order to make sure everything is working correctly.

The moderator also needs to decide whether, and to what extent, she or he will make written notes during the course of the focus group or just rely on audio or video recordings. Within the context of professional market research organizations, it is common for the focus group to be run by more than one moderator. One moderator actively facilitates the group while another observes and makes notes, sometimes from another room behind a two-way mirror and thus out of sight of the participants. Access to such facilities and resources to employ a second moderator are not always available to academic researchers, and they will often find themselves working on their own. I prefer not to make written notes during the course of the focus group. It takes my attention away from the discussion, and participants can feel you are not really listening if you are constantly looking down, making notes. However, in all cases—whether the researcher does or does not take notes during the group—it is advisable to make notes as soon as possible after the focus group has taken place. Technology is not infallible and can let you down. The researcher should always be prepared for such an eventuality and have notes for reference in the event of a technological failure.

Whatever type of recording method is used, the researcher must be aware of the ethical implications of the situation and ensure that informed consent to be recorded is obtained from all the participants. As previously stated, the question of ethics with regard to focus groups goes further than this one aspect, but here I highlight ethical issues involved with making a recording of a focus group. The researcher will be left with a permanent record of the proceedings, and this can make participants feel uneasy, particularly if the topic being researched is a sensitive one. The wishes of participants who do not want to be recorded should always be respected. In these cases, the researcher will have to rely on field notes. The moderator must also decide whether the presence of recording equipment influences the behavior of the participants (feeling intimidated and unwilling to speak, playing up to the camera, etc.). In my own research, I have used only audio recordings. By using a small, unobtrusive digital voice recorder and omnidirectional microphone, after some hesitation in the initial stages, participants have generally relaxed and forgotten that they are being recorded. I feel that being recorded has not significantly influenced the behavior of the participants. It could be argued that in contemporary society, where the use of such technology has become so commonplace, individuals are not unduly worried by the prospect of being recorded.

Advances in technology have changed the way focus groups are recorded, and they also provide new ways in which the groups can be conducted. Conducting focus groups via webcams and video conferences can help overcome the problems of needing to gather everyone together in one place in order to conduct the focus group. Online focus groups were being discussed as early as the late 1990s (Gaiser, 1997); yet Fox, Morris, and Rumsey (2007) comment that today those using focus groups still seem somewhat reluctant to exploit the advantages of new, online communication technologies. Fox and colleagues provide a discussion on the practicalities of hosting and moderating online synchronous focus groups, while Underhill and Olmsted (2003) and Schneider, Kerwin, Frechtling, and Vivari (2002) are concerned with comparing the data produced by online and face-to-face focus groups. Underhill and Olmsted argue that there is little difference between the data produced by online and face-to-face groups, while Schneider and colleagues found there were significant differences in the way people contributed and interacted—people, for example, tended to give shorter, less detailed responses in an online setting—leading to the suggestion that online and face-to-face groups may have different roles to play in qualitative research.

If, as has been argued throughout this chapter, process is as important as content within the context of focus groups, then it has to be seriously questioned how the nature of interaction between participants changes in an online setting compared to a situation where participants are physically present together. Does conducting a focus group using new communication technologies fundamentally change the nature of the focus group method itself? Will researchers still be able to make the same claims about the distinct ability and advantage that focus groups provide to the investigating process as well as the content?

From a feminist perspective, these technological advances create linkages between geographically dispersed and diverse groups of women; however, feminist researchers need to seriously consider whether using technology may disempower some women. Does conducting focus groups in this way disempower those women who do not have access to, or possess the necessary skills to use, such technology—thus resulting in the increasing marginalization of women who may already be particularly marginalized in society? These are particular issues that are going to become more and more pertinent and ever changing as technology advances and researchers increasingly use these new technologies in their work. While an explicitly feminist consideration of the impact of technology on focus groups has been provided by Pini and Previte (2004), these are issues that are going to need much further debate and consideration by feminist researchers.

Sampling and Recruitment

In any research project, choosing the right people to participate is an important part of the research process. Because focus groups are focused on a particular topic, participants need to have some kind of relationship to the issues being investigated. This makes random sampling inappropriate in most cases; rather, some kind of purposive sampling needs to be used. Snowball sampling may be particularly appropriate, especially if the researcher is trying to access hard to reach or marginalized groups or if the subject matter is a particularly sensitive one.

It is often the case that a research project will involve using more than one focus group. Sometimes the chosen participants are assigned randomly to one of the focus groups. However, it is common to organize participation along the lines of social characteristics so that data can be compared across groups. So participants might be split along the lines of gender, age, social class, or any other social category. Sometimes decisions about the composition of focus groups are influenced by the subject being researched. For example, if the aim of the project is to investigate opinions about domestic or sexual violence against women, then it may be advisable to hold separate focus groups for male and female participants.

As with all types of qualitative research, it can be difficult to find people who are willing to participate in the research process. Problems around recruitment can have a greater impact on focus groups than other types of qualitative interviews because focus groups require a number of participants to be present together at the same time and in the same place. Participants dropping out can be highly problematic in focus group research. It is often advisable to overrecruit in order to ensure that there will be enough participants to run the group successfully, even if some drop out at the last minute. To help lessen the chances of participants dropping out and to encourage people to participate, it is helpful if the focus group is held in a place that is easily accessible to all participants. If participants' travel expenses are met and other financial incentives can encourage participants to remain in the study, it is also advisable to contact the participants one or two days before the group is to be held in order to remind people about the practical details and to check that they are still willing to participate.

Problems around recruitment can also be eased through working with groups or organizations associated with the research topic. For example, I successfully worked with members of the WI and The Young Farmers organization, while Pini (2002, 2005) worked with the Canegrowers association. I found it advantageous to piggyback the focus group onto an already existing meeting, which participants were attending anyway—thus meaning that extra time, effort, and commitment on the part of the participants was minimized. This encouraged participation and lessened the chances of the focus group being affected by last minute dropouts.

Members of the group or organization can act as gatekeepers and help facilitate access to potential participants. Pini found the input from Canegrowers officials into the recruitment process extremely valuable. When Canegrowers played a part in the recruitment process, they actively influenced the composition of the groups because they knew the participants and could recommend which women might cause problems if included in the same group. For some of the focus groups, Pini did not have this input from Canegrowers officials. On one occasion, she inadvertently included a sister and sister-in-law who had a difficult relationship, which adversely impacted the focus group. Pini felt that neither participant would have found the experience empowering.

However, gatekeepers can also deny access and exercise power over which potential participants the researcher is introduced to and who is potentially excluded from the research process. I experienced particular problems when trying to recruit participants for a focus group consisting of foxhunters. I did not have any personal contacts within this community and so had to formally approach the officials of a local hunt—the Hunt Masters—in order to request access to the group and help to facilitate the recruitment of potential participants. The Hunt Masters were able to exert a considerable amount of control over this particular aspect of the research process, because they determined which people within the hunt I had access to and could make sure I spoke only to people who they felt would tell me the right things that corresponded to the official line of the organization.

Can the empowerment and involvement of participants in the recruitment stage be detrimental to the research? What different insights might I have gained if I had been able to talk to other members of the hunt? While the Hunt Master may have been empowered, what about those members he actively excluded from the research process?

With regard to the number of participants included in each focus group, market research orthodoxy suggests that the ideal number is between eight and twelve (Kitzinger & Barbour, 1999). The researcher can access a wide variety of attitudes and opinions with this number of participants. (A particularly important aim of much market research is to access as many different opinions as possible.) However, there is also the possibility that such a large group may become unwieldy to moderate and analyze. The group may lose cohesion, with participants breaking off into conversations with their immediate neighbors if they feel they do not have the opportunity to be heard by the group as a whole. There is the possibility that in a large group, not all participants will get the chance to participate and express their views as fully as they wish. While these problems may occur in both market research and social science focus groups, they may be more detrimental in social science research, which aims to analyze interaction as well as content, than in a market research setting where the priority is to access as many points of view as possible. In market research, the ambition to gain as many views as possible is usually the most important aim and generally overrides any potential disadvantages of working with a large number of participants.

Krueger and Casey (2000) comment that focus groups with four to six participants, often referred to as mini–focus groups, are becoming increasingly popular. There are advantages of smaller focus groups: greater opportunity for all participants to speak and fully express their views, ease of moderation, and analysis of the group. These advantages do need to be balanced against possible shortcomings, such as a lack of diversity of opinions. Ultimately the size of groups should be tailored to suit the needs of the particular project; and, when used in the right circumstances, small groups can be more effective than large ones. While there needs to be enough scope for meaningful interaction and discussion from different points of view to take place between participants, for social scientists whose aim is to produce rich, detailed, in-depth data that pays attention to process as well as content, the advantages of using small focus groups often outweigh any potential disadvantages. All of the focus groups I conducted were mini–focus groups consisting of four to seven participants. I purposely chose to use mini–focus groups because I wanted to give everyone as much opportunity as possible to participate. I also wanted to analyze the focus group for process as well as content. With this number of participants, there were enough people present for meaningful interaction to take place, but the group was still small enough to make analysis of this interaction possible.

Preparation for and Beginning the Focus Group

Preparation for a focus group usually involves the production of a questioning route or topic guide, which the moderator can use to help direct the discussion. Because of the interactive nature of focus groups and because feminist researchers wish to empower and give participants as much control as possible, a less restrictive topic guide is often more useful and appropriate than a directive questioning route. Rather than providing a set of specific questions, a topic guide merely provides a list of issues that need to be covered during the course of the focus group. Focus groups often take on a naturalistic conversational tone, which is more suited to a nondirective topic guide. However, if the researcher feels more confident and comfortable using specific preset questions then (as with all in-depth qualitative interview schedules) these should be open-ended questions designed to prompt discussion rather than closed questions that carry the danger of eliciting mere yes/no responses.

I used the following topics, questions, and prompts to form the topic guide that I used in all the focus groups in my research on British rural identity. The focus groups all had a casual, conversational tone, and I did not ask these questions word for word as they appear. Instead, I used the guide as a personal aid to remind myself of the areas I wanted to cover and as a prompt that I could fall back on should the discussion lag. The only exception to this is the first question, which I specifically used word for word to help me begin the discussion. As with most focus group topic guides, the guide begins with general topics before focusing in on the more specific issues that really get to the heart of the research question being investigated.

1. When you think about the countryside, what sort of things do you think about?

2. The Rural Way of Life.

    Is there a rural way of life? How would you describe it? Is there an urban way of life? What are the differences?

    [If participants do not talk about fox hunting/country sports, then I will raise the topic.]

3. Rural Identity and Belonging.

    Do you see yourself as having a rural identity? Is rural identity important to you? Does living in the countryside automatically make you a rural person?

[Remember to ask about other aspects of identity (e.g., class, gender, age, ethnicity). How do they intersect with rural identity? Ask about "the other." Who is the other of rural people?]

4. Rural Problems.

    What do you like/dislike about living in the countryside? Are there any particular problems that affect rural people—personal and general?

5. Rural Campaigning and Protest.

    What groups/organizations are you aware of? Do you belong to any? Have you participated in protest activity?

    [If participants do not mention Countryside Alliance, then I will—awareness of, attitudes toward, etc.]

6. Is there anything else you would like to tell me or any other issues you believe I should be thinking about?

Pini (2002) also used a topic guide and found that it alleviated her anxieties about making sure that all the important issues and topics were covered during her focus groups; conversation in focus groups can be meandering and circuitous. As a researcher, it is easy to feel anxious that you are not covering the most important topics. Most feminist researchers have the explicit aim of empowering their participants and giving them control over the research process, allowing them to take the conversation in the directions they choose. The reality is that this tactic can sometimes feel strange, and it can be hard for the researcher to step back and let go of the process. It can take a concerted effort on the part of the researcher to relinquish power and control over the process.

Directly before a focus group takes place there are a number of practical tasks that the researcher needs to perform. First, before the participants arrive, the researcher needs to set up the room for the focus group. Most commonly, focus groups will be conducted with participants and moderator sitting around a table. Particularly when the researcher does not know the participants, or the participants are themselves strangers to one another, it is useful for each participant to be given a name card that they can place in front of themselves. The moderator should also make a written plan of who is sitting where as part of the field notes; this can act as a useful aid when analyzing the data. Audio and video recording equipment also should be set up and checked to see that it is working properly. I have found myself in the somewhat embarrassing and very frustrating situation of turning on the voice recorder but forgetting to turn on the attached microphone and losing a whole group. If any visual aids or extra materials (film clips, photos, newspaper/magazine articles, etc.) designed to prompt discussion are being used, then these need to be prepared and ready for use.

Before the focus group can begin, there are a number of formalities that need to be carried out by the moderator. The moderator should introduce him- or herself; and participants should be introduced to one another (especially if they are strangers). The moderator should say something about the nature of the research project, explaining what it is about, what institutions or organizations (if any) are involved in overseeing or funding the research, and what will happen to the data produced during the course of the group. For many participants, this will be their first time participating in a focus group (academic or market research). The moderator should explain how the focus groups work, that they are interested in hearing from all participants, and that it doesn't matter if not everyone agrees with one another. Some researchers like to set ground rules for etiquette during the focus group. For example, they ask participants not to talk over one another, as this can affect the clarity of the recording, and they ask participants to respect each other and their views. The distinctive ethics of focus groups—that information is not just disclosed to the researcher but also to fellow participants—has been mentioned previously in this chapter, and it may be appropriate for the moderator to explicitly talk to participants about this issue. In every case, before the focus group begins, the moderator needs to gain informed consent from participants regarding their participation in the project, being recorded, and their right to pull out of the research at any time. At this stage, participants may also be asked to fill out a short questionnaire recording their personal details or social characteristics.

Moderating the Focus Group

When talking about the importance of interaction in a focus group, it is not just interaction between the participants that should be considered but also the interaction between the moderator and the participants. The moderator is also actively involved in the production of the research context and the generation of data (Munday, 2006).

The role played by the moderator is crucial to the successful running of a focus group. It is the job of the moderator to choose which topics to cover, to direct the conversation, and to manage the dynamics of the group—ensuring that everyone has the chance to participate and that the conversation does not veer wildly off track. This does not mean that the moderator has to exert a rigid form of control over the group; however, often focus group orthodoxy suggests that this should be the case. Bryman (2001) suggests that a major disadvantage of the focus group method is the potential for the moderator to lose control of the group and the research process. Many instructional books on the focus group method claim that a moderator should retake control of a group that has gotten out of hand. These books also provide practical techniques for doing this (see, e.g., Krueger, 1998b). However, focus groups do not have to be run in such a controlling way: People are used to interacting with one another and will generally cooperate and work to ensure the group runs smoothly, even when the moderator is not actively exercising control (Kitzinger & Barbour, 1999). For example, in the WI focus group, which formed part of my research, without any intervention on my part, all the participants worked together to ensure that one of the women who suffers from very poor hearing was involved and able to join in. Similarly, at one point, when two members of the group became involved in a heated exchange on the subject of fox hunting, it was the other participants, not me, who stepped in to manage the conflict and defuse the situation. It has also been suggested that it is possible to exert too much control over a group and that important insights can be obtained when participants are given the opportunity to direct the conversation, explore the topic as they wish, and exert some control over the research process (Munday, 2006).

Thus, focus groups are a method that has the potential to be used in a nonhierarchical manner that empowers and gives participants some degree of control over the research process, and it is this potential that is particularly appealing to feminist researchers (Wilkinson, 1999). As Jowett and O'Toole (2006) have documented, the disruption of the usual power relationships in the research process has been a constant aim of much feminist research practice. Simel (1997) argued that the focus group is the most egalitarian research method available and therefore is particularly appropriate as a tool for feminist research.

Focus groups can provide an environment that promotes the coconstruction of meaning, whereby meaning is negotiated and produced by the participants rather than having meanings imposed on them by the researcher (Wilkinson, 1998). However, even when feminist researchers aim to moderate in a nondirective manner, the actions of the moderator are still important to the success of the focus group. It is the role of the moderator to facilitate the group, both in terms of providing at least some direction to the discussion and helping to manage group dynamics. In particular, the moderator may need to have a more active role during the initial stages of the group as the participants take time to get to know one another and get used to what may seem to them to be a rather unusual situation. Additionally, as mentioned in the section "Preparation for and Beginning the Focus Group," there are some formal procedures that the moderator must undertake—for example, introducing and explaining the research project to the participants at the start of the group and ensuring that all ethical and informed consent requirements are met.

As Pini (2002, 2005) notes, in reality, it is somewhat erroneous to present the role that a moderator can adopt as being a sharp contrast between active-controlling and passive-nondirective. The reality will usually fall somewhere between the two. Sometimes the moderator will need to exert a high degree of control; at other times, the moderator can stand back and let the participants direct the discussion. While Pini aimed to conduct her focus groups in as noncontrolling and empowering a manner as possible, at times she found herself having to adjust her role in response to the changing dynamics of the group. Sometimes she needed to give more direction, while at other times she had to be not overly concerned about the conversation going off topic. As previously mentioned, she also felt slightly uneasy about handing over control to her participants and had to make a concerted effort to do this. This would indicate a possible conflict between the high ideals and aims of feminist research and praxis and what happens when researchers are out in the field, confronted by the practical realities of conducting research. Ultimately, the researchers come to the research process with a specific set of aims and objectives and a desire to produce knowledge about a particular topic of their own choosing. My own experience of conducting focus groups has led me to believe that the role of researcher will always carry an element of power that can never be fully removed.

Behind the Scenes With Jennie Munday

In keeping with my own commitment to feminist research practice, I made the decision to moderate the focus groups in a relaxed and nonhierarchical manner. The power over the focus group process and direction of discussion was with the participants. I did however use the same topic guide for all the groups because, while I ideally wanted my participants to take the conversation in whatever direction they chose, I wanted data on similar topics from all the groups so that I could compare and contrast the data produced across cases.

Within the context of each focus group, I tried to give participants as much freedom as possible to develop discussions and pursue topics as they wished. It was interesting to note, however, that even though I consciously tried to adopt a position whereby I intervened as little as possible, on reflection during the analysis of the transcripts, I often felt there were times when I had exerted too much control and intervened too quickly when I thought the discussion was going too much off topic. However, at other times, it was clear that participants did have control over the direction of the discussion and were free to construct and negotiate the meanings of their collective identity as they wished.

My relationship with the participants outside of the research process also impacted power relations during the focus groups. As previously stated, I knew many of the participants involved in the research personally. For much of my life, they were the ones who had power and responsibility over me; but now there was a role reversal. I was coming to these particular social contexts in the role of researcher; and however much I tried to facilitate the groups in a nonhierarchical manner, there was no denying that the role of research brought with it an element of power. I was the one with the topic guide, the voice recorder, and the set of research aims and objectives. Indeed, the participants seemed to expect me to be in charge in this context, even if this reversal of power did take some negotiating during the initial

> stages of the group. This often necessitated a period of negotiation and readjustment, sometimes quite awkward, often humorous, as we settled into these new roles and power dynamics.
>
> This raises the question whether participants will always wish to be empowered and be able to direct the research process, even if this is the moderator's aim. The role of researcher carries a level of status among the public. With some of the focus groups I conducted, participants actually expect and want the researcher to take control—ideas which can be hard for the researcher to challenge and break down.

Feminist focus groups may have the potential to be run in a nonhierarchical and empowering way; however, researchers have at times found that the reality does not always live up to these promises. For example, while I was consciously aiming to relinquish power to the participants, power relations that existed between them were present during the focus groups. For example, in one focus group, there was an awkward moment when a male participant revealed how much his wife earned—when she herself had refused to provide this information and did not want it disclosed in this context.

O'Toole (Jowett & O'Toole, 2006) found in her research that meaning was not built out of genuine consensus, but that conformity was imposed by dominant members of the group. O'Toole reported that a number of participants found the setting of the focus group unnatural and intimidating and it constrained their ability to participate—thus suggesting that the focus group might not necessarily be the supportive, empowering, collaborative environment it is often perceived to be.

Pini (2002, 2005) was similarly concerned that some participants may have silenced others, in particular lesbian women, in the focus groups. She also worried that she unwittingly, by trying to give a certain amount of control over the research process to her participants, had colluded with this silencing. During the initial stages of the research, Pini trialed a survey and sought feedback from her respondents as to what options should be available to choose from for the category marital status. The initial options available were married, single, divorced/separated, widowed, and other; but the "other" category was met with ridicule and hilarity. Two particularly vocal members stated that no woman in the sugar industry would fit into this category, and the other participants expressed agreement. Although Pini had concerns, she removed the category "other."

When feminists actively promote the focus group as a safe, participatory environment and encourage women to be open with one another, it may promote overdisclosure. Participants may find themselves revealing more than they intended or feel comfortable with. Pini (2002, 2005) was an insider, and she conducted research within small communities where everybody knew everybody else. She felt that this created particular problems with regard to overdisclosure. She was worried that as an insider, the participants might trust her too much and therefore disclose too much. She was also worried about the manner in which things said in the focus group could also go on to impact the relationships the women had in the wider community—that, for example, any offense inadvertently given in the focus group might then spill out into real life.

This again seems to highlight possible contradictions between the ideals of feminist research and praxis and the reality of actual research. Some participants may feel empowered, others may feel marginalized and silenced, and the focus group may not live up to the potential it initially promised. There are important points that need to be taken seriously, but feminist researchers should not abandon the focus group method because of these difficulties. Researchers must be realistic about what an individual method can achieve and must develop ways that can bring ideals and reality closer together.

So far, the discussion of the impact of the moderator on focus group research has considered the potential effects of the researcher having insider status or knowing the participants and how the choices made by the moderator as to how to run the group may impact the research process. Even when the researcher is not an insider, the identity of the researcher impacts the research process. While not wanting to be so crude as to suggest that because a researcher possesses certain social characteristics—gender, sexuality, marital status, ethnicity, age, social class, and so forth—that predetermine his or her identity and ways of behaving, participants can react differently because of assumptions they make about the social researcher's characteristics. For example, would lesbian participants feel more comfortable discussing issues with an openly lesbian researcher? When the researcher and participants do not share ethnicity and nationality, problems may develop around not sharing the same language. Some researchers advocate that the researcher and participants should be matched for social characteristics as closely as possible—however, as has already been discussed, being an insider is not without its problems and can lead to overdisclosure and assumptions that things are understood, when really more exploration and clarification is needed.

For many feminist researchers, conducting focus groups in a feminist manner that seeks to empower participants and disrupt research hierarchies means participants must be included and offered control over every stage of the project. Montell's (1999) participants played an active part in shaping the research process. Ritchie and Barker (2005) involved their participants in every stage of the research process, including the generating of research questions, facilitating the focus group discussions, and analyzing the transcripts. Ritchie and Barker describe their research as being participant led; participants were seen as collaborators rather than the passive object of the research process. Similarly Wright, Corner, Hopkindon, and Foster (2006) have used focus groups as part of a participatory research strategy in their work with cancer patients.

However, as Rose (2001) states, although focus groups are often seen as participatory and empowering, power relationships in the research process will always exist to some degree. The projects mentioned above are exceptions to the rule for, as Rose points out, it is usually the researcher alone who analyzes, writes up, reports, and publicizes the data generated by the focus group. Additionally, as has already been discussed with regard to my use of participants to help in the recruitment process and Pini's attempt to involve participants in designing the questionnaire that recorded participant's social characteristics, it cannot be assumed that involving participants in every stage of the research process will be unproblematic and necessarily empowering to all those who participate in the research.

While promoting the aims of feminist praxis and empowering and involving women in all aspects of the research process, academics must apply and compete for funding and achieve results that can be published or delivered as conference papers. If feminist researchers want to succeed in an academic environment, there are potential conflicts that must be taken seriously. They must combine the aims of feminist practice and praxis with the formal requirements of academia under circumstances where a feminist perspective may be seen as marginal or not properly understood.

Analysis and Writing Up of Data

Any methods of textual analysis—discourse, conversation, or content analysis—can be used to analyze focus group data. However, there are two particular problems that arise when analyzing focus group data. First, it involves the analysis of multiple voices, and second, interaction as well as speech content must be analyzed. Analyzing interaction requires paying attention to a number of elements: for example, body language, gestures, tone of voice, emotions (especially when they are shared, such as shared laughter at a commonly understood joke), and patterns of interaction such as who leads discussions, who gets interrupted, and who appears to have power and influence among the participants to direct conversations and achieve consensus around their own views.

Duggleby (2005) has noted that the analysis part of focus group data is often overlooked in instructional textbooks. She provides practical advice on how to analyze focus group data, particularly concentrating on how interaction between participants can be recorded, integrated into transcripts, and analyzed. As emphasized throughout this chapter, participant interactions are particularly important to focus group data and should be analyzed if the full potential of the focus group method is to be realized, yet it is this aspect that presents unique challenges that are rarely explored or addressed. Although interaction is often nonverbal in nature, indications of interaction will be apparent within a transcript of an audio recording of the group; and field notes taken by the moderator or observer can supplement this. It is now becoming increasingly common to use video recording in conjunction with audio recording for focus groups.

As Bloor and Wood (2006) comment, the use of video technology allows for greater accuracy in the recording and analysis of nonverbal behavior. Video as well as audio data can now be imported into CAQDAS software analysis packages such as NVivo.

Pini (2002) is one of the few researchers to provide details of how she analyzed her focus groups for both process and content. She made full transcripts of the focus groups and coded them using the NUD*IST VIVO software package. She split her analysis into two distinct phases of coding—the first being a thematic analysis and the second recording the dynamics that took place within the focus group, using codes such as "ironic laughter," "fun laughter," and "sharing the same experience."

I similarly made full transcripts of each of the focus groups I conducted, and I analyzed them for both content and process in much the same way as Pini. Although I did not make notes during the actual focus groups, I made notes as soon as possible after each group and paid particular attention to recording nonverbal elements, which proved useful during the analysis.

Behind the Scenes With Jennie Munday

Although I tried to run the focus groups in a nonhierarchical manner, this was not designed to be a fully participatory research project. My participants had no role in the subsequent processes of transcription, data analysis, writing up, or dissemination of the research. For me, analysis and writing up was a very solitary process. I still felt connected and committed to and ethically responsible for my participants. I still had strong relationships with participants whom I already knew, but at no time did I talk to them about the decisions I was making during analysis and writing up.

I am aware that during the process of analysis and writing up, I had total control over the research process and my participants were not involved in any way. During analysis, I assign categories to my participants that they themselves might not necessarily agree with—for example a particular social class position or labeling them as an "incomer" (a derogatory term used by rural people for those who do not fully belong to and are not fully accepted into the local community). When writing up the research, I had to make decisions about what data to include and what to leave out. I did not shy away from being critical of the views expressed by any of the participants, even those whom I know and love. Although participants were given scope within the actual focus group to explore meanings and understandings in their own terms, when writing up and disseminating the results of the project, it is my interpretation that predominates and is given status as academic knowledge. On reflection, I would think more carefully about how to maintain the active involvement of my participants in these areas of the research process in the future.

As far as I am aware, none of my participants have read the publications that were based on their own focus groups and none have ever asked to see them. I do not know what they would think of the results. Would they agree or disagree with what I have written? Would they recognize themselves in the writing? What sense would they make of the academic language I had to use? My father has read the article that was based on just the WI focus group and, while clearly proud that my work had been published, he seemed somewhat bemused by the academic style and language. He said that it did not sound like my voice, and he found it hard to believe that I could actually write in that way—again exemplifying that researchers must comply with certain academic expectations, conventions, and requirements.

Had I engaged in a fully participatory research project, where the participants were involved in analysis and writing up as well as the conducting of the actual focus group, this would have turned into a considerably different project, and I would have found it a very different experience to conduct.

CONCLUSION

As with any method, focus groups are not an inherently feminist research method. Initially, because of their association with market research, feminist researchers understandably avoided using focus groups in their research. However, it became increasingly apparent that focus groups possess certain characteristics that are useful to feminist researchers, including the ability to investigate process as well as content and the potential to conduct focus groups in a nonhierarchical, empowering manner. If used in an appropriate manner, which exploits these advantages and breaks away from commonly held assumptions about their use in market research, focus groups can be an important and valuable tool for feminist research and praxis. Focus groups do not provide all the answers, and their use is not totally without problems. While many researchers, including myself, have found focus groups to be a useful tool, for others they have been problematic. Researchers have experienced tensions between the ideal and the reality that led them to be somewhat disappointed that focus groups did not live up to their expectations. Advances in technology will continue to change the way focus groups can be recorded and conducted. This will not only provide new opportunities but will also pose new questions regarding participation and inclusion that feminist researchers will have to address. Additionally, given the increasing pressures on academics to gain funding and produce publications, feminist researchers will have to engage more with questions of how succeeding in academia can be combined with the aims of feminist praxis and the role focus groups can play in helping to resolve this potential conflict. However, feminist researchers have been adaptable and imaginative in their use of the focus group method. It is this ability to innovate and experiment, combined with the flexibility and robustness of the focus group method, that will enable feminist researchers to address these new situations—and any potential problems—to demonstrate that the focus group is indeed a valuable and useful tool for advancing the aims of both feminist research and praxis.

DISCUSSION QUESTIONS

1. What characteristics make focus groups different from other types of qualitative interviewing techniques? How might these characteristics contribute to the potential that focus groups have to be a feminist research method?

2. What topics do you think it would be appropriate to investigate using the focus group method? Assess the claim that focus groups are particularly useful for investigating sensitive topics and vulnerable or marginalized groups.

3. If you were to conduct a focus group, how would you choose to act in the role of moderator? How might your own position within the research impact the research process and data that is generated?

4. What role does technology play in running focus groups? What are the potential advantages and disadvantages that advances in new communication technologies may bring to conducting focus groups?

5. Do you feel that the advantages focus groups offer outweigh any potential disadvantages of using this method?

WEB RESOURCES

Surrey University's CAQDAS Networking Project provides guidance and a very good overview of the software packages available for analyzing qualitative data, including practical advice on packages that can be used for analyzing transcripts and both audio and video recordings of focus groups.

www.caqdas.soc.surrey.ac.uk

Graham R. Walden's (2008) "Focus Groups: Arts and Humanities, Social Sciences, and the Nonmedical Sciences," Lanham, MD: Scarecrow Press, is an extensive annotated bibliography covering all the recent major literature on focus groups. Extracts can be accessed via googlebooks:

http://books.google.co.uk/books/about/Focus_Groups_Art_and_humanities_social_s.html?id=DqodeJjzVpAC&redir_esc=y

An e-book version, "Focus Groups: A Selective Annotated Bibliography," is also available online from a variety of websites.

REFERENCES

Bertini, P. (2011). *Focus groups: Meaning making and quality data.* Retrieved from http://www.hpl.hp.com/breweb/encoreproject/other_publications_material/ItAIS2011_DefAUGwebsite.doc%20-%20NeoOffice%20Writer.pdf

Blee, K., & Taylor, V. (2002). Semi-structured interviewing in social movement research. In B. Klandermans & S. Staggenborg (Eds.), *Methods of social movement research* (pp. 92–117). Minneapolis: University of Minnesota Press.

Bloor, M., Frankland, J., Thomas, M., & Robson, K. (2001). *Focus groups in social research.* London, England: Sage.

Bloor, M., & Wood, F. (2006). *Key words in qualitative methods.* London, England: Sage.

Bryman, A. (2001). *Social research methods.* Oxford, England: Oxford University Press.

Castells, M. (1997). *The power of identity.* Cambridge, MA: Blackwell.

Catterall, M., Maclaran, P., & Stevens, L. (1999). Broadening the focus: Intervention and emancipatory possibilities in group research. In B. Dubois, T. M. Lowrey, L. J. Shrum, & M. Vanhuele (Eds.), *European advances in consumer research* (Vol. 4, pp. 347–352). Provo, UT: Association for Consumer Research.

Culley, L., Hudson, N., & Rapport, F. L. (n.d.). *Recruitment and reciprocity: Focus group method in health research with minority ethnic communities.* Retrieved from http://extra.shu.ac.uk/ethnichealth inequalities/seminar5/culleyextratext.pdf

Cunningham-Burley, S., Kerr, A., & Pavis, S. (1999). Theorizing subjects and subject matter in focus group research. In R. Barbour & J. Kitzinger (Eds.), *Developing focus group research: Politics, theory and practice* (pp.186–199). London, England: Sage.

Denmark, F., & Pauldi, M. (2008). *Psychology of women: A handbook of issues and theories.* Westport, CT: Praeger.

Duggleby, W. (2005). What about focus group interaction data? *Qualitative Health Research, 15,* 832–840.

Fielding, N. (1993). Qualitative interviewing. In N. Gilbert (Ed.), *Researching social life* (pp. 135–153). London, England: Sage.

Fox, F. E., Morris, M., & Rumsey, N. (2007). Doing synchronous online focus groups with young people: Methodological reflections. *Qualitative Health Research, 17,* 539–547.

Gaiser, T. J. (1997). Conducting on-line focus groups: A methodological discussion. *Social Science Computer Review, 15,* 135–144.

Gofton, L. (n.d.). *Review of the book advanced focus group research (2001), by E. F. Fern.* London, England: Sage. Retrieved from http://www.socresonline.org.uk/9/1/fern.html

Johnson, A. (1996). "It's good to talk": The focus group and the sociological imagination. *The Sociological Review, 44,* 517–538.

Jowett, M., & O'Toole, G. (2006). Focusing researchers' minds: Contrasting experiences of using focus groups in feminist qualitative research. *Qualitative Research, 6,* 453–472.

Kimmel, E., & Crawford, M. (1999). Promoting methodological diversity in feminist research. *Psychology of Women Quarterly, 23,* 1–6.

Kitzinger, J. (1994). The methodology of focus groups: The importance of interaction between research participants. *Sociology of Health and Illness, 16,* 103–121.

Kitzinger, J., & Barbour, R. (1999). Introduction: The challenge and promise of focus groups. In R. Barbour & J. Kitzinger (Eds.), *Developing focus group research: Politics, theory and practice* (pp. 1–20). London, England: Sage.

Krueger, R. (1998a). *Analyzing and reporting focus group results.* London, England: Sage.

Krueger, R. (1998b). *Developing questions for focus groups.* London, England: Sage.

Krueger, R., & Casey, M. A. (2000). *Focus groups: A practical guide for applied research* (3rd ed.). London, England: Sage.

Liamputtong, P. (2011). *Focus group methodology: Principle and practice.* London, England: Sage.

Madriz, E. (2000). Focus groups in feminist research. In N. Denzin & Y. Lincoln (Eds.), *The handbook of qualitative research* (2nd ed., pp. 835–850). Thousand Oaks, CA: Sage.

Melucci, A. (1989). *Nomads of the present: Social movements and individual needs in contemporary society.* London, England: Hutchinson Radius.

Melucci, A. (1996). *Challenging codes: Collective action in the information age.* Cambridge, England: Cambridge University Press.

Montell, F. (1999). Focus group interviews: A new feminist method. *NWSA Journal, 11(1),* 44–71.

Morgan, D. (1993). *Successful focus groups: Advancing the state of the art.* Newbury Park, CA: Sage.

Morgan, D. (1998). *The focus group guidebook.* Thousand Oaks, CA: Sage.

Munday, J. (2006). Identity in focus: The use of focus groups to study the construction of collective identity. *Sociology, 40,* 89–105.

Munday, J. (2008). *Identifications and oppositions: Rural identities and the political mobilisation of The Countryside Alliance* (Unpublished doctoral dissertation). Goldsmiths, University of London, England.

Owen, S. (2001). The practical, methodological and ethical dilemmas of conducting focus groups with vulnerable clients. *Journal of Advanced Nursing, 36,* 652–658.

Pini, B. (2002). Focus groups, feminist research and farm women: Opportunities for empowerment in rural social research. *Journal of Rural Studies, 18,* 339–351.

Pini, B. (2005). Farm women: Driving tractors and negotiating gender. *International Journal of Sociology of Agriculture and Food, 13(1),* 1–18.

Pini, B., & Previte, J. (2004, November). *Videoconferenced focus groups: Feminist methodological reflections.* Paper presented at QualIT2004: International Conference on Qualitative Research in IT & IT Qualitative Research, Brisbane, Australia.

Ritchie, A., & Barker, M. (2005). Explorations in feminist participant-led research: Conducting focus group discussions with polyamorous women. *Psychology of Women Section Review, 7*(2), 47–57.

Rose, D. (2001). *Revisiting feminist research methodologies* (Working Paper). Retrieved from http://www.publications.gc.ca/collections/Collection/SW21-142-2001E.pdf

Schneider, S. J., Kerwin, J., Frechtling, J., & Vivari, B. A. (2002). Characteristics of the discussion in online and face-to-face focus groups. *Social Science Computer Review, 20,* 31–42.

Simel, E. (1997). Can feminist methodology reduce power hierarchies in research settings? *Feminist Economics, 3*(2), 137–139. Retrieved from http://ilo.academia.edu/SimelEsim/Papers/885454/Can_Feminist_Methodology_Reduce_Power_Hierarchies_in_Research_Settings

Skeggs, B., & Woods, H. (n.d.). *Making class and self through televised ethical scenarios.* Retrieved from http://www.open.ac.uk/socialsciences/identities/findings/Skeggs.pdf

Stanley, L. (1990). *Feminist praxis: Research, theory and epistemology in feminist sociology.* London, England: Taylor & Francis.

Sunderland, P., & Denny, R. (2007). *Doing anthropology in consumer research.* Walnut Creek, CA: Left Coast Press.

Tonkiss, F. (2004). Using focus groups. In C. Seale (Ed.), *Researching society and culture* (pp. 193–206). London, England: Sage.

Touraine, A. (1981). *The voice and the eye: An analysis of social movements.* Cambridge, England: Cambridge University Press.

Underhill, C., & Olmsted, M. G. (2003). An experimental comparison of computer-mediated and face-to-face focus groups. *Social Science Computer Review, 21,* 506–512.

Wilkinson, S. (1998). Focus groups in feminist research: Power, interaction and the co-construction of meaning. *Women's Studies International Forum, 21,* 111–125.

Wilkinson, S. (1999). How useful are focus groups in feminist research? In R. Barbour & J. Kitzinger (Eds.), *Developing focus group research: Politics, theory and practice* (pp. 64–78). London, England: Sage.

Wright, D., Corner, J., Hopkindon, J., & Foster, C. (2006). Listening to the views of people affected by cancer about cancer research: An example of participatory research in setting the cancer research agenda. *Health Expectations, 9,* 3–12. Retrieved from http://onlinelibrary.wiley.com/doi/10.1111/j.1369-7625.2006.00353.x/full

CHAPTER 9

Feminist Media Research

Heather McIntosh and Lisa Cuklanz

It's Monday night, and you come home after a long day of classes and work and turn on the TV. On this night, CBS broadcasts several popular situation comedies, including at one time or another *Two and a Half Men*, *The Big Bang Theory*, and *Two Broke Girls*. This term, you are taking a course in feminist research approaches; and in learning the techniques and philosophical underpinnings of them, you have been looking at media with a more critical eye. In particular, you notice how women often are represented as sex objects or shopping addicts, and female characters are frequently co-dependent on males. Women of color are virtually absent, particularly as central characters. When they do appear, they adhere even more closely to exaggerated stereotypes. In *Two and a Half Men*, you notice how many of the women are just objects for the main character to chase, sleep with, and discard as he pleases. In both *The Big Bang Theory* and *Two Broke Girls*, the lack of money and the compulsion to buy frequently appear in the female characters' story lines.

At first, you thought these representations were just part of the story, meant to draw laughs from the audience and keep everyone entertained. You know that not *all* women are desperate for male attention or spend themselves broke over the latest shoe style, but you begin to notice how these shows rarely, if ever, waver from these stereotypes. Instead, the shows just adapt the stereotypes in new ways while reinforcing the same ideas over and over. Even one of the supposedly intelligent women on *The Big Bang Theory* downplays her intelligence in order to preserve her fiancee's masculinity. You see these patterns emerge in these programs and even in other shows you enjoy. But what research methods can you use to explore these themes for a sustained study? Many of the methods you have learned about so far, such as interviews and participant observation, involve getting data from *people* about various phenomena. How would you go about gathering systematic data from television shows or other media? And how might these representations be connected to the feminist ideas you are learning in your class?

Questions focused on the construction of gender and the uses of gender within texts, such as those observed above on these CBS shows, can be examined through the use of feminist media research. In this chapter, we will outline some key feminist theories that have proven useful in the examination of media; highlight central questions that these theories help to answer; and walk you through the application of feminist media research on several important types of media including print news, television, film, and the Internet. Feminist media research raises and provides answers to questions about patterns of gender within mediated texts. The patterns can be simple or complex, concrete or more abstract; but whatever their form, feminist media research provides a method of delimiting, analyzing, and explaining the power and significance of these patterns.

Feminist Media Theory

All research methods emerge and develop alongside theories that define and shape various disciplines. Feminist media research shares a strong relationship with cultural studies, which takes as its project the study of culture and its meanings, uncovering the political, social, and even economic implications of those meanings. For our purposes here, the term "feminism" refers to the wide range of ideas that inform feminist thought (Tong, 2008). Feminism and cultural studies share several features in that they both are "interdisciplinary, collaborative, self-reflexive, and politically engaged" (Stabile, 2011, p. 23). *Interdisciplinary* means that they work across different disciplines, such as sociology and communication. *Collaborative* means that researchers work together to engage and develop these ideas. *Self-reflexive* means that researchers maintain an awareness of their own influences in the research process, as described in the section below. Last, *politically engaged* means that researchers undertake research for motivations other than just personal ones, sometimes seeking to raise awareness about particular issues or even to bring about policy changes.

Feminist media analysis begins with discourses. According to Stuart Hall (1997), "Discourses are ways of referring to or constructing knowledge about a particular topic of practice: a cluster (or formation) of ideas, images and practices, which provide ways of talking about, forms of knowledge and conduct associated with, a particular topic, social activity, or institutional site in society" (p. 6). A discourse functions as a system of meanings created by a combination of texts and the social practices that inform them. By treating these systems as discourses, researchers are able to examine and question images and meanings that might otherwise go unexamined, and thus better to understand how power operates through ideas and representations. As Foucault (1972) writes, in explaining his concepts of the discursive archive, it is in discovering the patterns of what can and cannot be said that reveal to us the circulation of power within and through texts:

> The archive is first the law of what can be said, the system that governs the appearance of statements as unique events. . . . [T]he archive is also that which determines that all these things said do not accumulate endlessly in an amorphous mass . . . but they are grouped together with multiple relations, maintained or blurred in accordance with specific regularities. (p. 129)

The patterns of what can and cannot be said, or what is and is not said, form evidence of where power is located and how it is deployed. These patterns can be understood as derived from ideologies.

On the surface, some types of knowledge and meaning might appear "normal" or "natural" in their construction and thus go without question. For example, television commercials depicting women using household appliances such as vacuum cleaners, ovens, and washing machines appear frequently, and audiences might automatically associate women with those appliances and the domestic chores facilitated by them. This connection among women, appliances, and domestic chores thus appears "normal" or "natural." Real-life women and media-represented women who fail to use and even enjoy these appliances thus fail to be "normal" or "natural." In this way, mass media are understood to help construct and maintain cultural ideas. These ideas can be referred to as cultural norms, dominant ideologies, or mainstream concepts. The ability to define, convey, and uphold what is normal allows the inclusion of some ideas and the exclusion of other ideas. Through careful critical examination of these discourses, "[W]e can enquire into the structural conditions which make certain discourses possible and rule out others" (Milestone & Meyer, 2012, p. 23). This inquiry might push us to ask: Why do commercials show primarily women using household appliances and in some cases enjoying them? How do these associations in advertising discourses influence our dominant ideologies of the understanding of femininity? Of the norms of gendered behavior? Feminist media research carefully examines these conceptions and the ideologies to which they belong, as they relate specifically to gender and its intersection with other elements of subjectivity such as race, ethnicity, class, and sexuality.

What Is Feminist Media Research?

Feminist media research draws on the insights of feminist theories about media, and these theories differ according to what form of mediated text is under examination. Although there are important differences, all feminist media theories share the basic underlying tenet that mainstream mass media function through the dissemination, repetition, and support of central ideas that are accepted by the culture in which the medium under examination is produced. Thus, ideas about gender in mainstream mass mediated texts can tell us something about the dominant ideologies of their culture of origin. At the same time, the content of mainstream texts can also change over time, indicating important shifts in dominant ideas. Feminist media research is interested in examining and deconstructing the ideas about gender expressed in mainstream mediated texts, as well as in the process of change exhibited in these texts as cultural ideas about gender also shift. Feminist media research enacts a commitment to social justice, and is committed to contributing to our understanding of the operations of power within mediated texts. It seeks and brings to the foreground the expression of muted voices and critiques the patterned discourses that support and reflect dominant ideologies of gender.

Feminist research on mass media, whether film, television, or other forms, is usually focused on texts with an obvious dimension of gender. However, while not every text or group of texts can make a good subject for feminist media research, there is really a very broad range of possibilities. Some texts feature female and male characters in interaction with each other; others such as extreme action films, may have very few female characters, but may thus be very focused on constructions of masculinity as a concept. Any text or group of texts that has something to say about gendered characterizations of people, gender and relations of power, constructions of gender, or the intersections of gender sexuality, race, or class, can be the focus of feminist media research.

Feminist media research has several key goals. In addition to assessing the relations and expression of power within texts, this research aims to place central focus on the lives of women and members of other groups who have not traditionally held cultural and political power. Feminist media research provides critiques of media representations that support traditional power structures. It can also examine the ways in which mass media accept and convey subtle forms of ideological change over time. Thus, much feminist media research takes part in the project of instigating positive social change. Its ethical project is to discover and reveal the operation of power through ideology with texts, and to provide analysis that can in turn be used to inform the creation of new messages and meanings that challenge or break out of the traditional molds and advocate for the promotion of gender equality.

Assessing Texts and Relations of Power

Feminist media research offers a rich and flexible way in which to examine the complexities and reveal the implications of power relationships as they are represented in a range of multimediated environments, including print and electronic mediated texts and images. These multimedia communications contain overt and implied assertions of power as constructed within mediated texts. These power relationships emerge in representations of many themes, including

- Identity categories, such as gender, race/ethnicity, class, and sexuality
- Stereotyping, or the normalized representation of identity categories
- Voice, or the allowing or prohibiting of groups to speak for themselves
- Spectacle, or the privileging of the visual over other contexts
- Agency, or the ability to act on one's own behalf
- Symbolic annihilation, or the systematic silencing of various groups

Not all media texts and images exhibit all of these elements simultaneously, though many texts show intersections of several of them, such as stereotyping, gender, and sexuality. Further, not all texts demonstrate these power relationships in clear, neatly defined ways. In fact, the process of examining and deconstructing relations of power embedded within texts is a discursive one that requires consideration of multiple readings of nuanced relationships in texts that can at different points reflect, reassert, and even sometimes challenge power structures at work. Feminist media research can also be interested in identifying and understanding subjugated knowledges that are not readily available in mainstream mass media.

Cultural texts originate from motivations of information, entertainment, and advocacy. They include media texts such as newspapers, television shows, films, and even websites. They also include cultural products not only those created by media industries but also everyday objects that gain cultural significance through their uses, such as Barbie dolls, Nike shoes, Monopoly board games, and iPhones. While it might seem that *every* text is suitable for analysis, the process of selecting texts for inquiry is just as important as the process of their analysis.

Texts serve as important objects of inquiry. We live in a society overwhelmed with mediated messages, yet within their everyday uses they often go unnoticed. Because these texts are constructed within a particular set of cultural, social, economic, and political contexts, and they inform the values audiences receive about themselves, others, and the world around them, their analysis can reveal much about the social context in which they are produced and received. Feminist media analysis offers a way to access these ideas and experiences that would remain unavailable through other methods (Phillipov, 2012). A feminist approach to understanding multimedia communications involves an analysis or methodical exploration of a text or group of texts with the goal of revealing the power structures, their relationships, and the contradictions that inform them. Media analysis is a method that can be practiced by anyone without special resources because its objects of analysis include everyday messages available in our cultural environment. A researcher need only turn on the television to watch a show, do a search on YouTube, or even look around her dorm room for a possible object of research.

HOW DOES FEMINIST MEDIA ANALYSIS WORK IN DIFFERENT MEDIA?

Media analysis is a flexible form that offers the opportunity to uncover numerous insights in a variety of texts. With an emphasis on more recent scholarship, media addressed below include print, film, television, advertising, and new and convergence media.

We must note two important considerations here. First, while the following sections focus on a specific medium, the theories raised and the ideas discussed therein need not remain limited to that medium. Like the method itself, the concepts are flexible and apply to multiple texts. The concepts related to textual analyses of film studies also might work for television or for new media studies. The point here is to provide an overview of the method and to illustrate its current applications as a starting place for developing your own analyses.

Second, while this chapter addresses feminist media analysis primarily through the lens of textual analysis, analysis of media encompasses much more than texts. For example, analysis of media might consider different aspects of the industry, such as women's roles during innovation periods, gendering of different divisions of labor, and absences of women from key roles, such as directing and producing (Meehan & Riordan, 2002). Media industry also operates within particular modes of production, distribution, and exhibition; and media analysis might explore how the industry practices reduce the range of voices, rely on stereotypes, limit access to information, and overall turn everything into a commodity (Turow, 2011).

Media analysis also considers the idea of gender and audiences. Part of this analysis involves theorizing the ideas of spectatorship. Doane (1987) theorizes that the idea of spectatorship should expand to include a broader range of interpretations and possibilities. Another consideration of spectatorship includes the consideration of women's pleasures derived from engaging popular culture materials. Modleski (1982) analyzed soap operas and Harlequin novels for these ideas. Radway (1984) goes further and conducts extensive interviews with romance book club members to find that the women use the books to learn more about other places and time periods and to set examples of reading as pleasurable for their children.

Print News

The analysis of print media, especially news, is particularly common and fruitful because mainstream print media purport to be objective and, thus, the operation of power within print news is both unacknowledged and subconscious. While print media do adhere to a certain definition of objectivity and unquestionable professionalism, it is also an accepted truth for many scholars that one of the primary functions of print media is to support and purvey dominant ideologies to readers. In effect, mainstream news, while providing facts about specific events, selects and presents those facts within identifiably patterned modes. These patterns are derived from ideologies, such that mainstream news effectively tells its readers what to think about and, to some extent, what to think. Feminist research on print news focuses on gendered mediation, a general concept that refers to the ways in which news coverage presents people of different genders differently, or presents gendered material or concepts where none is needed. Gendered mediation provides a critical perspective on news media in its analysis of the gendered frameworks of meaning that often underlie reporting, particularly on political candidates and high-profile cases of gendered violence. Previous research has found that a very small percentage of quoted experts are female, that few stories about women appear on the front pages of newspapers, and that coverage of female political candidates focuses more on appearance and domestic interests than does coverage of male candidates. Coverage of gendered violence often questions the word of female victims while supporting males accused of crimes, particularly when the accused is a celebrity.

Analysis of print news is normally undertaken using the LexisNexis database, which includes major papers from the United States and Europe as well as transcripts of major news broadcasts. For students and faculty members, access to this database is normally free of charge, as long as the home institution subscribes. The database is searchable by keyword or subject, and can be further delimited by specific source title and/or date or publication. For news analysis, it is common to consider a large number of news stories on a specific topic, printed by different sources within a fixed time frame, as one single text.

The purpose of most analysis of print media, thus, is the elucidation and elaboration of how dominant ideologies are supported through patterns of repetition and omission. When undertaking print analysis, it is important to delimit a "text" that is appropriate for both the time frame available for the analysis (for example, from 20 to 40 stories could be plenty for a term paper assignment) as well as for the topic at hand. In cases in which thousands of stories were printed (such as the O. J. Simpson case), researchers normally limit their analysis to articles from major papers or, occasionally, to *The New York Times* only, since this paper is considered the most neutral and highest quality mainstream news publication, as well as the most widely read, within the United States. Because of the ease of searching within LexisNexis, dates and sources can be easily designated in ways that produce a manageable yet representative aggregated text for analysis. Transcripts of many news broadcasts can be obtained through LexisNexis, and videotapes of broadcast and cable news can be obtained, for a high price, from the Vanderbilt Television News Archive.

The most common approach to the analysis of print news is known as frame analysis. This method, which involves the identification of the central themes or "takes" on a particular topic can be found in the news, was adapted from Erving Goffman's (1974) work. Cuklanz (1996) examined news coverage of the Anita Hill/Clarence Thomas hearings, finding a very clear example of how news coverage supports not only dominant ideologies, but also the status quo of government power. The analysis shows how, before the hearings began, most central frames for the news story involved the idea that the primary reason to hold the hearings was for Anita Hill to tell her side of the story. Some articles directly stated, and may others implied, that the Senate Judiciary Committee would make a decision on the Thomas nomination based on the information that Anita Hill would present. However, at the end of the hearings, news frames shifted. At that point, instead of evaluating what Hill had said and how it would or could relate to the Senate's confirmation vote on Thomas, articles focused on the idea that Hill was not able to prove her allegations. Hill's voice and perspective were used to legitimate the hearings, but her words became irrelevant to the final decision about the Thomas confirmation. Both the identification of frames of meaning, and the establishment, through example, of the uniformity of various news sources within these frames, make up the basis of frame analysis.

Feminist research on print news has fruitfully examined coverage of specific cases of gendered violence (see Benedict, 1993) and issues related to gender in coverage of political candidates (see Falk, 2007). While analysts from the early 1990s starting with Faludi (1991) have examined mainstream news coverage of the so-called "mommy track," Vavrus (2007) uncovers a similar but more contemporary phenomenon in news coverage of "opting out moms," who allegedly turn solely to raising children after obtaining an education at high-priced, elite institutions. Vavrus examines the claims of news articles on this media-created phenomenon and shows how data and language are skewed in favor of an ideological message about the value of women's participation in the paid labor force and, particularly, around the concept of "choice" as explored in the articles she examines.

Internet

The digital environment refers primarily to the Internet, though more specifically most scholars consider the Web 2.0 environment when discussing not only convergence, but also social media and other Internet-based activities. Web 2.0 refers to the major shift in the Internet around 2004 to 2005 wherein new technologies and software enabled audiences to access, create, share, and otherwise interact with websites and with other people using those sites (Lister, Dovey, Giddings, Grant, & Kelly, 2009). This environment enables different types of participation, such as adding comments, offering ratings or rankings, sharing content, reposting content, and uploading content. In these cases, texts no longer possess easily delineated boundaries, as they seem to do with other media. A film's opening and closing credits might signal the start and end of a film, but a website possesses no singular, linear unspooling of credits and other materials that recurs each time. Instead, the user experience with a website might change for each and every person visiting that site. While one user might end up on the home page, another user might end up on an archived page. While one user might read a whole page from start to finish, another user might only watch the video embedded on that page, and still another might search for one word and, not finding it, click a link to go to another page or another site altogether.

The Internet has enabled the creation and dissemination of an enormous range of communications and, in doing so, has created new areas for feminist media analysis. A key difference between online spaces and traditional media is that more and more online spaces are created, developed, and maintained by women for purposes of expression, exploration, and connection, such as through blogging. These spaces often address women's issues in ways that other media overlook. Further, many of these sites enable participation, often bringing together women from around the world to collaborate on certain issues and missions, such as support and activism (Shade, 2002). Earlier examples of participative technologies include discussion boards and mailing lists, but more recent examples include Facebook, MySpace, Twitter, Tumblr, and Pinterest. For example, Haas (2009) engages in rhetorical analysis of infertility support communities, uncovering how men still hold positions of power within these communities even though the sharing of knowledge and experiences empowers some women. Other studies incorporate websites alongside traditional media to create a broader picture. Joseph (2009) considers the responses to Tyra Banks's weight gain and the media furor surrounding it, using Banks's website in particular.

Several studies explore the roles of eating disorder websites. One subject in particular that draws scholars is pro-eating-disorder websites, which represent anorexia and bulimia as "lifestyle choices" instead of medical conditions. Day and Keys (2008) use discourse analysis of these sites to uncover the ideas that inform this position, such as beauty ideals and eating behaviors. They gathered their materials by conducting multiple Internet searches to identify key sites and then downloading them. Further, they chose "to use public webpages and chat exchanges in publicly accessible forums only, avoiding 'lock and key' sites where greater privacy is assumed" (Day & Keys, 2008, p. 6). In other words, they opted to lurk on sites with publicly available information instead of trying to gain access to more restricted information. Day and Keys (2008) noted the different structures of the various sites, but they saw similar content appearing across the 13 sites they chose. These sites offered "tips" for obscuring an eating disorder, "rules" for following an eating disorder, a journal for sharing personal experiences, and a discussion board for interacting with others.

Day and Keys faced an interesting choice in that the websites included not only texts but also "images of emaciated women" (Day & Keys, 2008, p. 6). Instead of focusing on the images, they "decided to focus on the written text as this appeared to be the richest source of multiple discourses around food and its consumption (or non-consumption)" (Day & Keys, 2008, p. 6). After reading the sites carefully and in depth in order to gain familiarity with them, they then engaged in their analysis. They found two discursive patterns appearing across these sites. One centered on how starvation assisted in maintaining the thin ideal, and the other centered on the eating disorder as a form of rebellion against authorities and a means of control over themselves (Day & Keys, 2008, p. 7). They demonstrate how the sites and those using the sites occupy a conflicted subject position of both conformist to the beauty ideals and of resistance to other forms of authority.

Some feminist inquiries into social networking sites such as Facebook and MySpace explore questions of gendered self-representations. On these sites people can post pictures and information about themselves, such as their location, hobbies, political leanings, relationship status, occupation, and media interests. Through this profile, they can construct a self as they wish through what they post. In "A Critical Examination of Gender Representation on Facebook Profiles," Erin Bryant explores how college students in particular construct their online selves through these pages using the lenses of gender and self-stereotyping. Using Facebook's browse function, Bryant sampled 40 public profiles—20 from females and 20 from males—for her analysis. Specifically, "Textual analysis was used to provide more in-depth understanding of how members used their profiles to present a gender identity" (Bryant, 2008, p. 14). With a few exceptions, Bryant found that the dominant gender discourses continue on the site, even though users are somewhat free to challenge these discourses should they choose to do so.

Material Culture

Material culture offers a nonmediated way to undertake textual analysis, but these materials still emerge from and carry with them various social, political, and cultural contexts. Material culture, particularly works created by women, largely has been overlooked in favor of men's cultural production. This passing over in part comes from the connections of women's material culture with domestic duties. According to Kearney (2006), "Largely utilitarian in nature, the domestic arts of girls and women have long been disparaged as 'handicrafts,' products of manual household chores that allegedly do not require much intellect, reflection, or creativity to produce" (p. 25). By connecting women's material culture with the labor of women's traditional gender roles, the items under consideration become less valued in that a painting or a sculpture takes study and practice while a quilt or a candle is supposedly just an extension of what women already know.

Feminist analytical research on media offers the opportunity to reclaim the value of women's material culture. Foss and Foss (1991) offer a framework that suggests considering the "exigence of the text," the "audience of the text," the "nature of the communicator," the "nature of the text," the "functions of the text," and the "nature of the world created" (pp. 26–27). From there, they ask us to consider a wide variety of possible texts, including baking, graffiti, needlework, and quilting. Note how the texts become not just the object for analysis, but also the entry point into the contexts and rituals surrounding it.

Material culture also considers how items are used and understood in particular ways. Rand (2012) takes the color of ice skates as one of her key points in *Red Nails, Black Skates: Gender, Cash, and Pleasure on and off the Ice*. Rand took up ice skating in her 40s, and her book explores the gender implications of the sport and offers her own reflections on her participation within it. The color of the ice skates becomes a gendered issue. In general, men wear black skates, while women wear white skates (Rand, 2012). This association began in the 1930s, when white skates were introduced to match better with women's skating costumes and to improve the appearance of women's legs. Now, this gendered association of skate color is considered so normative that "rejecting them may be interpreted as a rejection of femininity" (Rand, 2012, pp. 74–75). Rand weaves interview data with her own observations about the gendering of these skate colors, noting her own desire to get black skates. She writes, "For the first five years I skated as an adult I really wanted black skates. It had nothing to do with gender bending, but with the kind of female I saw myself to be" (Rand, 2012, p. 89). For Rand, then, a physical feature of a material object, in this case the skate color, becomes a question for inquiry into gender systems both as constructed by social means and as negotiated by herself. In this case, the media analysis aids in bringing these multiple discourses together, thus reinforcing the importance of contexts in studying material culture. Feminist media research can include projects that analyze nontraditional forms of media such as clothing, toys, and furniture in relation to the discourses and meanings they generate with respect to gender.

Film

Originating with the work of Laura Mulvey (1975), feminist film theory brings together some of the concepts of psychoanalytic theory and ideas about the ways in which watching a film establishes the act of looking as a gendered (masculine) activity while the process of being looked at is gendered feminine. Entering a theater and watching a film resembles a dreamlike experience in which subconscious desires and needs are projected into the conscious realm. Films are understood as having the ability to capture and express elements of the cultural subconscious in much the same way that dreams reveal elements of the individual subconscious mind. For feminist film theorists, these ideas focus on the concepts of voyeurism and sexual fetish, two forms of sexual objectification of women through the male gaze. Relations of power between characters are often understood as metaphors for, or directly linked to, sexual relationships or fantasies of characters. Some elements of some films are understood in part as projections of sexual fantasies onto the big screen. Since feminist film theory focuses on these elements, feminist research on mainstream films often examines patterns of objectification of women, identification of viewers with male characters and points of view, and relationships that have developed in mainstream film between heterosexual male sexual expression and violence against women.

Feminist film researchers ask questions such as the following:

How are women's bodies examined or observed both by male characters and by members of the viewing audience?

What is the relationship between sexual objectification/sex and violence?

How are relations of power between characters related to sex and patterns of observation?

How do characters express and satisfy their desires?

How do powerful female characters present representational challenges in film?

What is the relationship between physical and sexual power?

For example, Chen (2012) offers an examination of the tensions between the restrictions created by the patriarchal order and the possibilities for women's agency within that order through the practice of martial arts and film.

Hilary Neroni's (2005) work on violent women in film provides an excellent extended analysis of several key themes in psychoanalytic feminist film research, including the relationship between masculinity and violence in film, the oppositional construction of femininity and masculinity, and the metaphorical and literal linkages between romance and aggressive and violent action. Neroni introduces the notion that femininity and masculinity are usually presented or understood implicitly in film as separate and distinct parts of a whole, with masculinity associated with action and femininity associated with passivity and objectification. Neroni argues that when female characters are violent and aggressive, the usual meanings in mainstream film are disrupted so much that there can be no successful resolution in their narratives. Violent female characters are either killed off by the end of the film, or returned back to the domestic realm of femininity and protection by male characters.

Television

The questions that feminist film theories point to in relation to mainstream films for a time also were applied to television texts, but with very limited success. The viewing situation for audiences of films is much different from that of television, and the extended, uninterrupted time frames of mainstream films have proven more amenable to psychoanalytic theories. Feminist research on television has focused more on stereotyping of characters and patterns of behavior and interaction in various genres of television programming. Because it is somewhat more concrete than feminist film theory, feminist television theory has been more likely to examine ancillary questions related to elements of identity such as race and especially class. The situation comedy is perhaps the genre on which the most feminist research has been done. As in other fields, comedy on television has often been the place where new roles and forms can be tried first. Thus, situation comedies have tended at times to be places for experimentation with new character types and new settings. Feminist research on television has also focused on other genres including cop/detective programs, makeover programs, soap operas, and talk shows. Feminist researchers in television studies tend to ask questions about patterns of representation that are related to gender including the following:

How are stereotypes utilized or avoided?

What is the function of stereotypes that are employed?

What is the ratio of male-to-female characters?

What are the basic roles for male versus female characters?

What are the patterns of interaction between characters around elements such as power, respect, attraction, and support?

What concepts of femininity and masculinity are projected? How?

What forms of sexuality and sexual relationships are found?

What are the limits of behavior of characters of different gender and sexuality?

Feminist television researchers generally understand the patterns they discover in tele-visual texts to be related to the dominant ideologies of the culture in which a particular program was produced. For example, Dow's 1990 work examining *The Mary Tyler Moore* show argues that the characters of Mary Richards and her colleagues mirror family roles in patriarchal society, with (for instances) Lou Grant as the benevolent patriarch and Mary as the dutiful daughter. Dow shows how Mary's role is limited in its power and scope to that of the daughter and/or wife to other characters. Feminist work has also examined roles in which women characters are often portrayed, including that of house-wife, sexual object, victim of violence, and love interest. And, since much feminist research has been done on fictional television programs, there is also a set of key themes related to gender that have proven historically significant. These include questions related to female friendship and support, which has usually been absent from television fictions; issues related to work–life balance (television programs have traditionally made it almost impossible for a character to have a satisfying family life and work life outside the home); and the portrayal of "mismatched" husbands and wives (with the wives being more attractive and intelligent but still subordinate to their husbands). Cuklanz and Moorti's 2006 work on *Law and Order: Special Victims Unit* provides a more recent example of feminist research on another television genre, the police drama. The following behind-the-scenes narrative describes the process through which the ideas in their article were initiated and developed.

Behind the Scenes With Lisa Cuklanz

Textual Analysis of *Law and Order: Special Victim's Unit*

I have been working for many years on textual analyses of the prime-time police drama *Law and Order: SVU*.[1] There are many ways to approach the relationship between the text you want to analyze and any theoretical concepts you want to bring to bear on the analysis. I always prefer to do a full reading of the text first, independent of the immediate constraints of having a specific set of concepts in mind. I look for patterns of repetition and omission, relations of gender, anything that stands out as a contrast to what I have seen or read about in other similar texts, or anything that is particularly appealing about a text. In this case, Sujata Moorti and I chose to analyze this series because it was the first prime-time

(Continued)

(Continued)

series in the United States that purported to focus specifically on "special victims," defined in much of the press surrounding the program as victims of sexual assault. Both of us had previously published books on representations of sexual assault in the mainstream media. We started by looking at the show and making observations in all of these areas.

At first, a number of elements seemed worth writing about; and in fact many of these elements that were noticeable at the very beginning stayed in the final product, which was not published until several years after the program first aired. For instance, it was immediately clear that the characterizations of Benson and Stabler reversed several primary associations with male and female characters in the workplace. Whereas most programs have historically presented women's work life and private life as presenting significant conflicts for the character, in *SVU* it is the male character Elliot Stabler who faces difficulties living a double life as a father and police detective. This time it is the father whose work creates problems for his home life. Stabler is often depicted as being out of touch with his children, angering his wife, and leading to arguments. Eventually, she leaves him. Although this simple narrative trajectory does not seem too extraordinary compared to lived experience, it was quite unique for prime-time television drama, and it was clear that this would be worth writing about.

Similarly, it was clear that the show tried to reverse several common tropes in the specific representation of sexual assault on television. The most important and perhaps most obvious was that the writers had made a commitment never to visually represent sexual assault on screen. This was an important departure from many programs of the past, and the absolute absence of images of sexual assault in a program dedicated to this subject was historically significant. This would be something that would necessarily make up part of any analysis of the *SVU* text. There were many other initial observations that proved central to the final analysis. These observations, while certainly informed by a knowledge of genre as well as of the history of representations of sexual assault in this genre and more broadly in mass media, did not rely on any specific theoretical approach. So, I certainly believe that it is possible to let your own interests and insights into a text serve as the initial guide to analysis. Once such areas of significance or interest have been identified, one can then always go to previously published scholarship with an eye to discovering the best way of explaining and arguing for the importance of what has been observed. Even starting with relatively little knowledge of the history of the genre or medium in which your text is situated, it is still possible to make observations first and then go back to the literature to better understand what you have discovered.

After deciding what stands out in your text, or what makes it special, and after going back to existing literature to further inform the significance and relevance of your insights within the genre and medium, the next thing to do is to collect examples. In this case, with the help of some student research assistants, we set to work making a thorough catalogue of specific examples of our more important insights. At first, every episode was thoroughly analyzed, since the series was new and there was no DVD database to access. This part of the process is very important because the collection of examples forces you as the analyst to define the parameters of the concepts you are developing.

For this project, the following questions needed to be answered in relation to just the two observations mentioned above: In what ways is Elliot's private life affected by his work? How is this similar to, or different from, the negative effects often shown for working female characters? In what ways can Elliot "get away" with expressing his attachments to his family that are seldom allowed for female characters? In what ways were gender representations for professional men and women reversed with respect to family/private life? Here we found one limitation: Although Elliot's private life was severely affected by his work life (an effect nearly always reserved for working women on television), the representation of Olivia still did not stray far from the accepted trade that female characters usually make (choose work or family, not both). Throughout many years of this series, Olivia has had no steady boyfriend, nor really any friends or family at all. Her alcoholic mother offers little support or comfort, and dies early on.

In relation to the other observation that sexual assault is not shown on screen, several clarifying questions were important to pursue through the discovery of examples within the text: Were there other ways in which the representation of sexual assault in *SVU* deviated from the usual prime-time fare? If so, what were the relationships among these? Was the ban on visualized sexual assault strictly observed? How close did individual episodes come to visual representation? Were there any patterns of representation that appeared to compensate for this absence of something that is usually present? In this case the emphasis on violated corpses and detailed crime scenes seemed significant. These elements led further to questions about the parameters of representation of dead bodies and forensic inquiry. In addition, it soon became clear that *SVU's* commitment to what could be considered feminist ideas about sexual assault did not carry over more broadly to representations of gender in other spheres. Most notably, once again through documentation of specific examples, it became clear that *SVU* evidenced a pattern of blaming female characters for many of the most significant individual and social problems depicted. These two seemingly contradictory forces, the commitment to feminist ideas about sexual assault and the contrasting willingness to depict female characters as villains of the worst kind, formed the basis of a central thesis in the article: While feminist in one sphere and at one level, in other spheres, and thus more pervasively, the program is in effect misogynist.

It is important to keep in mind that writing and analysis can be enjoyable processes, and that while there is a goal of completing an analysis, there is another way in which detailed analysis can be considered an unlimited endeavor. Each set of questions leads to another, and thorough knowledge of a single text can take many years. How do you know when you are finished? There are some things you can do to help yourself limit the scope

(Continued)

(Continued)

of your project. In the *SVU* case, when it seemed there was enough material to support the central thesis that had emerged, we decided to write the analysis and limit its scope to the first five seasons. For a classroom assignment, a smaller limit is perfectly acceptable. One season of a relatively new prime-time series, or a few episodes of each year of a long-running series, are perfectly sufficient as long as there are ample examples of the phenomena to support the focal point of the argument. It is more important to say something important, interesting, and well supported than to analyze an exhaustive amount of text.

In writing the actual analysis, it is important to provide the best possible examples of the patterns you wish to establish or concepts you wish to delimit. However, it is not necessary to hide or underplay counterexamples. Rather, it is important to be very honest about the character of the examples you have. In collecting examples to illustrate the blame placed on female characters, it became clear that male characters also commit heinous acts. This realization helped to push the argument toward delimitation of how male and female crimes differ, rather than on a one-sided argument that the series presents only women as villains. It is also useful, and actually strengthens the argument, to include one or two counterexamples in order to illustrate the conceptual limit of what you are presenting. It turned out to be the case that the show very seldom depicts males (fathers in this case) as turning their children into criminals, whereas mothers much more often receive this sort of blame. By including the few examples in which fathers are blamed along with the many depicting mothers as responsible for creating criminal children, the article is able to demonstrate the vast difference between the two. And, at this point, we went back to previously existing literature on the depiction of dangerous mothers in order to support, explain, and refine the discussion of what we had found.

Advertising

Advertising refers to messages that encourage consumers to buy companies' products or to think of those products in a positive light. Since advertising funds a majority of entertainment media, commercials and print advertisements clutter the media landscape. Visually, some advertising appears on the cutting edge, and some even will give nods to changing ideas about gender and society. For example, Gill (2007) discusses a reversal of the "sex object" stereotype, noting how advertising suggests that women dress provocatively in order to feel sexy themselves, not for others. Gill (2007) also notes the inclusion of more ethnic diversity within advertising. In the end, though, the messages become part of sales discourses and ultimately reinforce traditional ideas about gender roles.

The Process of Feminist Media Research

HOW TO CHOOSE TEXTS FOR ANALYSIS

Most often we think of industry-produced media texts including newspapers, films, television shows, magazines, books, advertisements, and music as key objects for media analysis. Other texts include more personal items, such as letters, diaries, and photographs. For example, Carroll Smith-Rosenberg (1975) analyzes female friendships of the eighteenth and nineteenth centuries through letters and diaries from 35 families. More official texts include documents, which range from governmental ones such as birth certificates and property titles to more procedural ones such as medical records and patient charts (Prior, 2003, 2011). Further, texts also include material culture, which refers to any artifact either produced or used by people (Lindlof & Taylor, 2011; Tilley, 2001). These artifacts might include toys, clothing, collectible items, and even what some might consider just plain junk. For example, Thomas (2003) explores the gendered forms of cemetery statues, yard art, and Barbie dolls, finding that female images get sexualized.

Many contemporary texts appear within a converged media environment. With the rapid growth of the Internet and the devices used to access it, we now listen to music through cell phones, portable music players, tablets, and computers. This access applies not just to music but also to multiple media, including television and film. We can interact with all of these forms on one device without owning a television, and film projector. This situation wherein different media "converge," or come together, occurs within a digital environment (Jenkins, 2006; Pavlik & McIntosh, 2013).

The Internet offers an enormous range of texts for study. For example, in her study *Storytelling Online: Talking Breast Cancer on the Internet*, Orgad (2005) uses a combination of online texts, including e-mail and discussion boards. In order to classify texts, Orgad (2009) suggests dividing the materials available on and about the Internet into two types: online data and offline data. Online data "are materials obtained using what have been often described as virtual methodologies: methods implemented by and through the internet" (Orgad, 2009, p. 35). For textual analysis, online data refer to texts such as word-based documents, still and moving images, and sounds found on the Internet, including blog posts, microblogs, discussion boards, social networking site posts, podcasts, and videos. Media analysis studies often focus on online data. Offline data include any materials generated within any environment offline (Orgad, 2009). While these two categories might suggest they are discrete, both Orgad (2009) and Bakardjieva (2009) note that these online and offline distinctions for data remain blurry.

Although online texts are abundant and easily available for analysis, one must avoid studying a text just because it is convenient or popular. Careful consideration must go into the texts chosen for analysis. Feminist inquiries pay particular attention to women, women's stories, and women's issues as they appear in media and other texts. For example, feminist television scholars use textual analysis to look more closely at strong female characters such as the protagonist in *Buffy the Vampire Slayer* (Boyle, 2008) and Carrie Bradshaw on *Sex and the City* (Arthurs, 2008). Smith-Shomade (2002) uses genres of situation comedies, talk shows, and others to frame her analysis of African American women's representations. They also look at texts created by women specifically, as some feminist film scholars do in considering the work of women directors. McHugh (2007), for example, examines the work of Jane Campion through how her films challenge the conventions of what have traditionally been called "women's films." In selecting a text or group of texts for focus through feminist research, the following questions could be important considerations:

- Is the text a historical or a contemporary one that has been overlooked previously because it is too feminine or contains mostly female characters?

- Does the text feature content that addresses or includes women, such as story lines, news items, viewpoints, and issues?

- Does the text focus on women or gender in a new way?

- Does the scholarship surrounding a text leave out important points pertaining to gender in regard to race, class, or sexuality, thus inviting further inquiry?

- Does the text offer a new approach to familiar themes or issues related to the televisual representation of gender?

These questions offer only starting places for thinking about choices of texts for textual analysis, and they are not wholly comprehensive by any means. Some texts might raise more than one of the questions above, while other texts might raise new ones. The point here is to avoid choosing texts for analysis just because of convenience or strong personal preference. The reasons generated for choosing a text for analysis must go beyond personal interests and must connect with larger feminist and cultural questions. A strong, well-reasoned answer to "Why this text?" is just as important as the analysis process itself.

Identifying and Developing Themes

The most basic starting point for much feminist media research is simply to observe and count the characters of different gender, sexuality, age, and so forth in the text(s). From there, it is important to examine and evaluate each of the characters and relationships contained in the text(s). The researcher needs to start with a clear understanding of the basic representations of gender and gender roles within the text, and is then in a position to move on to develop an idea of what about this particular text is worthy of further examination. The text should say something significant about gender, mark a departure from previous representations, offer gendered interactions whose examination illuminates the operation of power within the text, or contribute to the historical trajectory of some specific issue or theme. Key themes become the primary means of engaging a text, and determining these themes becomes the next step. A theme is an idea that repeats throughout a text, and can be suggested by previous scholarship on a particular medium, genre, or example. A theme is not random, though it might appear so on initial inquiries. After further inquiry, a theme begins to form a pattern that fluctuates in different ways throughout the text. The pattern might appear not only within a text, but also across multiple texts and even across multiple media platforms. For example, the sexualization of female form theme as employed in Thomas's (2003) study of material culture appears not only in films and on television, but also in video games and magazines.

Workable themes share several characteristics. A theme must be conceptually narrow enough in order to facilitate closer readings of texts. If a theme is too broad or vaguely defined, or encompasses too many features, systematic inquiry will become clumsy and cumbersome. It is best to search for a theme that can be clearly defined, or operationalized, so that both the writer and potential readers of the analysis will be able to apply it meaningfully to new examples within the text at hand and in other texts. It is important for the analyst to be able to identify the theme, to determine where examples of it exist in the chosen text, and to explain both clearly. Definitions of analytical themes or concepts, such as objectification, sexualization, and spectacle, may be borrowed or adapted from existing scholarship and applied to new texts. In gender analyses of advertising, for example, a recurring theme is the representation of traditional gender roles, with women shown within the home and dependent on a provider and with men shown in multiple occupations outside the home (Gill, 2007). Other themes center on the valuing of beauty standards, the lack of older women and nonwhite women, the fragmenting of women's bodies, and even the representation of violence (Gill, 2007). These themes occur across multiple media, including television, magazines, and websites.

An excellent example of thematic analysis related to gender representation is Battles and Hilton-Morrow's analysis of the television program *Will and Grace*. Battles and Hilton-Morrow (2002) argue that, although *Will and Grace* broke new ground in its representation of a gay man as attractive and likeable, the show's use of the trope of the friendship between a gay man and straight woman allows for the displacement of sexualized imagery from the gay couple (which is never visually represented on the show) to the heterosexual couple, as the characters of Will and Grace frequently embrace, kiss, and refer to each other in intimate terms. Similarly, Cuklanz and Moorti's 2006 work on *Law and Order: Special Victims Unit,* described above, centers on the theme of female criminality, arguing that while the program features both male and female criminals, the types of crimes and motive for them differ significantly depending on the gender of the criminal, with women's crimes being depicted as more damaging to their immediate victims and to the society as a whole. Esposito's 2009 work on *Ugly Betty* expands on the theme of privilege and postracialism on this program, arguing that one important episode manages to suggest that Betty, a young Mexican American woman from Queens, New York, is a beneficiary of affirmative action at the same time that it fails to interrogate notions of privilege. After depicting Betty as able to win a prestigious competition over her gay male competitor who has clearly worked much harder, the episode then includes dialogue about gay male disadvantage while at the same time suggesting that Betty was the recipient of unfair affirmative action. The show sidesteps difficult questions of white male privilege and fails to interrogate claims of unfair competition. All of these analyses focus on a particular theme that places gender in conceptual relation to other important thematic elements within a given program. Battles and Hilton-Morrow (2002) examine sexuality, gender, and visibility. Cuklanz and Moorti (2006) examine gender and criminality, and Esposito (2009) examines gender and racial discourses.

As the above examples illustrate, contemporary feminist research on mass media usually involves multiple themes and their interrelationships. These themes must avoid overlap. Textual phenomena must not fit within multiple categories, but instead should fit within only one. Berger (2011) describes this requirement through developing categories (another word for themes) related to violence:

> Categories must be mutually exclusive. You must not define your concept in a way that it can be applied to more than one kind of behavior. If you define violence too broadly or too narrowly, there will be problems. If your definition is too broad, researchers will argue that your measurements aren't reliable or of any value, because you deal with too many things. If your definition is too narrow, researchers will say you neglected important matters. (p. 210)

By ensuring themes remain mutually exclusive, they become workable and even more efficient in conducting your analysis.

Some themes, such as violence, are very important but also too prevalent to allow for comprehensive analysis. But limiting the examination of violence to how it appears within one program or one type of program still creates a theme that may be too broad to be useful. Once an important but broad theme, such as violence, has been identified, it needs to be conceptually divided into subcategories in some way. With the example of violence, subcategories could be based on specific behaviors, on who perpetrates the violence, on the identity of the victim of the violence, on the style of representation, on motivations for the act, and so forth (Berger, 2011, p. 212). Even simple conceptual schemes such as these make a start at developing a more sophisticated typography for the concept at hand.

While themes appear within a text, they also connect to cultural ideas *outside* texts. A text never emerges from a vacuum. Instead, it becomes the product of multiple contexts, including industrial, national, cultural, social, and political ones. These contexts influence not only a text's production and the ideas it represents, but also its uses and receptions. In *Where the Girls Are: Growing Up Female With the Mass Media*, Susan J. Douglas (1995) contrasts the rise of feminism with the media backlash that paralleled it. Just as the media, particularly the news media, mocked feminism, the media also exposed even more audiences to feminisms and their philosophies. Douglas (1995) writes, "Many reports were ambivalent and confused, taking feminism seriously one minute, mocking it the next. In this way, the news media exacerbated quite keenly the profound cultural schizophrenia about women's place in society that had been building since the 1940s and 1950s" (p. 165). Douglas develops her arguments through looking at key moments in the feminist movement alongside key news media productions of the era, revealing and examining the many manifestations of ambivalence found within them. Her consideration of these deeper contexts enriches her analysis of those period productions.

The path to developing themes starts at one of two points. Some scholars start with deriving the themes by closely watching the texts and looking for the patterns that way. Other scholars develop their themes through bringing together themes developed in other research, either using them wholesale or more likely using them as a starting point and honing them later. The path moving away from those starting points follows no straight line, however. No matter how the themes get developed, they change throughout the process of inquiry. As the analysis of the themes within the texts becomes more detailed, the researcher begins seeing patterns. These patterns may complement the existing themes, they may contradict the existing themes, or they may force an expansion or reduction of the existing themes. These patterns may illustrate the importance of some themes and the irrelevance of others. The process of analysis thus becomes more cyclical; and with each close reading of the texts, the themes become developed, refined, or discarded. The researcher can identify, select, delimit, and name the themes that are important or interesting within a given text based on many influences including historical knowledge, theoretical or scholarly debates and concepts, the function or reception of the text in its social context, and/or personal experience.

As the themes become refined, so might the definition of texts under consideration for analysis. Some researchers conduct textual analyses on single media texts. Many film scholars develop their ideas through in-depth inquiries into one film. Projansky (2011), for example, looks at *The Sisterhood of the Traveling Pants*, while Radner (2011) explores *13 Going on 30*. Esposito's work on *Ugly Betty* examines just one important episode of that program. In online contexts, Paasonen (2009) explores "the construction of *lifestyle* on corporate (doll) Web sites" (p. 23).

Documenting and Defining

Tracking thematic analysis involves keeping precise, detailed records. Starting with close reading of the texts toward developing themes, these records will involve the recording of thick description. *Thick description* (Geertz, 1973) refers to collecting relevant information—such as dialogue, physical characteristics, and plot events—from texts and making note of them and their locations in the texts. Those locations vary from text to text. For linear texts, that location might be a time stamp; while for online sites, that location might be a specific URL, such as www.feministing.com. If starting with a set of themes, then these records involve seeking details that fit within those themes and involve paying critical attention to the usefulness of those themes.

Several options exist for recording this information. One method involves keeping the information in a dedicated paper journal. For some researchers, this option brings them "closer" to the data, facilitating the analytical process. Other methods involve computer programs. One set of computer programs, such as the Microsoft Office, Apple's iWork, and OpenOffice's suites of programs, offers both word processing and spreadsheet options. Other programs are designed specifically for qualitative data analysis, such as the proprietary Atlas.ti, NVivo, and HyperRESEARCH. These proprietary programs are expensive, though many colleges and universities offer them to students and faculty for free due to site licensing. Open-source qualitative data analysis software includes RQDA, Textual Analysis Markup System (TAMS), and Tranana. These programs offer a less expensive alternative, but some offer fewer features than the proprietary ones.

Just as the process of developing themes follows a cyclical path, so does the process of data analysis, which involves culling through the data gathered, looking for important observations and ideas, and beginning to ask, "What does all this mean?" The most intensive data analysis occurs after the themes get narrowed down into a workable framework and the textual data get assigned to these different themes. However, data analysis really begins in the process of gathering the data and creating the themes as ideas about their significance and meanings appear along the way. Some scholars write research memos during these processes to help them keep ideas and insights organized. Research memos for some scholars refer to extra observations jotted down on a journal or field log page. Other scholars make research memos a more formal process by creating a computer document with dates, details, and other references. These memos prove particularly useful for keeping unexpected ideas recorded and accessible.

Data Analysis

Data analysis takes time, patience, and care to develop the key points and to choose the appropriate data to support those points. Researchers review their data multiple times, with various questions to guide them through each pass. Eventually, the passes provide no new insights or information, leading to saturation. The next step is writing up the results.

HOW TO UNDERSTAND THE RESEARCHER'S ROLE

In media analysis, the researcher becomes as connected to the text as to the contexts that surround it. A researcher becomes part of the power structures that inform the text. According to Hermes (2006), "Reading popular texts both ties us into the rules and structures of societal power and offers reflection on them. This dual process of actively becoming part of and simultaneously taking part in cultural practice, is an act of citizenship" (p. 159). In other words, the researcher, the texts, and the contexts that inform them all are part of the same cultural fabric.

Without the insights of interactions with audiences, the researcher becomes the primary arbiter of meaning in textual analysis. Some researchers speak from their own experiences and even maintain a personal connection to their subjects for analysis. For example, Haas (2009) writes in her chapter about online infertility support groups about how her own struggles with an endometriosis diagnosis led her to a personal exploration of and participation in these groups. After interaction with them, however, she "found that my initial sense of identification with most members of these forums soon wore off. After all, as a feminist, I am accustomed to first gaining an understanding of a technology and then revisioning it through a critical lens" (Haas, 2009, p. 64). Her experiences with these groups, her personal experiences with infertility, and her self-identification as a feminist all inform her textual analysis.

Researchers also speak about—and even for—those represented within those texts. Just as researchers follow ethical guidelines in speaking about interview subjects, they must follow similar guidelines in textual analysis. In particular, they must avoid making assumptions about the people shown, avoid making generalized statements about the people shown, and avoid misrepresenting them and their interests. Their discussions of the people and ideas represented in texts must be fair and well reasoned, not finely selected to emphasize some points at the expense of others.

Researchers further must recognize that multiple realities exist and that no single analysis will explain a text's deeper meanings. They must find a way to account for, acknowledge, and include those meanings within their analyses. Further, they must take care not to get too close to their texts through personal connections, as doing so might cause them to overlook something important or cause them to close off possible, viable meanings.

How do researchers try to address these issues? They do so by remaining reflexive throughout the research process. According to May and Perry (2011), reflexivity prevents "the assumption that there is an unproblematic relationship between the social scientific text and its valid and reliable representation of the 'real' world" (p. 15). In other words, what texts show or reveal offer no mirror of society, no direct connection between the two. Instead, processes occur in bringing reality into texts, and in those processes involve power relationships, as May and Perry (2011) explain further: "[Reflexivity] also guards against the assumption that textual openness reflects a fluid world in which choice is equally distributed between within and between different populations" (p. 15). Reflexivity helps researchers recognize these power relationships at work.

Reflexivity occurs throughout the research process, not just at the end as part of the writing process. Instead, researchers must remain open and questioning about their assumptions and ideas as they emerge. They must take care to avoid imposing their own meanings on textual representations, and thus not reading them through their own eyes. They must check and confirm their new ideas carefully through further data analysis, through outside research, and even through peer review. They must maintain a "double mind," conducting the research and asking questions of content and findings along the way.

What Are Some Advantages and Disadvantages of Doing Feminist Media Research?

For feminist researchers, media analysis offers a rich way of accessing and interrogating relations of power among different vectors of social hierarchy that intersect with gender, including race, class, sexuality, and age. Because of its thematic focus, this approach offers a limitless range of insights into mediated texts, and allows for the combination of several analytical elements in interaction with each other. Over time, feminist research on media has accumulated to create a record of the historical development of many genres of mainstream media with respect to gender and relations of power. The disadvantage of this approach is that when new texts are created, frameworks of analysis must be retested and often adjusted. Gender is constantly being constructed and reconstructed through mass media. Media analysis can never keep up with the pace and scope of change taking place, and is thus always a step behind the reality of gender construction in mainstream mass media.

Engaging with researching mediated communication offers multiple advantages. First, media analysis offers a key way to uncover multiple meanings within and around texts (Fürsich, 2009). While texts might appear to suggest just one meaning, they are in fact considered polysemic, which means they offer multiple meanings. Media analysis offers the means to get to those meanings and show how they interrelate. Second, this method is flexible in that it works with a wide variety of texts available. More practically, this method remains fairly inexpensive in that most materials are easily available (Berger, 2011). DVRs make recording television shows easy. YouTube offers an enormous archive of current and historical video. Further, materials available for study are abundant. Millions of websites invite users to interact with them and with each other, and numerous tools make recording the online data simple.

Media analysis is also considered "unobtrusive" (Berger, 2011, p. 213; Hesse-Biber & Leavy, 2006). Instead of observing or interviewing people as part of gathering data, texts already exist and require minimal, if any, interaction with people in order to study them.

The process of gathering data from people gets influenced both by researchers and by participants, whereas data exist without these layers of influence interfering.

While media analysis offers multiple advantages, it also draws several critiques. One critique centers on how media analysis offers little to no insight into other related contexts, such as production and audiences (Philo, 2007, cited in Fürsich, 2009). Claims based on production or based on potential audience reception and made through media analysis offer only speculation and raise the opportunity to make factual mistakes or gross assumptions, such as blaming a text's limitations on its broadcast contexts (Fürsich, 2009). A tendency emerges among new researchers to assert ideas as certainties based on analysis, when in effect, those supposed certainties offer just one possibility in a text's polysemy. Another critique of media analysis comes back to the perception of the incompleteness of its findings. According to Hermes (2006), "Textual analysis can never be taken to predict or explain how audiences will read, experience or interpret a text" (p. 156). However, Fürsich (2009) claims that this argument misses the possibilities the method offers. Further, Phillipov (2012) asserts the partiality of all research methods. No single method reveals all the potential insights available about a cultural phenomenon. A third critique comes back to the role of the researcher in media analysis. Unlike methods that draw insights from data gathered from audiences, textual analyses draw on the insights of researchers and the cultural positions informing those insights. As noted above, effective researchers undertaking textual analysis recognize that they must work toward a nuanced, multidimensional engagement of a text grounded in scholarship and data, and not just offer insights based exclusively on their own viewpoints.

The very polysemy of texts that makes media analysis an appealing method, can in another way be considered a limitation. Because texts are polysemic, it is important to acknowledge at some point within each work of media analysis that other readings or interpretations can be generated from the same text, and, thus, that the writer's interpretation is not to be taken as the absolute truth about a text. Texts generate meaning only through their interaction with audiences. Thus, while patterns of reception and understanding of most texts are quite predictable, it is simply not possible that all audiences will share interpretations of all elements of any given text. High-quality media analysis identifies and illuminates patterns within texts as well as their significance, but also acknowledges at least some of the limitations that multiple readings generate.

CONCLUSION

This chapter has offered an overview of feminist media research with its exploration of key terms, approaches, and theoretical underpinnings through traditional media, convergence media, and material culture. As the different examples throughout this chapter illustrate, media research is rich and versatile, and its objects for study are abundant and easily available. This flexibility and abundance, however, still requires rigor and reflexivity on the researcher's part.

Feminist media research provides several important functions that support the goals of feminism. Most significantly, feminist media research aims to discover, analyze, and critique the means through which mainstream media construct and maintain dominant ideas about gender. In doing so, feminist media research provides insights into the ways in which ideas that may seem "normal" or "natural" are actually socially constructed. By deconstructing these ideas, or showing how they are artificially supported in mediated texts, feminist media research can empower readers to think of new ways to understand gender as well as its intersections with categories such as race, class, and sexuality.

A second important function of feminist media research is to provide documentation of the subtle traces of social change surrounding our culture's accepted ideas about gender. As these dominant ideas shift, feminist media research documents the direction and degree of change, and also keeps track of points of particular resistance in this ongoing process. Thus, for instance, Crosby's work (2004) shows that while Buffy the Vampire Slayer and a few other recent female characters have been able to be strong, effective, and feminine, these heroines are still limited in that they do not want the power they have, try to give up their power, and are never able to become heads of female-centered communities apart from patriarchal power. These characters habitually relinquish either their power or their lives, while powerful and effective male characters can continue successfully throughout the run of their narratives' lives. Showing the ideological limit of concepts and/or conceptual shifts is a significant function of feminist media research. It illuminates the path toward further social change and empowerment for women.

Feminist media research focuses on muted voices and stories, bringing into focus those character types, generic forms, and characterizations that do not receive attention in other forums. It aims at social transformation and tries to locate forms of discursive power for femininity, feminine characters, and women either within or outside of mediated texts. It is rooted in commitment to social justice and dedicated to the discovery of inequality, imbalance, and progress within specific mediated products.

DISCUSSION QUESTIONS

1. While many textual analyses focus on media products, this method also works with understanding power discourses in elements of material culture. Think about the different objects you encounter from your life, your home, or your routines. What object(s) might be worth studying through this method? What object(s) in particular raise questions about feminism(s) and feminist issues?

2. Qualitative researchers often pair textual analysis with another method within longer studies. How might you use textual analysis with another method described in one of the other chapters of this book? What might be your motivations for doing so?

3. Media products usually come from large media industries, but the online content comes from a combination of media industries and everyday people. Feminist websites often make for rich online discussions that sometimes remain civil and other times get quite heated. What ethical concerns should you keep in mind when analyzing comments on these and other sites?

4. While convergence texts offer rich possibilities for textual analysis, they also pose some challenges in that they constantly change and even disappear. Say you found a popular blog about women's issues. How might you determine what aspects of the site to study?

5. Feminist inquiry requires questioning the role of the researcher and the power of the researcher within qualitative research methods. While other methods described in this book involve getting information from other people, textual analysis remains less intrusive, but no less open to ethical considerations. What ethical questions factor into textual analysis? What considerations must the researcher keep in mind when choosing texts, determining themes, and engaging interpretations?

WEB RESOURCES

- *Women's Media Center* addresses the problems of women's (mis)representations in the media: http://www.womensmediacenter.com/

- *Center for the Study of Women in Television and Film,* based at San Diego State University, pursues "an extensive agenda of original research documenting women's underrepresentation and investigating the reasons for the continuing gender inequities." http://women intvfilm.sdsu.edu/index.html

- *Feministing,* founded by Jessica Valenti, offers feminist commentary on media and other news events: http://feministing.com/

- *BlogHer* is an enormous consortium of women bloggers writing about media, feminism, women's roles, and many, many other related issues: http://www.blogher.com/

- *Media Praxis* is written by Alexandra Juhasz, a feminist documentary maker and media critic: http://aljean.wordpress.com/

- *The F Word: Feminist Media Collective* is a blog and radio broadcast that explores the feminist implications of media representations, sports, history, and other subjects: http://www.feminisms.org/

- *Feministe* is a blog that claims to be "in defense of the sanctimonious women's studies set" and offers commentary on media and news coverage: http://www.feministe.us/blog/

- *Bitch Magazine* is a feminist response to pop culture with some focus on media: http://bitchmagazine.org/

- *Ms. Magazine Blog* is a blog about the news and media, from the iconic magazine: http://msmagazine.com/blog/

NOTE

1. All of my work on this show is co-authored with Sujata Moorti of Middlebury College. Here, I offer my own perspective on the writing process apart from the joint authorship elements.

REFERENCES

Arthurs, J. (2008). *Sex and the City* and consumer culture: Remediating postfeminist drama. In C. Brunsdon & L. Spigel (Eds.), *Feminist television criticism: A reader* (pp. 29–40). New York, NY: Open University Press.

Bakardjieva, M. (2009). A response to Shani Orgad. In A. N. Markham & N. K. Byam (Eds.), *Internet inquiry: Conversations about method* (pp. 54–60). Thousand Oaks, CA: Sage.

Battles, K., & Hilton-Morrow, W. (2002). Gay characters in conventional spaces: *Will and Grace* and the situation comedy genre. *Critical Studies in Media Communication, 19,* 87–105.

Benedict, H. (1993). *Virgin or vamp: How the press covers sex crimes.* New York, NY: Oxford University Press.

Berger, A. A. (2011). *Media and communication research methods: An introduction to qualitative and quantitative approaches.* Thousand Oaks, CA: Sage.

Boyle, K. (2008). Feminism without men: Feminist media studies in a post-feminist age. In C. Brunsdon & L. Spigel (Eds.), *Feminist television criticism: A reader* (pp. 174–190). New York, NY: Open University Press.

Bryant, E. (2008, November). *A critical examination of gender representation on Facebook profiles.* Paper presented at the National Communication Association Conference, San Diego, CA.

Chen, Y. (2012). *Women in Chinese martial arts films of the new millennium: Narrative analyses and gender politics.* Lanham, MD: Lexington Books.

Crosby, S. (2004). The cruelest season: Female heroes snapped into sacrificial heroines. In S. A. Inness (Ed.), *Action chicks: New images of tough women in popular culture* (pp. 153–178). New York, NY: Palgrave Macmillan.

Cuklanz, L. M. (1996). Mainstream news frames the Hill/Thomas hearings. In P. Siegel & S. Drucker (Eds.), *Outsiders looking in: A communication perspective on the Hill/Thomas hearings* (pp. 167–182). New York, NY: Hampton Press.

Cuklanz, L. M., & Moorti, S. (2006). Television's "new" feminism: Prime-time representations of women and victimization. *Critical Studies in Media Communication 23*, 302–321.

Day, K., & Keys, T. (2008). Starving in cyberspace: A discourse analysis of pro-eating-disorder websites. *Journal of Gender Studies 17*, 1–15.

Doane, M. A. (1987). *The Desire to desire: The woman's film of the 1940s.* Bloomington: Indiana University Press.

Douglas, S. J. (1995). *Where the girls are: Growing up female with the mass media.* New York, NY: Three Rivers Press.

Dow, B. (1990). Hegemony, feminist criticism, and *The Mary Tyler Moore Show. Critical Studies in Mass Communication 7*, 261–274.

Esposito, J. (2009). What does race have to do with *Ugly Betty*? An analysis of privilege and post-tracial (?) representations on a television sitcom. *Television & New Media 10*, 521–535.

Falk, E. (2007). *Women for president: Media bias in eight campaigns.* Champaign: University of Illinois Press.

Faludi, S. (1991). *Backlash: The undeclared war on American women.* New York, NY: Anchor.

Foss, K. A., & Foss, S. K. (1991). *Women speak: The eloquence of women's lives.* Prospect Heights, IL: Waveland Press.

Foucault, M. (1972). *The archaeology of knowledge and the discourse on language* (A. M. Sheridan Smith, Trans.). New York, NY: Pantheon Books.

Fürsich, E. (2009). In defense of textual analysis: Restoring a challenged method for journalism and media studies. *Journalism Studies, 10*, 238–252.

Geertz, C. (1973). *The interpretation of cultures: Selected essays.* New York, NY: Basic Books.

Gill, R. (2007). *Gender and the media.* Malden, MA: Polity.

Goffman, E. (1974). *Frame analysis: An essay on the organization of experience.* New York, NY: Harper & Row.

Haas, A. M. (2009). Wired wombs: A rhetorical analysis of online infertility support communities. In K. Blair, R. Gajjala, & C. Tulley (Eds.), *Webbing cyberfeminist practice: Communities, pedagogies and social action* (pp. 61–84). Cresskill, NJ: Hampton Press.

Hall, S. (1997). Introduction. In S. Hall (Ed.), *Representation: Cultural representations and signifying practices* (pp. 1–12). Thousand Oaks, CA: Sage.

Hermes, J. (2006). Feminism and the politics of method. In M. White & J. Schwoch (Eds.), *Questions of method in cultural studies* (pp. 154–174). Malden, MA: Blackwell.

Hesse-Biber, S. N., & Leavy, P. (2006). *The practice of qualitative research.* Thousand Oaks, CA: Sage.

Jenkins, H. (2006). *Convergence culture: Where old and new media collide.* New York, NY: New York University Press.

Joseph, R. L. (2009). "Tyra Banks is fat": Reading (post-)racism and (post-)feminism in the new millennium. *Critical Studies in Media Communication 26*, 237–254.

Kearney, M. C. (2006). *Girls make media*. London, England: Routledge.

Lindlof, T. R., & Taylor, B. C. (2011). *Qualitative communication research methods*. Thousand Oaks, CA: Sage.

Lister, M., Dovey, J., Giddings, S., Grant, I., & Kelly, K. (2009). *New media: A critical introduction* (2nd ed.). New York, NY: Routledge.

May, T., & Perry, B. (2011). *Social research and reflexivity: Content, consequence, and context*. Thousand Oaks, CA: Sage.

McHugh, K. A. (2007). *Jane Campion* (Contemporary Film Directors Series). Urbana: University of Illinois Press.

Meehan, E. R., & Riordan, E. (2002). *Sex & money: Feminism and political economy in the media*. Minneapolis: University of Minnesota Press.

Milestone, K., & Meyer, A. (2012). *Gender and popular culture*. Malden, MA: Polity.

Modleski, T. (1982). *Loving with a vengeance: Mass produced fantasies for women*. New York, NY: Routledge.

Mulvey, L. (1975). Visual pleasure and narrative cinema. *Screen, 16*(3), 6–18.

Neroni, H. (2005). *The violent woman: Femininity, narrative, and violence in contemporary American cinema*. Albany: State University of New York Press.

Orgad, S. (2005). *Storytelling online: Talking breast cancer on the Internet*. New York, NY: Peter Lang.

Orgad, S. (2009). How can researchers make sense of the issues involved in collecting and interpreting online and offline data? In A. N. Markham & N. K. Byam (Eds.), *Internet inquiry: Conversations about method* (pp. 33–53). Thousand Oaks, CA: Sage.

Paasonen, S. (2009). "Yo! Wanna be part of our crew?" Girls, dolls, and online consumerism. In K. Blair, R. Gajjala, & C. Tulley (Eds.), *Webbing cyberfeminist practice: Communities, pedagogies and social action* (pp. 23–41). Cresskill, NJ: Hampton Press.

Pavlik, J. V., & McIntosh, S. (2013). *Converging media: A new introduction to mass communication* (3rd ed.). New York, NY: Oxford University Press.

Peirce, L. M. (2011). The American mother: A feminist analysis of the Kleenex "Get-Mommed" campaign. *Journal of Media and Communication Studies, 3*, 118–122.

Phillipov, M. (2012). In defense of textual analysis: Resisting methodological hegemony in media and cultural studies. *Critical Studies in Media Communication*. doi:10.1080/15295036.2011.639380

Prior, L. (2003). *Using documents in social research*. Thousand Oaks, CA: Sage.

Prior, L. (2011). Using documents in social research. In D. Silverman (Ed.), *Qualitative research* (pp. 93–110). Thousand Oaks, CA: Sage.

Projansky, S. (2011). Girls' sexualities in *The Sisterhood of the Traveling Pants* universe: Feminist challenges and missed opportunities. In H. Radner & R. Stringer (Eds.), *Feminism at the movies: Understanding gender in contemporary popular culture* (pp. 93–109). New York, NY: Routledge.

Radner, H. (2011). Speaking the name of the father in the neo-romantic comedy: *13 Going on 30* (2004). In H. Radner & R. Stringer (Eds.), *Feminism at the movies: Understanding gender in contemporary popular culture* (pp. 134–148). New York, NY: Routledge.

Radway, J. (1984). *Reading the romance: Women, patriarchy, and popular literature*. New York, NY: Verso.

Rand, E. (2012). *Red nails, black skates: Gender, cash, and pleasure on and off the ice.* Durham, NC: Duke University Press.

Shade, L. R. (2002). *Gender and community in the social construction of the Internet.* New York, NY: Peter Lang.

Smith-Rosenberg, C. (1975). The female world of love and ritual: Relations between women in nineteenth-century America. *Signs: Journal of Women in Culture and Society, 1*(1), 1–29.

Smith-Shomade, B. E. (2002). *Shaded lives: African American women and television.* New Brunswick, NJ: Rutgers University Press.

Stabile, C. A. (2011). The nightmare voice of feminism: Feminism and cultural studies. In P. Smith (Ed.), *The renewal of cultural studies* (pp. 17–27). Philadelphia, PA: Temple University Press.

Thomas, J. B. (2003). *Naked Barbies, Warrior Joes, and other forms of visible gender.* Urbana: University of Illinois Press.

Tilley, C. (2001). Ethnography and material culture. In P. Atkinson, A. Coffey, S. Delamont, J. Lofland, & L. Lofland (Eds.), *Handbook of ethnography* (pp. 258–272). Thousand Oaks, CA: Sage.

Tong, R. (2008). *Feminist thought: A more comprehensive introduction.* Boulder, CO: Westview Press.

Turow, J. (2011). *Media today.* New York, NY: Routledge.

Vavrus, M. D. (2007). Opting out moms in the news: Selling new traditionalism in the new millennium. *Feminist Media Studies, 7,* 47–63.

CHAPTER 10

Feminist Survey Research

Kathi Miner and Toby Jayaratne

Behind the Scenes With Kathi Miner and Toby Jayaratne

We are feminist psychologists who center our research programs on quantified data, primarily using survey methods to explore issues of importance to women and to those with a social justice orientation. As such, we are well aware that some feminist criticism has been directed toward survey research and quantitative research, more generally, with the claim that such research can be antithetical to feminist aims. We take an opposite view and instead consider quantitative research as one method of investigation that can make a significant contribution toward advancing feminist and social justice causes. What led both of us to hold this perspective and to merge our feminist values and our training as quantitative researchers?

For me, Kathi, they did not coincide initially. I was actually a feminist long before I began conducting quantitative research. During adolescence I started becoming aware of the inequities women faced and became angered by this realization. For example, I noticed that my mother did the cooking and laundry while my father watched television. I saw my sister's frustration when she learned she received less pay in her position as a staff reporter at the local newspaper than the similarly qualified male in the next office. I was angry when men whistled at me when I walked by and then called me a bitch when I ordered them to stop. I hated that I focused so much on what and how much I ate rather than doing well in school or learning about world events. It was not until I arrived at college that I realized that there was a name to what I was feeling: feminism. Feminism made sense to me and it became a part of my identity.

In college I also realized that people systematically studied these injustices. I was floored when I became aware that researchers could provide "hard data" to document what I was observing. What I observed back then still resonates: Women do significantly more housework and child care than men in heterosexual relationships (Bianchi, Milkie, & Sayer, 2000; Hook, 2010); white women make only 77% of what white men make in the same position, and this number is even lower for women of color (National Committee on Pay Equity, 2013); approximately 49% of college women have experienced some form of sexual victimization (e.g., rape, attempted rape; Fisher, Cullen, & Turner, 2000); 56% of adolescent girls have disordered eating patterns (Croll, Neumark-Sztainer, & Story, 2002); and 55% of girls 8 to 10 years old complain that they are too fat (Wood, Becker, & Thompson, 1996). These statistics moved me, and they move whomever I report them to. There is something powerful in quantification. When most people hear these statistics, they are in some way affected. And more often than not, these numbers convey in stark terms the social injustices that describe women's role in society.

As I became more proficient in statistics, I understood the compelling story numbers could tell about women's lives—not simply the proportion of women affected by this or that but the consequences of those experiences. For example, in my current research program I focus on the consequences for employees who observe harassing behavior targeted at women in their workplace. When I give talks about this research, I not only report the frequency of these behaviors, but also the consequences of these observations (such as significantly lowered job satisfaction and psychological well-being for observers). Importantly, I have noticed that people who would not call themselves feminists (and in fact would vehemently resist the label) listen when I explain these findings in quantified terms. Clearly, people respond to quantitative data. Numbers can inspire people to become social activists and they can influence those involved in public policy so that they enact legislation to improve the lives of women. With this in mind, a feminist quantitative survey researcher was born. My passion for social justice for women and my realization that numbers stirred people led me to want to conduct quantitative research on behalf of women.

I, Toby, grew up during the civil rights era in a family that was active in advancing a progressive political agenda. I learned from an early age the importance of understanding the factors that support policies of injustice, in order to challenge such practices. When I was in college, I had the opportunity to assist on studies of various social issues at my university. The people with whom I worked conducted their research specifically for the purpose of documenting inequalities and determining the most effective ways to promote social justice. It was inspiring being surrounded by those who had committed their entire careers to such work. For the most part, these researchers employed survey methods. Due to the high quality of their research and the respect that it garnered from others, findings from their studies were powerful in advocating for social change.

Given my activist upbringing, my identity as a feminist came easily in the 1960s. With my training in survey research, I decided that I could employ the quantitative skills I learned to investigate how sexism operated in our society and to explore the most productive means for achieving feminist goals. Once I started doing my own survey research, I found it to be a powerful technique for convincing others of the need to support various feminist causes.

(Continued)

(Continued)

However, one experience I had is particularly significant in informing my approach to research. Some years ago, when I was attending a women's studies conference, someone challenged the quantitative research methods I used, and suggested that such methods were not appropriate tools for feminist researchers. In response, I developed a critical eye with which to judge the methods I used, and I became aware of the value of various alternative, qualitative research strategies. However, rather than rejecting quantitative methods altogether, I came to believe that it was important for feminist researchers to remain open to using either (or both) of these methods, because they answer different types of research questions. As a social scientist whose main research topic focuses on the social and political implications of the public's genetic explanations for human characteristics and diseases, I attempt to follow this dictum. I use qualitative methods when I am attempting to gather initial information about an issue or to develop a more in-depth understanding of a topic. However, when I examine complex conceptual models or test theories, I use statistical (quantitative) methods, because they are best suited for that purpose. My professional experience has helped me realize that no one research technique works best in answering every research question, but rather, each new exploration requires a thoughtful, critical assessment in selecting an investigative strategy.

Although we have had different routes to a similar location, we both acknowledge the influence of our experiences and training on the development of our research perspectives. The guidance we received taught us to observe how the context of the research affects all aspects of the work we do and to maintain an awareness of the ethical and political issues associated with and implied by the research we undertake. Most importantly, however, we were educated to think about the research endeavor as a quest for knowledge in the service of social progress, a theme that we have carried with us as feminists and as survey researchers.

The point is not merely to describe the world but also to change it.

—Sherry Gorelick, 1996

Research is a search for answers to questions. Feminist research is a search for answers to questions that affect women's lives and promote social change for women. Those who engage in feminist research can select from a multitude of research methods, and there is no single, correct method that should be employed. Rather, the best way of doing feminist research completely depends on the specific questions to be addressed and the context of the research. In other words, to do quality feminist research (and all research), one should match the method with the question. To do that, it is necessary to become familiar with the various research techniques that are available.

This chapter will present one technique for conducting feminist research: survey methodology. More specifically, it will describe the survey research process, demonstrate how it can be applied to the exploration of feminist issues, and explain why it is an important, valuable resource for feminist researchers. Both historically and more recently, there are innumerable examples of how the results of survey research have made a difference in women's and other marginalized people's lives. These will be offered as examples throughout the chapter and will illustrate the unique and powerful effects survey research can have in understanding and alleviating gender oppression.

We come to this chapter schooled in the standards of mainstream social science research and with an appreciation for the utility of quantitative survey research. However, as feminists, we are also aware of feminist criticisms of quantitative research, and these inform our work in promoting social justice for women. Thus, bridging the disciplines of women's studies and psychology, we see ourselves as social justice scholars who come from a feminist perspective, striving to use survey research as a vehicle for advancing the feminist agenda.

The first section of this chapter focuses on several of the overarching issues regarding the use of quantitative methods generally, and survey research specifically, in feminist exploration. This section begins with a description of the historical development of survey research. Then it goes on to describe the major feminist criticisms of quantitative methods, including the primary differences between quantitative and qualitative research. The first section concludes by elucidating the unique benefits of quantitative survey research for feminist aims. In the second section, major components of survey research are introduced, highlighting significant issues that should be addressed in conducting quality feminist survey research.[1]

What Is the Historical Trajectory of Survey Research?

Perhaps the earliest and most well-known type of survey is the census, which began in the United States in 1790 and is conducted each decade by the federal government (U.S. Census Bureau, 1989). The census seeks to describe the characteristics (e.g., gender, race, average number of people per household) of an entire population (e.g., the United States) and was created to help determine how much representation each state should have in U.S. Congress. The most recent census was conducted in 2010, and more than 308 million Americans were surveyed (U.S. Census Bureau, 2011). The survey provided important information regarding a number of feminist concerns such as the number of women in poverty, the number of employed women, and the number of single mothers, and so on. This information is invaluable to feminists because it shows the current state of affairs for women in the United States.

Another purpose of surveys in their early development was to gain an understanding of social problems, and, indeed, even feminists employed such methods at that time. For example, during the late 1800s and early 1900s, feminists at the University of Chicago designed surveys and developed statistical techniques to assist social reform efforts (Deegan, cited in Spalter-Roth & Hartmann, 1996). This first generation of feminist survey researchers used the results of their surveys to educate the public and influence legislation supporting a host of progressive causes, such as reducing poverty, unemployment, and child labor. They differed from other feminists and survey researchers of the time in that they sought social change by employing empirical evidence to inform their goals. In contrast, most feminist social reformers during this period fought for social justice without necessarily utilizing such information and survey researchers typically conducted their work without an eye toward the advancement of social causes (Spalter-Roth & Hartmann, 1996).

A significant impetus for mainstream survey research development was World War II because the federal government was interested in assessing Americans' opinions and attitudes regarding the war and other social issues (Groves et al., 2009). This was a critical period in the evolution of such methods because survey researchers began to learn the importance of question wording, data collection techniques, interviewer training, and sampling procedures, and how these factors might affect the results of studies (Converse, 1987; Groves et al., 2009). Specifically, researchers found that certain methods were better than others for collecting and analyzing data so that they more accurately reflected public opinions and attitudes. This led to the establishment of accepted standards among researchers who conducted surveys. For example, researchers realized that during the interviewing process, evaluative comments by those conducting the survey (e.g., "good answer," "I agree") could dramatically influence a respondent's answers. Thus, proposed standards included the importance of limiting interviewers' remarks to those that are neutral so that the collected data was more likely to reflect respondents' true opinions.

During the 1960s and 1970s, a second generation of feminist survey researchers was, like those earlier, schooled in academic social science and had an interest in advancing social policy and social change for women (Spalter-Roth & Hartmann, 1996). This group of feminist researchers focused on social issues such as divorce, rape, employment discrimination, and women's health. However, this generation was generally critical of traditional science because it assumed that "truth" can be verified by observation and experimentation. These feminist scholars played an important role in pointing out how subtle (and sometimes not so subtle) factors continued to bias survey research in favor of the "male perspective." One common practice in this time period was to publish findings showing differences (e.g., in behavior, ability, attitudes) between men and women, without exploring the cultural and experiential factors that gave rise to these differences. This frequently implied that the differences (almost always favoring men) were inherent and could not be changed. Many of their concerns were addressed by mainstream survey researchers and survey research methods improved in response. However, some of these critiques still resonate today, and the dialogue about the best way to do research continues, because it is an ever-evolving process. Feminist survey researchers, then, have been influential in the broader effort to develop standards for conducting survey research that help to minimize bias and produce results that reflect social phenomena as accurately as possible.

What Are the Criticisms and Advantages of Quantitative Survey Research?

While there has been rapid growth in the use and sophistication of surveys, the survey research method, as a form of quantitative research, has been criticized by some feminist scholars. The major criticism of survey research has been that it is rooted in the tradition of *positivism*, which is a perspective that values objective and value-free science. Critics of positivism argue that it is impossible to conduct completely bias-free research. Interestingly, some feminist researchers have actually advocated objectivity as a way of incorporating feminist principles into their research. This strategy has been labeled *feminist empiricism* (Harding, 1987, 1998). Feminist empiricists argue that bias can be minimized only if the positivist principle of objectivity is rigorously upheld. They argue that adhering to the notion of objectivity will actually lead to data that are more, rather than less, representative of women's experiences because the research process will not be influenced by a particular perspective.

A somewhat different approach was recently termed *strong objectivity* by Harding (2004) and earlier was called *feminist objectivity* by Haraway (1988). This view recognizes that knowledge is situated, and in so doing, claims that objectivity is actually maximized. Hesse-Biber, Leavy, and Yaiser (2004) summarized feminist objectivity as

> knowledge and truth that is partial, situated, subjective, power imbued, and relational. [It] combines the goal of conventional objectivity—to conduct research completely free of social influence and or personal beliefs—with the reality that no one can achieve this goal . . . and recognizes that objectivity can only operate within the limitations of the scientists' personal beliefs and experiences. (p. 13)

Feminist quantitative researchers are often assumed to be feminist empiricists who wholeheartedly embrace positivism. However, in truth, feminist quantitative researchers actually have many different viewpoints regarding how to best conduct scientific research as do feminist researchers who utilize other types of research methods. For example, although we (the authors) both conduct quantitative research, which stems from the positivist tradition, we also distinguish ourselves from this tradition in that we do not agree with positivism's philosophical underpinning that there is an objective reality "out there" that is truly accessible. Nor do we believe that scientific research can and should be completely impartial. As such, we acknowledge and concur with most feminist criticisms of positivism. At the same time, we also recognize the importance of conducting research in such a way to reduce bias (error) as much as possible, whether that bias emanates from a sexist or a feminist perspective (or any other ideology). In other words, we maintain that if we are to understand clearly how the social structure is maintained (which will allow us to identify the best ways to alter it for purposes of social justice), we must attempt to remove bias in our research. Thus, although we conduct our research within a more traditional paradigm, we do so using feminist objectivity, with the ultimate goal of making a real difference in women's lives.

Feminists have expressed additional concerns about quantitative survey research. For example, feminists have sometimes claimed that in using quantitative methods, researchers reduce people simply to numbers while ignoring the contextualized lives in which they live. This sometimes leads feminists to conclude that qualitative research methods are "better" and "more feminist" than quantitative research methods. In fact, the debate over qualitative and quantitative research methods has been one of the most vigorous in feminist studies and some scholars have argued that conducting feminist research may *necessitate* the use of qualitative methods (e.g., Condor, 1986; Landrine, Klonoff, & Brown-Collins, 1992; Marecek, Fine, & Kidder, 1997; Sherif, 1979; Smith, 1987). We believe this is an exclusionary approach to research, rather than an inclusive one, and severely limits the options that are available for investigation. We contend that both qualitative and quantitative methods are useful in feminist research and, in the next section, describe how researchers should choose a research method that most effectively answers their research questions rather than the method considered to be the "most feminist." To make that choice, it is important to know the major differences between quantitative and qualitative research methods.

What Are the Differences Between Qualitative and Quantitative Research?

This section discusses the various distinctions between qualitative and quantitative techniques used in survey research. Although the section describes important differences between them, it emphasizes that these two categories of research sometimes overlap, with quantitative research incorporating some qualitative components and vice versa. Thus, quantitative and qualitative methodologies are described generally;

but the reader should recognize that in specific instances of survey research, there may be exceptions to the distinctions between these two methodologies.

When a researcher collects quantitative data, characteristics and experiences of the research participants are put into numerical categories, usually predefined by the researcher, and then evaluated using statistical analyses. For example, if a researcher is interested in the race of the study participants, she or he might include only two categories, such as white and nonwhite. It is also common for researchers to include only two categories when assessing sexual orientation: heterosexual and LGBT (lesbian, gay, bisexual, transgendered). Researchers might also ask participants how strongly they disagree or agree with some statements such as "Women should be able to make decisions about their own body," "Women are better at parenting than men," or "I often feel anxious" on a scale, say, from 1 (*strongly disagree*) to 5 (*strongly agree*). In these examples, research participants would need to make a very general assessment of their attitudes or beliefs, and would not be able to include more nuanced information (such as when or with whom they feel most anxious). Thus, the categories are often narrowly defined with most researchers deciding beforehand how detailed the responses can be. This decision is not arbitrary, but is based on many practical factors, such as the respondent's education level and the need to limit the time it takes someone to complete the survey. With the use of predefined categories, research participants have little influence on what information is analyzed (Jayaratne & Stewart, 1991). Moreover, because the categories are defined beforehand, researchers must know enough about the phenomena to construct relevant, inclusive categories. It is important to note, however, that not all quantitative research proceeds in this way. Sometimes researchers collect data without confining them to predetermined categories (e.g., asking race as a free-response, fill-in-the-blank question), and they later transform these responses into quantitative categories to be used in statistical analyses (e.g., collapsing responses "white" and "Euro-American" into the same category).

In contrast to quantification, qualitative data (e.g., data from interviews that is in the form of words rather than numbers) are generally evaluated through the use of themes or categories that emerge *after* data collection (although this practice is not universal in all qualitative methods). This process can increase the likelihood that the researcher will take into account all of the details and nuances of the respondents' answers and allows the researcher to explore a number of different interpretations of them. Thus, because the themes or categories are not narrowly defined beforehand by the researcher, participants often have the freedom to respond to research questions in ways that make sense to them. As a result, these data typically include information that participants themselves think is important. Proponents of qualitative research methods argue that this aspect of qualitative research is extremely important; participants should be able to describe their experiences as they perceive them, not through the researcher's preconceived notions about what their worlds are like (Landrine et al., 1992; Marecek et al., 1997; Wallston & Grady, 1992). This does not mean that qualitative data are somehow more accurate, however. Indeed, because the number of participants involved in qualitative research tends to be much smaller than in quantitative research, results may be less representative of the group the researcher is interested in understanding. Qualitative research is also subject to the researcher's interpretation, as Gorelick (1996) points out:

> After all, it is I who asked the questions, I who read the transcript, I who selected the materials to be placed in the text. . . . It is when I am trying to be most faithful to their meaning . . . that I am most painfully aware that simply "giving voice" is not so simple after all. . . . It is fraught with interpretation. (p. 38)

Thus, both quantitative and qualitative data have disadvantages in terms of the potential for altering the intended meaning of an individual's responses.

What Are the Advantages of Quantitative Methods?

Even though feminists have raised concerns about quantitative survey research, this method can serve as an effective tool for supporting feminist goals and philosophies and can offer a number of advantages not found in qualitative work. First, quantitative survey research can provide a vehicle for feminists to introduce sexism, racism, classism, heterosexism, and other social justice issues into mainstream discussions (e.g., public policy, legislation). This is perhaps the most significant benefit of quantitative research methods. Because social science research has traditionally been built on the ideal of objectivity, many mainstream researchers and the general public may be uncomfortable with research methods they tend to perceive as less objective (such as qualitative research), especially if the research is perceived as stemming from a partisan or controversial issue; such research may be seen as biased toward a particular political agenda (even though all research has some agenda). Quantitative research may have more appeal for these groups of individuals and thus they may be more apt to listen to and consider valid research that is quantitative (Spalter-Roth & Hartmann, 1996). The importance of this benefit cannot be overemphasized—for real social change for women to occur we must be able to report our research findings in a way that will attract people's attention and convince them of the need for social change. Numbers and statistics talk, and they talk loudly and persuasively. Indeed, findings that have the potential to promote social change for women need to be so influential that they cannot be ignored by nonfeminists and the lay public. Quantitative survey research can help us do that.

Second, the brevity of statistics makes them easy to remember and comprehend, and thus easy to communicate to others (Reinharz, 1992). One of the most compelling examples of this took place in the 1960s when the media reported that women earned 59 cents to every dollar that men made. This was a simple statistic, but it worked to inform the public about gender inequality in the workplace and, in some respects, became a rallying cry for feminists (e.g., bumper stickers and buttons were frequently seen with nothing but the words "59 cents"). More recently, in 2011, thousands of Americans were involved in "Occupy Wall Street" demonstrations protesting social and economic inequality, high unemployment, and corporate and governmental corruption, among other issues. The protesters' slogan, "We are the 99%," highlighted the stark discrepancy in wealth between the affluent 1% and the rest of the population: the lower 99%. Thus, quantitative data can effectively communicate important feminist and social justice concerns to the public in a relatively simple, but powerful, way.

Finally, quantitative methods are helpful when determining the best course of action in implementing social change for women because such techniques help us to identify patterns of gender oppression and they reveal how oppression operates. For example, quantitative survey research can document the psychological, physical health, and economic consequences associated with domestic violence, pay inequity, eating disorders, lack of medical care, and so on in large groups of women. If the results of quantitative survey research show that thousands (or millions) of women are similarly negatively affected by such experiences, it is more likely to result in legislation or policy advanced on women's behalf. Additionally, if researchers have differing opinions or are unsure about which type of legislative action to support to address such negative consequences for women, quantitative methods can help determine which changes will be most effective. This is the case because quantitative methods allow for the testing of mathematical models (tests of significance) that estimate such effects in an unbiased fashion.

There are undeniable benefits to using survey research and quantitative methods to advocate for feminist social change. You might now be wondering how to actually do survey research. The remainder of this chapter explains how to go about conducting survey research on feminist issues. The next section will explain the overarching framework for doing such research, describe the major components and decisions involved in each stage, and highlight how being a feminist affects the process.

What Is the Process of Conducting Survey Research?

Before we begin, it is important for you to know that doing survey research generally involves the same components and general decisions whether the researcher comes from a feminist or nonfeminist perspective. In other words, feminist survey researchers and those who conduct mainstream survey research, for the most part, engage in similar research activities. What distinguishes feminist survey research from other survey research is that, in the former, (1) the initial research questions that are explored (i.e., the main questions the survey will seek to answer) focus on issues of interest to feminists, and (2) the interpretation (i.e., how the researchers make sense of the results) and application of the results are conducted in a way that attempts to advance feminist values. In line with Kelly (1978), this means that the feminist perspective is most applicable during two specific points in the research process: the development of research questions and the interpretation of findings. These two points occur at the beginning and end stages of the survey research process, respectively. This applicability of the feminist perspective can best be conceptualized as the "bookends" of the survey research process; it holds the core of the research together (i.e., the "books") and gives individual components of the research process shape, structure, and meaning.

The components of the survey research method that come after the development of research questions and before the interpretation of findings (i.e., the middle stage or "books") involve decisions about choosing specific survey research techniques. For example, it is at this stage that the researcher must make a choice about the type of survey to use, whom to interview, the design of the survey, how to collect the data, and how to analyze data. In general, survey researchers (feminist and nonfeminist alike) must grapple with decisions regarding these components *before* the survey research process actually begins. Thus, much of the work occurs even before the data are collected! We also want to emphasize that to ensure good-quality data, it is extremely important that the decisions regarding the components in the middle phase of the research process be based on general principles of survey research (which in many ways are also fully consistent with feminist principles, as you'll see). The middle stage of the survey research process, then, should be the least influenced by the feminist (or any other) perspective, because it is during this stage that the accepted standards of survey researchers should be followed. The various components of the typical survey research process are presented in Figure 10.1.

What Are Research Questions and Hypotheses?

The first steps in the typical research process (not just survey research) are to formulate research questions and develop hypotheses. *Research questions* are simply the questions the research will attempt to answer. For feminists, research questions come from an interest in improving the lives of women and achieving social justice more broadly. For example, a feminist researcher might ask: "What is the best way to make academic environments more supportive for lesbian students?" "How does pay inequity between men

Figure 10.1 Major Components of the Survey Research Process

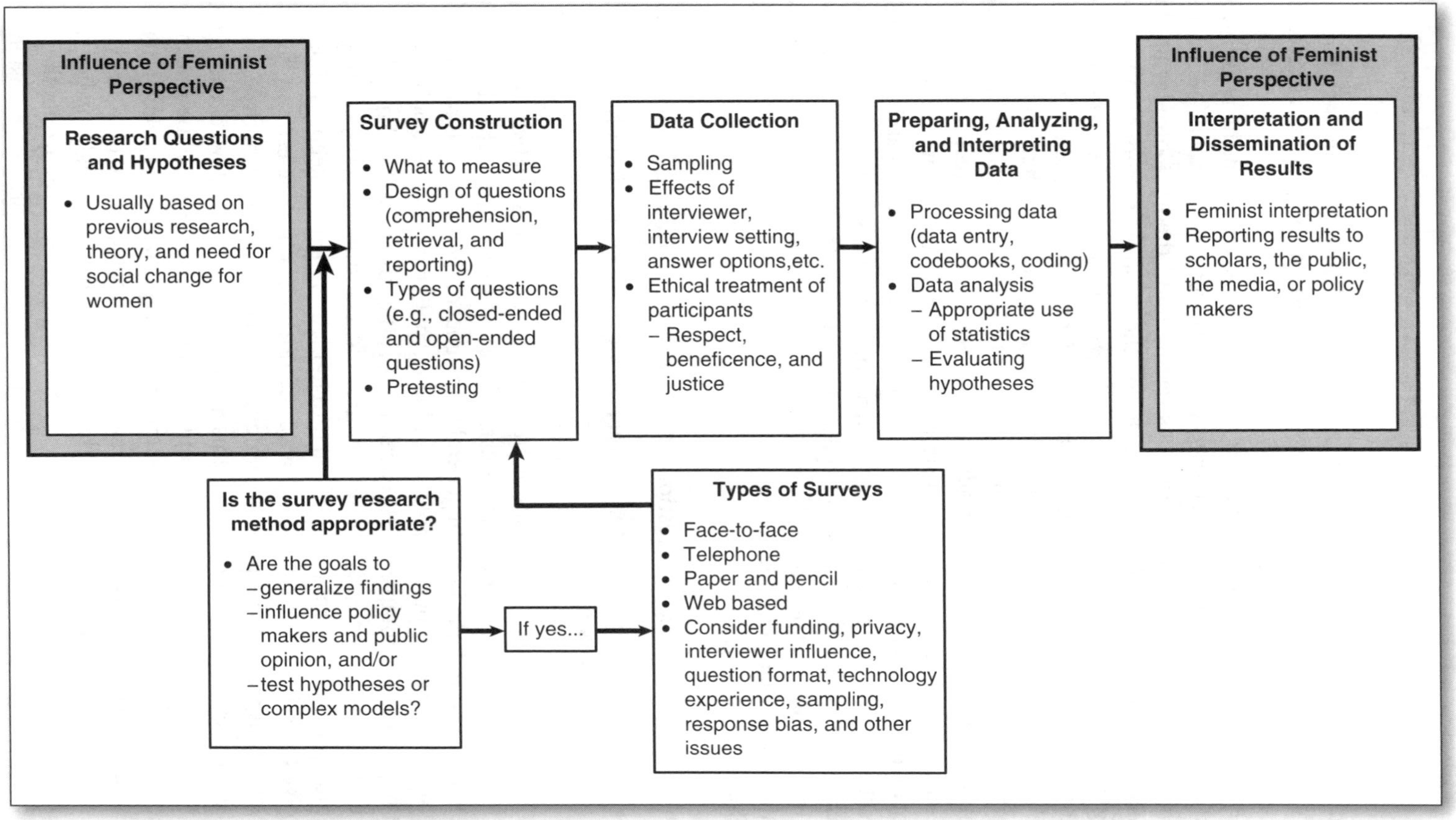

Note: From Miner, K. N., Jayarante, T., Pesonen, A., & Zurbrügg, L. (2011). Using survey research as a quantitative method for feminist social change. In S. N. Hesse-Biber (Ed.), *The handbook of feminist research: Theory and praxis* (2nd ed., pp. 237–261). Thousand Oaks, CA: Sage.

and women in the workplace affect children?" or "Why do some men batter women?" Of course, these are just a few examples of the multitude of questions a researcher might be interested in examining.

Hypotheses are the predictions that a researcher makes about the results of the study; that is, what they think the answer to their research question will be. Hypotheses are developed from an analysis of previous research and theory. Considering the research questions posed above, for example, based on the results of previous studies, a researcher might hypothesize that implementing policies denouncing the harassment of lesbian students leads to more supportive school environments for them, that pay inequity in the workplace affects children's scholastic achievement, or that some men are violent against women as a means of power and control. In some mainstream research, questions derive from an interest in advancing theory, without direct application to solving social problems. However, feminists are more likely to ask questions (such as those above) and develop hypotheses in a manner such that the research findings will have direct relevance to feminist social change. In this way, a feminist perspective directly affects the formulation of research questions as well as the way the hypotheses are articulated. The purpose of actually doing the research is to answer those research questions.

Questions that should be asked during the first phase of the survey research process include the following:

- What is my research question, and why is it important as a feminist issue?

- What is my hypothesis? Is it based on a careful evaluation of existing theory and empirical investigation?

Only after the research questions and hypotheses are formulated should one consider which specific research method to use. What factors influence the decision to employ the survey research method? In general, if the goal of the research is to apply the findings beyond the research participants, to influence policy makers and public opinion, or to test hypotheses or complex theoretical models, the survey method may be an appropriate choice. For example, Jayaratne, Thomas, and Trautmann (2003) employed the survey method to evaluate an intervention program designed to keep middle school girls involved in science. The specific goal of the research was to determine the effectiveness of various aspects of the program among minority and nonminority girls. The survey research method was chosen for this project because it allowed the researchers to (1) gather the opinions of a large number of girls, (2) generalize the findings to middle school girls, (3) influence policy makers on the importance of science interventions for girls, and (4) statistically test hypotheses about outcome differences between girls who participated in the intervention and those who did not. Although qualitative interviews were initially considered because they would have yielded more in-depth understanding of the girls' opinions of the program, the needs of the researchers, as listed above, were better addressed with the use of surveys than with other strategies. In particular, quantitative survey research could generate the necessary information to determine the most effective intervention programs for increasing both minority and nonminority girls' participation in science. In this way, quantitative methods served an important feminist goal.

How Is a Survey Constructed?

TYPES OF SURVEYS

Surveys are typically categorized by how they are administered; that is, how the data are collected. Traditional methods include face-to-face interviews (questions asked by an interviewer in person), telephone interviews (questions asked by an interviewer over the phone), and paper-and-pencil or mailed questionnaires (typically, when respondents fill in answers on paper and return the questionnaire to the researcher). Newer methods of survey administration employ computers in the data collection process, including Web surveys, which many survey researchers are now using to replace traditional paper-and-pencil questionnaires (Groves et al., 2009).

Each of these survey techniques has various benefits and drawbacks. Factors such as available funding, privacy issues, interaction between interviewer and respondent, question format, experience with technology, and response bias are all relevant aspects that should be taken into account. Many researchers employ multiple methods or combine methods to balance these factors. In some situations, the best type of survey will be determined by a single overriding factor, such as strict funding limitations. Below we briefly outline some of the major advantages and disadvantages of each type of survey.

Face-to-face interviews tend to be very costly, but they allow more direct involvement of the interviewer. This method is most appropriate for surveys that require extensive probing and clarification. However, when the topic of investigation is particularly sensitive, face-to-face interviews may yield data that are influenced by *social desirability*; that is, the presence of an interviewer may cause the respondent to reply with answers that put them in a positive light or that they believe the interviewer prefers (Paulhus, 1991). For example, a researcher interested in the sexual behavior of teen girls may find that girls are reluctant to admit the number of sexual partners they have had for fear that they will be judged negatively by the researcher for being sexually active. The possibility of social desirability is important to consider when conducting research on gender, race, or sexuality, which may involve sensitive and controversial matters. However, high-quality feminist research on very sensitive issues has been conducted using such interviewing techniques. Stewart and Dottolo's (2005) research provides a good example. In their work, diverse groups of students were interviewed regarding their experiences of sexism, racism, and heterosexism in college. In order to encourage students to respond honestly, the interview protocol included such measures as ensuring confidentiality to participants, taking steps to avoid participants being interviewed by someone they knew (as all interviewers were students as well), and, where possible, matching participants with interviewers of the same race.

Another example is the work of Beck and Britto (2006); they developed and implemented a sensitive-issues interview protocol and postinterview paper-and-pencil survey to better understand the experiences of family members of capital offenders, a group that has a history of trauma and negative feelings associated with the criminal justice system. Beck and Britto (2006) emphasized the importance of showing participants support and empathy during the interviews as well as maintaining a reciprocal relationship with participants by following up with them and informing them of the impact their experiences made on others. As a result, the researchers gained valuable information about respondents' experiences. In short, if done respectfully and ethically (that is, in a manner that does not exploit the participants or cause them harm or undue hardship through disclosure of sensitive information), face-to-face interviews can provide a wealth of information.

Telephone interviewing has been shown to produce results generally similar to those found with face-to-face interviewing methods (Groves & Kahn, 1979). Although telephone interviews are considerably less expensive and seem less intrusive, results can also be affected by respondent–interviewer interaction during the interview process. In recent years, the development of devices or services for screening telephone calls has resulted in lower rates of response for telephone surveys. Research shows that in general, these lower rates have not affected the types of individuals who answer telephone surveys (Pew Research Center, 2004). However, researchers should be aware of this issue and of how it might affect data collection.

Using computers to conduct surveys is quickly becoming the norm, with researchers collecting data via computers in many different situations. For example, researchers sometimes have participants complete surveys in a dedicated location (e.g., research laboratory, office), permitting researchers to closely observe data collection. This strategy allows researchers to ensure that participants complete the entire survey and answer survey questions in the correct order and under controlled conditions (e.g., without obvious distractions). Researchers are also available to answer any questions or address any concerns participants may have while completing the survey. More commonly, researchers administer surveys via the Web. With Web or online surveys, participants respond to the survey via the Internet using a computer in various settings (e.g., at home, in a coffee shop). Almost any type of research that can be done with a paper-and-pencil survey can be adapted for online use (Fraley, 2004).

There are many benefits to researchers' use of Web surveys. First, such surveys are typically much less expensive than either telephone or face-to-face surveys, since the cost is mainly for software or computer programming. Second, online surveys afford participants the ease of taking a survey when and where they prefer. Because of this, some samples can often be acquired more easily, such as single mothers who can take the survey when it is most convenient for them or sexual minorities who are concerned about anonymity (Harding & Peel, 2007). Third, Internet respondents tend to represent a greater range of people than is often possible with paper-and-pencil surveys. That said, individuals who have access to the Internet tend to be better educated than the average person, potentially excluding lower-income individuals, and Internet samples may be likely to attract a more restricted audience on certain demographic variables (Dunn, 2001; Reips, 2000). These differences are likely already diminishing as the Internet becomes more commonplace and, therefore, more representative of the population (Vaux & Briggs, 2006). A final benefit for researchers is that responses from Web surveys can often be downloaded directly from the data collection website into a database. This is not only convenient, but it also reduces human error associated with copying data from paper-and-pencil surveys or notes from phone conversations into a database (Groves et al., 2009).

Despite these benefits, there are also several potential disadvantages associated with Web surveys. For example, there is less influence over how they are administered because respondents often fill them out in unknown circumstances. This means that there is always the possibility that an individual other than the targeted respondent (e.g., a friend, family member) is answering the questions or influencing the responses. The presence of other people can also compromise respondents' privacy and level of honesty while completing the survey (Groves et al., 2009). As such, respondents should be instructed to complete the survey on their own without the help of others, informed that their honest answers are the most helpful to researchers, and told that their privacy will be protected. Additionally, there is no control over other distractions that might affect responses, such as a crying baby or having to rush through the survey if there is not enough time. Also, because it is easy for participants to decline to participate or to terminate the survey before they have answered all the questions, lower response rates can be a problem. Therefore, it is important that online surveys are kept brief and incentives (e.g., gift cards) for completing the survey are used when possible (Dillman, Smyth, & Christian, 2008). Obviously, the decision about which type of survey to employ is multifaceted, but it is significant in that it impacts all other aspects of the research and has major implications for the quality of the data collected.

SURVEY CONSTRUCTION

In the beginning stage of survey construction, it can be beneficial to conduct in-depth discussions (*focus groups*) with individuals who are representative of the population of interest. This can help the researcher understand the way people talk about the issues the survey will address and choose the appropriate vocabulary and phrasing of questions. This can also suggest issues, concerns, and ways of looking at the topic that the researcher has not considered (Fowler, 1984). Thus, these discussions can be a valuable tool to gain knowledge, especially about a subordinated group. For example, in their study of AIDS-related behaviors and attitudes, Quina and her colleagues (1999) conducted focus groups with two community samples of low-educated women who expressed their opinions on this topic. This allowed the population of interest (i.e., low-educated women) to participate in the research process and have a voice in the research; these aspects are central to feminist principles and values. Focus groups can be especially helpful when conducting cross-cultural survey research, as issues relevant in one cultural context may be irrelevant in another.

The process of survey construction concerns, first, decisions about what is important to *measure* (i.e., what questions will be asked) and then, *how* the questions will be asked (Fowler, 1984); these decisions should be based on what information is needed to evaluate the hypotheses. Determining what questions to include in a survey should be a fairly straightforward process. Suppose a researcher is interested in examining dating behavior in lesbian adolescents and her hypothesis is that girls who come from more accepting families will report more positive dating experiences compared with girls who come from less accepting families. The researcher should include questions about the girls' dating experiences and their family members' level of acceptance of their sexual orientation (plus any other issues of importance). However, the researcher must also decide *exactly* how those questions will be asked, a much more difficult task. How does the researcher go about doing this?

Designing questions. When established measures already exist in the relevant research literature it is preferable to use them, if they have been shown to be valid (Fowler, 1984). Valid measures are those that have been empirically evaluated and actually assess what they are supposed to access. For instance, a question about family income should make it clear to the participant that they report total income from all members of the family. If this is not made clear by the wording of the question, then the measure might actually be assessing the participant's income and it would not be a valid measure of family income. The issue of question validity is important to consider, whether using established measures or designing new ones.

If established measures are not available, or their exact format is not practical (e.g., they are too long, they have outdated wording), the researcher will need to design questions or adapt an existing measure suited to the population of interest. The major issues to address in designing questions are comprehension (the ease with which the respondent interprets and understands the question), retrieval (the degree to which the respondent can recall the information needed to answer the question), and reporting (the ability to formulate a response and put it in the format required by the questionnaire) (Groves et al., 2009). Clearly, if questions are not understood by the respondent, retrieval and reporting will also be inaccurate.

An excellent example of feminist research that adapted a survey for increased comprehension is Quina and colleagues' (1999) previously discussed work on AIDS behavior and attitudes. In the process of adapting their survey to their population of interest, they brought the readability level of the survey from the 12th-grade level (for which it was originally designed) to a 6th-grade level. They accomplished this with comments and feedback from groups of women who were similar to those that would be completing the survey (women with low literacy skills). This strategy allowed women in the population of interest to incorporate their voice into research that was ultimately about and for them—an important feminist concern in conducting research.

Research shows that respondents can and do sometimes have different interpretations of the same questions, especially when those questions are vague or contain technical terms (Groves et al., 2009; Schwarz, Groves, & Schuman, 1998). As a result, it is important to write questions so that all respondents are likely to interpret them similarly (Fowler, 1984). To minimize the likelihood of different interpretations, it is helpful to use everyday, nontechnical, unambiguous language when designing questions. Additionally, following the principles of feminist research, it is important to take into account differences between various social groups (e.g., different ethnicities, social classes, cultures) (Fowler, 1984) and to use nonoppressive (i.e., nonsexist, nonracist) language (Eichler, 1988). Landrine and her colleagues (1992) examined black and white women's interpretations of gender-related words and phrases (e.g., "I am feminine," "I am passive," "I am assertive") and found that different women associated very different meanings with the words, which influenced their responses to how well the words characterized themselves. For example, while black women defined the word "passive" as not saying what one really thinks, white women defined it as laid-back/easygoing, suggesting differences in question meaning and interpretation.

The issues surrounding designing survey questions become more complex when conducting cross-cultural research (Survey Research Center, 2010). One challenge is ensuring that the meaning of questions remains identical (or as similar as possible) across cultures. Because a common goal of cross-cultural research is the ability to compare people's experiences, attitudes, and beliefs in very different regions of the world, it is necessary that the questions assess the same thing; survey researchers call this *data equivalence*. This can be difficult when language translation is necessary (some words and sayings exist in some cultures but not others) or when cultural mores (e.g., participating in research, divulging private information to strangers, talking about oneself) are dissimilar. As such, some questions may need to be adapted or developed to better fit the new context, population, or language (Survey Research Center, 2010). For example, Gibbons, Hamby, and Dennis (1997) examined the meaningfulness and conceptual equivalence of questions assessing gender-role ideology for individuals from various cultures and found cultural differences among survey respondents. They recommended incorporating culturally specific questions into survey instruments and consulting with individuals in the culture when developing measures to be examined cross-culturally.

Types of questions. There are two different types of questions used in survey research: *closed-ended* questions and *open-ended* questions. Closed-ended questions present participants with a list of specific response options, while open-ended questions allow participants to provide their own answers. In survey research, open-ended questions are similar to fill-in-the-blank or short-answer questions, and closed questions are more like multiple-choice questions (Groves et al., 2009). For example, if researchers were interested in assessing feelings about gay men and lesbians serving in the military, they might ask respondents to choose between two alternatives in describing their views on this issue (e.g., "they should not be allowed to serve" or "they should be allowed to serve"). The researcher could also ask this as an open-ended question (such as "What are your views on gay men and lesbians in the military?"). Although closed-ended questions can limit richness and variety since they do not allow respondents to answer in their own words, they can also be beneficial because they are quicker and easier to answer, making individuals more likely to respond (Fowler, 1984).

One example that illustrates the use of both open- and closed-ended questions is Duncan's (2010) research on generational differences among women in their relationship to feminism. She had nearly 700 women from 31 states complete surveys while riding buses to a 1992 March on Washington for Women's Lives. Survey questions included open-ended questions assessing women's definitions of feminism (i.e., "How do you define feminism?") and close-ended questions assessing their feminist attitudes, gender consciousness, and political activism. She found that including both types of questions led to a more nuanced understanding of politically active women's definitions of feminism and self-labeling as feminists.

Pretesting. After the survey instrument is initially designed, it is helpful to pretest it; that is, to administer it to a small group of individuals (similar to those who will be included in the final sample) to determine if it requires further revision. In a pretest, the researcher typically asks individuals not only to respond to questions, but also to articulate their thoughts about the wording of questions themselves (e.g., if the questions were clear). This process can provide insights into interpretations of question meanings (Schwarz et al., 1998) and therefore may enhance the quality of the measure. Pretesting is particularly important in cross-cultural research to confirm that measures in a survey are equivalent across different cultural contexts (Survey Research Center, 2010).

Questions to be asked at this phase of the survey research process include:

- Which survey research method is best suited to answer my research question?

- What questions should I ask in my survey and how should I ask them?

HOW ARE RESPONDENTS SELECTED FOR A SURVEY?

After the type of survey has been chosen, the researcher must decide how she or he will select the people to participate in the survey. *Sampling* refers to the selection of people from a population to whom the survey will be administered (Stangor, 2004). A *population* is defined as the larger group of individuals the researcher wants to study. For example, a population might be all African American women aged more than 50 years in the United States, all incarcerated women in New Mexico, or all women who have given birth while attending Yale University. In contrast, a *sample* is the smaller subset of individuals that actually participates in the research. For example, following from the above, a sample might include African American women aged more than 50 years who live in the researcher's county and who answer an ad recruiting participants from the local newspaper, a small group of incarcerated women from each detention facility in New Mexico, or women who birthed a child while attending Yale University and whose current address was listed in the alumni directory. Researchers very often are interested in applying the findings based on the sample back to the larger group of interest—the population, a process called *generalizing*. This is particularly important because the findings of a study then have meaning for a larger group of individuals and not just those who participated in the study. Generalization is possible, however, only if the sample is *representative*—that is, approximately the same as the population in all-important respects (e.g., similarity by gender, age, ethnic background, education level). Here is where sampling comes in. How the research participants are selected determines if it is appropriate to generalize the research findings from a sample to a population.

The best way to ensure the generalizability of a sample is to select respondents from the population randomly, resulting in a *probability sample*. There are many different kinds of probability samples, but they all include some type of random selection of respondents (Czaja & Blair, 1996). For example, if a researcher was interested in the experiences of incarcerated women in New Mexico (the population), but could not conduct a survey using the entire population, she might instead obtain a probability sample of these women. One way to do this is to randomly select a small subset of women from each facility to participate in the survey. Because this technique would produce a probability sample, the researcher could generalize her findings to women in prison in that state as a whole. Because probability sampling has the distinct advantage of producing findings that can be confidently generalized to the population of interest and are thus persuasive, this sampling strategy is particularly useful if the goal of the research is to inform public policy regarding women's issues.

Despite this distinct advantage of probability sampling, sometimes a researcher is unable to use this method of selecting respondents. This may occur because the population is small (e.g., women of color who are CEOs of companies) or difficult to contact (e.g., sex workers). It can also be difficult to employ probability sampling simply because of lack of funding, since the methods to derive a probability sample can be costly. Because of these difficulties, many researchers use nonprobability samples in their research.

Nonprobability samples are those in which the sample is not representative of the population. In this case, the researcher can only apply the findings of the study to the particular group of individuals who participated, although she or he might speculate about how the findings apply to the broader population. The primary benefit of non-probability sampling is that it can be relatively inexpensive and can usually generate a large sample more quickly than probability sampling strategies (Biemer & Lyberg, 2003). To obtain a nonprobability sample, the researcher identifies the population of interest (e.g., all African American women aged more than 50 years), but then includes in the sample individuals based on some additional criteria (e.g., residing in Moscow, Idaho, because that is where the researcher lives). Thus, this type of sample would not represent the entire population of interest.

One common type of nonprobability sampling, and the one used in the example above, is *convenience sampling*. Convenience sampling consists of recruiting participants from places where they are easily accessible. For instance, much research in feminist social psychology uses samples of college students who attend the researcher's university (e.g., Smith & Frieze, 2003) and many researchers use samples of participants from their immediate geographical area. While convenience sampling can provide insights into the sampled population, researchers need to be cautious about generalizing their findings beyond the characteristics of their sample. For example, if a researcher conducts a study about the experiences of college women who have had a child while in school and selects women to participate in the research who attend the university where the researcher is a faculty member, she or he could undoubtedly learn valuable information about those students' experiences. However, it would be invalid for the researcher to generalize the findings to all women who have birthed a child in college. In fact, a researcher can only be confident about the generalization of findings if probability sampling is utilized. The choice of whether to use probability or nonprobability sampling, then, ultimately depends on the resources available to the researcher and importance of generalizing the results. Researchers should carefully choose the sampling method by weighing the advantages and disadvantages associated with various sampling techniques.

A variation of convenience sampling is *snowball sampling*, in which participants invite others in their social network to join the sample. The work of Konik and Stewart (2004) provides a good example of snowball sampling. This research was rooted in the feminist goal of illuminating the psychological strengths of sexual minorities, who have often been stigmatized by both mainstream psychology and the general public. This sampling method was utilized because minority group members (i.e., sexual minorities) can be difficult to identify in the larger population. By using this sampling technique, these researchers were able to increase the number of people included in their study because participants were encouraged to recruit their friends and acquaintances to also participate. Web surveys are particularly amenable to snowball sampling. For example, Syzmanski and Owens (2009), who were also interested in experiences of sexual minorities, utilized websites such as YahooGroups and Gayyellowpages.com to recruit participants who were sent e-mails that contained a link to their online survey. A single link to the survey website, which can be distributed among social networks, can facilitate the ease of access to the survey for interested participants. However, a major drawback of snowball sampling is that it can create systematic sources of sampling error because participants are likely to recruit others who share similar characteristics in addition to the characteristic of interest; for instance, sexual minorities may recruit other sexual minorities, but they may also recruit individuals of the same age, gender, or race, which would limit the ability to generalize the results to all sexual minorities.

The necessary question to be asked at this phase of the survey research process is:

- How should I select people to participate in my study?

How Do You Collect, Prepare, and Analyze Data From a Survey?

Data collection refers to the *process* of actually obtaining the information (i.e., attitudes, experiences, thoughts, feelings, etc.) that will help answer the research questions. It is important to understand how different factors related to data collection (e.g., the interviewer, the interview setting, the answer options, unrelated circumstances) may unintentionally influence the data, and ultimately affect the results of the study. Early survey research tended to ignore the effect of some of these elements, resulting in data that were often biased in favor of the researcher's viewpoint or the prevailing social discourse. This aspect of traditional survey research was a major focus of much feminist criticism, because it meant that a woman's viewpoint was sometimes distorted. Riessman (1987), for example, documented how both ethnicity and social class affect the interview process, and ultimately how the data are interpreted. In her research, a white, middle-class woman conducted interviews with both a middle-class white woman and a working-class Puerto Rican woman on the topic of marital separation and divorce. In describing their experiences, the narratives of the two women interviewees differed dramatically, representing their dissimilar backgrounds. From an evaluation of the transcripts of these interviews, Riessman found that the interviewer's comments (reflecting her own middle-class background) influenced the interview process. For example, during the interview the working-class woman offered a narrative of life events that was not chronologically ordered, but rather structured by theme. The interviewer had difficulty understanding this narrative due to her middle-class perspective that typically frames events temporally. By expressing confusion, the interviewer influenced the way the respondent told her story. Riessman showed how being from a different social class (despite being the same gender) can alter the meaning of the respondents' narrative, thus potentially increasing errors in the data. There are similar concerns when conducting cross-cultural research; it is critical that survey researchers are sensitive to cultural and social differences (e.g., in values, norms, laws, customs) that could influence participants' responses (Survey Research Center, 2010). Current survey techniques emphasize the value of minimizing such error effects during data collection (see Groves et al., 2009). Thus, both mainstream and feminist survey researchers promote awareness of how respondent attributes, interviewer attributes, and the setting in which the data are collected can affect the quality of the data.

ETHICAL TREATMENT OF PARTICIPANTS

Ethical principles are relevant to many aspects of the research process (e.g., truthful reporting of data, giving credit to those contributing to the research). Most discussions of research ethics, however, have tended to focus on how the participants in research are treated by the researcher. This emphasis is likely a result of serious abuses of research participants that have occurred in the not too distant past. Perhaps the most notorious, well-known examples are Milgram's (1974) obedience studies and the Tuskegee syphilis study (Jones, 1981). Milgram led participants to believe they were administering shocks to another person for purposes of "teaching," a procedure that greatly distressed many of the participants. In the Tuskegee experiment, the government studied the progress of syphilis in African American males without informing these men of their disease and without treating them, despite the existence of penicillin as an effective remedy. Although these are not examples of survey research, per se, an awareness of such exploitation resulted in a broad effort to prevent mistreatment of participants in all research on human participants.

Among the voices included in this movement to enact strict standards for the ethical treatment of research participants were feminist scholars. In fact, many initial feminist critiques of research targeted this particular aspect of the research process, since exploitation of research participants conflicted with basic humanistic values that are fundamental to feminists. These critiques often advocated decreasing or eliminating the power differential between the researcher and the researched (Du Bois, 1983; Fee, 1983). For example, Reinharz (1979) suggests that an equal relationship between the two would likely yield information that reflects the participant's reality rather than the researcher's reality. Feminists and social justice researchers more generally called for the need to redefine the process as "research with" or "research for" rather than "research on" (Stanley & Wise, 1983), thereby appreciating and valuing research participants, rather than considering them as "objects" of study. One result of the effort to ensure the ethical treatment of human subjects was the establishment of Institutional Review Boards (IRB) (now commonplace in most research organizations), which set mandatory standards for the conduct of research. These standards generally specify: (1) respect for persons (informed consent and protection from the risk of harm), (2) beneficence (maximizing benefits and minimizing risks to subjects), and (3) justice (fairness in the distribution of the benefits of research and equal treatment). While these guidelines cannot guarantee that all research involving humans will be ethical, they do go a long way in promoting these goals.

Because of the rise of Web surveys, it is important to consider the unique ethical implications of online research. In general, Internet research has some very tangible ethical benefits over paper-and-pencil surveys. For one, participation is fully voluntary—respondents can simply close their browser window at any time if they do not wish to participate in the survey; indeed, when administering online surveys, this option should be made explicit in the informed consent form. Respondents may also feel more comfortable completing a survey over the Internet because direct contact with the researcher is unnecessary. Additionally, researchers frequently do not collect personal identifying information from online survey participants, helping to bolster the confidentiality of the data (although this protocol tends to be subject to the unique IRB protocols of various universities; see Fraley, 2004). At the same time, however, maintaining respondents' privacy during Internet data collection offers unique challenges because respondents may fear that people other than the researchers may be able to access their responses in cyberspace, a legitimate concern when the survey covers sensitive or controversial issues (Israel & Hay, 2006). While Internet surveys generally do more to promote anonymity than to compromise it, it is advisable for researchers to statistically analyze responses of individuals who completed the survey as compared to individuals who dropped out before completing all measures, if possible. If differences are found between those who finished the survey and those who did not (for example, if men were more likely than women to complete the survey), we recommend that researchers evaluate the steps taken to assure participants of their anonymity to ensure that the steps were adequate. Additionally, some evidence exists that the initial interaction between the researcher and the participant heavily influences the participant's decision to respond or not (cf., Schwarz et al., 1998). Thus, when conducting online surveys, participants' first impressions of the survey (e.g., e-mail invitations, informed consent forms) should immediately assure participants that their privacy will be protected and that their responses are highly valued by the researcher.

Szymanski and Owens (2009), for example, employed several strategies for protecting confidentiality in their study of sexual minority women who completed an Internet survey on heterosexism and psychological distress. One strategy they offered was to have participants access the research survey via a hypertext link rather than e-mail to ensure their anonymity. Additionally, they used a separate raffle (i.e., a "lottery" for monetary rewards offered as an incentive for participation) database so there was no way to connect a woman's raffle submission with her survey. Furthermore, to ensure data integrity, they used a secure server protected with a firewall to prevent tampering with data and inadvertent access to confidential information of research participants. While these are excellent steps to take in order to ensure privacy, it is ultimately the researcher's task to evaluate the efficacy of such strategies, to be clear and open with participants about how their information is being protected, and to make a priority of managing data in an ethical manner.

PREPARING THE DATA FOR ANALYSIS

Once the data are collected, a series of procedures are frequently required before they can be analyzed. These involve data entry (entering the raw numeric data into computer files) and codebook construction (creating a guide that documents all questions and answer options). These procedures are routine and serve to minimize errors in the data while increasing the efficiency of the data analysis. One task that is more challenging during data preparation is the coding of open-ended questions. Because open-ended questions are often favored among feminist survey researchers, we briefly discuss coding this type of data below.

The goal when coding open-ended questions is to interpret and classify responses so that they can be assigned a numerical value in preparation for data analysis. Open-ended questions with relatively few answer options or with short, simple answers that are clearly interpreted (e.g., employment status) can be coded in a straightforward manner by assigning a number code to each category. For more complex open-ended answers, such as political opinions expressed in participants' own words, it is necessary to be more cautious about the coding process. On one hand, because the interpretive process can be highly subjective, applying a feminist perspective (or any other perspective) when coding can distort the *intended* meaning of the response. On the other hand, such interpretation may be seen as using a feminist lens through which to view the data and articulating a feminist viewpoint (which may otherwise be suppressed). This dialectical aspect of feminist survey research is an important issue in feminist scholarship, as the researcher attempts to maintain conventional objectivity, while at the same time giving voice to women or any subjugated group. Various methods are used by feminist survey researchers to balance both of these goals, such as having multiple people (called "raters") or those who are unaware of the study hypotheses code the responses, or training raters to take the literal meaning of responses rather than making assumptions. No method can guarantee, however, the accurate interpretation of the intended meaning, and therefore feminist survey researchers (as all researchers) need to be particularly careful when they code open-ended questions.

DATA ANALYSIS

Statistical analysis is a technique used to summarize and explain the information that participants report in a survey (e.g., a percentage, an average value). It is a necessary part of survey research because the information that is collected cannot be easily understood or reported in its raw form, as it typically represents the multiple diverse opinions or beliefs of many individuals. Without statistical analysis, determining the meaning of this information would be unwieldy and subject to a wide range of interpretations. Additionally, because statistics allow us to determine the probability or likelihood of certain outcomes based on the information we have gathered, they offer a way to judge various hypotheses (Jayaratne, 1983). For example, if two different but equally plausible strategies are proposed by feminists for persuading voters to support legislation upholding a woman's right to choose, a statistical analysis of data on voter attitudes can demonstrate which method is likely to be the most effective in accomplishing this goal.

Some feminists criticize the use of statistics and claim that the quantification of subjective personal experiences does not adequately convey the richness of women's lives (e.g., Marecek et al., 1997; Wallston & Grady, 1992) and therefore seems antithetical to feminist traditions. While we agree that the use of statistics, as summaries of information, does involve the loss of some in-depth meaning, we also argue that such use does not violate any feminist principles. Moreover, as mentioned previously, statistics can be used to effectively promote feminist goals. Consistent with our viewpoint, some feminist scholars point out that it is not statistics, per se, that are objectionable, but rather how they are used within the broader context of research that determines whether they violate feminist principles (e.g., Jayaratne & Stewart, 1991; Maynard, 1994; Peplau & Conrad, 1989). For example, statistics have been used to support sexist or racist theories (e.g., Buss, 1989; Herrnstein & Murray, 1994), but they have also documented the benefits of affirmative action and have been effective in shaping progressive social policies (e.g., Gurin, Dey, & Hurtado, 2002). We contend, therefore, that statistics can certainly be useful in advancing feminist goals.

Knowing which statistical techniques should be used to answer a specific research question is a significant issue, since using inappropriate statistics can not only distort the findings of a study but, in the worst-case scenario, can actually produce results that are opposite from those that accurately reflect the collected data. We therefore emphasize the importance of understanding statistics when doing (or evaluating) survey research.

Although we cannot explain these techniques here (large volumes have been written on the appropriate use of statistics), one illustration might help make our point. Suppose a feminist survey researcher wants to document and publicize the pervasiveness of poverty among women in a particular country where the majority of the women earn less than $1,000 a year but a small percentage earns more than $50,000 a year. If the researcher used a mean value (a statistic that is the average among all women) to describe women's incomes, it would appear that the average woman earns about $10,000 a year. This statistic might be correct, but misleading. An alternative statistic, the median (which represents the income level that divides the distribution of women's incomes in half, so that half the women are above that level and the other half below), might suggest that women's income is around $1,500. The mode (a statistic that represents the most common income level) could also be used and would suggest that most women earn less than $1,000. The median and mode would present a much clearer picture of women's earnings in this country than the mean. But an even better statistic is to simply give the percent distribution in various income categories. This example illustrates the value of having at least a basic knowledge of statistics, particularly in light of their frequent use in research that has feminist relevance.

EVALUATING THE HYPOTHESES

When statistical analyses are complete, researchers use the results to evaluate the hypotheses and determine if they are supported. Although this seems like a simple process, it rarely is straightforward. For example, it is not uncommon for statistical analyses to produce equivocal findings. Sometimes, one set of results contradicts other results. It might also be the case that the research findings appear to conflict with feminist ideals and interests. In this situation, it may be worthwhile to reevaluate the research to explore the possibility that such findings result from a deviation in accepted research protocol (e.g., misinterpretations of question wording). It may additionally be helpful to ask why a particular finding appears to conflict with feminist principles. This might lead to alternative understandings of the phenomena of interest that were previously not considered. Although it can seem frustrating to not have a clear-cut evaluation of a hypothesis, for many investigators studying complex phenomena without definitive answers is a valuable and rich part of the research process and often generates additional research questions that need to be explored.

Questions that must be asked at this phase of the survey research process include the following:

- How can I ensure that the people who participate in my study are treated ethically?
- What statistical technique would best test my research hypothesis?

How Are Survey Data Interpreted, Reported, and Disseminated?

In the final phase of survey research (the other "bookend"), the results are interpreted, reported, and disseminated. How a researcher interprets the overall results is the culmination of the investigation in the sense that it answers the research question put forth in the initial steps of the research process. We consider the feminist perspective to be especially applicable and necessary in this phase because it is at this point that the research is applied to the real world and can be used to improve women's lives. For feminists, then, the answer to the research question must also be given feminist meaning. That is, unlike the evaluation of the hypotheses using statistical information (a process that should follow accepted survey research practices), interpreting the overall research results should especially be subject to a feminist perspective.

To illustrate the significance of interpreting research findings, suppose a researcher conducted a study exploring differences between American women and men in mathematical performance, and the overall results of the study indicated that men performed significantly better than women. There are myriad interpretations of what that means. One could see this finding as indicating support for the "deficit hypothesis"; that is, it could indicate women are naturally inferior to men—an orientation seen frequently in earlier (and sometimes current) psychological and social research and much criticized by feminist scholars (Eichler, 1988; Jayaratne & Kaczala, 1983). Alternatively, one could interpret this difference as reflecting the effects of gender stereotypes on women's math performance (increasing performance anxiety), the educational system that puts limits on women's educational opportunities in math, or how parents encourage math achievement more in their sons than their daughters. These latter interpretations all point to the need for social change (improving the conditions that support and enhance women's math performance) rather than the acceptance of women's inferiority in this area. They also suggest the necessity for further research to pinpoint the most effective way to bring about that social change. These latter interpretations, then, would be much more likely to be put forth by a feminist than someone without an awareness of women's oppression or who does not support feminist goals. We should also note that in general, good research, rather than simply answering a question, often suggests new ideas and additional research questions. In sum, the feminist meanings we give our results are what mark the research endeavor as a significant feminist enterprise that works to improve women's lives.

The final step of the entire research process can be an exceptionally gratifying part of the research journey because it addresses the most fundamental goal of feminist research—to enact real-world social change for women. This step is the dissemination of findings, which refers to the reporting of results to scholars, the public, the media, or policy makers, by linking the results back to women's lives with a clear understanding of how they can benefit women. As such, the research acts as a catalyst for social change. As we have argued, feminist survey research can be particularly amenable to advocating for women, because it uses many mainstream research methods that are more acceptable to individuals who might distrust findings derived from alternative methods.

One excellent example of how survey research can be applied to real-world social change for women is the Supreme Court's rulings on affirmative action at the University of Michigan. In 2003, the American Psychological Association submitted an amicus curiae brief to the Supreme Court that supported the University of Michigan's policy of race- and gender-aware admissions in higher education in two court cases (*Gratz v. Bollinger*, 2003; *Grutter v. Bollinger*, 2003). This brief drew heavily on the work of feminist social psychologist Patricia Gurin's (as summarized in Gurin et al., 2002) survey research on the benefits of diversity in academia; her research demonstrated the benefits of a diverse academic environment for students. The Court's decision to uphold the principle of considering race and gender in college admissions is just one illustration of how survey data can be an effective way to change social policy, but it shows why feminist researchers should consider the use of survey methods as a valuable tool for social change.

Questions that must be asked during the final phase of the survey research process include:

- How do I interpret the results in such a way that they can be used to advance feminist goals?

- How should I disseminate my findings to put those goals into action?

CONCLUSION

Feminist research includes a multitude of methods, each of which can uniquely, or in combination, influence the social change effort to improve the lives of women. In this chapter, we focused on the survey research method and the important role it can play in this endeavor. We hope that this chapter provides budding feminist researchers with an understanding of why this method can be an effective tool in their work on behalf of women and other socially marginalized groups. We also hope that we have adequately stressed the importance of attending to those aspects of the survey research process that will yield information able to withstand critical scrutiny. Such research can most effectively advance feminist goals. Certainly, there are an immeasurable number of feminist issues that need investigating, many of which could be effectively addressed using survey research methods or other methods described in this volume. Each of us has the potential to contribute to the research effort to ultimately benefit women or other groups of individuals who suffer under the current social system. As members of the feminist community, we invite you to join us in this quest.

DISCUSSION QUESTIONS

1. How can conducting survey research help women? As the goal of feminist research is to produce knowledge that is for, rather than on, women, how can researchers ensure that this goal is achieved when they conduct surveys?

2. In what ways can objectivity benefit feminist goals? How might one respond to a nonfeminist accusation that the goal of social change makes feminist research inherently biased?

3. How can survey researchers ensure that women's unique experiences are conveyed to the public and policy makers via survey research?

WEB RESOURCES

- *ONTARIO INSTITUTE FOR STUDIES IN EDUCATION*

http://www.oise.utoronto.ca/rfr/pages/internet.html

This site was created by the Ontario Institute for Studies in Education at the University of Toronto. It provides excellent resources, such as lists of online feminist journals, newspapers, feminist and queer websites, and social research search tools.

- *SOCIAL PSYCHOLOGY NETWORK (SPN)*

http://www.socialpsychology.org/methods.htm#survey

This website has a wide array of information about social psychology and social psychology methods. The URL listed will take you to the specific section on survey methods. Studies can also be posted on this site.

- *THE WEB CENTER FOR SOCIAL RESEARCH METHODS*

http://www.socialresearchmethods.net/

Created by Cornell University, this website provides thorough, detailed information pertaining to research methods in the social sciences and covers a broad range of research designs and statistical tests.

AMERICAN ASSOCIATION FOR PUBLIC OPINION RESEARCH

http://www.aapor.org/Home.htm

As the website of a national association for public opinion and survey research professionals, this online resource provides a list of frequently asked questions about polls and conducting survey research.

NOTE

1. Although this chapter offers you a general introduction to survey research, we point out that if you are interested in using these methods or learning more about them, there are several excellent sources of additional information (e.g., Alreck & Settle, 1995; Czaja & Blair, 1996; Dillman, Smyth, & Christian, 2008; Groves, 1989; Groves et al., 2009; Tourangeau, Rips, & Rasinski, 2000).

REFERENCES

Alreck, P. L., & Settle, R. B. (1995). *The survey research handbook: Guidelines and strategies for conducting a survey*. Burr Ridge, IL: Irwin.

Beck, E., & Britto, S. (2006). Using feminist methods and restorative justice to interview capital offenders' family members. *Journal of Women and Social Work, 21*, 59–70.

Bianchi, S. M., Milkie, M. A., & Sayer, L. C. (2000). Is anyone doing the housework? Trends in the gender division of household labor. *Social Forces, 79*, 191–228.

Biemer, P. P., & Lyberg, L. E. (2003). *Introduction to survey quality*. Hoboken, NJ: Wiley.

Buss, D. M. (1989). Sex differences in human mate preferences: Evolutionary hypotheses tested in 37 cultures. *Behavioral and Brain Sciences, 12*, 1–49.

Condor, S. (1986). Sex role beliefs and "traditional" women: Feminist and intergroup perspectives. In S. Wilkinson (Ed.), *Feminist social psychology: Developing theory and practice* (pp. 97–118). Philadelphia, PA: Open University Press.

Converse, J. (1987). *Survey research in the United States*. Berkeley: University of California Press.

Croll, J. K., Neumark-Sztainer, D., & Story, M. (2002). Prevalence and risk and protective factors related to disordered eating behaviors among adolescents: Relationship to gender and ethnicity. *Journal of Adolescent Health, 31*, 166–175.

Czaja, R., & Blair, J. (1996). *Designing surveys: A guide to decisions and procedures*. Thousand Oaks, CA: Pine Forge Press.

Dillman, D. A., Smyth, J. D., & Christian, L. M. (2008). *Internet, mail, and mixed-mode surveys: The tailored design method*. New York, NY: Wiley.

Du Bois, B. (1983). Passionate scholarship: Notes on values, knowing and method in feminist social science. In G. Bowles & R. Duelli Klein (Eds.), *Theories of women's studies* (pp. 105–116). Boston, MA: Routledge & Kegan Paul.

Duncan, L. E. (2010). Women's relationship to feminism: Effects of generation and feminist self-labeling. *Psychology of Women Quarterly, 34,* 498–507.

Dunn, D. S. (2001). *Statistics and data analysis for the behavioral sciences.* New York, NY: McGraw-Hill.

Eichler, M. (1988). *Nonsexist research methods: A practical guide.* New York, NY: Routledge.

Fee, E. (1983). Women's nature and scientific objectivity. In M. Lowe & R. Hubbard (Eds.), *Woman's nature: Rationalizations of inequality* (pp. 9–27). New York, NY: Pergamon Press.

Fisher, B. S., Cullen, F. T., & Turner, M. G. (2000). *The sexual victimization of college women.* Washington, DC: National Institute of Justice, Bureau of Justice Statistics, Department of Justice.

Fowler, F. J. (1984). *Survey research methods.* Beverly Hills, CA: Sage.

Fraley, R. C. (2004). *How to conduct behavioral research over the Internet: A beginner's guide to HTML and CGI/Perl.* New York, NY: Guilford.

Gibbons, J. L., Hamby, B. A., & Dennis, W. D. (1997). Researching gender-role ideologies internationally and cross-culturally. *Psychology of Women Quarterly, 21,* 151–170.

Gorelick, S. (1996). Contradictions of feminist methodology. In H. Gottfried (Ed.), *Feminism and social change: Bridging theory and practice* (pp. 23–45). Urbana: University of Illinois Press.

Gratz v. Bollinger, 539 U.S. 244 (2003).

Groves, R. (1989). *Survey errors and survey costs.* New York, NY: Wiley.

Groves, R., Fowler, F. J., Couper, M. P., Lepkowski, J. M., Singer, E., & Tourangeau, R. (2009). *Survey methodology* (2nd ed.). New York, NY: Wiley.

Groves, R., & Kahn, R. (1979). *Surveys by telephone: A national comparison with personal interviews.* New York, NY: Academic Press.

Grutter v. Bollinger, 539 U.S. 306 (2003).

Gurin, P., Dey, E. L., & Hurtado, S. (2002). Diversity and higher education: Theory and impact on educational outcomes. *Harvard Educational Review, 72,* 330–366.

Haraway, D. (1988). Situated knowledges: The science question in feminism and the privilege of partial perspective. *Feminist Studies, 14,* 575–599.

Harding, R., & Peel, E. (2007). Heterosexism at work: Diversity training, discrimination law and the limits of liberal individualism. In V. Clarke & E. Peel (Eds.), *Out in psychology: Lesbian, gay, bisexual, trans and queer perspectives* (pp. 247–271). London, England: Wiley.

Harding, S. (1987). Introduction. Is there a feminist method? In S. Harding (Ed.), *Feminism and methodology* (pp. 1–14). Bloomington: Indiana University Press.

Harding, S. (1998). *Is science multicultural? Postcolonialisms, feminisms, and epistemologies.* Bloomington: Indiana University Press.

Harding, S. (2004). Rethinking standpoint epistemology: What is "strong objectivity"? In S. N. Hesse-Biber & M. L. Yaiser (Eds.), *Feminist perspectives on social research* (pp. 39–64). New York, NY: Oxford University Press.

Herrnstein, R. J., & Murray, C. (1994). *The bell curve: Intelligence and class structure in American life.* New York, NY: Simon and Schuster.

Hesse-Biber, S. N., Leavy, P., & Yaiser, M. L. (2004). Feminist approaches to research as a process: Reconceptualizing epistemology, methodology, and method. In S. N. Hesse-Biber & M. L. Yaiser (Eds.), *Feminist perspectives on social research* (pp. 3–26). New York, NY: Oxford University Press.

Hook, J. L. (2010). Gender inequality in the welfare state: Sex segregation in housework, 1965–2003. *American Journal of Sociology, 115,* 1480–1523.

Israel, M., & Hay, I. (2006). *Research ethics for social scientists.* Thousand Oaks, CA: Sage.

Jayaratne, T. E. (1983). The value of quantitative methodology for feminist research. In G. Bowles & R. Duelli Klein (Eds.), *Theories of women's studies* (pp. 140–161). Boston, MA: Routledge & Kegan Paul.

Jayaratne, T. E., & Kaczala, C. M. (1983). Social responsibility in sex difference research. *Journal of Educational Equity and Leadership, 3,* 305–316.

Jayaratne, T. E., & Stewart, A. J. (1991). Quantitative and qualitative methods in the social sciences: Current feminist issues and practical strategies. In M. M. Fonow & J. A. Cook (Eds.), *Beyond methodology: Feminist scholarship as lived research* (pp. 85–106). Bloomington: Indiana University Press.

Jayaratne, T. E., Thomas, N. G., & Trautmann, M. T. (2003). An intervention program to keep girls in the science pipeline: Outcome differences by ethnic status. *Journal of Research in Science Teaching, 40,* 393–414.

Jones, J. (1981). *Bad blood: The Tuskegee syphilis experiment.* New York, NY: Free Press.

Kelly, A. (1978). Feminism and research. *Women's Studies International Quarterly, 1,* 225–232.

Konik, J., & Stewart, A. J. (2004). Sexual identity development in the context of compulsory heterosexuality. *Journal of Personality, 72,* 815–844.

Landrine, H., Klonoff, E. A., & Brown-Collins, A. (1992). Cultural diversity and methodology in feminist psychology. *Psychology of Women Quarterly, 16,* 145–163.

Marecek, J., Fine, M., & Kidder, L. (1997). Working between worlds: Qualitative methods and social psychology. *Journal of Social Issues, 53,* 631–644.

Maynard, M. (1994). Methods, practice and epistemology: The debate about feminism and research. In M. Maynard & J. Purvis (Eds.), *Researching women's lives from a feminist perspective* (pp. 10–26). Bristol, PA: Taylor & Francis.

Milgram, S. (1974). *Obedience to authority.* New York, NY: Harper & Row.

National Committee on Pay Equity. (2013). *Wage gap statistically unchanged and still stagnant.* Retrieved from www.pay-equity.org/

Paulhus, D. L. (1991). Measurement and control of response bias. In J. P. Robinson, P. R. Shaver, & L. S. Wrightsman (Eds.), *Measures of personality and social psychological attitudes* (Vol. 1, pp. 17–59). San Diego, CA: Academic Press.

Peplau, L. A., & Conrad, E. (1989). Beyond nonsexist research: The perils of feminist methods in psychology. *Psychology on Women Quarterly, 13,* 379–400.

Pew Research Center. (2004). *Polls face growing resistance, but still representative survey experiment shows.* Retrieved from http://www.people-press.org/2004/04/20/polls-face-growing-resistance-but-still-representative/

Quina, K., Rose, J. S., Harlow, L. L., Morokoff, P. J., Deiter, P. J., Whitmire, L. E., . . . Schnoll, R. A. (1999). Focusing on participants: Feminist process model for survey modification. *Psychology of Women Quarterly, 23,* 459–493.

Reinharz, S. (1979). *On becoming a social scientist.* San Francisco, CA: Jossey-Bass.

Reinharz, S. (1992). *Feminist methods in social research.* New York, NY: Oxford University Press.

Reips, U. D. (2000). The Web experiment method: Advantages, disadvantages, and solutions. In M. H. Birnbaum (Ed.), *Psychological experiments on the Internet.* San Diego, CA: Academic Press.

Riessman, C. K. (1987). When gender is not enough: Women interviewing women. *Gender & Society, 1,* 172–207.

Schwarz, N., Groves, R. M., & Schuman, H. (1998). Survey methods. In D. T. Gilbert, S. T. Fiske, & G. Lindzey (Eds.), *The handbook of social psychology* (Vol. 1, pp. 143–179). New York, NY: McGraw-Hill.

Sherif, C. W. (1979). Bias in psychology. In J. Sherman & E. T. Back (Eds.), *The prism of sex: Essays in the sociology of knowledge* (pp. 93–133). Madison: University of Wisconsin Press.

Smith, C. A., & Frieze, I. H. (2003). Examining rape empathy from the perspective of the victim and the assailant. *Journal of Applied Social Psychology, 33,* 476–498.

Smith, D. E. (1987). *The everyday world as problematic: A sociology for women.* Boston, MA: Northeastern University Press.

Spalter-Roth, R., & Hartmann, H. (1996). Small happinesses: The feminist struggle to integrate social research and social activism. In H. Gottfried (Ed.), *Feminism and social change: Bridging theory and practice* (pp. 206–224). Urbana: University of Illinois Press.

Stangor, C. (2004). *Research methods for the behavioral sciences.* Boston, MA: Houghton Mifflin.

Stanley, L., & Wise, S. (1983). *Breaking out: Feminist consciousness and feminist research.* London, England: Routledge & Kegan Paul.

Stewart, A. J., & Dottolo, A. L. (2005). Socialization to the academy: Coping with competing social identities. In G. Downey, C. Dweck, J. Eccles, & C. Chatman (Eds.), *Social identity, coping and life tasks.* New York, NY: Russell Sage.

Survey Research Center. (2010). *Guidelines for best practice in cross-cultural surveys.* Ann Arbor, MI: Survey Research Center, Institute for Social Research, University of Michigan. Retrieved from http://www.ccsg.isr.umich.edu/

Szymanski D. M., & Owens, G. P. (2009). Group-level coping as a moderator between heterosexism and sexism and psychological distress in sexual minority women. *Psychology of Women Quarterly, 33,* 197–205.

Tourangeau, R., Rips, L., & Rasinski, K. (2000). *The psychology of survey response.* Cambridge, England: Cambridge University Press.

U.S. Census Bureau. (1989). *A century of population growth, from the first census of the United States to the twelfth, 1790–1900.* Baltimore, MD: Genealogical Publishing.

U.S. Census Bureau. (2011). *2010 census data.* Retrieved from http://2010.census.gov/2010census/

Vaux, A., & Briggs, C. S. (2006). Conducting mail and Internet surveys. In F. T. L. Leong & J. T. Austin (Eds.), *The psychology of research handbook: A guide for graduate students and research assistants* (pp. 186–209). Thousand Oaks, CA: Sage.

Wallston, B. S., & Grady, K. E. (1992). Integrating the feminist critique and the crisis in social psychology: Another look at research methods. In J. S. Bohan (Ed.), *Seldom seen, rarely heard: Women's place in psychology* (pp. 307–336). Boulder, CO: Westview Press.

Wood, K. C., Becker, J. A., & Thompson, J. K. (1996). Body image dissatisfaction in preadolescent children. *Journal of Applied Developmental Psychology, 17,* 85–100.

CHAPTER 11

The Feminist Practice of Program Evaluation

Donna M. Mertens and Nichole Stewart

Introduction

In an informal sense, we all engage in evaluation daily. For example, deciding what to eat for dinner or what clothes to wear to work or school requires such evaluation. We can even engage in more complex evaluation that involves gathering data to make a decision, such as reading *Consumer Reports* to decide what kind of car to buy, or researching acceptance rates when deciding where to apply to college. In contrast, the formal discipline of program evaluation is relatively young, having first emerged in the United States in the 1960s. Legislators used formal program evaluation to see if the federally funded initiatives from the War on Poverty were making a difference in the lives of poor people (Mertens & Wilson, 2012). Evaluation is an evolving field of study, and both its roots and current configuration give evaluation an enriching variety of perspectives. The presence of evaluation in real-world conditions further enhances its evolution as it is used to confront real-world challenges. Evaluators are called upon to evaluate a wide range of entities; they have developed a variety of strategies to depict what is being evaluated and how to conduct the evaluation. Now, evaluation is viewed as an essential part of the decision-making process for program development, revision, and demonstration of impact for many public and private agencies. The following definition of evaluation highlights its important components and provides grounding for comparing evaluation and research.

Evaluation is an applied inquiry process for collecting and synthesizing evidence that culminates in conclusions about the state of affairs, value, merit, worth, significance, or quality of a program, product, person, policy, proposal, or plan. Conclusions made in evaluation encompass both an empirical aspect (that something is the case) and a normative aspect (judgment about the value of something). This value feature distinguishes evaluation from other types of inquiry, such as basic science research, clinical epidemiology, investigative journalism, or public polling (Fournier, 2005, pp. 139–140). Several terms in the above definition require clarification and comment. The value feature of evaluation means that a judgment of the merit and worth of a project or program is made based on explicit values. Michael Patton (2008) provides insights into the meaning of two terms: merit and worth.

> *Merit* [emphasis added] refers to the intrinsic value of a program, for example, how effective it is in meeting the needs of those it is intended to help. *Worth* [emphasis added] refers to extrinsic value to those outside the program, for example, to the larger community or society. A welfare program that gets jobs for recipients has merit for those who move out of poverty and worth to society by reducing welfare costs. (p. 113)

Amy Wilson, a professor at Gallaudet University and coauthor of *Program Evaluation Theory and Practice* (Mertens & Wilson, 2012), gives us an illustration of the meaning of merit, worth, and evaluation as systematic. The following is her example from the evaluation of a program that trained women in the use of female condoms in order to reduce the spread of HIV/AIDS and other STDs.

Behind the Scenes With Amy Wilson

Defining Evaluation in Terms of Merit, Worth, and Systematic Inquiry

Recently, I was asked to evaluate a program for an HIV/AIDS Outreach Center. They were teaching women about the use of the female condom. The money came from the City Council, which was considering whether to continue funding for the Center's workshops or to move the money to support a faith-based coalition that proposed an abstinence-only model for prevention of HIV/AIDS. I chose to use a feminist evaluation lens, and so I decided to use the methods of surveys and interviews. This would allow the women in the program to express their feelings about the training they had received about use of the female condom. I knew there was a political context that was heating up because the Council was getting pressure from the faith-based coalition to reallocate the funds. They had to make up their minds before the next year's budget was approved.

When I was thinking about the *merit* of the program, I came up with a set of criteria that included ease of use, affordability, and women's willingness to actually use the condoms.

(Continued)

(Continued)

Evidence about the *worth* of the program would be in terms of the reduction of HIV/AIDS and other STDs. From the data I collected, I saw that many of the women found that the condoms were useful and reliable. However, they thought that the condoms cost too much, and they said they would use them only if they were free. In addition, some of the women said that they would not use the condom because it interfered with their pleasure during lovemaking. Even though data supports that the use of female condoms has worth in terms of the reduction of HIV/AIDS and other STDs, it is unlikely that this goal will be realized because of the lack of the intervention's *merit* for these women. I also used the evaluation data collection to explore what women want in terms of training for safer sex, with the faith-based initiative as one option. This allowed me to give information to the Council members about what they could consider if they chose to end the funding of the female condom program.

While evaluators may define merit and worth, the values upon which they are based should reflect real-world considerations—in Wilson's example, the circumstances and values of the women whom the intervention was intended to aid. This process of valuing distinguishes evaluators from other researchers, because evaluators "place value on data, their findings and . . . determine which outcomes to examine" (Alkin & Christie, 2004, p. 32).

OVERLAPPING AND DISTINCTIVE TERRITORIES IN EVALUATION AND RESEARCH

Mathison (2008) argues for the distinctive nature of evaluation, as compared to research. This argument is based on the importance of prioritizing stakeholder involvement in decisions throughout the inquiry process and using standards to make judgments about the utility, feasibility, and propriety of the inquiry. The standards that Mathison refers to are the *Program Evaluation Standards* (Yarbrough, Shulha, Hopson, & Caruthers, 2011), which direct evaluators to ensure that their work is useful to the stakeholders and is conducted in a rigorous, logistically feasible, and ethical manner. Stakeholders include anyone who has a stake in the program, including funders, administrators, service providers, and participants.

Evaluators emphasize the applications of their work in real-world contexts. In contrast, according to its traditional definition, research is a systematic process for the creation of knowledge. But not all research adheres to this strict definition. A notable exception is applied social research. In Mertens' coverage of the subject (2009), Trochim (2006) claims that evaluation is a form of social research that emphasizes the need to consider the organizational and political context in which the inquiry is conducted. Accordingly, evaluators must develop skills that may not be necessary in more traditional research studies, such as management, group processes, and political negotiating.

Based on the overlapping methods and goals in evaluation and applied social research, we acknowledge the significant overlap between evaluation and research, especially when research is conducted to determine "the need for, improvement of, or effects of programs or policies" (Mertens, 2009, p. 2). One of the key components of this overlapping territory addresses the need to be aware of the prevailing value systems that are used to make judgments in evaluation studies and the sources of such value systems. This linkage of values and issues of power in systematic inquiry for the purposes of contributing to social change leads us to the consideration of feminist evaluation.

FEMINIST EVALUATION

One caveat of feminist evaluation is that there are many different feminist traditions; this is exemplified in the other chapters of this text and is a common theme throughout feminist literature. Nevertheless, there are core characteristics that define feminism. All feminist traditions acknowledge that gender bias exists systemically, and it manifests in society in multiple ways. Feminists also acknowledge that the intersection of gender with race/ethnicity, disability, social class, sexuality, and other dimensions of diversity construct differential access to power and privilege.

Donna Podems (2010) explains: "[F]eminist evaluation is based on feminist research, which in turn is based on feminist theory" (p. 3). Essentially, it means that the evaluator brings a feminist lens to the evaluation process. This feminist lens is used when identifying what is to be evaluated, developing the evaluation questions, and collecting, analyzing, interpreting, and utilizing data. For further clarification, Podems adds that feminist evaluators recognize that women's experiences need to be accurately represented through a process that emphasizes participation, empowerment, and social justice. Thus, we offer the following definition of feminist evaluation:

> Feminist evaluation includes judgments of merit and worth, social science methods to determine effectiveness, achievement of program goals, and tools related to social justice for the oppressed, especially women. Its central focus is on gender inequities that lead to social injustice. It uses a collaborative, inclusive process and captures multiple perspectives to bring about social change. (Mertens, 2010a, p. 61)

Philosophical Framing for Feminist Evaluation: The Transformative Paradigm

Feminists recognize the intersections of various dimensions of diversity, in addition to gender, that are used as a basis for discrimination and oppression. Thus, a philosophical framing for feminist evaluation is needed. This framing must address the diversity found within targeted communities in evaluations, and determine how to appropriately include women who are oppressed because of a combination of factors including economic status, disability, deafness, and race. The transformative paradigm provides such a framework; it offers a broader umbrella that covers not only gender, but also the many other characteristics of women and oppressive societal structures. These characteristics and structures limit life opportunities for women and their families (Mertens, in press). The transformative paradigm prioritizes human rights and social justice and is commensurate with feminist theory and other theoretical frameworks that have evolved from oppressed communities.

The transformative paradigm is a metaphysical framework based on philosophical assumptions. Like feminist theory, these transformative assumptions focus on power differentials and diversities, including gender, that are associated with more or less access to privilege. It can be succinctly described as a framework that

> is applicable to people who experience discrimination and oppression on whatever basis, including (but not limited to) race/ethnicity, disability, immigrant status, political conflicts, sexual orientation, poverty, gender, age, or the multitude of other characteristics that are associated with less access to social justice. In addition, the transformative paradigm is applicable to the study of the power structures that perpetuate social inequities. Finally, indigenous peoples and scholars from marginalized communities have much to teach us about respect for culture and the generation of knowledge for social change. (Mertens, 2009, p. 4)

The components of the transformative paradigm reflect the structure of paradigms developed by Guba and Lincoln (2005). This structure holds that four major philosophical belief categories constitute a paradigm:

1. The axiological assumption refers to the nature of ethics.

2. The ontological assumption refers to the nature of reality.

3. The epistemological assumption refers to the nature of knowledge and the relationship between the knower and that which would be known.

4. The methodological assumption refers to the nature of systematic inquiry.

The transformative paradigm (Mertens, 2009, 2010a; Mertens & Wilson, 2012) is based on these four philosophical assumptions and provides a framework for exploring evaluation through a social justice lens. The transformative paradigm's philosophical assumptions are compatible with using a feminist lens to evaluate programs that address the needs of women in their full diversity. These include:

- *Axiological beliefs* reflect explicit goals to address issues of human rights, social justice, discrimination, oppression, and power differences.

- *Ontological beliefs* call for the recognition of power in the identification and privileging of various versions of reality. Such recognition must include a conscious effort to identify versions of reality that either support or hinder the pursuit of social justice.

- *Epistemological beliefs* address issues of cultural competence, respect, and establishment of appropriate relationships with the diverse stakeholders. These beliefs have a particular focus on voices that have traditionally been excluded.

- *Methodological beliefs* support the use of culturally appropriate methods that provide data viewed as credible by all stakeholders and that link that data to social action (Mertens, 2009).

TRANSFORMATIVE AXIOLOGICAL ASSUMPTION

The transformative axiological assumption includes the following concepts: respect for cultural norms, furtherance of social justice and human rights, reciprocity, and recognition of community strengths (Mertens, 2009). This assumption is in accord with the United Nations' declarations and resolutions that recognize the universality of human rights (1948), as well as the rights of racial minorities (1969), women (1979), children (1990a), migrant workers (1990b), people with disabilities (2006a), and indigenous peoples (2006b). Gender is one basis of discrimination, but there are many more. Relevant dimensions of diversity are contextually dependent; hence, there is a need to identify the dimensions that are relevant within each evaluation study. The transformative paradigm can be useful in raising questions about gender and other dimensions of diversity that are relevant within an evaluation context.

The transformative axiological assumption suggests that we need to have active engagement with members of the communities in which we work to have sufficient knowledge of their cultural norms and to know how to behave respectfully. As feminist evaluators, we can ask ourselves such questions as: How does positioning ourselves as working toward social justice and human rights change our work as evaluators? What would we do differently if we did not set these principles as primary definers of the ethics of what we do? What additional ethical issues arise when we use a feminist lens for our evaluation?

TRANSFORMATIVE ONTOLOGICAL ASSUMPTION

The transformative ontological assumption holds that multiple versions of reality arise from different social positions. The evaluator must investigate the sources of these different versions and highlight the consequences of privileging one version of reality over another. In evaluation contexts, this might be seen as persons in power who believe that women with disabilities are not capable of independent living. This might lead to keeping them at home rather than supporting them through transportation, education, or employment. This version of reality might be even stronger when women with disabilities are viewed either as an embarrassment to a family or as needing extra protection compared to men. However, women with disabilities may want to be and can be capable of being productive members of society. Thus, the investigation of issues of power and privilege can uncover versions of reality that have the greatest potential to ameliorate inequities based on gender.

TRANSFORMATIVE EPISTEMOLOGICAL ASSUMPTION

The transformative epistemological assumption recognizes the need for an interactive link between the evaluators and the full range of stakeholders. This is necessary to be responsive to the axiological and ontological assumptions that precede this assumption. Furthermore, evaluators must uncover the relevant dimensions of diversity, interact with all members of the stakeholder groups, and support appropriate interaction strategies. This assumption raises questions about the skills needed to interact appropriately in the evaluators' diverse cultural contexts. This epistemological assumption is particularly relevant to feminist evaluations because of the many cultural traditions that silence women. The American Evaluation Association's (AEA, 2011) statement on cultural competency provides guidance for this concept.

> Cultural competence is a stance taken toward culture. [It] is not a discrete status or simple mastery of particular knowledge and skills. A culturally competent evaluator is prepared to engage fully with communities to capture important cultural and contextual dimensions. (p. 1)

AEA's cultural competency statement includes this partial list of culturally significant factors: race/ethnicity, religion, social class, language, disability, sexual orientation, age, and gender. It also includes contextual dimensions, such as geographic region and socioeconomic circumstances. The statement identifies essential practices related to cultural competence, including awareness of the complexity of cultural identity, recognition of power dynamics, and recognition and elimination of bias in language. These practices and the transformative epistemological assumption both directly address the need to examine competencies for working within culturally complex communities in respectful ways.

TRANSFORMATIVE METHODOLOGICAL ASSUMPTION

The transformative methodological assumption suggests the need for an interactive link with communities as a starting point for methodological decision making and actions. The transformative paradigm's methodological assumption requires a cyclical approach to evaluation that begins with clarification of values and the involvement of communities, and continues to involve members of the communities in each stage of the evaluation. The initial methodological stage includes qualitative data collection that informs decisions about appropriate next steps. The information gained from this stage helps the evaluator decide whether to use quantitative, qualitative, or mixed methods. However, it is significant that the chosen methods must be rooted in culturally appropriate practices. Members of relevant communities examine the results of each cycle of data collection and use this information to determine the next steps of the data collection process. Such an approach allows evaluators to go beyond answering, "Are we doing the right things?" by allowing for responsive changes. This is especially important in the case of evaluations that use versions of reality to frame the "problem" or the intervention that do not provide fruitful avenues for advancing social justice and human rights.

These philosophical assumptions of the transformative paradigm provide a framework for feminist evaluation, as they are grounded in pursuing social justice, acknowledging the diversity of attributes and opinions, and facilitating culturally competent methods and uses for evaluation.

Principles of Feminist Evaluation

Principles of feminist evaluation were developed through a writing project that resulted in the publication of a special issue of *New Directions for Evaluation* titled "Feminist Evaluation: Explorations and Experiences" (Seigart & Brisolara, 2002). See, particularly, the principles set forth in the article titled "Exploring Feminist Evaluation: The Ground

From Which We Rise" by Sielbeck-Bowen, Brisolara, Seigart, Tischler, and Whitmore (2002). Brisolara (in press) updated these principles by discussing developments in thinking and adding questions for feminist evaluators to consider. (These questions are discussed later in this chapter.) Jennifer Brayton's (2011) depiction of feminist research also serves as an introduction to feminist evaluation principles.

> Overall, feminist research is uniquely feminist because it is feminist beliefs and concerns that act as the guiding framework to the research process. Methodologically, feminist research differs from traditional research for three reasons. It actively seeks to remove the power imbalance between research and subject; it is politically motivated and has a major role in changing social inequality; and it begins with the standpoints and experiences of women. (para. 1, section titled "Defining Feminist Research")

As you read the feminist principles below, think about how they reflect the philosophical assumptions of the transformative paradigm.

- Principle 1: Feminist evaluation has a central focus on the gender inequities that lead to social injustice (Brisolara, in press). According to Bowen (2011), feminist evaluators need to raise awareness related to the unique needs of women, point out disparities, and recommend changes in implementation strategies in the programs that they evaluate. If inequities are not made visible, it is unlikely that they will be addressed.

- Principle 2: Evaluation methods are social constructs, and many of their current forms reflect a dominant male/patriarchal ideology (Brisolara, in press). Bowen (2011) notes that some evaluation methods place greater value on concepts that may not align with feminist principles, such as objectivity, rigor, and the values of funding agencies. These evaluation methods reflect what such people were taught about evaluation without awareness of the damage that can be done by ignoring inequities based on gender. The feminist evaluator has a responsibility to bring to light the value of feminist principles in conducting evaluations in which gender-based inequities need to be made visible.

- Principle 3: Discrimination based on gender is systemic and structural (Brisolara, in press). Bowen (2011) asserts that we have a responsibility to clearly frame our own values, seek to understand the values of program stakeholders, and establish ways to communicate shared and divergent values in the process. This process can potentially help identify structural inequality that exists in the fabric of many organizations, institutions, governments, or social networks where embedded bias provides advantages for some members and disadvantages for others.

- Principle 4: Evaluation is a political activity; the contexts of evaluation are politicized, and the personal experiences, perspectives, and characteristics of evaluators lead to a particular political stance (Brisolara, in press). As was noted when discussing the definition of evaluation, evaluations occur in political contexts. Politicized contexts are imbued with asymmetrical power relations that need to be addressed in feminist evaluations.

- Principle 5: Knowledge is a powerful resource that serves an explicit or implicit purpose. Feminists hold that knowledge should be a resource for those who create, hold, and share it for informing social action to ameliorate inequities on the basis of gender (Brisolara, in press). The evaluation process can lead to significant negative or positive effects on the people involved in the evaluation. Power issues arise in terms of who controls the gathering and dissemination of knowledge and how that knowledge is used. Feminist evaluators have an ethical responsibility to use this knowledge for action and advocacy.

- Principle 6: There are multiple ways of knowing, and some of those ways are privileged over others in traditional evaluation approaches. Feminist evaluators value ways of knowing that emanate from personal experiences and feelings, in addition to those ways associated with quantitative data collection (Brisolara, in press).

- Principle 7: Knowledge and values are culturally, socially, and temporally contingent (Brisolara, in press). Thus, knowledge is filtered through the knower. Bowen (2011) notes that feminist evaluators seek to understand the perspectives of women with specific reference to their histories, daily lives, and their current positions in society. Evaluators also need to be critically self-reflexive. They must examine their own values in order to guide conversations across stakeholders to facilitate needed social changes.

Linda Thurston, a professor at the University of Kansas with an avid interest in the application of feminist principles to her work, provides us with this commentary that illustrates how she integrates feminist principles in her evaluation studies.

Behind the Scenes With Linda Thurston

Commentary on Feminist Principles of Evaluation

Workforce skill development programs for low-income women. Interventions for students with disabilities in urban preschool settings. University-level leadership studies programs. Training for child care workers. Workshops and summer camps to interest girls in science. Water quality management practices in the rural Midwest. Multilevel programs for students

(Continued)

(Continued)

with disabilities in postsecondary science and engineering education. K–12 STEM (science, technology, engineering, and mathematics) teacher professional development. Programs to advance women in postsecondary careers in math, science, and engineering.

These are all programs that I have helped evaluate; and they all have been evaluated, to some extent, using a feminist lens and feminist evaluation principles. Go back over the list in the first paragraph. You might think, "Okay, I can see using feminist evaluation principles for programs that relate specifically to women and girls." Or maybe you can see the application in settings that are clearly related to social inequities, such as urban settings. Or maybe it is also clear how a feminist lens is useful in evaluations that involve discrimination or social or structural inequities, such as the lack of representation of individuals with disabilities, women, and minorities in the STEM workforce. However, in my evaluation work, I go beyond the consideration of those obvious inequities. Social inequities, especially gender inequities, are part of the fabric of most societies, whether they are obvious or not. So university programs, interventions involving farmers and ranchers, and child care training programs all relate to that flaw in the fabric of our world. In addition, the focus of gender inequities is only one of the critical principles of feminist evaluation; I look at practically everything through my feminist lens.

Feminist principles are at the forefront when I work with others to develop evaluation questions, make decisions about appropriate methodologies for collecting and analyzing data, make judgments based on data, and even when reporting findings. Let me describe how this approach worked in the evaluation of one of these very diverse programs. You just read about seven specific principles of feminist evaluation. In my evaluation practice, I think of the principles of feminist evaluation that relate to my work as dealing with the focus of the evaluation; the methods of evaluation (including honoring and including multiple ways of knowing); attention to values (of the evaluator and the stakeholders); consideration of the political context of the evaluation and of the program being evaluated; the use of evaluation findings; and recognizing obvious or hidden biases, inequities, and privileges.

One of the overarching practices in operation for all of these evaluations is the inclusion of all stakeholders in several ways: in conversations preliminary to the planning of the evaluation, in forming the methodology, and in receiving and using the findings. This practice relates to many of the feminist evaluation principles. Considering the diverse needs, values, and stakes for all stakeholders helps us as evaluators to understand the political context of the evaluation. This consideration also assures that we are open to and respectful of the perspectives and experiences of everyone who is part of the program being evaluated. We do not base our evaluation plan, implementation, and reporting on the views of only the funder or the person/group in the power position. Many, many more people have a stake in the program being evaluated and in the results and the use of the findings.

Let me use one of my program evaluations as an example: the workforce development program for low-income women. In discussions about evaluation questions—What do we want to know about the program?—we needed to include *all* stakeholders: employers, social service staff, adult education personnel, and government program funders. But it also included women who took part or would take part in the training programs and their families. We knew they would not have the same questions about the program as other stakeholders. The funder had an entirely different perspective, history, and set of values and beliefs about program outcomes than the employer or the educator. Yet, we needed and valued the perspectives and opinions of them all.

There were some very obvious power differentials among the stakeholders, and this is one of the reasons that we did not meet with all of them together, as we sometimes do. We learned from experience that we could not bring program participants to the discussion with other stakeholders (at the beginning of the evaluation), as doing so led only to silenced voices. Yet, our feminist value of believing in the strengths of all women, no matter what their circumstances, guaranteed that the voices of the program participants and other stakeholders were heard equally. For the workforce development program, we asked all stakeholders what they wanted to know about the program and its impact on the participants (or themselves, in the case of the women in the program). We listened to and even corrected their language (e.g., "those women" became "our trainees") in our interviews and the wording of our questionnaires. Honoring and including all stakeholder voices, including the participants of programs or interventions, is basic to feminist evaluation.

Because of the varied educational experience and the power differentials between the participants and the evaluators, we chose methods that allowed us to collect data about their thoughts and experiences that were not based on educational level or language sophistication. Our data collection methods included interviews (women only, as interviewers), stories, art, and pictures. We used not only methods that collected data about specific workforce skills that developed in the program (for funders', employers', and educators' impact questions), but also other methods (such as those mentioned earlier) to learn about the women's experiences before, during, and after participation in the program. In these ways, we listened to all voices and used methods that were appropriate to the skills and strengths of individual stakeholders.

I believe that evaluation is about learning; the evaluator learns what questions to ask, what individuals to talk with, and what types of data collection to use in order to learn about all perspectives and experiences. Then the evaluator presents the findings in a usable form (which may differ from stakeholder to stakeholder) so that all stakeholders can learn about

(Continued)

(Continued)

their programs and then make appropriate changes in programming, policy, funding, social inequities, and so forth. We learned from the women about their concerns about working when their significant other was unemployed; we learned about their joy in showing their children they could work, in learning new skills, and in having homework time for mother and children together. The findings from evaluation of skills helped assure continued program funding and gave employers qualified, skilled workers. The findings from interviews gave the educators information about motivations for program participation and suggestions for issues to discuss with the program participants. Findings and the use of narratives from the program participants were used to advocate for alternative types of programming that would help women meet their goals for economic independence and make changes in public policy related to low-income families.

As an evaluator, I continually reflect on my own practice. Thus, I too learn from every evaluation in which I am involved. I continuously examine my own values and how they relate to the work I do. I was a feminist several decades before I was an evaluator, so the feminist perspective I bring to evaluation sometimes feels like the ocean might feel to a fish—it is so much a part of my life that I do not always recognize that it is separate. But, maybe it isn't.

Designing Transformative Feminist Evaluations

The design of transformative feminist evaluations involves conceptualizing each study in ways that align with the transformative paradigm's assumptions and that reflect the principles of feminist evaluation. To determine the design of the evaluation, the feminist evaluator would consider a number of questions that are associated with the transformative paradigm's assumptions. Examples of these questions are presented here for each of the assumptions.

TRANSFORMATIVE FEMINIST AXIOLOGICAL QUESTIONS:

- What are the ethical principles that guide my work?
- How do the ethical principles reflect issues of social justice, culture, and power differences?
- How are issues of gender addressed in terms of power differences?

- How can I design an evaluation that contributes to social justice and human rights?
- How can the evaluation design advance the rights of women as identified by the United Nations Convention on the Elimination of All Forms of Discrimination Against Women (CEDAW; United Nations, 1979) and the Millennium Development Goals (United Nations, 2000)?

TRANSFORMATIVE FEMINIST ONTOLOGICAL QUESTIONS:

- To what extent will the evaluation be designed to reveal different versions of reality?
- How will the experiences of men and women be made visible in terms of their different versions of reality?
- How will I design the evaluation in order to determine those versions of reality that have the potential to either support or impede progress toward social justice and human rights?
- How will the design allow me to identify the consequences of privileging one version of reality over another? How will I address the cultural norms and beliefs that have the potential to silence women?
- How can this evaluation contribute to the change in understandings of what is real and provide potential to address discrimination and oppression of women?

TRANSFORMATIVE FEMINIST EPISTEMOLOGICAL QUESTIONS

- How can I incorporate the development of the types of relationships needed to accomplish this work successfully? How can I take the positioning of women in a cultural context into account in designing the evaluation?
- How can I explicitly address issues of power differentials and ensure that the voices of the least powerful are accurately expressed and acted upon? What strategies can I use to enhance the opportunity for women's voices to be heard in contexts in which they are traditionally silenced? (Mertens, 2010b)

TRANSFORMATIVE FEMINIST METHODOLOGICAL QUESTIONS

- How can I use a cyclical design to make use of interim findings throughout the study?
- How can I incorporate the voices of women from diverse groups in establishing the focus and data collection plans for the evaluation?

- How can I engage with the full range of stakeholders to gather quantitative and/or qualitative data that enhance their understandings of the community?
- Will the design allow for the disaggregation of data by gender and other relevant dimensions of diversity?
- How can I be responsive in my data collection methods to the specific needs of the different stakeholder groups? How will the needs of diverse groups of women be addressed in order to give them access to full participation?
- How can I design the methods to enhance use of the evaluation findings to support the pursuit of social justice and human rights? How can the methodological lens contribute to identifying inequities on the basis of gender and other relevant dimensions of diversity? (Mertens, 2010b)

In the following section, we illustrate the design of feminist evaluations by using several examples from diverse sectors and regions of the world. These examples illustrate how feminist theory influences the evaluator's decisions about ways to understand the context in which the study was conducted, the evaluation questions, the nature of the design, and the data collection strategies that were used.

Establishing the Context Using a Feminist Lens

Researchers who reflect upon the methodological questions and feminist principles presented in the previous sections realize the importance of understanding the cultural context and the dimensions of diversity associated with gender that are relevant within that context. For example, Bowen (2011) conducted an evaluation of a rural mental health and substance abuse treatment program in Appalachia. She was aware of potential inequities based on gender associated with that region. The women came from lower socioeconomic levels. Many had traditional ideas about the woman's role as the caregiver for husbands, boyfriends, and children; as the housekeeper; and as another source of income. In this context, the man was viewed as the head of the household; the women generally married young and believed that they should stay married no matter what. The women in the program had co-occurring mental health and substance abuse problems. Research suggested that the root of these were unhealthy relationships that led to experiencing trauma through physical, sexual, and emotional abuse; deep poverty; and persistent racism. These women faced strong stigmas attached to accessing services; hence, they had successfully hidden or denied their problems until they became involved with the criminal justice system. Then, participation in the program became mandatory, under threat of losing custody of their children. Bowen's work illustrates the need to focus on gender inequities and to address the systemic nature of discrimination within this cultural context.

The second and third examples of using a feminist lens to identify important contextual variables are found in the work of Podems (2010) in Namibia and Magar (2012) in India, both of whom evaluated programs aimed at sex workers. A Namibian nonprofit organization (NPO) that serves to improve sex workers' rights and decriminalize adult sex work in Namibia asked Podems to conduct an evaluation. The evaluation focused on the NPO's intervention designed to influence policy makers to decriminalize sex work and protect sex workers in Namibia. Laws in the country that criminalized sex work had not changed after the NPO's intervention; and the political, cultural, and social environment made such a change doubtful. Hence, she needed to take into account existing legislation as part of the context for this evaluation, as well as the social dynamics around poverty that supported women's involvement in this trade. Magar (2012) also had to address the poverty, vulnerability, police violence, and criminalization of sex workers in India. She reviewed a program in which peer educators were doing both HIV prevention and antitrafficking. In these communities, sex workers have developed community-based groups (CBGs) that work to curb violence, stigma, and poverty to prevent HIV. In addition, some of the CBGs have begun antitrafficking initiatives to reduce underage sex work. She engaged with the feminist principles that acknowledge the larger political context as being critical to understanding the phenomenon under study. In addition, she recognized the importance of the cultural and social factors that influence a researcher's ability to support needed social change in order to protect the rights of women.

Even though two of the programs in Magar's study were run by feminists, conflicts arose in regard to the antitrafficking initiatives that used raid-and-rescue models to remove underage girls and women from brothels and return them to their homes. These conflicts arose because of the program administrators' different interpretations of the application of feminist principles. There are anti–sex work feminists and pro–sex work feminists. The anti–sex work feminists view sex workers as victims who are being exploited. The pro–sex work feminists acknowledge that females who are in sex work may want to remain in sex work. Magar's work illustrates the application of transformative feminist principles in her approach, in that she worked with communities with differing viewpoints about the rights of women to reveal their social positioning and to value the various groups' constructions of reality.

EVALUATION QUESTIONS USING A FEMINIST LENS

Feminists recognize that evaluation questions can be asked in ways that make the subjugated knowledge more likely to be either visible or invisible. If the questions do not focus on inequities on the basis of gender, it is quite possible that knowledge will not emanate from the evaluation that will address those inequities. Bowen (2011) found herself in the awkward position of having the evaluation questions formulated before a feminist perspective was brought to the evaluation design. Thus, the questions focused mainly on the impact and outcomes of the program. When a feminist lens was introduced in the second year of the program, questions were identified that related to the low enrollment of women in the part of the program that combined treatment for trauma and substance abuse. (The women were generally enrolled only in the substance abuse part of the program.) The combination program taught skills to prevent substance abuse and to control post-traumatic stress disorder (PTSD) symptoms so the women could address both their trauma and their substance abuse issues. Bowen based the expansion of the evaluation questions on her adherence to feminist principles that focus on structural inequities in terms of the perceived view of the role of women and their ability to access appropriate services.

In Podems's (2010) evaluation, the NPO and its donor provided the following evaluation question: "In what ways, if any, does the NPO's intervention impact sex workers and related legislation?" (p. 12). The NPO believed that this question could be answered by interviewing local policy makers, sex workers and their "bosses," university law professors, the local chief of police, other NPOs working in human rights, and national legislators. Using a feminist lens that focused on diversity in the sex worker community, Podems suggested that they expand the list to include police officers working in the most heavily trafficked areas of sex work and brothels not currently engaged with the NPO. She also wanted to expand the evaluation to ask about the experiences of male sex workers and transvestites. She negotiated adding an evaluation question about access to resources for these subgroups of sex workers, based on her recognition of the heterogeneity of the sex worker community and the need to be inclusive of those who are in more marginalized positions.

The questions used in Magar's (2012) feminist evaluation included:

- In what ways can sex workers be given critical voice in defining a proper response from the state that ensures their protection and agency?

- What are the unintended consequences of raid-and-rescue responses to trafficking?

These questions demonstrate the way a feminist lens is used to raise questions that have relevance to power differences and appropriate representation of marginalized women in evaluation studies.

EVALUATION DESIGNS AND DATA COLLECTION STRATEGIES USING A FEMINIST LENS

The transformative feminist methodological assumption leads evaluators to design their evaluations and data collection strategies in order to capture the complexity of the diverse experiences of women in their full cultural context. In Bowen's (2011) evaluation, she did not use a feminist lens to develop a design. Rather, the evaluators started with a quasi-experimental, one-group design with multiple standardized measures that were used to collect data at baseline, discharge, and 6 months after leaving the program. They also included interviews and observations of program activities. The evaluators added a feminist perspective during the second year of the evaluation in order to address the realities of women's lives in rural Tennessee, and to get a better idea of the challenges and strengths that these women brought with them into the program. The evaluators used multiple methods of data collection to understand the problem from a feminist perspective, including the women's histories and daily lives in order to make recommendations that the program could implement to better meet the needs of its female clients. The findings revealed that very few women either were informed about the combined treatment for trauma and substance abuse program, or were referred to it by their therapists. The therapists did not recommend the combination trauma and substance abuse program for the women because they believed that the women would not like the extra time, self-reflection, and self-work required in that program. The women also faced constraints in the form of transportation, child care, court appearances, and work schedules that made it more challenging to be in the more intense program. The evaluators concluded that they were diligent in understanding the female participants' values and experiences, but they had not developed sufficient understanding of the staff's values. The staff resisted making changes that would result in a gender-specific treatment because they believed that the general program was adequate for both men and women.

In Podems's (2010) evaluation in Namibia, she used semistructured interviews with police officers in their offices and on the street, and with sex workers that were served by the NPO and those that were not. Through these multiple sources, she was able to identify the power dynamics that affected different types of sex workers, such as the fact that those who worked in brothels were given more privilege than those who worked on the street. The sex workers who were most likely to run into trouble with the law were transsexuals and women who worked along highways or at truck stops. When presented with these findings, the NPO said it would consider expanding the populations that it worked with, as well as addressing laws that are used to unfairly target the sex workers from these further marginalized groups.

Magar's (2012) feminist lens led to an awareness of tensions that arose from two different feminist stances mentioned earlier with regard to the issue of trafficking and rescue operations. The evaluators used a combination of focus groups and open-ended interviews that yielded information about the raid-and-rescue missions, and about the consequences for the females who had been "rescued." The results indicate several unintended consequences: If the brothel owner bails out the rescued woman, she may end up deeper in debt to the owner. Some of the women had been sold by their families or husbands to brothel owners and were not welcomed back into their homes. Other women did not want to be rescued because they enjoyed their earning power and they wanted to contribute to the well-being of their families. These findings support the use of sex workers who are also peer educators, as they can build relationships with the brothel owners, police, and sex workers. Peer educators can play an important role in organizing around sex worker rights to decriminalize sex work and demand services from the state. At a minimum, underage sex workers should be given options and support to ensure they are safe and that their well-being is secure.

The preceding examples illustrate the application of feminist principles from a transformative stance through their focusing on gender inequities, making visible the structural and systematic discrimination that occurs based on gender, showing awareness of the political and power issues in their particular contexts, and valuing of personal experiences of diverse groups of women. Feminist evaluators have many tools that can add to their ability to make visible the experiences of women in many contexts. Evaluators are increasingly using emerging technologies for these purposes. Examples of the use of these technologies are presented in the following section.

Use of Technology in Feminist Evaluations

Technology is increasingly used among evaluation practitioners throughout the evaluation process, from needs assessment and concept mapping, to collection and analysis of data and the utilization of results. Within the transformative paradigm, geographic information systems (GIS) and other geospatial and visual technologies are tools and methods that can be used to facilitate the participation and collaboration of community stakeholders often marginalized in the process of evaluation based on race, class, sexual orientation, and gender (Mertens, 2009, 2010a). While critiques of GIS have described digital representations of spatial knowledge as politically driven, positivist, and inherently quantitative (Lake, 1993; Pickles, 1995; Martin & Wing, 2007), feminist geographers have advanced efforts to reenvision the technology as a feminist practice informed by feminist epistemologies (Kwan, 2002b). In feminist evaluations, data and information visualization technologies facilitate the first principle of feminist evaluation: identifying and making visible gender inequities and disparities that lead to social injustice.

Geographic information systems (GIS) can be used to visually represent a community's access to resources, neighborhood conditions, and the socioeconomic characteristics of residents. Data disaggregated by gender can lay bare the spatiality of inequality produced by the gendered nature of development and the differentiation of men and women in gendered spaces (see Figure 11.1). Figure 11.1 displays the Baltimore City census tracts with high female unemployment rates (greater than 15%), the density of job dispersed through the city and surrounding counties, along with the top work destinations for Baltimore City residents. Although these large, almost contiguous areas of Baltimore City have high female unemployment rates, jobs are not concentrated in these areas. Instead, they are located in the Central Business District and in major work destinations for Baltimore City residents along subway and light-rail routes. These examples illustrate some of the challenges unemployed women face in their distance from employment opportunities, and access by public transit.

This illustration shows the location of employment opportunities and their access pathways by public transit for the women in those communities.

Figure 11.1

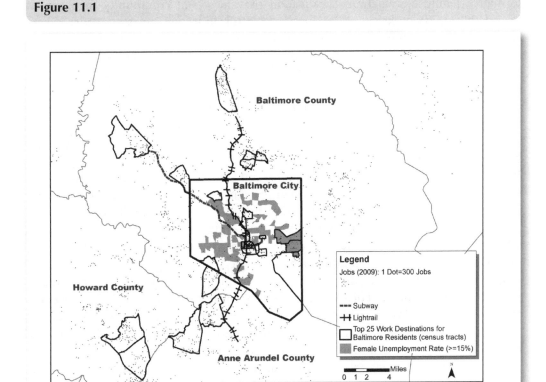

Source: U.S Census Bureau. LEHD Origin-Destination Employment Statistics. (2009). *American Community Survey (ACS) 5-year estimates (2005–2009)*. Baltimore: City EGIS.

McLafferty (2002) identifies an emerging "feminization of GIS" through three areas of innovation that strengthen the technology's potential usefulness in transformative evaluation:

1. New types of gendered data collected with a feminist lens and incorporated into GIS,

2. Critical self-awareness of GIS users, and

3. Feminist visualization to represent women's everyday lives and support women's activism.

GIS is largely associated with its ability to represent secondary quantitative data in quantitative analysis. However, qualitative approaches for using GIS have been, and continue to be developed in order to facilitate the methodological assumption in transformative feminist evaluation, clarification of values, and community involvement (Kwan, 2002a; Pavlovskaya, 2002). These uses can lead to new types of gendered data collection with a feminist lens. For example, multimedia GIS such as story mapping, spatial stories, biographical narratives of women's lives, life maps, and various audiovisual information such as graphics, photographs, videos, and voices have been combined with GIS (Bosak & Schroeder, 2005; Kwan, 2002a). In addition, GIS can represent "spatial configurations of networks, relationships, activities, meaning of places and events, flows that link people and places" (Pavlovskaya, 2002, p. 283).

Critical self-awareness can be enhanced for individuals and groups through visually based graphics that create visible inequities in terms of resources or safety issues. Reflexivity calls for researchers, evaluators, and those who teach the technology to community members to acknowledge the situated nature of spatial knowledge (Elwood, 2008) by understanding their own position in relation to community members and stakeholders, the research and evaluation process, and the knowledge produced (Kwan, 2002b). For example, volunteered graphic information (VGI; Goodchild, 2007) describes how Web 2.0 applications such as Google Maps, Google Earth, GPS technology, WikiMapia, and Microsoft's Bing Maps Platform increase the ability of community stakeholders to "gather and disseminate their observations and geographic knowledge" (Elwood, 2008, p. 173). Ultimately, creating user-generated content produces alternate representations of knowledge that challenge the status quo: commercially available data or data produced by institutions or government agencies (Pavlovskaya, 2002). These alternative representations can be important in empowering communities to pursue social justice.

The utilization of GIS for feminist visualization seeks to represent gendered experiences and spaces of women by using geographic data to link trajectories of women's everyday lives with geographical contexts, and to challenge traditional power relations to strengthen and empower women's activism (Kwan, 2002a). For example, Kwan used

3D GIS to "trace and visualize women's life paths in space-time" (Kwan, 2002a, p. 2) to reveal their constraints for spatial mobility and job locations. She combined these visual representations with data from personal interviews to portray what a woman goes through in a particular day in her life situation.

As an example of using GIS within a transformative feminist approach, a coalition of women in Long Island, New York, during the 1980s used the technology to help address high rates of breast cancer in their communities (McLafferty, 2002). They conducted their own surveys and created "pin maps," later depicted in GIS, to explore the spatial link between the incidence of breast cancer and environmental and social hazards. This effort ultimately gained political support and led to the creation of the National Cancer Institute's Long Island Breast Cancer Study Project.

Pavlovskaya (2002) sought to understand the effect of privatization and economic transition in Russia during the 1990s on individual household economic activities and on related class and gender processes that were not captured through analyzing only macroeconomic and national level data. Here, GIS was used as a technique in the methods to reveal the class and gender processes within households. Using GIS, information from interviews about the existence of informal economies, such as informal work for cash and unpaid domestic labor, was analyzed to identify urban change and underprivileged economic space. In this way, GIS was a transformative mapping strategy; it captured the communities' vision of urban change and enabled the creation of alternative knowledge about urban change.

Warren (2004) encountered the challenge of representing informal data from the community while attempting to map child care facilities for women entering into welfare-to-work programs. Public data about licensed facilities were available from the State Department of Health. However, the unlicensed facilities that serviced those poor women were excluded, so the community provided information about their locations that was later mapped in GIS.

Another example of a transformative feminist initiative's efforts to assist women transitioning from welfare to work demonstrates that GIS users should practice reflexivity and should use the technology in a way that reflects the perspectives and needs of community stakeholders, rather than those of the researchers (Gilbert & Masucci, 2006). Initial plans for creating a GIS resource for community organizations in North Philadelphia included assisting working mothers to develop technological and job-searching skills. This effort was refocused as it became clear the women entering the workforce did not have the time to engage in the technology the way the researchers had envisioned. Rather, they preferred that their children be exposed to using GIS. As a result, the geographers and the community organizations collaborated to develop an afterschool program to serve the women's children.

Within the transformative paradigm, GIS and other geospatial and visual technologies represent tools and methods to facilitate the methodological assumption in transformative evaluation—participation and collaboration of community stakeholders often marginalized in the process of evaluation based on race, class, sexual orientation, and gender (Mertens, 2009).

Benefits and Challenges of Using a Feminist Approach in Evaluation

Beyond the "how" involved in using a feminist lens in evaluation, labeling oneself or one's work as "feminist" is not always welcomed in evaluation by stakeholders such as funders, project administrators, or staff. Podems (2010) described how she discussed her feminist lens with a project director who was very supportive of the contribution that feminist thinking had on the evaluation, as long as Podems did not use the term "feminist" in her description of the approach. Bowen (2011) suggests that evaluators might overcome such resistance by describing the theoretical lens in terms of exploring social justice for women as a way to achieve healthy communities and equitable income distribution. In this way, the concepts of social justice for women, healthy communities, income, and equality are framed together in ways that are amenable to stimulating social change.

Rather than describe themselves as feminist evaluators, UN Women's evaluation office describes their work as "human rights and gender equity focused" (United Nations Evaluation Group, 2011). They identify three characteristics of this approach to evaluation:

1. The gendered nature of development and the importance of gender equality to economic and social development;

2. Poor and marginalized groups of people are gendered, and women and men are differentiated by race, ethnicity, age, disability, class, and caste; and

3. Power relations exist within the home/family, and these relationships intersect with power relationships in the society, policy, and economy.

Thus, while not labeling their work feminist, they reflect many of the same principles of equality and nondiscrimination, participation and inclusion, accountability and targeting structural causes for the nonrealization of rights that are associated with feminist evaluation.

POLITICAL FORCES AND THE USE OF THE FEMINIST LABEL

Bheda (2011) explored why many evaluators, even those who personally identify as feminists and whose work is reflective of feminist principles, do not always choose to identify their work as feminist. One reason is that the word "feminist" connotes a lot of baggage. Criticism is often directed at feminists from privileged positions for imposing a white, western, imperialist version of feminism on women of color and women from developing countries. In addition, "feminist" portrays feminists as strident revolutionaries who hate men; these stereotypical perceptions may lead to a lack of opportunity to get a contract to do work, or to a rejection or denigration of their work once completed. Some feminists use a strategy similar to that suggested by Bowen (2011) and describe their work in terms of social justice or human rights with a focus on gender issues.

Podems (2010) compared feminist evaluation principles to those associated with a gender approach, and concluded that the latter approach does not do justice to the issues of inequity experienced by women around the world. She explains that a gender approach helps identify differences between men and women, and records a woman's subordinate position in society—but it does not examine the reasons why these differences exist or challenge this positioning at all. A feminist approach does just that, and it focuses on the reasons for the inequities. A gender approach is designed to describe women's positions, but a feminist approach is designed to strategically change those positions. Podems concludes her critique of gender approaches with this statement.

> The written guidance provided on how to practically apply each approach varies drastically. For example, feminist evaluation encourages evaluators to be reflexive; recognize that evaluations are neither value free nor disinterested; consider and value different ways of knowing; hear multiple voices; stress the need to give voice to women within different social, political, and cultural contexts; and advocate for marginalized groups. Feminist evaluations *do not* provide frameworks that guide the evaluator. In contrast most GAD [Gender and Development] approaches provide a framework of how to collect specific gender data and do not include these critical feminist ideals in that framework. (p. 9)

Is it possible for gender analysis to be conceptualized and implemented in ways that are compatible with transformative feminist theory? UN Women, in cooperation with the International Labour Organization, developed gender analysis tools in attempts to answer some of these criticisms in their human rights and gender equity framework for evaluation. Commentary from two UN Women evaluators elucidates their position. They recommend that gender analysis be used as an integral part of evaluation strategies. They describe gender analysis as follows:

> The term "gender analysis" is used to describe a systematic approach to examining actors related to gender. It involves a deliberate effort to identify and understand the different roles, relationships, situations, resources, benefits, constraints, needs and interests of men and women in a given socio-cultural context. (International Training Centre of the International Labour Organization, 2009, p. 16)

Gender analysis focuses on the identification of variables that contribute to gender inequalities so they can be addressed. This might include differences in conditions, needs, participation rates, access to resources and development, control of assets, decision-making powers, and so forth between women and men. When used in this way, gender analysis questions both the need for different measures for men and women, and how gender equality presents at a variety of levels in the programs (e.g., grassroots, service delivery systems, the highest political levels).

Behind the Scenes With Inga Sniukaite and Belen Sanz

UN Women

There are political forces that are operating in the evaluation community to either avoid, or encourage the use of the feminist label. The UN Women Evaluation Office, together with other UN agencies with evaluation responsibilities, spearheaded the development of guidance on the integration of human rights and gender equality in evaluation (United Nations Evaluation Group, 2011). We encountered a number of challenges in finding the most suitable terminology to describe the approach that is responsive to the human rights agenda, takes into account the gendered nature of social reality, and seeks the transformative change for achieving social justice for diverse population groups. From the very outset, the drafters of the guidance agreed that the approach should build on the United Nations' mandate to protect, promote, and fulfill human rights and also to incorporate gender mainstreaming as a widely used strategy for the realization of gender equality. In addition, gender analysis, as it is conceived in development context (Kabeer, 1994; March, Smyth, & Mukhopadhyay, 1999), feminist evaluation (Seigart & Brisolara, 2002), and transformative approaches to evaluation (Mertens, 2009) were identified as conceptual frameworks that should inform the development of gender and human rights responsive evaluation. Interestingly, the word "feminist" did not make the headlines of this publication. Why?

In order to understand the choice of "human rights and gender equality responsive" versus "feminist," we should look more carefully at the political context of the organization as well as familiarity with and history of the use of specific concepts and terms. In addition, we argue that we have to look beyond the labels and focus on the set of principles and values that feminist, transformative, and human rights based approaches bring to conventional evaluation.

Human rights and gender equality are at the heart of the United Nations' mandate and its work. Negotiated in the form of conventions and international agreements, human rights and gender equality are very significant principles that guide UN work starting from environmental issues and development to peacekeeping and security.

There is a general consensus in the organization around human rights and gender equality that provides a platform for understanding and communicating the evaluation approach to UN agencies and their partners. The term "feminist" would be too broad for this specific political and organizational context. Feminism as a social movement and academic field is certainly useful for the advancement of human rights and gender equality, but the UN member states did not endorse it as an agreed agenda. The "labeling" of an approach should be informed and fit to the context. Therefore, we should not jump to a quick conclusion that there is a strong resistance to feminism as such in the evaluation community, but understand the context and use the term strategically. More significant is the application of the principles of transformation, empowerment, advocacy, reflexivity, diversity, and social change that are embedded in feminist and human rights and gender equality responsive evaluation.

The intersection between gender equality as a precondition for development, and human rights as a framework legitimates aspiration and promotes the mandate of the United Nations. The responsiveness of evaluation to human rights and gender equality makes it consistent with the principles of feminist evaluation, as this intersection does not allow "gender" to be treated as a technical category that counts men and women, but is used to interrogate the structural power relations within society that generate discrimination against women in relation with factors of structural discrimination and diversity. It also enables evaluators to ask questions on how programs and policies reverse inequalities and promote social and equitable justice, making this approach particularly powerful for empowerment transformative social change.

The United Nation's gender equity–focused approach to evaluation recognizes the gendered nature of development and differentiation and reflects the spatiality of inequality, or the spatial manifestation of power relations in society. Rooted in the pursuit of social justice, spatial justice specifically focuses on uneven development. According to Edward Soja (2010), spatial justice is the relationship between justice and geography, a sociospatial dialectic, whereby the spatiality of justice has a consequential geography that shapes and is shaped by social and political processes. Further, it can stimulate social activism and address inequality through coalition building.

By including gender analysis as a tool in evaluation, UN Women provide a mechanism to address inequities on the basis of gender. If this tool is placed within an evaluation conducted from a transformative stance, it becomes part of a cyclical process of examining relevant dimensions of diversity in addition to gender that need to be addressed in order to advance social justice and human rights. There is compatibility between the evaluation framework as it is conceptualized within UN Women, and the use of a transformative lens to plan and implement evaluations. When such a lens is brought to the evaluation, additional questions are raised that may increase UN Women's evaluations power to achieving their goals.

One possible solution to the tension found in the labeling of evaluation as either feminist or gender equity–focused comes in the form of transformational gender evaluation. Magar (2010) provides us with commentary about this positioning that she has found useful in her evaluation studies in South Asia.

Behind the Scenes With Veronica Magar

Transformational Gender

I believe that evaluators who address questions of gender inequity should recognize the political nature of evaluation in terms of larger social operations. This implies that evaluators need to be part of the social movement and social activist community. In my own work, I find that I must engage as an activist in order to see the transformational effects of evaluation that I desire to see based on my feminist beliefs. Evaluations can serve to inform policy makers about needed changes. In addition, evaluators can provide the knowledge needed for activists in the movement to learn and change as necessary. Inclusion of activists should be a part of the entire evaluation process. For example, they should be involved in decisions about the design and data collection, and in the data analysis and interpretation. In this way, the evaluator can contribute to the increase in a sense of agency amongt the members of the social movement and reduce the image of woman as victim.

In the context of evaluations of programs focused on women, activists should be viewed as important stakeholders. The evaluation process and findings should inform their work. When I did my own work with sex workers, I found I had to re-examine my own beliefs and recognize the rights of women to make choices and to consent to work in this area. I asked myself questions, such as:

What about sex workers who were trafficked against their will, but now claim that they do not want to be rescued? Are these trafficked women?

What about underage girls who want to continue in sex work? Should I not respect their choice as an emancipated minor? If not, what are the consequences of returning them to their homes? Are these more dangerous than allowing them to continue in sex work?

Am I not being complicit in trying to restrain women's sexuality, by imposing my values of what a woman should or should not do?

How can the evaluation contribute to a safer experience for those engaged in sex work?

What is my responsibility as an evaluator committed to an activist agenda?

How, as a feminist, can I support both movements to understand each other's positions and to work collectively to ensure women's rights to sexuality, work, and safety?

> I found that meeting with the activists as the findings emerged helped me work through many of these questions. They were able to provide me with insights about the potential consequences of reporting the results in different ways. We sought to present the findings in ways that respected the autonomy of the sex workers, but also had the potential to lead to changes that would increase their safety.

BENEFITS OF USING A FEMINIST EVALUATION APPROACH

Bheda (2011) found that feminists described several benefits to using and naming their work as feminist. First, it allows feminist evaluators to form a community where they feel safe and to explore the meaning of being a feminist evaluator. The American Evaluation Association has a "Feminist Issues in Evaluation" topical interest group, where these types of conversations and relationships develop. This is a site for critical self-reflection, sharing of ideas, frustrations, challenges, successes, and forming friendships. Something important is lost when evaluations with a feminist theoretical lens are not recognized as such. However, feminist evaluators are presently in a state of tension, having to make difficult decisions about when it is safe and appropriate to label our work as feminist and when it is better to use the feminist theory and to avoid the label.

Bowen (2011) noted that using a feminist lens in their evaluation revealed that women could have been better served and supported if they had focused more on past trauma. Women may have been more successful with maintaining sobriety if they had been able to address both their trauma and their addiction. Women's likelihood of maintaining sobriety could have been improved as well. Participation in the combined program was optional for women, and few women were actually referred or fully informed about it. Remarkably, of those participants with a formal diagnosis of PTSD, *none* were enrolled in the combined program. This is significant because 7% of women enrolled in the addiction treatment program reported histories of trauma, yet only 5% had a formal diagnosis of PTSD reflected in their electronic medical record. Bowen shared information with the staff about the prevalence of trauma histories among the women in the program; talked about linkages between trauma, addiction, and mental illness; and disseminated visual data that demonstrated the significant improvements among women who did enroll in the combined program when compared to those who participated only in the addiction program. Bowen's use of a feminist lens in interpreting the data led her to the question: Why was the program staff not encouraging participation in the combined program? The data and her conclusions supported at least two answers to this question. First, the logistical reasons cited earlier in this chapter, such as additional time and need for transportation, were seen as an impediment to enrolling the women in the dual program. Second, the women themselves separated their addiction from their trauma; they were unable to see the relationship between their husbands' beating and raping them and their dependence on illegal drugs.

CONCLUSION

Program evaluation is an approach to systematic inquiry that is an essential part of decision making for educational and social programs. As such, it is inherently political and value laden. These values are set forth as the foundation of the transformative paradigm; for example, the pursuit of social justice and the furtherance of human rights are commensurate with feminist theory. The transformative paradigm provides a philosophical framework that guides feminist evaluators to think about issues of equity on multiple bases. Furthermore, it guides them to think about issues of power and privilege on the basis of gender and other relevant dimensions of diversity, such as disability, deafness, race, ethnicity, and language. Feminist principles in evaluation are derived from feminist theories. Feminist evaluation focuses on gender inequities and social injustices. Feminist evaluators challenge the systemic nature of discrimination and the power invested in an uncritical application of inquiry methods. Recognition of contextual and cultural variables is essential to the conduct of feminist evaluation.

The benefits and challenges of feminist evaluation strategies are illustrated in the examples of feminist evaluation studies presented in this chapter. Feminist evaluators demonstrate an ability to bring to visibility inequities based on gender through their work, and especially through the use of technologically based strategies such as GIS. They provide information that can be used to improve the design and delivery of programs that target women in their full diversity. However, feminist evaluators face many challenges. One of the most notable challenges is whether they can openly label the work that they do "feminist." As seen in this chapter, there are situations in which the evaluator is asked not to use the word feminist, although the stakeholders appreciate the application of the feminist principles in the inquiry. There are other contexts in which political forces and legislative mandates recognize the importance of addressing gender-based inequities, but they do not allow the use of the term feminist. In addition, challenges arise because feminists do not speak with one voice. Feminists are not a homogenous group; at times, working from the same principles of addressing systemic discrimination on the basis of gender leads different feminists to different perspectives on appropriate social action. Feminist evaluators have an important role to play to make visible the different viewpoints and to provide a venue for critical dialogues about the implications of the various positions. This is not easy work, but it is important work.

DISCUSSION QUESTIONS

1. What is your opinion of the difference between research and evaluation? How does the emphasis on valuing and decision making come into your position about these two methods of systematic inquiry?

2. How would you explain the relationship between the philosophical assumptions of the transformative paradigm and the feminist principles for evaluation? What is gained or lost by bringing these two perspectives together?

3. Find an example of a feminist evaluation and examine it to determine how the evaluators applied the feminist principles found in this chapter.

4. What are your thoughts about the situation in which evaluators used feminist principles in their work but may or may not label their work as feminist evaluation? How do you characterize the arguments for doing so or not doing so?

5. In at least one of the examples in this chapter, there were diverse voices of feminists that caused tension in the evaluation. (Remember Magar's example of feminists who supported sex work and those who did not?) What other examples can you think of in which feminists might hold different values that could influence their application of feminist principles in their evaluation studies?

6. What are the benefits of UN Women using the terms human rights and gender equality to label their evaluation approach? What are the drawbacks of this labeling?

WEB RESOURCES

The United Nation's evaluation framework as it applies to gender-focused evaluation is most salient in the evaluation of sponsored programs and initiatives. The UN Women have a mission to foster women's empowerment and gender equality. They use a rights-based approach to strengthen women's economic security and rights, combat violence and HIV and AIDS, and promote gender equality.

- At this website, you will find resources developed by UN Women for the conduct of gender-focused, human rights–based evaluations: http://www.unwomen.org/about-us/evaluation/

- UNICEF and UN Women have a free electronic resource center on Equity, Gender Equality, and Human Rights responsive evaluation. This website allows access to the UN Women's guides to gender equity and human rights evaluations: http://www.mymande.org/index.php?q=human_rights_front

- The World Bank has a website dedicated to gender and development where you can find tools, examples, and databases related to women and development: http://web.worldbank.org/WBSITE/EXTERNAL/TOPICS/EXTGENDER/0,,menuPK:336874~pagePK:149018~piPK:149093~theSitePK:336868,00.html

- The World Bank also produced an atlas on gender and development that is available at this URL: http://www.app.collinsindicate.com/worldbankatlas-gender/en

- Google maps provides free access to different applications that allow the user to create maps that are interactive and can be used in websites to display data in graphic forms: http://code.google.com/apis/maps/index.html

- Prezi is a presentation application that allows for the combination of visual images that can be zoomed in and out to suggest the relative importance of concepts and how they relate to each other: http://prezi.com/

- IBM sponsors a website that allows users to create three-dimensional graphs to illustrate how data can be displayed in a dynamic way: http://www-958.ibm.com/software/data/cognos/manyeyes/

REFERENCES

Alkin, M. C., & Christie, C. A. (2004). An evaluation theory tree. In M. C. Alkin (Ed.), *Evaluation roots: Tracing theorists' views and influences* (pp. 12–65). Thousand Oaks, CA: Sage.

American Evaluation Association (AEA). (2011). *AEA public statement on cultural competence in evaluation*. Fairhaven, MA: Author. Retrieved from http://www.eval.org/aea.culturally.competent.evaluation.statement.pdf

Bheda, D. (2011). En "gendering" evaluation: Feminist evaluation but "I am NOT a feminist!" *New Directions for Evaluation, 2011*(131), 53–68.

Bosak, K., & Schroeder, K. (2005). Using geographic information systems (GIS) for gender and development. *Development in Practice, 15*, 233–239.

Bowen, K. (2011, November). *Evaluation of a rural methamphetamine treatment program: Intensive outpatient therapy using the matrix model retrospective gender analysis in an Appalachian context.* Paper presented at the annual meeting of the American Evaluation Association, Anaheim, CA.

Brayton, J. (2011). "What makes feminist research feminist?" Retrieved from http://www.unb.ca/par-l/win/feminmethod.htm

Brisolara, S. (in press). Feminist theory: Its domain and applications. In S. Brisolara, D. Seigart, & S. Sengupta (Eds.), *Feminist evaluation and research: Advances in understanding and implementation.* New York, NY: Guilford Press.

Elwood, S. (2008). Volunteered geographic information: Future research directions motivated by critical, participatory, and feminist GIS. *GeoJournal, 72*, 173–183.

Fournier, D. M. (2005). Evaluation. In S. Mathison (Ed.), *Encyclopedia of evaluation* (pp. 139–140). Thousand Oaks, CA: Sage.

Gilbert, M. R., & Masucci, M. (2006). The implications of including women's daily lives in a feminist GIScience. *Transactions in GIS, 10,* 751–761.

Goodchild, M. (2007). Citizens as sensors: The world of volunteered geography. *GeoJournal, 69,* 211–221.

Guba, E. G., & Lincoln, Y. S. (2005). Paradigmatic controversies, contradictions, and emerging confluence. In N. K. Denzin & Y. S. Lincoln (Eds.), *The Sage handbook of qualitative research* (3rd ed., pp. 191–215). Thousand Oaks, CA: Sage.

International Training Centre of the International Labour Organization. (2009). *Module on gender, poverty and employment.* Turin, Italy: Author.

Kabeer, N. (1994). *Reversed realities: Gender hierarchies in development thought.* New York, NY: Verso.

Kwan, M. P. (2002a). Feminist visualization: Re-envisioning GIS as a method in feminist geographic research. *Annals of the Association of American Geographers, 92,* 645–661.

Kwan, M. P. (2002b). Is GIS for women? Reflections on the critical discourse in the 1990s. *Gender, Place & Culture: A Journal of Feminist Geography, 9,* 271–279.

Lake, R. W. (1993). Planning and applied geography: Positivism, ethics, and geographic information systems. *Progress in Human Geography, 17,* 404–413.

Magar, V. (2010, October). *Evaluating gender for transformation.* Paper presented at the conference of the European Evaluation Society, Prague, Czech Republic.

Magar, V. (2012). Rescue and rehabilitation: A critical analysis of sex workers' antitrafficking response India. *Signs: Journal of Women in Culture and Society, 37,* 619–644.

March, C., Smyth, I., & Mukhopadhyay, M. (1999). *A guide to gender-analysis frameworks.* Oxford, England: Oxfam GB.

Mathison, S. (2008). What is the difference between evaluation and research—and why do we care? In N. L. Smith & P. R. Brandon (Eds.), *Fundamental issues in evaluation* (pp. 183–196). New York, NY: Guilford Press.

McLafferty, S. (2002). Women and GIS: Geospatial technologies and feminist geographies. *Cartographica: The International Journal for Geographic Information and Geovisualization, 40*(4), 37–45.

Mertens, D. M. (2009). *Transformative research and evaluation.* New York, NY: Guilford.

Mertens, D. M. (2010a). *Research and evaluation in education and psychology: Integrating diversity with quantitative, qualitative, and mixed methods.* (3rd ed.). Thousand Oaks, CA: Sage.

Mertens, D. M. (2010b). Social transformation and evaluation. *Evaluation Journal of Australasia, 10*(2), 3–10.

Mertens, D. M. (in press). A transformative feminist stance: Inclusion of multiple dimensions of diversity with gender. In S. Brisolara, D. Siegart, & S. Sengupta (Eds.), *Feminist evaluation and research: Advances in understanding and implementation.* New York, NY: Guilford Press.

Mertens, D. M., & Wilson, A. T. (2012). *Program evaluation theory and practice: A comprehensive guide.* New York, NY: Guilford Press.

Patton, M. Q. (2008). *Utilization focused evaluation.* Thousand Oaks, CA: Sage.

Pavlovskaya, M. E. (2002). Mapping urban change and changing GIS: Other views of economic restructuring. *Gender, Place and Culture: A Journal of Feminist Geography, 9*(3), 281–289.

Pickles, J. (1995). *Representations in an electronic age: Geography, GIS, and democracy.* New York, NY: Guilford Press.

Podems, D. (2010). Feminist evaluation and gender approaches: There's a difference? *Journal of MultiDisciplinary Evaluation, 6*(14), 1–17.

Seigart, D., & Brisolara, S. (Eds.). (2002). *Feminist evaluation*: Explorations and experiences [Special issue]. *New Directions for Evaluation, (2002)*96.

Sielbeck-Bowen, K. A., Brisolara, S., Seigart, D., Tischler, C., & Whitmore, E. (2002). Exploring feminist evaluation: The ground from which we rise. *New Directions for Evaluation, 2002*(96), 3–8.

Soja, E. (2010). City: Analysis of urban trends, culture, theory, policy, action. *Spatializing the urban, Part 1, 14*(6), 629–635.

St. Martin, K., & Wing, J. (2007). The discourse and discipline of GIS. *Cartographica: The International Journal for Geographic Information and Geovisualization, 42,* 235–248.

Trochim, W. (2006). *The research methods knowledge base* (2nd ed.). Ithaca, NY: Author.

United Nations. (1948). *Universal declaration of human rights.* New York, NY: Author. Retrieved from http://www.un.org/Overview/rights.html

United Nations. (1969). *The international convention on the elimination of all forms of racial discrimination.* New York, NY: Author. Retrieved from http://www.hrcr.org/docs/CERD/cerd2.html

United Nations. (1979). *The convention on the elimination of all forms of discrimination against women* (CEDAW). New York, NY: Author. Retrieved from http://www.un.org/womenwatch/daw/cedaw/text/econvention.htm

United Nations. (1990a). *Convention on the rights of the child.* New York, NY: Author. Retrieved from http://www.rightsofthechild.org/

United Nations. (1990b). *International convention on the protection of the rights of all migrant workers and members of their families.* New York, NY: Author. Retrieved from http://www.un.org/millennium/law/iv-13.htm

United Nations (2000). *Millennium declaration.* New York, NY: Author. Available at http://www.un.org/millenniumgoals/bkgd.shtml

United Nations. (2006a). *Convention on the rights of persons with disabilities.* New York, NY: Author. Retrieved from http://www.un.org/disabilities/default.asp?id=259

United Nations. (2006b). *Declaration on the rights of indigenous peoples.* New York, NY: Author. Retrieved from http://www.un.org/esa/socdev/unpfi i/en/declaration.html

United Nations Evaluation Group. (2011). *Integrating human rights and gender equality in evaluation— Towards UNEG guidance.* New York, NY: Author. Retrieved from http://www.unevaluation.org/HRGE_Guidance

Warren, S. (2004). The utopian potential of GIS. *Cartographica: The International Journal for Geographic Information and Geovisualization, 39*(1), 5–16.

Yarbrough, D. B., Shulha, L. M., Hopson, R. K., & Caruthers, F. A. (2011). *The program evaluation standards: A guide for evaluators and evaluation users* (3rd ed.). Thousand Oaks, CA: Sage.

CHAPTER 12

Feminist Approaches to Mixed Methods Research

Sharlene Hesse-Biber

What Is Mixed Methods Research?

Mixed methods research designs employ both quantitative and qualitative data collection and analysis techniques in the service of answering research questions. Mixed methods is a rich field for enhancing our understanding of the social world whereby researchers can, for example, combine data from a quantitative survey together with multimedia data—words, images, and graphics—with the goal of fostering as well as generalizing our understanding of the social world.

Mixed methods researchers often discuss how combining two different methods is synergistic in that one method enables the other to be more effective and together, both provide a fuller understanding of the research problem (Hesse-Biber, 2010b). Mixed methods research pioneers such as Jennifer Greene, Valerie Caracelli, and Sam Sieber, to mention just a few, provide an organizing framework for how mixed methods designs could promote research synergy:

- Qualitative data can add an "in-depth" understanding of quantitative survey research results that can allow researchers to explore anomalies or subgroups within their survey data.

- Qualitative data can serve to contextualize statistical results of a survey by adding a more complete understanding to a researcher's survey findings.

- Qualitative methods might facilitate in the construction of more valid survey research measures, for example, the development of quantitative measures such as a femininity–masculinity scale; by utilizing an in-depth qualitative method to query how well participants to the survey comprehended a given survey research measure, researchers may work the kinks out of their survey questionnaire.

- Qualitatively driven research approaches can benefit from mixing methods to enhance the validity of their qualitative findings; adding a quantitative data collection method can enable qualitative researchers to place their in-depth interview findings into a broader societal context with the goal of testing out a theory generated through the analysis of their qualitative interviews.

- Relying on the findings from a survey study may provide qualitative researchers with critical information regarding ways to identify representative cases for their in-depth qualitative studies.

All of these reasons and many others provide a strong argument for why a researcher might consider a mixed methods research design.

What Are Feminist Approaches to Mixed Methods Praxis?

Feminist researchers employ a range of methods to answer their research questions. They use both qualitative data-collection methods such as in-depth interviews and quantitative data-collection methods such as surveys (Chafetz, 2004; Miner, Jayaratne, Pesonen, & Zurbrugg, 2012). Feminist researchers' reasons for mixing methods are tightly linked to their research question or set of questions. Some feminists might choose mixed methods for the same reasons that nonfeminist researchers do. While qualitative methods and the use of multiple qualitative methods are an important part of feminist research praxis, mixed methods (qualitative and quantitative) research designs lend themselves to the following feminist research goals:

- Exploring women's subjugated knowledge by giving voice to women's experiences, in particular, knowledge ignored by traditional research approaches that leave out gender as a category of inquiry (see DeVault, 1990; Eichler & Lapointe, 1985; Haraway, 1991; Harding, 1986, 1987; Smith, 1978);

- Exploring multiple understandings of the nature of social reality, as this particularly pertains to women's issues and standpoints (Harding, 1986, 1987, 1991, 1993, 2007; Naples, 2007);

- Studying across differences in terms of race, class, gender, and so on (Collins, 1990; Mendez & Wolf, 2012; Mohanty, 1988; Wing, 2000; Zinn, Hondagneu-Sotelo, & Messner, 2008); and

- Fostering social justice and social change on behalf of women and other oppressed groups (Hesse-Biber & Carter, 2005; Lather, 1991; Spalter-Roth & Hartmann, 1996).

There are often multiple objectives contained within any given feminist research project and, as we shall see, feminist researchers employ a variety of mixed methods designs. This chapter explores how some feminist researchers tackle these major dimensions of feminist research and specifically how mixed methods can serve to further feminist research problems and perspectives.

Mixed methods are not inherently steeped in any one theoretical tradition, such as feminism; instead, they are a set of techniques by which researchers are able to approach specific research questions. While qualitative methods have been more associated with feminist research than quantitative methods, there is ongoing discussion about the advantages and disadvantages of different methods within the feminist community (Bowles & Duelli Klein, 1983; Cole & Stewart, 2012; Roberts, 1981). Miner, Jayaratne, Pesonen, and Zurbrugg (2012) note that some feminists believe that qualitative methods are generally "better" and "more feminist" than quantitative approaches because they see quantitative methods as methods that have been used to reinforce the "status quo." From this perspective, quantitative methods are said to be limited because some feminists believe they are patriarchal tools steeped in a positivistic theoretical tradition that serves to undermine social change and the goals of feminist research; in the words of Audre Lorde, "the master's tools will never dismantle the master's house" (Lorde, 1984, p. 13; Reinharz, 1985). However, many feminist researchers view the combination of qualitative and quantitative methods as a productive way of conducting research (see especially Cole & Stewart, 2012; Miner et al., 2012). They argue that quantitative methods such as survey research "are not inherently positivistic and, further, that they have the potential for concreted social change, which aligns them with feminist values" (Miner et al., 2012, p. 238).

Feminist researchers hail from many different theoretical approaches and have a wide spectrum of methodologies and methods. While some favor quantitative or qualitative methods, others turn to mixed methods or invent emergent methods (Hesse-Biber & Leavy, 2008), in order to best carry out their research. Although there are various strands of feminist inquiry, what unites them is their goal: knowledge building that focuses on the lives of women and other oppressed groups and that uncovers new voices and perspectives.

Mixed Methods Research Designs: A Brief Introduction to Basic Research Designs

David Morgan's (1998) work offers a set of mixed methods research designs for conducting a mixed methods study and provides a four-method research design based on the sequencing and relative importance (priority) of each method. Morgan suggests that researchers might ask the following questions as they contemplate mixing methods:

- What is your primary research method and what is the secondary (complementary) method?
- What method comes first? Second?

Morgan (1998) notes that answering these mixed methods design questions provides the researcher with four potential research designs as shown in Table 12.1.

The first design, as noted in Table 12.1, qual followed by QUAN, involves conducting the qualitative component of the research project first but keeping it secondary (designated by lowercase letters) to the project's goals. The quantitative method is primary (all upper case letters), but it is administered as a follow-up to the qualitative study. Using a qualitative design before a quantitative one is used when the researcher is unfamiliar with a given topic and would like to generate specific ideas or hypotheses that he or she might address more specifically in the quantitative part of the project.

In the second research design, quan followed by QUAL, the quantitative study is used secondarily (quan) with the qualitative study being primary (QUAL). In this case, the quantitative study is used to identify specific populations or issues that need to be further explored in-depth.

The third design, QUAN followed by qual, is often utilized when the researcher intends for the quantitative study to be his or her primary mode of inquiry with the qualitative study second. This type of design is used when there is a need to provide clarification or elaboration of research results from quantitative findings. The qualitative study assists in understanding such things as negative results, or what are

Table 12.1 Combining Qualitative and Quantitative Methods

Design 1	qual followed by QUAN (qual → QUAN)
Design 2	quan followed by QUAL (quan → QUAL)
Design 3	QUAN followed by qual (QUAN → qual)
Design 4	QUAL followed by quan (QUAL → quan)

Note: All lowercase means secondary method and all uppercase denotes primary method. Adapted from David Morgan (1998).

called "outliers," or findings that do not appear to fit the overall hypothesis or theoretical perspective.

The fourth design, QUAL followed by a quan, is used when the qualitative research study (QUAL) is primarily followed up with a smaller quantitative study (quan). The quantitative study is used to test results on different populations in order to ascertain whether or not the qualitative findings can be generalized to a wider population.

However, it is important to note that there are a multitude of other mixed methods designs that combine these methods and result in a wide range of additional research designs. Some mixed methods designs combine methods concurrently, that is, at the same time, but maintain the primary/secondary distinction. Others do away with this distinction and see both methods having an equal footing in the research design. Still others talk about issues of one method being embedded or nested within the other.

How Do Feminist Researchers Use Mixed Methods in the Service of Feminist Research Goals?

Mixed methods research designs offer feminist researchers some important knowledge excavation tools. This chapter explores, through in-depth case studies, how mixed methods research designs can serve to further feminist research perspectives and goals. I present case studies that exemplify how feminist researchers can harness the synergy contained in the promise of mixed methods research. These case studies are not exhaustive of the many other ways mixed methods can be successfully deployed by feminist researchers. They do, however, illustrate how mixed methods can enhance the major principles of feminist research praxis and goals.

As you approach each of these case studies, there are several sensitizing questions you might apply to each.

- What particular research problems interface well with a mixed methods design?

- What specific mixed methods research designs are utilized and why?

- At what stage(s) in the process of a research project (data collection stage? data analysis stage? data interpretation stage?) are the methods mixed, if at all?

- What are the specific advantages and disadvantages of using a mixed methods approach?

- What makes this research case study an example of a feminist approach to mixed methods?

Feminist Approaches to Mixed Methods Research: Case Studies

CASE STUDY 1. USING MIXED METHODS TO GET AT SUBJUGATED KNOWLEDGE: LAND FOREST USAGE IN NEPAL[1]

We start with a case study example of how a feminist geographer Andrea Nightingale (2003) employs *an iterative mixed methods approach,* in which both methods are on an equal footing and her analysis and interpretation are conducted as a dynamic interaction.

Geographic feminist researcher, Andrea Nightingale's work placed women's concerns at the center of her research project on the use of a community forest in Nepal. She employed a mixed methods research design to explore the silenced voices of women and other oppressed groups (based on class and caste) whose work and family lives comprise an integral part of land forest usage, yet their experiences are left out of social policy initiatives on forest usage among forestry policy planners.

Nightingale pointed out that prior to the 1990s, many feminist geographers were "feminist empiricists" who had engaged in making women visible in geographical studies by "adding women" into traditional research projects. Feminist empiricists' goal of eradicating sexist research, often "added women and stirred" them into a research project with little attention to gender differences in their analysis and interpretation of research findings.

Instead, Nightingale applies a "feminist standpoint" approach by placing women's issues and concerns about land usage as a central component in her overall understanding of land forest usage in Nepal.

Nightingale's specific research questions were twofold:

- How is the forest used by Nepali women?

- More specifically, in what sense do Nepali women shape the landscape of the forest and the meanings of how the environment is understood and used by women?

Nightingale's perspective on land usage combined both a feminist perspective on forest usage with a more traditional quantitative geographic approach. Traditional approaches to geography demanded a "correct" interpretation of land cover and land forms by checking areas on each photo with areas on the ground. Yet this simple method of comparison raised a central question for Nightingale's research, namely:

- Do the qualitative histories and the photos tell the same story?

Using a feminist standpoint perspective, Nightingale set out to determine how the forest landscape and the changes perceived in the photos are understood by women whose voices have often been left out of the traditional understandings of land usage over time.

Her research methods approach was twofold: she employed both quantitative and qualitative methods to explore her research questions. She used ethnographic techniques, more specifically ecological oral histories, to ascertain landscape change from the lived experience of those who use the land over time. She also conducted field observations and interviews with one community of villagers—inquiring of the community forest users within the Mugu district located in northwest Nepal. She asked her participants to talk about their past and present perceptions of the forest—their experiences with and assessment of ecological conditions of the forest environment. These narratives form snapshots of their experiences allowing a linking of present and past experiences. She also conducts aerial photo analysis, a quantitative approach, by systematically categorizing forest land—its textures, colors, and shades within the photos. She analyzed aerial photos from 1978 and 1996 by mapping changes of the forest area. She expressed some trepidation about using a mixed methods design by noting that while she felt both methods were equally valid—in that they each "correctly" relay the story of forest usage—she was concerned about the possibility of a contradictory result between the histories and the photos. What would that discrepancy reveal about both oral histories and aerial photo interpretations? The following diagram depicts how the various methods she used intersected and affected her overall interpretation.

For Nightingale, the decision to use a mixed methods iterative design (see Figure 12.1) allowed her to get at "the silences and discrepancies" between her qualitative and quantitative findings (Nightingale, 2003, p. 81). Nightingale's reasoning for using a mixed methods approach stemmed directly from a feminist epistemology on knowledge building—meaning that all knowledge is socially situated—and it is from this epistemology that she developed a series of research questions that stressed the importance of understanding the experiences of women and other oppressed groups regarding forest use. She notes:

> In my own work on community forestry in Nepal, I used qualitative, ethnographic techniques, such as oral histories, participant-observation and in-depth interviewing as well as aerial photo interpretation and quantitative vegetation inventory. In addition to highlighting the situatedness and partiality of knowledge, the Nepali case study also helps to show the importance of challenging "dominant" representations of forest change—in this case, aerial photo interpretations—not by rejecting them outright, but by demonstrating explicitly how they provide only one part of the story of forest change. This is a particularly important project in Nepal where increasingly remote sense data are used to determine changes in forest cover, land use and environmental degradation. (2003, p. 80)

Figure 12.1   Nightingale's Mixed Methods Iterative Design

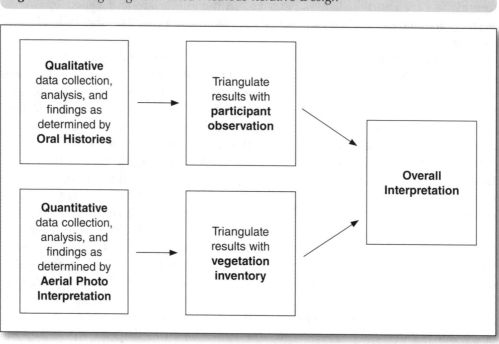

Nightingale notes that pursuing a mixed methods approach was done with some trepidation, as this research was work she was doing for her doctoral dissertation. Let's go behind the scenes to get a glimpse of the tensions she experienced in employing a mixed methods design in her research project.

Behind the Scenes

Interview With Andrea Nightingale

Nightingale: I thought that working across the social and natural sciences necessarily entailed using mixed methods.... [O]ne of the people on my committee had said to me, "Oh, that would be really interesting because you could use like aerial interpretations to validate your interviews." And I said, "No, I don't want to do that because I think that both these forms of knowledge are valid, and I don't want to uphold one over the other." And so it was more interesting to me to kind of think about...why.... Were they the

	same or weren't they the same, and what did it mean if they weren't? Not to sort of say, "Oh, well, people must have been lying to me."
Hesse-Biber:	So he actually wanted you to do what is known as mixed methods for the purpose of triangulation?
Nightingale:	Exactly.
Hesse-Biber:	It seems to me that this member of your committee was coming from more of a positivistic perspective of reality where there is the truth out there, right?
Nightingale:	Yes. [A]nd certainly triangulation was part of the agenda in terms of the kind of work I was doing. It makes a lot of sense to triangulate different kinds of data, whether that's participant observation or in-depth interviews or some of the ambulatory interviews that I use.... But I really felt very strongly that there were different ways of understanding what was happening with forest change. And I didn't want to privilege one of those understandings over the other, but rather I wanted to kind of put them side by side and see what they said to one another.
Hesse-Biber:	Right.... So it seems to me that underlying this uneasiness with your dissertation advisor was in a sense . . . a different theoretical perspective on knowledge building that you were going after.
Nightingale:	[M]y approach to knowledge would sort of suggest that knowledge is partial and situated, . . . and the work of Donna Haraway has been hugely influential on me . . . . But even some of Judith Butler's work and the way she conceptualizes how we come to know about the world, through bodily performances, and repetitive interactions.

Not only did Nightingale mix methods in the data collection stage of her mixed methods project, but she also mixed the analysis of her data (QUAL and QUANT data analysis). She used one type of data analysis to inform the other and then compared inconsistencies in her findings, rather than trying to triangulate the data in order to fit a given story or "truth." Nightingale used both her data sets, including aerial photos and oral histories of forest usage, "on equal terms" to answer questions "at roughly the same scale" (2003, p. 86). Both data sets were equally important to her research, and one did not preempt the other.

Nightingale's feminist approach allowed her not just to see nature as something "out there" in an aerial photo, but to look at the nature–society boundary. Nature is also socially and physically constructed by society—the basic interactions of the individual with the natural landscape.

Let's go behind the scenes again to listen to part of my interview with Nightingale that touches upon the shifting nature–society boundary:

Behind the Scenes

Interview With Andrea Nightingale

Hesse-Biber: The questions that you are asking in your research, it seems to me, go beyond geographic methods that require a very quantitative understanding of gathering data. [I]t sounds to me as if the way in which you thought of these issues entails an interaction of the environment with its surrounding social context of people using it and their ideas about it. The forest becomes part of kind of a living space, right? Where people are interacting in many different ways that deal with issues of power and social control and gender and all of those things to create the forest that you see in any given picture.

Nightingale: Absolutely, that's a really nice way to put it. And I was very much influenced by some kind of postmodern thinking around class.... Thinking not so much rigidly and linearly about class as something you were born into, but rather that class is performed. And so, the kinds of economic activities you engage in determine your class position. And those things change over time, and for many people they can be involved in multiple class processes ... even in one given day.... So they go sell some firewood, till their field, and then go work for somebody else.

Hesse-Biber: Right.

Nightingale: And so I collected a census, which ... was more, to some degree, a quantitative measure, where I hired some teenaged boys who were pretty well educated in the village who went around and collected information on everyone's landholdings, the amount of livestock they had, the amount of education that each different family member had obtained, the number of people in each household in different age categories, ... and just the different kinds of occupations that they were involved in.

And that ended up being an incredibly interesting, useful look at class. Because I know, for example, one of the key statistics that came out of that had to do with education and people with educational attainment. Which I had a vague idea of just from interviewing people, chatting with them; but I didn't get the same picture of it that I got once I'd done that census.... I guess kind of the bottom line in thinking about mixing methods is it's so much driven by the question you're asking.

And, you know, being very careful that you're able to . . . have a . . . meaningful picture, whatever phenomena it is you're attempting to understand.

You know, when it came to class, it did make sense to have what I treated as relative numbers. I didn't actually believe . . . say, the total hectares of land that everybody said was accurate, but at least it was proportionally accurate. Because the two guys who collected it knew everybody, had an idea of everybody's landholdings, and they were able to standardize, if you will, the measures of how much land everybody had.

Nightingale's mixed methods research then, opens up new conceptual space to rethink the nature–society boundary. What appears hidden in the aerial photos of the forest is a set of societal relationships embedded in caste, class, race, and gendered relationships, as well as cultural beliefs about the natural environment that, in turn, repurpose forest land usage and serve to change the physical landscape that is observed in the aerial photos over time.

Nightingale's mixed methods research project mixes methods at the data collection as well as at the data analysis and interpretation phases of her project. She places her quantitative and qualitative analyses on an equal plane, and both sets of findings are interwoven to produce her final research results. She used one type of data to inform the other. She compared inconsistencies among her qualitative and quantitative data, by going back and forth between both types of data sets. She notes:

A different research design might have used photos merely to set the context for forest change and then use the histories to detail the cultural and political aspects of that change. Instead, by setting the data sets in relation to each other, I have allowed for both to be acknowledged as partial and situated. (2003, p. 86)

Applying a feminist standpoint lens to her mixed methods project allows Nightingale to observe nature, not as something "out there" in an aerial photo, but to delve below the image she observes in order to look at the nature–society boundary. Nature, she notes, is socially and physically constructed by society—the basic interactions of the individual with the natural landscape. What appears hidden in the aerial photos of the forest is a set of the societal (the web of social relations and interweaving of caste, class, race, and gender relationships with regard to the nature environment) and the cultural (the set of beliefs about nature and how the nature environment is conceptualized by individuals—factors that interface with the forest landscape).

CASE STUDY 2. GETTING AT SUBJUGATED KNOWLEDGE: SEX WORK IN TIJUANA[2]

Like Andrea Nightingale, ethnographer Yasmina Katsulis focuses her research on the lived experiences and voices of women when seeking to uncover knowledge about the day-to-day experiences of girls and women who work in Tijuana, Mexico's sex industry.

She focuses her research on issues of violence and stereotyping of women who work in the sex industry (Katsulis, 2009). Unlike previous research of sex workers that assumed a "deviant model"—wherein female sex workers are "prostitutes" and stigmatized as "disease vectors"—Katsulis's research deploys a feminist orientation that seeks to uncover subjugated knowledge in service of transforming the social situation of women who work in the sex industry (p. 3). Katsulis's feminist theoretical background informs the research questions she asks and the methods she selects. She notes that at first, her research started out as a primarily qualitative study. However, over time, she turned it into a mixed method research project:

> It was not until I had been living in Tijuana for a number of months that I realized how structurally diverse the commercial sex industry is. My goal of writing a purely qualitative study shifted as I began to strategize about how to incorporate this diversity and, more specifically, to identify patterns in the relationships between social diversity, social hierarchy, and health outcomes. (p. 12)

Incorporating a quantitative perspective and quantitative method allows her to ask new questions about the macro-level social and economic power hierarchies within the Tijuana sex industry. Katsulis expands her set of research questions to now include information that requires the collection of quantitative data in order to generalize her findings to reveal the social and economic workings of the sex industry itself within which sex workers are employed.

Katsulis's research began with her initial field observations at several sex worker sites. Her fieldwork observations led her to target a sample that included "customers, professionals, researchers, and policy makers." This sample allowed her to "explore potential themes within a broad range of diverse work experiences" (p. 12). Her data collection, in large part, consisted of in-depth interviews with "sex workers themselves," as she "carried out 251 formal interviews with sex workers, 88 of whom worked legally (86 females, 2 transgendered females) and 160 of whom worked illegally (107 females, 14 transgendered females, 42 males)" (p. 12).

As Figure 12.2 shows, Katsulis does not begin her research with a mixed methods design. The addition of a quantitative method (the survey interview) was integrated as she began her in-depth interview process. Katsulis interviewed women who came to a clinic in Tijuana for HIV/AIDS prevention but realized that because these women were working in the "legal" sector of the sex trade, their experience was not representative of other kinds of sex workers in Tijuana. Her chosen quantitative component, survey interviews, was added to her research design in order to include the experiences of sex workers from the "illegal" sector of the sex industry as well, so as to make some generalizations about the diversity of sex workers' lived experiences and the social and economic factors that they perceive within their work situation. Katsulis reflects on the design of her research: "I used a combination of participant observation, informal conversational interviews, semistructured interviews, and surveys conducted in a variety of settings" (2009, p. 12). Katsulis was better able to pursue research that accounts for a wider range of lived experience by using both quantitative and qualitative research.

Her sequential, exploratory, mixed methods design is depicted in Figure 12.2.

Katsulis's reflection on her study's design demonstrates how mixed methods data can be integrated at various stages of the research process. She began her study with participant observation at a variety of sites over a course of 18 months, and these initial observations shaped her study in two ways: (1) they allowed her to target a sample for further semistructured interviewing, and (2) they revealed possible questionnaire items (the next qualitative phase of her study). The data gleaned from these semistructured interviews with "legal" sex workers in a clinic setting allowed her to expand her study to include the experiences of "illegal" sex workers from a range of work in the Tijuana sex industry—strippers, brothel workers, street hookers, massage parlor workers, and call/escort services. Additional funding from the National Science Foundation also facilitated the expansion of her research, as she was able to interview sex workers beyond the clinic setting. The final component of her mixed methods design was the surveying of "illegal" workers; because the ratio of "illegal" to "legal" sex workers is 2 to 1, this final component made her research more inclusive of a wider range of experiences across the spectrum of the sex industry in Tijuana. Further, funding from her grant allows her to provide free HIV testing to all participants.

Katsulis's mixed methods research yields several advantages. First, her integrated analysis brings several sets of data into dialogue with each other in a way that sheds light on macro-level social patterns as well as on individual experiences. Second, her feminist approach to mixed methods allows her not only to uncover the lived experiences of sex workers, but also to pursue those areas of sex work that had been previously neglected. Third, the use of both qualitative data (from interviews) with quantitative data (from the survey) provides a "dualistic perspective" that combines women's voices with broader findings. With the addition of quantitative data, she is able to frame her qualitative data to argue for social change and policy initiatives. For a fuller discussion regarding the persuasive power of numbers (connoting "scientific method" and "rigor") in policy making, see Spalter-Roth and Hartman, 1996.

Figure 12.2   Katsulis's (2009) Sequential, Exploratory, Mixed Methods Design

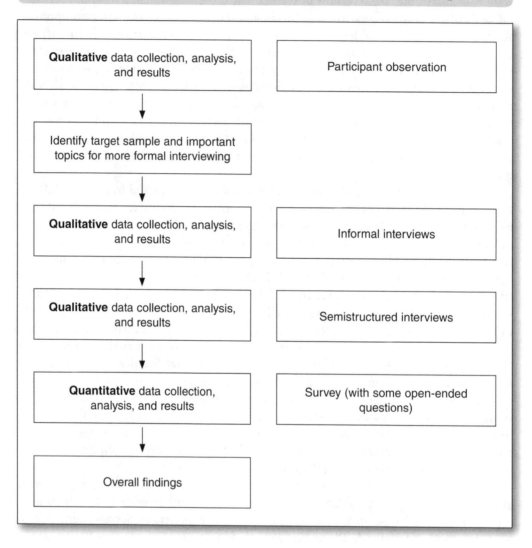

CASE STUDY 3. UNCOVERING SUBJUGATED KNOWLEDGE AND GENERATING/TESTING THEORIES OF INEQUALITY: STUDYING THE GENDER GAP IN PUBLIC OPINION IN CANADA[3]

Brenda O'Neill's (2009) research resides in the interface between feminism, religion, and women's political opinions. As a feminist empiricist political science researcher whose goals are similar to those of early feminist empiricists, O'Neill seeks to explore subjugated knowledge with regard to women's political opinions that had been left out of academic research in her field of political science.

O'Neill's research focuses on the following question:

- What is the role of religious beliefs and feminist identification in shaping women's political attitudes?

Because the field-specific quantitative data sets available to her do not contain information regarding gender, O'Neill has to gather her own data about women's political opinions relating to the issues in which she is interested. This lack of available secondary data makes doing mixed methods troublesome, even before she began this particular project; in the early stages of her professional career, then, she came up against the enormous upfront costs of acquiring a quantitative data set and the difficulties of obtaining funding for her study.

Her exploratory sequential mixed methods design began with a qualitative component (a focus group). She gathered data from nine focus groups of women (8 to 10 women each)—ethnic- and age-diverse groups from a sample of Canadian cities varying by size and region. Within the focus groups, O'Neill nested a quantitative component of demographic data (age, social class, religious affiliation).

The next step was a quantitative telephone survey of a random sample of 1,264 women aged 18 or older, drawn from ten Canadian provinces. The survey gathered, in addition to standard demographic data (socioeconomic status [SES], religious denomination, etc.), data about women's attitudes and beliefs regarding politics, feminism, and religion.

O'Neill's rationale for conducting both types of studies is directly connected to her feminist perspective. Overall, she hoped to "set the record straight" by unearthing knowledge about women's political attitudes and beliefs, but she also aimed to transform

Figure 12.3 O'Neill's (2009) Sequential, Exploratory, Mixed Methods Design

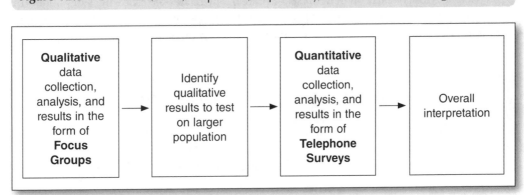

research methods, measures, and concepts to include women's voices. Her research question emerged from her dissatisfaction with the manner by which the concept of religion had been measured. From her focus groups, she recognized that "faith needed to be conceptualized beyond the narrow concepts of membership in a religious denomination and attendance at services." As opposed to "how more quantitative approaches to the study of political behaviour have conceptualized religion: denomination (including a measure for evangelicalism), salience and attendance at services," O'Neill's research was oriented toward broadening the definition of religion in a way that included women's voices (2009, p. 11).

Furthermore, O'Neill wanted to generate theory about women's political participation in relation to religion and feminism from the qualitative data and "test" the theory against the quantitative data. In order to ground her quantitative measures in women's lived experiences, she inductively produced quantitative measures based on the collected qualitative data. Her goal was to develop nonandrocentric measures of political participation and a richer understanding of religion and feminism to shape the questions developed for the quantitative survey. O'Neill discusses the ways in which qualitative and quantitative components complement one another:

> By starting with a more qualitative method, I was able to incorporate the rich discussions into the construction of survey questions. And indeed, the ability to better capture the multi-dimensionality of concepts by using the Qual/Quant design has been identified by others (Leckenby & Hesse-Biber, 2007). More than this, however, the focus groups established the importance of a concept that I would have completely missed had I jumped immediately into the more quantitative method (e.g., the importance of spirituality). The focus groups also provided assistance with the choice of vocabulary and the phrasing of new questions that deviated from those employed in existing surveys. (pp. 11–12)

Before leaving this case study, let's join feminist political scientist Brenda O'Neill "Behind the Scenes," as she relates to us how her passion for doing feminist research was galvanized and became stronger early on in her research career. She relates the following story about the strong negative reaction she received from some of her colleagues who sought to marginalize her feminist approach as well as her openness to utilizing qualitative methods.

Behind the Scenes With Brenda O'Neill

I believe that the research question ought to dictate the appropriate method to employ. The dominance of quantitative techniques in my work stems from my statistical training in the disciplines of economics and political science. I additionally identify as a feminist and my openness to qualitative methods stems from independent learning, research, and reading. My first academic invitation to contribute to an edited collection involved writing a chapter on the use of quantitative methods within feminist research (O'Neill, 1995). At the workshop where we were asked to deliver the papers, my presentation was interrupted by a researcher who turned to the editors and asked why my chapter was included in the volume given that feminists had largely discredited quantitative research methods. That experience galvanized my interest in methods, methodology, and epistemology. (O'Neill, 2009, p. 1)

Important lessons are contained in Brenda O'Neill's account of her research workshop experience, especially for those researchers who are just starting out their careers with a commitment to a feminist research approach. Not everyone in your field will welcome your perspective and may not respect or legitimate the use of nonquantitative tools. Her story also reminds us of the importance of getting in touch with the courage of our convictions, getting in touch with our values and commitments to social change that can fuel our continued commitment to going after knowledge that lies hidden and whose uncovering, in fact, may serve to upend dominant ideas as well as traditional methods practices.

CASE STUDY 4. THE POTENTIAL CONUNDRUMS IN USING A MIXED METHODS EXPLANATORY DESIGN FOR FEMINIST RESEARCH: A CAUTIONARY CASE STUDY[4]

In her mixed methods project, Suzanne Hodgkin (2008) applies a feminist transformative approach to understanding women's acquisition of "social capital." Two questions guide her study:

- Do men and women have different social capital profiles?
- Why do women participate more in social and community activities than in civic activities? (p. 301)

More specifically, Hodgkin wants to show the synergistic impact of using a mixed methods design: to "bring both depth and texture to" feminist research (p. 297). The vehicle she uses to do this is to center gender as a major explanatory variable in her data analysis. Like feminist empiricists before her, she seeks to address the lack of gender focus in studies of social capital, that is, "the norms and networks that enable people to work collectively together to address and resolve problems they face in common," (p. 297) as well as to make visible women's motivations for investing in particular types of social capital acquisition. Her goal was "to develop an understanding of what motivates women's involvement in social, civic, and community life and the social realities of their experiences" (p. 304).

Hodgkin selects a sequential explanatory mixed methods research design a priori in order to show how mixed methods research can be complementary to feminist research goals. She begins her research with a quantitative component and ends with a qualitative component that is used to help explain complexities she discovers in her quantitative data findings (see Figure 12.4).

In the quantitative phase, she sent a survey to 4,000 random households in Australia. Four hundred three men and 998 women replied, with a mean age of 48.7 (only those 18 and older were eligible to participate). The majority of participants were employed, living in a household as a couple, and educated at least through secondary school (p. 302). The goal of the study was to identify any gender differences between men and women's social capital profiles. Hodgkin used a previously generated measure of social capital developed by the South Australian Community Research Unit that she claims could "make a distinction between informal and formal types of participation" that would highlight women's involvement in nonpublic activities (p. 301). She states that this instrument is "sufficiently sensitive to gender issues, particularly its focus on caring. . . . The researcher particularly favored the distinction made between [social and civic activities]" (p. 303). However, unlike O'Neill's study discussed earlier, Hodgkin does little to question the *androcentric biases* that might be present in the social capital measurement variable. The survey also measures levels of participation, computed in scores of "informal social participation, social participation in public places, social participation in groups, individual civic participation, collective civic participation, and community group participation" (p. 304).

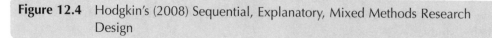

Figure 12.4   Hodgkin's (2008) Sequential, Explanatory, Mixed Methods Research Design

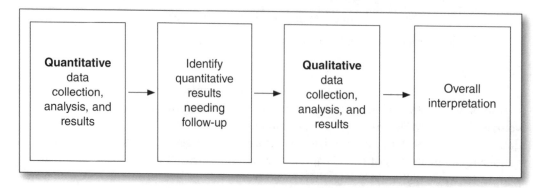

Next, she conducted a qualitative phase involving interviews. Using random cluster sampling, twelve women aged 29 to 49 were selected from the women who had agreed to interviews when completing the questionnaire. The first six participants within the age range to respond were chosen; in addition, six more participants were also interviewed, after which "the researcher felt comfortable that saturation had been achieved" (p. 302). The qualitative component explored women's viewpoints regarding their motivations and social realities, asking them to describe a week in their lives; differences between their experiences and their partner's; how they felt about certain activities they were involved in; the impact of caring for children on other experiences; and other such questions. This phase consisted of an interview, one week of diary writing (or written reflections), and a second interview (which included reflections on the first).

In analyzing Hodgkin's mixed methods data, there appears to be little dialogue between the quantitative and qualitative elements, except that the qualitative findings are in the service of the quantitative findings. Quantitative data were then analyzed to determine differences in types of participation based on gender. Here, gender was employed as a *nominal level variable*, with no differentiation among women in terms of specific differences that might matter, such as social class, age, and number of children. She notes that women as a categorical variable "reported higher levels of informal social participation, social participation in groups, and community group participation" (p. 307). In addition, women were involved more in informal sociability and activities with a group/community focus or focus on children. Men were more involved with civic and "formal" activities (e.g., sporting clubs, trade union groups; p. 308).

Analysis of the qualitative data results in three narratives—"wanting to be a 'good mother,' wanting to avoid social isolation, and wanting to be an active citizen" (p. 312)— that motivate women's participation in social, community, and civic activities. Hodgkin notes: "[T]he quantitative findings provide evidence of women's predominance in formal sociability and to a lesser extent men's predominance in associational life. . . . The researcher used the narratives to delve more into the motivations behind the range of participation" (p. 313).

Within her analysis stage, each method plays a distinct role, with one level layered on top of the other. She notes that the quantitative data provides "the big picture, revealing a different pattern of participation for men and women. The qualitative data assists in developing and sharpening this picture" (p. 313). There is no back and forth tension between the two data sets, nor any questioning of findings from either data set.

The author explicitly states that her research project is "located in the transformative paradigm" and is conducted in the tradition of feminist empiricist research (p. 299). Her research question is transformative in that it seeks to obtain subjugated knowledge regarding women's motivations and degree of social capital. However, Hodgkin does not push on the boundaries of this paradigm enough, nor use mixed methods to their full potential in this study. There is no attempt to discuss how her findings can serve to transform our understanding of women's social participation and its implications for actually improving women's condition.

In addition, the category of woman is treated as a universal category with no way for her to distinguish among the types of women and men in her study (i.e., with regard to differences in race, class, age, etc.). When gender is treated as a nominal level variable with little attention to differences among women and men, we need to be concerned that we do not begin to assume we are capturing the range of differences among both men and women's lived experiences.

This study is a cautionary one that reminds the researcher of the importance of reflecting on issues of difference as well as the validity of measures and variables we employ in our research. We need to ask, for example: "Do our measures measure what they are intended to?" Validity of measures becomes a critical factor in employing a sequential explanatory design in feminist research. There is the assumption that we are working with a "full deck" of variables and their dimensions with regard to gender (and, for that matter, a range of other differences). If we ignore doing so, we may unwittingly wind up stereotyping our perception of gendered experiences.

CONCLUSION[5]

THE PROMISE OF MIXED METHODS RESEARCH FOR FEMINISM

For feminists testing out their theories and generalizing their research findings, mixed methods designs may allow for integrating and contextualizing women's lived experiences with macro-level social patterns. O'Neill's mixed methods study does this by placing her research findings from both components in conversation with each other.

> By starting with a more qualitative method, I was able incorporate the rich discussions into the construction of survey questions. And indeed, the ability to better capture the multi-dimensionality of concepts by using the Qual/Quant design has been identified by others. (O'Neill, 2009, p. 11)

Mixed methods studies can generate the knowledge feminist researchers need to pursue social justice goals for women and other oppressed groups. For those social policy decision makers who expect researchers to have both numbers and words in their data, mixed methods projects are powerful tools for social change. This aim of social justice—and, particularly, the transformation of women's lives—is present in the case studies this chapter has covered.

Feminist perspectives, in turn, can enrich mixed methods praxis by adding to its validity. For example, feminist praxis provides strategies for dealing with gender bias by tending to issues of androcentrism, racism, classism, and so forth throughout the research process. Feminists stress the importance of taking into account the values and attitudes we bring to a research endeavor; thereby, we have a better chance of addressing these biases and thus strengthening the validity of our project.

The practice of "strong objectivity" can make these biases visible. When researchers disclose their values, attitudes, and biases regarding a set of research questions, their findings can maintain a higher degree of validity. There are a number of aspects of "strong objectivity" that can be important to a researcher. For example, be conscious of difference and how your research does or does not focus on difference (this will depend on your research question). Feminist researchers are typically aware of difference and, in particular, of the ways in which women's experiences will differ given their various locations in social structures and historic trends. A feminist approach makes central gender as it intersects with other differences such as race, class, sexuality, and so forth. O'Neill's case study highlights her awareness of the possible bias of measurement tools. By choosing not to use a secondary measure that neglected women's viewpoints, O'Neill challenges the standard conceptualization of religiosity within her discipline by developing a grounded set of measures that come out of her qualitative focus group component. The focus group allows her access to women's experiences regarding religion and their sense of spirituality. Specifically, her feminist perspective guides her mixed methods design in terms of "assistance with the choice of vocabulary and the phrasing of new questions that deviated from those employed in existing surveys" (O'Neill, 2009, p. 12).

Feminist mixed methods research grounds the research question in the chosen method(s) used. Mixed methods research design is not in itself "methods-centric," as the design usually unfolds as the process of data collection unfolds. The design takes shape as the researcher iteratively gathers data, analyzes and interprets it, and decides on the next steps. Katsulis's case study began with a qualitative component: ethnographic observations and interviews. As she analyzed the data she had gathered, she then expanded her project to include other sectors of sex industry workers in Tijuana.

Feminist research often destabilizes dualistic variables like sex/gender by examining the interconnections between categories. The constructedness of the sex/gender category and the heightened awareness of difference are two emphases in feminist research processes. Additionally, feminist researchers push mixed methods research to find purposes beyond triangulation. For example, Nightingale's research made use of mixed methods designs to uncover the silenced voices of women of various castes. In addition to collecting oral histories and forestry documents, she integrated a more quantitative approach (aerial photo analysis) to unearth women's experiences.

Researchers who are interested in mixed methods at the data analysis and data interpretation stage can look to feminist approaches for strategies. Nightingale's project is an excellent example of how the different levels of data analysis can and should be brought into dialogue with each other. Noting its inability to discover the causalities underlying forest changes, she did not rely on GPS data alone. Had she, like traditional geographic researchers, used GPS data alone as primary evidence of forest usage, she would have been limited to its single viewpoint.

Feminist perspectives are not constrained by a single methodology; instead, they are applicable across a spectrum of views on reality, from positivism to postmodernism. A feminist approach to mixed methods encourages researchers to push beyond triangulation and accommodates the tensions and ambiguities that arise from the use of diverse qualitative and quantitative methods in feminist research projects. Such an approach does not suggest that researchers should discontinue inquiry with the emergence of ambiguous findings but instead suggests that new knowledge is discovered in ambiguities. Marginalized knowledge can be brought to the foreground in the course of allowing tensions to remain in the research data.

THE CHALLENGE OF MIXED METHODS RESEARCH FOR FEMINIST RESEARCHERS

As seen in the case studies, feminist approaches to mixed methods research can run into obstacles when using both quantitative and qualitative methods. For example, feminist researchers may inadvertently introduce androcentric biases to their projects when they choose to work with the limited measures available to them. This obstacle was found in O'Neill's study; she was able to circumnavigate this because of the fortuitous timing of her grant and alternatively develop her own measures based on women's lived experiences. Other feminist researchers may need to rely on "the master's tools" and thereby unintentionally subvert their own attempts to disrupt gender stereotypes.

Additionally, some of the limitations of the case studies have shown how feminist researchers at times do not go far enough to connect their quantitative and qualitative components. A lack of synergy can be absent due to this neglect, as the tensions and ambiguities that arise between the two sets of separate data may not be accounted for or explored. The possibilities for social change and transformation are narrowed when the quantitative and qualitative sets of data are not integrated to their fullest extent.

PARTING THOUGHTS

Mixed methods research can unite women's lived experiences across macro and micro levels and can unearth diverse understandings of women's lives. In order for these levels to be brought together, mixed methods research requires its researchers to pay attention to dialogue. Developing good communication and listening skills, and taking differences into account will improve understanding. Feminist researchers must (1) orient research toward understanding rather than "winning," (2) reflect and confront our assumptions (especially those related to gender and sex), (3) accept and embrace difference, (4) suspend judgment, and (5) listen in order to build new sets of shared assumptions and culture.

Practicing these research skills will maintain the synergistic promise of mixed methods research. As social researchers increasingly acquire and use mixed methods, they also magnify the importance of the research question. Further, acknowledging and thinking through the "context of discovery" will impact the choice of methods. It remains true that two methods are not necessarily better than one, even though mixed methods projects have some clear advantages. Feminist researchers should continue to seek methods that are flexible, adaptable, and that foster awareness of potential androcentric bias, as finding such tools will allow feminists to work toward social justice.

DISCUSSION QUESTIONS

1. What are some problems that feminists identify in traditional research processes, and in what ways do feminists hope to alleviate these problems?

2. What unique advantages do mixed methods offer to feminist researchers?

3. What is the definition of "strong objectivity" in relation to research praxis, and what does it mean for feminist research? For mixed methods research?

4. Coming from a feminist perspective, how do the following research projects use mixed methods? What advantages do mixed methods lend to these projects? What do these research designs look like? How were they formulated? How do they compare?

   - Nightingale's (2003) forest usage study in Nepal, India
   - Katsulis's (2009) sex work study in Tijuana, Mexico
   - O'Neill's (2009) study of public opinion in Canada
   - Hodgkin's (2008) work on social capital in Australia

5. Define reflexivity. Why is it so important to feminist researchers? Provide an example to support your answer.

WEB RESOURCES

- Best Practices for Mixed Methods Research in the Health Sciences

  http://obssr.od.nih.gov/scientific_areas/methodology/mixed_methods_research/index.aspx

  Website contains some very useful "guidelines" you might peruse when thinking about conducting a mixed methods research project. The website was prepared by the Office of Behavioral and Social Sciences Research Division of the National Institutes of Health (NIH), U.S. Department of Health & Human Services. These guidelines are particularly helpful to follow if you are considering obtaining research funding from NIH.

- Glossary of Mixed Methods Terms/Concepts

  http://www2.fiu.edu/~bridges/glossary.htm

  A dictionary of terms and concepts related to mixed methods research.

NOTES

1. Part of this case study example is adapted from S. Hesse-Biber, *Mixed Methods Research: Merging Theory with Practice* (Guilford, 2010b).
2. This case study was adapted from Hesse-Biber, 2010a.
3. This case study was adapted from Hesse-Biber, 2010a.
4. This case study was adapted from Hesse-Biber, 2010a.
5. Part of this conclusion is adapted from Hesse-Biber, 2010a.

REFERENCES

Bowles, G., & Duelli Klein, R. (Eds.). (1983). *Theories of women's studies.* London, England: Routledge & Kegan Paul.

Chafetz, J. S. (2004). Some thoughts by an unrepentant "positivist" who considers herself a feminist nonetheless. In S. Hesse-Biber & M. L. Yaiser (Eds.), *Feminist perspectives on social research* (pp. 302–329). New York, NY: Oxford University Press.

Cole, E. R., & Stewart, A. J. (2012). Narratives and numbers: Feminist multiple methods research. In S. Hesse-Biber (Ed.), *Handbook of feminist research: Theory and praxis* (2nd ed., pp. 368–387). Thousand Oaks, CA: Sage.

Collins, P. H. (1990). *Black feminist thought: Knowledge, consciousness, and the politics of empowerment*. New York, NY: Routledge.

DeVault, M. (1990). Talking and listening from women's standpoint: Feminist strategies for interviewing and analysis. *Social Problems, 37,* 96–116.

Eichler, M., & Lapointe, J. (1985). *On the treatment of the sexes in research.* Ottawa, Ontario: Social Sciences and Humanities Research Council of Canada.

Haraway, D. (1991). Situated knowledges: The science question in feminism and the privilege of partial perspective. In *Simians, cyborgs, and women* (pp. 183–202). New York, NY: Routledge.

Harding, S. (1986). *The science question in feminism.* Ithaca, NY: Cornell University Press.

Harding, S. (1987). Introduction: Is there a feminist method? In S. Harding (Ed.), *Feminism and Methodology* (pp. 1–14). Bloomington: Indiana University Press.

Harding, S. (1991). *Whose science? Whose knowledge?* Ithaca, NY: Cornell University Press.

Harding, S. (1993). Rethinking standpoint epistemology: What is "strong Objectivity"? In L. Alcoff & E. Potter (Eds.), *Feminist epistemologies* (pp. 49–82). New York, NY: Routledge.

Harding, S. (2007). Feminist standpoints. In S. Hesse-Biber (Ed.), *Handbook of feminist research: Theory and praxis,* (pp. 45–69). Thousand Oaks, CA: Sage.

Hesse-Biber, S. (2010a). Feminist approaches to mixed methods research: Linking theory and praxis. In A. Tashakkori & C. Teddlie (Eds.), *SAGE handbook of mixed methods in social & behavioral research* (2nd ed., pp. 169–192). Thousand Oaks, CA: Sage.

Hesse-Biber, S. (2010b). *Mixed methods research: Merging theory with practice.* New York, NY: Guilford.

Hesse-Biber, S., & Carter, G. L. (2005). *Working women in America: Split dreams.* New York, NY: Oxford University Press.

Hesse-Biber, S., & Leavy, P. (2008). *Handbook of emergent methods.* New York, NY: Guilford.

Hodgkin, S. (2008). Telling it all: A story of women's social capital using a mixed methods approach. *Journal of Mixed Methods Research, 2,* 296–316.

Katsulis, Y. (2009). *Sex work and the city: The social geography of health and safety in Tijuana, Mexico.* Austin: University of Texas Press.

Lather, P. (1991). *Getting smart: Feminist research and pedagogy with/in the postmodern.* New York, NY: Routledge.

Leckenby, D., & Hesse-Biber, S. (2007). Feminist approaches to mixed methods research. In S. Hesse-Biber & P. Leavy (Eds.), *Feminist research practice: A primer* (pp. 249–291.) Thousand Oaks, CA: Sage.

Lorde, A. (1984). *Sister outsider: Essays and speeches.* Berkeley, CA: The Crossing Press.

Mendez, J. B., & Wolf, D. L. (2012). Feminizing global research/globalizing feminist research: Methods and practice under globalization. In S. Hesse-Biber (Ed.), *Handbook of feminist research: Theory and praxis* (2nd ed., pp. 641–658). Thousand Oaks, CA: Sage.

Miner, K. N., Jayaratne, T. E., Pesonen, A., & Zurbrugg, L. (2012). Using survey research as a quantitative method for feminist social change. In S. Hesse-Biber (Ed.), *Handbook of feminist research: Theory and praxis* (2nd ed., pp. 237–263). Thousand Oaks, CA: Sage.

Mohanty, C. T. (1988). Under Western eyes: Feminist scholarship and colonial discourses. *Feminist Review, 30,* 61–88.

Morgan, D. (1998). Practical strategies for combining qualitative and quantitative methods: Applications to health research. *Qualitative Health Research, 8,* 362–376.

Naples, N. (2007). Standpoint epistemology and beyond. In S. Hesse-Biber (Ed.), *Handbook of feminist research: Theory and praxis* (pp. 579–589). Thousand Oaks, CA: Sage.

Nightingale, A. (2003). A feminist in the forest: Situated knowledges and mixing methods in natural resource management. *ACME, 2*(1), 77–90.

O'Neill, B. (1995). The gender gap: Re-evaluating theory and method. In S. Peterborough (Ed.), *Changing methods: Feminists reflect on practice* (pp. 327–355). Ontario, Canada: Broadview Press.

O'Neill, B. (2009, January). *A mixed methods approach to studying women's political opinions.* Prepared for delivery at the First European Conference on Politics and Gender, Queen's University of Belfast, UK.

Reinharz, S. (1985). Feminist distrust: Problems of context and content in sociological work. In D. Berg & K. Smith (Eds.), *Exploring clinical methods for social research*, (pp. 63–84). New York, NY: Wiley.

Roberts, H. (1981). *Doing feminist research.* Boston, MA: Routledge & Kegan Paul.

Smith, D. (1978). A peculiar eclipsing: Women's exclusion from man's culture. *Women's Studies International Quarterly, 1,* 281-296.

Spalter-Roth, R., & Hartmann, H. (1996). Small happinesses: The feminist struggle to integrate social research with social activism. In H. Gottfried (Ed.), *Feminism and social change* (pp. 206–224). Urbana: University of Illinois Press.

Wing, A. K. (2000). *Global critical race feminism: An international reader.* New York: New York University Press.

Zinn, M. B., Hondagneu-Sotelo, P., & Messner, M. A. (2008). *Gender through the prism of difference.* New York, NY: Allyn & Bacon.

CHAPTER 13
Conclusion

Putting Together Your Research Project

Sharlene Hesse-Biber

Conducting a Feminist Research Project

In this chapter, I bring together a series of building blocks for thinking about how to put together a research project with an emphasis on feminist research issues and praxis.

The basic premise of this entire book has been to provide you with the theoretical and empirical tools for conducting research from a feminist perspective. The book provides you with a detailed analysis of a range of methods that feminists have employed in their research projects from survey research to ethnography, from in-depth interviewing and focus groups to mixed methods research.

I leave you with a "hands-on" research example that illustrates the genesis, analysis, and interpretation as well as the writing up of a feminist research project. While I cannot tackle all the methods you have learned in this book, I will select one method and follow that from the research question I address. I also provide you with a general checklist of things to consider once your project is complete.

What Are the Steps to Consider as You Begin Any Feminist Research Project?

STEP 1. DEVELOPING IDEAS

Deciding on a research problem. One way to discover a problem that you feel passionate about is to practice reflexivity. What social justice causes resonate with you? What kinds of communities are you interested in working with? What broad goals do you hope to achieve with your research? When figuring out just what type of researcher you are and what exactly it is that you want to research, I suggest that you complete the short exercise that follows:

(1) Write down your research problem in one sentence.

(2) Write two questions that are related to this problem.

A generalized research problem is usually contained in a single sentence. Research questions are more specific and detailed, and should directly flow from your research problem. Thinking through the relationship between your research problem and potential research questions will help you to choose a research question to pursue.

Again, reflexivity is an important feminist research strategy that provides you a way to connect with your particular research interests. Further, reflexivity asks you to be conscious of your own researcher standpoint by considering the specific values and attitudes you bring to the research problem at hand. What assumptions are you making about social reality? Some sensitizing questions you might ask yourself are:

- In what sense is reality knowable?

- How do I perceive the social world?

- Do I perceive that meaning is multiple and subjective, or do I assume that there is a "truth," out there waiting to be found?

If there are stakeholders who have funded your study and who have determined what research problem they want to fund, you might apply the same reflexive questions to those who are sponsoring your study. How you answer these philosophical questions is important because they will greatly influence not only the formulation of your research question, but also the selection of methods and data analysis strategies that you will use to answer your research question.

Role of literature review. Once you have honed in on a specific research area and/or topic, begin to review the research literature. This is usually a good first step in enabling you to fine-tune exactly what type of research question or set of questions you want to pursue.

First, if you are interested in a general topic, but feel vague about how to narrow down your interest to a specific research question, conducting a literature review in your area of interest might be a good way to begin. You might first want to familiarize yourself with the computerized literature retrieval systems that may be available to you, including the large variety of databases available online and offline. Many of these databases contain abstracts (summaries) of articles and reports that will enable you to quickly obtain an overview of these works. You may also want to think of some important "key words" or phrases that you can input into these databases that will best describe the topic under consideration.

- How do the authors of these articles define their topic?
- What key terms and phrases do they employ?

As you progress in your literature review, it will be helpful to keep a list of these key words, phrases, and definitions so that you can build up a useful set of terms to input into your databases and, later, use to anchor your own research. While conducting your review of related literature, you may want to keep the following questions in mind, as their answers will give you a sense of what has and has not been researched in your chosen area and how such research has been conducted:

- How have other researchers approached your topic? With what questions?
- What has been the history of research on this topic?
- What are the research controversies within this literature?
- What is known? Which findings seem most relevant to your interests?
- What remains to be done—that is, which burning questions still need to be addressed concerning your topic?

You might think about the literature review as a network of expert information that you tap into from time to time throughout your research project to help you "answer" many of these questions. Each time you query this knowledge network, you are given an opportunity to read about and ultimately be part of the conversation about a given research topic. If you have already narrowed down your topic to some specific questions, the literature review can provide you a context within which to place these questions and will allow you to "tweak" them on the basis of what you find out in your literature review. Perhaps you will discover that several researchers have already asked a similar question. How will this affect how you pursue your topic? Will you decide to replicate their study, extend your study to a different population, or alter your question somewhat to pursue an uncharted area?

You might also peruse the research literature about your research problem and identify the set of questions others have focused on regarding the research problem of interest to you and what specific research findings impact your problem. What issues in the literature regarding your research problem have not been addressed? What gaps can you discern in the current research thinking/findings with regard to your research problem?

While doing this, also look at the types of issues other scholars tackle regarding your research problem area and the way they specify their study in terms of asking specific research questions. How are these questions linked or not linked to their research design (methods used/sample/analysis) and interpretation of their data? What skills are required to answer these research questions? How much time and money do you think it took to finish this study? Write up a reflexive memo about how this study has impacted your thinking about how you want to proceed with your own research. Do you have the time and research skills to carry out this research problem as it is stated in your research questions? What additional resources will you need to carry out this research, and are they readily available to you?

In a qualitative research design, it is important not to think of the literature review as occurring at a fixed point within the research process (see Figure 13.1).

It is often the case in quantitative research that the literature review is conducted at the beginning of a research project and serves as a justification for the researcher's choice of particular questions and their research significance. Given the cyclical and iterative nature of the qualitative research process, with its emphasis on discovery, the

Figure 13.1 Cyclical and Iterative Nature of the Literature Review in Qualitatively Driven Research Projects

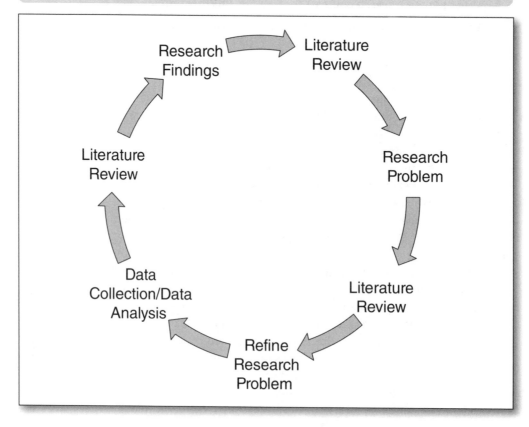

literature review may need to be conducted at multiple points in the research process as new discoveries are made within the data; in this case, the researchers can look to the literature to provide a context within which to understand their findings. The function of an initial literature review in qualitative research is primarily to formulate a set of relevant and sometimes general exploratory questions about a topic or phenomenon, unlike in quantitative research where the literature review serves to generate a specific set of hypotheses that can be tested. For this reason, an initial literature review for a qualitative study may not have to be as lengthy or exhaustive as is expected for a quantitative study. This is especially true in qualitative research because the initial research questions may change early on in the research process in response to new discoveries in the field that shift the researcher's understanding of the phenomenon.

Additional strategies for formulating a research problem include finding out about the work that faculty and students are working on in your discipline or profession. When possible, network among these research scholars. You might want to make a list of faculty/advanced graduate students in your department/program who might assist you in refining your research problem.

Set up a general meeting with at least two scholars to brainstorm about your research problem. Before this meeting it is important to come up with an agenda of what specific things you want to ask each scholar and also set aside time to brainstorm with them about your research interests. Discuss potential research problems you have been thinking about and get feedback from them. Ask them about how they chose their research problem and if they have any tips for you. The research problem and questions you listed from going through the exercise I suggested at the beginning of this step will be useful when discussing your potential research interests with faculty members and graduate students.

STEP 2. DECIDING ON YOUR RESEARCH DESIGN

Once you've tackled the major questions contained in Step 1, you will have a question or set of questions to answer in the research project. Remember that depending upon your particular methodology (theoretical perspective), your question or set of questions may change over the course of your research. As you begin to collect data, you may find you are constantly tweaking your question as new data is collected.

Next, I address some strategies for selecting a methods design that best suits your research project by offering a set of research strategies you might think about as you decide on your research design.

- Be sure to maintain a tight link between your research problem and the research method. In what sense does your research problem lend itself to a particular method of data collection, such as a survey or an in-depth interview or perhaps a mixed methods research design?

- Are you open to changing the design if needed?

In posing this question, the researcher acknowledges that methods are tightly linked to research problems, and a feminist researcher needs to make a conscious effort not to de-link the research problem from methods praxis (Figure 13.2). An example of this tight link is provided later in the chapter when we study the phenomenon of the "Freshman 15." If you choose to mix methods, another set of research design issues/questions will come to the forefront, namely, what will be your primary and secondary method? Will they both be primary? How will you sequence the methods in time? Will you collect the qualitative and quantitative methods at the same time (a parallel mixed methods study)? Will you sequence the data collection over time—first collect one method, then the other? Remember it is important to ask yourself: Why this mixed methods design? Will it serve to answer the questions that flow from my research problem? In what sense?

Sample. How will you decide on the target sample? Should you consider diversity within your target sample? Is getting a diverse sample by gender, race, class, and so on critical to your research problem? The type of sample also depends on the methods selected. Do you seek a representative sample of a given population? This will require you to become familiar with random sampling procedures (see survey Chapter 10). How important is it that you generalize your research findings to a wider population? If so, you will need to gain skills in how to gather a representative sample of the wider target population you seek to generalize about. If you then collect qualitative data, what type of sample will you need for the qualitative component of your mixed methods project? Do you need this sample to be representative? Why or why not?

STEP 3. WHAT TYPE OF DATA ANALYSIS?

In order to determine the type of data analysis you will employ on each type of data collected in answering your research question or questions, it is important to ask yourself

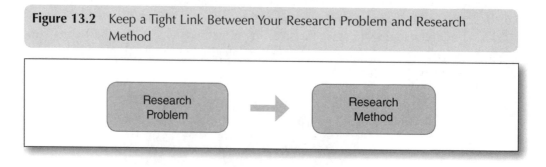

Figure 13.2   Keep a Tight Link Between Your Research Problem and Research Method

what type of data analysis strategy (i.e., grounded theory analysis, statistical analysis, etc.) will best serve to answer your research question or set of questions. The research question, then, is your guide to determining the type or types of data analysis you will employ in answering your research problem.

A grounded theory data analysis, which I use in the in-depth research example that follows and discuss at length here, provides a way into understanding meaning in your data. It is a method of analysis in that it provides a way to develop "progressively more abstract conceptual codes that are called "categories" to synthesize, to explain and to understand" data (Charmaz, 1995, p. 28). A grounded theory analysis begins with a close reading of your interview data. Charmaz (1995) suggests that one begins with "open coding." This consists of reading the data "line by line" and meticulously coding each line. The questions one should ask during this process as noted by Charmaz (1995) are:

- What is going on?
- What are people doing?
- What is the person doing?
- What do these actions and statements take for granted? (Charmaz, 1995, p. 38)

A grounded theory analysis consists of cycles of coding and memoing. Figure 13.3 illustrates the dynamic process between these two techniques.

Both codes and memos are pathways into your data. When coding the data, a researcher is doing some of these things:

1. Assigning words to segments of text

2. Sorting coded text segments in new ways

Figure 13.3 Maintain a Tight Link Between Memoing and Coding of Your Qualitative Data

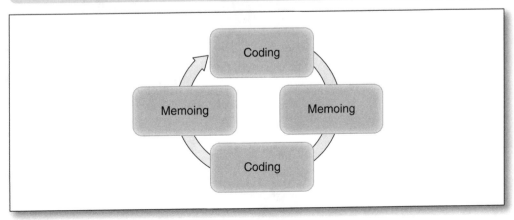

3. Condensing data into analyzable segments

4. Generating analytical concepts

When a researcher is memoing (see Figure 13.4), he or she is doing some of the following things:

1. Summarizing data through description

2. Including key quotes

3. Reflexively writing ideas about your analysis and interpretation of your data

4. Asking questions like: "What is going on here? How are these codes/categories related? What is not related? What does all this mean?" (See Charmaz, 2004.)

Figure 13.4   The Memoing Process

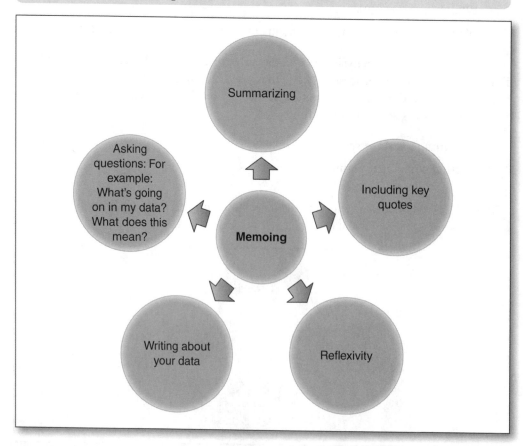

Sticking close to the data (by coding and memoing) allows you to "hear" the voices of the participants and, as Kathy Charmaz (1995) suggests, memoing about your data will help keep you grounded to your participants' meanings. Charmaz notes that by memoing, the researcher will "elaborate processes, assumptions and actions" that are embedded in codes (Charmaz, pp. 42–43). Writing memos serves to elevate a literal code to a "category." It is the interaction between coding and memoing that is what is at the heart of a grounded analysis. I literally ground my ideas in the data through this process. Ideally, the memo-writing process should occur all along the analysis process. Just as one reads the interview, one also reads and sorts through memos. This process of reading and sorting of memos is crucial to the development of one's ideas and theories. Memos allow me to see what are the relationships between code categories, what are my hunches about what is going on in my data, and what these codes mean; their ideas may even serve to bring up new ideas and relationships within the data.

Having said this, I am not "theory-less" in pursuing my topic. I may have some ideas about my given research project even before I begin to collect data, and it is important to remember that we bring these ideas into our research. In fact, our very interest in a topic and our own pet theories about what is going on can enter into our research. That's why it is also critical to be reflexive on your own "researcher standpoint" as you enter into any project and be aware of the range of biases you bring with you regarding the research topic.

While I utilized a grounded theory approach in my research example to follow, there is a multitude of other ways into your data. You might decide to do a narrative analysis— whereby you would not begin with "line by line" coding, but instead you would be interested in the ways in which participants frame meaning in terms of the stories they relate to you in their interviews. You would be interested in examining the structure of the narrative: Is it, for example, episodic or chronological? Is the meaning of specific stories contained within their interview? How do participants represent their lived reality in a story form? The unit of analysis of your interview is not the line, but the beginning and endings of stories contained within their interviews.

STEP 4. HOW WILL I INTERPRET FINDINGS FROM MY ANALYSIS OF THE DATA COLLECTED?

It is important to note that analysis and interpretation are not necessarily two distinct phases in the qualitative research process, as we have seen in the case of grounded theory analysis. The process is much more fluid, as the researcher often engages simultaneously in the processes of data collection, data analysis, and interpretation of research findings.

Memo writing is an important link between analysis and interpretation. With early observations in the field or with the first interviews conducted, early memo writing will allow the researchers to look at what interpretations of the data seem plausible and which ones they ought to revise.

David Karp notes the following concerning memo writing:

> Especially at the beginning you will hear people say things that you just hadn't thought about. Look carefully for major directions that it just had not occurred to you to take. The pace of short memo writing ought to be especially great toward the beginning of your work. I would advocate the "idea" or "concept" memos that introduce an emerging idea. Such memos typically run 2 to 3 pages.

> By this [a data memo] I mean a memo that integrates the theme with data and any available literature that fits. By a data memo, I mean something that begins to look like a paper. In a data memo, always array more data on a point than you would actually use in a research paper. If you make a broad point and feel that you have 10 good pieces of data that fit that point, lay them all out for inspection and later use. Also, make sure to lay out the words of people who do *not fit the pattern*. (Karp, personal correspondence, 2004)

Working with qualitative data, whether those data are collected from fieldwork observations or intensive interviewing, the researcher is constantly involved with the data at an intimate level. As we transition from problems with data collection and coding to issues of writing up research results, other questions begin to emerge concerning the interpretation of qualitative data. At the heart of this questioning are issues of power and control over the interpretation process.

As we mention in many chapters, some qualitative researchers follow a scientific model of research, using patterned research procedures along the lines of the natural sciences and following the tenets of positivism. Under this framework, it is imperative that the researcher be objective—that is, not allow his or her values to enter into the research process. In this model of research, the scientist remains objective in order to gain a "true" understanding of reality. In this tradition, it is as if "reality" or the "true" picture will emerge only if the researcher is true to the scientific tenet of objectivity.

Much of qualitative research, however, deals with observation and interviewing, methods that require constant interaction between the researcher and the researched. The researcher can impact the research process at multiple points along the research path—from the choice of research project and problem to the analysis and interpretation of findings. There are important power dynamics within the interviewer/interviewee relationship that can affect the interpretation of research results.

In the chapter on in-depth interviewing, I noted that certain social attributes of researcher and researched can impact issues of power and authority in the research process (see Chapter 7). We also saw in the Feminist Ethnography chapter how these attributes can guide one's entire research project, from gaining access to the setting, to the social relations in the setting, to how one exits the setting (see Chapter 5).

One of the central issues to examine in this discussion of the interpretation of findings is the extent to which power differences between the researcher and researched impact the research findings and the researcher's assessment of what they mean (the interpretation process).

What power does the researcher have in determining whose voice will be heard in the interpretation of research findings?

This question is of central importance in the work of Katherine Borland (1991). She explores the range of interpretive conflicts in the oral narrative she conducts with her grandmother, Beatrice Hanson. She asks her grandmother to talk about the time she accompanied her father to the racetrack at the fairgrounds in Bangor, Maine, an event that happened more than 42 years earlier.

Borland is interested in understanding the different levels of meaning making that take place in the telling and interpretation of oral narratives. She recognizes that there are multiple levels of interpreting narratives. A first-level narrative story—that is, the story her grandmother tells her—conveys the particular way her grandmother constitutes the meaning of the event (pp. 63–64). There is, however, a second level of meaning to the narrative: the meaning the researcher constructs, filtered through the personal experience and expertise of the researcher. Borland listens to her grandmother's story and reshapes it by filtering the story through her own personal life experiences and outward experiences—keeping in mind the expectations of her scholarly peers, to whom, she notes, "we must display a degree of scholarly competence" (p. 73).

Borland (1991) uses a gender-specific theoretical lens to interpret her grandmother's story as a feminist account. However, her grandmother does not agree with her interpretation. In dealing with these issues of authority or ownership of the narrative, Borland raises issues about who has the authority to interpret narrative accounts. For Borland, the answer lies in a type of delicate balancing act. Borland shows her interpretation to her grandmother, and the process of exchanging ideas and interpretations begins. It is clear that no story should remain unmediated. In other words, the storyteller's viewpoint ought to be present within the interpretation. While not all conflicts can be resolved, it is important that the researcher be challenged by the narrator's point of view. The exchange of points of view might provide new ways of understanding the data. In the case of Borland's research, what came out of the exchange between Borland and her grandmother was a more nuanced understanding that included her grandmother's interpretation and Borland's creation of a more nuanced understanding of the research data.

STEP 5. HOW WILL YOU WRITE UP YOUR METHODS PROJECT?

How you write up your mixed methods project results should also be tightly linked to your original research problem and the questions that flowed from them. Some important decisions need to be made as you begin to write up your research findings.

It is important for you to be transparent about how you went about conducting your research project. The reader needs to follow the logic you employed to analyze your data and to understand the rationale behind your selection of a given set of methods to answer your research problem. The reader should also be able to understand how the set of analytical methods you selected is related to the meaning of both your qualitative and quantitative data. You might want to consult the research literature on your topic/problem to explore exactly how researchers tackle a specific problem, focusing on how they analyze and interpret their data using a specific method.

Gaining credibility for your research findings also means that the conclusions you draw from your data don't overreach what you actually found in your data. A common issue in many research write-ups is researchers claiming they did more than they actually did. The reader needs to see that you in fact provide credible evidence in answering each of your research questions without overstating your accomplishments. It's also important to let the reader know the drawbacks of your research project: what you didn't do. This, too, will lend more credibility to your study in the eyes of your reader. Every study has weaknesses—knowing them and claiming them is an important part of building credible evidence for what you did do and that you know its limitations.

Summary of Steps:

Step 1. Formulate a research question or problem.

Step 2. Create a mixed methods design that will address your research question.

Step 3. Determine what set of tools you will use to analyze and interpret your data.

Step 4. Decide how you will integrate your collected data sets in the analysis stage.

Step 5. Figure out how you will best convey your findings in your write-up.

In addition to these specific steps, there are some additional factors you might want to consider before you launch into a mixed methods project.

STEP 6. OTHER CONSIDERATIONS

Ethical considerations. Have you met the requirements of an IRB (Institutional Review Board) that is responsible for the ethical research conduct at your college or university or worksite? What ethical issues do you foresee in your research project, given your research problem and mixed methods design? What ethical framework informs how you conduct your own research beyond those requirements you must meet to obtain approval to conduct your study from an IRB? For example, think about how your study might benefit the participants who agreed to be part of your study, and how much do you go out of your way to provide some type of reciprocity for the time and effort they gave in making your study a reality? You might consider providing your participants with a copy of their transcripts if you conducted an interview with them, or you might send them a copy of your research findings.

Methods training. Do you have the required methods training to conduct your study? This is especially the case if you decide to select a mixed methods research design. For example, qualitative researchers who add a survey to their design may find it difficult to analyze their quantitative survey results if they lack basic training in the gathering and analysis of quantitative data. The same issue applies for those quantitative researchers who add a qualitative method to their research design. Without these methods skills, the mixing of methods may not provide the "synergistic" promise of mixed methods research designs.

Putting a Feminist Research Project Together: An Example[1]

This section of the chapter provides a holistic example of putting your own research ideas into practice, following the steps I just outlined for you.

While this example by no means tackles all the methods presented in this book, I have selected one method that follows from my initial research questions. I will also discuss the use of computer software programs as an option for contemplating the analysis of your data. I also address some general issues you might consider when you're interpreting and writing up your research results.

CONDUCTING A RESEARCH PROJECT: SETTING THE SCENE

The following excerpts are the voices of college women who were interviewed about their body image during their freshman year of college, and more specifically about their feelings regarding the infamous "Freshman 15," the fifteen pounds that college-age women frequently gain during their first-year experience at college. Let's listen to some of their comments.

Pam: I remember when I was in freshman year I came to school and gained that weight and when I went home for Christmas I remember my dad remarked that I was getting a little chubbier especially in my butt. And I think that was one of the main reasons when I came back to school I started excessively losing weight.

Emily: I gained it quick. When I went home for Christmas I had gained 15 pounds!

And somebody noticed it?

Emily: Yeah, my whole family.

So what happened then?

Emily: After that I came back from my semester break. I noticed that my friends who had gone to school hadn't really gained weight. My parents had noticed, and my brothers. And so when I came back I stopped eating between meals and I rarely ate breakfast. I ran 2 miles a day. . . . I wanted to lose weight. To avoid eating at night I would go to the library and study. That's what I did. Studying in the library, I'm not in my room. When I came back I would say I have to go to bed because I had been sick and so I was conscious about going to bed early.

Judy: You know, when I overate it was my freshman year. The most I ever ate in my life. I never vomited it out. I wouldn't know how to do that. I did do it sort of secretly you could say. My freshman year roommate, you know she was thin and fine and she could eat what she wanted. She didn't overeat. She could eat a hamburger and french fries for lunch. She just wouldn't go out and have a sundae and everything on top of it. She was just that type of metabolism. And freshman year when you have the points, and you got the store, and you got the cookies, and the candy bars. My mother never really bought that stuff, which is great. We never had any kind of junk food like that around. Once in a while my mother would buy it and we'd gobble it up. We'd have ice cream, plenty of that, so I wasn't like a hog over that. I didn't need that. When I went to college, I did buy like cookies and candy and when she wasn't there I was eating them. I was eating alone.

THE RESEARCH PROBLEM

What is the lived experience of college freshman women regarding their perceptions of their body image in college?

The goal for this project is exploratory in nature. I am interested in understanding what the specific body image issues college freshman women may have. I have read some literature on this topic and found that few research studies on this are focused on college women's "subjective experiences." Most studies were based on survey research data whose goals were to test out specific hypotheses using quantitative measures that looked at specific factors, such as "levels of body dissatisfaction" measures, using a set of scales whereby a participant had to select from a limited range of answers. While some studies noted a relationship between body dissatisfaction and eating issues, there was little discussion of: "Why" was this the case? How did women's own feelings about their college life have an impact on being dissatisfied with their bodies? and How might this, in turn, have led to their eating issues? This form of inquiry, led me to focus on under-standing women's subjective experiences. I have some general agenda items I am partic-ularly interested in, such as whether or not college freshman women experience what has been termed the "Freshman 15," the fifteen pounds that many college women are alleged to gain during their first year at college.

RESEARCH DESIGN

I decide to conduct a *convenience sample* of college freshman women who attend the university at which I am also a professor. I decide to recruit women by putting up signs around the campus, including the local women's resource center. I want to obtain a *pur-posive sample* of college freshman women with diverse backgrounds. So I am interested in having representation of freshman women by race and ethnic background and social class, where possible. I am interested in obtaining 25 interviews in order to make some statements about differences among women by race and ethnicity, and, where possible, by class status. I have obtained approval to conduct this study from my college's institutional review board (IRB).

I decide as well to conduct in-depth interviews as my method as I want to get at the lived experience of women. I would probably start out my interview with a set of general open-ended interview questions with the goal of gaining insight into and understanding the lives of freshman women. I follow the guidelines on interviewing that we have talked about in the in-depth interviewing chapter. I am mindful that I am an "outsider" as well as an "insider" in the college community. As a white, middle-class female college professor, I am interviewing college students; and there is an inherent power dynamic in my relationship with them. In my interviews with women of color, there will be differences to consider in terms of my race/ethnicity and class status. It would be important at this point for me to reflect in a research memo on these differences and how they might impact the research situation. How do my unique differences bump up against those I interview? What biases do I bring to the interview situation?

I gather my data by using a digital recorder with the permission of my participant. I am careful at the end of each interview to ask each participant if there is something they would like to talk about that we have not touched upon. I am also aware that when I turn off the recorder and continue to talk with my participant, this is also valuable data, and I can use it as long as my participant has agreed to let me do so in my consent form. I do my best to recall what transpired without the recorder running right after I leave the interview. I am careful to follow what I have learned about the importance of establishing rapport with my participants and being careful to listen intently to what they are telling me, mindful of any muted language contained within their dialogue.

I am mindful as I plan my project to reflect on its ethical implications by following the IRB guidelines of my university's ethics board, along with a set of open-ended questions I prepared to provide the IRB with an idea of the types of questions I will be asking each participant. I have written up a detailed consent form for IRB approval, as well; and I am especially mindful to make sure I have a consent form signed by my research participant and agreed to before the interview begins.

DATA ANALYSIS[2]

I decide to use a grounded theory analysis of my data because it enables me to listen closely to the meanings the participants in my study relate to me regarding their first-year college experience especially around issues of body image. After each interview, I immerse myself in the data I collect by playing back the recording of my interview with my participant. As I begin to transcribe the interview, I am also beginning to analyze and interpret my data. That is, I am writing down any ideas that come to mind (memoing), looking for themes that I find particularly important. After a few interviews, I especially look for the common pathways or patterns of behavior whereby individuals experience their bodies within a college culture. I would be particularly mindful to write down my ideas as a set of data memos.

When I talk about data analysis, this means that I am looking for meaning within my data. As I mentioned earlier, *memoing* and *coding* are two important ways to get at meaning within my data. In Figure 13.5, I have taken an excerpt from one of my interviews with college freshman women concerning their eating patterns and disordered eating habits.

You can see from this excerpt above, I have "coded" the first few lines of text from one interview using a "literal" coding procedure that uses the participant's own words. These are descriptive code categories. If we proceed down the code list, the codes become more "analytical," for example, the term "positive body image." Nowhere does the participant say this, but the researcher generates the code "body image," which is a more conceptual category that appears to fit what the participant is saying when she notes, "I'm going to have so many boyfriends, and boys are going to be so in love with me." As we go further down the code list, the codes become much more interpretative.

Figure 13.5   Coding an Interview: Pam, College Freshman Interview Excerpt

(Text/Segment/Chunk)		Code
I always wanted to be the thinnest, the	→	Thinnest, prettiest
prettiest. I wanted to look like the girls	→	Look like girls in magazines
in the magazines. I'm going to have so	→	Boys will love me
many boyfriends, and boys are going	→	Positive body image
to be so in love with me, I won't have	→	Provides economic resources
to work, and I'll be taken care of for the	→	Thin rationale
rest of my life.	→	Thin as a means of security
	→	Media creates standards

Adapted from Hesse-Biber and Leavy (2004, p. 412).

To code means to take a segment of text and give it a "name," or sometimes a number. There are many ways to "code" a given text. I began by doing some "literal" coding and moved quickly to a more "focused" coding procedure. Sociologist Kathy Charmaz uses the term "focused" coding. She notes that when doing this, the researcher would look at all the coded data (for example, "positive body image"); look at all the pieces of text associated with that code for each interview; and compare each segment to the other in order to come up with a clearly delineated working idea of what the concept "positive body image" means (Charmaz, 1983, p.117).

Focused coding differs from "literal" coding in that you are not placing a "label" on something to describe what it is, but you are looking for a code description that allows you to develop an understanding or interpretation of what each of your participants is saying about their body image. To engage in "focused coding" means that you sort your "literal codes" into more abstract categories. This is a process of modification of code categories that moves your analysis from a literal to a more abstract level. This process is important in order to generate theoretical ideas.

You might begin this process in earnest after coding a number of interviews with college freshmen and retrieving the text associated with specific codes. Let's refer to the above segment of text. Suppose that I retrieved all the text associated with the code "thin." Reading through all the text segments associated with this code reveals, in fact, that participants are talking about thinness in a variety of ways. For example, in the text segment above, I note at the bottom of the segment—"thinness as a means of security" and "media creates standards." Thinness as a means of security is capturing what my participant is voicing when she says that she wants to have a boyfriend, love, money, and to be taken care of. In fact, examining other interviews uncovered a range of other reasons participants wanted to be thin, such as "thin as healthy," "thin as empowering," and so on. This eventually led me to develop an even larger code category I termed "Thin Rationales" of which the code category "thinness as a means of security," was a subset. A second larger category—"media creates standards" of behavior—was developed in a similar manner.

I eventually came up with a whole series of codes that I modified and that evolved into more abstract codes. So, for example, in the body image study with freshmen, we can see that the code "Clothing made for thin people" evolved into the code category "Clothing that fits" (see Figure 13.6).

Eventually, this category morphed into part of a still larger code titled "Body Surveillance." This represents the idea that women are constantly watching their bodies through checking on whether or not their clothing fits them, watching their image in the mirror, weighing themselves several times during the day, and so on, in addition to comparing their image to those super-thin models in the media. These initial codes then became part of a larger conceptual category that overall captures the importance of surveillance as a "control" mechanism used to coax women's bodies toward the thin idea initiated by the self and by society. You can see we are moving our analysis from the literal plane to a more abstract and theoretical understanding of women's body image concerns and to what might be some of the factors that help us understand their need to be thin. We might then begin to look at differences

Figure 13.6   Changes to Initial Codes in the Body Image Study

From	To
Clothing made for thin people	Clothing that fits
Minimal diet	Control over body and eating
Magazines	Media creates standards
Will always want to be thin	Values thinness
1. Thin as a means of security	All 4 characterized as "Thin Rationales"
2. Thin and healthy	
3. Thin as part of identity	
4. Thin/beauty is empowering	

among the sample in terms of whether or not women differ on these issues by race/ethnicity and, where possible, by class.

AN ASIDE: DATA ANALYSIS USING A COMPUTER-ASSISTED SOFTWARE PROGRAM

A researcher's analysis can be enhanced by the use of computer software packages. As Fielding and Lee (1998) note, the work of researchers over the past two decades is being transformed by computerized software programs. Software programs can be categorized into two main types. The first type consists of "generic software" that was not specifically designed for qualitative research. There are three types of software in this category. (1) "Word processors" assist the researcher with the typing and organizing of field notes and interviews as well as with developing an organizing scheme for these data. (2) "Text retrievers" can also quickly sort through a range of data to find a specific pattern or "string" of characters in the data to enable the researcher to identify themes and/or topics within a large body of data. (3) The last generic software mentioned is that of "textbase" managers. These are large database systems that allow for the retrieval of semistructured information that is entered into "records" and "fields."

There is a second main type of software that is specifically designed for qualitative data analysis. Hesse-Biber and Leavy (2006) note:

> These packages fall into four types: (1) "code and retrieve programs," (2) "code-based theory building programs," (3) "conceptual network building," and (4) "textual mapping software." Code and retrieve programs allow codes to be assigned to particular segments of text and make for easy retrieval of code categories using sophisticated "Boolean search functions." Code-based theory building programs allow the researcher to analyze the systematic relationships among the data, the codes, and code categories. Some programs provide a rule-based systems approach that allows for the testing of hypotheses in the data, while others allow for a visual representation of the data. Conceptual network building and textual mapping software programs allow the researchers to draw links between code categories in their data, and they see this as an "add-on" feature to their code-based theory building programs. (p. 361)

Fielding and Lee (1998) note that the field of qualitative software development has grown over time and there is a growing and extensive national and international community of software users. In addition, as Hesse-Biber and Leavy (2006) note:

> Computers hold out the promise of revolutionizing the way researchers conduct their analysis, but they also hold out a set of caveats for the qualitative analyst. The researcher who uses these programs should assess their strengths and weaknesses as well as the

implications of using computer software programs to analyze qualitative data. We recommend that you try these programs when appropriate and see how they work for you. (pp. 364–365)

INTERPRETATION AND WRITING UP OF YOUR RESEARCH PROJECT

In the next sections, I will provide you with a general overview regarding issues of interpretation and writing up of your research project. Norman K. Denzin (2004) suggests that there is an "art of interpretation."

This may also be described as moving from the field to the text to the reader. The practice of this art allows the field-worker-as-bricoler . . . to translate what has been learned into a body of textual work that communicates these understandings to the reader. (p. 447)

Figure 13.7   Process in the Analysis and Interpretation of Data

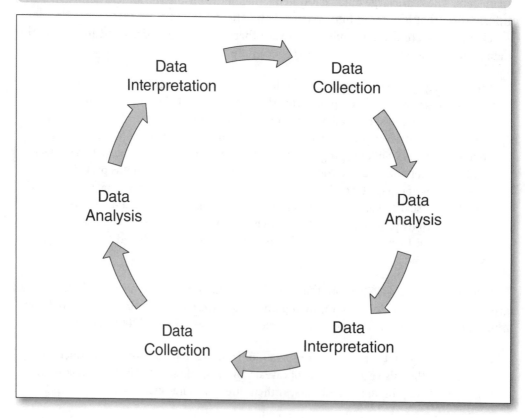

There is no specific path to interpreting your data. In fact, the researcher often goes back and forth from data analysis to data interpretation that leads to the collection, where appropriate, of more data. These are not separate phases of the research endeavor. The process is depicted in diagram in Figure 13.7.

Diagram of the "Iterative" Process in the Analysis and Interpretation of Data

As we can see in the diagram in Figure 13.7, the research process is fluid—with the researcher engaging in data collection, data analysis, and interpretation of research findings in a dynamic way. Memo writing is the link between analysis (What did I find?) and interpretation (What does it mean?). Early memo writing is the place where I ask: What does it mean? Which of my ideas seems to be supported by the data? What additional questions do I need to ask that I haven't asked? Who else should I interview? What have I not followed up on? What new data do I need to collect?

More questions begin to rise to the surface as we begin to put together the story of what we have found. What rises to the surface are specific issues of how we go about representing our respondents' subjective understandings of their lived experiences. What is at the center of this phase of the research process concerns issues of whose story we are in fact representing.

When you are ready to begin the writing phase of your project, be mindful of how connected your writing will be to the process of interpretation with which you are constantly engaged. In effect, writing and interpretation can be considered one and the same process. As there can be multiple analyses from any given research project, your task is to explore how the data you collected sheds meaning onto your research question.

CONCLUSION

As I end this chapter, I provide you with a "checklist" you might consult as you begin to undertake your research project. This list of questions is not exhaustive, but is meant to highlight some of the important factors you might consider in undertaking your own evaluation of your research project as a whole.

Evaluation Checklist of Questions you might ask yourself as you evaluate your research project.

- **Overall Research Question and Literature Review**

  Ask: Is the question clearly stated? Is the question clear and focused? Does it take into account ethical issues? Is it significant? Tip: In dealing with the question of significance of your problem, your review of the literature needs to make it clear to the reader exactly why this particular problem is important to your field. Show the reader, through your review of the research literature, how pursuing your particular problem will make a contribution.

- **Issues of Credibility**

  Ask: What are some criteria for assessing the validity of your research study? Do participants recognize their own experiences in your analysis and interpretation of the data? Why or why not? Do you provide an "audit trail" of your work? Can the reader follow the analytical steps you provide as evidence of credibility?

- **Research Design**

  Ask: Did you clearly describe your sampling procedure? Did you justify your selection of your sample procedure, given your research question? More specifically, is this sampling procedure a valid choice for this research problem?

  Did you clearly explain your rationale for selecting your method(s)? Did you justify how this particular research method will address your research question effectively?

- **Ethics**

  Ask: Did you state the ethical issues and considerations in conducting your research project? Did you address these ethical considerations clearly in your research project?

- **Analysis**

  Ask: Did you clearly justify how the analytical techniques you selected will serve to answer your research question? Did you fully describe your data analysis procedure? Have you done what you said you would do?

- **Interpretation**

  Ask: Can the reader get a sense (gestalt) of the meaning of your data from your written findings? Are your research findings placed in context of the literature on the topic?

  Ask: Does the evidence fit my data? Are the data congruent with your research question?

- **Conclusions/Recommendations**

  Ask: Do conclusions reflect your research findings? Do you provide some recommendations for future research?

  Ask: Have I discussed important limitations of my research project?

- **Significance of Your Work**

  Ask: What is the significance of your research?

As we have seen throughout this chapter, research is an iterative—back and forth—process, somewhat like fitting together the pieces of a puzzle. A little bit of data can go a long way in gathering meaning, and one should not be tempted to gather too much data while failing to reflect on the data bit by bit. What are required are a creative spirit and a set of analytical and interpretative skills. Coding and memoing are two powerful techniques you might employ to the process of understanding and interpreting your data. You may encounter false starts as well as moments of discovery and generation of theoretical insights into the analysis and interpretation of your data. This type of work is not for the "fainthearted." It often requires an attention to detail, and perseverance in the face of chaos, as well as a knack for tolerating ambiguity. The writing up of your research also requires that you, the researcher, be reflective of your own positionality—the set of social and economic attributes you bring to bear in analyzing and interpreting your data. It is a journey well worth taking, for the journey leads to our understanding and capturing the lived reality of those whom we research.

As we end this book, it's important to remind ourselves of the range of gains the women's movement and feminism have accomplished over these many decades—making gains toward gender equality. But there are major social issues and problems that remain resistant to change. There continues to be a growing violence against women across the globe. The feminization of poverty is still with us, and its consequences are devastating for women and their children. Global hunger continues to rise. Women who are employed in the workforce still experience the gender gap in wages, such that while women's wages have increased, the wage gap is still present and remains resistant to change. At home, women still find they are doing the majority of the housework, and the number of women who are heads of families continues to grow (see Hesse-Biber & Carter, 2005, for more details).

Feminist research offers a set of perspectives and praxis tools to address these and other issues resistant to change. The direction of feminist research, as we move into the next decades, must keep women's concerns and those of other oppressed groups central to its research mission. The field of feminist research also needs to maintain its strong interdisciplinarity that offers a multitheoretical perspective onto a range of societal and global issues. Feminist principles of praxis need to continue to foster social activism, social justice, and transformation around these increasingly global problems, issues, and concerns. While the feminist movement and feminist researchers have met with some success over the last decades, this should not mean that feminism and feminist research are irrelevant—quite to the contrary. They are the driving forces that must continue to provide findings and solutions to eradicate these social injustices. That is a goal worth striving for, supporting, and growing.

WEB RESOURCES

FEMINIST RESEARCH

- **Methodological and Epistemological Issues**

http://www.socresonline.org.uk/2/3/3.html

Covers a range of issues raised when doing feminist research. A paper from *Sociological Research Online* by D. Millen.

http://www.qualitative-research.net/fqs-texte/1-01/1-01westmarland-e.htm

Discusses the appropriateness of qualitative and quantitative methods for feminist research. A paper by Nicole Westmarland in *Forum: Qualitative Social Research.*

- **Feminist Research Design and Institutional Gatekeeping Mechanisms**

http://culturecat.net/node/460

A blog entry from Clancy Ratliff of the Department of English at East Carolina University discussing the problems posed by institutional gatekeeping mechanisms.

GROUNDED THEORY

- **Introductions to Grounded Theory**

www.analytictech.com/mb870/introtoGT.htm

A straightforward account of what grounded theory is and how to use it, by Steve Borgatti. The paper outlines the key principles of grounded theorizing and then goes on to discuss open, axial, and selective coding in turn, using worked examples of qualitative data.

NOTES

1. Portions of this section are adapted from Hesse-Biber & Leavy (2006), *The Practice of Qualitative Research,* Sage Publications, Inc. The parts presented are apart from the joint coauthorship.

2. Parts of this data analysis section are adapted from S. N. Hesse-Biber & P. Leavy (2004), Analysis, Interpretation, and the Writing of Qualitative Data, in S. N. Hesse-Biber & P. Leavy (Eds.), *Approaches to Qualitative Research: A Reader on Theory and Practice* (pp. 409–425), New York, NY: Oxford University Press. The parts presented are apart from the joint coauthorship.

REFERENCES

Borland, K. (1991). That's not what I said: Interpretive conflict in oral narrative research. In S. Gluck & D. Patai (Eds.), *Women's words: The feminist practice of oral history* (pp. 63–75). New York, NY: Routledge.

Charmaz, K. (1983). The grounded theory method: An explication and interpretation. In R. M. Emerson (Ed.), *Contemporary field research: A collection of readings* (pp. 109–126). Prospect Heights, IL: Waveland Press.

Charmaz, K. (1995). Grounded theory. In J. Smith, R. Harre, & L. Van Langenhove (Eds.), *Rethinking methods in psychology* (pp. 27–49). London, England: Sage.

Charmaz, K. (2004). Grounded theory. In S. Hesse-Biber & P. Leavy (Eds.), *Approaches to qualitative research: A reader on theory and practice* (pp. 496-521). New York, NY: Oxford University Press.

Denzin, N. K. (2004). The art and politics of interpretation. In S. Hesse-Biber & P. Leavy (Eds.), *Approaches to qualitative research: A reader on theory and practice* (pp. 447–472). New York, NY: Oxford University Press.

Fielding, N., & Lee, R. (1998). Introduction: Computer analysis and qualitative research. In N. Fielding & R. Lee (Eds.), *Computer analysis and qualitative research* (pp. 1–21). London, England: Sage.

Hesse-Biber, S., & Carter, G. L. (2005). *Working women in America: Split dreams.* New York, NY: Oxford University Press.

Hesse-Biber, S. N., & Leavy, P. (2004). *Approaches to qualitative research: A reader on theory and practice.* New York, NY: Oxford University Press.

Hesse-Biber, S. N., & Leavy, P. (2006). *The practice of qualitative research.* Thousand Oaks, CA: Sage.

Author Index

Subject Index

⑤SAGE research**methods**

The essential online tool for researchers from the world's leading methods publisher

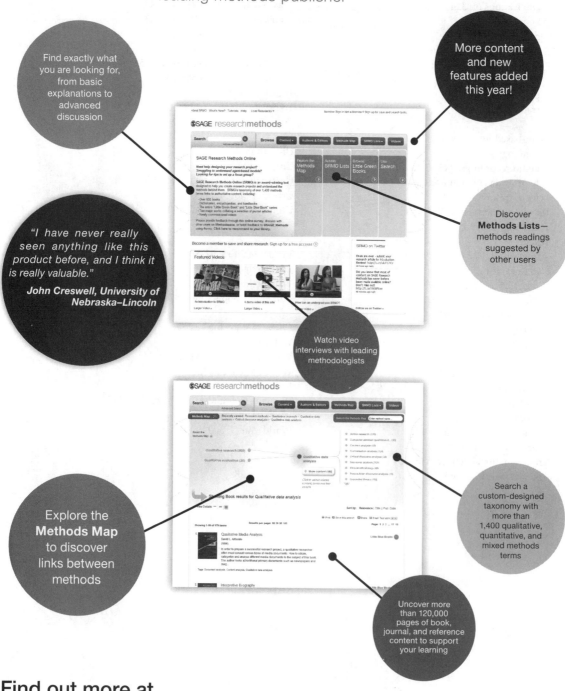

Find exactly what you are looking for, from basic explanations to advanced discussion

More content and new features added this year!

"I have never really seen anything like this product before, and I think it is really valuable."

John Creswell, University of Nebraska–Lincoln

Discover Methods Lists—methods readings suggested by other users

Watch video interviews with leading methodologists

Explore the Methods Map to discover links between methods

Search a custom-designed taxonomy with more than 1,400 qualitative, quantitative, and mixed methods terms

Uncover more than 120,000 pages of book, journal, and reference content to support your learning

Find out more at
www.sageresearchmethods.com